The IMF and its Critics

The IMF is the first economic institution in line to protect countries from the effects of financial crises and to insulate the world economy from possible systemic risk. However, many argue that the IMF is insufficiently equipped to do this job, while others argue almost the opposite: the IMF's well-intentioned actions induce other countries to take risks which increase their exposure to the same problems. This book, written by leading economists from both universities and the multilateral agencies, combines rigorous economic analysis with insider perspectives on key policy debates. It analyses the Asian and Argentine financial crises of the late 1990s, issues of policy ownership, the more general quest for financial stability and governance of the IMF. It is an essential reference for anyone interested in the role of international financial institutions in our globalised economy.

DAVID VINES is Professor of Economics at Oxford University, Adjunct Professor of Economics at the Australian National University and a Research Fellow of CEPR. He is co-editor of *The Asian Financial Crisis: Causes, Contagion and Consequences* (Cambridge University Press, 2000), *The World Bank: Structure and Policies* (Cambridge University Press, 2000), and *Europe, East Asia and APEC* (Cambridge University Press, 1998).

CHRISTOPHER L. GILBERT is Professor of Finance in the Department of Finance at Vrije University, Amsterdam, Professor of Econometrics at the Università degli Studi di Trento, and a Fellow of the Tinbergen Institute. He is co-editor of *The World Bank: Structure and Policies* (Cambridge University Press, 2000).

The IMF and its Critics

Reform of Global Financial Architecture

---

edited by

David Vines and Christopher L. Gilbert

CAMBRIDGE
UNIVERSITY PRESS

CAMBRIDGE UNIVERSITY PRESS
Cambridge, New York, Melbourne, Madrid, Cape Town, Singapore, São Paulo

Cambridge University Press
The Edinburgh Building, Cambridge CB2 8RU, UK

Published in the United States of America by Cambridge University Press, New York

www.cambridge.org
Information on this title: www.cambridge.org/9780521821544

First published 2004

A catalogue record for this publication is available from the British Library

Library of Congress Cataloguing in Publication data
The IMF and its critics: reform of global financial architecture/edited by David Vines
and Christopher L. Gilbert.
   p.   cm. – (Global economic institutions)
Includes bibliographical references and index.
ISBN 0 521 82154 1
1. International Monetary Fund.   2. Financial institutions, International.
3. International economic relations.   4. Financial crises – Case studies.   I. Vines,
David.   II. Gilbert, C. L.   III. Series.
HG3881.5.I581384   2004
332.1′52 – dc21   2003051539

ISBN 978-0-521-82154-4 hardback

Transferred to digital printing 2007

Global Economic Institutions

This is the fifth of a series of books produced under the auspices of the Global Economic Institutions Research Programme of the UK Economic and Social Research Council. The earlier titles have been on Europe, East Asia and regionalism, on the Asian Financial Crisis, on the World Bank and on international financial governance.

Centre for Economic Policy Research

The Centre for Economic Policy Research (CEPR) was founded in 1983 to enhance the quality of economic policy-making within Europe and beyond, by creating excellent, policy-relevant economic research, and disseminating it widely to policy influencers in the public and private sectors and civil society. A second goal was to unify and integrate the European economics research community.

CEPR is based on a new model of organisation, called a 'thinknet': a distributed network of economists, who are affiliated with, but not employed by, the Centre, collaborating through CEPR on a wide range of policy-relevant research projects and dissemination activities. CEPR's network of Research Fellows and Affiliates comprises nearly 600 economists, based primarily in Europe in universities, research institutes, Central Bank research departments and international organisations. No research is performed at CEPR's London headquarters, which serve a purely administrative function, defining research initiatives with the network, seeking funding, organising research-related activities, such as meetings and publications, and working to disseminate the findings of project teams.

This distinguishes CEPR from traditional thinktanks, which employ researchers directly, and typically take an institutional position. In contrast, CEPR has a pluralist and non-partisan stance: the Centre takes no institutional policy positions, and its publications carry a wide range of policy conclusions and recommendations. The opinions expressed in this book and all other CEPR publications are those of the authors and not necessarily those of CEPR or its supporting funders.

Chairman	Guillermo de la Dehesa
President	Richard Portes
Chief Executive Officer	Hilary Beech
Research Director	Mathias Dewatripont

Centre for Economic Policy Research
90–98 Goswell Road
London, EC1V 7RR
UK
Tel: 44 (0)20 7878 2900   Fax: 44 (0)20 7878 2999
Email: cepr@cepr.org   Website: http://www.cepr.org

Contents

Figures

Tables

Contributors

Graham Bird is Professor of Economics at the University of Surrey and Director of the Surrey Centre for International Economic Studies. He is a Visiting Professor at The Fletcher School of Law and Diplomacy, Tufts University in the USA, and has acted as a consultant to many international organisations. He has recently been a high-level expert adviser to the Independent Evaluation Office of the IMF, and has also been a Visiting Scholar with the Fund's Research Department. He has published 22 books and monographs and more than 150 articles in leading academic journals. His most recent book is *The IMF and the Future: Issues and Options Facing the Fund* (Routledge, 2003).

James M. Boughton is Assistant Director of the Policy Development and Review Department at the International Monetary Fund (IMF). He also has been an Advisor in the Research Department at the IMF, and from 1992–2001 he was the Fund's Historian. His publications include a textbook on money and banking, a book on the US Federal funds market, two IMF books that he co-edited, and articles in professional journals on international finance, monetary theory and policy and international policy coordination. His latest book, *Silent Revolution*, on the history of the IMF from 1979 to 1989, was published in October 2001.

Michel Camdessus is President of the Board of the CEPII and former Managing Director of the IMF. He has held numerous appointments in the French Civil Service, culminating in his appointment as Director of the Treasury in the Ministry of Finance and Economic Policies. He has served as Financial Attaché to the French delegation at the European Economic Community, Chairman of the Paris Club, Chairman of the Monetary Committee of the European Economic Community, Deputy Governor of the Bank of France, and he was appointed Governor of the Bank of France in November 1984, a position he held until his appointment as Managing Director of the IMF in January 1987. Michel Camdessus is also President of the Semaines Sociales de France.

Andrew Crockett was appointed President, JP Morgan Chase International, with effect from 1 October 2003. Before that, he was General Manager of the Bank for International Settlements (BIS) from January 1994 to March 2003, and was Chairman of the Financial Stability Forum from April 1999 to March 2003. From 1972 to 1989 he was a staff member of the IMF, and from 1989 to 1993, an Executive Director of the Bank of England. In the latter capacity, he was a member of the Monetary Committee of the European Union, Alternate Governor of the IMF for the United Kingdom and a member (subsequently Chairman) of Working Party 3 of the OECD. He is a member of the Group of Thirty and of the Board of Trustees of the International Accounting Standards Board.

Gordon de Brouwer is Professor of Economics in the Asia Pacific School of Economics and Government at the Australian National University. He is Executive Director of the Australia–Japan Research Centre within the School. He previously worked as Chief Manager, International Markets and Relations at the Reserve Bank of Australia, and was Visiting Professor at the Australian Treasury in 2002. His interests include: open economy macroeconomics; the economies of Australia, Japan and East Asia; financial markets; central banking and monetary policy; the economics of national security; and international relations.

Brian M. Doyle is an Economist in the Division of International Finance at the Federal Reserve Board. He was educated at Queens University at Kingston (BA) and Princeton University (PhD). He has served as an Adjunct Professor of Economics at Johns Hopkins University and Syracuse University. His research work includes articles on business cycle co-movement, causes of business cycles and new open economy macroeconomics.

Joseph E. Gagnon is an Assistant Director in the Division of International Finance at the Federal Reserve Board. He was educated at Harvard University (BA) and Stanford University (PhD). Previously, he was Director of the Office of Industrial Nations and Global Analyses at the US Department of the Treasury and a Lecturer in Economics at the University of California at Berkeley. His research focuses on international trade and capital flows and the macroeconomic linkages between the United States and foreign economies.

Christopher L. Gilbert is Professor of Finance in the Department of Finance at Vrije University, Amsterdam, Professor of Econometrics at the Università degli Studi di Trento and a Fellow of the Tinbergen Institute. He was previously Professor of Applied Econometrics at Queen Mary, University of London, and prior to that a Fellow of Wadham College, Oxford. His academic research falls into four areas: primary commodity and commodity futures markets (on which he has worked extensively with the World Bank), global economic institutions (he was joint editor with David Vines of a Global Economic Institutions Research volume on the World Bank), applied finance and financial econometrics, and the history and methodology of econometrics.

Andrew G. Haldane is Head of the Division of International Finance at the Bank of England, focusing on emerging market risks and the redesign of the international financial architecture. His research interests include monetary and financial stability frameworks, monetary policy rules and the international financial architecture on which he has published extensively, including books on inflation-targeting and crisis resolution.

Dale W. Henderson is a Senior Adviser in the Division of International Finance at the Federal Reserve Board and an Adjunct Professor of Economics at Georgetown University. He was educated at Wesleyan University (BA), the London School of Economics (MSc Econ) and Yale University (PhD). Previously, he was a Professor of Economics at Georgetown University and a Lecturer in Economics at the University of Pennsylvania and held visiting positions at the University of Virginia, Georgetown University, and Yale University. His research work includes books on pollution control and on monetary policy in open economies and articles on the gold market and on several topics in macroeconomics, including stabilisation policy and foreign exchange market intervention.

Gregor Irwin is an Economic Adviser at HM Treasury. Previously he was a Fellow in Economics at University College, Oxford and at Lady Margaret Hall, Oxford.

Malcolm Knight is General Manager of the Bank for International Settlements (BIS). From 1999 to 2003 he was Senior Deputy Governor of the Bank of Canada, responsible for overseeing strategic planning and coordinating all the Bank's operations as well as acting for the Governor and sharing responsibility for the conduct of monetary policy as a member of the Bank's Governing Council.

Mark Kruger is currently an Advisor to the Executive Director for Canada, Ireland and the Caribbean at the International Monetary Fund. He is on leave from the Bank of Canada, where he was an Assistant Chief in the International Department. His research interests are international policy issues and international finance.

Allan H. Meltzer is University Professor of Political Economy and Public Policy at Carnegie Mellon University. Since 1989, he has also been a Visiting

Scholar at the American Enterprise Institute in Washington. In 1999–2000, he served as Chairman of the International Financial Institution Advisory Commission, known as the Meltzer Commission, which proposed major reforms of the IMF and the development banks. His writings have appeared in numerous journals; he is the author of several books and more than 300 papers on economic theory and policy. From 1973 to 1996, he was co-editor of the *Carnegie-Rochester Conference Series on Public Policy*, the *Journal of Economic Literature* and the *Journal of Finance.*

Laurence H. Meyer is a Distinguished Scholar at the Center for Strategic and International Studies in Washington, DC and Senior Advisor and Director for Macroeconomic Advisors. He served as a member of the Board of Governors of the Federal Reserve System from June 1996 to January 2002. He was educated at Yale University (BA) and the Massachusetts Institute of Technology (PhD). Previously, he was a Professor of Economics at Washington University and co-founder and President of Laurence H. Meyer & Associates. He has written numerous articles in professional journals, has authored a textbook on macroeconomic modelling and has testified before the Congress on macroeconomic policy issues.

Paul Mosley is Professor and Head of the Department of Economics at Sheffield University, and was President of the Development Studies Association from 1998 to 2001. He is author of *Overseas Aid; Its Defence and Reform* (1987) and co-author of *Aid and Power* (2nd edn., 1995) and *Finance against Poverty* (1996).

Alex Mourmouras is Deputy Chief of the European Division in the IMF Institute. His current areas of research include the political economy of international financial institutions, IMF conditionality and the effectiveness of Fund-supported programmes, and problems of real and nominal convergence of transition and other developing countries. He has previously served as an economist in the IMF's Fiscal Affairs Department and as Associate Professor and Director of Graduate Studies at the University of Cincinnati.

Michael Mussa is a Senior Fellow at the Institute for International Economics and former Director of Research at the IMF. He served as a member of the US Council of Economic Advisors from August 1986 to September 1988, and has been a member of the faculty at the University of Rochester and the Graduate School of Business of the University of Chicago.

Andrew Powell is Professor in the Universidad Torcoauto Di Tella Business School and is Director of graduate programmes in Finance in the Business

School. Previous to that he was the Chief Economist of the Central Bank of Argentina, joining the Central Bank in March 1995 and leaving at the end of April 2001. During this period at the Central Bank he was directly responsible for the areas of research and regulation and was intimately involved in the banking sector reforms in the post-Tequila period. He represented Argentina as a member of a G10 working party on emerging debt market instability, as a G20/G22 deputy and member of all three G22 working groups (on crisis resolution, financial system strengthening and transparency) and was a member of a Financial Stability Forum working group on incentives. He has published widely and recently completed papers on inflation targeting, on the Argentine crisis, on the role of the IMF, on the effect of Basel II on emerging countries and on the role of foreign banks in Latin America.

James Powell is Chief of the International Department of the Bank of Canada, focusing on international financial architecture and exchange rate regimes. Recent published work includes research on dollarisation in Canada as well as a history of the Canadian dollar.

Lawrence Schembri is Director of Research in the International Department of the Bank of Canada and Adjunct Professor of Economics at Carleton University. He was educated at the University of Toronto (BCom), London School of Economics (MSc) and the Massachusetts Institute of Technology (PhD). He has published research in the areas of international macroeconomics and international trade.

David Vines is Professor of Economics at the University of Oxford and a Fellow of Balliol College. He is also Adjunct Professor of Economics in the Research School of Pacific and Asian Studies at the Australian National University, and a Research Fellow of CEPR. From 1994 onwards he was Director of the ESRC Research Programme on Global Economic Institutions. His research is on macroeconomics and international economics, European monetary union, and regional integration in the Asia-Pacific region. He is also working on global economic institutions and was editor, with Pierre-Richard Agénor, Marcus Miller and Axel Weber, of a volume on the Asian Financial Crisis, and with Christopher Gilbert of a volume on the World Bank, both for the Global Economic Institutions Programme.

Dominic Wilson is a Senior Global Economist at Goldman Sachs & Co., where he is primarily responsible for the firm's research on global thematic issues and the world economy. His published work covers a range of topics including the links between trade and development in East Asia, the management of international capital flows, and Japan's economic crisis.

Ngaire Woods is Director of the Global Economic Governance Programme and Fellow in Politics and International Relations at University College, Oxford. She has a forthcoming book, *The Economic Missionaries: The IMF, The World Bank and International Relations*, having previously published *The Political Economy of Globalization* (Macmillan, 2000), *Inequality, Globalization and World Politics* (with Andrew Hurrell, Oxford University Press, 1999), *Explaining International Relations since 1945* (Oxford University Press, 1986) and numerous articles on international institutions, globalization and governance.

Acknowledgements

From 1994 until 2000, the UK Economic and Social Research Council (the ESRC) funded the Global Economic Institutions (GEI) Research Programme, whose objectives were to fund academic research on the functioning of multilateral economic organisations and about the global institutional structures within which economic activity takes place. As part of this programme, a group of researchers considered reform of the policies of the IMF. Some of that work was published in *The Asian Financial Crisis: Causes, Contagion, and Consequences* (edited by Pierre-Richard Agénor, Marcus Miller, David Vines and Axel Weber, Cambridge University Press, 1999). This book brings together further work on this theme. It was edited by Christopher L. Gilbert (Vrije Universiteit, Amsterdam) and David Vines (Balliol College, Oxford, Australian National University and CEPR) who was Director of the GEI Programme.

The initial presentation of some of the chapters in this volume took place at the final conference of the GEI Programme which was held at the Bank of England in June 2000. We are extremely grateful to the Bank for acting as host to that meeting, to those who presented papers at the meeting, and to others who attended and made the meeting such a success. That conference ranged widely over the future of global economic institutions as a whole, and we took the view that the perspective of papers at that meeting was too wide to make a useful book. Instead, discussion there suggested to us that it would be valuable to bring together some of the presenters of papers at that conference with others to produce a volume specifically focused on the future of the IMF within the international financial architecture.

We are glad to acknowledge the funding by the ESRC of work in this important area. We are also much indebted to Andrew Crockett, Chairman of the Steering Committee of the GEI Programme and then General Manager of the Bank for International Settlements, and Jim Rollo, also a member of the Steering Committee of the GEI Programme, then Chief Economist at the UK Foreign and Commonwealth Office and now Professor of Economics at

Sussex University, for jointly hosting the June 2000 meeting at the Bank of England.

Some of our first chapter makes use of work which Gregor Irwin has done with David Vines, and we are very grateful to be able to build on that work. In addition David Vines worked on this volume while at the Bank of England as a Houblon Norman Fellow during 2002 and we are happy to acknowledge the Bank's support in this additional respect.

We thank the IIE for permission to reproduce figures 8.1–8.8 from *IIE Policy Analyses in International Economics*, 76 (2002).

At Cambridge University Press, Chris Harrison has worked hard to expedite our plans, and arranged for referees to comment on initial drafts of a set of chapters. We are grateful for those comments, since they helped us to improve considerably the general shape of the book. The production of the book would also not have been possible without the continuing assistance and enthusiasm of the Publications staff at CEPR, in particular Anil Shamdasani.

Introduction

CHRISTOPHER L. GILBERT AND DAVID VINES

In 1994, the UK Economic and Social Research Council (ESRC) launched the Global Economic Institutions (GEI) Research Programme, with the objective of funding academic research on the functioning of multilateral economic organisations and about the global institutions within which economic activity takes place. The IMF and the World Bank are the two major global institutions established at the 1944 Bretton Woods Conference, and they have now been joined by the World Trade Organization (WTO). An earlier volume (Gilbert and Vines, 2000) arising out of the GEI Programme was devoted to the World Bank. In this volume, which will be the final publication from the programme, which ended in 2000, we move to the IMF.

This book began with a conference on the future of the Global Economic Institutions, held at the Bank of England, in May 2000 at which a number of the papers included as chapters in this volume were presented. We are very grateful to the Bank of England for hosting the conference. The conference discussion suggested to us that it would be valuable to bring together some of the presenters of papers at that conference and others to produce a book on the future of the IMF within international financial architecture.

The process of assembling the book has been overtaken by the crisis in Argentina. This crisis has hardened attitudes about the IMF, in that all wish to avoid repeat events like the Argentine crisis. This followed the crisis in East Asia in the late 1990s which had led to a sense that all was not well, either with policies recommended to prevent financial crisis or with the crisis resolution measures that the world was able to deploy. Much, too, was learned from looking back at that crisis.[1] Further, in September 1995, the crisis in Russia also led to a re-examination of the IMF's role. In the case of Russia there are many deep political questions which can obscure the economic lessons to be learned. But in the case of Argentina the entire set of 'moral hazard' issues come to the

---

[1] See Agenor, Miller, Vines and Weber (1999) for a discussion of what we learned, a book published as part of the GEI Programme.

fore – the sense that the position of the IMF on policy advice and crisis management may actually make things worse. All observers now believe that the IMF needs to change its position, at least in certain respects.

How should this be done? Chapter 1, by David Vines and Christopher L. Gilbert, reviews the changing position of the IMF in the international financial architecture in the light of these questions. It differentiates between the IMF's role in dealing with advanced countries, its position in assisting the least developed countries (who have limited international capital market access) and its stance *vis-à-vis* emerging-market economies with access to international capital markets and the vulnerability to international financial crisis which this brings. The chapter argues the need for a policy on the part of the international community which distinguishes between countries which are in a state of solvency crisis, for whom it may be appropriate to engineer a debt write-down, and the appropriate solution in the case of liquidity crisis – where it is argued that the appropriate response will be the provision of finance, within the constraints available, supplemented, if need be, by lending, by capital flow standstills and by lending into arrears.

Chapter 2, by Andrew Crockett, on progress towards greater international financial stability, was written before the Argentine crisis. It brings together lessons to be learned from the European crisis of the early 1990s, Mexico in 1994, the East Asian crisis and Russia. He suggests incremental reform of the system in two ways. Macroeconomic policies in potential crisis countries should concentrate on a move towards greater exchange rate flexibility within a stable macroeconomic framework (a proposal taken up by others) and with a greater degree of financial stabilisation. This requires, Crockett argues, the strengthening of key institutions (not just banks but also other financial institutions), ensuring that they operate in open and transparent markets, and establishing that the infrastructure within which they operate is robust and well understood. Crockett also offers suggestions as to how the IMF should manage financial crises, including the need to help countries reach understandings with their creditors about debt rescheduling, a topic taken up elsewhere in the book.

Chapter 3, by Laurence H. Meyer, Brian M. Doyle, Joseph E. Gagnon and Dale W. Henderson, discusses international policy coordination among the developed countries and what we can expect from this in contributing towards greater international financial stability. This is a very useful review of what coordination has achieved in the past, pointing towards a need to continue this work and to give more effort to the joint modelling of monetary and fiscal policies and how they might be combined to solve international policy needs. Greater care is also needed in specifying policy objectives in a world in which the current account of the balance of payments is not clearly an objective. What should replace this? (A target for national savings?) And what role should fiscal policy play, and what are the appropriate moves for actual international cooperation within this framework? This last is a question which has come to the fore in the wake of the downturn which began in 2001.

Allan H. Meltzer, in chapter 4, takes up one possible response to the problems of financial instability in emerging markets, raised in Crockett's chapter. He reviews the work of international financial institutions (IFIs), and the role of the IMF, in the light of the work of the 'Meltzer Commission' which reported in late 1999. He suggests that the IMF might continue to function as a lender of last resort (LOLR), but with severe constraints imposed around its operations by pre-qualifications – lending would take place only to countries which had satisfied the international communities as to the appropriateness of their financial policies and macroeconomic framework. Others, including ourselves, are critical of this approach, but it is helpful to have it set out clearly, providing the basis for discussion. It seems that all would agree that if the IMF is to continue to operate in a way not circumscribed in the manner proposed by Meltzer, then changes really will be needed in its practice to avoid the moral hazard problems described at the beginning of this introduction.

Chapter 5 by Malcolm Knight, Lawrence Schembri and James Powell, proposes a very different response to these issues. The authors suggest that fundamental reform is necessary in emerging markets to provide the increased financial stability advocated by Crockett. Their argument is that the crises in emerging market economies have been due to the incomplete and distorted market structures in these economies, and which were not ready to receive the large amounts of capital which were directed towards them. In developed countries risk management practices are well developed, even allowing for the inadequacies which have become evident in 2001–2. In emerging markets, by contrast, lenders from the industrial countries and borrowers from the emerging markets themselves have relied heavily on guarantees provided by the government to mitigate the inadequacy of local risk management. It is these guarantees which lead to moral hazard behaviour, and thus to the risk of crisis. Such analysis focuses on reform in potential borrowing countries designed to create deeper, broader and better regulated financial markets. Once reforms become enacted, the need for explicit guarantees by government will diminish and the risk of crises will be reduced.

In chapter 6, Dominic Wilson suggests a degree of caution in moving in this direction. An open capital account is, he argues, desirable when domestic distortions are relatively minor. But distortions may drive a wedge between private and social costs and in the presence of these the costs of capital account liberalisation may outweight benefits. This may suggest delay in such liberalisation, an approach which, in the first instance, attempts to raise the price of particular transactions or indeed limits certain kinds of capital flows entirely. Although this is a different approach to capital account liberalisation from that of Knight, Schembri and Powell, it may be complementary to theirs.

The greater deepening which those three authors describe may take time, and limits on capital account movement during the interim, in the way described by Wilson, may be necessary. Chapter 7, by Gregor Irwin, Christopher L. Gilbert and David Vines, adds to Wilson's view. It further documents the way in which distortions, and inappropriate institutions and policies, can lead to difficulties in the process of capital account liberalisation and in so doing present further reasons for caution in this liberalisation process.

Chapter 8, by Andrew G. Haldane and Mark Kruger, sets forth in detail the kind of approach to crisis resolution discussed by Vines and Gilbert in chapter 1. They suggest there should be a presumption of limited initial finance to help weaken the moral hazard problem. Private sector involvement should happen more regularly. There should be more regular use made of standstills, not to relieve debtors of their obligations to service debts in full and on time, but instead to enhance the effectiveness of the crisis management process, where necessary. There should be clear guidelines for invocation of standstills, as part of a transparent process in which the reconstruction of sovereign debt is managed. This should include equal treatment of creditors and seniority for any new money which is brought in. There should be a clear timescale. Because there are potential costs of such standstills this process should be used with caution. The chapter presents a clear framework for IMF intervention.

Chapter 9 by James M. Boughton and Alex Mourmouras, surveys recent contributions to the political economy of the IFIs in relation to the concept of ownership. It surveys how ownership of policies might augment the strength of policy response to crises, and how it might relate to conditionality. The general view is that, because the Fund does crisis prevention and resolution it is particularly exposed to ownership conflicts with countries' governments. This in turn raises the question of what the role is for IMF conditionality when a government fully owns a policy reform, and the further question of whether, when a government does not fully own a reform, conditionality can ensure success of the reform process (or whether it is merely a way of limiting the financial commitment of the IMF).

Gordon de Brouwer, in chapter 10, presents a regional perspective on IMF reform. He documents East Asian dissatisfaction with the IMF in the aftermath of the 1997–9 Asian crisis. He claims that the IMF is seen as promoting US interests and ideology and as being insufficiently sensitive to Asian concerns. What is needed, he suggests, is a specifically East Asian forum which would encourage dialogue between regional governments and would be able to respond to future regional crises. He claims that a forum of this sort would complement and not compete with the IMF and other currently existing IFIs. Three major issues are raised in this review. First, were IMF policies in the Asian crisis really inappropriate or misconceived, and possibly ideologically motivated, or were they poor because the IMF needed to develop the macroeconomic theory of the Asian crisis on the hoof as the crisis developed? Initially, the crises were viewed through the spectacles of the 1995 Mexican crisis. But it is well known that armies always fight the previous war. Could an Asian organisation have done any better, or would it be able now to do better in the face of future crises? Second, what would such an Asian organisation do? Would it provide a forum for consultation? Or would it become an agency which could actually lend money at a time of crisis? Third, are proposals for an Asian currency union a way to take forward policies for managing crisis? As the EU Maastricht Treaty makes clear, currency union requires high levels of fiscal coordination and monitoring. These measures clearly do detract from national sovereignty. Countries will be willing to make this order of sacrifice only if their citizens are able to identify at least to some extent with a federal polity. This does not seem to be a likely outcome in East Asia, and the chapter appears to support this view. As a result, it leads to the conclusion that continued discussion of regional monetary cooperation might result in something short of monetary union in the region, but this will need further elaboration as to details.

Chapter 11, by Graham Bird and Paul Mosley, contains a defence of current IMF practice. The authors argue that Fund programmes concentrate on demand contraction, rather than on structural adjustment and on attracting other capital flows, because this is inevitable when crises arise. But along with this they argue that moral hazard arguments are overblown, conditionality is effective to some degree, and – because work on long-term poverty reduction and growth is valuable – it is inevitable that the Fund does such work to some degree. Bird and Mosley imply that the Fund should continue broadly as it has been doing, and not narrow its work as the authors of earlier chapters have suggested.

In our view, this description of useful things done does not adequately engage with the core argument of those earlier studies. It is not only important that the Fund avoids moral hazard, or has useful conditionality, or that it can help with poverty reduction. It is also that the Fund cannot act as a LOLR in the presence of really large-scale financial crises. So it must be in a position to be able to withdraw from the support of countries in difficulty, at an earlier stage than that at which it withdrew from Argentina. At such a stage the Fund cannot simultaneously be all of (1) the country's ally, working with it on poverty reduction, (2) the judge that the country's adjustment efforts are inadequate and (3) the mediator, manager and judge of the legal conflicts involved in a debt write-down on the country's foreign debt. If, as the authors believe necessary, the Fund continues to work on role (1) then how can it act as judge as in role (2) And if not, then who can? And surely it cannot play role (3) if it is also an ally of the country because it is playing role (1)? But if it does not, who will? Do the authors want a country in these circumstances to be left at the mercy of vulture bond funds? Or do they actually want another, brand-new international financial institution, to carry out roles (2) and (3)? Might it not be better to have the Fund concentrate on roles (2) and (3), as even Anne Krueger (2001) has now been arguing, and give role (1) to the World Bank?

These issues were brought to a head by the Argentine crisis. Argentina was the star pupil who flunked the final examination. Who is to blame? The examination system may be arbitrary or the teacher's faith in the pupil may have been misplaced. Either way, the pupil suffers. If she is strong, she will bear up and recover. By contrast, it is the academy's reputation which may be permanently affected.

The Argentine crisis differs from other recent crises because this was a crisis of the Fund's making. It is arguable that the IMF and the World Bank wasted large amounts of money in Russia, and that they did so knowingly, but the responsibility for those decisions lies largely with the governments that made the decision that a nuclear post-communist Russia must be supported financially. As during the 1980s debt crisis, the Washington-based institutions bent their criteria to generate the politically required lending. And while it is possible to argue that IMF policy may have exacerbated the East Asian crisis, we have not seen it asserted that the crisis was actually provoked by IMF actions. By contrast, until quite late in the 1990s, the Argentine Currency Board was held up by the IMF as an example of a successful anti-inflation peg and a possible model for other developing countries in similar circumstances. Argentina and Chile were the two Latin American success stories and, of the two, it was Argentina which had benefited most from Fund support and advice. The consequence was that continued success of the Argentine stabilisation programme became as important for the IMF as it was for the country itself. Its failure has been very important, in different ways, for both.

In chapters 12 and 13, Michael Mussa and Andrew Powell offer two contrasting views of the Argentine episode. For Mussa, the inevitability of eventual failure of the currency peg was predicated by the inability of the government to control its fiscal balance. That inability stemmed from the constitutional relationship between the federal government and the provincial authorities which allowed the latter to commit the former to expenditures without providing the required tax revenues. Mussa recognises the success of the currency peg in eliminating inflation but argues that, once this had happened, the IMF should have urged the government to move to a floating rate which would have resulted in fiscal imbalance becoming rapidly reflected in the exchange rate. For Powell, by contrast, there was no inevitability either in fiscal latitude or crisis. Argentine policy and IMF support were *ex ante* rational but Argentina suffered from an unfortunate roll of the dice. At that point, it became *ex post* rational for the government to fiscally cut and run, and for the IMF to withdraw support. Argentina is seen as an IMF failure and Brazil as a success, but it might have been otherwise. IMF policies should be judged in the aggregate and not on the basis of particular accidental episodes.

Much of this volume is concerned with relatively technical issues of how the IMF should operate. The fact that these questions can even be posed relies on a prior acceptance of the requirement for a global, membership-based, supra-governmental financial institution, and the implications of that structure. These issues are addressed in the final two chapters.

Economists' analysis of institutional performance is generally in terms of outcomes and not processes. Different processes may be more or less efficient in generating required outcomes. This can often give rise to a useful division of responsibilities – the economists discuss policy alternatives leaving discussion by others of how these decisions can be put into effect. But in other cases, it can result in a dangerous over-simplification of the policy alternatives. This is an implication of Ngaire Woods' analysis of the IMF's governance in chapter 14. The IMF is a membership organisation but one in which the developed countries in general and the United States in particular play a dominant role. Reform proposals must respect this consensual structure but, at the same time, ensure that it continues to command assent. A club which attempts to deny certain members access to club facilities (perhaps because they have failed to 'pre-qualify' for assistance) is likely to lose the support of those members. On the other hand, it is also important to ensure that the more powerful members continue to see merit in acting within the club rather than unilaterally or through their own group (perhaps the G7). The incentive to use the IMF is that it confers legitimacy on actions which might otherwise be seen as interfering excessively in a country's domestic affairs, but legitimacy comes at the cost of accountability, and this involves a wider constituency than developed country taxpayers.

This view locates the IMF as a core institutional component of the humanistic vision for a free and democratic world order. Woods' discussion of accountability links directly to the final chapter 15, which amplifies that humanistic perspective. This is the text of the 2000 Cyril Foster Lecture given at the University of Oxford by Michel Camdessus, shortly after his retirement as Managing Director of the IMF. In his lecture, Camdessus, quoting Václav Havel, emphasises the need for a sense of responsibility for and solidarity with the world. It is that sense which will be required as the IMF moves forward to meet the challenges that the new century will throw up.

REFERENCES

Agénor, R., M. Miller, D. Vines and A. Weber (1999). *The Asian Financial Crises: Causes, Contagion, and Consequences*. Cambridge, Cambridge University Press

Gilbert, C. L. and D. Vines (2000). *The World Bank: Structure and Policies*. Cambridge, Cambridge University Press

Kruger, A. (2001). 'International Financial Architecture for 2002. A New Approach to foreign debt Restructuring', IMF, mimeo

1 The IMF and international financial architecture: solvency and liquidity

DAVID VINES AND CHRISTOPHER L. GILBERT

1 The emergence of the current global architecture

The starting point of our discussion is the global framework of international institutions, set up at the 1944 Bretton Woods Conference. The IMF was perhaps the chief element of this framework and passed its initial two decades within its confines. In this framework, the IMF helped to manage balance of payments adjustment within a global system of pegged but adjustable exchange rates. The IMF now does something looser than this – it exercises surveillance over and influence on macroeconomic policies worldwide. In this section we set out how and why this change came about, describing how the Fund's role has changed as the overall framework has changed. In subsequent sections we consider the role for the Fund within this new framework. Its central role has come to be that of helping to manage macroeconomic stability in developing countries, and, in particular, the management of international financial crises. Crucial to this is its role in responding in appropriate and differentiated ways to liquidity and solvency crises. A discussion of this role will form the focus of this chapter.

The global architecture of the golden age

The post-war world into which the Bretton Woods' twins (the IMF and the World Bank) and the GATT were born was one in which the main issues were: to prevent a collapse in economic activity and employment; to promote growth; to avoid the emergence of payments imbalances; to promote the growth of international trade and avoid a slide back into the protectionism of the 1930s; and to promote economic development through international lending.

We are grateful to Vijay Joshi for helpful comments. The later part of the chapter draws on Irwin and Vines (2004). We are grateful to Gregor Irwin for his major part in that work.

Table 1.1 *International institutional and policy framework in the Bretton Woods era*

Objective	Instrument(s)	Responsible authority
Full employment (and low inflation)	Demand management (mainly fiscal)	National governments
Economic growth	Low interest rates	Central Banks
Balance of payments adjustment	Pegged but adjustable IMF exchange rates	IMF (with national governments)
Promotion of international trade	Tariff reductions	GATT
Economic development	Official international lending	World Bank

The policy framework in which these institutions were located is shown in table 1.1. Central to this was the promotion of high levels of employment and output by means of national macroeconomic policies. It was believed that the management of demand, mainly using fiscal policy, would prevent slumps in demand and prevent the re-emergence of periods of global depression like that in the 1930s.

A clear and internally coherent international institutional and policy structure was established around this central preoccupation.[1] The IMF presided over a system of fixed exchange rates, the adjustment of which was to take place so that external balance – a satisfactory balance of trade – could be made consistent with the achievement of full employment The World Bank lent money, first for reconstruction and then to the developing countries for development projects. This was to enable them to get access to investment resources from abroad – to run balance of trade deficits, to borrow, invest and grow, in the expectation that such borrowing could be repaid out of the increased export proceeds that

---

[1] For discussions, from a British point of view, of the establishment of this world, see volumes 25, 26, and 27 of the *Keynes Papers* (Keynes, 1971), and also Harrod (1952). For a brief discussion of the role played by one key British player, James Meade, see Meade (1988). Gardiner (1956) and van Doormael (1978) also present valuable transatlantic accounts. Opinions now differ on how clearly the participants understood the nature of the framework that they were creating. It is our view that at least some of the British participants understood this framework with great clarity. One of us was first shown the taxonomy displayed in table 1.1 by James Meade. Meade described how much time and effort the young group of economists at the UK Treasury (consisting of Denis Robertson, Marcus Fleming and Meade himself) spent in trying to persuade Keynes away from the protectionism which Keynes initially thought some countries might need to resort to, so as to avoid a collapse in aggregate demand after the war, at a time of projected extreme dollar scarcity. (The pages of the Keynes papers referred to above bear testimony to that effort.) Meade also said that he first saw such a taxonomic diagram when, during a particularly tedious wartime meeting, Keynes drew something like it on the back of an envelope, saying, as he did so, 'At last, I am convinced'.

would accompany this growth. A series of GATT rounds brought about tariff reductions, creating markets for the exports as required. The period when this policy framework was in place was one of extraordinary dynamism, although there is disagreement as to how much this setup was actually responsible for the so-called 'golden age' (Matthews, Feinstein and Odling Smee, 1982; Matthews and Bowen, 1988).

There were positive cumulative interactions. With demand management and exchange rate adjustment jointly assigned to the achievement of macroeconomic equilibrium, the politics of trade liberalisation was facilitated. It stimulated the international reallocation of production, and promoted investment and growth.

The collapse of this architecture, and its reconfiguration in the 1990s

Despite its major successes, the Bretton Woods framework contained within itself three important seeds of its own destruction. These became apparent in the 1970s and the 1980s. The recognition of these three problems, and the response to them, led to a reconfiguration of global architecture in the 1990s.

Prevention of inflation

First, it was a framework which contained no clear responsibility for preventing inflation. Although there were periods of (generally unsuccessful) price controls or 'incomes policy', the seeds of incipient inflation were sown. Eventually, tension generated by the great inflation of the 1970s killed the interventionist demand-managing macroeconomic policies, designed to promote high employment, which were at the centre of the 'golden age' architecture. It also led to the increased acceptance of monetarist theories, in both politics and the economics profession, and to the abandonment of the simple Hansen–Hicks version of Keynesian economics which had underpinned the full employment policies.[2] This acceptance was seldom justifiable in terms of clear empirical evidence. Initially the response was in the form of monetarist policies, which attempted to replace management of demand with non-interventionist rules fixing the money supply. These were generally unsuccessful. With great difficulty, macroeconomic theory and policies have been reconfigured, over a period of two decades, around anti-inflation policies pursued by means of inflation targets. These

---

[2] Although this point is separable from the first one, the collapse of full employment polices largely happened by means of the collapse of pegged exchange rates. The case of France in the early 1980s is perhaps the most striking example.

policies hark back to the earlier era. They are again interventionist, since they manage the level of demand in the economy through interest rate changes. They can be analysed with a generalisation of the Hicks–Hansen framework. But they are conducted through monetary policy rather than fiscal policy, and they are directed at stabilising the price level (or its rate of growth) rather than the level of output or employment.

Growth of international capital flows

Second, the growth of international capital flows – which was in part a result of the international stability associated with the 'golden age' – helped to undermine the role of the IMF. As first demonstrated by the 1967 sterling devaluation, it was no longer possible for the IMF and national governments to set exchange rates without reference to market perceptions of the sustainable rate. With increasingly mobile capital, once demand management policies generated a suspicion that there would (or might) be a need to devalue the exchange rate to preserve external balance, speculation could make it difficult or impossible for Central Banks to defend the existing rate. In 1971, the even greater problems caused by dollar inflation and the Vietnam war-driven US balance of payments deficit led to capital flows which caused the breakdown of the entire pegged exchange rate system and a reluctant move to floating exchange rates. In addition, the emergence of interventionist monetary policy dedicated to the pursuit of inflation targets, as described in the previous paragraph, led to countries adopting different interest rates, necessarily causing changes in exchange rates.[3] In the face of these changes, the IMF appeared to lack a coherent role. Despite this, there were few suggestions for abolition of the IMF, and the increased uncertainty in the new environment, together with the perception of a greater need for explicit coordination in government policies, suggested the evolution of a new role. As discussed in what follows, this came to be thought of as the exercise of surveillance and influence over macroeconomic policies, supported by conditionality-based lending.

Growth in the mobility of international capital flows

Third, the growth in the mobility of international capital flows also led to private foreign investment replacing official international capital flows from advanced

---

[3] In this new world, if capital were highly mobile then (real) interest rates would need to converge in the long run, but differences in (real) interest rates would be required during any period in which (for example) high real interest rates were required in a country to reduce inflation back to target. The (real) exchange rate of a country in this position would need to appreciate to the point where expected depreciation back to equilibrium exactly offset the expected stream of higher real returns from holding interest-bearing assets than those obtainable abroad.

Table 1.2 *International institutional and policy framework in the 1990s*

Objective	Instrument(s)	Responsible authority
Low inflation	Monetary policy	Central Banks
Structural employment policies and growth	Fiscal policy	National governments
International macro policy coordination	G3 fiscal and monetary policies	IMF and G7/G8 summits
Global financial stability	Regulatory standards and requirements	BIS, IMF
Trade liberalisation	Legal rules governing microeconomic policies relating to trade	WTO
Resource allocation and growth in developed countries	Microeconomic policies (but 'best endeavours' only; no enforcement)	OECD
Macroeconomic stability in LDCs	Fiscal and monetary policy advice and assistance; lending with conditionality, crisis resolution	IMF
Development in LDCs	Development policy advice and assistance; lending	World Bank

countries to the capital-scarce areas of the world economy – whether in the form of bank and bond-based lending, or equity purchases, or foreign direct investment (FDI). In the face of this the World Bank also needed to modify its role. This initially came to be thought of as the exercise of influence over development policies, again supported by conditionality-based lending. Action to combat poverty subsequently also became a dominant objective and, indeed, one of the major stated *raisons d'être* for the Bank's operations.

These developments transformed the two Washington-based institutions. On the trade side in Geneva, trade liberalisation became harder as the world moved beyond the relatively simple menu of tariff reduction and as governments became more adept at responding to protectionist pressures by devising and strengthening non-tariff measures. This induced other developments which eventually led to the GATT being superseded by the World Trade Organisation (WTO). As a result of these changes we now have a much less clear arrangement of international institutions and their responsibilities, set out in table 1.2.

How these responsibilities are to be exercised is also much less clear. For the Fund to exercise surveillance over and influence on macroeconomic policies is much less straightforward than presiding over a system of exchange rate pegs. For the Bank to exercise influence over development strategies is much less straightforward than lending money for projects. For the WTO to be drawn, as it increasingly is, into the exercise of surveillance over and influence on a complex of trade, regulatory and industrial policies gives it a mandate which is much less straightforward than that of brokering tariff reductions. These uncertainties about purpose and function lead to more difficult questions about legitimacy and about governance, compared with the time when the institutions had simpler agendas.

The role of the IMF in this architecture

The IMF began life as a multilateral institution which administered the international monetary system, but now does something looser than this – it exercises surveillance over and influence on macroeconomic policies worldwide. It pursues its objectives through a bundled mixture of rather different activities: research and economic analysis; policy advice and technical assistance; and lending subject to conditionality. It also needs to provide these activities in rather different ways to different kinds of countries.

Following Knight, Schembri and Powell (chapter 5 in this volume) we may distinguish between countries with modern and sophisticated financial markets, a high degree of international capital market access, and good policy-making capability, which we call advanced countries, and a second group of countries which do not fully meet these criteria, which are the developing or emerging market countries. For the former group of advanced countries the role of the Fund is now a limited one. The IMF operates some surveillance over, and seeks to influence, macroeconomic conditions in these countries. This work is the subject of the Fund's regular consultations with all countries and is reflected in the Fund's *World Economic Outlook*. We discuss this activity in section 2. Other than this, the Fund's operations have become concentrated on providing macroeconomic assistance for the developing countries. We discuss the issues concerning how the Fund should deal with these countries in sections 3–6.

The activities for these two groups of countries are two rather different types of activity for one institution to carry out. The first involves having some – highly limited – global responsibility for the internalisation of the externalities created by foreign spillovers in macroeconomic policy. The second is one in which the core richer countries in the world economy assist in the solution of macroeconomic problems in the poorer countries, where both financial markets and policy-making capacity are much less well developed, while at the same time enabling these richer countries to hold back from direct bilateral intervention in the internal decisions of these poorer countries.

2 The IMF and advanced countries: policy cooperation

We have noted that use of monetary policy for inflation stabilisation conflicts directly with the use of monetary policy for exchange rate stabilisation.
This is the main reason for the unwillingness of governments to commit to
'target zones' for exchange rates, despite extensive discussion in the 1980s.
Nevertheless, even if national monetary policies are directed at a domestic
anti-inflationary objective, by means of interest rate movements, with conse-
quential exchange rate variability, there is scope for international surveillance
over, and pressure for cooperation in, national macroeconomic policies. We
identify two forms that the Fund's surveillance activities have taken since the
1970s.

First, there is scope for surveillance over the conduct of monetary policy.
Policies of national governments primarily reflect their own domestic agenda
and priorities. In the event of a common world inflation or demand shock,
externalities imply that suboptimal interest rate cooperation will result:[4] all
countries have an interest in the nature of the anti-inflation rule which any one
country pursues. This issue emerged in the late 1990s in discussion of the extent
to which the ECB was prepared to assist the Fed in responding to the transmitted
effects of the Asia crisis.

Second, governments appear to have a (possibly electorally based) tendency
towards excessive deficit financing – see Alesina (1988, 1989). This tendency
is currently apparent both in Europe and North America. It suggests that there
is scope for international oversight and coordination of fiscal policies. In the
presence of effective anti-inflationary monetary policies, the consequences of
such excess deficits is higher real interest rates. However, with integrated international capital markets the consequence of any *one* country doing this will
be pressure towards higher interest rates *worldwide*, augmented if this happens in a number of major countries. The world as a whole therefore has an
interest in some form of pressure on countries to constrain these international
externalities. This is a longer-term pressure, arising out of an unwillingness to
keep national savings sufficiently high by taxing at a high enough rate. Some
form of coordination (a type of intercontinental Maastricht Treaty) could help
to reduce this coordination problem (see McKibbin, 1996). By contrast, there
may be shorter-term pressures in the opposite direction: if the current downturn
persists there may be need for relaxed fiscal positions which would push in the
opposite direction; making moves in this opposite way may also be assisted by
policy cooperation.

---

[4] See Currie, Levine and Pearlman (1995, 1996).

What can be the role of the IMF in this process? Arriazu, Crow and Thygesen (1999) discuss the conduct and impact of Fund surveillance on a country-by-country basis in article IV consultations. They argue (1999, chapter IV) that this has been 'taken seriously' but that, at the same time, it does not appear that the Fund had more than an occasional impact on national policy decisions through this means. Also, this influence is exerted on a country-by-country basis, so it is difficult to configure it in such a way as to promote international policy co-ordination. Furthermore, for policies to be influenced in other-country-serving directions requires cooperation between finance ministers. So long as the Fund's activities are overseen by country Executive Directors who lack the power and influence to make the relevant tradeoffs and agreements, it will be unable to exercise this responsibility. It is therefore inevitable that any actual coordination of policies will be concentrated in the G7. However, the G7 does not have a research or policy analysis capacity. The Fund provides this facility. This puts the Fund in the position of attempting to influence international macroeconomic policy without giving it any particular cards to play.

Meyer *et al.* (chapter 3 in this volume) review the practice of such G7 surveillance over fiscal and monetary policies. In doing so, they examine the Fund's important input, which includes the preparation of surveillance papers for discussion, and in effect involves acting partly as a secretariat. The suggestion, for example, in the Report of the International Financial Institution Advisory Commission, or Meltzer Commission (henceforth IFIAC, 2000), that article IV consultations be discontinued for OECD countries in order to save resources, seems mistaken. It would lead to a diminution of resources available for, and reduced capability in, pursuing this objective. In the current global architecture, it is only the Fund which can carry out the analytical work to feed into this process. In our view, any weakening of the Fund's ability to do this is undesirable.

3 Developing countries: research assistance and policy advice

Knight, Schembri and Powell (chapter 5 in this volume) argue that the IMF has an important role to play in the provision of the best-quality advice on the advancement of technical skills for use in the promotion of strong macroeconomic policies. For richer G7 and OECD countries there is a presumption that this work is done domestically and through international intellectual connections. But there are many countries in which such policy-making capacity is limited or, in some cases, non-existent. There are four main reasons why an institution like the Fund appears important in the provision of this research and policy advice to such countries.

First, many national governments of poorer countries cannot afford or cannot get access to the necessary resources themselves. Thus the advice becomes a form of technical assistance. Second, there are economies of learning-by-doing in the making of macroeconomic policy – it is not a skill likely to be learned in the private sector. Third, there are significant economies of scale and scope in the provision of such analysis and this analysis is also an international public good (because the theory of macroeconomic policy is partly comparative). Finally, to be useful, Fund advice must stress frankly both weaknesses and required remedies; Fund assistance, when successful, consists in working with a country to help it solve its problems, including the building of policy credibility. This involves not merely one-off advice, but continuing policy assistance.

If only the first feature were important, then there might be a temptation to provide aid resources for governments of poorer countries so that they could purchase from private suppliers. But the second, third and fourth features imply that it is difficult to see how private suppliers could effectively provide this technical assistance to the required degree if it were not provided by the Fund. Learning-by-doing, economies of scale and scope and the need for a continuing relationship suggest that any attempt to substitute in this way would be dogged by market failure. Alternatively, if there were an attempt to provide this by the governments of advanced countries, then the result would be direct bilateral relationships of a quite possibly unacceptable kind. The Fund is a *multilateral* membership institution: one which gives the richer countries, and in particular the United States, a degree of legitimacy which they otherwise lack when they assist in the solution of developing country policy problems (see Woods, chapter 14 in this volume). This fact implies that proposals to weaken the ability of the Fund to provide this technical assistance, on a continuing basis, or proposals which would have this effect, should be viewed with caution. Indeed, all the crisis-prevention proposals we discuss below require a strengthening of this capability.

How should this support be provided by the IMF?

For some poorer countries, in which policy-making capability is weak, direct IMF involvement can strengthen the position of those policy-makers able to deliver good policy. Research and analysis by the IMF, and assistance with policy development, will by itself be inadequate; actual engagement in the policy-making process will be of value. Such engagement offers a route towards obtaining detailed Fund assistance in the construction of credible and coherent macroeconomic policy. What is required in these circumstances is an ongoing Fund programme, with conditionality attached. This is a means of locking in and guaranteeing good programmes in an environment in which unassisted policy-making cannot be relied upon. Fund lending is also a way of ensuring the continued engagement of the Fund. These countries are also member countries of the Fund and a direct commitment on the part of the Fund with their policy-making gives them a direct return from the organisation to which they belong. The Meltzer Commission (IFIAC, 2000) failed to acknowledge this important concern.

For countries whose policy-making capability is better developed, and in which there are not immediate adjustment problems or crises, direct IMF involvement may not be necessary. Instead research and analysis, and assistance with policy development, may be all that a country actually needs from the IMF. Although article IV Consultations are a way in which this can be provided, these lead to infrequent one-off interactions and there are other, more direct ways which will lead to more continuous involvement. In such circumstances a country does not require an IMF programme and the conditionality which accompanies it. At present a Fund programme is the only way to obtain *detailed* Fund assistance in the construction of credible and coherent macroeconomic policy-making. But many have argued that, for countries which have already partly developed policy-making capabilities, and do not have an immediate adjustment difficulty or financial crisis, this undermines ownership of policies and might, perversely, retard the very building of the policy-making capacity which is sought. This strongly suggests that a way should be found of getting more support for countries in such a position, without them remaining for long periods of time within a full Fund programme, with Fund lending and full Fund conditionality, and with all policies subject to negotiation with, and needing agreement with, the IMF. Proposals to move the Fund's long-term lending facility (the Poverty and Growth Facility) to the Bank (see Williamson, 2000) would have part of the desired effect. These proposals should be combined with a means of continuing engagement with policy-making assistance from the Fund, for countries which do not have a Fund programme.[5]

[5] There is a separate problem with conditionality not considered here. This is that increasingly the range of aspects included in conditionality has been growing beyond what is required for macroeconomic adjustment, including in particular an explicit concern with poverty reduction. This appears to have come about partly as a result of political pressures from advanced countries, arising through the Fund's multilateral governance mechanism. Many observers, including Arriazu, Crow and Thygesen (1999), IFIAC (2000) and Williamson (2000) question the wisdom of this. We concur. Indeed, there has been much work at the IMF since 2000 on reformulating conditionality, pulling back from too wide a spread of concerns on structural issues. This has led to a careful restatement during 2002 of the principles governing the IMF's implementation of conditionality, which focuses specifically on ensuring the appropriate policy for macroeconomic adjustment. See IMF (2002a, 2002b). The principles point in the direction of the IMF promoting macroeconomic adjustment policies which are poverty-reducing, but not making the IMF lending conditional on the implementation of such policies. Moves in this direction can be designed so

Crucial to the policy advice that needs to be offered is that on exchange rate regimes. This is discussed below.

4 Countries with limited capital account access: adjustment assistance

The Fund's traditional role in developing countries has been in the provision of adjustment assistance to countries with limited international capital market access. It is again useful to distinguish between countries with modern and sophisticated financial markets, and poorer developing countries with poorly developed financial markets and limited international capital market access.[6] The IMF has traditionally had an important role in the provision of adjustment assistance to such countries. We consider those countries in this section. We postpone to section 6 consideration of emerging-market economies with a high degree of international capital market access. In those countries there may be a vulnerability to capital account crisis. Assistance from the IMF may also be important, for different reasons.

For those countries with poorly developed financial markets and limited international capital market access, a worsened current account position will give rise to serious difficulties. In countries in which there is a low degree of international capital market access, in which financial markets are not well developed, policy-making capacity is poor and, crucially, policies lack credibility, external support from the IMF may be important during an adjustment period. The IMF provides liquidity support and so enables the country to spread the burden of adjustment over time, in a way which would not be possible without such lending.

For countries in this position where there is also *some* degree of capital market access, *both* such liquidity support *and* conditionality may be important. This is the position of many developing countries. For them, credibility will be partial and limited funding will be available only from private markets at a price reflecting the perceived riskiness of this lending. In these circumstances, liquidity support will lower the amount which must be borrowed from private markets, reducing its cost. In addition, the conditionality attached to the liquidity support will provide a commitment device which the borrowing government can offer to private markets, lowering the risk premium on foreign borrowing.[7] This

---

as to encourage domestic engagement as discussed in chapter 9 in this volume by Boughton and Mourmouras.

[6] Partly because of the absence of policy-making capacity discussed in section 3, and the credibility which this brings.

[7] As noted in n. 5, there has been much work at the IMF since 2000 on reformulating conditionality, which makes it more appropriate for this purpose.

reduces the costs of private inflows, enabling further intertemporal spreading of the adjustment burden and/or a lowering of the cost of adjustment by means of borrowing from the private sector. Thus, an IMF programme can spread out and/or reduce the costs of adjustment, both because of the liquidity that it offers and because of the signalling effect of that offer of liquidity (Marchesi and Thomas, 1999).

More than this, without the commitment device which conditionality brings, the country may be unable to give credible commitments to its creditors that loans will in fact be used for adjustment. The outcome of relying on private creditors at a time of adjustment difficulty may then be no private loans, leading to adjustment which is so costly that it is delayed, with the possible result of a full-scale debt crisis of the kind discussed below. Thus, more than just offering the spreading of adjustment, submitting to conditionality may enable successful adjustment where otherwise this would not be possible. In effect, the availability of conditionality can help to solve a multiple-equilibrium credibility problem. In circumstances in which policy-making capacity is not fully developed, adjustment policies can become too costly to pursue, precisely because it is feared that they will not be pursued. The outcome may be that they are not in fact pursued. Suggestions that conditionality be removed from the Fund's armoury – like those advanced by the Meltzer Commission (IFIAC, 2000) – miss this aspect of its effect. (See also chapter 4 in this volume.)

This ability to combine financial assistance with conditionality is something which private financial markets cannot match. There have been few attempts to apply such conditionality by private financial markets and we do not know of a single example of private markets doing this effectively.[8] Nor is it possible for individual advanced countries to establish and enforce such conditionality on developing countries. Neither the private sector nor developed country governments have the legitimacy to impose conditions on other governments. The Fund's ability to impose conditionality arises fundamentally from its legitimacy as a multilateral membership institution.

Crucial to the policy choices required for such countries, within such conditionality, is the choice on exchange rate regimes. Although support for quasi-fixed exchange rates has been much eroded by the Asian crises – and in a different way by the crisis in Argentina – it may be that for countries of the kind discussed in this section with limited capital market access, quasi-fixed exchange rate pegs remain possible. These could be supported in regional

---

[8] Rodrik (1995) discusses one example when in 1976 the Peruvian government allowed a consortium of US banks to impose conditions on it, and to monitor their implementation, in return for a $240 million loan. The conditions were not met, the adjustment programme was a failure and the IMF was called in the following year.

arrangements, the most successful example being that of Francophone West and Central Africa.

5 Emerging-market economies: capital account crises

We now turn to the emerging-market developing economies with open financial markets. The crises in Mexico, East Asia, Russia, Brazil, Turkey and Argentina have been precisely in those economies more integrated with the international financial system than those discussed in section 4. The opening of emerging-market economies such as these to international capital market access, while undoubtedly a precondition for long-term growth and prosperity, has increased rather than diminished their vulnerability to medium-term crisis.

The design of crisis-avoidance policy is complicated by the diversity of the crises which have overtaken middle-income countries since 1990. All of these crises were driven by problems with macroeconomic fundamentals, but in different ways. The 1995 Mexican crisis is analysable in terms of an over-valued exchange rate sustained by capital account inflows. However, the Asian crises, apart partially from the crisis in Thailand, were not caused by obvious current account imbalances. In Asia, the general problem was one of excessive, and hence unprofitable, investment financed by excessive bank lending. This was exacerbated by the use of historic cost accounting and an associated unwillingness by banks to mark loan books to market. The Russian crisis involved a sharp fall in the price of oil exports, which engendered fears about fiscal sustainability, in the presence of fiscal institutions which required oil revenue to sustain tax receipts (Kirsanaova and Vines, 2002).

In Argentina, the story is one of domestic political institutions being insufficiently strong to sustain solvency (Mussa, chapter 12 in this volume; but see Powell, chapter 13 in this volume, for a more sympathetic view). The federal government lacked the powers to control spending by provincial governments which was nevertheless financed, at the margin, out of the federal deficit. Governments were unwilling to tax sufficiently to make this deficit manageable, and the Central Bank lacked the power to regulate inefficient provincial banks. Furthermore, when crisis came, the constitutional independence of the Central Bank proved nugatory. The currency peg was only in part unsustainable for reasons of competitiveness. More important, the private sector's nominal dollar wealth at the pegged exchange rate exceeded the dollar value of the assets available in the economy. In Brazil, and in Turkey, there have been similar fears about solvency, fears which so far appear are much less firmly based.

The common element in these stories is that an open capital account exposes a country's macroeconomic policies to surveillance by the international financial markets (see Irwin, Gilbert and Vines, chapter 7 in this volume). This 'disciplining' function is far more rigorous than any surveillance by the IMF, even though there is a danger that countries may be disciplined for economic fundamentals offences of which they are not guilty.

We can summarise the circumstances by saying that crisis can develop when it becomes apparent that dollar-financed enterprises in a country might not be able to repay borrowing obligations. There are, in these circumstances, two very different types of crisis which can arise. *Solvency* crises emerge in which firms have profitable opportunities for continuing investment, but these are blocked because potential profits are not large enough to cover the interest obligations on an overhang of debt. As a result there can be bankruptcies leading to efficient investment projects being terminated early. But beyond this, *liquidity* crises can occur, even when there is solvency and no debt overhang: if all lenders roll over their loans, profitable investment can take place, but if they do not, firms are unable to meet their obligations and so they default. That is, in the presence of profitable investment opportunities, and without any debt overhang, there is nevertheless the possibility of a default which can be self-fulfilling. Countries can suffer from what is, in effect, a form of 'bank-run'.

Vulnerability to solvency crises can be enhanced by the widespread use of implicit guarantees, including those of pegged exchange rates (Corbett and Vines, 1999a, 1999b; Dooley, 1999). Knight, Schembri and Powell (chapter 5 in this volume) argue that these guarantees arise through the attempts of emerging-market governments to manage the intermediation between the virtually complete financial markets of industrial countries and the distorted financial market structures in their own countries. A solvency crisis can develop when it becomes apparent that firms will not be able to repay borrowing obligations because governments might not be able to meet guarantees on them. It has become clear that quasi-fixed exchange rates are unmanageable in such regimes and that the guarantee of quasi-fixed exchange rate regimes adds to the problems just described. The pressure towards crisis grows when it becomes apparent that Central Banks might not be able to meet the guarantees embodied in fixing the exchange rate.

The risks involved in borrowing in foreign currency were downplayed in Asia because of implicit guarantees that the fixed exchange rates of currencies in the region would not be changed. The problem was exacerbated by the use of interest rates above world rates to restrain booming domestic demand. The result was a build-up of unhedged short-term foreign- currency-denominated debt, as companies sought to escape high domestic interest rates by borrowing at lower rates in dollars: firms had high debt to equity ratios, and the debt was liquid and in foreign currencies. When weaknesses became apparent, dollar creditors became unwilling to roll over loans and attempted to enforce repayment in dollars, ahead of other creditors.[9] In Korea, Indonesia and Malaysia contagion seems to have been a central cause: a belief that if currency collapse could happen in Thailand it could also happen elsewhere. As the crises developed and currencies fell, the value of outstanding obligations in terms of domestic currency rose beyond what companies could afford to pay, making creditors all the more unwilling to roll loans over.[10] But it may also have reflected a view that some of the fundamental problems evident in Thailand were also present, perhaps to a lesser extent, in these other countries.

Crisis resolution

In the face of the vulnerability to crisis described above, there is a natural wish on the part of both governments and the electorates that support them for an international financial architecture in which these crises can be managed and in which the likelihood of future crises can be reduced (Institute for International Finance, 2002). The IMF and the G7 are the two institutions which have been in a position to respond to this perceived demand.

There is a need for greater clarity in this new architecture about the required role for the IMF. The US Treasury and the IMF have both argued that there should be a more straightforward and efficient process for sovereign debt restructuring, either through collective action clauses in sovereign bonds

[9] The impossibility of using monetary policy to stabilise the economy, when there are both fixed exchange rates and a high degree of capital mobility, has been clear for a long time. The Asian experience has strengthened the understanding that this is true for lower degrees of capital mobility, and that the resulting problems are connected with the emergence of foreign currency-denominated debt. Stabilisation of the economy under fixed exchange rate requires a greater degree of fiscal activism than was contemplated at the time in Asia.

[10] The risk of currency crises is exacerbated by the potential for multiple equilibria in determining whether there is a solvency crisis. Suppose that the risk of default is low and that the interest rate which must be paid on foreign borrowing is low. Let there be a negative shock to the economy. Then, because of the low interest rate, the government can afford to pay its guarantees to those firms which default. It is possible that this good equilibrium is the only equilibrium, even in the short run. This will be the case if the stock of outstanding guarantees is 'not too large'. But it may be that there is also the possibility of another bad, crisis, equilibrium. If foreign banks fear that there is a range of potentially bad shocks to the country, sufficiently bad that the government might renege on its guarantees in the event that such bad shocks materialise, then they will raise the interest rate (to an extent dependent, of course, on the probability of these bad shocks). But by doing so they increase the cost to the government of meeting its guarantees. It might be the case that if they do this there is a range of shocks sufficiently bad that the government has no choice but to renege on its promises. This validates the fear of the foreign banks, implying that the crisis is an equilibrium outcome (see Irwin and Vines, 2003).

(Taylor, 2002), or through the institution of a sovereign debt reconstruction mechanism (SDRM) (Krueger, 2001, 2002). The Bank of England and Bank of Canada have argued for an enhanced role for debt standstills and lending into arrears by the IMF (Haldane and Kruger, chapter 8 in this volume). All of these sets of proposals have been put forward as an alternative to the IMF attempting to act as a lender of last resort (Fischer, 1999). The following discussion draws upon Haldane, Irwin and Saporta (2002) and Irwin and Vines (2004).

Liquidity crises

We have described two potential kinds of crisis above. Liquidity crises differ from 'solvency crises' in which there is the difficulty that borrowers cannot repay their loans. In a liquidity crisis it is short-term debt service and not long-term repayment that is at issue. Korea in 1997 may be an example. In such a liquidity crisis the belief held by the international lenders that firms in the borrowing country will default is self-fulfilling: because the international banks expect a firm to default they stop lending, and as a result the firm is forced to default. But if they were to continue to lend the full amount in the second period the investment would be sufficiently profitable for the firm to repay its loans with interest. Essentially there is a *coordination problem* among international lenders. The challenge is to ensure that sufficient financing is available in the second period. One way of sharpening criticisms of the IMF's responses to the Asian crisis (for example, Stiglitz, 2001) is to argue that the Fund mistakenly saw the entire group of countries as subject to a solvency crisis. By contrast, Malaysian Prime Minister Mahatir correctly viewed the problem in Malaysia as primarily one of maintaining liquidity.

There are three possible responses to liquidity crises which, on the face of it, are equally effective in dealing with the problem: creditor committees, IMF financing and standstills. We consider each in turn. Creditor committees enable the international banks lending to each individual firm to coordinate their lending decisions in the period after a crisis emerges. The outcome will be efficient *ex post*. Of course, ensuring the coordination required for creditor committees will be difficult.[11]

The second possibility, in response to this, might be provided by IMF lending. Suppose that international banks call in their loans in response to a crisis. If the IMF bridges the full financing gap by lending to the firms, either directly or through the government, the international banks can receive a full repayment of their first-period loans with interest, and the full investment can be maintained

---

[11] Haldane, Irwin and Saporta (2002) demonstrate that an aggregation problem may arise when coordination is required across firms. This means that creditor committees can provide only a partial solution to the liquidity crisis problem.

by the firms. The investment would be sufficiently profitable for the IMF to be repaid in due course with interest at the market rate, which would cover the opportunity cost of the Fund's lending. This financing does not involve any element of a subsidy. With this intervention all of the parties are made better off and any inefficiency from the early liquidation of the investment projects is avoided. The outcome will also be efficient *ex post*. The difficulty with this approach may be the inability of the IMF to mobilise sufficient funds to provide what is required. But in the face of a liquidity crisis, an expansion in the ability of the IMF to lend is what is needed.

Difficulties in achieving this lead us to the third possibility – that of a standstill. Under a standstill the international banks are prevented from calling in their loans and are therefore forced to roll over their lending. However, on its own this may be insufficient to ensure that investments are sustained after a crisis. This is because, in order for this to be possible, a net inflow of capital may be required, just to cover the operating costs of existing development projects, in the period until these projects have become self-financing and then profitable. If there is no additional financing and just a standstill, the size of investment activity will have to be curtailed, making it less likely that all borrowing costs will be able to be recovered. For this reason, standstills alone will reduce, but not eliminate, the range over which liquidity crises occur. A solution to this problem could be found if, at the same time as the standstill is called, IMF lending into arrears provided the extra funding. This would require a greater willingness by the IMF to engage in lending into arrears than appears to be the case at present.

Solvency crises

In a solvency crisis international lenders call in their loans and bankruptcies emerge in the borrowing country. This outcome is clearly inefficient. To achieve an efficient outcome sufficient financing must be available to make it possible for investment to be maintained – some means must be found for dealing with the overhang of debt. Clearly, standstills and creditor committees will, by themselves, be insufficient to deal with the problem since what is needed is an injection of money to cover the debt overhang.

By contrast, IMF financing can potentially provide a solution, providing that (1) the lending is at a sufficiently subsidised rate to deal with the overhang, so that firms do not default, or (2) the borrowing government repays the IMF in due course, *and* injects the required extra funds into the balance sheets of the failed investments which led to the crisis circumstances. There is obviously a cost of doing this which must be borne by the governments of the creditor countries which effectively finance the IMF, or by the governments of the borrowing countries. However, one or other of these parties may be willing to bear the costs. The governments of lending countries may be willing to bear this cost, because of the benefit to the international banks. Alternatively, the governments of borrowing countries may be willing to bear the costs, because of the benefits from avoiding crisis.

The final possibility is for the borrowers[12] in the developing country and international banks to negotiate a write-down of the first-period debt. If this write-down is sufficiently large, borrowing firms in the indebted country will not default, and so international banks will be willing to provide sufficient financing to allow their investment to continue. When will it be possible to write down debt so as to prevent a default? Clearly we require that, with continued financing, the firms have a positive value, and so the owners of the firms are better off than if they defaulted. The international banks are also better off lending in the period after the crisis, providing that they get more than they would if the firms simply defaulted. It can be shown (Irwin and Vines, 2002) that both of these things are possible provided the investments are profitable, looking into the future, after the write-down has dealt with the debt overhang.[13]

We have argued that both IMF financing at a subsidised rate and write-downs can provide alternative, but equally effective, responses to solvency crises: either can enable investments to go forward and reduce the inefficiencies caused by the crisis. However, the use of these devices is likely to be constrained. The use of IMF lending to solve solvency crises would be constrained if there were limits on the scale of IMF lending to a particular country at a time of crisis. Furthermore, debt write-downs might lead to collective-action problems between the creditors. There is the risk of litigation by creditors against the debtor (Krueger, 2002), and also a risk of some creditors holding out against an agreed write-down of debts in the hope of a more favourable settlement (Haldane, Irwin and Saporta, 2002).

More than this, the methods chosen to resolve crises may create incentives, *ex ante*, for inefficiencies in the decision to invest by firms or in the form of investment financing which results. If the IMF is expected to provide subsidised financing in the event of a solvency crisis, lenders have an incentive to *minimise* the amount of the investment that is financed by their own equity and to maximise the amount which is financed by borrowing which will be bailed out

---

[12] There will be differences depending on whether the majority of outstanding debt is owned by the government or by private firms. These cases will merge into each other to the extent that, as happened to a large extent in the Asian crisis, a large proportion of the outstanding private debt is taken over by the government.

[13] There will be major differences if the outstanding debt is owed mainly by the government or mainly by the private sector. Lenders to public institutions cannot take equity positions in exchange for non-performing debt, and also it will not normally be possible to realise assets. This makes it much harder to resolve sovereign rather than private sector crises, and provides a further argument against the acquisition of private risks by the public sector.

if there is a crisis (Irwin and Vines, 2002). This is because doing this increases the expected value of the subsidy they receive in the event of a solvency crisis: lending is bailed out whereas equity investment bears the risk of loss in the kind of bad outcome which leads to crisis. IMF lending, designed as a way of solving solvency crises, generates moral hazard. This is a fundamental reason for moving in the direction of debt write-downs and away from the expectation of continued bailout at the time of crisis.

Repositioning Fund response in the face of crises

A lender of last resort (LOLR) is one which lends freely against good collateral (King, 1999). It is impossible to avoid the conclusion from the above that the IMF is not in a position to provide LOLR financing. The IMF lacks the resources to do this, but in any case, it is undesirable that it should act in this way.

The above discussion has drawn the distinction between liquidity crises and solvency crises. In the first of these we have argued that financing should if possible be forthcoming. In this case, investments in the country are profitable, looking forward. The revenue from them provides collateral: and borrowers will be able to repay in due course. In such a crisis, an effective LOLR must be willing to lend whatever it takes to prevent a run on liquidity. However the IMF may not be able to lend freely in such circumstances: the IMF lacks both sufficient resources to obtain the needed funds and the power to command taxation to gain these resources. The current resources of the IMF – between $125 billion and $150 billion, depending on how they are measured – are wholly inadequate for an international LOLR. It is clear that the IMF does not have the resources to make loans, of the size made in the East Asian crisis, in the face of future crises. In a world with a very high degree of capital mobility, the IMF may not have sufficient resources to deal with a crisis simply through the provision of 'jumbo loans'; what the IMF can lend may be dwarfed by what those withdrawing funds from a country will be able to mobilise.[14] This suggests that, in the case of a liquidity crisis, there may not be the capability for the continued lending which would be desirable. Instead there may be a need for standstills and lending into arrears (rather than the write-down which, it has been argued, is what is required in the case of a solvency crisis).

---

[14] This problem is complicated by the fact that, in the East Asian crisis, lending was organised from the World Bank as well as from the IMF. Injecting large sums of money into short-run financial crises is not the function of the World Bank. Its lending role involves the provision of long-term loans for long-term development purposes (see Gilbert, Powell and Vines 1999). Beyond this, lending was concerted from a group of OECD countries. But arrangements for doing this were vague and informal. It does not seem that there is the willingness to make large loans in this way in the face of future crises (King, 1999).

There is an important analogy here with US Chapter 11 bankruptcy. In Chapter 11 bankruptcy proceedings it is possible for a firm to escape from the crisis without its assets actually being written down; but the proceedings are still important because they enable the company to be given a stay of respite from its creditors. We need the Fund to help make possible standstills on interest and debt repayments, and to do 'lending into arrears'. The Fund needs to be able to do this even when there is not the prospect of sovereign debt restructuring at the end of the process.

The lesson from the Korean crisis at the end of 1997 is that, if successful, standstills can benefit all parties. The Korean crisis was one of liquidity, with no underlying solvency problem. Although payments were not formally suspended, considerable pressure was collectively applied on banks to roll over lending which had fallen due. However, in the fullness of time, Korean debt has been repaid and the banks collectively have not suffered. Once the possibility of standstills becomes institutionally formalised, this may raise lending rates to all emerging-market economies. Nevertheless, we believe that this fear is likely to be exaggerated.

By contrast in the case of a solvency crisis, the IMF should *not* lend freely. In this case, there will not be good collateral. IMF lending will solve the crisis only if it is subsidised (or if the government of the borrowing country meets a proportion of the cost out of its tax revenues). The discussion above suggested that the preferred outcome in such circumstances is a debt write-down: there needs to be clear limits on how much the Fund will normally lend to a country in such a solvency crisis before the need for a debt reconstruction is triggered. Establishment of such clear limits is clearly difficult. But without such limits, lenders see the possibility of the IMF lending saving them from the need for a reduction in the value of their debt in the case of such solvency crises. This sets up *ex ante* pressures for excess willingness to lend by lenders. These are moral hazard pressures, created by the belief that such crises will be solved by IMF lending. Borrowing countries also hope that there will be continuing loans rather than a need to declare a standstill, or to default and renegotiate their debt. This sets up further moral hazard pressures: *ex ante* pressures for excess borrowing by countries. Such an approach identifies the Fund's discretion to act as part of the problem, rather than part of the solution. The imposition of lending limits – which act as a barrier against attempting to act as a LOLR in the face of solvency crises – is thus necessary to solve the moral hazard problem. Creditors would know that if a solvency difficulty developed then they would suffer write-downs.

This has clear implications for requests for the IMF to become a LOLR. To others it should have the resources to lend in the face of liquidity crises. But it may lack these currently, and this is something which would need to be remedied. By contrast, an attempt to lend in this way in the face of solvency crises may create moral hazard. Limits on IMF lending, and its replacement by standstills, coupled by lending into arrears, may thus be needed in the face of liquidity crises, even though such lending would in principle be desirable. Limits on lending in the face of solvency crises will be desirable, to avoid moral hazard problems.

This discussion raises a difficult signal extraction problem. As the proposed approach requires different responses to liquidity and solvency crises, it is important that the IMF is able to distinguish between different types of crisis. But this may not always be possible; a lack of timely information might make this judgement subjective and probabilistic. A mistake could have consequences more serious than those already discussed. It will be the case that dealing with a liquidity crisis speedily is important – to prevent a worsening of the fundamentals and so make a future solvency crisis less likely. Such arguments have been used recently in the case of Brazil. But if the perceived liquidity crisis is in fact an emerging solvency crisis, then dealing with it as a liquidity crisis may delay the onset of the solvency crisis and may make the cost much worse. This appears to be what happened in the case of Argentina.[15] This suggests that much more work is required on what to do if there are signs of an emerging crisis but insufficient indication of which kind.

In the light of this difficulty in determining the nature of a crisis, those representing borrowing countries always lobby for liquidity support, and those representing lending countries (effectively, the United States and some Western European governments) do this too, to prevent borrowing countries having to declare standstills or defaulting on loans. The result is likely to be a form of continual 'denial' which will be perpetuated in the absence of some institutional reform at this level. The Fund, even though it has insufficient money, finds itself under pressure to make larger and larger loans in the hope of providing at least some partial alleviation of the crisis in the short term. Furthermore, these demands extend to the World Bank, threatening funding for longer-term development. This is a classic time-inconsistency problem: in the long term, financial stability would be better served by recognising this weakness. But simply promising that intervention on a similar scale will not occur in the future lacks credibility: the Fund will always be under pressure, in the event of another crisis, to act 'one last time', especially if it is not clear what kind of crisis is at hand. In these circumstances, the Fund is at risk of assisting countries in 'gambling for resurrection'. Unlimited liquidity support will enable the borrower to postpone adjustment, in the hope of a better outcome, but risking the development of further debt which may lead to a need for sovereign debt crisis in subsequent periods. This is the analysis of Mussa (chapter 12

[15] Matters are even more complex if, as discussed above, the question as to whether a crisis is a solvency crisis partly depends on the government's response on whether to meet the outstanding interest obligations of domestic firms.

in this volume) concerning Argentina. Earlier adjustment would avoid this, but IMF lending in the earlier stages may make it possible to postpone this adjustment.

This discussion suggests a role for IMF 'conditionality'. If the Fund sets clear limits on how much it will normally lend to any country in such a crisis, and this is combined with standstills or a debt write-down, the country in crisis must set in train processes of adjustment. Conditionality becomes the means of ensuring that borrowing countries can live within the standstills or requirements of debt write-down until they regain access to the international credit market.

Setting limits and imposing conditionality is difficult. But, without the commitment device which conditionality brings, the country may be unable to give credible commitments to its creditors that there will in fact be adjustment. The outcome of relying on private creditors at a time of adjustment difficulty may then be very high interest rates which bring forward the solvency crisis. Thus, more than just offering the spreading of adjustment in return for loans, as in section 4, submitting to conditionality may enable successful adjustment where otherwise this would not be possible. In effect, the availability of conditionality can help to solve a multiple-equilibrium credibility problem.[16]

Significant steps have been taken in formalising the position of the Fund in the last two years. It is now generally accepted that the IMF cannot be a LOLR, and the Fund is itself working on the SDRM and Collective Action Mechanisms for countries facing solvency crises. But these mechanisms will not deal with liquidity crises. The challenge for the IMF over the coming years will be not just to solve problems of solvency crisis. It will also need to move forward to elucidate whether and how it can obtain the funds necessary to lend in the face of liquidity crises. It will further need to be clear on the circumstances in which, when it cannot obtain the required finances, it will endorse the suspension of payments by countries facing a liquidity crisis, and to make clear when it will lend into arrears in such circumstances, and by how much. This will require the establishment of *ex ante* criteria for the imposition of payments standstills, in order to give private sector lenders a greater degree of clarity about when this will happen, and so make the process an orderly one when it does occur. There is now a commitment on the part of the G7 countries to work in the direction of formalising how such 'constrained discretion' would operate in the solution of crises.

If such a framework can be devised, then how the IMF operates in a crisis will become more formalised. Progress on the SDRM and Collective Action Mechanisms for countries will be needed. But, in addition, the IMF will need

[16] See IMF (2002a, 2002b) and the discussion of this issue in nn. 5 and 7. See also Blejer *et al.* (2002) for a discussion of how to modify IMF conditionality, traditionally specified in terms of monetary aggregates and international reserves, for economies with open international financial markets.

to commit credibly to assisting a debtor with liquidity support, beyond a certain limit, only in truly exceptional circumstances. At the same time, it will need a credible commitment to keeping open the option of allowing a payments standstill. Some means must be found to ward off undue pressure against this outcome, pressure which is likely to come from the United States and the governments of other countries in which lending banks and bondholders are located. Such a mechanism, if it can be found, will prevent the burden of liquidity crises from falling entirely on borrowing countries. It will spread the burden of crisis-without-liquidity-support onto lenders, and lessen debt overhangs.

Crisis prevention

What should be done to *prevent* crises? If crises are driven by poor fundamentals, the governments of middle-income countries must take the long-term coherence of their macroeconomic policies and the strength of their institutional structures more seriously. This was a lesson painfully learned by the governments and electorates of the developed economies in the 1970s and 1980s. Middle-income countries can benefit from the experience of the developed economies. This will involve movement towards floating exchange rate regimes. Monetary policy should be based around inflation targeting in an environment in which Central Banks are fully independent.

Despite this, there will be further crises in the future. To the extent that crisis prevention is not possible, attention should focus on minimising the pain that these crises cause. An important reason why the developed economies have, since 1929, and at least until the present, appeared immune to financial crisis, is that developed economy financial systems have proved able to cushion these economies against very severe contractions. This was true of the United Kingdom in 1976 and the US Savings and Loans (S&L) crisis in the mid-1980s (although it has been less true of Japan since 1990). This points to the conclusion of Knight, Schembri and Powell (chapter 5 in this volume) that 'emerging-market economies must take bold steps to vastly broaden and improve the efficiency of their domestic financial markets', in such a way as to improve this cushioning. This will require the support, encouragement and assistance of the industrial countries and the international financial institutions.

The limited significance of the Meltzer Commission proposals

An alternative response to the evolution of the IMF in a crisis-prone world was developed in the 'Meltzer Commission' Report (IFIAC, 2000) – see also chapter 4 in this volume. At its core this report identified the Fund's discretion to act as part of the problem to be dealt with, because it creates moral hazard. In this there is similarity with the argument presented above. But the Meltzer Commission's proposed solution to this problem is very different from ours, and from the solutions currently being worked on at the IMF. Specifically, the Commission proposed formal constraints around a remaining LOLR function for the Fund. We believe this approach to be fundamentally misguided.

The Meltzer Report favoured 'quasi-LOLR lending' in the case of macroeconomic imbalances and of financial crisis. But it presented a list of qualifications which would hedge in this lending to the extent of making the Fund a LOLR in name only. The restrictive features proposed were as follows.

(a) Pre-qualification for assistance would substitute for negotiation of policy reforms upon the onset of crisis; lending programmes would therefore no longer need to involve conditionality.
(b) Lending would be confined to solvent countries with 'fundamentally sound policies and finances', i.e. to solvent countries.
(c) Lending would be for a short term only, e.g. 'a maximum of 120 days with only one allowable rollover'. This is premised on the view that any crisis would be one of liquidity.
(d) Credit limits would 'restrict the amount of assistance that a country can receive from the IMF'. These would 'reflect the capacity of the sovereign to repay its debt to the IMF'. 'A borrowing limit equal to one year's tax revenues might be a reasonable credit limit.'
(e) When crises occur, governments and the private sector should be left to resolve claims, unimpeded by any IMF intervention, or payments standstills.

We regard these proposals as highly problematic for four reasons.

(1) Pre-qualification fails to deal with the moral hazard problem. Williamson (2000) points out that problems would arise if circumstances began to deteriorate, or good policies began to be abandoned, in a country which had pre-qualified. In these circumstances it would be very difficult to withdraw pre-qualification, because that in itself might provoke crisis, and this could promote moral hazard. Also, pre-qualification fails to deal with the consequences of a crisis in an important non-qualifying country; it would be much better to attempt to prevent the crisis from developing instead of having to prevent contagion in other qualified countries. As a result, countries in breach of pre-qualification conditions would remain pre-qualified and would receive loans, *and* the commitment to deny lending to important non-qualifying countries would be incredible. We believe that the pre-qualification system would almost completely unravel.

(2) The proposals fail to make the distinction between liquidity and solvency crises. At best, its proposals would address liquidity crises since insolvent countries would fail to pre-qualify for assistance. However, as we have noted, it may be difficult to be confident *ex ante* whether a country is solvent since this will depend partly on what shocks the country experiences and partly on its policy responses to these shocks. Some pre-qualified countries are therefore likely to turn out to be insolvent, and non-conditional limited-term lending will be insufficient to allow them to resolve this problem. In any case, the IMF does not have, and is unlikely ever to have, sufficient funds to act as a lender of last resort.

(3) The Meltzer Report fails to recognise the importance of the fact that the IMF is a membership organisation, and that its legitimacy stems from the fact that, in joining the IMF, governments accept the obligation to act in accordance with the IMF's rules (see Woods, chapter 14 in this volume). IMF membership is not obligatory and some governments prefer not to accept these obligations. Those governments that do join must expect some return, and will not always regard a contingent return as acceptable. This effectively rules out pre-qualification and requires the Fund to provide regular advice and consultation to those countries which express a requirement for this form of assistance.

(4) The Meltzer proposals offer very little to the poorest countries, most of whom are likely to find difficulty in pre-qualifying for assistance. Further, there is little likelihood that any crises that these countries experience will be regarded as having systemic implications. It is therefore unlikely that, under the Meltzer Commission proposals, they will have any possibility of availing themselves of the LOLR facility.

None of this is to minimise the importance of the moral hazard issue. However, by focusing on the elimination of moral hazard, implementation of the Meltzer proposals would substantially reduce the effectiveness of the IMF and thereby leave the world more exposed to crises than currently.

6 Implications for the IMF

The IMF as an institution now finds itself with important strategic choices reviewed in this chapter, and in the present volume.

First, the Fund needs to sustain its role in the international coordination of macroeconomic policies with the G7. The position of fiscal policy in this may be important. If the downturn which has characterised the initial years of the twenty-first century persists over a longer period, there may be need for a more relaxed fiscal position, which may also be assisted by such policy cooperation. Second, the Fund should also find a better way of continuing to work on policy development with countries over the longer term, including with countries which do not have a continuing Fund programme.

Third, the Fund needs to solve problems relating to the prevention and resolution of crises. This has been the major focus of this chapter. King (1999) writes with regard to this 'the present system is not sustainable. The danger is that we have the worst of both worlds. The IMF may lend large amounts, create moral hazard in doing so, and still not be able to ward off the threat of financial crises'. There needs to be a mechanism for declaring debts to be excessive and either by collective creditor action, enabled by collective action clauses, or through the sovereign debt reconstruction mechanism, writing down the value of debts. There also needs to be a mechanism which goes beyond this and allows the Fund to help to deal with liquidity crises, even if there is not a prospect of ultimate debt write-downs and reconstruction. Finally, there needs to be more clarity about what the Fund will do in the face of crises. This involves limiting what it will do in the case of solvency crises. In the case of liquidity crises, doing this involves ensuring that the Fund is able to lend enough to help resolve such crises. It also involves being clear about what the IMF will do with regard to standstills, and about lending into arrears, if it cannot lend enough. Clarifying what the Fund does in crisis circumstances is the central challenge facing it as an institution.

REFERENCES

Alesina, A. (1988). 'Macroeconomics and Politics', *NBER Macroeconomics Annual*, 3, 13–62

(1989). 'Politics and Business Cycles in Industrial Democracies', *Economic Policy*, 8, 55–98

Arriazu, R., J. Crow and N. Thygesen (1999). 'External Evaluation of IMF Surveillance'. Washington: International Monetary Fund

Blejer, M., A. Leone, P. Rabanal and G. Schwartz (2002). 'Inflation Targeting in the Context of IMF-Supported Adjustment Programs', IMF Staff Papers, 49 (3)

Corbett, J. and D. Vines (1999a). 'Asian Currency and Financial Crises: Lessons from Vulnerability, Crisis, and Collapse', *World Economy*, 22(2), 155–77

(1999b). 'The Asian Crisis: Lessons from the Collapse of Financial Systems, Exchange Rates, and Macroeconomic Policy', in R. Agénor, M. Miller, D. Vines and A. Weber, *The Asian Financial Crises: Causes, Contagion, and Consequences*. Cambridge, Cambridge University Press

Currie, D. D. A., P. Levine and J. Pearlman (1995). 'Can Delegation be Counterproductive? The Choice of Conservative Bankers in Open Economies', CEPR Discussion Paper, 1148

(1996). 'The Choice of Conservative Bankers in Open Economies: Monetary Policy Options for Europe', *Economic Journal*, 106, 3245–58

Dooley, M. P. (1999). 'Are Recent Capital Inflows to Developing Countries a Vote for or Against Economic Policy Reforms?', reprinted in a revised form in R. Agénor, M. Miller, D. Vines and A. Weber (eds), *The Asian Financial Crises: Causes, Contagion, and Consequences*, Cambridge, Cambridge University Press

Fischer, S. (1999). 'On the Need for an International Lender of Last Resort', revised version of address to American Economic Association, www.imf.org

Gardiner, R. N. (1956). *Sterling-Dollar Diplomacy*, Oxford, Clarendon Press

Gilbert, C. L., A. Powell and D. Vines (1999). 'Positioning the World Bank', *Economic Journal*, 109 (459), 598–634

Haldane, A. G., G. Irwin and V. Saporta (2002). 'Bail-Out or Work-Out?: Theoretical Considerations', Bank of England, mimeo

Harrod, R. (1952) *The Life of John Maynard Keynes*. London, Macmillan

IFIAC (2000). *Report of the International Financial Institution Advisory Commission* (Meltzer Commission). Washington, DC, Department of the Treasury

International Monetary Fund (2000a). 'Conditionality in Fund Supported Programmes – Policy Issues', available at http://www.imf.org/External/np/pdr/cond/2002/eng/guid/092302.htm

(2000b). 'Guidelines on Conditionality', available at http://www.imf.org/external/np/pdr/cond/ 2001/eng/policy/021601.pdf

Irwin, G. and D. Vines (2003). 'Government Guarantees, Investment, and Vulnerability to Financial Crises', *Review of International Economics*, forthcoming

(2004). 'The Efficient Resolution of International Capital Account Crises: How to avoid Moral Hazard', London, Bank of England, Working Papers, forthcoming

Keynes, J. M. (1971). *The Collected Writings of John Maynard Keynes,* ed. D. Moggridge, London, Macmillan

King, M. (1999). 'Reforming the International Financial System: The Middle Way', speech delivered to a session of the Money Marketeers at the Federal Reserve Bank of New York, 9 September

Kirsanaova, T. and D. Vines (2002). 'Government Budget, Oil Prices and Currency Crises in Russia', mimeo

Krueger, A. (2001). 'International Financial Architecture for 2002: A New Approach to Sovereign Debt Restructuring', IMF, mimeo

(2002). "A New Approach to Sovereign Debt Restructuring", IMF

McKibbin, W. (1996). 'Disinflation, Fiscal Consolidation, and the Role of Monetary and Fiscal Regimes', Australian National University, Canberra, mimeo

Marchesi, S. and J. P. Thomas (1999). 'IMF Conditionality as a Screening Device', *Economic Journal*, 109, C111–25

Matthews, R. C. O. and A. Bowen (1988). 'Keynesian and Other Explanations of Postwar Macroeconomic Trends', in W. A. Eltis and P. J. N. Sinclair (eds.), *Keynes and Economic Policy*. London, NEDO

Matthews, R. C. O., C. H. Feinstein and J. C. Odling-Smee (1982). *British Economic Growth 1956–73*. Oxford, Clarendon Press

Meade, J. E. (1988). *Collected Papers, Volume IV: The Cabinet Office Diary of James Meade, 1944–46,* eds. S. Howson and D. Moggridge. London, Unwin Hyman

Moggridge, D. (1986). 'Keynes and the International Monetary System, 1909–1946', in J. S. Cohen and G. C. Harcourt (eds.), *International Monetary Problems and Supply Side Economics: Essays in Honour of Lorie Tarshis.* London, Macmillan (1992). *Maynard Keynes: An Economists' Biography.* London, Routledge

Rodrik, D. (1995). 'Why is there Multilateral Lending?', CEPR Discussion Papers, 1207

Stiglitz, J. E. (2001). *Globalization and its Discontents.* Harmondsworth, Allen Lane

Taylor, J. (2002). 'Sovereign Debt Restructuring – A US Perspective', Washington, DC, US Department of the Treasury

van Doormael, A. (1978). *Bretton Woods: Birth of a Monetary System.* London, Macmillan

Williamson, J. (2000). 'The Role of the IMF: A Guide to the Reports', Washington, DC, Institute for International Economics, mimeo

2 Progress towards greater international financial stability

ANDREW CROCKETT

1 Introduction

The decade of the 1990s saw a series of international financial crises on a scale and frequency unprecedented in the post-war period. The economic costs were high, spillover effects were widespread and the political and social consequences were severe. Not surprisingly, calls for the reform of the international financial architecture mounted.

Since 1998 there has been a plethora of international conferences devoted to this general theme. To those who expected them to result in a new 'system', comparable in its coherence and comprehensiveness to the Bretton Woods arrangements, the outcome of these deliberations is no doubt a disappointment.

But this would be to set the wrong standard. There is no brand new 'system' waiting to be discovered. What has been achieved (*inter alia* through programmes such as the one sponsored by the ESRC), however, is a better understanding of the strengths and weaknesses of current arrangements. From this flows an agenda of incremental reforms that, if carefully pursued, should result in a stronger and more efficient international monetary system.

There is no realistic alternative to an economic system based on decentralised market forces. This has been virtually universally accepted at the national level since the collapse of centrally planned economic systems in the late 1980s. And it applies equally at the international level. When governments attempt to control decisions about the allocation of real resources, they typically introduce rigidities and inefficiencies that outweigh any benefits stemming from the pursuit of social objectives in economic decisions.

But this does not mean that markets can be left to themselves, either nationally or internationally. Economics teaches us that free markets allocate resources efficiently only under conditions of perfect competition, and these rarely apply in their most rigorous form. Public policy therefore has to deal with circumstances of market failure.

36

Some forms of market failure have been well understood for a long time. Perhaps the best known is monopoly. Nobody disputes the need for governments to either break up monopolies or to regulate them in the public interest. But there are other types of market failure, particularly common in markets for the intertemporal exchange of value, that have been analysed in depth only more recently. Many of them fall under the general heading of 'asymmetric information'.

Asymmetric information introduces inefficiencies into markets that lead to suboptimal outcomes, and in some cases to volatility and multiple equilibria. Capital markets are particularly prone to problems of asymmetric information. This is unfortunate, since financial markets have come to play the central role in the international monetary system. Exchange rates for most currencies are now determined by supply and demand in private markets. Liquidity is created as a by-product of credit granted in private markets. And the adjustment process is largely governed by private capital flows. If capital markets function inefficiently, or are subject to volatility, the consequences are potentially widespread.

All of this has major implications for the architecture of the international monetary system. It means that the rules that govern international financial relations, and the institutions that monitor them, have to be directed towards making capital markets function better, rather than to supplanting private markets with officially directed flows.

In what follows, I will begin by looking at the recent history of financial crises. This will provide the background against which to analyse the causes and consequences of financial market failures. Next, I will consider how international financial arrangements have evolved over the post-war period and what are the central features of the present architecture. After that I will discuss how the architecture needs to be reformed, both with regard to the 'rules of the game' that govern international financial relations, and with regard to the institutional structure for managing, monitoring and adapting these rules. Finally, I will have something to say about whether changes are needed in the way we handle the periodic crises that are bound to afflict the system.

2 Recent financial crises

Four serious crises occurred in the 1990s that warrant attention for the lessons they convey about vulnerabilities in international financial arrangements. They are the ERM crisis in 1992–3; the Mexican crisis of 1994–5; the East Asian crisis of 1997–8; and the Russian/LTCM crisis of Autumn 1998. (There were of course a host of other crises of lesser magnitude, or confined to one country.)

The ERM crisis, 1992–1993

The *ERM crisis* occurred when market participants lost confidence in the willingness of European countries to maintain currency parities against the D-Mark. Up until the middle of 1992, expectations of a smooth transition to monetary union had given rise to strong stabilising capital flows. These 'convergence plays' had caused interest rates spreads to narrow, in effect creating easier monetary conditions in certain countries with pre-existing inflationary pressures. Divergences in economic circumstances, resulting from the reunification of Germany, were largely discounted.

Following the negative result of the Danish referendum on the Maastricht Treaty, doubts about the process of monetary union began to mount. Capital flows tended to be reversed and could be contained only through a renewed widening of spreads. Widened spreads, however, far from demonstrating countries' commitment to stick to their ERM parities, served to cast doubt on the sustainability of the arrangement. In some cases – Italy, for example – higher interest rates meant that the cost of servicing the high outstanding debt level rose alarmingly. In others – such as Britain – rising interest rates further intensified the depression in the housing sector, and placed severe strains on mortgage-holders.

Eventually, several ERM member countries, as well as some non-members that had pegged their exchange rate to the DM, were forced by massive speculative pressure to either realign or to abandon pegging arrangements altogether. The following year, speculative pressures returned, and resulted in a widening of the exchange rate bands to ±15 per cent.

The ERM crisis was an example of what came in the literature to be called a 'second-generation' type of exchange rate crisis. That is to say, it was caused not by an unsustainable balance of payments position (France had a comfortable surplus, but was still the victim of massive outflows) but by a perception that the domestic policies required to maintain the exchange rate would ultimately prove unsustainable. The markets were in effect betting that there was a dual equilibrium and that the authorities would be unwilling to pay the price of adhering to their preferred equilibrium and would be forced to accept the second best.

The Mexican crisis, 1994–1995

The Mexican peso crisis that broke out at the end of 1994 had some of the same elements. Mexico had experienced heavy capital flows and upward pressure on its currency for several years until early 1994. External investors had been impressed by the pace of economic liberalisation in the country, and had (too) readily accepted the argument (advanced by Finance Minister Pedro Aspe, and endorsed by a wide spectrum of influential opinion) that because the government had no significant budget deficit, it was protected against a currency crisis. Not enough attention was paid to the dangers of rapid expansion of bank credit by newly privatised banks, and the very weak supervisory system then in place.

The build-up to the crisis started in early 1994, when a series of political events (a violent uprising in one province, and the assassination of the ruling party's presidential candidate) caused foreign investors to reduce and subsequently reverse capital inflows to the country. The authorities financed this reversal of confidence by running down reserves and borrowing in foreign currency. Following the change in the presidency, a modest devaluation was undertaken as a means of strengthening the balance of payments.

The devaluation was clumsily handled and led to a collapse in the currency. The value of the peso more than halved, and its slide was halted only by a coordinated support package of some $50 billion. This was another case of multiple equilibrium. A small change in the exchange rate did not restore confidence, because the short-term effect on the balance sheet of the government and financial institutions, both of which were heavily exposed in dollars, far outweighed the longer-run effect on competitiveness. Moreover, uncertainties about how much and how rapidly devaluation would be passed through in higher inflation cast doubt on the sustainability of almost any exchange rate. Such doubts also attached to the currencies of other countries in Latin America, which as a result faced markedly higher financing costs in international markets (the 'tequila' effect).

The East Asian crisis, 1997–1998

Damaging though the Mexican crisis was, the East Asian crisis that started in Thailand in 1997 had even greater and more widespread consequences. In one sense, the crisis was a surprise. The growth rates of most of the countries that were affected had been spectacular. Moreover, growth seemed to be solidly underpinned by high rates of domestic saving and investment, low inflation and reasonably prudent fiscal policies.

Once again, volatile capital flows played a role, both in the build-up to the crisis and in triggering it. And once again, an excessive expansion of bank credit and inadequate prudential standards sowed the seeds of future trouble. Foreign investors (especially foreign banks), impressed by the economic performance of these countries, lent uncritically amounts that, with hindsight, were greater than the countries' absorptive capacities. Balance of payments deficits rose and a substantial part of investment went into 'conspicuous construction'. The easy availability of funds and rising property prices dulled financial institutions' critical instincts. Add the cosy expectation that the government–private sector nexus would protect both lenders and borrowers and the environment was created for massive misallocation of investment resources.

In Thailand, as in Mexico, the government tried to deal with what appeared to be a modest over-valuation of the currency by a modest devaluation. Once again the result was a spiral in which devaluation weakened the position of financial institutions and the weakening of the financial sector led to a further loss of confidence in the currency.

An ingredient that was much more virulent than in the Mexican case was *contagion.* The crisis spread in the ensuing six months to almost every country in East Asia, including some, such as Indonesia and Korea, that were thought to have sound macroeconomic fundamentals. The situation was eventually stabilised with the help of massive loan packages coordinated by the IMF. But stabilisation did not come quickly, nor without initial depreciations in currencies that were far beyond any estimates of what was needed to restore medium-term competitiveness.

Russia/LTCM, 1998

The last crisis of the 1990s that I want to consider is that which began with the Russian devaluation and unilateral debt moratorium in August 1998. This triggered the turbulence in financial markets in industrial countries that led to the near-collapse of the hedge fund Long Term Capital Management (LTCM). The Russian crisis was the clearest example, though not the only one, of the power of moral hazard. It is hard to believe that the substantial flows of funds to Russia in the two years preceding its default were not at least partly induced by an expectation that Western countries were in some sense committed to the support of Russia. That expectation disappeared with the Russian default in late summer 1998.

What happened then was a clear example of contagion. The Russian economy in 1998 was small in size (smaller than that of the Netherlands) and had modest trade links with other countries. Moreover, no significant financial institution was materially endangered as a result of its exposure to Russia. However, Russia's unilateral declaration of a debt moratorium created a pervasive increase in perceived uncertainty. The result was a flight both to quality and liquidity. The desire for quality led to a widening in spreads on lower-grade credits, while the flight to liquidity meant that high-quality but less liquid assets also lost value.

This had profound implications for all highly leveraged institutions who managed their portfolios on the basis of the continuous availability of liquidity. LTCM would have been unable to unwind its portfolio without incurring massive losses. Moreover, the prospect of the unwinding would have led to serious losses for other players. In the event, the danger was averted by timely reductions in interest rates and an officially encouraged rescue of LTCM by its principal creditors. Nevertheless, it had been a close call. It was hardly comforting for the resilience of the international financial system.

3 Lessons of the crises

It is now time to draw together what can be learned from these episodes and consider what they demonstrate about weaknesses in the international financial system. How are they related to the present 'architecture'? To anticipate the argument, I will suggest that, while the roots of each crisis lay in domestic policy mistakes, all of them were triggered and intensified by the greater freedom of capital flows. Open capital markets, in turn, are the key element of an international financial architecture based on decentralised decision-taking.

I will group the symptoms of shortcomings in the present arrangements under four headings. These symptoms are, as will be apparent, interrelated. First comes volatility in international capital flows. Second, unsustainable exchange rate regimes. Third, chronic weaknesses in national financial systems. And fourth, contagion across national boundaries.

Volatility of capital flows

All of the episodes of crisis listed above have seen excess volatility in international capital flows. Periods of optimism have led to substantial inflows. These inflows have not simply been used to finance longer-term direct investment. A substantial part of them have been in financial form, intended to take advantage of interest differentials, or rising equity prices, or in some cases the possibility of currency appreciation. Larger inflows presented difficult problems of absorption for the receiving countries. Sometimes they added to domestic liquidity, pushing up demand and generating inflationary pressures. In such circumstances, asset prices often rose dramatically. An associated development was to stimulate imports and weaken export competitiveness. And by increasing the availability of funds to the domestic financial system, incentives for prudent financial intermediation were blunted.

The problems of excessive inflows are, however, small in comparison to those that occur when the flows are reversed. Central Banks find their reserves depleted and are often unable to borrow. Devaluation or floating worsens

Table 2.1 *Capital flows[a] in Asian countries, 1996–1999, billion dollars*

	1996	1997	1998	1999
	Net private capital flows			
Indonesia	11.5	−9.2	−9.9	−8.3
Korea	24.9	−21.2	−21.2	7.1
Malaysia	7.9	1.4	0.8	−8.8
Thailand	16.6	−14.1	−16.1	−6.8
Crisis-hit Asia	60.9	−43.1	−46.4	−16.8
	Net official capital flows			
Indonesia	0.6	8.9	7.9	6.6
Korea	−0.4	17.5	11.6	−9.1
Malaysia	−0.8	−0.5	0.4	1.0
Thailand	0.3	7.2	3.5	0.3
Crisis-hit Asia	−0.3	33.2	23.4	−1.2
	Swing in private flows as a percentage of imports			
Indonesia	13.9	−49.6	−2.7	6.7
Korea	4.9	−31.9	0.0	23.6
Malaysia	1.1	−8.2	−1.1	−14.7
Thailand	−3.2	−48.8	−4.6	18.4
Crisis-hit Asia	3.4	−31.7	−1.5	11.4
	Swing in private flows as a percentage of GDP			
Indonesia	2.6	−9.6	−0.8	1.1
Korea	1.4	−9.7	0.0	6.9
Malaysia	0.8	−6.7	−0.9	−12.5
Thailand	−1.2	−20.6	−1.8	7.5
Crisis-hit Asia	1.1	−11.1	−0.6	3.9

Note: [a] Capital flows are calculated as the difference between the current account and the changes in reserves; private flows are calculated as a residual from an estimate of official flows.

inflationary pressures and exposes the weaknesses in the balance sheet of the financial system. A currency crisis and a domestic banking crisis interact with one another in a downward spiral. No satisfactory mechanisms exist to halt the process through a lender of last resort (LOLR) or a temporary interruption in the freedom of investors to withdraw funds.

Some indication of the volatility of flows can be gained from table 2.1, which shows flows of funds to selected Asian countries before, during and after the recent crisis. The 1996–7 swing in flows to these countries represented about 11 per cent of their current GDP (and about one-fifth in the case of Thailand), or one-third of their total import payments. Inevitably a swing of such magnitude, even if partly replaced by official balance of payments assistance, provokes a massive contraction of domestic demand.

Unsustainable exchange rate regimes

Another common feature of recent crises has been unsustainable exchange rate regimes. Despite the abandonment of the Bretton Woods system in 1973, many countries maintained some form of fixed-but-adjustable exchange rate peg in much of the period since then. The justification was that stable exchange rates remove an element of uncertainty from private sector decision-making, provide a better environment for macroeconomic policy formulation and protect external competitiveness.

All these considerations have importance. On the other side, however, is the fact that *some* mechanism has to exist for balancing the supply and demand for currencies over time. In a system where the demand for and supply of foreign exchange is simply the counterpart of current account transactions, the authorities can afford to meet short-run imbalances through changes in reserves, deciding only later whether to respond to longer-lasting imbalances through an exchange rate adjustment or by changes in domestic demand.

By now, however, short-run changes in foreign exchange supply and demand are dominated by capital transactions. Any possibility that an exchange rate will adjust creates a profit opportunity that market participants are bound to try to exploit. A fixed-but-adjustable exchange rate regime is liable to become unstable, unless a credible mechanism exists to ensure that the necessary domestic measures to preserve the parity will always be undertaken.

Another problem with fixed-but-adjustable exchange rates is the lack of an 'exit strategy'. As soon as a question mark arises over the balance of payments, the country will face a dilemma. To devalue at the first hint of difficulty undermines the rationale for having a fixed rate in the first place. But once a country has begun to resist downward pressures on the rate, there will be political and economic objections to yielding. Virtually every country that devalued or abandoned a fixed rate in the 1990s did so only after a costly resistance and at considerable reputational cost.

Weaknesses in financial systems

Weaknesses in national financial systems have imposed severe costs on the countries concerned. They have also been an element propagating financial difficulties across national boundaries, for two reasons. First, with free movement of capital, the international financial system can be thought of as the aggregation of all the participating national financial systems. Second, domestic financial weakness can act as a constraint on national authorities' ability to pursue needed adjustment policies.

A typical way to dampen pressure on a domestic currency is to raise interest rates. This provides an incentive to holders of the currency not to sell, and it restrains domestic demand, thus strengthening the underlying balance of payments. But if the authorities are concerned about the fragility of domestic financial institutions, they may be unwilling to raise rates. Even if they are willing, market participants will know there is a limit to how far they can go. Devaluation may not be a much more palatable option. If the domestic banking system is exposed in foreign currency, it may be unable to withstand a devaluation. As we have seen, this dilemma was faced in acute form in Thailand.

Contagion

Lastly, the present international financial system has shown itself particularly prone to contagion. On each occasion when a crisis has affected one country, it has quickly spread to other countries or markets. The ERM crisis began in the associated Scandinavian countries, led to a devaluation of the lira and shortly afterwards toppled sterling and other currencies. The after-effects were still being felt almost a year later when the French franc came under attack, despite having relatively strong fundamentals.

Similarly in the case of Mexico, a number of other Latin American countries felt pressures and were forced to intervene and/or raise interest rates. This despite the fact that they had virtually no trade and investment links with Mexico. In East Asia, the crisis that began in Thailand spread throughout the region and had echoes as far away as South Africa, the Czech Republic and South America. And as we have seen, the Russian default had severe repercussions on the New York money markets.

Contagion seems to exist for real, financial and purely psychological reasons. Ironically, the least important cause seems to be real trade linkages. It is true that when one country is forced to devalue, the competitive position of its trading partners (especially in third markets) will be adversely affected. But this does not seem to have been a major factor in the spread of recent crises. More important has been financial contagion. Lenders to countries that have got into difficulties have often used risk management models that mechanically require them to sell assets in the same asset class ('proxy hedging'). Psychological contagion occurs when problems in one country serve as a 'wake-up call' to investors to reassess their exposure in countries with similar non-financial characteristics.

Regardless of how contagion gets started it can be rational for investors to take it into account in their behaviour. If the withdrawal of funds by an 'irrational' investor reduces the likelihood that a 'rational' investor will be repaid, then the rational investor will have an incentive to withdraw early. This phenomenon is familiar from the literature on bank runs. It is usually used as the justification for having a LOLR, to prevent a liquidity crisis turning into a solvency crisis. Because national banking systems have a LOLR, bank runs hardly ever get started. In the international financial system, however, there is no comparable mechanism to guard against currency runs.

Financial contagion, like physical disease, tends to affect first those that are most vulnerable. So it is true that in most recent episodes, countries affected by contagion have usually had certain inherent weaknesses. This was true in the ERM crisis, and it was true in the Asian crisis. Countries with stronger fundamentals, such as France in the ERM and Hong Kong, Singapore and Taiwan in Asia, generally survived the crisis with less cost. This does not detract from the point, however, that the difficulties created by contagion were disproportionate to the underlying economic weaknesses in the countries concerned.

4 The changing financial architecture

The sources of crisis identified above are all, in one way or another, connected to the greater role played by integrated capital markets in the current financial architecture. It is therefore worth pausing to consider how this came to be. How has the architecture evolved over the post-war period? What are its strengths and weaknesses? This will provide a basis for discussing reforms aimed at tackling the weaknesses while preserving the strengths.

The monetary arrangements devised at Brettons Woods gave governments substantial influence over international financial flows and left relatively little to private markets. It was, in the words of Padoa-Schioppa and Saccomanni[1] a 'government-led' international monetary system. A key objective of the system was to liberalise trade flows and to provide convertibility for current payments. Fixed exchange rates were assumed to facilitate the growth of trade and any changes in exchange rates had to be multilaterally agreed. If imports and exports were not in balance (net of flows of long-term capital), the difference would be reflected in changes in foreign exchange reserves. Countries were expected to respond to movements in reserves by adjusting macroeconomic policies so

[1] Padoa-Schioppa and Saccomanni (1994).

as to restore payments equilibrium at the given exchange rate. If necessary, the resources of the IMF (and its policy conditionality) were available to assist the process. In extreme cases of 'fundamental disequilibria', an exchange rate adjustment could be undertaken, approved by the IMF.

This system worked reasonably well so long as national capital markets were insulated from one another, and long-term capital flows were of an official nature. But as private capital flows grew in importance they began to play a much greater role in the adjustment process. The growth of the euro-dollar market in the 1960s signalled the beginning of a period in which mobile capital would flow into (and out of) countries based on expectations of relative short-term yields.

The first consequence of this trend was to undermine the regime of fixed-but-adjustable exchange rates. Market participants could see the emergence of unsustainable payments positions, and could form expectations as to whether they would have to be corrected by an exchange rate adjustment. By so doing, of course, they brought forward the need for governments to take action. Reserves could less easily be used to 'buy time' to decide on adjustment policies. Either credible action had to be taken at once to demonstrate the sustainability of an exchange rate, or else speculative outflows would soon force a change in parity.

This characteristic of capital markets is to introduce what has been called 'the non-linearity of time'.[2] Capital markets concentrate at a moment in time the received consequences of past events (the assets and liabilities created by past transactions) and the expected consequences of future developments (the flows of claims implicit in current policies, and the price expectations they engender).

What is the implication of this 'non-linearity of time'? Most importantly, it means that it is harder to sustain disequilibria in prices and quantities. If market participants have confidence in the sustainability of the policies of a government or a private borrower, then capital flows will help reinforce the status quo; if not, they will quickly undermine it.

With open capital markets, governments cannot easily manage either exchange rates *or* the adjustment process *or* liquidity creation. What they *can* manage is their domestic macroeconomic and structural policies. In the new international financial architecture, it is the markets' perception of these that drives the pattern and volatility of capital flows and the associated developments in the exchange rates and liquidity.

How should we judge this fundamental change in the international financial architecture? Is it a matter of regret that governments can no longer set exchange rates, limit capital flows and prevent the emergence of the kind of crises we have experienced in recent years? Or should we be glad that resources are now

---

[2] Jakob Frenkel.

allocated by the market's 'hidden hand', even if this leads to periodic spectacular episodes of turbulence?

As in all such questions, the answer is neither one nor the other. As a practical matter, however, there is no turning the clock back to an era where capital flows were of minor importance. The sophistication of our financial infrastructure has simply progressed too far to make it possible, even if it were desirable. Yet it is almost certainly not desirable either. Private capital markets have facilitated an enormous resource transfer to emerging markets. Although not always used wisely, this has contributed materially to faster rates of capital formation and output growth. Capital flows have also encouraged the transfer of technological and managerial know-how. And they can act as a source of discipline on borrowers and the policies of borrowing countries. All this is to the good and should not be lightly compromised.

On the other hand, it cannot be denied that free capital mobility has contributed on occasion to serious resource misallocation and to damaging instability. And a major weakness is that the exercise of discipline on borrowing countries' policies is all too often exerted much too late. So the answer, 'leave it to the market', cannot be accepted either.

Instead, I believe the approach has to be one of dealing better with cases in which private markets are inefficient, or lead to instability. The approach to the new architecture, in other words, has to be to focus on helping markets allocate resources effectively, rather than on *supplanting* market judgements. This is analogous to the role that is increasingly accepted for governments in national economies. In most advanced countries, governments no longer have a major role in enterprise ownership or in price setting. But they do have a growing role in *regulating* the conditions in which the private sector operates and monitoring how it behaves. And there is a growing, sophisticated literature on how regulation needs to be designed so as to enhance competitive market forces, rather than stifle them.

5 Reform: new rules?

Against this general background, what can be said that is more specific about the conventions and guidelines that should govern international economic and financial relations? I will discuss that in this section before going on to institutional questions in section 6.

The rules and conventions that I suggest are needed share certain important elements of continuity with the past. Clear support should be given to free trade and a multilateral approach to the management of the international financial system. But whereas past rules have sought to define the *international interface* between governments' policies (exchange rates, liquidity provision, adjustment obligations, and so on), the new conventions will have to define *domestic requirements* relating to the sustainability of structural and macroeconomic policies – and, most importantly, the prudent and efficient operation of financial systems. If the job of pursuing sustainable and appropriate domestic policies in these areas is achieved, much of the task of managing international financial flows can be left to private markets. (Not all, however, for there will remain the task of dealing with shocks and breakdowns in the functioning of private markets.)

Macroeconomic policies

Since domestic macroeconomic policies are a sovereign responsibility, it might be thought unnecessary, and even inappropriate, to try to devise internationally applicable rules. However, shifts in macroeconomic policies have effects on savings – investment balances, and hence on exchange rates and on international flows of goods and capital. They therefore have an international dimension that justifies an attempt to at least provide some framework or general guidelines. This is not unprecedented. Such a framework is explicitly apparent in the Maastricht treaty, which lays down fiscal deficit and debt limits for participants in monetary union.

There is now little dissent from the proposition that countries should aim at a low and stable rate of inflation (1–3 per cent is probably the range that is most generally favoured[3]). This is widely viewed as being in the national interest as well as being consistent with stable international relations, so is not particularly controversial.

A prudent budgetary policy is likewise widely supported. The Maastricht treaty puts a limit of 3 per cent of GDP on budget deficits and 60 per cent as the upper band of the debt to GDP ratio. Economists have quibbled with the mechanical application of these ratios (with good grounds), but few have disputed the general objective they embody. So international understandings here too should be relatively easy to reach, without the need for formal agreements.

A more problematic issue is the exchange rate regime. For obvious reasons, countries have wanted to have stability in their exchange rates. It facilitates the formation of monetary policy and it provides a stable environment for the development of export-oriented industries. But as already noted, fixed exchange rates pose particular difficulties in an environment of free capital flows. If markets perceive that domestic economic policies are inconsistent with the

[3] Bernanke *et al.* (1999); Fischer (1996).

chosen exchange rate, they will speculate on a change. If the government resists, but does not change its domestic policy priorities sufficiently, the subsequent adjustment can be abrupt and painful.

As a result of experiences with currency crises, it is now increasingly believed that governments have to pursue one of three courses. First, they can credibly make clear that the domestic economy will be allowed to adjust to take the strain of pressures on the exchange rates. This variant can be referred to as 'strong fixing' and can be given institutional strength through a currency board, or the adoption of a currency union. Secondly, they can strengthen administrative restrictions on capital flows. Thirdly, they can allow their currency to float, so that a movement in the exchange rate can absorb the incipient impact of changes in payments flows.

The first option, 'strong fixing' is practicable only for a country that has flexible domestic institutions and a demonstrable will to accept domestic 'pain' to preserve the fixed peg. This means that relatively few countries will find this the preferable option. Those that have a history of domestic monetary misman-agement (Argentina, for example) may be able to mobilise political support for 'strong fixing' as a way to escape their hyper-inflation legacy. And countries with highly flexible markets (such as Hong Kong) can also be successful in this strategy.

The second option, capital controls, is also of limited applicability. Controls will be neither desirable nor feasible in the longer term for countries with devel-oping financial sectors, and they will over time forfeit some of the advantages from integrated capital markets.

This means that the third option, greater flexibility in the exchange rate, is likely to be the preferable option for most countries. It is clearly not without disadvantages, but it is the only one that significantly reduces the potential for currency crises of the type that have plagued the international financial system. It is important to note that exchange rate regimes that are in principle flexible can be supported by policies designed to impart a good deal of stability *ex post*. But not of course in all circumstances.

Financial stability policies

The key lesson from the financial crises of the 1990s is the need to strengthen domestic financial systems. Weaknesses in financial systems have been inde-pendent sources of instability in many countries, and have compounded the effects of currency crises in others.[4] Table 2.2, updated from a book by Morris

---

[4] Kaminsky and Reinhart (1999).

Table 2.2 *Cost of banking crises, 1980–1999*

Country (time period of crisis)	Estimate of total losses/costs (percentage of GDP)
Latin America	
Argentina (1980–2)	55
Chile (1981–3)	41[a]
Venezuela (1994–5)	18
Mexico (1995)	12–15[b]
Africa	
Benin (1988–90)	17
Côte d'Ivoire (1988–91)	25
Mauritania (1984–93)	15
Senegal (1988–91)	17
Tanzania (1987–95)	10[c]
Middle East	
Israel (1977–83)	30[d]
Transition countries	
Bulgaria (1990s)	14
Hungary (1995)	10
Asia	
Indonesia (1997–)	59
Korea (1997–)	17
Malaysia (1997–)	10
Thailand (1997–)	24
Industrial countries	
Spain (1977–85)	17
Japan (1990s)	10[e]

[a] 1982–5.
[b] Accumulated losses to date.
[c] 1987.
[d] 1983.
[e] Estimate of potential losses.
Sources: Caprio and Klingebiel (1996); World Bank (1999).

Goldstein,[5] shows the resolution costs of recent banking crises, expressed in relation to the GDP of the country concerned.

How can the international community set about the task of strengthening national financial systems? This is a large question, and I will try to break it down into manageable components. I will discuss first the coverage of the concept of financial stability, noting that it goes well beyond the, admittedly important, subject of financial sector supervision. Then I will describe the broad approach to improving the stable functioning of the financial sector which is now being pursued through the development of codes of best practice and prudent behaviour. These can serve as a benchmark for regulatory efforts and a standard to which individual countries can aspire to converge. Next, I will say something about

[5] Goldstein (1997).

how these standards can be developed, monitored and, if necessary, amended. Finally, I will comment on the management of the process – how to ensure that countries have the right kind of incentives to pursue international standards, what to do if progress is inadequate, how to identify gaps in regulations and vulnerabilities in the system, and so on.

The coverage of financial stability

For the financial system of a country to be stable and efficient, three separable elements have to work well. First, the key institutional intermediaries (banks, securities issuers, insurance companies and fund managers) have to operate efficiently and prudently. Second, the markets in which they transact (equity, fixed income, foreign exchange and commodities) have to be open and transparent. And third, the infrastructure within which financial transactions take place (accounting conventions, contract law, enforcement of property rights, bankruptcy arrangements, corporate governance, payment and settlements arrangements, etc.) has to be robust and well understood.

requirements

Shortcomings in any one area can undermine the stability of the financial system more broadly. Prudent rules for capital holding by financial institutions are of little use if accounting rules allow bad loans to be concealed. Valuation of financial claims is very difficult if uncertainty surrounds how property rights will be treated in a bankruptcy procedure. Investment decisions become risky when markets are not transparent, and so on. A first step therefore, is to recognise that the new financial architecture requires a large number of bricks to be laid. There is no substitute for painstaking work on a number of fronts if the financial sector of emerging economies is to be brought to a level in which it is resilient to most potential shocks.

The approach to strengthening systems

Recognising that there are multiple aspects to a robust and well-functioning financial system, it is now widely accepted that best practice needs to be defined in each of these aspects, and a strategy developed for its implementation.

Standards need to be global in their application, because the financial industry is global. There is always a risk that financial intermediation will gravitate to centres with weaker standards (regulatory arbitrage) or that disturbances in weaker centres will spill over to other countries (contagion).

As the same time, standards have to be applicable to countries with widely different histories and institutional structures. It would be unreasonable to expect an emerging or developing country with a rudimentary financial sector to comply with standards that an advanced financial centre has reached only after decades of development. Sensitivity will be required to balance the desire to move quickly to best practice with the need to recognise practical constraints.

How to develop standards

It would be possible to imagine standards being developed and applied by an international financial institution, either the IMF or a new institution created for the purpose. However, the balance of advantage seems to lie in allowing committees of national experts to develop standards in their respective spheres. In the first place, they are closer, in their day-to-day activities, to the practical issues that arise in regulating financial activity. Secondly, once they have debated and agreed an international standard, they are more likely to understand and 'buy in' to its practical implications.

There remains an issue of representativeness. Giving all countries a share in the development of standards is at first sight attractive, but it has to be recognised that it is often a recipe for paralysis. On the other hand, attempting to force on the many standards designed by the few will produce resentment at best and active resistance at worst. How can this problem be overcome? One way, which has been found to work reasonably well by the Basel Committee on Banking Supervision, is for the key financial centres to get together to work out rules which they voluntarily agree to abide by themselves. If these rules are well designed, they will then, through peer pressure and market forces, acquire wider applicability.

Two requirements are necessary for this process to have effectiveness and acceptability. First, there must be a genuine process of consultation, whereby those not directly represented in the standard-setting body can have their views considered in reaching recommendations. Second, recommendations have to be applicable not only to the small group that designs them but also to the broader population of countries that will have to apply them.

It is noteworthy that those standard-setters that reach agreement in small groups (with consultative procedures) such as the Basel Committee, have generally speaking managed to implement standards faster than those that have had more outwardly 'democratic' procedures. Moreover, it does not seem as though the Basel Committee's recommendations have had significant difficulty being accepted outside the standard-setting group.

How should standards be implemented?

The question of implementation is key to the success of an approach based on development of codes of best practice. The requirements here are (1) effective prioritisation of standards (there are now 60+ standards on the website of the Financial Stability Forum, so some prioritisation is essential); (2) incentives to encourage the speedy adoption and implementation of codes; (3) the provision of a mechanism to monitor progress in implementation (and to disseminate the results); and (4) the provision of resources to help countries identify and deal with shortcomings in their financial systems.

The most effective tool in implementation is the market. When the market rewards high standards of financial regulation with greater market access and lower borrowing costs, there is little doubt that countries will pursue higher standards without the need for outside pressure. To do this, however, it will be necessary to ascertain which standards are of key importance. Countries can make their own 'audit' of their systems, and this will undoubtedly be helpful in raising consciousness about underlying weaknesses. However, it seems likely that they will often need expert assistance to identify problem areas, then to remedy them and finally to attest credibly that standards have indeed been upgraded.

All of this is an appropriate mission for the IMF and the World Bank in the new financial architecture. Indeed, in some sense it could be seen as their key function: equipping national authorities and private markets with the capacity to handle international financial relations in an efficient and stabilising way. The purely *financial* role of the two institutions would then be to deal with the much smaller range of cases where market failures led either to inefficient outcomes or to financial instability.

The management of the process

To recapitulate the argument so far: the new architecture is based on resources allocated by national and international capital markets. A key requirement is the improved functioning of markets, and the removal of sources of market failure. This requires an upgrading of standards across a wide range of areas. A large number of standard-setters are involved, as are national authorities and the international financial institutions.

With such a wide range of actors, some coordination is required. The key ministerial level committees are the G7, the G20 and the International Monetary and Financial Committee. These provide the overarching framework for monitoring the architecture.

With regard to the more specific task of identifying potential vulnerabilities in financial systems, and proposing approaches to dealing with them, the Financial Stability Forum (FSF) created in 1999 has a key role to play. I will come to this in the next part of the chapter.

6 Reform: new institutional mechanisms

The broad implication of the preceding analysis is that the role of international financial institutions is to deal with *market failures* in private markets, not to replace private capital flows. This is a considerable change from the focus of these institutions when they were set up. It is *not*, as I will try to show, a diminution in the importance of their respective roles.

The International Monetary Fund

The IMF has for a long time been centrally involved in policy advice to its member countries (I have always thought it unfortunate that the term 'surveillance' has been attached to this activity). The need for policy advice is likely to continue, though the nature of the dialogue changes as national authorities increase their own complement of highly trained economists.

The focus of the Fund's ongoing work (i.e. outside crisis situations) must be to help markets work better and to avoid the build-up of unsustainable imbalances. One way in which it can do that is by acting as a standard-setter in areas of its expertise (macroeconomic policies). It has already usefully developed standards of data transparency and could perform a similar function in the, admittedly more judgemental, areas of fiscal and monetary policy guidelines.

Another important role of the Fund is to help in the dissemination and implementation of standards developed by others. As already pointed out, building a safe and efficient financial system is a complex and time-consuming task. It requires sensitivity to differing institutional structures across countries. Countries will undoubtedly require help to: first, assess the weaknesses in their financial systems; second, develop a strategy for dealing with them; and third, secure technical assistance to implement the strategy. Finally, it will be important for the Fund to certify that high standards are being maintained on an ongoing basis.

The World Bank

The World Bank's role will also change. Indeed it has already changed substantially since the 1970s. Instead of being the principal source of foreign capital for many developing countries, it is now, in aggregate terms, a relatively minor player.

The role of the Bank can be seen as being to enhance the effectiveness of private flows and to replace them only when they are not adequate or appropriate to particular public policy objectives. There are four important ways in which the Bank can improve the effectiveness of capital flows coming through market channels.

First, just as one of the Fund's most important contributions is policy advice, so the Bank's expertise can help developing countries design better overall strategies. Its involvement in such a broad cross-section of countries gives it a unique perspective on how to tailor development strategies to different institutional and economic settings.

Second, it can lend to specific sectors and programmes with important positive externalities (education, health, infrastructure). These are often neglected, especially in countries facing stringent budgetary positives.

Third, it can help upgrade the financial system through which resources are mobilised and allocated. Financial sector weaknesses act as a drag on countries' capacity to mobilise investable resources and allocate them efficiently.

Fourth, it can act as a direct provider of funds when economic and political risks inhibit the private market from playing an adequate role.

The Bank for International Settlements

Next something should be said about the role of the Bank for International Settlements (BIS) and more generally of the Basel process. The BIS is a forum for cooperation among all the leading Central Banks in the world. This cooperation has become more important as the role of Central Banks in promoting monetary and financial stability has become more prominent. The 'Basel Process' refers to a variety of committees and informal contacts that oversee cooperation in a number of different areas.

In the field of monetary and foreign exchange policies, regular meetings among governors and other senior officials provide the basis for in-depth information-sharing. This stops short of policy coordination but is a necessary basis to ensure that national policies are not inadvertently inconsistent or destabilising. It also provides a kind of 'early warning system' to raise consciousness about impending sources of strain in the system.

As far as the financial system is concerned, Central Banks are looked to in most countries for an overarching responsibility for stability. This includes their role as a LOLR, but goes considerably further than that. The BIS can provide a venue at which the international implications of market developments can be discussed. This enables Central Banks to share perspectives on changing market structures and dynamics and to discuss possible responses to sources of tension. This, too, falls short of policy coordination, but is probably necessary to make the 'soft law' of codes and standards operationally effective.

Other institutional actors

Looking beyond the central institutions in the International Financial Architecture, a greater role will have to be played by *other actors and groupings*, such as private sector financial institutions, international standard-setters and national regulatory authorities. Since the bulk of financial flows are now private, policy-makers in the official sector would do well to find imaginative ways to involve the private sector institutions in devising ways to prevent and deal with crises. Standard-setters have generally come together as a result of a felt need to impose consistent standards (a 'level playing field') across national boundaries. They need to be more directly involved in the debate about how to protect global financial stability more generally. For similar reasons, national supervisors, whose actions affect the international activities of the major regulated financial institutions, should also be drawn into the issue of managing global financial stability.

This brings me back to the role of the Financial Stability Forum. The Forum was established in early 1999 following a report by Hans Tietmeyer, commissioned by the G7. Underlying the Forum's creation was the recognition that a wide range of national and international authorities now have responsibility for one or another aspect of international financial stability. Yet there existed relatively few mechanisms for information exchange among them, or for consultation on matters of potential systemic vulnerability. The Forum therefore brings together Deputy Finance Ministers, Deputy Central Bank governors and Heads of Supervision from G7 countries; Central Bank governors from four additional countries with major financial markets; the heads of the key international standard-setting bodies and senior representatives from the principal international financial institutions. Its mandate is to assess vulnerabilities affecting the international financial system, to identify and oversee action needed to address these vulnerabilities and to improve coordination and information exchange among the authorities responsible for financial stability.

One of the functions of the Forum is to help coordinate the activities of the diverse set of institutions represented in its membership. This should help ensure an overall approach to the design and implementation of standards aimed at enhancing financial stability. The senior level of the Forum's members should help it give impetus to ongoing work in other bodies, whether represented in the Forum or not. And finally, the Forum can work through ministerial-level bodies, such as the G7, G20 and IMFCs to help resolve difficult issues.

7 Handling of financial crises

However much success is achieved in strengthening financial systems, it will, as I have just said, be unrealistic to expect that financial crises will become a thing of the past. It will still be necessary to have a strategy for when countries get into serious financial difficulty.

Over the past several years, criticism of IMF-supported economic pro-grammes has multiplied. The critics often have diverse reasons for disagreeing with Fund policies, so a clear-cut response is not possible.

One line of criticism is that Fund-supported programmes interfere with the effective working of market mechanisms. According to this line of argument, the Fund is a potent source of moral hazard. If the Fund did not exist, markets would find an appropriate way of disciplining bad policies and imprudent behaviour. The Fund should therefore be abolished. Support for abolition is not widespread, but has attracted support from such influential names as George Schultz and Walter Wriston.

It is hard to believe, however, that the world would be better off with *no mechanism to manage crises*. It will be impossible to eradicate all sources of market failure and unexpected disturbances will continue to occur. A means is needed to deal with multiple equilibria, to prevent liquidity crises becoming solvency crises, to handle contagion, herd behaviour and the like.

A second line of criticism, reflected in the Meltzer report (2000)[6] is to try to replicate the traditional approach to the LOLR in domestic economies. In this approach, the Fund's lending would become less judgemental (or conditional). It would lend more or less unlimited amounts to countries that had pre-qualified through the pursuit of appropriate macroeconomic and financial policies. But in other respects, including its involvement in smaller countries, its role would be curtailed.

Although there are many interesting and useful ideas in the Meltzer report (to which I have not done justice here), it seems likely to be an unduly mechanical approach to dealing with crises. These come in many different forms. It is easy to imagine cases in which additional policy measures, beyond providing finance, are needed to resolve a crisis. It is also easy to imagine situations where outside finance would be useful, and where it is precluded because the country has not pre-qualified.

If the above reasoning is accepted, the Fund's assistance will therefore con-tinue to be needed in a variety of crisis circumstances, even if the number of such crises is reduced in the future. However, the way in which Fund resources are provided, and the size of packages, needs careful consideration. Such con-sideration is of course already under way, but will need to be carried further.

To simplify somewhat, the standard approach to financial programming in the Fund in the past was to estimate an overall balance of payments deficit that needed to be covered by external sources of finance. Measures, largely of a macroeconomic nature, were agreed with a country that would eliminate this overall deficit within a given timeframe – say, three years. The need for Fund resources was the cumulative balance of payments deficit in the interim.

[6] IFIAC (2000).

The liberalisation of capital flows has made this model outdated. The balance of payments 'gap' needing official finance is virtually impossible to quantify. If domestic and foreign residents have lost confidence in one or more elements of a country's economic policies (say, its exchange rate commitment or its financial sector's solvency), the volume of capital outflows can be many times greater than the 'overall' deficit. On the other hand, if confidence is regained, private short-term flows will relatively easily cover a deficit.

If the amounts of external assistance a country may need to reassure external creditors are hard to calculate, they are also large. Larger, in fact, than creditor countries are willing to provide very frequently, either bilaterally or through the IMF. And even if the amounts were not too large, the consequences of providing finance to, in effect, finance capital flight raises serious moral hazard issues.

The broad consequences of this analysis are ineluctable, even if the precise implications are not yet clear. The Fund's role in a crisis-hit country cannot be to provide finance to underwrite private claims. This is now widely agreed. Instead, it will typically have three main elements: (1) helping a country design a policy package judged sufficient to restore medium-term viability; (2) providing financial resources that cover part of the prospective financing need and (3) helping the country reach understandings with its other creditors to reschedule claims falling due. Exactly how element (3) of the Fund's role will be designed is, however, a matter that will take time and ingenuity to specify.

REFERENCES

Bernanke, B., T. Laubach, F. Mishkin and A. Posen (1999). *Inflation Targeting: Lessons from the International Experience*. Princeton, NJ, Princeton University Press

Caprio, G. and D. Klingbiel (1996). 'Bank Insolvencies: Cross-Country Experience', Washington, DC, World Bank, unpublished

Fischer, S. (1996). 'Why are the Central Banks Pursuing Long-Run Price Stability?', in Federal Reserve Bank of Kansas City, Jackson Hole Symposium, 'Achieving Price Stability'

Goldstein, M. (1997). 'The Case for an International Banking Standard', *Policy Analyses in International Economics*, Washington, DC, Institute for International Economics, April

IFIAC (2000). 'Report to Congress', International Financial Institution Advisory Commission, US Congress, March

Kaminsky, G. and C. Reinhart (1999). 'The Twin Crises: The Causes of Banking and Balance-of-Payments Problems', *American Economic Review*, 89(3), 473–500

Padoa-Schioppa, T. and E. Saccomanni (1994). 'Managing a Market-Led Global Financial System', in P. B. Kenen (ed.), *Managing the World Economy: Fifty Years After Bretton Woods*. Washington, DC, Institute for International Economics

World Bank (1999). *Global Economic Review*. Washington, DC, World Bank

3 International coordination of macroeconomic policies: still alive in the new millennium?

LAURENCE H. MEYER, BRIAN M. DOYLE, JOSEPH E. GAGNON
AND DALE W. HENDERSON

1 Introduction

The subject of this chapter is macroeconomic policy coordination among developed countries.[1] The chapter covers both the findings of theoretical models of policy coordination and the historical experience of coordination between policy-makers in different countries.[2] Most importantly, the chapter assesses the extent to which models of policy coordination capture the key features of

This version of the chapter is essentially unchanged from the version that was prepared for and presented at the 'Reforming the Architecture of Global Economic Institutions' end-of-programme conference of the Global Economic Institutions programme, at the Bank of England on 5–6 May 2000. As such, it only reflects events, both in the theory and in the practice of international policy coordination, up to that date. At the time this chapter was written, Meyer was a Governor of the Federal Reserve System. Doyle, Gagnon, and Henderson are staff economists in the Division of International Finance at the Federal Reserve Board. The authors thank Ralph Bryant, C. Randall Henning, Andrew Hughes-Hallet, Karen Johnson, Steven Kamin, Peter Kenen, James Lister, Ellen Meade, Louellen Stedman and Edwin Truman for helpful comments and advice. The authors also thank Hayden Smith for research assistance. The views expressed in this chapter are solely the responsibility of the authors and should not be interpreted as reflecting those of the Board of Governors of the Federal Reserve System or any other person associated with the Federal Reserve System.

[1] Therefore, there is no discussion of the theoretical and practical considerations raised by recent attempts to coordinate both the management of the financial crises in emerging markets and the design of an international financial system in which such crises occur less frequently and have less serious effects.

[2] The terms 'cooperation' and 'coordination' are used in different ways in different analyses of interactions among macroeconomic policy-makers. In this chapter, we use 'cooperation' to refer to an agreement among policy-makers in two or more nations that involves achieving a Pareto efficient outcome and that is credibly enforced, for example, by a supranational authority. In cases in which there is a set of two or more self-enforcing equilibria, we use 'coordination' to refer to an attempt to achieve one particular equilibrium out of the set. These uses follow the conventions of game theory. Otherwise, we use 'coordination' as a general term to refer to attempts by policy-makers to achieve improved outcomes.

practical experience. For areas where the models and experience diverge, we attempt to draw some lessons for both modellers and policy-makers.

The past few decades have seen the development of theoretical and empirical models designed to explore the benefits of international macroeconomic policy coordination. The models highlight the fact that macroeconomic policy actions in one country affect economic welfare in other countries; that is, they have *externalities* for other countries. The key insight of the models is that coordination of policies among countries that takes into account these externalities may lead to higher welfare for all countries. Starting with this key insight, the modelling of international policy coordination has moved in many different directions addressing such issues as the types of problems that coordination is best suited to address, which policies are best suited to address which problems, the means of enforcing international agreements, the roles that uncertainty and information sharing play in the coordination process and the measurement of the gains from policy coordination.

The decades since the breakdown of the Bretton Woods system in 1971 have witnessed a proliferation of attempts to discuss and coordinate macroeconomic policies among the major industrial nations and within Europe. Informal discussions in the early 1970s among a few finance ministers have evolved into regular meetings, involving several layers of leadership, in what are now referred to as the G7 countries. These meetings have led to such high-profile international agreements as the Plaza Agreement of September 1985 and the Louvre Accord of February 1987. Discussions among economic policy-makers also take place on a regular basis at the Bank for International Settlements (BIS), the International Monetary Fund (IMF), the Organisation for Economic Cooperation and Development (OECD) and in numerous regional entities. While such meetings generally do not lead to formal agreements on coordinated macroeconomic policies, the exchange of information and views that takes place on these occasions is considered an important vehicle for enhancing the quality of economic policy-making among participating nations. Within Europe, an even more formalised process has led to the adoption of a common monetary policy for eleven countries in the European Union (EU), with explicit rules limiting fiscal policy independence as well.

There are several good surveys of models of policy coordination and many worthwhile discussions of the experience with such coordination. However, there have been very few investigations of the correspondence between the models and experience.[3] The main contributions of this chapter are a further investigation of the correspondence and an attempt to draw lessons for both the modellers and practitioners of policy coordination.

---

[3] One very useful investigation is Bryant (1995).

Has the practical experience of international policy coordination generated the gains suggested by the models? From this perspective, it is the practical process of international policy cooperation that is put under the magnifying glass, and we consider what types of obstacles might be operating to prevent this process from achieving its hypothetical potential.

To what extent have the models captured the most salient aspects of macroeconomic policy coordination in practice? In this context, a disconnect between models and practice represents a failure of the modellers to specify properly the objectives and constraints facing policy-makers.

The remainder of the chapter is divided into four sections. Section 2 is a review of the theory of policy coordination. This section includes an attempt to summarise the contributions of some of the papers produced in connection with the Global Economic Institutions (GEI) project. Section 3 is a discussion of the experience with policy coordination since the breakdown of the Bretton Woods System, both among G7 countries and within Europe. In section 4, there is an attempt to draw lessons based on both theory and experience. Section 5 concludes. There are three appendices: appendix 1 contains support for a proposition in the text, appendix 2 contains a chronology of major events in the history of policy coordination and appendix 3 provides a list of some regular international policy coordination meetings.

2 Models of policy coordination

In theory, international policy coordination raises welfare for all countries. Each country is concerned only with its own welfare. However, policy actions of each country affect the welfare of others; that is, they generate 'externalities'. Externalities give rise to policy conflicts. Each country would like the others to take policy actions different from those dictated by pure self-interest. Without coordination, these policy conflicts lead to (Pareto) inefficient outcomes, but with coordination, outcomes may be efficient.

A canonical example

As an example, consider two symmetric countries, *A* and *B*, which face a symmetric negative productivity shock. With unchanged policies, this shock increases inflation in each country. Each country has an incentive to tighten monetary policy in order to lower inflation and raise welfare. However, tightening by one country causes its currency to appreciate, thereby increasing inflation in

Figure 3.1 *The Prisoner's dilemma*

		Country B	
		'Tighten Less'	'Tighten More'
	'Tighten Less'	3,3	0,4
Country A			
	'Tighten More'	4,0	1,1

the other country further. When one country takes an action that improves its own welfare and that action reduces the welfare of the other country, the country taking the action generates a negative externality for the other country.[4] The policy conflict is that each country would like the other to expand not contract.

The payoffs for the two countries can be arrayed in a payoff matrix that has the same form as the payoff matrix for the well-known 'prisoner's dilemma' game (figure 3.1).

The first number in any pair is the payoff to country A. If A thinks that B is going to tighten less, A has an incentive to tighten more, get a payoff of 4, and leave B with a payoff of 0 and vice versa. For each country, 'Tighten More' is a 'dominant strategy' because it generates a larger payoff no matter what the other country does. If each country plays its dominant strategy, the outcome is the Nash equilibrium in which both countries receive payoffs of 1. The Nash equilibrium is clearly inefficient. In the Nash equilibrium each country ignores the negative externality that it generates for the other, so each country adjusts its instrument by more than the amount consistent with efficiency.[5]

If the two countries could credibly commit to coordinate their policies, they could both choose 'Tighten Less' and achieve the efficient outcome in which both would receive payoffs of 3. However, each country has an incentive to renege on a commitment to choose 'Tighten Less'. If one country assumes the other will choose 'Tighten Less', then it can do better by choosing 'Tighten More'. In other words, a credible commitment to coordinate policies is not possible, so the efficient equilibrium is not achievable.

The simple productivity-shock game just considered is an example of a 'one-shot' game with complete information. Most of the basic elements of the analysis of international policy coordination and the refinements of this analysis can be illustrated by altering or relaxing the assumptions underlying this simple example.[6] For simplicity, it is assumed throughout the discussion of the theory of policy coordination that the world economy consists of two symmetric countries.

---

[4] And if the action increases the welfare of the other country, the country taking the action generates a positive externality for the other country.

[5] And if the externalities were positive, each country would adjust its instrument by less than the amount consistent with efficiency.

[6] See Hamada (1974, 1976, 1979, 1985) and Canzoneri and Henderson (1991) which contain the basic analysis and some refinements.

Types of policy conflicts

Policy conflicts that create an incentive for policy coordination are of two main types: stabilisation conflicts and ongoing conflicts. Stabilisation conflicts are temporary; they occur because of wage and price inertia and eventually disappear as wages and prices adjust. Stabilisation conflicts can arise as a result of either disturbances or exogenous policy changes. Ongoing conflicts are permanent; they occur even if wages and prices are perfectly flexible and never disappear. Ongoing conflicts arise when countries have inconsistent objectives such as different desired values for the same bilateral current account or the same real exchange rate between two currencies.

Possible causes of stabilisation conflicts in theory and experience

In theoretical analyses, it is usually assumed that stabilisation conflicts arise because of exogenous shocks. Attention is usually focused on three basic configurations of shocks: symmetric shocks, (perfectly) asymmetric shocks and country-specific shocks.[7] Symmetric shocks affect each of the two countries in exactly the same way; the example of equal negative productivity shocks in each of the two countries is considered above. Asymmetric shocks affect each of the two countries in equal and opposite ways. A country-specific shock affects one country and not the other. Stabilisation conflicts for monetary policy can also arise because of initial conditions that one or more country regards as suboptimal and changes in fiscal policy that are driven by political or other non-stabilisation considerations such that they are effectively exogenous. Suboptimal initial conditions and exogenous changes in fiscal policy can be divided into the same three configurations as purely exogenous shocks, as described above.

Oil price shocks exemplify approximately symmetric shocks for most industrial countries. Inflation rates in Europe in the early 1980s can be thought of as symmetric suboptimal initial conditions. The simultaneous fiscal expansion in the United States and contraction in Europe and Japan in the early 1980s can be viewed as an asymmetric shock for the monetary authorities. The upward movement in the dollar in early 1985 can be interpreted as having resulted from an asymmetric shock that raised the demand for dollar assets and lowered the demand for assets denominated in the other major currencies. Finally, German unification in the early 1990s and the Japanese asset bubble are good examples of country-specific shocks.

[7] The three basic configurations are not independent. A country-specific shock is the sum of pairs of symmetric and asymmetric shocks that are equal in absolute value. Nonetheless, dividing shocks into three configurations (instead of two) simplifies the exposition.

Commitment and cooperation

In the terminology of the policy coordination literature, efficient outcomes in one-shot games can be achieved through 'cooperation'. Cooperation involves commitments by two or more countries to follow efficient policies. Commitment is possible when there is a supranational authority that can punish departures from announced policies so severely that departures are unthinkable. If countries can commit themselves, they can act, in effect, as a single entity and choose their policies by joint maximisation. That is, they can internalise the externalities that they generate for one another and achieve efficient outcomes. The threat of punishment causes each country to choose the efficient policy even though each country has an incentive to choose a policy other than its efficient policy if the other chooses its efficient policy.

In the special case of symmetric countries and symmetric shocks, efficient outcomes in monetary policy games can also be achieved by commitment to 'fixed exchange rate leadership' (Canzoneri and Gray, 1985). One country commits to fix its money supply at the efficient value and the others agree to fix their exchange rates with that country. Of course, a common monetary policy is not optimal in the cases of asymmetric or country-specific shocks.

It may be difficult to convince countries to surrender their sovereignty to a supranational organisation, so commitment and, therefore, the achievement of efficient outcomes through cooperation, may not be possible. However, there are cases in which nations have surrendered some of their powers to supranational organisations with the intention of improving outcomes. In the area of trade relations, the General Agreement on Tariffs and Trade (GATT) and its successor the World Trade Organisation (WTO) have had the power to punish deviations from agreed rules of behaviour. In the area of monetary policy, the countries of the euro area have turned over the responsibility for setting monetary policy to the European Central Bank (ECB), so there is no need to consider the possibility of deviations and punishment. GATT, the WTO and the ECB are all the result of formal agreements among nations.

Repeated contact and self-enforcing agreements: trigger mechanisms

Even if commitment is not possible, the fact that countries will face the same or a similar problem in the future may be enough to make it possible to achieve efficient outcomes. For example, if the game considered above is repeated every period, the countries may have different incentives than if the game is played only once. Suppose Country *A* plays 'Tighten Less' in the first period and in every subsequent period as long as Country B has always played 'Tighten Less'. If Country B ever plays 'Tighten More', then Country A plays 'Tighten More' forever thereafter. If Country A follows this 'trigger strategy' and B an analogous one, then both countries will play 'Tighten Less' unless they discount the future 'too much'. The short-run benefits of cheating in one period by playing 'Tighten More' when the other country plays 'Tighten Less' are outweighed by the costs of having both countries play 'Tighten More' forever. Country A may play 'Tighten Less' in each period because it believes that if it does so Country B will play 'Tighten Less' in the next period and if B does not, Country A will play 'Tighten More' in every future period, and Country B may do the same. The assumption by each country that the other is following such a 'trigger strategy' may be enough to ensure that A will always play 'Tighten Less' and vice versa.[8]

The reason why trigger strategies can support repeated play of efficient policies is that for each country the value of deviating from the efficient policy in each period is outweighed by the discounted value of having efficient policies played in the future. Therefore, for trigger strategies to work, there must be at least some probability each period that the game will continue, and outcomes in the future must not be discounted 'too heavily'.

Even if this condition is met, the 'Folk Theorem' tells us that there are many possible Nash equilibria in repeated games including both repeated play of efficient policies (like 'Tighten Less') and repeated play of the non-cooperative policies (like 'Tighten More'). Therefore, one function of international policy coordination fora might be to coordinate on the Nash equilibrium of the repeated game that involves repeated play of efficient policies.

Contact in several areas

It has been pointed out that countries interact on other important kinds of policies besides macroeconomic policy, such as trade and defence policy.[9] The gains

---

[8] Repeated interaction with incomplete information, a finite horizon and no coordination can lead to outcomes similar to those under repeated interaction with complete information, an infinite horizon and coordination on efficient policies. Countries may not know each other's 'types', that is, each other's preferences. Repeated interaction makes it possible for countries to build 'reputations' for being of a certain type. A country may have an incentive to play the efficient policy for much of the finite horizon even if it intends eventually to deviate from that policy, because it can gain more from deviating if it first builds up a reputation for choosing the efficient policy (Canzoneri and Henderson, 1991).

[9] Putnam and Henning (1989) discuss the implications of the fact that countries interact on several kinds of policies. Basevi, Delbono and Delnicolo (1990) consider interactions on both trade policy and macroeconomic policy.

from coordinating several kinds of policies may be significant even if the gains from coordinating any one kind of policy are not. Also the opportunities for coordinating the different kinds of policies are staggered, so countries can verify what has happened to one kind of policy before deciding what to do in another. It would be useful to have more analysis of the implications of interactions on several kinds of policies.

Model uncertainty

There is also uncertainty over what the model of the economy is; what its parameters are; what its structure is and the type of shocks it faces. Not only do nations not necessarily know the 'true' model of the economy, they also do not necessarily know the model that other countries believe to be true. While Frankel and Rockett (1988) first pointed out that nations might lose by working together under uncertainty *ex post*, Ghosh and Masson (1991, 1994) show that uncertainty is likely to increase the potential gains *ex ante*. First, countries may have different information sets that they can share, and by doing so get better expected outcomes. In models where policy-makers must set their policies before uncertainty is resolved, the expected gain from coordination is greater whenever there is multiplicative or parameter uncertainty. Ghosh and Masson further argue that uncertainty provides a rationale for episodic efforts at coordination, since crises generate large uncertainties, and hence potential gains, and are also, fortunately, infrequent.

'Counterproductive coordination'

Several analysts have put forward examples in which what they define as co-ordination is counterproductive.[10] As stated above, in the terminology of the policy coordination literature, cooperation is possible only when commitment is possible. In the examples designed to show that coordination can be counterproductive, it is assumed that the participants in the policy game cannot credibly make all of the commitments necessary for achieving the efficient equilibrium but that some participants can commit to jointly maximise and play Nash against others. This type of commitment is called 'coordination',

---

[10] Rogoff (1985a) and Oudiz and Sachs (1985) produced the earliest examples, and Canzoneri and Henderson (1991) produced another. Tabellini (1990) produced an important example involving two political parties in each of two countries.

and this type of coordination can be counterproductive for those who engage in it.

In the example of Rogoff (1985a), the authorities in each of two countries have an 'inflation bias' problem because desired outputs are above natural outputs. Even though inflation is costly, the equilibrium rate of inflation must be high enough that the incentive to increase the money supply in order to raise output is just offset by the extra cost of additional consumer price index (CPI) inflation. In a two-country world with non-cooperative behaviour, an increase in the money supply in one country increases its inflation both by increasing its output price inflation and by causing its currency to depreciate in real terms, making imports more expensive.[11] With joint maximisation between monetary authorities and non-cooperative play against the private sector, when one country expands its money supply the additional real depreciation of its currency helps the other country by lowering CPI inflation there. Therefore, the extra cost of CPI inflation for the two countries taken together is lower and the equilibrium rate of inflation must be higher if the incentive to try to raise output is to be matched by additional joint costs of CPI inflation. Thus, the inflation bias in both countries is higher.

Existing examples of counterproductive coordination leave a key question unanswered. The commitment of some of the participants to jointly maximise and play Nash against other participants must be taken seriously and acted on by the other participants. If this kind of commitment is credible, why is it not credible to commit to deliver an efficient outcome? Both kinds of commitment require those making the commitment to be off their Nash reaction functions. Since existing examples provide no answer to the key question, in our view they are not convincing. Indeed, we regard them as examples of the kind of outcomes that would never occur. The agents who can make credible commitments have an incentive to avoid commitments that lead to these outcomes and to make other kinds of commitments which can improve outcomes or at least not worsen them, and the other agents have every reason to take these other commitments seriously.

Monetary policy and fiscal policy

The analysis of stabilisation policy often proceeds under the assumption that monetary policy is the only policy instrument.[12] There are several explanations

---

[11] The first-order conditions for a monetary authority with non-cooperative behaviour and with joint maximisation are given in appendix 1 (p. 97).

[12] From, for example, the survey of Persson and Tabellini (1995), it is evident that for the most part monetary policy and fiscal policy have been studied separately in the policy coordination

for why this assumption is made. First, the general criticism of stabilisation policy in the 1970s and thereafter fell most heavily on fiscal policy, at least in part because fiscal policy had played a major role as a stabilisation instrument in the 1950s and 1960s. Second, monetary policy is more flexible and it became conventional wisdom that fiscal policy is too inflexible to be useful as a stabilisation tool. Third, the analysis of stabilisation conflicts among countries is much simpler when it is assumed that there is only one instrument in each country and, given other considerations just mentioned, it is natural to choose monetary policy as that instrument.

In a closed economy, if the only two targets of policy are the output gap and CPI inflation, then there is a need for either monetary policy or fiscal policy as a stabilisation instrument, but not both.[13] In the short run, the output gap and the inflation rate are linked by the aggregate supply curve or Phillips curve. Therefore, choosing the output gap is the same thing as choosing the inflation rate. Both monetary policy and fiscal policy affect only the aggregate demand schedule. If shocks are known before policy is set, shocks to the aggregate demand curve (money demand shocks or goods demand shocks) can be exactly offset by either monetary or fiscal policy. Shocks to aggregate supply cannot be exactly offset but the best attainable output-gap/inflation pair can be achieved by either monetary or fiscal policy through shifts in the aggregate demand schedule. In order to make the problem of choosing the optimal mix of monetary policy and fiscal policy meaningful, it is necessary to add another target for policy such as a desired level of government spending based on public finance considerations or a desired level of investment (or, as a proxy, the real interest rate) based on long-run growth considerations.

In a two-country world economy, if the only two targets of policy are the output gap and CPI inflation, the situation is somewhat more complicated. First suppose that the only shocks are money demand and goods demand shocks in each of the two countries. If both monetary policy and fiscal policy are available in both of the two countries, then bliss is attainable and, in general, all four policies are needed.[14] In each country, monetary policy offsets the money demand shock and fiscal policy offsets the goods demand shock. Now suppose that the only shocks are productivity shocks. If both monetary and fiscal policy are available in both countries, there is no Nash equilibrium. In each country, CPI inflation depends only on the output gap and the real exchange rate (the

literature. As stated in the text, in analyses of stabilisation conflicts it is usually assumed that monetary policies are the only instruments. In the complementary analyses of ongoing conflicts over spending priorities and tax collections at full employment, it is usually assumed that fiscal policies are the only policy instruments.

[13] The output gap and the employment gap can be used interchangeably. If it is assumed that supply of labour is perfectly inelastic, then variation in the employment gap is the same as variation in employment.

[14] This result and the other result stated in this paragraph are proved in appendix 1.

price of one country's goods in terms of the other's). Thus, each country can use one instrument to keep the output gap at zero and use the other to attempt to move the real exchange rate to the value that it prefers. The values of the real exchange rate desired by the two countries will be different, so each country finds it in its interest to move its instruments without limit in an attempt to achieve its desired real exchange rate while always keeping its output gap at zero.

It is clear that the output gap and CPI inflation are not the only targets of macroeconomic policy. As indicated above in the discussion of a closed economy, countries may have targets for government spending or investment. In addition, countries may have targets for actual or structural government deficits, ratios of government debt to gross domestic product (GDP), or current account balances. For example, the Maastricht Treaty establishes norms for actual deficits and debt ratios for the members of EMU. In general, when countries have target variables other than the output gap and CPI inflation, no matter what the source of shocks, bliss is not attainable so there are stabilisation policy conflicts, and a Nash non-cooperative equilibrium exists.

There are several notable exceptions to the general practice of ignoring fiscal policy in analyses of international stabilisation conflicts. In all of the contributions that allow for both monetary and fiscal policy, countries have targets in addition to the output gap and inflation. However, there is as yet not complete agreement about what the additional targets of macroeconomic policy should be. A non-exhaustive list of candidate variables includes the current account, government spending, domestic goods consumption, imported goods consumption, the total taxation rate, the non-indexed government debt to GDP ratio, the government deficit to GDP ratio, the public sector borrowing requirement (PSBR), the short-term interest rate, the direct taxation rate and autonomous taxation.[15] To make progress in analysing the international coordination of monetary and fiscal policy, it will be necessary to devote more effort to deciding exactly what the targets of macroeconomic policy should be.

When countries have more than two target variables, models become considerably more complex. Frequently, it is either not informative to rely on analytical results or not even possible obtain such results, so simulation results

---

[15] In the seminal paper of Oudiz and Sachs (1984), the target variables include the current account. In Eichengreen and Ghironi (1999), Levine and Pearlman (1997, 2002) and Alesina and Tabellini (1987), the target variables include government spending. In each of two works by McKibbin and Sachs (1988, 1991) and in each of the four papers in the volume edited by Currie and Levine (1993) (Krichel, Levine and Pearlman; Christodoulakis, Gaines and Levine; Levine and Currie; and Currie and Levine), the target variables include a subset of domestic goods consumption, imported goods consumption, government spending, the total taxation rate, the non-indexed government debt to GDP ratio, the deficit to GDP ratio, the public sector borrowing requirement (PSBR), the current account, the short-term interest rate, the direct taxation rate and autonomous taxation.

are reported instead. The one very important but not very surprising conclusion that emerges from these studies is that to achieve the best results, both monetary and fiscal policy must be coordinated among countries. To make progress in analysing international macroeconomic policy coordination it will be necessary to rely heavily on estimated or calibrated economic models. As yet it is not clear whether the appropriate analysis will yield a few very general precepts or results that depend heavily on the particular shocks and model under consideration.

Information exchange

As is well known, one of the major activities at actual meetings on policy coordination is the exchange of information. As is also well known, in much of the early theoretical work on policy coordination there is no need for the exchange of information. It is assumed that all the agents have all relevant information, as in the simple example at the beginning of this chapter.

In some of the later theoretical work, there is scope for the exchange of information. As pointed out above, in infinitely repeated games when trigger strategies are considered, there are multiple equilibria which include both the efficient equilibrium and many inefficient equilibria. Thus, there is scope for the countries to communicate about which of the possible equilibria are better and what strategies they intend to follow. When one country says it will follow some strategy which is in its own best interest given that the other country follows some other strategy, the first country has every incentive to follow through on what it says if the second country does also. In game theory, exchange of such information is referred to as 'cheap talk'.[16] Cheap talk may make possible coordination on the efficient equilibrium.

Ghosh and Masson (1994) provide examples in which exchanging information may lead to either better or worse outcomes when countries act non-cooperatively. Their findings are another example of the general principle that when there are two distortions removing one distortion may not improve the outcome. For example, in a non-cooperative setting with externalities like our canonical example and with lack of full information, exchanging information does not necessarily lead to a better outcome because the Nash equilibrium is still inefficient. Of course, when nations coordinate policies, exchanging information always improves outcomes.

---

[16] For a discussion of the application of the 'cheap talk' concept in economic models, see Farrell and Rabin (1996) who define 'cheap talk' as 'costless, nonbinding, nonverifiable, messages that may affect the listener's beliefs'.

Recently there have been advances in the analysis of information exchange in the game theory literature. It would be useful to investigate the extent to which these advances can be applied to the analysis of policy coordination.

Quantitative analysis

There is an extensive literature on the quantitative analysis of policy coordination. A comprehensive survey of that literature is beyond the scope of this chapter.[17] Instead we summarise what we take to be the conventional wisdom regarding the gains from achieving cooperative (efficient) outcomes instead of conventional non-cooperative outcomes.[18] This conventional wisdom is consistent with the conclusions of many but not all studies.[19] We also discuss extensions of the quantitative analysis in which both the approach and the conclusions are somewhat different.

Oudiz and Sachs (1984) (hereafter, OS) are the first to estimate the gains from cooperation. They use the reduced forms of two econometric models and (quadratic) country welfare functions. In these welfare functions the target variables are the output gap, inflation and the current account surplus; and the relative weights were inferred from a baseline forecast for the years 1984–6. OS find gains of between 0.5 and 1 per cent of GDP per year for each of the country blocs considered.

Over the ensuing nineteen years there have been many other estimates of the welfare gains between cooperative and conventional non-cooperative outcomes. Each set of estimates is based on a quantitative model and country welfare functions. In some cases, the parameters of the quantitative model are determined by estimation, and in others they are determined by calibration. Sometimes the country welfare functions include different variables from those used by OS.

---

[17] McKibbin (1997) provides such a survey. Bryant *et al.* (1988) and Bryant, Hooper and Mann (1993) provide an extensive comparison of policy multipliers and policy rules in a host of large macroeconomic models – many models that are used in the empirical work on policy coordination.

[18] Efficient outcomes can always be achieved by cooperation. However, they can sometimes be achieved without cooperation, for example by using trigger strategies. For simplicity, in this section we refer to efficient outcomes as cooperative outcomes, as is conventional in the quantitative coordination literature.

[19] There is a closely related literature on the comparison of alternative policy regimes. A regime is a specification of simple policy rules for two or more countries, usually the same rule. Using quantitative models, countries are subjected to several types of shocks under alternative regimes. The objective is to determine which regime performs best for which types of shocks and whether any regime seems to be preferable for most kinds of shocks. McKibbin (1997) also provides a thorough survey of this literature.

Often the weights for the target variables are chosen by the analyst rather than inferred from a baseline forecast.

What is remarkable is that despite some differences among the methods used to obtain them, many of the estimates of the welfare gains from cooperation have been close to the OS estimates. However, there are some notable exceptions with considerably higher estimates, from an average of 2.8 to an average of 7.4 times as high as the OS estimates.[20] Despite these exceptions, the conventional wisdom is that the gains from cooperation are roughly between 0.5 and 1 per cent of GDP per year, as confirmed by McKibbin (1997).

Whether the welfare gains from cooperation found by OS and the many studies that followed are large or small is to a large extent in the eye of the beholder. Gains of 0.5 to 1 per cent a year are of the same order of magnitude as estimated gains from the Uruguay Round of trade agreements. In any case, most analysts regard the gains from cooperation as small.[21] When the gains arise from cooperative responses to shocks, they are usually deemed to be small relative to the size of the shocks.[22]

A handful of authors have extended the quantitative analysis of policy co-ordination to include outcomes other than the cooperative and conventional non-cooperative outcomes. They have considered three types of gains: Type I gains are realised by moving to the cooperative outcome from the conventional non-cooperative outcome, Type II gains are realised by moving to the conventional non-cooperative outcome from a constrained non-cooperative outcome and Type III gains are realised by moving to a constrained non-cooperative outcome from the historical outcome. Type I gains are measured by OS and most other investigators. Type II and Type III gains are measured in the extensions. The main conclusion of the extensions is that the sum of Type II and Type III gains are often an order of magnitude larger than Type I gains, because at least one component of the sum is an order of magnitude larger.[23] In other words, taking the final step from the conventional noncooperative

---

[20] Hughes-Hallet (1986) finds gains from cooperation of 0.47 and 1.35 percentage points of annual GDP growth for five years for the United States and Europe, respectively. Translated into level terms to make them comparable with OS, these gains are 1.4 and 4.1 per cent of GDP per year on average. Becker *et al.* (1986) find gains ranging from 1.8 to 3.3 percentage points of unemployment per year for five years for the United States and five European countries. Translated into terms of GDP using an Okun's law coefficient of 3, these gains range from 5.4 to 9.9 per cent of GDP per year.

[21] Similarly, according to Feenstra (1992), the estimated gains from trade agreements, which are on the order of 1 per cent or less of GDP per year, are regarded as small by most trade economists.

[22] Obstfeld and Rogoff (2001) have reinforced the conventional wisdom that the gains from cooperation are small. The authors use a model that exemplifies the 'new open economy macroeconomics'. Several other authors have used similar models to analyse policy coordination, but it is beyond the scope of this chapter to survey these recent contributions.

[23] See nn. 24–26.

outcome to cooperation is less important than taking one or the other of the earlier steps.

The justification for considering Type II and Type III gains is that countries can attain the conventional non-cooperative outcome only under quite strong assumptions. Each country must have the same considerable amount of information about the structure of the world economy, any shocks and the tastes and actions of all countries. In addition each country must use this information in a relatively sophisticated way: using its own welfare function, it must calculate its optimal policy response for any given policy responses by all the other countries. It is argued that these assumptions may often not be met and that countries may have to communicate more or become more sophisticated in their use of information if they are to realise Type II and Type III gains.

The challenge in considering Type II and Type III gains is to construct plausible alternatives to the conventional non-cooperative outcome. History is a clear alternative as long as it can be argued convincingly that history should not be regarded as conventional non-cooperative outcome.[24] It is certainly true that historical outcomes are sometimes quite different from those implied by the plausible welfare functions and the mainstream quantitative models used by investigators. Other alternatives are generated by relaxing one or another of the strong assumptions that underlie the conventional non-cooperative outcome. One such alternative is a 'limited information' non-cooperative outcome.[25] This kind of outcome arises when countries do not combine their information to make, for example, the best possible estimates of current shocks. Another such alternative is an 'insular' or 'isolationist' non-cooperative outcome.[26] This kind of outcome arises when there is a shock and each country maximises its own welfare assuming (counterfactually) that the others will stick to their pre-shock policies rather than make the optimal response to the shock.

---

[24] Hughes-Hallet (1986) finds that for the United States and Europe Type III gains are roughly 9.5 and 8 times as large as Type I gains, respectively. See also n. 20.

[25] In their 'US Deficit Game', Canzoneri and Edison (1990) compare a 'coordinated' non-cooperative outcome based on correct information about the US deficit with an 'uncoodinated' non-cooperative equilibrium based on an estimate of the US deficit constructed by putting equal weights on the correct information and a plausible alternative. Moving from the uncoordinated outcome to the coordinated outcome reduces loss from 25 to 31 per cent of the uncoordinated loss for one quantitative model and from 6 to 20 per cent for another. In contrast, moving from the coordinated non-cooperative outcome to cooperation reduces loss by less than 1 per cent of the coordinated non-cooperative loss.

[26] Hughes-Hallet (1986) finds that for the United States and Europe Type II gains are roughly 29 and 2 times as large as Type I gains, respectively. See also n. 20. In their US and Europe disinflation example, Canzoneri and Minford (1989) find that for the United States and Europe Type II gains are roughly 2 and 7 times as large as Type I gains, respectively.

Two other pairs of authors have extended the quantitative analysis of policy coordination in yet other ways. Ghosh and Masson (1994) provide a thorough analysis of the implications of model uncertainty for the gains from cooperation. They find that with model certainty the gains from cooperation are considerably larger than those found by OS and that with model uncertainty the gains are increased substantially.[27] Sachs and McKibbin (1985) find that although industrialised country cooperation generates relatively small gains for these countries, it may generate 'substantial' gains for the developing world.[28] For example a cooperative disinflation by the industrialised countries yields a significantly lower world interest rate than a non-cooperative disinflation, thereby raising the welfare of the developing world.

According to conventional wisdom, the gains from cooperation are small. However, several investigators have found significant gains from cooperation or coordination on better non-cooperative outcomes. It appears that the case is not closed and that, therefore, there is scope for further quantitative analysis of policy coordination.

Papers produced in connection with the GEI Project

Five papers produced in connection with the Global Economic Institutions (GEI) Project are also relevant here. Two of the papers are empirical. Bai and Hall (1996) use a common factor approach to try to test for the degree of symmetry in the shocks to output, employment and interest rates in Europe, the United States and Japan. They find that there is some evidence of common shocks to the United States and the European Union, with little common persistence but similar common volatility. They also find that there is little to no relationship between the shocks in the United States and Japan. This work is particularly interesting since countries should react and cooperate differently depending on the degree of symmetry of shocks. Caporale *et al.* (1998a, 1998b) look at the gains to coordination among the G3 where the 'shock' is a unilateral monetary or fiscal tightening in the United States. They report gains to coordination which are similar to those in the literature within a three-year horizon.

The remaining three papers are theoretical and show that delegation of the type proposed by Rogoff (1985b) can be counterproductive for policy

---

[27] According to Ghosh and Masson (1994), with model certainty and with model uncertainty, respectively, the gains from cooperation average 6 per cent and 10 per cent of GDP per year forever.

[28] Sachs and McKibbin (1985) estimate gains for the developing countries that they characterise as substantial. Unfortunately, they do not present their estimates in a way that makes it easy to evaluate their characterisation.

coordination.[29] Rogoff shows that a closed economy with a social welfare function that implies inflation bias can reduce that bias by delegating monetary policy to a 'conservative' central banker, one whose personal welfare function has a higher weight on an inflation objective than the social welfare function. However, the conservative central banker does not respond optimally to productivity shocks because he lets the output gap vary more than would be desirable and lets inflation vary too little. Thus, there is a tradeoff between the average level of inflation and stabilisation performance.

Currie, Levine and Pearlman (1996a, 1996b) argue that if each of two countries delegates monetary policy to Rogoff-type conservative central bankers, stabilisation performance may be compromised, and if shocks are symmetric, international policy coordination may be counterproductive.[30] These findings seem to follow naturally from Rogoff's finding for a closed economy. In the context of our above game (i.e. in the face of a symmetric productivity shock) coordinated monetary policy leads to less tightening than non-cooperative monetary policy. Conservative central bankers coordinating and, therefore, acting like a single authority contract less than they would if they acted non-cooperatively, but they still contract more than would be implied by the social welfare function. Levine and Pearlman (1997) expand on Currie, Levine and Pearlman (1996b) by taking account of the fiscal authorities of both countries. When fiscal policy has an additional externality, delegating to conservative central bankers may be even more counterproductive. The paper further demonstrates that commitment to joint maximisation among a subset of agents who then play non-cooperatively against the rest may not be welfare-enhancing.

To provide some perspective on the GEI papers it is important to consider the findings of Walsh (1995). He shows that under the usual assumptions there is a contract for the head of the Central Bank that completely eliminates inflation bias without compromising stabilisation performance. Thus, with Walsh-type contracts, there is no tradeoff between the average inflation rate and stabilisation performance. Walsh-type contracts involve linking the compensation of the head of the Central Bank to inflation performance. There is much disagreement about whether it is feasible to implement Walsh-type contracts and, therefore, about whether there is a tradeoff between the average inflation rate and stabilisation performance. Coordination among policy authorities subject to Walsh-type contracts is not counterproductive.

---

[29] In an another paper, Rogoff (1985a) showed that what he called coordination could be counterproductive.

[30] The primary focus of these papers is that delegating to a conservative central banker and then playing non-cooperatively can be worse than not delegating, for the same reasons as in the cooperation case. They also show that if the nations cooperate when choosing the type of central banker before then playing non-cooperatively, the countries will choose 'anti-conservative' central bankers when the shocks are symmetric.

3 Experience of policy coordination since 1973[31]

This section is a selective review of the experience with policy coordination since the breakdown of the Bretton Woods System. It focuses on two areas in which policy coordination has received the most public attention, namely the global G7 process which includes the largest industrialised countries, and the European process of Economic and Monetary Union (EMU).[32]

The Group of Seven (G7)

Evolution of the G7

The G7 traces its roots to ad hoc, and often secretive, meetings of the Group of Five finance ministers and Central Bank governors.[33] In March 1973, US Treasury Secretary George Shultz invited the German, French and British Finance Ministers (Helmut Schmidt, Valéry Giscard d'Estaing and Anthony Barber) to an informal meeting in the ground floor library of the White House. At the first meeting of what was initially called the 'Library Group', participants agreed to abandon attempts to re-establish fixed parities between the dollar and European currencies, thereby helping to usher in the floating rate era. The Japanese Finance Minister was invited to join the group in the autumn and Central Bank governors were invited soon afterward, thus establishing the G5 process.

The process gained added momentum with the launching of annual economic summits. Soon after they became Heads of their respective governments, original Library Group members Schmidt and Giscard invited the leaders of the other G5 countries plus Italy to Rambouillet, France in November 1975. Canada attended the 1976 summit in Puerto Rico to complete the Group of Seven at the Head of State/Government level. Despite the participation of seven countries at the Leaders' summits ever since 1976, the ministerial process remained largely limited to the G5 during the 1970s and early 1980s.

---

[31] This section and appendix 2 are based largely on historical accounts contained in Solomon (1982, 1999), Ainley (1984), Cooper *et al.* (1989), Hajnal (1999), Putnam and Henning (1989), Dobson (1991), *The Twenty G7 Summits* (1994), Bryant (1995), Stark (1995), Bergsten and Henning (1996), James (1996), Kenen (1996), as well as the texts of G7 and Economic and Financial Committee (Ecofin) statements.

[32] Other fora for macro policy discussions among the major economies include the Economic Policy Committee (EPC) and its Working Party 3 (WP-3) of the OECD, the Executive Board and International Monetary and Financial Committee of the IMF and the G10 Central Bank governors' meetings and other meetings at the BIS.

[33] The G5 countries are the United States, Japan, Germany, France and the United Kingdom. The G7 adds Italy and Canada.

The G5 Finance Ministers and Central Bank governors released their first of-ficial statement in January 1985 and they attracted worldwide attention with the Plaza Agreement of September 1985. Shortly afterwards, the group expanded to become the G7 with the addition of Italy and Canada in 1986.[34] The G7 Finance Ministers and Central Bank governors have met regularly every year since 1986, always immediately before the IMF/World Bank spring and autumn meetings, and often in January or February.

Deputy Finance Ministers have participated in the process since the begin-ning, while there was no equivalent at first on the Central Bank side. Over time the finance deputies have taken on a greater role in steering the process. Central Bank deputies have long been invited to participate in biannual surveillance discussions with their finance deputy colleagues. In recent years, Central Bank deputy governors have begun to meet or call each other regularly to coordinate Central Bank participation in the G7 process more broadly.

At the Leaders' summits, the President of the European Commission has attended regularly since 1977 and he has been joined by the President of the European Council since 1986. The President of Russia was invited to meet with the G7 leaders at the end of their 1991 summit and Russia's participation has increased over time such that the summit is now called the G8 Summit. However, during the summit, the leaders of the original seven arrange some time to meet without Russia to discuss macroeconomic policies and certain other IMF-centred issues, such as debt relief.

The summit process is guided by 'sherpas' representing the leaders of each country and 'sous-sherpas' from the finance and foreign ministries of the par-ticipating countries plus the European Commission. Despite much overlap be-tween sous-sherpas and G7 Deputy Finance Ministers, the G7 finance ministry and Central Bank process still does not include European Commission or Russian participation on a regular basis. With the launch of the euro in 1999, the President of the ECB and the Chair of the Euro-11 Council have assumed a limited role in the G7 process while the group considers the issue of euro area representation in the long term.

Macro policy coordination in the G7

The G5's first attempt at policy coordination occurred in the wake of the oil price shock of December 1973. As each country began to experience higher inflation and a deteriorating balance of payments, the world faced the danger of excessive monetary and fiscal contraction as each country's tighter policies tended to raise inflation and reduce net exports in its neighbours. This is one of

---

[34] For some time after the creation of the G7 ministerial process, the G5 ministers and governors continued to meet occasionally. Indeed, Italy boycotted the Louvre Accord of 1987 because it was discussed within the G5 first before it was to be discussed by the G7.

the classic examples in the literature for gains from international coordination by taking account of externalities. Rather than agree on specific macro policies, however, the G5 decided to push for a new oil adjustment facility in the IMF to give countries an alternative to fiscal tightening.[35] In addition, the G5 agreed to establish the International Energy Agency (IEA), affiliated with the OECD, as a forum for oil importing nations to discuss energy strategies.

The next attempt at macro policy coordination took place at the London summit of 1977, when leaders agreed on unspecified, but widely acknowledged, growth targets. Failure to achieve the London growth targets led to specific policy pledges at Bonn in 1978 that appeared to be a classic example of cooperative game playing. The United States pledged to decontrol domestic oil prices, while France, Germany and Japan pledged specific fiscal expansions. A formula to conclude the Tokyo Round of trade negotiations was also part of the bargain. It is important to recognise that there was a pre-existing domestic faction in each country pushing for these policies, especially the fiscal expansions. For the United States on oil and France on trade, the summit agreement may have helped tip the balance of domestic forces, but it could never have succeeded without the domestic pressure groups. In Germany and Japan, politics were already strongly heading toward fiscal expansion even before the summit. All of the participants essentially carried through with the agreements reached in Bonn.[36]

Many commentators have viewed the burst of global inflation and subsequent recession in 1979–81 as evidence that the Bonn summit was a failure because it promoted misguided policies. In particular, it has been argued that by the time coordinated policies were agreed upon the economic problems had already changed. However, it is also true that the Iranian revolution and the Organisation of Petroleum Exporting Countries (OPEC) oil shock of 1979 could not reasonably have been predicted in 1978, so that the poor outcomes of 1979–81 were only partly due to mistimed policies adopted in Bonn.

The elections of Margaret Thatcher and Ronald Reagan led to a cessation of serious attempts at policy coordination in the early 1980s, as these leaders tended to favour unilateral action and were generally suspicious of international coordination in all spheres. By 1985, however, the relentless rise of the dollar and the burgeoning US current account deficit led to a change of heart.

The Plaza Agreement of September 1985 and the Louvre Accord of February 1987 marked the high-water-marks of policy coordination in the post-Bretton Woods era. Each of the G5 (later G7) countries promised to undertake a list

---

[35] In its first two years of operation, the oil adjustment facility lent a total of $8.3 billion to 55 countries. After 1977, the oil adjustment facility was wound down, but the principle of lending more flexibly in the face of oil and other commodity price shocks was incorporated into other IMF facilities.

[36] For a careful treatment of the Bonn summit and its outcomes, see Putnam and Henning (1989).

of specified policy actions and to cooperate in currency intervention. (Currency intervention will be discussed in section 4.) Formal statements by the G7 during this period indicated that there was broad satisfaction with growth and inflation performance in the major economies. The primary area of concern was the large external imbalances between the major regions, which were raising protectionist pressures that the leaders feared they could not resist.

Under the Plaza Agreement, specific commitments included:

- The United States promised to reduce its fiscal deficit by more than 1 per cent of GDP in FY 1986 and to continue further reductions in the future.
- Japan promised to liberalise its financial markets to ease consumer credit, to facilitate the internationalisation and strengthening of the yen, and to conduct monetary policy 'with due attention to the yen rate'.
- Germany promised tax cuts and a progressive reduction of the share of the public sector in the economy.
- All countries promised to resist protectionist pressures and to pursue unspecified structural reforms in a variety of sectors to increase economic efficiency.

Under the Louvre Accord, specific commitments included:

- The United States promised to reduce its fiscal deficit from 3.9 per cent of GDP in FY1987 to 2.3 per cent in FY1988.
- Japan promised to cut its discount rate by 0.5 per cent.
- France promised to cut taxes by 1 per cent of GDP while lowering the fiscal deficit by the same amount between 1986 and 1988.

Many of the promises not listed above were so vaguely worded that it is pointless to discuss whether they were implemented. In the more specific monetary and fiscal areas, the monetary commitments were fulfilled, at least for a short while. The fiscal commitments were largely not achieved, particularly French promises to reduce taxes, Japanese promises on fiscal stimulus and US pledges on deficit reduction.[37]

Many Japanese observers regard the Louvre Accord as the beginning of Japan's bubble economy because it contained a brief reference to Bank of Japan (BOJ) plans to lower the discount rate by 50 basis points and because Treasury Secretary Baker spoke out against looming interest rate increases in Germany and Japan later that year. In fact, pressure on Japan to ease monetary policy

---

[37] Assessing the fulfilment of the fiscal pledges is complicated by the existence of many different revenue and spending programmes at all levels of government, by different fiscal years and because of the unpredictable effect of economic activity on revenues and entitlement spending. This assessment is based on general government revenues and balances tabulated in the *OECD Economic Outlook*, December 1999, as well as the discussion in Dobson (1991).

started much earlier and was already evident in the language of the Plaza Agreement.[38] However there was no pressure evident in public statements from US officials or in G7 communiqués to ease Japanese monetary policy during the 1988–90 period when the bubble was most pronounced.

Beginning at the end of the 1980s and continuing to the present day, G7 statements have avoided specific macro policy obligations in favour of a general sense of the desired direction of individual policies in the different regions. At the same time, more effort has been placed on ensuring that participants have a common understanding of the problems to be addressed. The macroeconomic surveillance process was formalised to cover specific indicators of growth, inflation, monetary and fiscal conditions and external imbalances on a regular basis. The role of the IMF was enhanced in the late 1980s to support this surveillance process, including the preparation of surveillance papers for discussion. The purpose of these changes was to monitor consistency in policies across countries and to encourage participants to consider the medium-term implications of policy stances.

The large current account imbalances of Japan and the United States have continued to be a major focus of discussion. The IMF took on the role of impartial observer both in keeping track of the effects of past policies and in assessing the likely impacts of current and proposed future policies. Statements released by the G7 in the early-to-mid-1990s tended to focus on the need for the United States and other countries with large fiscal deficits to reduce them. Europe and Japan acknowledged the need for structural reforms to raise employment and private investment. At times, the G7 also endorsed Japanese announcements of fiscal stimulus plans and encouraged further actions to strengthen the banking system.

The common thrust of these agreed policies was to moderate domestic demand growth in the United States and accelerate domestic demand in Europe and especially Japan. To a large extent, the macroeconomic components of these policies were implemented, particularly the substantial reduction in fiscal deficits in most countries and the substantial increase in Japanese fiscal deficits. Low and stable inflation rates are another area of shared success. However, it is not clear that much credit for these outcomes can be given to the G7 coordination process, since domestic pressure also existed for these policies. Moreover, continental Europe and Japan clearly did not succeed in stimulating growth through structural reform, the implementation of Japanese fiscal expansion was erratic and the record of the 1990s shows little success in achieving the goal of reducing external imbalances.

---

[38] Japanese money and credit growth did pick up very slightly in late 1985 and more substantially in late 1987.

G7 currency intervention

Perhaps the greatest focus of the public has been on the implications of the G7 process, and specifically the Plaza Agreement and Louvre Accord, for exchange rates. The Plaza Agreement specifically called for further dollar depreciation. The Louvre Accord declared that dollar depreciation had gone far enough. Both announcements described participants as being ready to cooperate closely to encourage the desired exchange rate adjustment whenever it was appropriate. In this context, 'cooperate' is generally accepted as code for concerted intervention. Over time, language affirming 'close cooperation in the exchange markets where appropriate' has been a frequent, but not universal, element of G7 statements.

The motivation for currency intervention is to avoid large swings in exchange rates that bring about unsustainable current account imbalances and impose large adjustment costs on the economy. To the extent that these swings are induced by the fundamental macroeconomic policy mix, currency intervention is ineffective at best and harmful at worst. However, when financial markets overshoot the exchange rates consistent with fundamental policies, intervention may be able to help restore equilibrium, although such a presumption is not universally accepted.

While they have not publicly committed to specific currency interventions in advance, G7 participants have engaged in concerted intervention on occasion ever since the original G5 in the 1970s.[39] In 1985, intervention associated with the Plaza Agreement aimed at hastening the dollar's depreciation. In 1987, intervention aimed at preventing further depreciation. In 1989, intervention sought to limit the dollar's appreciation. From the US perspective, intervention peaked in 1989, when US authorities sold over $22 billion to purchase DM and yen, largely in concert with Germany and Japan.

Coordinated intervention declined markedly in 1990 and 1991, and US and German authorities virtually ceased intervention in 1992 and 1993. Coordinated intervention picked up modestly in 1994 and 1995 in an attempt to restrain the rise of the yen, and to a lesser extent, the DM. After the dollar's rebound in late 1995, the US authorities ceased intervention entirely in 1996 and 1997. The only instance of coordinated intervention since 1995 occurred in 1998, when the United States joined Japan on one day in June to halt the sharp depreciation of the yen.

Despite the virtual abandonment of coordinated intervention in recent years, Japanese authorities have continued to intervene frequently on a unilateral basis.

[39] The Jurgensen Report – published in 1983, but whose conclusions had already been accepted by much of the economics profession – cast doubt on the effectiveness of sterilised exchange rate intervention and may have been partly responsible for the lull in intervention activity in the early 1980s.

Moreover, G7 statements regularly repeat the threat of possible future coordinated intervention if warranted by the circumstances. At the September 1999 G7 meeting, participants hinted that coordinated intervention to deflect the yen's appreciation might be forthcoming in conjunction with further steps to ease monetary conditions by the Bank of Japan. While the language of the January 2000 statement on exchange rates was little changed from September, participants seemed less inclined to consider coordinated intervention, as the BOJ judged that prospects for recovery lessened the need to consider easing monetary policy further. Many Japanese officials do not want to repeat the perceived mistake of bowing to international pressure for loose monetary policy, such as has been attributed to the Louvre Accord.

Other policies in the G7

Over time the G7 has expanded its interests beyond macroeconomic surveillance and exchange markets to include the full range of IMF policies and other international economic issues such as the transition of former socialist economies, debt reduction for poor and heavily indebted countries, environmental issues, corruption and money laundering and reform of the international financial system. Concrete outcomes of this process include increased IMF lending to Russia, adoption of the OECD anti-bribery convention, the HIPC initiative and the Financial Stability Forum (FSF). The G7 is also the core of the new G20 mechanism for dialogue with key emerging markets on global financial and economic developments and institutions.

In addition, the network of contacts built up by the G7 process proved invaluable in addressing fast-breaking crises such as the need to secure funding for the Gulf War effort in 1990–1, the rescue package for Mexico in 1994–5, and similar packages for Thailand, Korea and Indonesia in 1997–8.

European economic and monetary union

Evolution of coordination in the euro area

In December 1969, the European Council appointed Pierre Werner of Luxembourg to draft a report on the feasibility of economic and monetary union. The Werner Report of 1970 outlined the path to monetary union. In 1971, the finance ministers of the European Community endorsed the goal of economic and monetary union by 1980.

The first concrete step down this path was the creation of the European currency 'snake', which was limited to a small core of countries that pledged to keep their currencies within $2\frac{1}{4}$ per cent of each other. The snake was launched in March 1972. The original members were the six European Community (EC) countries (Germany, France, Italy, the Netherlands, Belgium and Luxembourg) plus Denmark. The United Kingdom joined two months later. Within a year, the United Kingdom and Italy dropped out of the snake. France dropped out in 1974, rejoined in 1975, and dropped out again in 1976.

In 1979 the snake was transformed into the Exchange Rate Mechanism (ERM) at the heart of the new European Monetary System (EMS). France and Italy joined the ERM at its inception, although Italy was given a wide band of ±6 per cent whereas France and the snake legacy countries had bands of $\pm2\frac{1}{4}$ per cent. In the first three years there were several exchange rate realignments, but over time parity changes become less frequent. Membership in the ERM grew during the following decade, most notably when the United Kingdom joined in 1990.

The aftermath of German unification in 1990 led to policy strains that brought on speculative currency attacks that forced the United Kingdom and Italy out of the ERM by 1992. France persevered, but was forced to accept wider bands in 1993.

The Maastricht Treaty, signed in 1991, succeeded in forcing major fiscal consolidations in all EU countries by the middle-to-late 1990s. The Stability and Growth Pact of 1996 aimed to cement fiscal gains by establishing goals and incentives for fiscal deficits after monetary union. Italy rejoined the ERM in late 1996 in a bid to qualify for EMU. In May 1998, eleven countries were ratified as initial members of the monetary union based on their fulfilment of the convergence criteria during 1997. Shortly afterward, a subset of the Ecofin, the Euro-11 Council, began to meet to discuss financial and exchange rate policies in the euro area. On 1 July 1998, the European Monetary Institute (EMI) metamorphosed into the European Central Bank (ECB). On 1 January 1999 the euro came into being.

Macro policy coordination experience

The snake era marked an increase in international macro policy coordination within Europe beyond that achieved through supranational institutions such as the European Commission, the OECD and the IMF and through direct contacts between governments. Finance Ministers and Central Bank governors of the snake countries and their deputies had to communicate frequently both bilaterally and in meetings on the margins of the Ecofin (which normally includes only Finance Ministers) and its deputy-level counterpart, the Monetary Committee, which includes both finance ministry and Central Bank deputies.

The driving force behind increasingly tight monetary links in Europe has been a desire to achieve three objectives: (1) facilitate greater integration of markets by trade; (2) bolster the political integration of Europe via a powerful symbol of unity; and (3) prevent rounds of competitive devaluation that ultimately lead to trade barriers and higher inflation. Whether reducing exchange rate volatility can have a significant impact in achieving objective (1) is an empirical question that is open to debate. The role of monetary union in achieving objective (2) is outside the scope of economic analysis. However, the role of monetary coordination in achieving objective (3) is precisely the focus of much of the theoretical literature on policy coordination.

As discussed in section 2 of this chapter, a common monetary response is optimal in the case of shocks that affect all countries symmetrically. Examples of such symmetric shocks, to a reasonable approximation, are energy price shocks, shocks emanating from US or Japanese macro policies, and developing country financial crises. In addition, when countries agree that they desire to move together to a lower inflation rate, as has been the case for Europe since the mid-1980s, a coordinated monetary policy can yield better outcomes.

A common monetary response is generally not optimal in the case of a shock that affects countries asymmetrically. German unification in 1990 introduced a big, persistent and slow-building asymmetric shock. Loose fiscal policy and high autonomous consumption and investment demand in Germany forced the Bundesbank to increase interest rates much higher than its ERM partners would have preferred. Despite this pressure, Germany's partners refused to accept the Bundesbank's proposal to revalue the DM.[40] The result was temporarily slower growth and rising unemployment outside of Germany. While the experience of the United Kingdom after it left the ERM demonstrates the benefits of monetary independence in the face of asymmetric shocks, policy-makers in the euro area argue that large asymmetric shocks such as German unification are sufficiently rare that the costs associated with them under monetary union are not likely to exceed the benefits from union.

One important aspect of monetary union in Europe is that the ECB is the first institutionalised example of symmetric monetary policy cooperation (as opposed to asymmetric pegged exchange rate regimes). In the face of an asymmetric shock like German unification, the ECB will tend to spread the costs around the entire union, whereas under the EMS, the Bundesbank set policy from a German perspective and the other countries faced the unattractive choice of either following suit or risking a loss of monetary credibility by devaluing.

Now that monetary union is a reality in Europe, attention increasingly has focused on coordinating fiscal policies. The Maastricht Treaty placed

[40] James (1996, p. 485) provides an interesting discussion of the events of September 1992.

significant emphasis on limiting the scope for fiscal deficits. This emphasis arose from fears that under monetary union with an expanded common financial market, profligate governments will find it easier to finance large deficits, thereby imposing the externality of higher interest rates on all member countries. The Stability and Growth Pact enshrines a mechanism for punishing such profligate behaviour, but it does so by putting obstacles in the way of counter-cyclical fiscal policy (at least unless and until countries achieve structural fiscal deficits low enough to 'reload the fiscal cannon').

Some observations on the historical experience

Probably the most striking aspect of the foregoing history is the very different directions taken by policy coordination within Europe, as opposed to within the G7. While the G7 has moved away from specific policy pledges to a more general sense of the desired direction of policy, the core of Europe has moved toward ever tighter monetary and fiscal policy coordination. To a large extent this divergence reflects the strong desire for political union in Europe, but it also reflects a greater commonality of economic philosophy within continental Europe than across the G7.

However, even across the G7 countries there has been a convergence of economic understanding over time and the process of policy dialogue probably helped to advance this common understanding. In the 1990s, there was broad agreement on the need to reduce fiscal deficits in most countries and the desirability of giving Central Banks the primary goal of price stability. (Japan was the primary outlier, where it was agreed that both monetary and fiscal policy should focus on supporting growth.) Both Japan and the euro area countries agreed on the need for structural reforms to increase competition and flexibility of financial, labour and product markets. Monetary and fiscal policies moved in the agreed directions to a substantial, even surprising, extent, although progress on structural reforms was often disappointing.

In the field of currency intervention, most G7 countries have come to perceive important limitations in the efficacy of such intervention as a policy tool and have been unwilling to engage in the really large operations that might be required to make this tool effective.[41] This development has had the beneficial effect of reinforcing the focus of policy coordination on

---

[41] Japan has been more willing to intervene regularly than other G7 countries, but the magnitude of Japanese intervention, although increasing in recent years, continues to be modest relative to the size of the yen–dollar and yen–euro foreign exchange markets.

macroeconomic fundamentals. However, it is possible that intervention could play some role in the future if currencies moved sufficiently far from their perceived fundamentals.

It remains to be seen whether future opportunities for explicit policy deals may present themselves and how the G7 will respond to such opportunities. There are reasons to believe that explicit deals will be harder to come by in the future. Countries (outside of the euro area) have been increasingly reluctant to make specific policy pledges owing to the uncertain ability of at least some of the participants to persuade their legislatures to enact the required fiscal or structural legislation. Monetary authorities have become less willing to tie their hands in a public forum both out of concern about appearing to jeopardise their independence from governments and because they prefer to be able to react quickly to incoming news. Indeed the modern consensus that Central Banks should be independent and focused solely on macroeconomic stabilisation – primarily price stabilisation – has greatly reduced the attention on monetary policy in the context of the G7.[42] Consequently, fiscal and structural policies have received greater emphasis over time.

Despite the potential existence of policy tradeoffs, trade negotiations have rarely played a role in macroeconomic policy coordination.[43] This is probably due to the slow and complicated nature of trade discussions and the glacial speed with which they are implemented. Nevertheless, there may be scope for incorporating trade policy as one element of the policy coordination dialogue, especially given the attention already devoted to current account imbalances.

From the point of view of each country's own output and inflation objectives, the 1990s outcomes were considered largely successful in terms of what macroeconomic policies can do, although European and Japanese policy-makers admitted that earlier structural reforms would have led to higher growth rates. Some US policy-makers believed that macro policies could have yielded higher growth in Europe and Japan, but the level of concern was lower than at times in previous decades. All sides viewed the current account imbalances between

---

[42] Central Bank governors meet monthly at the BIS, providing a forum for cooperation in which they can maintain their independence from their respective governments. However, even in this forum, there has been a reluctance to commit to specific policy 'deals', and the discussion has been primarily of the information-sharing type. This reluctance presumably stems from the desire to retain maximum freedom to manoeuvre rapidly in response to news. Building a consensus for specific coordinated policies is likely to take longer than a single meeting, so that even with monthly meetings coordinated policy-making would be much slower than most Central Banks are willing to accept.

[43] The 1978 Bonn Summit was the primary exception. Since then, G7 statements have routinely noted the importance of maintaining an open and free trading system, but have not pledged specific trade policy changes.

the three regions as a major problem. Given the difficulty of achieving internal political consensus on major fiscal and structural policy agendas, it seems unlikely that international policy coordination could have accomplished more on these fronts.

4 Correspondence between models and experience: some lessons

Where have the models and experience coincided well?

The central insight of the modelling literature is that when each country's policies generate externalities on other countries' welfare, there will be gains from international policy coordination. As we have seen, taking account of externalities does appear to be a major factor behind international coordination history, from the initial response to the 1973 oil price shock, through the Bonn Agreement of 1978, attempts to deal with external imbalances of the 1980s and 1990s, and the formation of monetary union within Europe.

Experience has generated examples of economic shocks that can be fairly characterised according to the standard categories of symmetric, asymmetric and idiosyncratic shocks. Various oil shocks can be viewed as approximately symmetric shocks from the point of view of the industrial countries. Undesirably high inflation rates in European countries in the early 1980s can be viewed as approximately symmetric shifts in initial conditions (resulting from past shocks and mistaken policy responses). The fiscal expansion in the United States and fiscal contraction in Europe and Japan in the early 1980s can be viewed as an asymmetric fiscal policy shock, at least from the point of view of monetary authorities that were forced to respond to it. German reunification is a classic example of a country-specific shock.

The models have focused on macroeconomic policy coordination, and this area has received the most attention historically, especially within Europe. However, other areas, such as structural policies, have received increased attention over time. Indeed, some of the most interesting episodes of international policy coordination in the 1990s have occurred in non-macroeconomic areas such as responding to financial crises and providing debt relief to poor countries. These are areas where cooperation is important because of externalities and the 'free rider' problem. To an individual creditor, debt relief mainly benefits other creditors, so joint action is needed in order to help the debtor. More generally, policy-makers within the G7 and within the EU have never felt constrained as to the areas of policy that can usefully be coordinated, and that is probably a good thing.

Where have the models and experience not coincided well?

Treatment of exchange rates and current account balances

In most of the models of policy coordination, it is assumed that the policy-maker in each country minimises a loss function that depends on the output gap and inflation.[44] The current account and the exchange rate are usually not included in the loss function. The focus of the analysis is how to choose monetary policy (and sometimes also fiscal policy) in the two countries to achieve the best possible outcomes for the output gap and inflation.

However, in international meetings of macroeconomic policy-makers, much time is spent discussing the appropriateness of current account and exchange rate developments and what should be done to attempt to influence them if they are judged to be inappropriate. There are five possible reasons why so much time is spent discussing current account and exchange rate developments in international fora:

- First, external variables are obviously legitimate topics for discussion in such fora, as they constitute the transmission channel by which one country's policies affect other countries. Some countries may find it more expedient to cast international policy coordination in terms of these variables than in terms of internal variables such as the output gap and inflation rate.
- Second, current accounts and exchange rates can be regarded as information variables or indicators of the appropriateness of macroeconomic policies given the current shocks, even if they are not target variables.
- Third, for some countries, exchange rate depreciations can lead to immediate and substantial upward pressures on inflation.
- Fourth, foreign exchange markets may be subject to inappropriate and irrational movements, and these markets may be susceptible to influence by the public statements of macroeconomic policy-makers.
- Finally, the current account may actually be a target variable along with the output gap and inflation.

Indeed, the record of official statements over the years leaves the strong impression that policy-makers view non-zero current account balances, and the large exchange rate movements that often precede current account imbalances, as undesirable *per se*. There are two main reasons why policy-makers may take this view. First, sharp swings in current accounts produce dislocations and incur adjustment costs, and these costs are viewed as especially pernicious if

---

[44] The most common functional form is a weighted sum of squared deviations of output from potential output and squared deviations of inflation from a target value.

the current account is expected to be reversed in the near future. Second, current account imbalances may give rise to protectionist pressures in deficit countries that could threaten global free trade.

However, it is important to recognise that current account imbalances often redirect demand from overheated to stagnant economies and improve macro outcomes globally. Moreover, the capital flows associated with current account imbalances are the mechanism by which rates of return are equalised across countries, leading to a more efficient global allocation of capital.

A possible example of a beneficial current account imbalance is the present situation in which the United States is experiencing a large positive productivity shock. It may be appropriate for there to be a large swing in the real value of the dollar and the US current account, as the United States borrows abroad now to finance investment and consumption justified by the productivity increase, but must later service the increase in debt out of future earnings on the (more productive) capital stock.

In some cases, a current account imbalance may signal an inappropriate policy mix, even though the imbalance itself is beneficial given the policy mix in place. One example is the early 1980s when there was fiscal expansion in the United States and fiscal contraction in many of the other OECD countries. While it might have been best if the US fiscal expansion had never taken place, it seems clear that given the paths of fiscal policies, the monetary policies chosen (which implied large swings in the real value of the dollar and the US current account deficit) were more appropriate than a looser monetary policy in the United States and tighter monetary policies abroad (which would have implied smaller swings). The current account deficit enabled the United States to maintain a relatively stable path of output and prices without sacrificing investment in future productivity.

Finally, an example of an undesirable current account imbalance is one caused by financial market irrationality that propels a country's exchange rate far from its fundamental equilibrium. In such a case, capital is misallocated and trade adjustment costs are wasted because the exchange rate, and hence the current account, are not in equilibrium. This example provides the best case for currency intervention to offset exchange rate swings.

The case for policy action is strongest when the current account imbalance is unsustainable in the sense that the implied future changes in international asset portfolios are implausibly large. Unsustainable imbalances can arise either because of large structural fiscal deficits or because of a long-lasting asset market disequilibrium. By definition, unsustainable imbalances cannot persist indefinitely. The mechanism by which they eventually end is typically a sharp change in the exchange rate. Policy action to address the fundamental source of the imbalance at an early stage can help to minimise the disruption that would be caused by a sharp change later on.

Unfortunately, it is not easy to know when a given current account imbalance is unsustainable. In light of the persistence of what were thought to be unsustainable imbalances between the United States, Japan and Europe for the better part of two decades, and given the lack of any significant return to protectionism, policy-makers perhaps need to reconsider the attention devoted to minimising current account imbalances.

Role of fiscal policy in stabilisation

In the model literature of the 1980s and 1990s on stabilisation conflicts, attention was focused primarily on monetary policy. It was usual to regard fiscal policy as one of the givens to which monetary policy had to react. Why fiscal policy was almost completely discounted as a stabilisation tool is not completely clear, but there are four possible reasons:

- First, fiscal policy played an important role in stabilisation policy in the 1960s and 1970s and may have suffered disproportionately from the general disillusionment with stabilisation policy in the 1980s and 1990s, when it was referred to pejoratively as 'fine tuning'.
- Second, it has been argued that fiscal policy cannot be changed in a timely enough fashion for it to be effective in responding to changing macroeconomic conditions.
- Third, temporary tax changes may have only a small effect on stabilising output.
- Fourth, for political reasons, fiscal policy may focus on long-term goals, such as the Reagan Administration's desire to secure higher potential output from supply-side tax cuts.

Four other considerations suggest that it may be time to re-evaluate the presumption that fiscal policy is not useful as a stabilisation tool:

- First, while it may be difficult to change fiscal policy in a timely fashion in the United States, it is not as difficult to so do in the parliamentary systems of the other major industrial countries. Moreover, it may be possible to design more 'automatic stabilisers' that do not require ad hoc legislative action.
- Second, even if fiscal policy changes take longer to achieve than monetary policy changes, fiscal policy may affect the economy with a shorter lag.
- Third, when economic activity is weak and short-term interest rates reach a zero lower bound, as they have in Japan, it may be appropriate for fiscal policy to play an increased role in stimulating economic activity.
- Finally, with the inception of EMU, the member countries have no scope for using monetary policy to deal with stabilisation conflicts caused by asymmetric or country-specific shocks, so it may be desirable to rely more heavily on fiscal policy.

Non-optimal policies

While the models typically consider that ongoing conflicts arise from inconsistent objectives between two countries, in practice misguided policies are more often the source of ongoing conflict. A recent example was the persistence of high fiscal deficits in many countries long after policy-makers realised that these deficits were not optimal even in the absence of harmful externalities across countries. Indeed, it may be argued that persistent and misguided fiscal policies were the fundamental issue behind most of the practical coordination dialogue in the 1980s and 1990s, since they often are the major source of large swings in exchange rates and current account balances.

In this vein, some critics of policy coordination have argued that there are much bigger gains to be had from countries moving to the frontier of their own optimal policy set (without coordination) than from there to a coordinated outcome.[45] This follows simply from the quantitative model work, where the gains to policy coordination are typically relatively modest. Feldstein (1988) claims that based on his experience in the Reagan Administration, policy coordination sometimes distracts policy-makers from necessary domestic policy responses and sometimes the policies under discussion would have a harmful or negligible effect on the economy. The actions of other governments may become the scapegoat for one's own inability to take actions at home. He and others further note that policy coordination may be very difficult to do because of domestic political constraints, either because of political considerations or because 'government' is not a single agent but rather several bodies having responsibilities over different areas of policy (there is more on this issue below).

Internal political dynamics

It is clear from the historical record that no policy dialogue has persuaded a country to undertake a policy shift unless a significant constituency for that shift already existed within the country. The modelling literature would benefit from greater attention to the interaction between internal and external policy dialogues. While the literature has explored the issue of enforcement of international agreements, it has tended to do so from the point of view of a single agent who is tempted to cheat on her agreement. In practice, however, the parties negotiating an international agreement have almost always made a good faith effort to live up to their commitments. The difficulty is typically in obtaining the necessary internal approval to implement the external agreement.

---

[45] See, for example, Fischer (1988) and Feldstein (1988).

Information exchange

In all of the various fora for international economic policy coordination, probably the most consistent activity is information exchange, both concerning the perceived state of the world and the internal policy debate within each country. This helps to ensure that policy-makers are fully informed. To the extent that the group compares the record of past discussions with actual economic outcomes, it can provide a 'reality check' both on whether policy-makers do as they say they will do and on whether their models of the world make sense.

The literature on model uncertainty and information-sharing provides interesting insights on when such activities would be expected to be welfare-improving and when they might not be. In practice, behaviour such as wilful provision of misinformation is not realistic since almost all data become public eventually and most data become available to everyone at the same time. Similarly, it is highly unlikely that policy-makers could convincingly deceive one another about their objectives or their internal models of the economy. In practice, the dialogue is one of education and moving toward a more common understanding of the international economy.

Monetary policy coordination

As noted previously in this chapter, stabilisation models of international macroeconomic policy coordination have generally focused upon monetary policy coordination, with fiscal policy generally being characterised as one of the elements in the Central Banks' policy environment. Yet, as also noted earlier, there have been relatively few episodes of overt and explicit monetary policy coordination since the passing of the Bretton Woods system, and particularly in recent years, monetary authorities have been reluctant to commit to concrete, publicly announced plans of action. Given that monetary policy actions in one country can generate externalities for other countries, what accounts for the relative paucity of international agreements on monetary policy outside of Europe? There are three explanations that might answer this question to some extent:

- First, Central Banks zealously guard their independence, and entering into international policy commitments either entails, or might be perceived by the public to entail, a loss of that independence. While it is true that Central Bank independence is generally defined as independence from the government or the Finance Ministry, some Central Banks may view any commitment of their policies to an external party as infringing on their prerogatives and responsibilities.
- Second, in a rapidly changing economic environment, commitments to future monetary policy actions may be undesirable or infeasible.

- Third, relative to the overall volatility of the economic environment, the externalities for one country associated with a monetary policy action in a second country may be relatively small. It may only be in the face of particularly large shocks – such as the oil price shocks of the 1970s – that the gains to coordination become sufficiently large to merit the effort required to achieve them.

The considerations listed above imply that international monetary policy coordination on the global level, to the extent that it occurs, probably is implemented in a more subtle and less overt fashion than is contemplated in at least the simplest of the policy coordination models. While monetary policy-makers rarely reach explicit public agreement on how their monetary policies should be determined, in the course of frequent meetings in which their countries' economic situations and monetary stances are discussed, informal consensuses may evolve concerning the direction of policy and the appropriate responses to shocks going forward.

For example, at present, many industrial country monetary authorities are in a tightening posture as efforts are made to ensure that strengthening activity and the still-high level of oil prices are not reflected in sustained gains to inflation. In principle, this situation could lead to a tighter-than-optimal stance of global monetary policy as tightening in each country, through its effects on exchange rates, will prompt additional tightening in the other countries. In practice, this situation will not likely lead to a formal agreement on monetary policy coordination, but it may lead to an informal consensus that tightening should proceed tentatively and with the prospective reactions of other Central Banks in mind as well. This informal consensus can be monitored on a frequent basis, insofar as the discussion at international meetings could unfavourably highlight the actions of countries not adhering to this consensus.

Hence, in practice, monetary policy coordination might be hard to distinguish from the information exchange process described on p. 82 above. Or, to put it another way, the information being exchanged is (1) a description of the current and prospective reaction functions adhered to by the different national monetary authorities, and (2) views on the appropriate reaction functions to implement moving forward. This type of exchange is sufficiently subtle, private and non-binding to satisfy the Central Banks' need for independence and scope to address unexpected contingencies, and yet at the same time may accomplish much of the coordination required in order to exploit policy externalities.

It is interesting to note that the formation of the euro area addresses some of the same concerns described above (Central Bank independence, freedom to manoeuvre and externalities) in a very different manner. First, the independence of the new ECB is enshrined in the Maastricht Treaty, which cannot be changed by a simple majority of the European Parliament (EP) or any national parliament.

Second, the problem of reaching explicit agreement without losing the ability to respond quickly to new developments is solved by imposing an integrated institutional structure, known as the European System of Central Banks (ESCB), onto the existing national Central Banks of member countries, with the ECB as headquarters. Finally, the externalities associated with independent monetary policies within the euro area are generally greater than the externalities across G7 countries, owing to the very close economic linkages within Europe.

Exchange rate target zones

Some modellers have argued for exchange rate target zones as a mechanism for enforcing macroeconomic policy coordination. If target zones are viewed as a variant of fixed exchange rates then they can lead to better outcomes in the case of symmetric shocks. However, in the case of asymmetric or country-specific shocks, the optimal policy response will generally involve movements in exchange rates. Proponents of target zones argue that the limited flexibility of exchange rates within the zones provides some cushion in the case of asymmetric or country-specific shocks, and that countries could agree to alter the zones in the event of a sufficiently large shock of this kind. However, if altering the zones in response to shocks is a recurrent option, it is not clear what benefit is gained by having zones in the first place.

The experience of Europe – a relatively integrated and homogeneous area – with different exchange rate regimes casts severe doubt on the practicality of target zones across the G7 countries. Dissatisfaction with experience under the target zone systems of the snake and the ERM led European countries to engage in increasingly close monetary and fiscal coordination, culminating in monetary union. Such explicit and restrictive institutional links are highly improbable among the other G7 countries. Even if they were politically feasible, economic shocks across the G7 countries are far less symmetric than among the countries of the euro area.

5 Conclusions

What have we learned?

Based on the foregoing analysis of both models of, and experience with, international macroeconomic policy coordination, we would like to point out some areas where modellers could devote further efforts most fruitfully and where policy-makers could learn from both the insights of the models and the historical experience.

Areas for further modelling effort:

- Practical policy coordination almost always involves more than one type of policy, and usually involves several types of policies. At a minimum, more effort should be devoted to joint modelling of monetary and fiscal policies.
- Internal political divisions within countries have a major impact on the international coordination process. Macro policy modellers should draw from models in microeconomic areas that have considered the impact of internal factions on the cross-country coordination process.
- Modelling the process of information exchange is still in its early stages and could yield a large payoff since information exchange is the most universal feature of practical policy coordination.
- Economic modellers in general have not fully explored the implications of market irrationality and bubbles for both internal and external policies.

Issues for policy-makers:

- Policy-makers should think carefully about their ultimate objectives. In particular, should the current account be considered an objective, and, if so, should the target for the current account always be zero?
- International coordination will be more relevant and productive if policy-makers can achieve better internal policies first, as inappropriate domestic policies have sometimes become the main focus of international policy discussions. In particular, a structural fiscal deficit is often responsible for an over-valued currency and a persistent current account deficit.
- Policy-makers may have discounted the role of fiscal policy in stabilisation too much, because past attempts to use it led to unsustainable budget deficits. Rather than ignore fiscal policy as a stabilisation tool, there should perhaps be more effort toward designing a sustainable framework for countercyclical fiscal policy, at least in those countries where the fiscal process allows a sufficiently timely response to shocks.

So is policy coordination among the developed countries alive in the new millennium? First, it is clear that information exchange is very active, perhaps even to excess. There are many opportunities for such exchanges and much time is consumed by government officials (and their staffs) in preparing for and travelling to these meetings. As we suggested earlier, particularly in the case of monetary policies, such exchanges can lead to an implicit form of policy coordination in the context of repeated interactions. In addition, information exchange helps policy-makers to advance to a more common understanding of the global economy.

Second, the moves in the euro area to a single currency, to a supranational Central Bank, and to binding guidelines on fiscal policies, have taken policy coordination to a new level.

Third, policy coordination in the G7 has evolved in at least two ways. There is less focus on specific policy agreements and more on the general direction of policy in the G7 countries. This reflects domestic political constraints in being able to deliver very specific policy commitments. And there has also been less willingness to participate in coordinated intervention and more attention to the fundamental policies that may be the source of undesired swings in exchange rates and current account balances. In general, the focus has been to achieve cyclical convergence among the G7 economies to minimise swings in exchange rates and current accounts and to encourage policy mixes within countries that also contribute to that objective.

Coordination issues today

In the past few years, there has been an unusually wide divergence in the cyclical positions of the G7 economies – with US growth surprisingly robust, Japan exceptionally weak and the euro area in between. This is an example of a 'stabilisation problem', though an unusually persistent one. In effect, it also represents initial conditions that have the effect of asymmetric shocks. This disparity has been the source of recent swings in exchange rates and current account balances. The latter developments are desirable in response to the cyclical divergence – in effect, open economy versions of built-in stabilisers – but cyclical convergence, achieved with an appropriate mix of policies, could reduce the swings in exchange rates and current account balances. In moving toward cyclical convergence, the emphasis has therefore been on policy choices that at least would not themselves widen the swings in exchange rates and current accounts. With respect to Japan, that meant an emphasis on fiscal policy and domestic demand-led growth, as oppose to policies that relied on currency depreciation and external stimulus. This is a perfect example of avoiding negative externalities. With respect to the United States, there has been some emphasis on holding onto the budget surpluses – both to avoid further stimulus to demand and to avoid further deterioration in the current account.

A second issue is the G7 response to the global financial turmoil and crises among emerging-market economies – in effect, a symmetric shock to the G7 economies. From the standpoint of macro policy, the key has been to ensure that aggregate demand in the G7 was maintained in order to be a stabilising force in the global economy. While this was primarily an issue of each country/area responding to domestic stabilisation needs, there was also a focus on ensuring that the policy choices within the G7 did not increase G7 growth at the expense of other economies.

A third important issue is the productivity shock. The question here is what kind of a shock this is – a country-specific shock or a symmetric shock? At the moment it appears to be a country-specific shock and as a result has added secular divergence to the remaining cyclical divergence, further feeding, for a while, both the appreciation of the dollar and the widening of the US current account deficit. If this turns out to be a symmetric shock, with productivity picking up over time elsewhere, the effects on exchange rates, capital flows and current accounts will presumably unwind. There has been some attention in G7 discussions to focusing on structural reforms in the euro area and Japan that might strengthen sustainable growth rates in those areas, reducing the prevailing secular divergence.

A fourth issue is the weakness in the euro. To a degree the depreciation of the euro has reflected the cyclical and secular disparities discussed above and to some extent may have been reinforced by the unexpected strength of euro liability issue. But many believe that the depreciation in the euro is greater than can be accounted for by fundamentals, making it a topic of G7 rhetoric, at least.

A fifth issue – which has received relatively little attention in the G7 – is the sharp rise in oil prices in 1999 and into early 2000. This is another example of a symmetric shock to the G7 economies that potentially could call for calibrated responses, in light of the changes in each country's policies. However, in part because this was a rebound from a level that was not perceived as sustainable and because of the reduced vulnerability of G7 economies to changes in oil prices, there has been relatively little focus on this shock.

Appendix 1 Outcomes in a two-country model with both monetary and fiscal policy

Consider a one-shot game in a standard model with two countries, unstarred and starred, in which each country has employment and CPI inflation as objectives and has both monetary and fiscal policies as instruments. For shocks to money or goods demands both countries can attain bliss, but for productivity shocks no Nash non-cooperative equilibrium exists. All variables (except interest rates) are natural logarithms. Variables with bars over them represent natural values. Natural values of employments are inelastic notional supplies, and natural values of all other variables are zero-disturbance, flexible-wage values. Let variables with hats over them represent deviations of variables from their natural values.

Production functions imply that outputs, y and y^*, rise with the employments, n and n^*, and fall with the productivity shocks, x and x^*, so

$$\hat{y} = (1 - \alpha)\hat{n} - x, \quad \hat{y}^* = (1 - \alpha)\hat{n}^* - x^* \tag{A.1}$$

Nominal wages minus output prices, p or p^*, must equal marginal products of labour. Since nominal wages are set at their zero-disturbance, flexible-wage value, rearranging yields

$$\hat{p} = \alpha\hat{n} + x, \quad \hat{p}^* = \alpha\hat{n}^* + x^* \tag{A.2}$$

Consumer price indices, q and q^*, and the real exchange rate, z, in deviation form are

$$\hat{q} = \hat{p} + \beta\hat{z}, \quad \hat{q}^* = \hat{p}^* - \beta\hat{z}, \quad \hat{z} = \hat{e} + \hat{p}^* - \hat{p} \tag{A.3}$$

where β is the common propensity to import, and e is the nominal exchange rate.

Outputs must equal demands. Unstarred (starred) demand rises with outputs and unstarred (starred) government expenditures net of a demand shock, g (g^*), falls with real interest rates, r and r^*, and rises (falls) with real depreciation of the unstarred currency:

$$\hat{y} = (1 - \beta)\varepsilon\hat{y} + \beta\varepsilon\hat{y}^* - (1 - \beta)v\hat{r} - \beta v\hat{r}^* + \delta\hat{z} + \hat{g}$$
$$\hat{y}^* = \beta\varepsilon\hat{y} + (1 - \beta)\varepsilon\hat{y}^* - \beta v\hat{r} - (1 - \beta)v\hat{r}^* - \delta\hat{z} + \hat{g}^* \tag{A.4}$$

Money supplies net of money demand shocks, m or m^*, must equal money demands which rise with outputs and output prices and fall with nominal interest rates, i or i^*; furthermore, open interest parity and Fisher equations hold:

$$\hat{m} = \hat{p} + \hat{y} - \lambda\hat{i}, \quad \hat{m}^* = \hat{p}^* + \hat{y}^* - \lambda\hat{i}^*$$
$$\hat{i} = \hat{i}^* - \hat{e}, \quad \hat{i} = \hat{r} - \hat{q}, \quad \hat{i}^* = \hat{r}^* - \hat{q}^* \tag{A.5}$$

The reduced form for employments and the real exchange rate are[46]

$$\hat{n} = \psi_1\hat{m} + \psi_2\hat{m}^* + \psi_3\hat{g} + \psi_4\hat{g}^* + \psi_5 x + \psi_6 x^*$$
$$\hat{n}^* = \psi_2\hat{m} + \psi_1\hat{m}^* + \psi_4\hat{g} + \psi_3\hat{g}^* + \psi_6 x + \psi_5 x^*$$
$$\hat{z} = \psi_7(\hat{m} - \hat{m}^*) - \gamma\psi_3(\hat{g} - \hat{g}^*) + \psi_8(x - x^*) \tag{A.6}$$

---

[46] The coefficients of the reduced forms are

$$\Delta\psi_1 = \theta_1(\theta_5 - \theta_6) + \theta_2\theta_5 > 0, \Delta\psi_2 = \theta_1\theta_6 + \theta_2\theta_5 \gtrless 0,$$

$$\Delta\psi_3 = \theta_1 + \theta_2 > 0, \Delta\psi_4 = \theta_2, \Delta\psi_5 = \theta_1(\theta_3 + \theta_4) + \theta_2\theta_3,$$

$$\Delta\psi_6 = \theta_2\theta_3 - \theta_1\theta_4, \Delta\psi_7 = \theta_1\left[\frac{1}{\lambda}(\theta_1 + \theta_2) + \gamma(2\theta_6 - \theta_5)\right] > 0,$$

$$\Delta\psi_8 = \Delta\theta_1[1 + 2\theta_2 - \gamma(\theta_3 + 2\theta_4)], \Delta = \theta_1^2 + 2\theta_1\theta_2 > 0,$$

$$\theta_1 = (1 - \varepsilon)(1 - \alpha) + \gamma\delta, \theta_2 = \beta\varepsilon(1 - \alpha) - \kappa\gamma, \theta_3 = 1 - \varepsilon + v,$$

$$\theta_4 = \beta\varepsilon + \kappa, \theta_5 = \frac{v - \kappa}{\lambda}, \theta_6 = \frac{\kappa}{\lambda}, \kappa = 2\beta(1 - \beta)v - \delta, \gamma = \alpha + \frac{1}{\lambda}$$

The reduced forms for $\hat{q}$ and $\hat{q}^*$ can be obtained using (A.3), (A.2), and (A.6). Each government seeks to minimise a loss function,

$$L = \frac{1}{2}\left[\sigma(k - \hat{n})^2 + (\hat{q} + \overline{q} - q_{-1})^2\right]$$

$$L^* = \frac{1}{2}\left[-\sigma(k - \hat{n}^*)^2 + (\hat{q}^* + \overline{q}^* - q_{-1}^*)^2\right] \tag{A.7}$$

where the target value of employment is greater than or equal to the natural rate if $k \geq 0$, and the target values for CPI inflation rates are zero.

When $k = 0$, the first-order conditions with non-cooperative behaviour are a system of four equations in the three variables, n, n^*, and z which can be shown to be independent:

$$\frac{\partial L}{fm} = \psi_1\sigma\hat{n} + (\alpha\psi_1 + \beta\psi_7)(\alpha\hat{n} + \beta\hat{z} + x + \overline{q} - q_{-1}) = 0$$

$$\frac{\partial L}{fg} = \psi_3\sigma\hat{n} + (\alpha\psi_3 - \gamma\psi_3)(\alpha\hat{n} + \beta\hat{z} + x + \overline{q} - q_{-1}) = 0$$

$$\frac{\partial L^*}{fm^*} = \psi_1\sigma\hat{n}^* + (\alpha\psi_1 + \beta\psi_7)(\alpha\hat{n}^* - \beta\hat{z} + x^* + \overline{q}^* - q_{-1}^*) = 0$$

$$\frac{\partial L^*}{fg^*} = \psi_3\sigma\hat{n}^* + (\alpha\psi_3 + \gamma\psi_3)(\alpha\hat{n}^* + \beta\hat{z} + x^* + \overline{q}^* - q_{-1}^*) = 0$$

(A.8)

With no productivity shocks ($x = x^* = 0$), there is a Nash equilibrium and bliss can be attained. The natural money supplies, $\overline{m}$ and $\overline{m}^*$, are set so that $\overline{q} = q_{-1}$ and $\overline{q}^* = q_{-1}^*$. In this situation, the system of equations (A.8) is homogeneous and, thus, is satisfied by $\hat{n} = \hat{n}^* = \hat{z} = 0$. From (A.2) and (A.3) it follows that $\hat{p} = \hat{p}^* = 0$ and $\hat{q} = \hat{q}^* = 0$, so bliss is attained. However, with productivity shocks, there is no Nash equilibrium. The system of equations (A.8) is not homogeneous and, therefore, has no solution. These conclusions follow whether or not there are money demand and goods demand shocks.

When $k \geq 0$, $\psi_2 = 0$, and disturbances are zero so that the deviations of all variables from their natural levels are zero, the first-order conditions for the unstarred country with non-cooperative behaviour and with joint maximisation are, respectively,

$$\frac{\partial L}{\partial m} = [-\sigma k\psi_1 + (\overline{q} - q_{-1})(\alpha\psi_1 + \beta\psi_7)] = 0$$

$$\frac{\partial(L + L^*)}{\partial m} = [-\sigma k\psi_1 + (\overline{q} - q_{-1})(\alpha\psi_1 + \beta\psi_7)]$$

$$-(\overline{q}^* - q_{-1}^*)(\beta\psi_7) = 0$$

(A.9)

Since the two countries are symmetric, in equilibrium $\overline{q} - q_{-1} = \overline{q}^* - q^*_{-1}$. Therefore, with joint maximisation, the natural money supply $\overline{m}$ must be set so that $\overline{q} - q_{-1}$ is greater and inflation bias is higher. An analogous argument applies to $\overline{m}^*$ and $\overline{q}^* - q^*_{-1}$.

Appendix 2 Chronology of international macroeconomic policy coordination

1940s   Establishment of IMF to administer fixed exchange rate system. Marshall Plan administered by the Organization for European Economic Cooperation, predecessor of the OECD. European Payments Union (EPU) facilitates intra-European trade.

1950s   IMF is locus of macro policy discussion. European Coal and Steel Community (ECSC) established in 1952 and evolved into European Economic Community (EEC) in 1958 (Treaty of Rome).

1962   Foundation of the General Arrangements to Borrow (GAB) and the G10 to supplement IMF resources. Working Party Three begins a process of dialogue about balance of payments developments among the G10 countries at the OECD.

1970   The Werner Report outlines path to European Economic and Monetary Union.

1971–2   Repeated negotiations (including Smithsonian Agreement of 1971) to salvage fixed exchange rates. In 1972, six EC countries plus Denmark and the United Kingdom join currency 'snake'. The United Kingdom and Italy leave the snake within a year.

1973   Finance ministers of the United States, France, Germany and the United Kingdom (the Library Group) meet in the White House library. The G5 (adding Japan) Finance Ministers and Central Bank governors process begins later in the year. United Kingdom joins EEC.

1974   The G5 spearhead collective response to oil shock. Launch of oil adjustment facility at the IMF. Establishment of IEA. France drops out of snake.

1975   Giscard and Schmidt (original Library Group members) decide to elevate the G5 process to the Head of State level and add Italy at the Rambouillet summit. France rejoins snake.

1976   Canada attends the summit in Puerto Rico to form the G7, but ministerial process remains the G5.
France drops out of snake.

1977   President of European Commission attends London Summit. G3 countries adopt unspecified, but widely acknowledged, growth targets.

1978   Bonn summit trades off US oil price decontrol with fiscal expansion in Germany and Japan.

1979   France and Italy join the snake countries to form the ERM.

1980–4   Thatcher and Reagan administrations ideologically opposed to international coordination. Jurgensen Report (1983) questions effectiveness of sterilised intervention.

1985   Plaza Agreement aims to hasten dollar depreciation. Coordinated intervention.
Single European Act (SEA) drafted. The Act was ratified in 1986 and took effect in 1987.

1987   Louvre Accord aims to stabilise dollar. Italy and Canada become permanent members of G7 ministerial process. Coordinated intervention.

1988–9   Frequent coordinated intervention in the face of continued currency volatility.
Delors Report sets the stage for EMU.

1990–1   G7 organises payments for Gulf War.
German unification. United Kingdom joins ERM in 1990.
Maastricht Treaty signed in 1991.

1992   United Kingdom and Italy forced out of ERM.

1993   ERM bands widened under pressure from speculative attack.

1994–9   Rising concern about Japanese recession and yen bubble.
Agreement on need for fiscal consolidation in G7 exc. Japan.
General satisfaction on inflation.
EU Stability and Growth Pact agreed. ECB established and euro launched.

Appendix 3 Extant fora

Global: IMF, BIS, G10, OECD (WP-3), G7.
European: EU Commission, Ecofin, Euro-11 Council, ECB.

Appendix 4 Some regular international policy coordination meetings (global level, excludes regional meetings)

- G7 Leaders' Summits: 1 per year
- G7 Finance Ministers (FMs) and Central Bank Governors (CBGs): 3 per year
- G7 Deputy FMs: at least 1 before each FM/CBG meeting
- G10 CBGs at BIS: 10 per year
- G10 FMs and CBGs: 2 per year
- G10 Deputy FMs and Deputy CBGs: 4 per year
- OECD Economic Policy Committee: 2 per year (Sub-Deputy)
- OECD Working Party Three of EPC: 4 per year (Deputy/Sub-Deputy)
- IMF International Monetary and Financial Committee: 2 per year (Ministerial)
- IMF Executive Board: at least weekly (Sub-Deputy)
- BIS and OECD Expert-Level Meetings of Various Kinds

REFERENCES

Ainley, M. (1984). 'The General Arrangements to Borrow', pamphlet Series, 41. Washington, DC, International Monetary Fund

Alesina, A. and G. Tabellini (1987). 'Rules and Discretion with Noncoordinated Monetary and Fiscal Policies', *Economic Inquiry*, 25 (October), 619–30

Bai, H. and S. Hall (1996). 'Testing the Symmetry of Shocks among the G3 Countries', Global Economic Institutions Working Paper 14, ESRC

Basevi, G., F. Delbono and V. Delnicolo (1990). 'International Monetary Cooperation under Tariff Threat', *Journal of International Economics*, 28, 1–23

Becker, R. *et al.* (1986). 'Optimal Policy Design with Non-Linear Models', *Journal of Economic Dynamics and Control*, 10, 27–31

Bergsten C. F. and C. R. Henning (1996). *Global Economic Leadership and the Group of Seven.* Washington, DC, Institute for International Economics

Bryant, R. (1995). *International Coordination of National Stabilization Policies.* Washington, DC, Brookings Institution

Bryant, R., D. Henderson, G. Holtham, P. Hooper and S. Symansky (1988). *Empirical Macroeconomics for Interdependent Economies.* Washington, DC, Brookings Institution

Bryant, R., P. Hooper and C. Mann (1993). *Evaluating Policy Regimes: New Research in Empirical Macroeconomics.* Washington, DC, Brookings Institution

Canzoneri, M. B. and H. Edison (1990). 'A New Interpretation of the Coordination Problem and Its Empirical Significance', in P. Hooper *et al.* (eds.), *Financial Sectors in Open Economies: Empirical Analysis and Policy Issues.* Washington, DC, Board of Governors of the Federal Reserve System, 399–436

Canzoneri, M. and J. A. Gray (1985). 'Monetary Policy Games and the Consequences of Non-Cooperative Behaviour', *International Economic Review*, 26(3), 547–64

Canzoneri, M. B. and D. Henderson (1991). *Monetary Policy in Interdependent Economies: A Game Theoretic Approach*. Cambridge, MA, MIT Press

Canzoneri, M. and P. Minford (1989). 'Policy Interdependence: Does Strategic Behavior Pay? An Empirical Investigation Using the Liverpool World Model', in D. Hodgman and G. Woods (eds.), *Macroeconomic Policy and Economic Interdependence*. London, Macmillan, 158–79

Caporale, G. M., M. Chui, S. Hall and B. Henry (1998a). 'Fiscal Consolidation: An Exercise in the Methodology of Coordination', Global Economic Institutions Working Paper, 38 ESRC

(1998b). 'Evaluating the Gains to Cooperation in the G3', Global Economic Institutions Working Paper, 39, ESRC

Cooper, R., B. Eichengreen, C. R. Henning, G. Holtham and R. Putnam (1989). *Can Nations Agree?: Issues in International Economic Cooperation*. Washington, DC, Brookings Institution

Currie, D. and P. Levine (1993). *Rules, Reputation and Macroeconomic Policy Coordination*. New York, Cambridge University Press

Currie, D., P. Levine and J. Pearlman (1996a). 'The Choice of "Conservative Central Banker" in Open Economies: Monetary Regime Options for Europe', *Economic Journal*, 106, 345–58

(1996b). 'Can Delegation Be Counterproductive? The Choice of "Conservative" Bankers in Open Economies', Global Economic Institutions Working Paper, 13, ESRC

Dobson, W. (1991). 'Economic Policy Coordination: Requiem or Prologue?', Policy Analyses in International Economics, 30. Washington, DC, Institute for International Economics

Eichengreen, B. and F. Ghironi (1999). 'Macroeconomic Tradeoffs in the United States and Europe: Fiscal Distortions and the International Monetary Regime', Federal Reserve Bank of New York, mimeo, November.

Farrell, J. and M. Rabin (1996). 'Cheap Talk', *Journal of Economic Perspectives*, 10 (3), 103–18

Feenstra, R. C. (1992). 'How Costly is Protectionism?', *Journal of Economic Perspectives*, 6, 159–78

Feldstein, M. (1988). 'Distinguished Lecture on Economics in Government: Thinking about International Economic Coordination', *Journal of Economic Perspectives*, 2, 3–13

Fischer, S. (1988). 'International Macroeconomic Policy Coordination', in M. Feldstein (ed.), *International Economic Cooperation*. Chicago, University of Chicago Press for NBER

Frankel, J. A. and K. E. Rockett (1988). 'International Macroeconomic Policy Coordination when Policymakers Do Not Agree on the True Model', *American Economic Review*, 78(3), 318–40

Ghosh, A. R. and P. R. Masson (1991). 'Model Uncertainty, Learning and the Gains from Coordination', *American Economic Review*, 81(3), 465–79

(1994). *Economic Cooperation in an Uncertain World*. Oxford, Blackwell

Hajnal, P. I. (1999). *The G7/G8 System: Evolution, Role and Documentation*. Aldershot, Ashgate

Hamada, K. (1974). 'Alternative Exchange Rate Systems and the Interdependence of Monetary Policies', in R. Aliber (ed.), *National Monetary Policies and the International Financial System*. Chicago, University of Chicago Press

(1976). 'A Strategic Analysis for Monetary Interdependence', *Journal of Political Economy*, 84, 677–700

(1979). 'Macroeconomic Strategy Coordination under Alternative Exchange Rates', in R. Dornbusch and J. Frenkel (eds.), *International Economic Policy*. Baltimore, MD, Johns Hopkins University Press

(1985). *The Political Economy of International Monetary Interdependence*. Cambridge, MA, MIT Press

(1986). 'Strategic Aspects of International Fiscal Interdependence', *Economic Studies Quarterly*, 37, 165–80

Hughes-Hallet, A. (1986). 'International Policy Design and the Sustainability of Policy Bargains', *Journal of Economic Dynamics and Control*, 10, 467–94

James, H. (1996). *International Monetary Cooperation Since Bretton Woods*. Washington, DC, International Monetary Fund

Kenen, P. B. (1996). *The International Economy*, 3rd edn. (with corrections). Cambridge, Cambridge University Press

Keohane, R. O. (1984). *After Hegemony: Cooperation and Discord in the World Political Economy*. Princeton, Princeton University

Levine, P. and J. Pearlman (1997). 'Delegation and Fiscal Policy in the Open Economy: More Bad News for Rogoff's Delegation Game', Global Economic Institutions Working Paper, 25, ESRC

(2002). 'Delegation and Fiscal Policy in the Open Economy: More Bad News for Rogoff's Delegation Game', *Open Economy Review* 13(2), 153–74

McKibbin, W. (1997). 'Empirical Evidence on International Economic Policy Coordination', in M. U. Fratianni, D. Salvatore and J. von Hagen (eds.), *Handbook of Comparative Economic Policies, 5: Macroeconomic Policies in Open Economies*. Westport, CT, Greenwood Press

McKibbin, W. J., and J. D. Sachs (1988). 'Coordination of Monetary and Fiscal Policies in the Industrial Economies', in J. Frenkel (ed.), *International Aspects of Fiscal Policies*. Chicago, University of Chicago Press for NBER

(1991). *Global Linkages: Macroeconomic Interdependence and Cooperation in the World Economy*. Washington, DC, Brookings Institution

Obstfeld, M. and K. S. Rogoff (2001). 'Global Implications of Self-Oriented National Monetary Rules', *Quarterly Journal of Economics*, 117 (2), 503–35

Oudiz, G. and J. Sachs (1984). 'Macroeconomic Policy Coordination Among the Industrial Economies', *Brookings Papers on Economic Activity*, 1, 1–64

(1985). 'Intertemporal Policy Coordination in Dynamic Macroeconomic Models', in W. Buiter and R. Marston (eds.), *International Economic Policy Coordination*. Cambridge, Cambridge University Press

Persson, T. and G. Tabellini (1995). 'Double-Edged Incentives: Institutions and Policy Coordination', in K. S. Rogoff and G. Grossman. *Handbook of International Economics*, Amsterdam, North-Holland

Putnam, R. D. and C. R. Hennning (1989). 'The Bonn Summit of 1978: A Case Study in Coordination', in R. N. Cooper *et al.* (eds.), *Can Nations Agree? Issues in International Economic Cooperation*. Washington, DC, Brookings Institution

Rogoff, K. S. (1985a). 'Can International Monetary Policy Coordination Be Counterproductive?', *Journal of International Economics*, 18, 199–217

(1985b). 'The Optimal Degree of Commitment to an Intermediate Monetary Target', *Quarterly Journal of Economics*, 100, 1169–89

Sachs, J. and W. McKibbin (1985). 'Macroeconomic Policies in the OECD and LDC External Adjustment', NBER Working Paper, 1534

Solomon, R. (1982). *The International Monetary System, 1945–1981*. New York, Harper & Row

(1999). *Money on the Move: The Revolution in International Finance Since 1980*. Princeton, Princeton University Press

Stark, J. (1995). 'The G7 At Work', *The International Economy*, September–October, 52–4

Tabellini, G. (1990). 'Domestic Policies and the International Coordination of Fiscal Policies', *Journal of International Economics*, 28, 245–65.

The Twenty G7 Summits: On the Occasion of the Twentieth Summit, Naples, July 8/10, 1994 (1994), Adnkronos Libri, Rome

Walsh, C. (1995). 'Optimal Contracts for Central Bankers', *American Economic Review*, 85, 150–67

4 The Report of the International Financial Institution Advisory Commission: comments on the critics

ALLAN H. MELTZER

When the US Congress approved $18 billion of additional funding for the International Monetary Fund (IMF) in November 1998, it authorised a study of international financial institutions. Congressional concerns included the growing frequency, severity and cost of financial disturbances, the fragility of the international monetary system, the ineffectiveness of development banks, and corruption in Russia, Indonesia, Africa and elsewhere. But Congress also expressed concern about whether international financial institutions (IFIs) had adapted appropriately to the many changes since the Bretton Woods Agreement in 1944.

In July 1999, Congress completed appointment of the members of the International Financial Institution Advisory Commission (usually called the Meltzer Commission). Between 9 September 1999 and 8 March 2000, the Commission met twelve times and, in addition, held three days of public hearings. On 8 March 2000, it presented its Report to the Speaker and the Majority Leader of the House of Representatives (International Advisory Commission, 2000). The Report stimulated active discussion of issues that might have been addressed at the fiftieth anniversary of the Bretton Woods Conference, in 1994, but were not.

Discussion was overdue. As the US Congress recognised, the world economy and the international financial system are very different from the world envisioned at Bretton Woods in 1944. The principal international financial institutions responded to many past changes and crises by expanding their mandate and adding new facilities and programmes. New regional institutions opened to serve the needs of regional populations. Many of the activities of these agencies overlap with those of the World Bank.

The Commission had a very broad mandate and a very short life. The US Congress asked the Commission to evaluate seven major institutions and

I am grateful to Adam Lerrick and Valeriano Garcia for many helpful suggestions. A version of this chapter is also included as the introduction to the Spanish edition of the Report of the International Financial Institution Advisory Commission (2000).

recommend changes in only six months. The Commission chose to concentrate on the IMF, the World Bank, and the three regional development banks. It gave less attention to the Bank for International Settlements (BIS) and the World Trade Organisation (WTO).

There were two broad sets of issues, organisational and functional. The former includes the structure of the institutions and the incentives that motivate individuals. Performance can be improved only by changing the incentives under which the staff work and member countries operate. A frequent criticism, discussed in 1992 in the Wapenhans Report, but still not fully addressed, is that the World Bank rewards lending, not poverty alleviation or successful economic and social development (World Bank, 1992). A different set of incentives in a restructured organisation would focus more attention on benefits to the citizens of client states.

The Commission started work with ten members, including six economists, so it seemed appropriate to focus attention on economic themes.[1] There was not enough time to treat all issues adequately. As Chairman, I chose to emphasise the role of the multilateral institutions in supplying services that the private market would not provide and developing infrastructure that would permit market solutions where feasible and non-market solutions elsewhere. An economist's reflex response is to ask: What are the public goods that these institutions can supply effectively? What is their comparative advantage? Where do markets fail? Can an international financial institution effectively and efficiently supply the missing services?

A second set of issues soon became apparent. There is considerable overlap between the Bank and the IMF and between the Bank and the regional banks. The overlap might be justified as a type of competition to provide services to client states at lowest cost. Unfortunately, the overlap and duplication arise for reasons that have little to do with competition or efficiency. With the banks and the IMF involved in the two principal tasks – reducing risk and enhancing development – reform proposals must discuss the IMF and the development banks together.

1 The framework

In setting the Commission's charge, the US Congress recognised that two major changes in international financial arrangements required changes in the

[1] The members were: Professor Charles Calomiris, Congressman Tom Campbell, Dr Edwin Feulner, Jr, Dr Lee Hoskins, Mr Richard Huber, Dr Manuel Johnson, Professor Jerry Levinson, Professor Allan Meltzer, Professor Jeffrey Sachs and Congressman Esteban Torres. The eleventh member, Dr C. Fred Bergsten, also an economist, joined in January 2000, after most of the Commission's hearings had ended.

responsibilities of the IFIs. First, the fixed but adjustable exchange rate system, agreed to at the Bretton Woods Conference, ended in 1973. Second, private financial institutions, corporations and individuals in the developed countries now supply the largest part of the capital flow to emerging markets economies. The IFIs' share is now less than 5 per cent of the total. The percentage varies across countries, however. Many of the poorest countries remain dependent on the IFIs.

Major problems of the system follow from these changes. Many developing countries rely excessively on short-term capital inflows to finance long-term development, a very risky approach that has caused crises throughout history. Financial systems in developing countries are, too often, used to subsidise favoured industries or individuals, weakening the financial institutions and eroding their capital. This, too, increases the risk of crises and failures. Pegged exchange rates replaced the fixed exchange rate system in many developing countries, opening the countries to speculative attacks. With weak financial systems dependent on short-term capital, the system became subject to frequent, severe crises.

Further, the IFIs lend to governments and have very little influence over the use of funds. Often projects are not completed, funds are misappropriated and promised reforms are not implemented. Instead of improving their performance as development agencies, the development banks have expanded their programmes to overlap with the IMF. The reverse is also true. The IMF makes long-term loans for structural reform and poverty alleviation. Some countries remain permanently in debt to the IMF.

The majority report responds to these fundamental problems by proposing structural changes in the institutions. The Report recommends separate roles for the IMF and the development banks. It sees the proper role of the IMF as preventing financial crises and preventing the spread of crises that occur. This is a classic public responsibility – to reduce risk to the minimum inherent in nature and trading practices. It is very different from the role that the IMF has assumed. Crisis-prevention does not mean, and in the Commission's majority view should not mean, that the IMF continues to 'bail out' all lenders, or lend large amounts to maintain pegged exchange rates, or dictate the policies followed in client countries. Financial stability does not require that all countries follow a 'Washington Consensus' or that the IMF lend for institutional reform. The IMF should give advice, but it should not tie the advice to assistance.[2]

---

[2] Private consultants charge for advice. The IFIs pay or subsidise countries. Many critics of the Commission report argue that countries would not accept advice if it were given without subsidised lending (see US Treasury, 2000). This is a peculiar argument. Must countries be bribed to take the advice? Or, do they take the subsidised loan, ignore the advice, or give it lip service only? Russia is an extraordinarily bad example of a country that took the money but not the advice. There are many others.

Lending for institutional reform is one of the tasks of the development banks. The majority believes that their mission should have four parts: promoting economic and social development, improving the quality of life, reducing poverty and providing global and regional public goods. These institutions should not be banks. Their job should not be to increase the number and size of loans or to lend to creditworthy countries. To recognise that their mission is development, not lending, the Commission's majority recommended that the names of these institutions should be changed from development banks to development agencies.

The World Bank has started to create field offices in recipient countries. The majority believes that this is another waste of resources by an overly large and ineffective bureaucracy. The Inter-American (IDB), Asian (ADB) and African Development Banks have offices in all of the relevant countries. Many governments, and their constituents, have closer ties of language, culture and understanding to the regional agencies. The majority believes that effectiveness would be improved, and costly overlap reduced, if the regional banks assumed sole responsibility for many of the programmes in their regions. The World Bank's direct role in transferring resources would be limited to regions without a development bank and to Africa, where poverty problems are most severe and difficult to solve and where the regional bank has less experience. The World Bank would continue to supply technical assistance and promote knowledge transfer in all regions.

Critics contend that this proposal would 'undermine the effectiveness of the overall development effort' (US Treasury, 2000, p. 8), although they have not elaborated this argument.[3] This criticism avoids discussing the waste from duplication between the World Bank and the regional development banks, but this is not its main omission. The aim of the Commission recommendation is to force the World Bank to concentrate its financial resources on the region with the largest number of very poor countries. The Bank lends mostly to middle-income countries that have investment grade ratings and can, therefore, finance development in the market place. The Commission's majority believe that this change is overdue.

World Bank management argues that the proposed change would reduce its ability to learn from diverse experience in many parts of the world. This argument is puzzling. Often the most objective and useful examinations are made by those who are not directly involved in a project. They have less incentive to cover over failures and mistakes.

The more important reason, I believe, for opposing the transfer of programme responsibilities from the World Bank to the ADB and IDB is very different. The

---

[3] There have been many criticisms and comments. Most of the principal criticisms are in the Treasury's mandated response. We refer to it wherever applicable.

United States has more direct influence over the World Bank. The US Treasury does not wish to see power and responsibility shift to the countries in the region. I believe a shift of this kind is likely in coming years, and it is best to make the transfer in an orderly way. Indeed, in Europe and Asia the movement toward greater regional control is well under way. South America seems likely to follow.

Organisational and structural changes are important, but they are not sufficient to increase operational or programme effectiveness. Incentives to make programmes work and to reduce waste and corruption must increase. The majority report gives considerable attention to these issues. The World Bank's current administration deserves credit for commenting publicly on corruption, but it has not developed effective programmes to create the incentives to succeed. Public comment and exhortation are not enough to create lasting change. Incentives give people reasons to change their behaviour. The majority report replaces exhortation and subsidies with strong incentives to improve performance and reform institutions.

The specific proposals in the majority report implement this framework. Our goal was to provide public goods efficiently, effectively and in ways that give countries and the IFIs incentives to increase economic stability, raise living standards, improve the quality of life for their citizens and cooperate in providing regional and global public goods. The Bush administration adopted one of the Commission's principal recommendations by proposing to replace loans with grants to the poorest countries.

2 The IMF

The majority proposed that the IMF focus its efforts on four main tasks: crisis prevention, crisis management, improved quality and increased quantity of public information, and macroeconomic advice to developing countries. The Treasury's response endorsed these objectives. Our differences are limited to means, not ends.

Each of the serious crises since 1982 has its own special features and some common features. Before the crisis breaks out, investors begin to withdraw funds. The country often guarantees the foreign exchange value of the funds in an attempt to forestall the withdrawals. This postpones the crisis but does not prevent it. The IMF tries to help the country maintain its exchange rate by lending foreign currency to defend the exchange rate. The country may increase interest rates and promise reforms, but investors see increased risk. If the financial system depends on short-term capital inflows, it may collapse with the exchange rate. The most damaging crises are of this kind. Brazil in 1998 and Argentina in 2001 show the benefit of opening the financial system, as the Commission urged. Some depositors withdrew from local banks but deposited in branches of foreign banks. This reduced the drain to currency, and prevented a banking collapse.

The majority does not believe that all crises can be prevented. It does believe that the frequency and severity of crises can be reduced by reforming country and IMF practices to increase incentives for policies and behaviour that enhance stability. The IMF should be a quasi-lender of last resort (LOLR), not first resort, providing liquidity when markets close.[4] It should work to prevent crises, act to mitigate them and leave structural reform and development to the capital markets and the development banks.

The majority proposed to establish preconditions for IMF assistance. Countries that met the conditions would not have to wait, as they presently do, while negotiators agree on a long list of structural, institutional and financial changes. Crises worsen during these delays, so we propose immediate assistance to qualifying countries.

The conditions must be straightforward, clear, easily monitored and enforced. The majority proposed four conditions, but the list could be altered or expanded slightly. Most important, I believe, are that the financial system is adequately capitalised, government financial policies are prudent, information on the maturity structure of foreign debt becomes available promptly and foreign banks are allowed to compete in local financial markets. Members of the WTO have agreed to phase-in this last condition and several have done so. The majority would speed up implementation as Mexico, Brazil, Argentina, Hungary, Chile, Poland, Czech Republic, Venezuela, Peru and others have done (see *The Economist*, 2000, p. 118). The majority recommended that the exchange rate system be either firmly fixed or floating, but it did not include that recommendation as a precondition. After further reflection, I would include that condition.

Countries would have strong incentives to meet and maintain the preconditions. Once a country qualifies, it would obtain more foreign capital on more favourable terms. IMF acceptance of the country as qualified for automatic assistance would serve as a seal of approval and reduce expected losses. The market would have a list of countries that qualified, and a list of those that did not. The latter would get fewer loans and would pay higher interest rates to compensate for the additional risk. Thus, preconditions redirect private sector flows away from high-risk borrowers toward those that pursue stabilising policies. This reduces the risk in the entire system.

---

[4] A LOLR must have unlimited ability to create money. The IMF does not have that power, so its ability to act like a LOLR is limited. The Commission recommended that the IMF have commitments from principal Central Banks to lend to the IMF against collateral.

Preconditions are not a panacea. They will not increase incentives for stability or induce countries to reform if the IMF bails out all countries and limits creditors' losses.[5] Countries that are crisis-prone because they follow profligate policies or use their financial system to finance politically favoured projects must have an incentive to change their ways. If the IMF does not allow countries to fail, markets will not distinguish sufficiently between countries with proper and improper policies and standards except in time of crisis. Lenders will not have to bear the full risk of their decisions, so they will not charge enough to encourage governments to reform.

Argentina offers an example of how much a country can change if the IMF does not bail out the lenders. In March 2001 Mr López-Murphy became Economy Minister. His programme called for expenditure reduction, a major change from the previous calls for tax rate increases under IMF programmes. The government came close to collapse, so Minister López-Murphy resigned without enacting his programme. The IMF gave no additional assistance at the time. In less than five months, the new Economy Minister, Domingo Cavallo, got agreement on a policy of zero deficits, computed monthly, and much greater reductions in public employee wages, transfers to the provinces and other items than Minister López-Murphy had proposed. Changes that had been 'unacceptable and unthinkable' became the law of the land.[6]

What about third countries, countries that are harmed by the collapse of a trading partner? The majority would assist such countries automatically, if they met the preconditions. In all other cases, it would help them only if were a systemic crisis. We recognise that the IMF would have discretionary power. They could, and likely would, stretch the meaning of 'systemic'. The main risk is not, as several critics suggest, that the IMF would do too little. The more serious risk is they will continue to bail out most countries, thereby reducing the incentive to reform.

Some of the Report's critics claimed that the majority proposal was an effort to curtail the IMF's activities. Much too often, this claim attacks the members' motives and misrepresents the Report. The IMF's activities would decline if crises declined, as the majority believes they would. The main reasons for reduced lending would be that there would be less need for lending, if there

---

[5] Several critics (including Treasury, 2000) either ignore or miss the role of incentives. The underlying theme of the majority report is that proper incentives are both more powerful than exhortation and, because they are adopted by the country through its own processes, more likely to be accepted. It is not the same to say, 'we did this so we could get more investment on better terms' instead of 'the IMF insisted that we do this'.

[6] Unfortunately the changes came late and were piecemeal. The government did not have a comprehensive programme for growth and increased employment to accompany these changes. At the time of writing, the country is in default on its debt and has blocked foreign exchange transactions and frozen most bank accounts.

were fewer crises. And there would be fewer crises if preconditions were met.[7] Financial sectors would be solvent and open to competition from foreign banks, governments would be prudent, and exchange rates would either float, even if not freely, or be firmly fixed and supported by adequate reserves and appropriate policies. Lenders to countries that did not adopt the preconditions would bear the losses they undertook. Hence, they would limit loans to non-qualifying countries increasing incentives for reform.

Treasury and other critics argue correctly that all crises are not liquidity or financial crises. They then claim that the majority report does nothing about other, non-liquidity crises (US Treasury, 2000, p. 7). This is a misunderstanding. First, the majority required prudent fiscal policies to remove this source of disturbance.[8] Second, the majority did not neglect structural problems. It assigned these problems to the development banks and, as noted below, proposed to increase incentives for introducing and continuing structural reforms for ten or more years so that the reforms became institutionalised. Removing structural problems from the IMF's mandate is based on a well-known proposition: money can solve liquidity problems, not real structural problems. In developing countries, structural problems arise because of regulation, tariffs, inadequate financial supervision, absence of the rule of law and other impediments to investment (Burnside and Dollar, 2000). As recent experience in Argentina and Asia, and earlier experience in Mexico, Argentina, Russia, Ukraine and elsewhere demonstrates, loans and liquid resources often allow countries to delay reform. More systematic research shows that foreign aid and liquidity do not produce development, and may retard development unless a country decides to implement structural reforms (Burnside and Dollar, 2000).

Critics also made much of the elimination of (*ex post*) conditionality (Frankel and Roubini, 2001, p. 73). There are three main reasons behind this decision. First, as the Report notes, there is no evidence that conditionality makes a difference on average. There are well-known problems in testing for the effects of conditionality, but the tests that have been reported, both within the IMF and outside, do not show economically important effects on output or economic

---

[7] A frequent criticism is that, if the majority report had been adopted, the IMF would not have been able to assist countries in the Asian crisis (US Treasury, 2000, p. 6). This criticism is not correct. The majority endorsed discretionary authority to act in a systemic crisis. Also, the critics do not say whether the reforms had been in place for the five-year phase-in that the majority report proposed. If the Asian countries had met the preconditions for five years, they would have been much less vulnerable. The problem would have been smaller because countries would have had safer financial institutions and floating exchange rates.

[8] It is easy to see how fiscal profligacy can waste resources and slow growth. Argentina provides the most recent example of a country that allowed an unbalanced budget to destroy a fixed exchange rate system. More difficult is how fiscal profligacy can continue in developing countries if it is not financed by domestic banks or foreign lenders.

growth. (Significant effects on the balance of trade or payments are found, but the 'improvement' is certain to occur because the country cannot borrow when it has a crisis.) Second, the majority believes that local decisions should be encouraged in the interests of democratic accountability. Crises have become the occasion for IFIs to demand reforms that domestic majorities do not want and that governments will not enforce. Third, negotiating a long list of conditions delays action at times of crisis, deepening and spreading it. Delay was very damaging to Mexico, Korea and others.

The Clinton Treasury claimed that the majority proposal 'would preclude the IMF from being able to respond to financial emergencies in a potentially large number of its member countries' (US Treasury, 2000, p. 7). This statement brings out clearly the principal difference in orientation between the Commission majority and many of its critics. The Treasury claims that countries would not respond to the incentives to reform despite the fact that private lenders and investors annually provide 50–100 times the amount of financial resources advanced by all the IFIs. They would not reform to meet the preconditions, so they would not qualify for assistance.

If it were true that most countries would not reform to gain access to financial markets and to enhance stability, what reason is there to believe that these countries will reform because the IFIs exhort them to do so and offer a tiny fraction of the resources they could acquire by reforming?

The majority report proposes to use market discipline in place of conditionality. Publication of timely, accurate information on economic, financial and political developments permits lenders and investors to make informed decisions. The IMF has a major role in improving the quality and increasing the quantity and timeliness of country data. Publication of reports of IMF missions and the IMF's recommendations is a welcome development. Improved information reduces uncertainty and improves lenders' decisions. Release of information encourages reform and permits investors to make continuous marginal adjustments instead of rushing to exit when anticipations change quickly. Further, improving information and opening the economy to foreign banks reduces reliance on renewable, short-term loans. Thus, it reduces one of the major problems of development finance, excessive reliance on short-term loans.

Many of the Commission's critics want to continue conditional lending after crises occur. Few, if any, defend the large number of conditions, often more than twenty but reaching 140 separate conditions on Indonesia's loan in the late 1990s. None show that the conditions are not in conflict, are enforced, are helpful to the country, or are related to macroeconomic stability. It is gratifying to report that the IMF has decided to shorten the list of conditions that countries must meet to receive assistance. Like the majority, it proposes to shift its emphasis toward crisis-prevention and reform of financial systems, and it will urge countries to avoid adjustable, pegged exchange rates. The IMF has greatly increased publicly available information about its decisions and actions, and it has encouraged member governments to do the same. The Clinton Treasury endorsed these changes.

Unfortunately, the IMF has not accepted the full logic of the Commission Report. Its members debate whether and how lenders can be 'bailed-in' to force them to share the cost of a financial crisis. In practice, investors are 'bailed in' unless the IMF helps the country support a pegged exchange rate by lending enough to allow creditors to leave. A floating exchange rate raises the cost to the lenders who decide to bail out. In Argentina in 2001, the new IMF and US Treasury administrations allowed creditors to take their sizeable losses either by selling their bonds at a loss or renegotiating after default. No international crisis or contagion occurred. This suggests that markets distinguished more effectively between Argentina's problems and conditions in other countries than discussions of contagion presume. It remains to be seen whether recognition of risk will reduce capital flows to developing countries.

Under the majority proposal, countries that failed to satisfy preconditions for stability would not receive assistance until they implemented reforms. Higher interest rates compensate lenders for taking the risk of lending to countries with weak financial systems or profligate policies. The lenders should bear the losses in a crisis so that they, and others, will know that the risk premiums they collect are payments that compensate for expected losses that they will bear. They would then price loans and assets correctly.

A related issue, known as 'moral hazard', arises in international lending when governments or IFIs permit lenders to believe that they will be bailed out in a crisis. Most critics of the Report's discussion of moral hazard accept that it was encouraged by official policies in the 1994 Mexican crisis and contributed to the Russian débâcle in 1998. Lenders received large payments for bearing risk, but they believed that the principal governments or the IFIs would prevent a Russian default.

Critics deny that moral hazard was present in Asia. They point to the lack of evidence in interest spreads and other market measures. Such data are not compelling, in part because they do not address whether the loans were correctly priced. These data are consistent with moral hazard. If lenders priced the risk correctly, spreads would not change significantly.

There is an additional problem. In Mexico, Thailand and Korea the government responded to the first large withdrawals by guaranteeing the dollar value of loans to foreign, private sector lenders. The guarantee took different forms. What matters is that the local government could not honour the guarantee in the event of a run unless foreign governments or IFIs provided the dollars. The guarantee postpones or prevents capital from leaving only if the lenders believe that the guarantee will be honoured by the IMF (or others). In most cases, this assumption has been at least partly correct. The Finance Minister knows that he must depend on assistance. The lenders act on the presumption that they will collect the risk premium but will not bear the full risk. This is moral hazard.

A related criticism is that the majority's approach requires the IMF to impose a 'standstill', to prevent lenders from withdrawing from countries in crisis. This is false. The majority relies instead on a flexible exchange rate. The government would not borrow and pay out foreign exchange; the Central Bank would not support the currency. The exchange rate would fall until those who chose to exit were matched by private investors willing to lend or acquire assets at what they think are bargain prices. Settlement of the outstanding foreign currency claims of bondholders and lenders would be left to negotiation by the parties, as the Report notes. Experience in Ecuador suggests that agreements can be reached within a reasonably short time.

The majority does not believe that its proposals are painless. There are costs for the lenders and for the country. The answer does not lie in short-term solutions that force lenders to remain by imposing a 'standstill'. That policy would lead to an excessive reduction in the flow of loans and development finance. There are better policies.[9]

Part of the solution lies in letting financial institutions compete in the local market. They would hold both assets and liabilities denominated in local currency, so they would be less exposed to exchange rate risk. Opening the financial system would encourage entrants with a long-term commitment, thereby reducing the current excessive reliance on short-term capital. And, foreign banks would bring expertise in risk management and act as relatively safe havens if a crisis arises.

The IMF's Poverty Reduction and Growth Facility (PRGF) makes long-term loans at concessional interest rates to relatively poor countries. Development lending is the responsibility of the development banks. If these banks did a better job, there would be no need for the PRGF. The majority solution is to strengthen the development banks instead of adding another development institution within the IMF.

IMF staff are reluctant to criticise the development banks publicly, so they offer another rationale for the PRGF. The countries receiving long-term assistance do not require other types of IMF lending; PRGF makes membership attractive. The majority believes that duplication, without effective competition is costly. The IMF does not have the experience or expertise and should

---

[9] The Treasury and other critics are right when they claim that limiting IMF loans to 90 days with one renewal, as the majority recommended, is too short. The Commission made this recommendation after testimony and discussion with lawyers who raised issues about subordination of other debt to IMF loans of longer maturity. They suggested 90-day loans as a way around this problem. I accept this criticism. A year would have been a better choice.

not develop it. The proper solution is to make the development banks more effective.

3 The development banks

The development banks' main problems are that their programmes lack focus, are often loosely related, or unrelated, to their stated goals and all too frequently fail to accomplish their objectives. After decades of programmes and billions of dollars, many of the poorest nations have lower living standards than in the past. The World Bank's education programme has failed dramatically. After years of educational assistance, Guatemala has a 33 per cent illiteracy rate. Programmes to improve health are no more successful. Overall, the World Bank's own assessments, though flawed, show very little achievement in the poorest countries. All of the fault does not lie with the development banks, but they have not found ways around the obstacles that some governments create. They continue to lend despite the obstacles and the resulting failures, and they give most of their loans to countries that can borrow in the capital markets, many of which do not require subsidies.

Countries have made substantial progress where they have strengthened institutions and the role of markets and little if any progress in many of the poorest countries where they have not reformed. Most of the very poor countries have large debts that cannot be serviced or repaid. The Commission voted unanimously to forgive the debts entirely, after countries institute reforms. The IFIs have more than enough accumulated reserves and provisions for loss to write off all debts of the poorest countries. I believe that reform of the IFIs and the recipient nations should be a precondition for donor country funding of debt forgiveness.

The majority favoured major changes to focus efforts on three broad areas and improve incentives in the countries and the development banks. First, the development banks should work to improve the quality of life, even in countries where corruption or institutional arrangements prevent or hinder economic development. The majority proposed grants, instead of loans, to pay up to 90 per cent of project costs approved by the development banks. To increase achievement and reduce waste, grants would be given after competitive bidding and would require independent monitoring and auditing of results. Payments would be made, after performance is certified, directly to providers or suppliers instead of governments. The suppliers would have an incentive to assure that inoculations are made, potable water is supplied, sanitation is improved, literacy rates increased and that these and other programmes produce measurable results. Before leaving office, Treasury Secretary Summers endorsed the use of grants in place of loans, and the Bush administration adopted his proposal. The Bank opposed it, perhaps because it called for monitoring results.

Second, long-term subsidised loans to develop effective institutions would assist countries that willingly adopt and sustain the necessary reforms. Here, too, independent auditors must certify that progress continues. This proposal replaces the command and control measures mandated by the development banks with incentives that encourage local support for development.

Third, many problems that prevent development or reduce the quality of life are common to many different countries. The development banks have maintained a country-specific focus. They have not tried to find solutions to common problems such as malaria, measles, tropical agriculture and many others. Research is costly, and individual market demand is too small to induce companies to do the research. By joining countries together and subsidising research efforts, the development banks can close the gap between social and private rates of return.

The majority also recommended that scarce official financial resources be concentrated on poor countries without access to alternative funds and that countries graduate automatically and regularly from the programmes. Graduation would release more money to help the poorest countries. The development banks should continue to offer technical assistance to countries that graduate, but these countries should borrow in the market and be subject to market discipline.

The World Bank and others responded to the majority proposals by claiming that ending loans to middle-income countries would harm the poorest countries by reducing the Bank's income (Gilbert, Powell and Vines, 1999). This claim has no merit. The Bank lends at a rate very little above its own cost of funds; it adds a fractional fee to cover administrative expense. The only 'profit' on the loan comes from the allocation of a portion of the Bank's costless equity capital. The same capital would be available to support grants. There would be no diminution of resources.

At times, some Bank officials claim that the Bank has unlimited borrowing capacity in the capital market. Hence, its loans could be increased indefinitely, and there is no reason to shift loans from middle-income countries toward the poorest countries. This is either a misstatement or an error. The Bank's borrowing limit is set by its industrialised member callable capital – the amount that countries have pledged to the Bank. Lender's risk increases once the Bank's loans approach the amount of its industrialised country callable capital, so lenders would demand higher interest rates to cover the increased risk. Given its history of rolling over uncollectable debts, the risk premium would rise rapidly. The Bank's borrowing capacity is unlimited only if the industrialised countries are willing to supply unlimited contributions to the Bank.

In his testimony before the Commission and in subsequent comments, the Bank's president claimed that replacing loans to poor countries with grants was a good idea in principle, but impractical.[10] He claimed it would require a large increase in support by donor countries. This claim is the very opposite of 'unlimited borrowing capacity', but it, too, is incorrect.

The Bank earns all of its net income by investing funds it has not disbursed and its own costless, paid-in capital in the securities market. These earnings would remain. As outstanding concessional loans are repaid, the volume of earning assets would increase. Would the available resources be large enough to support a large grants programme?

After the Report was published, a senior staff member analysed the amount of development programmes that the Bank could support with current resources, if it replaced loans with grants, as the majority proposed. The calculation showed that the value of programmes that could be financed with grants greatly exceeded the amount provided by traditional concessional loans now made (Lerrick, 2000). Hence the amount of assistance would increase. Effectiveness would improve. Theft and misappropriation would be reduced. And there would be no debt burden for the poorest countries.

Several months after the Report appeared, a private foundation adopted the Commission's grants proposal, with monitoring, as part of a new health programme for African nations. Former Treasury Secretary Summers also shifted the Clinton Treasury's position. His statements at the time of the Prague meeting of the IMF and the World Bank favoured increased use of grants. In 2001, the Bush Administration formally adopted the proposal to shift funding from loans to grants.

The Bank's president offered another defence of Bank loans to middle-income countries that can borrow in the capital markets. He claims that the Bank finances socially useful projects that do not earn monetary returns. Further, he claims that the capital markets would not finance these projects.

This argument overlooks an important difference. The Bank receives a government guarantee of principal and interest. If private lenders received the same guarantee, they would not care how the country used the loan proceeds.

In fact, the Bank does not know what its loans to middle-income countries finance on the margin. Money is fungible. No outsider can know reliably which project or projects were financed by development aid. It is in the interest of the

[10] US Treasury (2000, p. 8) opposes the proposed automatic graduation rule ($4000 *per capita* income or investment grade rating). It does not make its own graduation proposal, but argues that most of the world's poor live in countries like China that would have graduated under the Commission's proposal. One of the Commission's minority endorsed the grants proposal in testimony after the report was published. (Reform of the International Monetary Fund, 2000, p. 38).

country and the Bank's officers to claim high marginal social returns. In most cases, projects with high returns could be financed without assistance from the IFIs, especially if the country guarantees repayment.

This problem arises in all but the poorest countries where there is true additionality. That's another reason why the development banks should focus on poor countries without access to financial markets.

4 Perspective: the IMF two years after the Commission's Report

Much has changed at the IMF in the nearly two years since the Commission report appeared. Interest rates are higher; the number of lending programmes has been reduced; there is greater transparency, more information, a less opaque accounting system and more information about member countries available for interested parties.

A new team is in charge. They appear to agree on some of the principles that the Commission highlighted, including the substitution of incentives for command and control in country programmes. The Commission's majority believed that countries do not reform because they get loans from the IFIs. Lasting reform occurs when the country's parliament or government becomes convinced that reform is in their economic and political interest and that it benefits their constituents.

After giving Argentina substantial assistance in December 2000, the IMF changed course. In March 2001, a new Argentine Minister of Economy, Mr López-Murphy, announced his intention to reduce government spending. The Vice President resigned in protest; there was little political support, and López-Murphy resigned within two weeks of his appointment. By mid-summer, the government and parliament had accepted reductions in spending much larger and more encompassing than López-Murphy had proposed. The Congress voted, reluctantly, for a balanced budget. Adversity accomplished reforms that IMF lending did not achieve.

Although the IMF loaned an additional $5 billion in August 2001, it insisted that Argentina meet the budget targets that it had promised to meet. Argentina defaulted on its debt, the largest nominal default ever recorded. Unlike Korea, Thailand, Indonesia and Mexico, the IMF did not rush in with a new programme to 'bail-out' the creditors. It had discovered that the easiest way to 'bail-in' a lender is to avoid bailing them out by providing additional loans to support an over-valued currency and excessive debt.

The IMF was not passive. During the summer, it agreed to lend money to Brazil to prevent the consequences of an Argentine default from spreading, as the Commission had proposed. And it advised Argentina that it had to adopt a comprehensive framework for its debt, exchange rate, monetary and fiscal policies. At the time of writing, in the winter of 2002, Argentina's government has not developed a comprehensive, consistent plan to restore growth, and the IMF has not offered any money.

One case is not much evidence. In time, we will know whether there is a new set of rules that emphasises incentives to reform and the responsibility of the troubled country to adopt them. Nevertheless, the IMF's response to Argentina's problems is markedly different than its earlier responses to Argentina or its approach to many other countries. It permitted a default by a major country after permitting smaller defaults by Ecuador, Pakistan and Ukraine. Default and restructuring aligns risk and return. It is the single best means of reducing moral hazard in international lending.

Turkey is another change, but of lesser magnitude. Turkey's problems were mainly domestic. Turkey's debt was mainly internal, its banking problems overdue for reforms that Turkey's political system would not undertake. The IMF's role in Turkey continued decades of support for an important US and G7 ally. This time, however, the IMF insisted that the promised reforms be adopted, not just promised.

On the other hand, the IMF failed to create the incentives for reform that the Commission majority favoured. The IMF's Contingent Credit Line (CCL) is the closest analogue to the Commission's recommendation of precommitment to support countries that meet and maintain a small number of reforms that are essential for stability. The problem is not that the IMF bureaucracy is unwilling to accept countries into the CCL. On the contrary, the Managing Director seems committed, and the Fund is officially eager. The problem is that the bureaucracy cannot produce a CCL programme that attracts member governments. A main difficulty is that the IMF bureaucracy is reluctant to make assistance automatic.

5 Conclusion

The international economy has experienced several prolonged, deep financial crises since 1980. At the same time, economic development has bypassed the poorest countries. Many of them are in Africa, but extreme poverty can be found also in Latin America, Asia and southern and eastern Europe.

Reform of the IFIs is needed to increase economic stability, improve the flow of information, encourage economic development, support institutional reform, reduce moral hazard, reduce poverty and support provision of regional and global public goods. The Report of the International Financial Institution Advisory Commission offers an integrated approach to many of these problems.

This chapter develops the Commission majority's main recommendations and responds to criticisms by the US Treasury and others. It is useful to conclude by putting these criticisms into context in two ways. First, although the Treasury was critical of many of the majority's recommendations, they wrote: '[W]e share the Commission's desire to find new ways to encourage countries to reduce their vulnerability before crisis strikes. In this context, we agree with the report that it is critical for countries to strengthen the financial sector, improve the quality of disclosure, and reinforce the resilience of the exchange rate regime' (US Treasury, 2000, p. 8).

Second, it is encouraging that, with the passage of time, and new Treasury officials, the Treasury has endorsed, and the IMF has adopted or considered, some of the majority's recommendations. The changes already adopted include reduction in the number of different lending arrangements, incentives for countries to repay more quickly, penalties in the form of higher interest rates for countries that remain in debt and agreement that the IMF will emphasise short-term lending.

An interview with a senior IMF official suggests how much the IMF has changed. The IMF now aims for 'a minimum amount of conditionality' instead of the lengthy list of reforms. Then, he added, 'the IMF needs to be more flexible, not dictating to a country what policies are needed. The country should be allowed to present a program to the IMF . . . And the IMF needs to be selective, patiently waiting for the country to be ready' (IMF, 2002, p. 14).

More remains to be done. The most difficult, but most important, changes are (1) to recognise that reform can work only if lenders to non-reformed countries are required to take the losses implied by the risk premiums they receive, and (2) to replace command and control orders from Washington with incentives that encourage reform at the local level.

Finally, I would welcome the opportunity to cite important reforms at the World Bank and the development banks. Regrettably, the development banks have moved more slowly, or not at all. One must hope that they will shift from a policy based on 'bribe and exhort' to incentive-based policies before there is another crisis.

REFERENCES

Burnside, C. and D. Dollar (2000). 'Aid Policies and Growth', *American Economic Review*, 90, 847–68

Economist, The (2000). 'Emerging Market Indicators', 4 November, 118

Frankel, J. A. and N. Roubini (2001). 'The Role of Industrial Country Policies in Emerging Market Crises', National Bureau of Economic Research, Working Paper, 8634, 1–110

Gilbert, C. L., A. Powell and D. Vines (1999). 'Positioning the World Bank', *Economic Journal*, 109, F598–F633

International Advisory Commission (2000). *Report of the International Financial Institution Advisory Commission*, Washington, DC, US Government Printing Office

International Monetary Fund (2002). 'IMF Conditionality' *IMF Survey*, 31(1), 14 January, 14–16

Lerrick, A. (2000). 'Development Grant Financing: More Aid per Dollar', *Hearing before the Joint Economic Committee*, Washington, DC, Government Printing Office, 12 April

Reform of the International Monetary Fund (2000). *Hearing before the Subcommittee on International Trade and Finance*, 106th Congress, 2nd session. Washington, DC, Government Printing Office, 27 April

US Treasury (2000). Response to the Report of the International Financial Institution Advisory Commission, Washington, DC, Department of the Treasury, 9 June

World Bank (1992) (Wapenhans Report). 'Effective Implementation: Key to Development Impact', World Bank, internal document

5 Reforming the global financial architecture: just tinkering around the edges?

MALCOLM KNIGHT, LAWRENCE SCHEMBRI
AND JAMES POWELL

1 Introduction

The 1990s was a tumultuous decade for the international financial system, especially for emerging-market countries. Capital flows to those countries increased dramatically in the first few years of the decade. But from 1994 to 1999, the world economy was shaken by a series of financial crises in Mexico, East Asia, Russia and in a number of other emerging markets. These crises caused major recessions in the affected countries. But they were a wake-up call to policymakers that the existing international financial architecture must be reformed.

The surge in capital inflows to emerging-market economies during the first half of the 1990s was driven by high rates of investment relative to saving in these countries and associated high expected returns, financial liberalisation and innovation and lower transactions costs. Simultaneously, investors in the industrial countries increased their supply of financial capital in the belief that international diversification, the explicit or implicit guarantees offered by the governments of developing countries and the prospect of international bailouts if things went wrong had mitigated the risks of increased exposures to emerging markets. In retrospect, it is evident that many of the same structural changes that facilitated large capital inflows to these economies also exacerbated outflows when expectations shifted. In such circumstances, pegged exchange rate regimes collapsed and weak banking systems imploded. The international financial architecture failed to forestall these crises or limit contagion. As a result, economic expansions in many emerging-market countries were suddenly thrown into reverse.

This chapter has benefited from detailed comments and suggestions provided by its discussants, Sir Nigel Wicks, Mervyn King and Michael Dooley as well as Christopher Gilbert. Additional comments and suggestions from Paul Jenkins, Charles Freedman, John Murray, Mark Kruger and Mark Zelmer are also gratefully acknowledged. Debi Kirwan provided helpful technical assistance. We are grateful to Francine Rioux for her invaluable secretarial services.

124

From the perspective of the late 1990s, it appeared that emerging-market economies were riddled by crises and that the process of capital account liberalisation that many of them had embarked upon was a mistake. Indeed, some commentators have claimed that the benefits of free capital mobility were grossly over-sold.[1] We argue that the basic problem was not excessively rapid financial liberalisation in emerging-market countries, but rather the inconsistency in the international financial system between the largely complete markets investors in the capital exporting industrial countries had become accustomed to for risk management and the incomplete and distorted market structures in the emerging-market countries to which vast amounts of capital were being directed. To resolve this dichotomy, both lenders in the industrial countries and governments and corporate borrowers in emerging markets relied heavily on implicit and explicit guarantees to mitigate the inadequacy of local markets for managing risk. This attempt to paper over a fundamental fissure in the architecture of the international financial system contributed to the abruptness and severity of the financial crises of the 1990s, as well as the striking extent of the contagion that they engendered.

This view of the shortcomings of the current international financial architecture is summarised in the first half of this chapter. Such an analysis leads directly to a suggested approach to reform that entails working systematically to develop a system of broad, deep and well-regulated financial markets that can more effectively price and manage the risks inherent in capital transfers from industrial to emerging-market countries. This approach, which is outlined in the second half of the chapter, addresses the reform of the International Monetary Fund (IMF) and other financial institutions, but goes further. It deals with the relationship between the choice of exchange rate regime by individual countries and the arrangements for providing liquidity to the international financial system, under normal conditions and in times of crisis. Only by pursuing a comprehensive approach to reform can the international community eventually achieve a more stable and robust global financial architecture.

Section 2 focuses on the role of financial markets in emerging economies and on the lessons learned from recent crises. It seeks to explain why, under current international financial arrangements, both emerging-market borrowers and industrial country lenders have had a strong incentive to resort to government guarantees as a way of encouraging capital inflows. It considers how such behaviour worked to increase the moral hazard inherent in the system. Section 3 broadly outlines our proposals for a comprehensive, market-based approach to reform of the international financial architecture. It describes several broad avenues for change in emerging-market countries: financial sector strengthening; improvements in the implementation of macroeconomic policy; associated

---

[1] See, for example, Bhagwati (1998) and Radelet and Sachs (1999).

changes in exchange rate regimes and monetary policy targets; and a consistent programme of financial market deepening and capital account liberalisation. It considers the role that governments and private sector lenders in industrial countries can play in strengthening the international financial system and in mitigating the effects of crises when they occur. Section 4 describes reforms for the IMF and other international financial institutions that would reinforce the proposals made in Section 3. It includes a discussion of how possible changes in the arrangements for private sector involvement in the prevention and resolution of financial crises fit into a comprehensive market-based approach to reform of the international financial architecture. Section 5 summarises our main conclusions.

2 The international financial crises of the 1990s

Incomplete financial markets and the management of risks

Although many observers claim that the international financial crises in emerging-market economies of the 1990s were caused by financial markets that were too unencumbered, we argue that the main underlying cause of these crises was the risks created by the dichotomy between the largely complete and highly transparent financial markets of the industrial countries and the incomplete and distorted financial market structures in the developing world. It is useful to consider how this dichotomy arose.

During the 1960s and 1970s, mathematical economists were preoccupied with determining why the structure of markets, even in the industrial countries, remained incomplete. Following Arrow and Debreu (1954), they reasoned that if more complete spot and forward markets existed, economies would be able to allocate resources much more efficiently. Why then, in the late 1960s and early 1970s, were virtually the only forward markets those for a few major currencies?

These puzzles have gradually been resolved since the 1960s. Forward and derivatives markets were either rudimentary in nature or non-existent in the 1960s for several reasons: governments and private firms did not make enough timely and accurate information available to permit markets to assess risks effectively; certain key prices in the system, particularly the exchange rates of the major currencies, were held fixed; international capital transactions were heavily regulated even in the most advanced countries; and the pricing formulas and raw calculating power needed to process financial information and establish the prices of many financial derivatives did not exist.

In the industrial countries, these gaps in the structure of financial markets were progressively and largely eliminated over the next thirty years. The shift to flexible exchange rates in the 1970s for the major currencies made spot and forward foreign exchange markets much more responsive as sensitive signalling devices for transactors' expectations of future events. Secondary markets and derivatives markets for domestic government and other securities broadened and deepened. Flows of timely market information increased tremendously. As private transactors in industrial countries discovered that virtually any forward contract could be duplicated by a combination of spot market and credit market transactions, there was a tremendous expansion in the availability of financial markets to allow economic agents to manage, hedge, or lay off risks. The legal and informational framework that is essential for efficient markets was greatly extended and refined.[2] Algorithms, most importantly the option pricing methodology developed in the early 1970s by Black, Scholes and Merton, opened the door to the creation of complex financial instruments. As a result, markets in the industrial countries have become largely complete, making them hugely more efficient in allocating resources, across sectors and regions and over time, and much less susceptible to financial crises.

What does all this have to do with the current debate on the future international financial architecture? A lot. While some might claim that financial market liberalisation has increased market instability and financial contagion by reducing the cost of speculation, we argue that the emerging-market crises that occurred during the 1990s were a result of the way in which the virtually complete markets of industrial countries *interacted* with the incomplete, weakly regulated and distorted financial markets of capital importing countries in the developing world. The incomplete financial market structures and weak banking systems in emerging-market economies created strong pressures for developing country governments to provide, and industrial country creditors to seek, certain types of implicit and explicit guarantees.

---

[2] In many cases, these refinements were introduced to redress the effects of financial crises in industrial countries that were themselves caused by residual gaps that remained in their financial market structures. Examples are legion: the collapse of the Bretton Woods exchange rate system of fixed par values between the late 1960s and the early 1970s; the suspension of the US dollar's convertibility into gold as a result of the Smithsonian Agreement of 1971; the elimination of controls on international capital movements by the United Kingdom in 1979 and by most other European countries by the mid-1980s; the major improvements in the regulation of the US financial system in the wake of the crisis in the savings and loan institutions (S & Ls) in the early 1980s; the measures taken to strengthen equity market regulation following the stock market crash of 1987; the Basel Capital Accord of 1988; and the improvements in disclosure rules in the Nordic countries' financial systems in the wake of the crises in the early 1990s.

Table 5.1 *Net capital flows to emerging-market economies,*
1973–1999 (period averages of annual flows, US $ billions)

	1973–7	1978–82	1983–8	1989–95	1996–9
FDI	3.6	9.0	12.6	39.8	133.3
Portfolio investment	0.2	1.7	4.3	41.5	38.5
Other	6.4	15.3	−5.2	33.1	−62.1
Total private	10.2	26.0	11.6	114.3	109.7
Total official	*11.0*	*25.5*	*29.5*	*11.7*	*18.0*
Total flows	**21.2**	**51.5**	**41.1**	**136.0**	**127.7**

Sources: IMF, *International Capital Markets* and *World Economic Outlook.*

Financial flows to emerging markets

The seeds of the financial crises that struck a number of developing countries in
the mid-1990s were planted by the dramatic growth in capital inflows to emerging markets that began to accelerate in 1991. Table 5.1 shows that net private
capital flows to emerging markets increased more than tenfold between the
mid-1970s and the late 1990s. Whereas official capital flows had been a major,
and sometimes principal, source of emerging-market finance in the 1970s and
1980s, by the 1990s they were dwarfed by private capital inflows. The causes of
this remarkable surge have been widely discussed.[3] Owing to rapid growth in
Asia and more market-oriented policies in Latin America, these regions became
increasingly attractive to foreign investors. Furthermore, because the amount
of international investment in emerging markets had been low throughout the
1980s, international portfolio diversification to emerging-market countries was
attractive to investors in industrial countries, particularly with the development
of diversified emerging-market index funds, the securitisation of bank loans
and the development of the 'Brady bond' market and other financial innova-
tions. Whereas bank lending dominated the flows in the late 1970s, foreign
direct investment (FDI) had become an important source of finance by the late
1990s.

   If foreign capital is invested wisely, over the long term it raises labour productivity, economic growth and national welfare. Capital inflows, especially FDI,
also yield dynamic benefits in the form of technology transfers and positive
externalities, such as a more highly trained labour force. Thus, governments
in developing countries, many of which had already initiated programmes for
economic reform and were under great pressure to deliver the promised results

[3] See IMF (1998). See also Schadler *et al.* (1993).

quickly, implemented a number of measures designed to encourage foreign borrowing.

However, rather than undertake the time-consuming and costly reforms needed to fundamentally transform their financial markets as a way of attracting and managing these inflows, governments in developing countries tended to adopt various implicit and explicit guarantees in an attempt to overcome financial sector deficiencies and reduce risk.[4] These guarantees were welcomed by large institutional creditors in industrial countries, who saw them as a means of limiting risks that could not be hedged because the borrowing countries lacked the markets for doing so. As discussed below, these guarantees aggravated the liquidity, currency and maturity mismatches, thus weakening the risk–return profile that sustained these inflows and setting the stage for the financial crises of 1997–8. The existence of these guarantees stunted the natural growth of financial market. Corbett and Vines (1999) underscore the importance of insufficient institutional development as the principal underlying factor of the Asian crisis. We strongly subscribe to this view.

Lessons learned

Over-reliance on the banking sector for intermediation

An important lesson from the emerging-market financial crises of the 1990s is that a resilient national financial system requires financial intermediation to be based not only on a well-developed and well-regulated banking system but also on competition among banks, non-bank financial institutions (NBFIs), and domestic debt and equity markets in channelling funds from foreigners and domestic savers to borrowers in the home economy (Knight, 1998, 1999). Since many, if not most, emerging-market economies lack the structure of financial institutions and markets that can compete with banks to intermediate savings, weaknesses in their banking sectors have been rightly viewed as a critical factor contributing to the recent crises (Kaminsky and Reinhart, 1999). These weaknesses have been discussed extensively since the Asian crisis. We will summarise them, as illustrations of this chapter's argument that the dichotomy between complete markets in the industrial countries and incomplete markets elsewhere lies at the heart of the problem with today's international financial architecture.

Miller (1998), among many others, argues that much of the recent financial instability in emerging-market countries is due to an over-reliance on the banking

---

[4] Krueger (2000) makes similar arguments and cites specific examples. See also Mishkin (2000).

sector to intermediate savings. In the crises of 1997–8, the maturity and currency mismatches on the balance sheets of banks in a number of borrowing countries, coupled with the fact that the first creditors to run were the most likely to be able to avoid capital losses, made banks in those countries highly vulnerable. As funds were withdrawn from banks perceived to be weak, and converted into foreign exchange, interest rates had to be increased to maintain currency pegs. Given the maturity and currency mismatches, these increased interest rates quickly rendered important segments of the banking system insolvent in the afflicted countries, either directly or via effects on borrowers' balance sheets.

Lack of competition in the banking sector of the emerging countries has also been identified as a significant weakness. This problem has often been closely linked to government intervention: nationalisation; ownership restrictions, particularly on holdings by foreigners;[5] and lax rules on connections between banks and industrial conglomerates. As a result, banking systems in emerging-market countries tend to be concentrated, with a large proportion of deposits held in a relatively small number of institutions. This oligopolistic structure has not only led to less efficient intermediation, it has also affected the soundness and stability of the banking systems in emerging markets. Oligopolistic banking systems charge higher spreads between loan and deposit rates and provide lower levels of intermediation than competitive banking systems (Knight, 1998). Weak competition also results in less-effective credit assessment and loan management by such banks.

During the 1990s, many emerging-market countries exacerbated these problems by abruptly liberalising their banking sectors – through the removal of administrative controls on interest rates, bank-by-bank credit ceilings and limits on new entry – and by liberalising short-term interbank claims while retaining tight controls on longer-term inflows of debt, FDI and equity capital. By maximising the mismatch between short-term external liabilities and long-term domestic assets, these actions created severe vulnerabilities in the banking systems of developing countries (Knight, 1999). And these fundamental changes often occured when banking supervision and regulation and the banks' own risk-management techniques were extremely weak (Caprio and Honohan, 1999). The banking sectors in the emerging-market countries were ripe for the crises that befell them in 1997–8.

---

[5] The Meltzer Commission Report (Meltzer 2000) identifies the lack of foreign participation in the banking sectors of emerging-market countries as a further factor that reduces competition. The Report recommends that foreign participation in the domestic banking sector be one of the eligibility conditions for emergency IMF lending (see also chapter 4 in this volume). Using data for Argentina and Mexico, Goldberg, Dages and Kinney (2000) find that foreign banks maintained credit growth during crisis periods while domestic banks did not.

Capital markets

Most developing countries lack the depth and breadth of capital markets found in industrialised countries, and the capital markets that do exist are typically thin and illiquid, particularly at longer maturities. Since such gaps in financial markets limit the information available for risk assessment and risk pooling, they prevent the efficient transfer of risk across market participants. The most serious gaps and deficiencies include:

- limited markets for domestic currency government and corporate debt
- thin markets for foreign currency government and corporate debt, especially long-term
- limited forward markets for foreign exchange
- thin and opaque equity markets.

These gaps and deficiencies lead to excessive reliance on short-term debt rather than equity flows. In most emerging-market countries, only governments and the largest corporations can issue foreign currency debt, and then only at relatively high interest rate spreads over London Interbank Offer Rate (LIBOR) and short maturities.[6] The proceeds of these loans, even when they are optimally employed, are typically used to finance investment in highly illiquid forms of fixed capital or imported intermediate inputs. The short maturity of emerging-market debt, coupled with the long gestation period for investment projects, creates an increased risk of maturity mismatches that usually cannot be hedged in domestic financial markets. This imbalance has often been a source of national balance sheet risk that cannot be easily transferred to other agents, providing yet another factor that contributed to the recent financial crises.

Greater recourse to FDI or inflows of portfolio equity would have alleviated these severe vulnerabilities. Because equity investors are bailed in when a crisis arises, and because equity flows are industry- and even firm-specific, they tend to be more stable than debt flows in times of volatility. This was true of the emerging markets during the recent crisis. While net bank lending dried up and reversed, non-debt-creating flows remained strong.

Canada's experience is relevant here. External current account deficits were high in Canada during the early twentieth century, at one point reaching almost 18 per cent of GDP. But because these large differences between domestic saving and domestic investment were financed by inflows of FDI attracted by high expected returns on real capital (rather than by a contractual obligation to pay interest), they did not lead to exchange rate instability.

---

[6] The bulk of the foreign currency debt issued by emerging-market countries has an average maturity of less than five years. Some of the larger countries have however, been able to issue longer-term debt. For example, Brazil, which in the aftermath of its 1998–9 currency crisis adopted fiscal reform and a flexible exchange rate, has issued thirty-year bonds.

Table 5.2 *Stock market capitalisation, selected countries, 1980–1998 (per cent of GDP)*

	1980	1985	1990	1995	1996	1997	1998
Developed markets							
Canada	44.6	42.0	42.2	62.3	79.5	89.9	90.0
Germany	8.9	29.6	23.6	23.9	28.2	39.0	50.9
Hong Kong	137.2	99.0	111.5	218.1	291.6	241.6	209.8
Japan	35.8	70.6	98.2	71.4	67.2	52.8	66.0
United Kingdom	38.5	72.2	86.2	125.2	147.8	151.7	169.9
United States	51.8	55.2	52.7	92.7	108.6	136.2	153.6
Emerging markets							
Brazil	3.8	18.7	3.5	21.0	28.0	31.1	20.7
Korea	6.1	8.5	43.6	39.9	28.6	9.5	35.7
Malaysia	50.6	52.0	113.6	255.0	309.4	95.1	131.7
Mexico	6.7	2.1	12.4	31.7	32.3	38.9	23.3
Thailand	3.8	5.0	28.0	84.2	55.0	15.3	31.4

Sources: International Financial Corporation, *Emerging Stock Markets Factbook*, 1999. IMF, *International Financial Statistics.*

Although equity markets in emerging-market economies have experienced dramatic growth since 1980, they are generally small by the standards of industrial countries (table 5.2).[7] Furthermore, the equities traded in the local stock markets of emerging economies are predominantly those of the largest local companies or subsidiaries of multinational corporations. Since equity markets in these countries are, in general, not a major factor in intermediating savings flows, domestic firms have high debt to equity ratios. The heavy dependence of the non-financial sector on fixed interest loans from the domestic banking system is an important source of vulnerability. Finally, in the presence of an explicit or implicit guarantee that the country's exchange rate will remain unchanged, the incentive for domestic borrowers to obtain lower interest rates by borrowing in foreign currency, even when they are non-exporters who are not 'naturally hedged', creates strong inducements for domestic banks to borrow foreign currency abroad at short terms to make these foreign currency loans to domestic residents – a practice that the current Basel capital rules inadvertently encourages. Thus, even when such banks show a fully matched foreign currency position, they often bear very large unhedged risks *vis-à-vis* their domestic borrowers.

The absence of the necessary legal infrastructure (accounting and auditing standards, bankruptcy law, etc.) is another reason why incomplete markets

[7] The exception is Malaysia.

persist in developing countries. In advanced economies, well-functioning financial institutions and markets strengthen market discipline by monitoring firm managers and exerting corporate control. In emerging economies, weak or non-existent market discipline makes it difficult for potential investors to assess risks accurately. Thin and opaque equity markets, combined with explicit government policies to limit foreign direct and portfolio investment, led emerging economies to rely disproportionately on debt flows instead of equity (table 5.1, p. 128) until the early 1990s. A reliance on debt financing contributed to the magnitude of the crises in emerging markets in the 1990s.

To summarise, excessive reliance on banks and major gaps in the structure of financial markets have limited the scope for economic agents in emerging-market economies to use market mechanisms to hedge or diversify risk, and have exacerbated financial instability.

Government guarantees

The process of transferring capital from industrial to developing countries, though essential to growth, is highly risky. Because of incomplete information and incomplete markets, the quantitative extent of the risks (and the capital that should be held against them) is virtually impossible to calculate and to hedge. The best way to manage risks in the emerging economies will be to develop well-regulated and efficient market structures. To do so, it is necessary to have accurate and timely information, and a full range of well-functioning markets that allows agents to diversify risks, supported by a well-functioning legal and regulatory framework. When this comprehensive structure of markets is allowed to take root, risks can be characterised by reasonably well-defined probability distributions, which can be handled by modern pricing formulae for futures and options markets.

As the discussion on p. 132 illustrated, what happened in emerging markets in the 1990s was quite different. Too often in developing countries the legal structures to support markets were deficient and lacking in due process; the main banks and other financial institutions employed accounting practices that were anything but transparent, giving rise to uncertainties such as transfer risk, political risk and convertibility risk. These are not the sorts of risks that can be characterised by neat probability distributions. Incomplete and imperfect financial markets in the emerging-market countries made the assessment and management of these risks extremely difficult, if not impossible. Under these circumstances, industrial country and domestic lenders were typically willing to supply capital only if they were offered some sort of guarantee. The authorities of many emerging-market countries were quick to do so. Rather than undertake fundamental financial sector reform, they provided explicit and implicit guarantees to international lenders, particularly large institutional lenders who thought that if crises occurred they could influence host and home governments to reduce the risks associated with their loans to emerging markets.[8] (See Appendix 1, p. 150 for a conceptual framework.)

Chain of guarantees

Dooley (1994) uses the term 'chain of guarantees' to describe this behaviour. In his view, and ours, these guarantees were the trigger for the financial crises of the 1990s. In emerging economies, domestic depositors were often insured by deposit insurance (usually implicit), while foreign lenders to domestic banks or firms were insured by the implicit guarantee that the debts would be assumed by the government should the domestic borrowers default. Furthermore, lenders and borrowers were often also insured against foreign exchange risk by the government's commitment to a pegged exchange rate, which entailed an implicit promise to protect domestic borrowers from foreign exchange losses. Domestic banks were insured against credit risk on loans directed to or guaranteed by the government, and against maturity and liquidity risk, because the Central Bank would act as a lender of last resort and the government would not allow the banking system to fail because it was too important to the domestic economy. Hence, the chain of guarantees began with savers and extended through the intermediaries to the ultimate borrowers. Governments were committed to protecting them all. This not only created a moral hazard, which led to excessive risk-taking and eventual collapse, but also precluded the longer-term development of markets to hedge these risks.

To summarise, in the absence of complete markets, industrial country lenders and emerging-country borrowers and governments had strong incentives to use guarantees to attempt to limit risk. But when such guarantees were no longer credible, the result was inevitably a crisis as lenders rushed for the exits, creating contagion across whole classes of emerging-country borrowers that were viewed as similar risks, regardless of their individual circumstances. The chain of guarantees lubricated the mechanism that encouraged huge capital flows from industrial to developing countries during the 1990s. But in doing so, it vastly increased the degree of moral hazard on the part of both creditors and debtors.

---

[8] Dooley (1997, pp. 5–6) makes a similar argument. In his insurance model of currency crises, governments want to increase their net reserve position and thus provide guarantees to increase the expected yield on domestic liabilities held by foreign investors.

3 Towards a new global financial architecture

If countries are to reap the benefits of the globalisation of financial markets, tinkering around the edges of the international financial architecture is not sufficient. With the support, encouragement and assistance of the industrialised countries and the IFIs, emerging-market countries must take bold steps to broaden the scope and improve the efficiency of their domestic financial markets. Because a broader and deeper set of financial markets will generate more information, improve risk assessment, contribute to more efficient intermediation of domestic and foreign savings and lead to a more resilient financial system, such efforts will ultimately stabilise capital flows and foster higher and more stable rates of economic growth. Simultaneously, emerging-market countries must undertake the institutional reforms needed to create sustainable exchange rate regimes, supported by a prudent fiscal policy, a low-inflation monetary policy and reforms to further enhance the development of sound and efficient financial systems.

From this perspective, some recent papers that offer plans for the reform of the international financial architecture are too narrowly focused on detailed proposals for changes to international institutions, such as the IMF and the World Bank, and not focused enough on the reform of the broader global financial architecture. An approach that focuses exclusively on organisational changes to the international financial institutions really is 'just tinkering'.

Consider the early 1970s when the Bretton Woods system of 'pegged-but-adjustable' exchange rates was under stress. Years earlier, Triffin (1960) had predicted that the Bretton Woods system of fixed par value exchange rates would eventually collapse. He felt that with exchange rates pegged to the US dollar, and the dollar fixed in terms of gold, the United States would have to run net balance of payments deficits over time to provide liquidity to the international monetary system as world GDP expanded. But these deficits would eventually undermine the credibility of the dollar's convertibility into gold.

As Triffin predicted, the system of fixed par values did collapse, in the early 1970s. Following that collapse, the plans to reform the international monetary system that were discussed in the mid-1970s explicitly recognised that a system where the exchange rates of most countries remained fixed would continue to require an ultimate provider of international liquidity. Conversely, if exchange rates were fully flexible, movements in each country's exchange rate would depend on its own monetary policies and on the shocks to which it was subjected. While it was argued that an emergency lender of last resort (LOLR) would still be needed for countries that were solvent but illiquid, the system would generally not require the provision of a secularly increasing stock of ultimate international liquidity. References to the international financial system as a *system* are surprisingly absent these days. But because of the close linkage between international exchange rate arrangements and the need for a provider of international liquidity, the choices that countries make concerning their exchange rate regimes are an essential aspect of the reform of the international financial architecture. Indeed, to the extent that countries adopt flexible exchange rates, the need for an ultimate provider of international liquidity is reduced.

We take it as given that the key objectives for reform of the global financial architecture should be to: (1) minimise instances of international financial crises in all countries; (2) limit the degree of contagion that occurs when a crisis in one country is transmitted to other countries in the same 'asset class' whose external positions would otherwise be viable; and (3) resolve crises, when they occur, in ways that avoid moral hazard on the one hand and an excessively severe macroeconomic adjustment burden in the crisis countries on the other.

To provide an adequate plan for an international financial system that will achieve these objectives, we must look not only at reform of IFIs like the IMF and the World Bank, but also at the way financial markets, exchange rate regimes and macroeconomic policies function in the world economy. Much ink has been spilled on this topic, and few of the suggestions offered here are original. However, our proposals will show that our conclusions flow logically from the preceding analysis, which emphasises the dichotomy that exists when substantial amounts of capital are transferred over long periods from regions that have largely complete markets to those that have serious gaps in their market structures. Hopefully, this line of reasoning may shed more light on these fascinating questions.

Our proposals for reform emphasise the need to foster an increased role for market forces in managing the large net flows of capital from industrialised to emerging-market countries that are likely to occur for decades to come. We reject proposals to reintroduce capital controls. Such controls, even in the rare cases where they are effective, create severe economywide distortions, encourage corruption and can expand the underground economy.[9]

Our proposals underscore the importance of encouraging the development of more complete markets in emerging economies. This will require considerable effort and time on the part of emerging markets themselves, and on the part of industrialised countries and IFIs. Emerging markets, supported by the international community, need to work steadily towards upgrading their financial infrastructure (e.g. their legal frameworks, accounting standards and disclosure requirements) and strengthening the regulation and supervision of financial systems. Such improvements are essential for the development of effective markets. Borrowers and lenders must be weaned from their reliance on government guarantees. Through a better alignment of risk and reward, the

---

[9] See Mathieson and Rojas-Suárez (1993), pp. 18–19.

elimination of such guarantees will permit markets to function properly. These proposals also inevitably provide for the development of a stable macroeconomic policy environment, including a sustainable exchange rate regime that will facilitate non-inflationary long-run growth, and provide the underpinnings for further deepening of the financial systems in emerging markets. Finally, the roles that international financial institutions and the private sector can play within this proposed structure are articulated.

By implementing these proposals, the emerging-market countries can turn financial market globalisation to their advantage by benefiting not only from access to less expensive capital but also from stronger market discipline which, along with strengthened prudential oversight, will serve to improve the stability and resilience of domestic financial systems. Thus the silver lining of the recent crises in emerging markets is the impetus for governments to overcome the political obstacles to fundamental market-enhancing reforms.

Domestic financial sector reform

Financial infrastructure reform

The key areas for financial infrastructure reform are well known: accounting and auditing practices; stronger corporate governance and insolvency laws; timely and accurate public disclosure of financial data; more effectively risk-proofed payment and settlement systems; strengthened supervision and regulation; and more effective market discipline. The purpose of such reform is not just to improve the intermediation of foreign capital inflows but also to strengthen the ability of financial institutions in emerging markets to intermediate between domestic savers and borrowers. Of course, a basic step is for the emerging-market countries to strive to undertake the reforms necessary to implement the international standards and best practices that are being formulated in various fora. The draft report of the Financial Stability Forum (2000) catalogues the standards and codes that have been developed over the past several years. While the Basel Committee's core principles for effective banking supervision and the IMF's codes of transparency for fiscal policies and for monetary and financial policies are central elements, the Forum's catalogue lists a large number of standards and best practices that pertain to most aspects of a country's financial system.

Although the adoption of these standards should be voluntary, recognition by market participants that a country is implementing such codes and standards can enhance its reputation as a well-managed destination country for international capital flows. Linking progress on the implementation of standards to eligibility for IMF assistance (for example, to qualify for access to contingent lines of credit) may also provide a strong incentive for emerging markets to take action. The IMF is already extending its work to assess compliance to these standards, often at the request of the member country concerned, or in the context of its regular article IV consultations and Financial System Stability Assessments for individual member countries. We believe these assessments should eventually be made public.[10] Many recent papers on international financial reform have called on the IMF and the World Bank to play a larger role in accelerating these reforms by providing or coordinating technical support. This is appropriate. But the extensive work that these two institutions have already done, since the early 1990s, to strengthen financial systems in emerging-market countries should not be overlooked. To cite just two examples, starting in 1996 the IMF and the World Bank were actively encouraging the Basel Committee's efforts to develop its core principles of effective banking supervision. Similarly, Knight, Petersen and Price (1999) describe the work done by the IMF since 1991 in coordinating a major technical assistance programme provided by experts from Central Banks in advanced countries, the IMF and the World Bank to all fifteen countries of the former Soviet Union (FSU) to help them develop their central banking institutions and to establish modern, well-regulated financial systems.

Banking sector reform

The first step in strengthening emerging-market financial systems is to eliminate implicit and explicit guarantees made by governments to, or on behalf of, domestic banks. Directed lending by domestic banks to preferred domestic firms and guarantees on foreign loans to private borrowers should also end immediately. Reasonable economic arguments can be made for limited deposit insurance and the LOLR functions. Deposit insurance schemes should, however, be self-financing, LOLR facilities should be subject to explicit and transparent rules and the exposure of the Central Bank and the government should be limited.

In the wake of recent crises, the banking sectors in a large number of emerging-market countries remain weak and vulnerable. The most pressing reform in the affected countries is the recapitalisation and restructuring of the banking sector, as well as a fundamental strengthening of regulation, prudential supervision, disclosure and market discipline. To accelerate this process, countries are encouraged to permit foreign banks more scope to enter the domestic

---

[10] The IMF has begun to undertake Financial System Stability Assessments (FSSAs) in the context of its article IV consultations with selected countries. Peer review by experts in various aspects of financial system stability is an important aspect of the IMF's work in this area. Canada was the first of the G7 industrial countries to accept an IMF FSSA.

banking sector and to acquire under-capitalised or otherwise troubled domestic banks. Foreign banks can inject the capital needed to return domestic banks to viability, thus potentially lowering the burden for local taxpayers. They bring with them the strong accounting standards, disclosure requirements and risk assessment and management practices that are required by supervisors and private investors in their home country.[11] Foreign entry encourages competition, thus instilling stronger market discipline and greater resilience to shocks, by forming asset pools that are more diversified across countries, industries and asset classes. Simultaneously with recapitalisation, significant steps must be taken to improve bank regulation and supervision along the lines of the Basel Committee's *Core Principles for Effective Banking Supervision* (1997) and its other, more detailed, standards. Perhaps the most important caveat is to prevent the owners and managers of banks that became insolvent from retaining a financial interest and/or operational control of the restructured institutions.

Capital market broadening and deepening

The financial infrastructure reforms described above will have a large impact on capital markets because those markets trade standardised instruments whose values depend critically on transparent and enforceable regulations governing accounting and auditing practices, bankruptcy and corporate governance. Capital markets can operate efficiently only if investors believe that they have reasonable access to fundamental information about the financial situations of debtor governments and firms. Again, the rules on disclosure and governance are critical.[12] Also critical is the elimination of government guarantees which have stunted the growth of markets in emerging economies. Markets are likely to develop spontaneously, and possibly in short order, once such distortions are eliminated.

Some commentators, most notably Hausmann (2000), have argued that, for the foreseeable future, many emerging-market countries, primarily those in Latin America, will not be able to issue long-term debt in their own currencies, because of 'original sin'. That is, past macroeconomic policies have been so ineffective that even if the authorities try to institute the appropriate reforms they will not be able to undo past mistakes for at least a generation.[13] But this

---

[11] Gavin and Hausmann (1996) make a similar argument.

[12] Standards have also been proposed for the regulation and supervision of securities and insurance markets: *Objectives and Principles of Securities Regulation* by the International Organization of Securities Commissions, and *Insurance Supervisory Principles* by the International Association of Insurance Supervision.

[13] Hausmann thus recommends that these countries should dollarise because reforms will not have any immediate and substantial effect on interest rate spreads.

conclusion may be excessively pessimistic. Chile and Mexico have successfully expanded and deepened their capital markets in recent years, and they have made progress in developing markets for domestic currency-denominated instruments and in lengthening the maturity of their debt. Brazil, too, has experienced considerable success with its new monetary framework consisting of a flexible exchange rate and inflation targets.

Macroeconomic policy reforms in emerging-market countries

The objective of domestic macroeconomic policy reform is to construct a coherent and transparent framework to help ensure a stable low-inflation environment that is conducive to long-term economic growth. This means implementing a sustainable fiscal policy, a monetary policy that targets an appropriate nominal anchor and an exchange rate regime that is consistent with the monetary policy framework.

Sustainable fiscal policy

The fundamental starting point for credible macroeconomic policy reform is the implementation of a firm fiscal policy that establishes a 'virtuous' set of debt dynamics. Until the Asian crisis in 1997, by far the most frequent cause of economic problems in developing countries was excessive fiscal deficits financed by money creation. Unfortunately, it normally takes a lengthy period of poor economic performance for fundamental changes in fiscal policy to be achieved (Eichengreen, 2000). The simple rules of thumb are that government debt should not be increasing as a proportion of GDP (ideally it should be falling), and that any fiscal deficit should be financed by government borrowing from the private sector rather than by monetary expansion.

The exchange rate regime

If there is a sustainable fiscal policy, the Central Bank can choose and credibly commit to a nominal anchor from the following set of options: a permanently fixed exchange rate, a growth path for the monetary aggregates, or a price-level/inflation rate target.

For many emerging-market countries, a significant factor in the recent crises and their propagation was the commitment to a pegged exchange rate. Whenever a crisis arose, this commitment provided a one-way bet to speculators so that speculative outflows became self-fulfilling. As stated earlier, the implicit guarantee afforded by the pegged exchange rate also encouraged excessive borrowing in foreign currency by domestic residents, making them highly vulnerable to devaluation.[14] The danger of the pegged exchange rate trap is an important lesson from these crises, and forms the basis for one of the central and most widely accepted recommendations for the reform of the global architecture: emerging countries should adopt a polar exchange rate regime, either permanently fixed or fully flexible.[15]

For each country, the choice of exchange rate regime will depend on a number of factors. Typically, countries that are small, have small non-traded goods and services sectors, have a sizeable share of their trade with a large currency bloc and are unlikely to be subjected to real shocks that differ from those that affect their principal trade and financial partners, may choose a fixed exchange rate as their nominal anchor. Given recent negative experience with traditional adjustable pegged arrangements, such countries should choose either a currency union, a unilateral adoption of their main trading bloc's currency, or a currency board.[16] Provided that the trading bloc can maintain reasonable price stability, this approach will stabilise the consumer price deflator in the small country. The small country will reap microeconomic gains from being part of a large bloc that uses a single vehicle currency as a medium of exchange and store of value. However, these microeconomic gains, while significant, are probably smaller than in the past, before information technology and market development have sharply reduced the cost of making exchanges from one currency to another.

Conversely, if a country has a reasonably large non-traded goods and services sector and is likely to be subject to asymmetric real shocks (shocks that affect its production and consumption patterns differently than they affect its major trading partners), and if it has the institutions and instruments needed to target a domestic nominal anchor, a flexible exchange rate is a better choice.

A flexible exchange rate anchored by a credible monetary policy has many attractions, not only for industrial countries such as Canada, but for a growing number of the larger, more sophisticated emerging economies. If the domestic

---

[14] During the 1990s, private agents seemed to act on the basis that exchange rates in a number of emerging-market countries would remain fixed, despite the fact that interest rate spreads generally implied that there was a non-zero probability of devaluation. Although this behaviour may seem irrational, past experience and government pronouncements may have led them to believe that the government's commitment to the peg was credible, or that in the event a devaluation took place, political pressure would force the government to bail out domestic borrowers.

[15] For example, the Council on Foreign Relations Task Force Report (Goldstein, 1999) recommends a managed flexible exchange rate for most emerging markets with a currency board or common currency reserved for special situations.

[16] While the choice of exchange rate regime is as much a political decision as an economic one, of the three rigidly fixed arrangements, a currency union is likely to be preferred on economic grounds since the small country would retain at least some influence on the conduct of monetary policy. It would also share in the seigniorage.

price level is well tethered, a flexible exchange rate facilitates adjustment to external capital flows and demand shocks, output, employment and consumption.[17] Given an asymmetric shock – for example, a fall in the terms of trade – a decline in the real exchange rate can be a key element of the adjustment process. It makes the export sector and import substituting sectors more profitable, while import activities become less profitable, so that economic activities are redirected in ways that offset the effects of the negative external shock. Moreover, during periods of large capital inflows, letting the real exchange rate appreciate via an appreciating nominal exchange rate rather than through higher domestic prices under a fixed or pegged rate reduces the likelihood of persistent over-valuation when circumstances change and domestic assets are less attractive.[18] Ortiz (2000) has discussed the useful role that Mexico's flexible exchange rate played in external adjustment during the slump in world commodity prices.

A flexible exchange rate allows a country to choose its own inflation rate within a coherent and transparent monetary policy framework. It eliminates the implicit exchange rate guarantee on foreign borrowing and the associated moral hazard. Thus, it obliges domestic borrowers and foreign lenders in emerging markets to manage risk more effectively, and tends to foster the development of forward and futures markets, as has taken place in Chile and Mexico.[19]

From a global perspective, flexible exchange rates provide a public good because the need for an ultimate provider of international liquidity is reduced *pari passu* with the extent of floating. And since a flexible rate reduces the likelihood of financial crises, calls for emergency bailouts of afflicted countries by creditor countries or the IMF will be less frequent, thereby significantly reducing the degree of moral hazard in the system.

A clear domestic nominal anchor

A country that wishes to pursue an independent monetary policy and, consequently, chooses a flexible exchange rate, must find a clear, domestic monetary policy anchor. Canada's experience with direct inflation targets since 1991 may be relevant to emerging-market countries. Although it is an advanced industrial country, primary commodities constitute a relatively large proportion of Canada's output and exports. The combination of a flexible exchange rate, which Canada has had in all but thirteen of the past fifty-five years, and inflation-control targets, in place since 1991, has served Canada very well. This combination

---

[17] Osakwe and Schembri (1999) demonstrate, using a sticky-price rational expectations model, that a flexible exchange rate will generate more stable output than either a permanently fixed exchange rate or a collapsing fixed exchange rate.

[18] Murray (1999) provides a good assessment of the benefits of a flexible exchange regime for Canada, an industrialised country that experiences large external demand shocks.

[19] Obstfeld (1989) and Mishkin (1999) offer similar arguments.

has successfully reduced inflation from relatively high levels in the 1980s and at the same time promoted solid economic growth. It is a transparent monetary framework that a number of emerging-market countries may find attractive.

Canada's inflation-control target range of 1–3 per cent underpins the Bank of Canada's objective of achieving a low and stable rate of inflation that will create the necessary environment for a well-functioning economy. An explicit inflation target has many benefits. In particular, it clarifies the Central Bank's objective and thereby helps to anchor inflation expectations. The Canadian experience strongly suggests that inflation targeting and a flexible exchange rate provides a powerful policy framework for achieving domestic monetary stability with external balance. In Canada, direct inflation targeting now provides a transparent nominal anchor while the exchange rate is permitted to vary. This has helped the economy to adjust to asymmetric shocks to the terms of trade or to changes in the demand for Canadian assets by foreign investors.

An important question is whether the monetary framework and experience of Canada and other industrial countries, such as New Zealand, Sweden, or the United Kingdom, can be extended to emerging-market countries. It is unrealistic to assume that countries with a history of fiscal imbalances, inflationary monetary policies and financial instability can achieve overnight the economic and financial stability of an industrialised country. However, the relevance of direct inflation targeting does not appear to be limited to industrial countries. It is now being tried, with solid early success, by emerging-market countries such as Mexico, and more recently by Brazil and Chile.

The success of those three countries suggests that credible macroeconomic policy reforms can yield good results in a relatively short period of time. Nonetheless, even if this policy framework cannot be adopted initially, it may be worth achieving over the medium term. The market structures needed to implement monetary policy and to deepen the financial system may develop more effectively under a regime of direct inflation targeting.

Monetary policy credibility in an emerging-market country is an essential prerequisite for developing fixed income markets, particularly at the longer end. Ultimately, this will give the authorities better objective indicators of market expectations and more information with which to undertake their monetary operations. It will make them aware that – with a flexible exchange rate and an independent monetary policy that targets price stability – changes in fiscal policy that are not considered to be sustainable will have an immediate impact on the exchange rate. Thus, directly targeting a low stable rate of inflation imposes considerable discipline on the domestic fiscal authority.

If a country has a flexible exchange rate and a credible monetary policy, capital account liberalisation is much easier to achieve. Relatively free capital mobility is important to help ensure that large but temporary real shocks do not result in excessive or prolonged appreciations or depreciations of the real exchange rate. Thus, freer capital mobility can be an important element in a smooth external adjustment process.

In summary, in a globalised financial system, countries should adopt either a permanent fixed or a flexible exchange rate regime. However, based on the experience of a number of countries, both industrial and developing, the adoption by more countries of a monetary framework with explicit inflation targets and a flexible exchange rate would improve the international financial architecture by extending market structures, reducing or eliminating the use of guarantees to encourage capital flows and limiting the need for an ultimate provider of international liquidity, either on an ongoing basis or in crisis situations. Choosing such a monetary framework, therefore, carries the prospect of profoundly reducing moral hazard.

4 The role of international financial institutions

We strongly believe that in an interconnected global economy there is a continuing need for IFIs. Notwithstanding large private capital flows, the World Bank and the regional banks can play a useful role by helping to finance projects in developing countries that have a high social rate of return. They can provide invaluable technical assistance in institution-building and good governance. But central to the whole system is an international surveillance institution, and the IMF fulfils that role. We see the IMF's role more as a provider of surveillance, of information on macroeconomic conditions and as a neutral third-party adviser, not a lender. Its own lending should be limited in the future, with emphasis placed on creditors and debtors resolving their financial problems themselves.

The role of the IMF in a globalised financial system

The increasing adoption of floating exchange rates and the surge in international capital flows in the 1990s led to numerous calls for IMF reform. Opinions on this subject range from advocating the abolition of the IMF to turning it into a *bona fide* international LOLR (see Sachs, 1995, Calomiris, 1998, Schultz, Simon and Wriston, 1998, Fischer, 1999a; Summers, 1999 for a range of a views on the role of the IMF). One's view of the scope of the IMF's role as a provider of liquidity to the international financial system depends on one's view of how well financial markets can be made to operate, particularly in the emerging countries. We believe that financial markets generally work well in allocating capital if incentives are not distorted. This suggests that the IMF should play a limited, catalytic role in providing financial assistance for the resolution of crises.

Surveillance and advice

We emphasise the IMF's large comparative advantage in undertaking the surveillance of the macroeconomic policies of its member countries, collecting and disseminating data, assisting financial negotiations during crises and providing technical assistance to less-developed members. The IMF is uniquely placed to exercise economic and financial surveillance by evaluating the macroeconomic policies of its member countries in the context of its article IV consultations and its programme negotiations and programme reviews. In recent years, however, pressure from member governments has obliged the IMF to address an increasing number of issues that are ancillary to its central role in assessing macroeconomic performance. We believe that the IMF should be allowed and encouraged to focus on its acknowledged areas of expertise: monetary and fiscal policy and policies relating to the national balance sheet and debt sustainability. It is desirable for the IMF to play a major role in assessing its member countries' financial systems, because of the close link between financial system weakness and macroeconomic stability.[20] Finally, given its universal membership and existing surveillance procedures, the IMF is best placed to be the agency to monitor and publicly disseminate information on countries' compliance with international codes and standards. This includes the codes of conduct that it has developed itself, such as those on data transparency and on fiscal, monetary and financial policies, as well as those developed by specialised groups in areas outside the IMF's competence. To date, more than sixty such standards have been drafted or are under development. Because these specialised groups were established as rule-making bodies, they do not have the resources to monitor and encourage compliance. Consequently, this task is likely by default to fall to the IMF.

In 1999 the Financial Stability Forum (FSF) – comprising financial regulators, Central Banks and Treasury officials of G7 countries – was established to exchange views on international vulnerabilities and establish priorities and action programmes. To help emerging markets set priorities, one FSF work group focused on determining which codes and standards were the most important and how to implement them. Key standards for sound financial systems have been identified covering macroeconomic fundamentals, institutional and market infrastructure and financial regulation and supervision. Other FSF work groups have completed useful work on highly leveraged institutions, offshore centres and capital flows. The G20 group of industrial and systemically important emerging-market countries provides a useful forum for developing the international consensus, political support and direction needed to implement

---

[20] See Lindgren, Garcia and Saal (1996). Our recommendations concur with those of the 1999 external evaluation of IMF surveillance. See also Crow, Arriaza and Thygesen (1999).

standards and codes, as well as other key elements of reform, such as sustainable exchange rate regimes and sound asset–liability management.

Crisis management

Owing to its role in assessing macroeconomic policies, balance of payments and debt sustainability in each of its member countries, the IMF should continue to play a central role in resolving financial crises when they occur. But, particularly for countries that have been accessing private capital markets, this does not mean that the IMF should be the only, or the first, or the largest, lender in crisis situations. As Goldstein (1999) recommends, the IMF should encourage the formation of standing steering committees composed of holders of emerging-market bonds and bank loans. It should work with these committees and with representatives of the borrowing country during liquidity crises and debt-rescheduling negotiations. Litan (1998) argues that the IMF's relatively scarce financial resources in the face of massive capital flows make its role as a crisis manager even more important than its role as an international lender.[21] In summary, for market-borrowing emerging economies that experience crises, the IMF's primary role should be as a *facilitator*, assessing the prospects for macroeconomic adjustment, debt sustainability and external financing as a means of carrying forward negotiations between creditors and debtor countries.

Lending

The foregoing suggests that depending on the extent to which a reformed international financial system includes a larger number of countries that practise exchange rate flexibility, the role of the IMF in surveillance will deepen and expand, but its role as a large-scale and long-term lender will atrophy. This, indeed, was the case for the industrial countries when, with Canada in the lead, they adopted widespread floating in the first half of the 1970s.

Some have argued that the frequency, virulence and spread of financial crises in emerging markets suggests a need to turn the IMF into an international LOLR.[22] Parallels are often drawn between the IMF and a national Central Bank providing liquidity to solvent, but illiquid, banks. However, the parallel is imperfect. Unlike banks, governments are sovereign. They cannot be taken over and closed. Moreover, the scale of lending contemplated by a true international lender of last resort would vastly dwarf that of a Central Bank.

---

[21] See Litan (1998).
[22] See Fischer (1999). See also Rogoff (1999) for a brief review of the literature.

We believe that moral hazard concerns as well as practical considerations militate against such an extension of the IMF's role. The prospect of using international assistance to supplement international reserves to defend a pegged rate or to bail out foreign lenders is yet another link in the chain of guarantees discussed earlier that can distort the actions of borrowing countries in favour of more expansionary policies (debtor moral hazard) and, more importantly, bias the credit allocation decisions of private lenders (creditor moral hazard).[23] In addition, when a crisis occurs, as long as official money is on the table, there is reduced incentive on the part of the debtor and its creditors to sit down and negotiate a debt restructuring. Indeed, access to official funds might only accentuate the race for the exits by providing a willing counterparty. In such circumstances, the IMF acts as the lender of first, rather than last, resort.

The solution to this problem lies in establishing a framework for greater private sector involvement in the resolution of crises. Strict limits on the scope of IMF lending (and of the official sector more generally, either through other IFIs or through coordinated bilateral support) to countries in crisis would limit creditor moral hazard and would help address private sector pressures in a crisis for more public assistance. Large official financial assistance packages would no longer exist, and countries would not have extensive access to public funds to try to sustain pegged exchange rates that were no longer appropriate. By the same token, consideration should be given to a penalty interest rate that would escalate over time, as well as to short maturities for IMF assistance to limit debtor moral hazard and ensure that countries exhaust private options before approaching the official sector. (See appendix 2, p. 152 for suggestions on arrangements for IMF lending.)

Private sector involvement in crisis resolution

As King (1999) emphasises, in an international financial system dominated by flexible exchange rates, a country is most likely to experience a crisis when it has mismanaged some aspect of the liquidity, maturity, or currency structure of its national balance sheet. In such circumstances, how can the international community best address financial crises? When a country has been accessing private international capital markets, the onus must be on the debtor country

---

[23] The most egregious case of creditor moral hazard occurred in Russia which was viewed as being too geopolitically important to fail prior to the summer of 1998. Indeed, lending to Russia was called the moral hazard play. More subtly, private credit raters explicitly take into account the prospect of receiving international assistance when awarding ratings to countries.

and its private creditors to find a solution. The IMF can play a key role as a broker in assisting this process, as long as it is not itself a large lender. The IMF is the entity with the expertise and objectivity to assess the appropriate path of macroeconomic adjustment, as well as to determine the debt profile that would be sustainable over the medium term.

A voluntary rescheduling of debts is the preferred outcome of any negotiation between a debtor and its private creditors. However, it is conceivable that a debtor might be forced to declare a temporary standstill, including the introduction of temporary capital controls, to limit capital outflows and provide an opportunity for negotiations on a debt-restructuring programme, or even debt reduction if the problems are very serious. As international borrowing is a 'repeated game', a debtor is unlikely to call a standstill frivolously. The cost of being shut out of international capital markets would have to be weighed against the economic, political and social benefits associated with a temporary suspension of debt-servicing.

Temporary standstills are one way of dealing with the coordination problem in the presence of a restive group of private creditors, all with differing interests. It is important to underscore, however, that a standstill can benefit the debtor and creditors. It provides time for the debtor to get its house in order, thereby poten-tially preserving value for creditors. Consequently, the inclusion of temporary standstills in the crisis resolution 'tool kit' ought not to reduce unwarrentedly the flow of resources to emerging economies nor exacerbate contagion when exercised in the event of a crisis.

Additional mechanisms to address the collective action problem should be considered, such as ongoing communications between a debtor and its private sector creditors and the establishment of standing creditor associations. The introduction of collective-action clauses in sovereign debt instruments should also be encouraged. While collective-action clauses would not have been of much help in dealing with the crises in Asia and Brazil, they were useful in helping to restructure the debts of Ukraine. As countries rely more on bond financing relative to bank loans, the value of collective-action clauses is likely to rise. Reflecting the importance of this issue and the merit in leading by example, Canada agreed in 2000 to introduce such clauses in its own foreign bond covenants.

In sum, while the case for an international LOLR is superficially appealing, it is not convincing. Instead, reliance should be placed squarely on the shoulders of the debtor and its creditors to resolve financial problems. Only then will the incentives be in the right place. While the IMF can provide limited amounts of resources to help grease the wheels, its role in crisis management should be primarily to provide information, analysis, and advice and to play a coordinating role to bring debtors and creditors together.

5 Concluding remarks

What is truly new about the new global economy is the unprecedented and growing influence of global capital markets, a development that is likely to continue for years to come. To cope well with this new reality, further substantial steps to strengthen the international financial system are needed. Fundamental reform is essential. This cannot involve just tinkering around the edges if we are to meet our objectives of minimising the occurrence of future crises and the risk of contagion, as well as resolving crises when they occur in an expeditious fashion that avoids moral hazard on the one hand and excessive macroeconomic adjustment in crisis countries on the other.

The suggestions here provide for a market-based approach to reform that is broadly acceptable, reasonable and comprehensive. The approach will lead to the development of more complete markets in emerging economies and will place the responsibility for crisis prevention and resolution on the shoulders of debtors and creditors, with the IFIs, and the international community more generally, showing the way rather than trying to carry the burden. Emerging-market economies must break new ground in their efforts to reform their financial sectors and their monetary frameworks and, wherever possible, industrial countries should provide effective technical assistance. Government guarantees and other government-induced distortions in the financial sector should be removed and international standards and codes on disclosure, financial sector regulation, insolvency and corporate governance implemented. To strengthen the domestic financial sector, and indeed the rest of the economy, macroeconomic institutions and policies should be reinforced. In this regard, we favour the adoption of a flexible exchange rate and inflation targets by the larger, more sophisticated emerging-market economies.

The IFIs, chiefly the IMF, should support these changes by providing surveillance and policy advice and by collecting and disseminating data. The IMF should encourage the adoption of internationally developed codes and standards by releasing surveillance reports. With the assistance of the IFIs and the rest of the international community, reforms aimed at achieving more complete financial markets, low inflation and a flexible exchange rate should greatly reduce the number of financial crises. If crises occur, however, IMF lending should be in the form of short-term emergency loans in limited amounts. The large bailout packages of the 1990s should be replaced by mechanisms, possibly including standstills, that ensure that risks as well as the rewards of lending are borne by creditors and debtors instead of the international community.

The reform agenda is large and requires widespread support to be realised fully. But the potential gains in terms of world welfare are also large and should provide the incentive for countries to overcome any political obstacles to reform of the global financial architecture.

Appendix 1 Emerging-market economies and the incentive for guarantees: a simple conceptual framework

To understand the incentives to seek and grant government guarantees, we can use a simple one-period model. Consider figure 5A.1; the vertical axis represents the expected rate of return on domestic assets less the return on the risk-free international asset, say US Treasury bills. On the right-hand side, an upward-sloping risk–return frontier is shown for the available set of domestic assets with the standard deviation of the return on the horizontal axis. For convenience, the risk–return frontier is assumed to be continuous, but in practice it may not be, because the set of domestic assets available for foreign investors may not be sufficiently large. It slopes upward because in an efficient market a higher expected return can be obtained only by taking on more risk. On the left-hand side, the foreign capital supply curve is drawn with the amount of foreign capital inflow (net) on the horizontal axis. It slopes downward, implying that to attract more foreign capital the expected return differential on domestic assets must be higher.[24]

Also on the right-hand side, a set of indifference curves can be added reflecting the risk–return preferences of a representative foreign investor. Given the risk–return frontier, the optimal portfolio of domestic assets held by foreigners is given by the point of tangency between the frontier and the highest indifference curve, represented by point A. This point gives the equilibrium expected return differential and the level of foreign capital inflow.

Suppose that this level of capital inflow is below the desired level. To increase capital inflows given the preferences of foreign investor, the national authority must find a way to shift the risk–return frontier upwards to the left, that is, some mix of increasing expected returns and reducing risk. Consider these two extremes: (1) undertake economic reforms, particularly with respect to the financial sector that could raise expected returns by increasing economic efficiency and reduce risk by providing efficient risk transfer; or (2) provide guarantees to limit the risk to foreign investors. (Government guarantees may not ultimately reduce the risk because those guarantees may not be sustained under certain outcomes.) Such guarantees could be represented by a horizontal

[24] Given that foreign capital inflows will also depend on risk, which increases with expected return, it is possible that for high levels of risk the curve may bend and become upward-sloping. For simplicity, we assume that this possibility is outside our range of interest.

Figure 5A.1 *Capital inflows and the risk–return tradeoff*

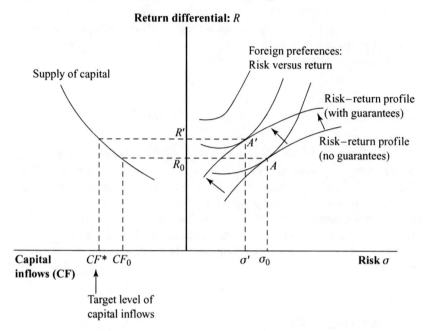

shift in the risk–return frontier. The expectation of an IMF bailout would have a similar effect since investors would perceive a reduction in risk and take on more risky investments.

This 'quick-fix' approach of guarantees to attract foreign capital and accelerate the rate of economic development led national authorities to neglect the difficult longer-term task of strengthening their financial systems to manage capital inflows so that they would be a stable, assured source of external financing over the longer term. Instead, the focus of public policy in these countries was to encourage inflows over the short to medium term, rather than make the substantial long-term investment in legal and financial infrastructure required to ensure that the flows were being efficiently intermediated and sustainable. As long as expected returns in these countries were relatively high and the guarantees remained credible, these stop-gap measures seemed to work well. Capital inflows and economic growth increased throughout the early 1990s. When coupled with the commitment to pegged nominal exchange rates, however, this approach often resulted in over-valued real exchange rates that reduced expected returns, altering expectations and increasing the volatility of inflows. When shifts in sentiment occurred, the guarantees on liabilities were tested, creditors ran for the exits, capital flows reversed and the scramble by large international creditors to reduce exposure spread contagion as loans were called from all countries perceived to be in the same asset class. The recent crises have highlighted the failure of these guarantees, their link to contagion and the need for fundamental financial market reform.

Appendix 2 Suggestions on arrangements for IMF lending

Consideration should be given to rationalising IMF financing to have two principal types of arrangements at its disposal: a standby arrangement (SBA) linked to an IMF adjustment programme with macroeconomic conditionality and a precautionary arrangement for a member country that has satisfied certain stringent eligibility criteria. Both types of arrangements would be short-term in nature, strictly limited in terms of access and involve rates of charge sufficiently high to ensure that official lending is not a substitute for private capital.

Standby arrangements

Traditional SBAs would continue to be used for member countries that approached the IMF with balance of payments problems, and that had not previously qualified through prior actions for access to a precautionary facility. A country would be eligible for an SBA, assuming it agreed with the required conditionality, regardless of whether the problem originated in the current account or the capital account. However, access would be strictly limited to, say, the existing cumulative access limit of up to 300 per cent of quota. If this proved insufficient to deal with the problem, external debt service could be rescheduled, if necessary with the help of a standstill.

The 300 per cent of quota would not be an automatic entitlement. Should a country's external debt profile appear to be unsustainable under reasonable assumptions for external sector adjustment, the IMF should not lend. Additional official assistance for a country in such a position would only add to the country's debt burden. Moreover, since the IMF is considered to be a preferred creditor, additional IMF loans would reduce the value of existing claims. Lending into arrears could be considered if a debtor country were negotiating in good faith with its creditors for debt reduction.

The SBA could be priced at a penalty interest rate that would rise over time to discourage misuse and to encourage early repayment. One could, for example, use the rate of interest for drawings under the existing Supplementary Reserve Facility. Repayment would be obligatory after 2–2.5 years.

Precautionary arrangements

A precautionary arrangement, such as the existing contingent credit line (CCL), could be useful for countries willing to adhere to tough eligibility requirements. Such requirements should include adherence to key international codes and standards, a sustainable exchange rate regime and the willingness to include collective-action clauses in its bond covenants. Given the need to satisfy the eligibility requirements, countries could be rewarded with a larger access limit, say 500 per cent of quota, and a more attractive interest rate, say beginning at 200 basis points above the normal rate of charge. Access would be automatic in the event of a crisis. Again, should 500 per cent of quota not be sufficient to satisfy a country's foreign exchange needs, it would have to negotiate a rescheduling, which might involve a standstill. As with purchases under SBA we would recommend a short maturity of 2–2.5 years.

Concerns have been raised about the usefulness of the CCL because of the exit problem – how to disqualify a country whose policies have slipped. This should be not viewed as a serious impediment. The potential to publicly disqualify a country would put teeth into the process. If publication should provoke a crisis, so be it. Hopefully, however, serious crises would be infrequent, since more timely and complete flow of information about a country's circumstances should permit markets to adjust more smoothly than in the past. Moreover, the country in question could always apply for an SBA, thereby indicating to markets its determination to correct its shortcomings.

REFERENCES

Arrow, K. and G. Debreu (1954). 'Existence of an Equilibrium for a Competitive Economy', *Econometrica*, 22

Basel Committee on Banking Supervision (1997). *Core Principles for Effective Banking Supervision*, Bank for International Settlements

Bernanke, B., T. Laubach, F. Mishkin and A. Posen (1999). *Inflation Targeting: Lessons from the International Experience*. Princeton, NJ, Princeton University Press

Bhagwati, J. (1998). 'Why Free Capital Mobility may be Hazardous to Your Health: Lessons from the Latest Financial Crisis', paper presented at the NBER Conference on 'Capital Controls', Cambridge, MA, 7 November

Calomiris, C. (1998). 'The IMF's Imprudent Role as Lender of Last Resort', *Cato Journal*, 17, 275–94

Caprio, G., Jr. and P. Honohan (1999). 'Beyond Capital Ideas; Restoring Bank Stability', *Journal of Economic Perspectives*, 13, 43–64

Corbett, J. and D. Vines (1999). 'The Asian Crisis Lessons from the Collapse of Financial Systems, Exchange Rates and Macroeconomic Policy', in P.-R. Agénor, M. Miller, D. Vines and A. Weber (eds.), *The Asian Financial Crisis: Causes, Contagion and Consequences*. Cambridge, Cambridge University Press

Crow, J. (Chair), R. Arriazu and N. Thygesen (1999). *External Evaluation of IMF Surveillance: Report by a Group of Independent Experts*. Washington, DC, International Monetary Fund

Dooley, M. (1994). 'Are Recent Capital Inflows to Developing Countries a Vote for or Against Economic Policy Reforms?', Working Paper, 295, University of California, Santa Cruz, May

(1997). 'A Model of Crises in Emerging Markets', NBER Working Paper, 6300.

Eichengreen, B. (2000). 'When to Dollarize?', paper presented at the Dallas Federal Reserve Bank Conference, 'Dollarization: A Common Currency for the Americas', 6–8 March

Financial Stability Forum (2000). 'Draft Issues Paper on the Task Force on Implementation of Standards', mimeo

Fischer, S. (1999a). 'Reforming the International Financial System', *Economic Journal*, 109, F557–F576

(1999b). 'On the Need for an International Lender of Last Resort', speech delivered to the Joint Luncheon of the American Economic Association and the American Finance Association, New York, 3 January

Gavin, M. and R. Hausmann (1996). 'The Roots of Banking Crises: The Macroeconomic Context', in R. Hausmann and L. Rojas-Suárez (eds.), *Banking Crises in Latin America*. Baltimore, MD, Johns Hopkins University Press

Goldberg, L., B. G. Dages and D. Kinney (2000). 'Foreign and Domestic Bank Participation in Emerging Markets: Lessons from Mexico and Argentina', Federal Reserve Bank of New York, mimeo

Goldstein, M. (1999). 'Safeguarding Prosperity in a Global Financial System. The Future International Financial Architecture', Institute for International Economics, Report of an Independent Task Force Sponsored by the Council on Foreign Relations

Hausmann, R. (2000). 'On the Pros and Cons of Dollarization', paper presented at the Dallas Federal Reserve Bank Conference 'Dollarization: A Common Currency for the Americas', 6–8 March

IMF (1998). *International Capital Markets: Developments, Prospects and Key Policy Issues*, Washington, DC, IMF

Kaminsky, G. and C. Reinhart (1999). 'The Twin Crises: The Causes of Banking and Balance-of-Payment Problem', *American Economic Review*, 89(3), 473–500

Kim, E. 1998. 'Globalization of Capital Markets and the Asian Financial Crisis', *Journal of Applied Corporate Finance* 11, 30–9

King, M. (1999). 'Reforming the International Financial System: The Middle Way', speech to a session of the Money Marketeers of the Federal Reserve Bank of New York, 9 September

Knight, M. (1998). 'Developing Countries and the Globalization of Financial Markets', *World Development*, 26, 1185–1200

(1999). 'Developing and Transition Countries Confront Financial Globalization', *Finance and Development*, June, 32–5

Knight, M., A. Petersen and R. Price (eds.) (1999). *Transforming Financial Systems in the Baltics, Russia and other Countries of the Former Soviet Union*. Washington, DC, IMF

Krueger, A. (2000). 'IMF Stabilization Programs', Conference on Economic and Financial Crises in Emerging Market Economies, Woodstock

Lindgren, C.-J., G. Garcia and M. Saal (1996). *Bank Soundness and Macroeconomic Policy*. Washington, DC, IMF

Litan, R.E. (1998). 'Does the IMF Have a Future? What Should it Be?', October, mimeo

Mathieson, D. and L. Rojas-Suárez (1993). *Liberalization of the Capital Account: Experiences and Issues*. Washington, DC, IMF

Meltzer, A. (Chair) (2000). 'Report of International Financial Institution Advisory Commission', US Congress mimeo

Miller, M. (1998). 'Financial Markets and Economic Growth', *Journal of Applied Corporate Finance*, 11, 8–15

Mishkin, F. M. (1999). 'Global Financial Instability', *Journal of Economic Perspectives*, 13, 3–20

(2000). 'Financial Policies and the Prevention of Financial Crises in Emerging Market Countries', Woodstock

Murray, J. (1999). 'Why Canada Needs a Flexible Rate', Bank of Canada Working Paper, 99–12

Obstfeld, M. (1998). 'The Global Capital Market: Benefactor or Menace?', *Journal of Economic Perspectives*, 12, 9–30

Ortiz, G. (2000). Speech at Dallas Federal Reserve Bank Conference, 'Dollarization: A Common Currency for the Americas', 6–8 March

Osakwe, P. and L. Schembri (1999). 'Real Effects of Collapsing Exchange Rate Regimes: An Application to Mexico', Bank of Canada, Working Paper, 99–10

Radelet, S. and J. Sachs (1999). 'What Have We Learned, So Far, From the Asian Financial Crisis?', US Agency for International Development mimeo

Rogoff, K. (1999). 'International Institutions for Reducing Global Financial Instability', NBER Working Paper, 7265

Sachs, J. (1995). 'Do We Need an International Lender of Last Resort?', Princeton University, mimeo

Schadler, S., M. Carkovic, A. Bennet and R. Kahn (1993). 'Recent Experiences with Surges in Capital Inflows', Occasional Paper, 108, Washington, DC, IMF, December

Schultz, G., W. Simon and W. Wriston (1998). 'Who Needs the IMF?' *Wall Street Journal*, 3 February

Summers, L. (1999). 'The Right Kind of IMF for a Stable Global Financial System', US Treasury, Address to the London Business School, London, 14 December

Triffin, R. (1960). *Gold and the Dollar Crisis*. New Haven, CT, Yale University Press

6 The IMF and capital account liberalisation

DOMINIC WILSON

1 Introduction

In mid-1997, the IMF's Interim Committee issued a statement announcing that the time had come 'to add a new chapter to the Bretton Woods agreement'. The statement called for the establishment of a 'multilateral and non-discriminatory system to promote the liberalization of capital movements'. The Committee invited the Executive Board to complete work on a proposed amendment of the IMF's Articles that would make the 'liberalization of capital movements one of the purposes of the IMF' and extend the IMF's jurisdiction to enforce those obligations on its members.

The timing of this statement was not propitious. The massive reversal in capital flows to East Asia that followed the floating of the Thai baht on 2 July 1997, and which accelerated in the months after the IMF statement was issued, turned out to be unprecedented in its speed and scale. Although the crisis initially centred on the East Asian economies, the turbulence in emerging markets was much more widely felt. In June 1998, Russia was added to the critical list when its announcement of a debt moratorium prompted an unwinding of positions in Russian and other emerging markets. And in January 1999 the Brazilian government abandoned the peg on its exchange rate, a move which was prompted by rapid capital flight and which precipitated a large currency depreciation and further capital withdrawal. These crises prompted economists once again to take a harder look at the risks as well as the benefits of an open capital account. Within a year of the Asian crisis, the strong support for promoting capital account liberalisation as a core goal for developing countries had come under severe challenge and the IMF's own role in promoting open capital accounts was also under criticism (Bhagwati, 1998; Rodrik, 1998).

The views expressed here are the personal views of the author and should not be attributed to Goldman Sachs.

156

Some of the vigour has faded from the debate but questions remain. What should the IMF's attitude be towards capital account liberalisation? Should it move back to adopt the formal promotion of capital account convertibility through its articles? And, more broadly, what advice should the Fund be giving to developing countries with regard to the capital account?

Our argument is that there is currently little reason for the IMF to promote a formal commitment to capital account liberalisation, or to seek the powers to require capital account convertibility, even presuming that the support for that position among its members could still be mustered. The case for capital account liberalisation, and the form in which it should be implemented, is likely to be highly contingent on conditions in domestic markets. It may thus be more helpful to focus on a framework that helps governments to decide when and where various kinds of restrictions may be appropriate policy responses and which are the best available policy options in different circumstances. The systematic ranking of regimes and policy tools under different assumptions about underlying market conditions has long been a part of the trade literature. The work of Bhagwati (1971) and Corden (1957), among others, has illustrated how the ordering of trade regimes might alter in the presence of various distortions and provided a framework to assess and rank the various possible policy responses.

To illustrate this case, this chapter sketches a similar kind of approach to the problems arising from international capital flows. A simple diagrammatic approach is used to illustrate that in the presence of distortions, a relaxation of capital account restrictions is likely to have two opposing effects. On the one hand, reduced borrowing costs will increase the efficiency of intermediation and tend to raise welfare. On the other, the ability to borrow abroad will tend to increase the deadweight costs from distortions. The tension between these two effects means that the case for capital account liberalisation is likely to be more finely balanced than has often been acknowledged. In the absence of offsetting action to address distortions, the optimal degree of capital account liberalisation will also vary according to the degree to which domestic markets are distorted. In economies where distortions are particularly severe, financial autarky may be optimal.

Analysing the problems of managing capital flows in terms of underlying distortions may be helpful because it influences the form of the policy discussion in a particular direction. The work on distortions and welfare in the trade field highlighted the fact that though restrictions on the current account might succeed in addressing a range of domestic distortions, there were generally less costly ways of achieving the same objectives. Similar arguments apply to the capital account. Moving directly to restrict capital flows would almost certainly reduce the incidence of capital account crises, but in many cases is an extremely costly way of ensuring financial stability. The general lesson from the earlier literature is to tackle distortions as close as possible to their source (Corden,

1957). As a result, the 'first-best' solution in efficiency terms is almost always to remove the distortion. In some cases, this will involve governments reducing their involvement in the market, but in others it may imply increased regulatory activism. In some situations, it may not be possible or desirable to eliminate the distortion itself. This may happen if the distortion arises from a policy that serves another important purpose or if the removal of the distortion takes time. In that case, there is a case for 'second-best' policies that alter the cost of the distorted activity in a manner that directly offsets the distortion. In these cases, the burden should lie on those who want to introduce restrictions to identify precisely the market failure or policy distortion that they are seeking to redress.

Although a 'distortions' approach leads to a presumption that capital account restrictions would often be suboptimal policy responses, a brief survey of the East Asian experience suggests that a relatively wide range of distortions may drive a wedge between the social costs and benefits of borrowing decisions in developing countries. Identifying these distortions also suggests that in many cases their removal may take a considerable amount of time and that in their presence, the case for restrictions on capital transactions on second-best grounds may be hard to ignore. While it makes both theoretical and empirical sense to treat the 'developed country paradigm' of open capital accounts as a desirable endpoint, the appropriate policy positions for the IMF to promote are likely to be more nuanced.

Section 2 provides a very simple sketch of how the costs and benefits of capital account liberalisation are likely to depend on the severity of distortions in domestic markets. Section 3 identifies a number of distortions that may have contributed to vulnerability in East Asia. Sections 4 and 5 discuss the possible policy responses suggested by the distortions approach and revisits the appropriate role of the IMF in this context.

2 Capital account liberalisation in the presence of distortions

A diagrammatic approach

The argument that full capital account liberalisation may not be desirable in the presence of distortions can be sketched in simple diagrammatic terms. Figure 6.1 depicts the marginal expected costs and benefits of units of borrowing for an economy that has not opened its capital account (financial autarky). The marginal cost and benefit schedules essentially represent supply and demand curves for credit.[1]

---

[1] This is essentially a partial equilibrium approach. A more rigorous representation can be derived in a general equilibrium context from fundamental principles, by considering the cost of current

Figure 6.1 *The economy before liberalisation*

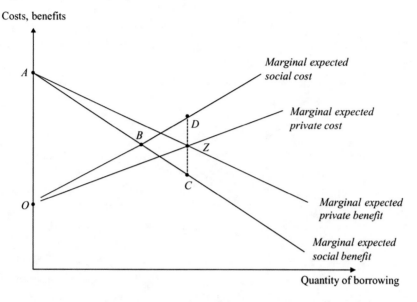

In the absence of distortions social and private costs and benefits are equal and the resulting equilibrium will be Pareto efficient. But the presence of distortions drives a wedge between the costs and benefits perceived by individual borrowers and lenders and the costs and benefits to the economy as a whole. These distortions can take a number of forms. Subsidies to investment activities might, for instance, pull the marginal social benefit of additional borrowing below its marginal private benefit. Subsidies to credit, tax breaks or external costs to individual borrowing decisions will push marginal private costs below marginal social costs. We shall consider the various possibilities in detail below. For the moment, it is sufficient to consider the implications of distortions in general, whatever they may be. Figure 6.1 indicates that the presence of distortions leads to an equilibrium at Z, where marginal private costs and benefits intersect. There is over-borrowing relative to the social optimum B, and an associated deadweight loss equal to $\triangle BCD$. In the financially autarkic economy, the tendency for interest rates to rise helps to choke off the increased demand for borrowing. The more inelastic the supply of credit, the smaller the deadweight loss will be.

Now imagine that the economy implements full capital account liberalisation. Liberalising the capital account, as in Figure 6.2, has two main effects.

relative to future consumption. McKinnon and Pill (1998) use a two-period framework to analyse overborrowing in this way.

Figure 6.2 *The economy after liberalisation*

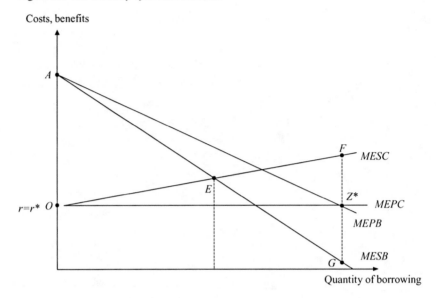

First, it will make the marginal private cost of credit more elastic (for the small open economy, the supply curve will become perfectly elastic at the world real interest rate, r^*). Second, as we discuss in more detail below, the move towards foreign borrowing may itself introduce new sources of market failure that affect the wedge between private and social costs of borrowing. In particular, there are grounds for thinking that there are particular externalities associated with foreign (and foreign currency) borrowing, that would not constitute a policy issue under financial autarky. Once again, the equilibrium, Z^*, is characterised by over-borrowing relative to the optimum, E. The amount of borrowing (and of over-borrowing) is greater after capital account liberalisation, since the interest rate does not now rise to choke off increased credit demand.

What are the welfare consequences of a move to capital account liberalisation in the presence of distortions? Welfare can be measured in terms of changes to the implied Marshallian surplus in the two different situations. Figure 6.3 replicates Figures 6.1 and 6.2 on a single diagram to allow comparison. It is obvious that in the absence of distortions, there are clear gains from international liberalisation, since $\triangle OAE > \triangle OAB$. These gains represent the efficiency benefits that arise from a lower cost of borrowing and a more elastic credit supply schedule and lie behind the conventional case for the move to capital account liberalisation.

Figure 6.3 *The costs and benefits of liberalisation*

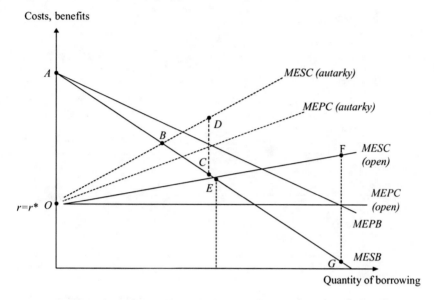

In the presence of distortions, however, the case is less clear. There are now two offsetting effects to capital account liberalisation. The first – the 'efficiency' effect – captures the same benefits that arise in the absence of distortions, which we have seen are clearly positive ($\Delta OAE > \Delta OAB$). But there is now an offsetting 'distortion' effect, which measures the increase in the deadweight loss from over-borrowing. From Figure 6.3, this is clearly negative since $\Delta EFG > \Delta BCD$. Because the supply of credit is now highly elastic, there is greater potential for over-borrowing than before capital account liberalisation. If access to foreign borrowing introduces new sources of market failure, or exacerbates existing ones, this will further increase the 'distortion' effect from liberalisation.

Thus, there is a tension at the heart of the case for capital account opening where domestic markets are distorted. The ability to borrow abroad increases the scope for socially beneficial borrowing, but it also expands the opportunity to borrow for projects that are not worthwhile from a social perspective. If domestic distortions are relatively low, the 'efficiency' effect will exceed the 'distortion' effect. But if the level of distortions is high, the 'distortion effect' may come to dominate and a move to an unrestricted capital account could lower welfare. Comparing the 'efficiency' and 'distortion' effects of an incremental move towards full capital account liberalisation means that the optimal capital account policy is likely to be contingent on the level of distortions in the domestic economy.

Figure 6.4 *Taxes as a means of replicating the social optimum*

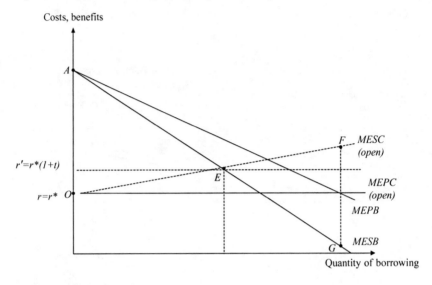

There are also no clear theoretical grounds to rule out the possibility that some intermediate position by which capital account transactions were taxed or restricted would in some cases be the optimal policy, akin to the arguments for optimal tariffs or quotas on the current account. The analogy with trade theory also suggests that if distortions cannot be removed, measures to alter the price or quantity of available capital flows may help to bring the social costs and benefits back into line. For instance, in figure 6.4, a tax on borrowing (t), that raised the effective interest rate from r to r' could in theory serve to raise the private cost of borrowing in a way that replicated the socially optimal equilibrium E.

Empirical evidence

These ambiguities in the theoretical case for free capital movements are reflected in the empirical evidence. The potential benefits of foreign direct investment (FDI) as a means of technology transfer have long been recognised and there is substantial empirical evidence that FDI raises total factor productivity (TFP), capital accumulation and growth.[2] There are, however, few clear findings relating

[2] Borenzstein, de Gregorio and Lee (1995), for instance, use cross-country growth regressions to demonstrate that FDI raises growth in the host economy, through complementarity with domestic investment and human capital. Similar evidence on the productivity of FDI and its role in promoting domestic investment and growth can be found in country studies (e.g. Warr, 1998, for Thailand).

broader capital account liberalisation to economic performance and growth. The most rigorous way to investigate these issues would be to compare the path of an economy with and without capital account restrictions in a fully specified model. McKibbin (1998) carried out preliminary work in this vein, which illustrates the gains predicted by orthodox theory. But McKibbin acknowledges that the magnitudes are highly sensitive and that the model's structure eliminates by assumption many of the market failures that would weaken the case for capital account liberalisation. Simple regression analyses, which do not rely on assumptions of this kind, give much more ambiguous results. Rodrik (1998) regresses an index of capital account restrictions on GDP growth and finds no clear link between unrestricted capital accounts and growth or inflation performance, after controlling for initial conditions. The World Bank (1998) reports further evidence along similar lines. What neither study notes is the strong negative relationship between black market premia on exchange rates and growth, a relationship that is one of the most robust in the growth literature (Lee, 1993; Sala-i-Martin, 1997). Since these exchange rate distortions are associated with extensive controls on capital and foreign exchange, they indicate the dangers posed by restrictive regimes, at least if the exchange rate is not managed in a way that validates fundamentals.

In practice, the move towards freer capital movement has been based as much on pragmatism as on proof. As international trade has increased, so have the opportunities for disguised capital movements through misinvoicing and delayed payment. The difficulties of controlling capital flows in open economies were illustrated by a succession of balance of payments crises under the Bretton Woods system and helped lead to its collapse (Obstfeld, 1998). In developed countries with strong institutions and relatively undistorted markets, the orthodox theory of the benefits of unrestricted capital flows is likely to be reasonably close to the truth. Together with the practical difficulties of restraining capital flows, this creates a powerful case for liberalisation. But in developing economies, where domestic distortions are more severe, the presumption that full capital account liberalisation is appropriate is less clear.

3 Identifying distortions

Two kinds of distortion

If the strength of the case for capital account liberalisation is contingent on distortions that affect the costs and benefits of borrowing, then the identification of correction of relevant distortions is likely to be a central part of the process of assessing the prospects for capital account liberalisation. The diagrammatic sketch of liberalisation in figure 6.1 noted two separate ways in which capital account liberalisation might alter the balance between private and social costs and benefits. The first was that capital account liberalisation might exacerbate the impact of existing distortions on the allocation of resources. The second was that the process of expanding foreign borrowing might itself introduce new opportunities for distortions or market failure that could drive a wedge between private and social returns.

This distinction may be helpful in considering policies towards liberalisation, since the two types of distortion essentially relate to two different kinds of policy problem. The identification of existing distortions is really a question of readiness: can an economy make productive use of additional inflows of capital or will capital inflows be allocated towards areas of low return? The identification of distortions associated with foreign inflows themselves is more an issue of regime choice for the capital account: given readiness to open the capital account, can arrangements be put into place which reduce the risks intrinsic to foreign capital flows?

The two main schools of thought in the latest generation of crisis models generally also reflect this delineation. In the first category are those models that emphasise the existing misallocation of resources in the pre-crisis period towards activities where expected returns were low. Much of this discussion has highlighted the role of moral hazard in a poorly regulated financial sector as a critical distortion that encouraged firms to invest in overly risky projects, gambling on the chance of high returns (Krugman, 1998). The best-known formal exposition of the problems of overborrowing in the presence of moral hazard comes from McKinnon and Pill (1997, 1998). In the presence of deposit guarantees, banks effectively discount the lower tails of the distribution of returns and so face incentives to make higher-risk lending decisions. Since the expected private benefits from investing in risky projects are higher than the expected social benefits, the result is over-borrowing relative to the optimum. As in the diagrammatic approach in figure 6.3, the impact of market failure on over-borrowing in McKinnon and Pill's model is less severe in the financially autarkic economy since interest rate rises raise the cost of excess borrowing. Aizenman (1998) develops a more sophisticated model in the same spirit, in which banks mitigate the problems of excessive risk by engaging in costly monitoring. He finds that economies with inefficient banking systems and poor prudential supervision will engage in excessive risk-taking. In this model, capital account liberalisation may magnify the impact of severe distortions not just by increasing the opportunity for poor investments, but also because by reducing the cost of funds it reduces the level of monitoring and exacerbates the underlying distortion itself.

In the second category are those models that emphasise the external costs associated with the process of foreign borrowing itself. Chang and Velasco (1998) have drawn attention to the problems of financial sector illiquidity, using a version of the well-known Diamond–Dybvig (1983) model of bank runs.

In their model, capital account liberalisation brings efficiency gains for inter-mediation, but increases the risk that the financial system will suffer a liquidity crisis. In particular, a build-up of short-term foreign debt may sharply increase both the risks of a liquidity crisis and the costs of such a crisis should it occur. If these risks are not fully internalised in the cost of borrowing, then the private cost of borrowing will not reflect its true social cost and the resulting situation may again be suboptimal. Creditors may be particularly inclined to refuse to roll over debt if information about the quality of borrowers or their balance sheets is highly uncertain (Baccheta and Wincoops, 1998) or if bankruptcy procedures make the collection of assets after default costly. In a similar vein, Krugman (1998) has drawn attention to the problems of unhedged foreign currency-denominated borrowing in leaving firms' balance sheets vulnerable to currency depreciation. Again, the implication is that there are external costs to foreign borrowing decisions that are not reflected in the cost to individual firms.

Although their focus is generally both narrower and more rigorous, many of these models can be interpreted as specific variants on the general theme of capital account liberalisation in the presence of distortions set out in the diagrammatic approach on pp. 159–62. A thorough analysis of the experience of the East Asian financial crisis indicates that both kinds of distortions are likely to be important in assessing the case for (and the form of) capital account liberalisation in developing markets. A selective list of the most important distortions are considered below (for a more comprehensive discussion see Corsetti, Pesenti and Roubini, 1998).

Distortions to the underlying allocation of capital

In the first category, two main types of existing distortion appear to have been important in East Asia, both of which raised the private benefit of some forms of borrowing above its social benefit:

- *Subsidies and related party lending*   Governments in many of the East Asian countries historically subsidised certain sectors and certain firms, either im-plicitly or explicitly. In Korea, for instance, certain industries, particularly producers of capital-intensive goods and tradable goods, received implicit and explicit subsidies from the government either in the form of direct tax concessions or directed credit. In addition, 'related-party' or politically mo-tivated lending was widespread in several economies. Since these practices meant that the allocation of resources was not based on intrinsic profitability, investment finance was not always allocated to projects that were socially efficient.

- *Market failure in the financial sector*   As noted above, the problems of moral hazard in the financial sector have featured prominently in recent crisis models and appear to have posed significant problems in East Asia. Weakly capitalised and poorly supervised financial institutions had little of their own money at stake and so faced stronger incentives to take risks. Prudential supervision was generally inadequate and prudential regulations were poorly enforced (Fane, 1998). There was a widespread perception that governments would guarantee deposits and that financial institutions would not be permitted to fail. Of course, some kinds of guarantees to financial institutions can be desirable on the grounds of financial stability and the integral place of banks in the domestic financial and payments system. The corollary is that prudential supervision is needed tightly to control the risks banks take. In the absence of proper prudential regulation, deposit insurance and other guarantees that limit liability can act as a general subsidy to risk-taking. Where lenders can safely ignore the lower ends of the distribution of returns on the projects that they finance, the expected return from the project *faced by the lender* will exceeds the project's *actual* expected return. These risks may be particularly severe after episodes of financial liberalisation. Increased competition is likely to erode the franchise value of existing banks, which if it occurs rapidly may further encourage risk-taking and 'gambling for redemption' (World Bank, 1998).

Distortions associated with foreign borrowing

On top of these existing distortions were a number of market failures that appear to have been intrinsically related to the process of foreign borrowing. In the majority of cases, these market failures pushed the private cost of foreign borrowing below its true social cost:

- *Explicit subsidies to particular forms of foreign borrowing*   A number of the East Asian economies provided explicit subsidies to foreign borrowing through preferential tax treatment. The Bangkok International Banking Facility gave special tax breaks to foreign currency dealing (Radelet and Sachs, 1998), as did the Malaysian Financial Centre on Labuan Island. In both cases, policies were aimed at promoting a regional offshore banking centre. In the Philippines, onshore income from foreign exchange loans was taxed at 10 per cent compared to a 35 per cent rate on other loan income. Philippine banks also faced no reserve requirements on foreign currency deposits. These subsidies reduced the costs of borrowing abroad faced by borrowers relative to their true social cost and clearly encouraged the accumulation of foreign debt.

As well as price incentives, the differential pace at which restrictions on different kinds of foreign borrowing also channelled borrowers towards bank borrowing, where existing distortions were arguably particularly severe. In general, it was common practice to loosen restrictions on foreign bank debt earlier and more comprehensively than limits on foreign equity. Thailand and Malaysia, in particular, maintained extensive restrictions on portfolio investments while greatly relaxing restrictions on foreign bank borrowing. In Korea, too, restrictions on bank borrowing were lifted more comprehensively than restrictions on equity purchases by foreigners. Regulations limiting the issues of securities to entities with high ratings also meant that in practice most foreign borrowing was intermediated through banks (IMF, 1998).

- *External costs of individual borrowing decisions*   The private and social costs of financial activities will diverge when there are external costs to individual borrowing decisions. For instance, borrowers may not take into account the effect of individual risk-taking or individual failure on credit conditions for others, though these external effects may be significant particularly in the presence of imperfect information. An individual's decision to borrow may also increase the vulnerability of the economy (or at least of other borrowers) to particular events or shocks, particularly in the presence of other distortions. The externalities posed by systemic risks are likely to operate regardless of whether economies are open to foreign capital inflows. But foreign borrowing can increase the significance of this kind of externality by raising both the probability of crisis and the costs incurred if it should occur. Where borrowing is foreign currency-denominated, a withdrawal of funds is potentially more destructive since the Central Bank cannot act as a lender of last resort (LOLR). In domestic financial crises, substantial injections of funds could stabilise the banking sector in the event of a crisis and prevent further withdrawals. It might be argued that creditors should take account of these kinds of risks and impose higher costs on marginal lenders as the ratio of short-term debt to reserves increases, as compensation for additional risk. This is a less likely outcome if creditors face moral hazard problems of their own (e.g. from the expectation of domestic or international bailouts) or if information on overall reserve and debt levels is not publicly available or costly to collect.

- *Assumption of exchange rate risk by Central Banks*   The combination of stable exchange rates and large nominal interest rate differentials provided a fertile environment for excessive foreign borrowing. All of the affected economies pegged or stabilised their currencies to varying degrees. In the face of large capital inflows in the early 1990s, monetary authorities conducted sterilised intervention. There is room for some debate over the degree to which exchange rate regimes themselves constituted a distortion. Between 1990 and 1997, Thailand, Malaysia, Indonesia and the Philippines maintained large nominal interest rate differentials relative to developed countries accompanied by only small movements in exchange rates.[3] These persistent differences in foreign and local currency returns suggest that market participants acknowledged a risk of abnormal depreciation and are hard to reconcile with the notion that exchange rates enjoyed 'excess credibility', as some authors have suggested (Eichengreen, 2000, pp. 40–91). The important issue then is why the failure to cover exchange risk was so widespread. It is possible that borrowers simply accepted higher risk in exchange for higher returns. In that case, the fact that investors took on risks should not in itself be cause for concern. But if risk-taking or foreign borrowing is subsidised in other ways, or if there are external costs to it, then widespread acceptance of exchange risk may still be undesirable. Where large parts of the corporate and financial sector is exposed to the same risk (i.e. are taking the same gamble), the systemic consequences of foreign currency borrowing may be severe, even if foreign borrowing is optimal at an individual level. A second issue is that Central Banks' policies of reserve accumulation in the face of rising foreign borrowing by the private sector may effectively lead the Central Bank to assume the foreign currency risk that the borrowers should be facing. If borrowers believe that the Central Bank has sufficient reserves to cover their foreign borrowing, private borrowers will be comfortable borrowing in foreign currency on an unhedged basis. The cost of hedging is then effectively borne by the Central Bank which purchases lower-yielding foreign reserves in exchange for higher-yielding domestic securities. The fact that borrowers do not face the true social cost of their borrowing decisions will again likely lead to overborrowing relative to the optimum.

4 Tackling the problem

Section 3 illustrated that it is easy to identify a fairly wide range of distortions that may make even relatively advanced developing economies, like the East Asian economies, vulnerable to crisis. The framework set out in section 2 suggests that any sensible approach to capital account liberalisation must take account of these distortions and address them where possible. In doing this, the general principle should be to make individuals face the true costs of their decisions. In that regard, the necessary measures should be seen as part of a broader sequence of financial reform that seeks to align the private and social costs and benefits of financial activities.

---

[3] In Korea, these incentives were markedly smaller. Smaller interest rate differentials were accompanied by significant depreciation in the won.

The 'first-best' solution: the developed country paradigm

The ideal response to the problems identified above would generally involve removal of the underlying distortions. Figures 6.1–6.3 illustrated that distortions impose deadweight losses regardless of capital account policy and that a situation with no distortions and full capital account liberalisation is in general clearly superior to any other.

The identification of some of the most obvious distortions in East Asia suggests that in most developing economies this would require a number of policy changes. First, domestic distortions to the allocation of resources (tariffs, subsidies to different industry groups) should, as far as possible, be removed. By far the most important distortions in many developing economies are focused in the financial sector. Moral hazard is an intrinsic feature of a financial system in which safety nets are provided to financial institutions. In general, the costs of financial crisis are sufficiently great that in practice safety nets do operate, even where deposits have not been explicitly guaranteed. Without eliminating these guarantees, moral hazard can be removed (or limited) only by prudential regulation. The traditional regulatory solution mimics an insurance contract (Fane, 1998). Minimum capital adequacy ratios (CARs) operate like the 'deductible' component of the contract, since the bank loses its capital if it fails even when deposits are guaranteed. Reserve requirements then operate like the insurance premium, raising the private cost of providing loans to a level that includes the implicit costs of deposit insurance provision. Essentially, the reserve requirement operates as a tax on risk-taking activity that balances the subsidy to risk provided by safety net provision.[4] This implies that reserve requirements are likely to be optimal for all risk-taking activities that are subject to moral hazard, not simply for domestic deposits. But the success of tight CARs and reserve requirements to limit moral hazard depends on the ability of prudential authorities to enforce regulations swiftly and actively.

Second, favourable tax and regulatory treatment for foreign borrowing would need to be abolished. This would remove explicit subsidies to accumulate foreign ahead of domestic liabilities. Ideally, restrictions on foreign access to domestic equity markets would not be retained long after restrictions on bank borrowing were relaxed.

Third, steps would need to be taken to internalise the externalities identified in foreign borrowing. In East Asia, these externalities arose principally from the build-up of short-term foreign currency debts in excess of liquid assets and the substantial costs of a sudden withdrawal of capital posed substantial risks

---

[4] The use of prudential regulation to limit moral hazard may arguably be better viewed as a 'second-best' policy. Since moral hazard can be viewed as 'fundamental' to financial systems, I deal with it here as a distortion that cannot be directly removed.

given the absence of an international LOLR. Section 3 indicated that external effects may have been exacerbated by uncertainty over the true financial position of domestic borrowers or by moral hazard in creditor nations. Increasing the provision of financial information and raising the risk weighting on short-term interbank lending might give creditors greater incentives to monitor these dangers and price these risks into loans. But although improving disclosure requirements and tightening prudential regulations on cross-border lending in creditor nations could reduce the external costs of currency exposure, it will not eliminate them. To that extent, there is a strong case for raising the costs of accumulating short-term currency exposures relative to other forms of risk.

Finally, authorities should arguably move towards more flexible exchange rate regimes.[5] By exposing borrowers directly to exchange risk and allowing the exchange rate to appreciate in the wake of capital account liberalisation, the incentives for excessive foreign borrowing are likely to be reduced. The IMF found that increased exchange rate flexibility in Chile after its financial crisis in 1982 was useful in discouraging short-term speculative flows (IMF, 1998). Floating the exchange rate is no panacea. Over-borrowing episodes have occurred under flexible regimes and the sharp appreciations that can follow capital account liberalisation will continue to present difficult policy dilemmas.[6] But a more flexible exchange rate is more likely to encourage borrowers to take account of exchange risk (Reisen, 1999) and less likely to tempt borrowers into betting on currency stability through unhedged foreign borrowing.[7]

Applying these remedies to the various distortions would essentially bring developing economies to the position of most developed countries. Developed countries typically do not provide preferential tax treatment to foreign borrowing or extensive domestic subsidies. They generally operate floating exchange rates.[8] They retain few restrictions on overseas bank borrowing or

---

[5] The debate over appropriate exchange rate regimes continues to be vigorous. In advocating greater flexibility we do not rule out the possibility of 'intermediate' regimes like the Basket, Band and Crawl advocated by Williamson (2001). But it is critical that sufficient movement in the exchange rate be countenanced to discourage borrowers from ignoring exchange rate risk.

[6] The textbook response to an appreciation that results from a massive capital inflow is to contract fiscal policy. In practice, this may be politically difficult and in some circumstances may induce further inflows by signalling greater credibility of the government's reform programmes.

[7] Some doubt has been cast (e.g. Grenville and Gruen, 1999) on the idea that exchange rate flexibility will reduce unhedged foreign borrowing or provide greater flexibility, largely on the basis of Latin American experiences. The Latin American cases, where economies are *de facto* dollarised and so authorities are reluctant to allow exchange rate movements even under flexible regimes, present special problems that do not generally apply in East Asia.

[8] The establishment of European Economic and Monetary Union (EMU) on 1 January 1999 does not invalidate this. All participants retain floating exchange rates relative to foreign currencies, although they share a common currency with other participants.

portfolio equity purchases by foreigners. They enforce strict CARs and reserve requirements, backed up by strong prudential supervision. And, to a growing extent, they require banks and securities firms to hold additional capital against short-term currency exposure (Abrams and Beato, 1998).[9] Within the East Asian region, Singapore and Hong Kong broadly conform to this position, though of course in Hong Kong the dollar is pegged through a currency board arrangement.

Undoubtedly, even with these 'first-best' solutions to existing distortions, large (and possibly irrational) movements in asset prices and capital flows remain possible. But with the social and private costs of financial activities more effectively aligned, economies can in general be made robust to adverse developments and the benefits of an open capital account are relatively clear-cut. Theory and evidence thus support the notion that capital account liberalisation is likely to be a desirable endpoint as economies develop. *Prima facie* evidence comes from the fact that developed countries have not been strong advocates of limiting their own capital movements in recent years. The absence of serious capital account crises in developed economies also suggests that in the absence of severe *domestic* distortions, the intrinsic problems of foreign borrowing and related systemic issues may be of a second order.

Reducing vulnerability: policies for the short and medium term

Implicit in these 'best-practice' recommendations is that the removal of existing distortions is both feasible and does not conflict with other objectives that the economy is unwilling to abandon. The removal of explicit subsidies to foreign borrowing and moves towards greater exchange rate flexibility are easily instituted and have already occurred in most cases in the East Asian economies (see Hernandez and Montiel, 2001, for a good discussion of changes in East Asian exchange rate regimes). But the removal of distortions in the financial sector and the establishment of an effective system of enforceable prudential regulations are unlikely to be possible overnight (Macfarlane, 1998). Resolving financial sector weakness requires greater technical expertise among financial institutions, efficient legal procedures and experienced regulators.

Even if the correct procedures can be introduced, authorities must have the will and the capacity to enforce them. The problem, for instance, in the South East Asian economies was less that the necessary regulations had not been

---

[9] The European Union, for instance, introduced a Directive in 1993 that required an 8 per cent capital charge against the overall foreign exchange position of banks and securities firms. France Germany, the Netherlands and Spain now operate systems along these lines.

enacted but that they had not been enforced. These are huge tasks and as a consequence, developing economies are likely to continue to have seriously distorted financial sectors at least over the period in which financial reform is being completed. Where financial systems are weaker, problems of excessive moral hazard will be more severe and the probability and cost of a banking crisis will be higher than in developed countries. As a result, the social costs of various risky financial activities may continue to exceed the private incentives faced by banks even after attempts to institute 'best-practice' measures have been made.

If, as seems likely, developing economies will go through substantial periods of time where these kinds of distortions continue to be significant, capital account liberalisation is likely to be optimal only if other offsetting action can be taken to align private and social costs. In other words, if in the short term these distortions cannot be tackled directly by adequate prudential supervision, there may be a strong 'second-best' case for raising the cost of certain risky activities beyond the levels required in developed countries, along the lines crudely illustrated in figure. 6.4. The vulnerabilities associated with the East Asian crisis suggest that there may be a particularly strong case for raising the costs of foreign borrowing above domestic borrowing and for raising the costs of short-term, and foreign currency-denominated, bank debt relative to other forms of foreign funding.

The issue then becomes one of how best to align social and private costs. Direct prohibitions or controls on certain kinds of activity may be an inefficient way of doing this, since they will exclude some transactions where the social benefit exceeds the social cost as well as some where it does not. In general, it will be more efficient to raise the *price* of these activities so that they reflect their true social costs. In doing this, efforts must be made to ensure that all those who undertake particular kinds of risky activity are treated equally, otherwise attempts to discourage particular transactions in one part of the economy may simply divert it to another.

A simple way to counter excessive moral hazard in relation to all risky *bank-related* activities is simply to raise the required minimum CARs above the 8 per cent set out by the Basel Accord (Fane, 1998) or to raise reserve requirements. These measures raise the price of risk-taking activities generally. But the higher risks and greater external costs imposed by unhedged foreign currency borrowing may justify additional prudential requirements which recognise the additional risks it carries. There are a number of ways to affect the incentives of banks in the affected economies to borrow and lend in foreign currencies and to build up foreign exchange exposure. 'Best-practice' arguments for imposing additional asset requirements on open foreign exchange positions have already been considered and are likely to be reinforced by second-best considerations.

These would help to limit the build-up of exchange risk by financial institutions themselves.

But regulations that focus on the foreign exchange positions of *banks* would not (indeed, did not) prevent financial institutions from borrowing abroad and lending on in foreign currency, balancing their own books but transferring exchange risk to the corporate sector, as happened in Thailand. Measures to discourage on-lending of this kind would need to raise the costs of borrowing and lending in foreign currency directly. Increasing the risk-weightings in calculating CARs for foreign currency lending to the private sector would raise the cost of domestic banks' lending to the private sector in foreign currency. Since the importance of these measures may vary at different stages of development, there is an argument for leaving such measures to the discretion of individual economies rather than instituting them in a generalised fashion through the Basel Accords.

Measures along these lines would raise the cost of bank-intermediated foreign currency borrowing. With proper prudential design, non-bank financial intermediaries could also be regulated in a similar fashion. But even a broad range of CARs will do nothing to prevent direct borrowing or the accumulation of exchange risk by the private sector, although this represents a large part of the problem in some countries. One approach is simply to leave the monitoring of the private sector to the banks that lend to them. If banks both at home and abroad take full account of the risks of lending to corporate borrowers and if domestic authorities are prepared to allow bankruptcies to occur, this should deliver an efficient solution. Moves to tighten CARs for developed country banks that lend in foreign currency to the private sector in developing countries could help in this regard.

Yet the risks posed by widespread foreign borrowing suggest that such a laissez-faire attitude may be risky. At the other end of the spectrum, strict limits on non-bank borrowing abroad might be maintained to ensure that foreign borrowing is largely channelled through more heavily regulated financial firms. The Czech Republic operates this kind of policy, requiring strict case-by-case approval on non-bank foreign borrowing. This aims to ensure that foreign borrowing is largely intermediated by domestic banks that are subject to domestic prudential control. There will be some costs to this kind of policy in terms of disintermediation, but these may be worth bearing.

A much-discussed alternative that would raise the cost of foreign borrowing for financial and corporate borrowers alike would be to introduce large compulsory reserve requirements for all foreign loans. The version of this system introduced in Chile, and widely discussed, required that 30 per cent of any foreign loan had to be deposited for one year in a non-interest paying account. Less extreme differential reserve requirements for foreign and domestic deposits could still raise the relative cost of foreign borrowing substantially. This kind of requirement is a cruder and more direct form of tax on foreign borrowing than most of the prudential measures described above. The evidence from Chile on the success of this kind of measure is mixed. The Chilean tax appears to have succeeded in discouraging short-term capital flows only after controls were strengthened in 1993 and there is considerable debate over whether their effectiveness has been eroded. Several commentators have argued that the greater stability in Chile's financial sector owes more to improvements in its banking system than the disincentives to foreign borrowing (IMF, 1998). In fact, Chile's experience in this regard is illustrative of the advantages and disadvantages of all of these 'second-best' measures. According to 'Goodhart's Law' financial regulations that seek to raise the costs of certain kinds of financial activity tend to be circumvented over time. They are best seen as temporary measures that can be justified only alongside vigorous measures to reach the 'first-best' scenario of a prudent and well-regulated financial system.

Sequencing and prohibitions: policies for the less developed

As we noted earlier, there is nothing in theory to exclude the possibility that in economies where distortions are very severe, even small moves towards capital account opening might lead to increases in deadweight losses that outweigh the associated efficiency gains. Where the financial sector is so weak, domestic distortions so large and the possibility of effective supervision so remote that these distortions cannot be adequately addressed, it may be desirable to prohibit certain types of foreign capital inflow altogether. The conditions under which this proves optimal are likely to be restrictive. Not only must domestic distortions be severe but the prospects for removing them rapidly (which would be a superior solution) must be low. The argument is then essentially one of sequencing. In countries with severe financial weakness, the logical sequence of measures is to reform the financial sector before liberalising the capital account.

The case for direct controls is most likely to hold for countries with extremely basic domestic institutions that have not already opened to foreign capital and so does not apply to many developing economies. But for the least developed economies, there may be good reasons to work rapidly to strengthen financial systems before liberalising foreign borrowing greatly. Even then, there are huge issues of practicality, particularly as these economies become more open to trade. The risk that continued exchange controls will prove increasingly ineffective and that considerable distortions will emerge as borrowers seek to circumvent them will rise over time. This makes the task of moving to 'second-best' and 'best-practice' regimes more urgent.

Another situation where direct prohibitions may be desirable arises when there is considerable uncertainty about the exact risks of capital inflow or foreign currency exposure and when the costs of a bad outcome rise rapidly. In this case, it can be shown that direct quantity limits are likely to be preferable to attempting to influence decisions by price, using an argument first elaborated by Weitzman (1974). The basic idea is that a policy design based on an under-estimate of the wedge between private and social costs could expose the economy to sharply rising risk. One area where this appears most likely to be relevant is in containing currency exposure. Particularly following episodes of financial liberalisation, financial institutions and regulators may face considerable uncertainty over the risks of foreign currency borrowing. As a result attempts to influence the cost of taking on foreign currency risk, along the lines already described, might still leave the economy open to considerable risk of over-borrowing. This creates an argument for direct limits on foreign currency exposure. Although limits of this sort are being replaced by capital requirements in many developed economies, they still have a role to play in many developing countries.

The problems of transition: short cuts to avoiding financial sector distortions

The solutions suggested so far have focused on addressing or counteracting distortions in the financial sector, through prudential regulation or other means. In practice, installing, operating and enforcing these kinds of systems effectively is a demanding and time-consuming task. Many developing countries lack the technical expertise and institutional capacity that would make it easy to operate even the kinds of second-best prudential and regulatory measures discussed above. Against this background, it may be sensible to consider ways in which distortions and deficiencies in the domestic financial system can effectively be bypassed.

   Greater international participation in the banking sector provides one way of rapidly importing expertise and prudent management systems though it re-mains one that many economies (and not just the developing ones) are reluc-tant to embrace. Through ties to their parents, domestic affiliates effectively have their own private lenders of last resort and since the parent's asset base is in general highly diversified they are less likely to be destabilised by adverse domestic conditions or exposures to particular parts of the local econ-omy. As a result, a highly internationalised financial sector is likely to be less exposed to the kinds of risk management problems and more of the external costs associated with foreign borrowing may be internalised. More broadly, the continued liberalisation of foreign direct investment and equity investment and the deepening of bond and equity markets allows economies to borrow from abroad in ways that avoid the market failures implicit in their banking system. A greater tendency to use local equity markets to mobilise foreign savings would also limit the exposure to foreign currency risk that is an unavoidable part of bank borrowing.

5 The IMF and capital account liberalisation

The main thrust of the analysis above is that the strength of the case for capital account liberalisation, and the extent to which various kinds of capital account restrictions are appropriate, is likely to be highly contingent on the state of the domestic economy. To summarise the six key points:

(1) Where domestic distortions are relatively minor, an open capital account appears to be the optimal position, both in theory and in terms of the revealed preference of the most advanced economies. The developed country paradigm is thus a desirable endpoint.

(2) There is substantial evidence that in many developing countries, distortions that may drive a wedge between the private and social costs and benefits of borrowing are severe. Some of these distortions affect the underlying allocation of capital, some appear to be intrinsic to the regimes for foreign borrowing themselves.

(3) In the presence of significant distortions, the costs for capital account liberalisation may outweigh their benefits. Because the removal of distortions in some areas, particularly in the domestic financial sector, is a difficult and time-consuming process, 'second-best' arguments for measures to limit capital movements that are not applicable to developed countries may be applicable in developing economies.

(4) In general, these restrictions may be best implemented by attempting to raise the price of particular transactions rather than prohibit them altogether. In many cases, this might be done through increased prudential requirements for particular activities.

(5) Where domestic distortions are very severe, or where prudential infrastructure is so basic that the ability to implement and enforce prudential solutions effectively is very weak, it may be desirable to limit certain kinds of capital inflow altogether.

(6) Since the reduction or removal of domestic distortions is likely to be welfare-enhancing regardless of capital account policies, identifying and addressing these distortions is likely to be an important part of the policy process.

What do these conclusions imply about the appropriate attitude for the IMF towards capital account liberalisation? The basic answer is that the IMF's stance on capital account liberalisation should reflect the ambiguity of the theory and evidence in favour of open capital accounts and the contingent nature of that case. This requires a greater focus on sequencing issues and a willingness to acknowledge that in many developing economies the case for some kinds of capital account restrictions on a temporary basis may be powerful. Against the background of this more cautious stance, it remains desirable that the IMF continues to promote the notion that the desirable endpoint both in theory and practice is likely to be a fully open capital account regime, as instituted by the most advanced economies. But in reality, this goal may be some way off for the weakest economies.

This shift in emphasis implies that the IMF should consider in greater detail *how* capital movements could be controlled rather than *whether* they should be. Moves to manage capital flows span a broad spectrum from prudential regulations of the kind operated by developed country financial systems to outright prohibitions on capital movements. By tackling the symptom rather than the source of the problems, the danger is that as governments step into regulate or tax capital flows, they will fail to do so in the most efficient way and risk introducing new distortions to replace the old ones. Advice and technical assistance from the IFIs is likely to be important in minimising this risk, but requires a willingness to take a more flexible approach to capital account policy. A reluctance to enter the debate on the appropriate forms of capital controls (or a perception of inflexibility on this issue) raises the risks that the international institutions cede the field to those who promote what are clearly suboptimal solutions.

In providing advice to developing countries on capital account regimes, there may also be value in promoting a framework that focuses firmly on the identification and correction of underlying distortions that present an obstacle to capital account liberalisation. Influencing the terms on which the policy debate takes place can be an important step to the promotion of sensible policy outcomes. The vigorous attacks on the use of trade restrictions to fulfil policy objectives that were more effectively fulfilled by other means by Corden, Bhagwati and others did serve to increase pressure on governments that sought to justify trade barriers. They also placed the burden of proof on those who wished to restrict trade to identify the policy problem that they hoped to solve and to explain why it could not be tackled directly.

In our view, this more nuanced approach is unlikely to be helped by a formal commitment to capital account liberalisation in the IMF's goals or to the instatement of capital account convertibility in the IMF's Articles. Some commentators (Eichengreen, 2000) have argued that there need not be a conflict between making capital account liberalisation an explicit objective of IMF policy and some kinds of capital account restrictions. Just as the commitment to current account convertibility does not rule out the imposition of price-based restrictions like tariffs, so capital account convertibility would mean the removal of foreign exchange and other capital controls, but not necessarily all tax-based instruments on capital transactions. But a commitment of this kind would compromise the perception if not the reality of flexibility on this issue, even assuming that sufficient support from IMF members could now be obtained. In addition, this kind of commitment would appear to rule out support for quantitative restrictions under any circumstance, an option that it seems unwise to preclude for the least developed economies at least for particular kinds of capital flow.

The sophistication of the debate over capital account liberalisation has already increased substantially. Policy-makers, both nationally and in international institutions like the IMF, are now recognising that greater care must be taken in assessing the appropriate regimes for capital inflows in developing countries. In particular, it is widely accepted that the efficiency of the allocation of capital flows and the extent to which they lead to sustained improvements in economic performance will depend heavily on the development and efficiency of the financial system (IMF, 1998). The IMF has shown considerable willingness to adopt a flexible attitude in its discussion of capital account issues with a 2001 Fund Survey acknowledging explicitly that 'it is important to meet certain preconditions before the capital account is fully opened'. Fund research continues to make a critical contribution to ongoing research into the efficacy of various kinds of capital account restrictions (IMF, 2000). With our understanding of the sources and solutions to international capital market instability still quite under-developed, this more pragmatic approach is likely to be more sensible than renewed steps towards making the IMF a torch-bearer for capital account liberalisation.

REFERENCES

Abrams, R. and P. Beato (1998). 'The Prudential Regulation and Management of Foreign Exchange Risk', IMF Working Paper, 98/37

Aizenman, J. (1998). 'Capital Mobility in a Second Best World', NBER Working Paper, 6703

Bachetta, P. and E. van Wincoop (1998). Capital Flows to Emerging Markets: Liberalization, Overshooting and Volatility', NBER Working Paper, 6530

Bhagwati, J. (1971). 'The Generalized Theory of Distortions and Welfare', in J. Bhagwati et al. (eds.), *Trade, Balance of Payments and Growth*. Amsterdam, North-Holland
(1998). 'The Capital Myth: The Difference between Trade in Widgets and Trade in Dollars', *Foreign Affairs*, 77(3), 7–12

Borenzstein, E., J. de Gregorio and J. Lee (1995). 'How Does Foreign Direct Investment Affect Economic Growth?', NBER Working Paper, 5057

Chang, R. and A. Velasco (1998). 'Financial Fragility and the Exchange Rate Regime', NBER Working Paper, 6469

Corden, W. M. (1957). 'Tariffs, Subsidies and the Terms of Trade', *Economica*, 24

Corsetti, G., P. Pesenti and N. Roubini (1998). 'What Caused the Asian Currency and Financial Crisis?', unpublished manuscript

Diamond, D. and P. Dybreg (1983). 'Bank Runs Deposit Insurance and Liquidity', *Journal of Political Economy*, 91, 401–19

Eichengreen, B. (2000). 'The International Monetary Fund in the Wave of the Asian Crisis', in G. W. Noble and J. Ravenhill (eds.), *The Asian Financial Crisis and the Architecture of Global Finance*. Cambridge, Cambridge University Press

Fane, G. (1998). 'Prudential Regulation of Financial Institutions in the 1997–98 Crises in Southeast Asia', in *The East Asian Crisis: From being a Miracle to Needing One?*, London and New York, Routledge

Grenville, S. and D. Gruen (1999). 'Capital Flows and Exchange Rates', RBA Conference on 'Capital Flows and the International Financial System', Sydney, 9–10 August

Hernandez, L. and P. Montiel (2001). 'Post-Crisis Exchange Rate Policy in Five Asian Countries: Filling in the "Hollow Middle"', IMF Working Paper, 01/170

IMF (1998). *International Capital Markets: Developments, Prospects and Key Policy Issues*. Washington, DC, IMF

IMF (2000).

JP Morgan (1999). *Asian Financial Markets Report*, 1st quarter 1998

Krugman, P. (1998). 'What happened to Asia?', www.mit.edu/people/krugman, January

Lee, J. (1993). 'Trade, Distortions and Growth', IMF Staff Papers, 40(2), 299–328

MacFarlane, I. (1998). Speech to Financial Regulators, Sydney, November

McKibbin, W. (1998). 'Some Global Consequences of Financial Market Liberalisation in the Asia Pacific Region', Paper presented at ANU Conference on 'Financial Reform in Japan and Australia', August

McKinnon R. and H. Pill (1997). 'Credible Economic Liberalizations and Overborrowing', *American Economic Review*, 87(2), 189–203

   (1998). 'International Overborrowing: A Decomposition of Credit and Currency Risks', unpublished manuscript

Obstfeld, M. (1998). 'The Global Capital Market: Benefactor or Menace?', NBER Working Paper, 6659

Radelet, S. and J. Sachs (1998). 'The Onset of the East Asian Financial Crisis', HIID, unpublished paper

Reisen, H. (1999). 'After the Great Asian Slump: Towards a Coherent Approach to Global Capital Flows', OECD Development Centre, Policy Brief, 16

Rodrik, D. (1998). 'Who Needs Capital-Account Convertibility?', Harvard University, mimeo, February

Sala-i-Martin, X. (1997). 'I just Ran 2 Million Regressions', *American Economic Review*, 87(2), 178–82

Warr, P. (1998). 'Thailand', *The East Asian Crisis: From Being a Miracle to Needing One?*. London and New York, Routledge

Weitzman, M. (1974). 'Prices vs. Quantities', *Review of Economics and Statistics*, 41(4), 471–91

Williamson, J. (2001). 'The Case for a Basket, Band and Crawl (BBC) Regime for East Africa', in D. Gruen (ed.), *Future Directions for Monetary Policies in East Asia*. Canberra, Reserve Bank of Australia

World Bank (1998). *Global Economic Prospects*. Washington, DC, World Bank

7 How should the IMF view capital controls?

GREGOR IRWIN, CHRISTOPHER L. GILBERT AND DAVID VINES

1 Introduction

This chapter is a substantially revised version of Gilbert, Irwin and Vines (2001).
in which the focus is on the implications of capital account liberalisation for
the poorest developing countries.

The articles of agreement of the IMF, first drafted in 1945, include among their
primary purposes the achievement of current account convertibility and trade
liberalisation. In April 1997, the IMF announced its intention to alter its articles
of agreement to widen its mandate to include capital account liberalisation.
Since then a succession of financial and currency crises worldwide have led
some to call into question the desirability of free international capital mobility
and to advocate restrictions on capital flows (Rodrik, 1998). In this chapter, we
assess how the IMF should view capital controls.

First, we discuss the extent to which countries should move towards capital
account liberalisation. The focus is on developing countries as full capital account convertibility already exists in the developed countries. Our argument – in
line with the climate of opinion since the crises in East Asia and elsewhere – is
one in favour of caution. The reasons are partly sequencing (or 'second-best')
ones, and partly that liberalisation can increase the vulnerability to financial
crisis. Second, we discuss what role the IMF should play in facilitating the policy and institutional development identified in the first part of this chapter as
necessary for the successful liberalisation of the capital account. We argue that
the IMF is well placed to provide the technical assistance, analysis and advice
which is essential.

The plan of the chapter is as follows. In section 2 we review the arguments in
favour of liberalisation, and in particular how these relate to developing countries. The most important of these arguments are those relating to allocational
efficiency and macroeconomic discipline. We also argue that capital account
liberalisation can accelerate the development and coverage of the domestic

banking sector. Finally we consider the effect of capital liberalisation on fixed investment.

In section 3 we present the arguments for caution. First, although there is widespread agreement that if capital account controls were the only 'distortion' the first-best policy would always be liberalisation, the fact is that in developing countries there will be many distortions, both in markets and as the result of government policy, and this therefore weakens the case for liberalisation. Second, the experiences in the 1990s of countries moving towards financial liberalisation shows that those which have opened up their markets to international capital flows have been exposed to financial and currency crises, and in particular the risk of a rapid withdrawal of liquid funds. This experience serves as a warning to liberalising countries of the dangers of inadequate management of the liberalisation process.

Our assessment in section 4, which is in accordance with the consensus among professional economists, is that capital account liberalisation provides potential net benefits, but sequencing arguments are very important. Within a cost-benefit framework, the benefits of liberalisation are seen as more modest than had previously been supposed, while the East Asian crisis has increased our estimates of the potential costs of poorly managed liberalisation and of the crises which liberalisation can bring. We identify a role for the IMF in promoting the orderly liberalisation of capital accounts within the context of a comprehensive and carefully sequenced economic reform package. We support the proposed extension of the Fund's purposes to include capital account liberalisation, but we argue against giving the Fund jurisdiction over capital payments in the same way as it presently has jurisdiction over current payments. Section 5 concludes.

2 Arguments for capital account liberalisation

General arguments

It is natural for market-oriented economists to regard capital market liberalisation as an integral component of the overall liberalisation process in developing countries. This was true of post-war adjustment in Europe, and has been extrapolated to the fast-growing East Asian economies and now to the remainder of the developing world. Fischer (1998, p. 2) wrote that 'capital account liberalization is an inevitable step on the path of international development, which cannot be avoided and should be embraced. After all, the most advanced economies all have open capital accounts'.

A number of different arguments have been advanced for capital account liberalisation. These have been well summarised by Schneider (2001). The arguments for liberalisation fall into two main classes – those which emphasise efficient microeconomic allocation of resources, and those which emphasise improved quality of macroeconomic and financial policy.

Microeconomic arguments

These arguments have been most cogently advanced by Cooper (1998). At the most simple level, he argued (p. 12) that a free capital market will result in efficient capital allocation – 'maximising efficiency in the world's use of capital, a scarce resource'. Capital account liberalisation reduces interest rate differentials across currencies and countries and thereby reduces international differences in the cost of capital. As a consequence, investment becomes more efficient. This argument is identical to standard arguments on the gains from free trade in goods and services.

This argument stresses production efficiency, but one can make a similar argument in terms of households. Capital market controls prevent households diversifying their asset portfolios. This prevents their obtaining insurance against poor domestic economic performance. It seriously reduces the value of pension and other long-term insurance provision. Portfolio diversification, facilitated by the abolition of capital controls, permits individuals to insure against country specific risks by diversifying their asset portfolios.

In a similar but less concrete vein, Cooper (1998, p. 12) urged the importance of individual freedom – 'individuals should be free to dispose of their income and wealth as they see fit'. Cooper (1998) also argued that capital market controls can, in line with all forms of regulation, result in increased rent extraction. He states (p. 12) that 'the discretion given to officials to give exceptions to general provisions on international capital movements, [gives] rise to favouritism and corruption'. Corruption increases the arbitrariness arising from capital market controls and thereby generates costly additional uncertainty. Resources are redistributed in ways which are unlikely to reduce inequality or poverty, or to contribute to faster growth.

Macroeconomic and financial argument

This set of arguments has been stressed by Dornbusch (1998), who emphasises the impact of capital market liberalisation on the quality of macroeconomic and financial management. The mechanism is the inflows and outflows of capital in response to financial market expectations of the future path of the economy in relation to their perceptions of government policy. On this view, the markets are seen as 'disciplining' governments. Under a floating exchange rate regime, the major impact of these capital flows will be via their effects on the country's exchange rate while in a regime in which the currency is regulated, the impact will be via the country's gold and foreign exchange reserves.

Dornbusch (1998, p. 20) saw two aspects to this market discipline. In terms of macroeconomic policy, 'countries stand to gain by enlisting the capital markets in support of good policies'. Because capital markets are forward-looking, the possibility of large inward or outward capital flows imposes an element of constraint on government policies, requiring that these be feasible over the longer term. This discipline is a means for obtaining commitment to sound policies from governments which may be subject to short-term electoral or other political pressures. Second, a liberalised capital account will generate financial market discipline – 'intense capital mobility puts greater burdens on a country to ensure that its financial system is well supervised and regulated' (Dornbusch, 1998, p. 20). The mechanism here is that, if countries are to compete in free international capital markets, they will be required to conform to international standards with regard to reporting and to financial regulation.

Dornbusch (1998, p. 20) also argued, we believe inconsistently, that 'the scope for discretionary action has become extremely limited'. He suggested that capital market controls may be evaded through exploitation of special provisions and loopholes or by black or grey market operations. The net effect of controls is therefore only to increase costs. However, if these costs are large, the microeconomic costs to the economy will be substantial, and since many firms and individuals will prefer to comply with the regulations than to bear the costs and risks associated with evasion, the capital controls will in large measure be effective. We take it that controls are sufficiently effective for governments to wish to maintain them, since otherwise there is no point to any discussion. Furthermore, the evidence from Chile and Malaysia, among other countries, demonstrates that controls can have significant effects.[1]

Capital account liberalisation, investment and growth

Dornbusch's (1998) arguments focus on the indirect effects of capital account liberalisation on growth as the consequence of disciplining governments to adopt more coherent macroeconomic policies and more rigorous final market regulation. These arguments raise important questions about sequencing, which we discuss below. It may also be the case that market discipline is subject to a form of Type I error in which governments are disciplined for 'offences' which they have not committed or which they may only be considering. On this view, the markets may constrain governments from adopting, or even actively considering, quite reasonable policies simply because the financial markets cannot be persuaded of their efficacy. In that case, capital account liberalisation

---

[1] See also the evidence on black market exchange rates in Cooper (1999).

will limit the possibilities open to governments and may thereby constrain growth. Although Dornbusch's arguments will resonate with those who take a market view of economic policy, they are unlikely to persuade those who see merit in more interventionist approaches.

For these reasons, there is also merit in investigating the possible direct effects of capital market liberalisation on growth. We now consider in detail two such potential benefits. First, we argue that capital liberalisation might hasten the development of the local financial sector, and in so doing alleviate the financial repression which frequently constrains growth, especially in the poorest developing countries. Second, we consider the link between capital liberalisation and fixed investment in developing countries. We are circumspect on this. We argue that capital liberalisation, in itself, has little effect on foreign direct investment (FDI), and we note that the correlation between portfolio flows and actual fixed investment rates is low.

Development of the domestic financial sector

Acceleration of growth rates, particularly in the poorest developing countries, will require a higher level of savings and investment. Yet it is a characteristic of such countries that there is widespread financial repression. There is a shortage of savings at prevailing interest rates, and what saving is done is undertaken primarily by enterprises, rather than households, and is not intermediated (McKinnon, 1973; Shaw, 1973). This is likely to reduce investment and the evidence suggests that such distortion constrains growth rates (King and Levine, 1993).

In much of Sub-Saharan Africa, for example, the coverage of the banking sector is actually lower than at the end of the colonial period, largely as the consequence of the politicisation of bank lending. The presence of international banks goes some way in offsetting this, but these seldom extend their operations outside the capital city. Rural banking, in particular, is often very weak. Deaton (1992a, 1992b) shows that households attempt to smooth consumption, but poor access to liquid assets limits their ability to do this. In circumstances of this sort, household saving typically takes the form of the purchase of physical assets, with the consequence that windfall gains may be dissipated in asset price inflation (Bevan, Collier and Gunning, 1990).[2] Households resort to social mechanisms for risk management based on the village or extended family

---

[2] Dehn (2000) shows that initial positive investment responses to temporary shocks fail to lead to permanent increases in growth, while large shocks are actually associated with declines in investment.

(Collier and Gunning, 1999). There is little possibility of borrowing to finance investment.

Banking arrangements of this sort offer low returns to savers who in any case often put little trust in the banking institutions. Offered the choice, savers would prefer to deposit money abroad ('capital flight') or in the domestic branches of international banks. Traditional restrictive banking arrangements can therefore seldom compete with international banks. Capital account controls reinforce financial repression by enabling non-competitive arrangements to be sustained. Liberalisation will place domestic banks under greater pressure to compete and this may eventually result in the growth of a modern banking sector. Evidence to support this is provided by Williamson and Mahar (1998) who find increased financial depth, as measured by the ratio of M2 to GDP, in developing countries which have liberalised the domestic financial sector and the capital account.

Financial repression also has implications for macroeconomic performance in that it implies that there is little practical distinction between fiscal and monetary policy. With capital controls, the shallowness of the market for domestic debt will imply high interest rate volatility. If capital controls are eliminated, governments can borrow on international markets. That, too, will bring benefits. We regard these direct impacts of capital account liberalisation on the financial sector as being one of the most important reasons for regarding liberalisation as being an important plank of development policy.

Fixed investment

We have already noted that one of the most important arguments in favour of capital liberalisation is that it results in a more efficient international allocation of capital. An important concern for developing countries is whether this will result in greater fixed investment and, as a result, faster economic growth. This might be expected if the marginal return on capital is higher in developing countries and if it is the existence of capital controls that prevents the exploitation of such opportunities by international investors. In this subsection we take a closer look at this issue.

Both foreign direct investment (FDI) and portfolio investment in developing countries rose dramatically during the 1990s, with some decline after 1997 following the onset of the East Asian crisis.[3] Both have now partially recovered, and there is every prospect that the first decade of the twenty-first century will

---

[3] It is conventional to break down inward capital flows into three components: FDI; portfolio investment; and other flows, which include loans, aid flows and official funding. We do not discuss the third component in this chapter.

continue to show a high level of inward capital flows into developing countries. Both FDI and portfolio investment give countries access to international technology, enabling them to participate in a process of transformation and growth to an extent which would not be possible if confined to domestic technology. Both have the potential to raise growth rates and thereby reduce levels of poverty.

At the same time, the growth in both portfolio investment and FDI has been patchy, with many countries receiving very little inward investment; and volatile, so that those countries which have been recipients have suffered from periodic 'emerging market crises' during which flows dry up. Bosworth and Collins (1999, p. 148) record that five countries accounted for nearly two-thirds of financial flows into developing countries over the period 1990–5 (China, Mexico, Korea, Thailand and Brazil, in that order).

The distinction between FDI and portfolio investment flows is important:

(a) FDI and portfolio investment are not significantly correlated. Bosworth and Collins (1999, p. 151) report a correlation coefficient over the period 1978–95 of 0.01, rising to 0.06 in the subsample of emerging markets To cite specific important instances, China, which was the largest recipient of FDI, obtained very little portfolio investment, while Brazil, which was the largest recipient of portfolio investment, obtained little FDI.
(b) Portfolio investment flows are much more volatile than FDI flows – it is much easier to sell shares in a Thai company and withdraw the capital, than it is to sell a factory in Thailand with the same objective. Although FDI can decline in a crisis, it is unlikely to reverse.
(c) Econometric evidence shows that FDI translates directly into fixed investment with a near unit coefficient. By contrast, the multiplier for portfolio investment is much smaller. The panel estimates reported by Bosworth and Collins (1999, p. 162) give a coefficient of 0.90 (standard error 0.22) for FDI over their emerging market sample to be compared with 0.15 (standard error 0.08) for portfolio investment.
(d) Countries do not need to fully liberalise their capital accounts in order to benefit from FDI since both inflows and outflows can be accommodated through special provisions. Portfolio investment does, however, require capital account liberalisation.

Taken together, these remarks imply that openness to portfolio investment offers fewer benefits and imposes higher costs than does openness to FDI, and that many of the benefits from access to FDI can be obtained without full liberalisation. According to Rodrik (1998), there is in fact little econometric evidence that capital market liberalisation has any effect on developing country growth, although Quinn (1997), who uses a measure which takes into account the extent as well as the presence of controls, does find evidence of positive effects.

FDI is driven by expected profitability, in relation to risk, as it affects shareholder values. We suppose that shareholders are interested in dollar returns. Since funds for FDI derive from international markets, capital account liberalisation will have only minor effects on the costs of FDI. However, it will affect the perceived ability of investors to repatriate profits and the risk associated with repatriation. Investors will also interest themselves in the macroeconomic environment, so the indirect effects of liberalisation on macroeconomic policy will be important. Capital account liberalisation, together with the confidence that capital movements will remain free over the relevant investment horizon, should therefore contribute to FDI. However, it is doubtful that this is a major determinant of the direction of FDI, and there is a large number of examples of countries, the most notable of which is China, which are major recipients of FDI despite maintenance of capital market restrictions.

The major reason for the apparent small effect of capital account liberalisation on FDI is that it directly affects neither relative prices nor institutional quality. It is a characteristic of many economies with low degrees of trade openness that distortions of relative prices in relation to border prices arise out of pressure to protect domestic industries rather than local factor abundances. It is unlikely that international investors will find investment in such environments attractive, particularly when indigenous firms maintain the ability to seek reinforcement of protection if they deem this necessary. This indicates that FDI will be more dependent on the liberalisation of goods and services, and on the strengthening of those institutions which will ensure a level playing field for indigenous and international firms. Capital account liberalisation can contribute to the stimulation of FDI, but the fact that this contribution will be small without institution-building and liberalisation of the markets in goods and services indicates that it should fall relatively late in the sequencing of reforms.

This argument does not imply that there are few benefits from capital account liberalisation, but only that the benefits arising out of better allocation of world capital are unlikely to be large until other reforms are at least in progress. It suggests that financial market development and the quality of macroeconomic policy are the principal objectives likely to be attained through liberalisation.

3 Arguments for caution in capital account liberalisation

Capital liberalisation also imposes costs on developing countries. Understanding the nature of these costs not only permits an informed and balanced assessment of the merits of liberalisation, but is also instructive in determining how the process of liberalisation can best be managed. Arguments against capital account liberalisation can be grouped under two categories (Dooley, 1996). First, capital controls can be justified as a second-best response to a market failure: while the first-best response is to correct this market failure directly, where this is impracticable it may be welfare-improving to create an additional distortion (in the market for international capital) to offset this. It follows that capital account liberalisation, in the absence of other institutional reform, may lead to reductions in welfare. Second, where capital account liberalisation can give rise to vulnerability to crisis, government intervention can be justified to reduce this vulnerability. Capital controls can provide one way for the government to do this.

In the following subsections we consider each of these arguments in turn, but we also show how vulnerability problems may be rooted in some pre-existing distortion. The two arguments of this section are therefore interconnected. In these subsections we draw heavily on the experience of liberalising economies in the 1990s.

Second-best arguments

As Dooley (1996) and Wilson (2000) point out, there are many distortions which can provide the basis for second-best arguments in favour of capital controls.

Protection and subsidies

Suppose that the current account is not liberalised and that certain sectors have significant protection from foreign competition which increases the price domestic producers receive relative to world prices. Capital account liberalisation could encourage investment in these protected sectors which is welfare-reducing; if the protection in these industries is sufficiently great, investment may even occur in situations where the value of the investments at world prices is negative. A similar argument can be made in the situation where production in certain sectors is subsidised by the government through an active industrial policy. This argument implies that there are circumstances in which increased FDI reduces welfare.

Moral hazard

A common first step in the growth of financial systems is the development of a banking system insured by (and often owned by) the government. This is a natural response, in a risky environment, to the absence of financial systems strong enough to undertake proper risk management. Such an institutional structure can distort investment incentives, since (explicit or implicit) government guarantees remove some of the downside risk from investment. Firms will stand to gain if investments turn out well, but they do not bear the full cost if things turn out badly. That creates an incentive for 'over-investment', in the sense that investment will be undertaken for which the expected return is less than the expected cost (McKinnon and Pill, 1997; Krugman, 2001). Capital account liberalisation, which permits access to a large supply of funds for potential investment projects, will lead to a greater number of investment projects being feasible given the guarantee, and thus a greater amount of investment being undertaken for which the expected return is less than the expected cost (Wilson, chapter 6 in this volume). Many see accounts along these lines as providing a simple account of the pre-crisis Asian economies.

Unreformed tax systems

There are two main problems. First, many developing countries have a relatively narrow tax base. Difficulties in taxing overseas earnings make it attractive to countries to prohibit the export of domestic capital (Razin and Sadka, 1991). Capital account liberalisation imposes costs on these countries by further reducing the tax base. Second, there is empirical evidence that countries with capital controls tend to exhibit relatively high inflation (Dooley, 1996, p. 656), resulting in lower real interest rates, and hence low real service costs, on domestic debt. Capital account liberalisation therefore entails either increases in explicit tax rates or reductions in government expenditure (Giovannini and de Melo, 1993). Liberalisation prior to solution of these two problems can exacerbate budget deficit problems and result in restrictive macroeconomic policies which do little to encourage development.

Fixed exchange rates

Suppose that the authorities have a commitment to a fixed exchange rate as a form of nominal anchor, as remains true in many developing countries. Suppose further that the authorities are in the practice of regulating the economy through monetary policy, raising interest rates at time of boom and vice versa. The viability of this type of regime is underpinned by capital account controls (Wyplosz, 1986), and undermined by capital account liberalisation. One way of making this clear is to note that there is an 'impossible trinity' of fixed exchange rates, independent monetary policy, and capital mobility: one of these will have to go.[4] The East Asian crisis has shifted the majority view in the economics

---

[4] See Warr (1998) who shows how the exchange rate peg prevented the pre-crisis boom in Thailand being choked off, with the consequence that price increases were unchecked, making the export sector increasingly uncompetitive.

profession towards a strong preference for floating rate regimes as a way of resolving this choice. But, as discussed below, the institutional reforms necessary for a transformation of monetary policy are very large. The construction of such institutions can currently only be an aspiration in many developing countries. A move to capital account liberalisation, along with a move to floating exchange rates, prior to the construction of these monetary institutions, may leave the economy exposed to severe monetary instability.[5] This point seriously qualifies the macroeconomic discipline argument for capital market liberalisation, and suggests that, for many developing countries, liberalisation can be only a long-term objective. That is, if macroeconomic policy-making institutions are not strong enough to stand the scrutiny of forward-looking capital markets then capital controls may be desirable as a second-best response.

Reforms suggested by second-best arguments

This discussion suggests that there are a number of important preconditions for financial liberalisation. For each distortion or market failure we have identified above we can determine the reforms necessary as a precursor to capital account liberalisation.

Current account liberalisation and reform of industrial policy

We have already argued that such policy reforms are necessary as otherwise capital account liberalisation might: (1) exacerbate existing distortions; or (2) entrench opposition to reform in these areas.

Improved regulation of the financial sector and removal of implicit guarantees

The East Asian crisis demonstrated that guarantees to the banking system can result in a tendency towards excessive risk-taking, and that capital account liberalisation can exacerbate this by providing access to an elastic supply of cheap foreign funds. Such guarantees are a common response in the developing countries to the problems caused by an institutionally under-developed banking system. They should be replaced by modern methods of risk management implemented by the banking sector itself, and both donor countries and multilateral agencies may be able to assist in this process. These systems should

[5] Stiglitz (2002, p. 7) states 'Western banks benefited from the loosening of capital controls in Latin America and Asia, but those regions suffered when inflows of speculative hot money . . . that had poured into countries suddenly reversed. The abrupt outflow of money left behind collapsed currencies and weakened banking systems.'

be buttressed by prudential regulation. In particular, capital adequacy ratios (CARs) will typically need to be raised, probably to levels well above those in OECD countries. Enhanced loan loss provisioning is required in order to prevent banks from carrying bad loans on their books which should be written off (see Fane, 1998). Once such reforms are introduced it will be possible to reform the system of guarantees given to the financial sector.

Fiscal reform

This is required to broaden the tax base and in so doing to reduce the dependency of the government on forms of finance which are underwritten by capital controls. This may require major institutional reforms – in particular, tax evasion is often facilitated by current bank regulatory regimes.

Central Bank independence

Capital account liberalisation spells the end for pegged exchange rate regimes. The transition to a floating exchange rate regime requires the creation of a new form of nominal anchor: the nominal anchor must be provided by the Central Bank's monetary policy. In turn that requires strong monetary institutions – Central Bank independence, coupled with a credible commitment to some form of inflation targeting. This is a strong requirement. We note that a number of developed market economies have experienced difficulties in this regard. Eichengreen *et al.* (1999) discuss the moves which are required.

Vulnerability arguments

There is a further reason for caution in the advocacy of capital account liberalisation. The experience of the 1990s has shown that developing countries which liberalise are vulnerable to financial crisis: the financial crises of the 1990s have been intrinsically crises of capital mobility in which countries are subject to a panic withdrawal of large amounts of liquid funds. This is in contrast to the financial crises of the 1980s in Latin America, at the core of which were government budgetary problems.

Vulnerability may be viewed as reflecting the existence of structural nonlinearities: a state of affairs is vulnerable when, even if there are only small changes in fundamentals, there can be a big shift to some sort of bad outcome. There are many ways to make this general idea specific (Dooley and Walsh, 1999); the easiest way of doing so is in terms of the idea of multiple equilibria.[6] The financial system is vulnerable to crisis when both a good equilibrium and a bad equilibrium is possible; a crisis occurs when the economy shifts from the good to the bad equilibrium. In what follows we discuss how vulnerability can arise when the capital account has been liberalised before sufficient of the reforms already discussed have been implemented.

Vulnerability and unreformed financial systems

As discussed on p. 185, most developing countries are characterised by under-developed financial systems and the poorest countries by financial repression. We have argued that a common first step in the growth of financial systems is the development of a banking system insured by the government, and that this can promote over-investment. The East Asian crisis has made clear just how vulnerable countries are to financial crisis if the capital account is liberalised in these circumstances. The archetypal East Asian financial system functioned by channelling domestic savings into particular forms of investment and growth, via a banking system operating under state guarantees.

In this environment firms become highly geared. They, and the banks which lend to them, become exposed to the effects of a revenue downturn; and in aggregate the whole of the financial system becomes so exposed. In countries experiencing successful growth the possibility of a downturn can be seriously under-estimated. Firms, and the financial system that lends to them, suppose that they are implicitly guaranteed against such bad outcomes. Liberalisation, without reforming the financial system, implies that foreign suppliers of capital obtain access to these guarantees. Over-investment is encouraged and there is a rapid increase in the stock of implicit guarantees to the financial system (Krugman, 2001). The mere statement by government that rescues will not take place will seldom be credible unless accompanied by institutional reforms which tie the government's hands (Diaz-Alejandro, 1985).

Economies of this type are subject to multiple equilibria: if foreign lenders believe that the government can honour its guarantees they will set low interest rates (the risk premium is low) with the result that the government will in fact be able to afford to honour the guarantees; but if foreign lenders believe that the government will not be able to honour its guarantees, they will set high interest rates, such that the government will not in fact be able to afford to honour the guarantees. The expectation that the government will renege can therefore become self-fulfilling. When this happens there will be a financial

---

[6] Seminal multiple-equilibrium analyses are to be found in Diamond and Dybvig (1983) and Obstfeld (1986, 1991, 1994, 1995). These papers analyse, respectively, bank runs and exchange rate crises, and use very different kinds of analysis. They share the generic idea that one can locate vulnerability in the existence of multiple equilibria.

crisis in which a rapid reversal of international capital flows occurs. This is because once the government is forced to renege it is difficult to see how it can credibly promise similar guarantees in the future. But without such guarantees much of the investment undertaken will become unprofitable, and funds will be withdrawn from the country. See Corbett, Irwin and Vines (1999) and Irwin and Vines (2000).

Vulnerability and fixed exchange rates

A high proportion of developing countries continue to operate pegged exchange rates. Pegged exchange rates exacerbate vulnerability once the capital account is liberalised. This is because they result in a large outstanding stock of un-hedged foreign debt. It is easy to see why private investors should choose not to hedge – a fixed exchange rate reassures investors that the exchange rate will not be devalued. The fact that foreign debt is unhedged raises the domestic currency value of the stock of outstanding government guarantees to the financial system in the event of a currency depreciation, making it more expensive for government to meet these guarantees.

Governments operating fixed exchange rate regimes are prone to resist depreciations which are in the long-term interests of the country because of the short-term capital losses that depreciation will impose. Free cross-exchange movement of capital reduces the possibilities of this. It may imply that, when they do occur, depreciations are larger than would have been the case in a floating regime in which market participants would have held more hedged positions. Depreciations of this sort may be characterised in terms of a shift between multiple equilibria, or alternatively in terms of more or less favourable adjustment paths. In either case, it is clear that the fixed exchange rate regime meshes poorly with a free capital account. Any move towards capital market liberalisation must be predicated on an acceptance of a floating exchange rate regime, either on a stand-alone basis, or as part of a currency union (such as the CFA zone in francophone Africa).

Irrationality and contagion

A final set of arguments questions the rationality of market expectations. At its most extreme, this view sees markets as driven by whim and irrational fads. For example, Stiglitz (2002, p. 100) writes – 'Capital market liberalization made the developing countries subject to both the rational and irrational whims of the investor community, to their irrational exuberance or pessimism.'

A less extreme version of the argument sees markets as unable or unwilling to discriminate between different emerging market economies, with the effect that problems in one country are generalised across other related or unrelated countries. There was a widespread view during the Asian crisis that financial markets appeared to exhibit contagion of this sort. For example, Cooper (1998, p. 15) claimed 'the large outflows from Malaysia following the Thai crisis in July 1997 was a case of pure contagion; it was economically disruptive, with little useful allocative or signalling effect. From London or New York, all of South-East Asia is a blurred spot in the world and traders . . . issued their sell orders before asking discriminating questions.'

Market irrationality and contagion arguments have the opposite implication from Dornbusch's (1998) market discipline arguments. In effect, they imply that governments may be disciplined for offences they did not commit, or perhaps were only considering.

The fact that a number of countries simultaneously experience similar problems does not in itself imply contagion. However, one does not need to subscribe to the view that traders in the world's leading investment institutions are less bright than academics to understand the possibility of contagion. The crucial elements in a model which has this implication are set out by De Long *et al.* (1990) (see also Shleifer, 2000). These models are developed in relation to equities but the translation to international portfolio investment is immediate. The crucial assumption is that there is a group of poorly informed investors who form expectations extrapolatively and not rationally. We might also suppose, in the context of the Asian crisis, that they incorrectly regarded South-East Asia as homogeneous. Informed traders will have been aware of the different circumstances of different countries, but were also aware of the misperceptions of the remainder of the market. Consider a speculatively based outflow of a country with solid fundamentals. With sufficiently long horizons, the informed investors would have taken advantage of the outflow to buy the mispriced assets. However, the De Long *et al.* model implies that, if the informed traders were constrained to produce short-term returns, they might not be able to risk the possibility of a failure of prices to revert over the required horizon. In this case, they would also have withdrawn their funds despite their knowledge that there was no fundamental basis for this. In essence, they speculate on the behaviour of the irrational or uninformed investors. This model is reminiscent of the Keynesian 'beauty contest'.[7]

Can countries with liberalised capital accounts avoid contagion? The examples of Singapore, and to a lesser extent Hong Kong, suggest an affirmative

---

[7] An alternative arbitrage pricing theory (APT) route to the same conclusion is to see investors as thinking of their portfolio allocation in terms of different asset classes reflecting different dimensions of risk. A rise in the price of emerging-market risk will affect their required returns, and hence their holdings, of portfolio investments in all emerging markets. This prompts the question of whether there is indeed a common emerging-market risk component, or whether this is an irrational perception.

answer. The crucial element is to reduce public misperceptions with regard to asset values. The Asian countries which suffered most from contagion were those which scored relatively poorly on corporate transparency and financial supervision. Lack of transparency increases the scope for misinformed trading while poor financial supervision can make it difficult for investors to distinguish between problems arising out of inadequate liquidity and from those deriving from low profitability. But although capital market liberalisation requires financial discipline, it appears doubtful that this will ever completely insulate a country from contagion.

As such, this is not an argument against capital account liberalisation but an indication that countries which do liberalise must have policies and institutional arrangements which allow them to pursue sensible economic policies without being deflected by irrational capital market movements. Because fixed exchange rates both encourage short-term flows (by lowering the speculative downside risk) and increase the costs of these flows, a floating exchange rate and a clear and transparent monetary regime are the most important of these arrangements.

4 Our assessment

The argument of this chapter is that the advanced country paradigm – well-regulated financial markets, strong macroeconomic policy-making institutions (with an independent Central Bank, floating exchange rate and low budget deficits), well-regulated financial institutions and a liberalised capital account – is the end to which all countries will ultimately be aiming (Knight, Schembri and Powell, chapter 5 in this volume). If countries have the capacity to undertake this full economic liberalisation package, capital account liberalisation will be an integral part of this first-best policy and will be welfare-enhancing. But if countries do not have the capacity to undertake full economic liberalisation, capital account liberalisation may not only be impracticable – the second-best argument suggests that it may lead to a reduction in welfare. It could also increase vulnerability to financial crises.

Concerns of this sort have focused attention on the optimal sequencing of economic reform. McKinnon (1993) argues that capital account liberalisation should come after fiscal reform, liberalisation of the domestic capital market and current account liberalisation. We agree that these are necessary *conditions* for the successful liberalisation of the capital account. Indeed, we would add two further requirements to this list. A successful liberalisation of the capital account requires a modern financial system with a move away from an over-guaranteed, bank-based system. It also requires a floating exchange rate (see Irwin and Vines, 2004). However, these conclusions about the sequencing of economic reform require qualification in two respects:

(a) Some of the reforms which are necessary conditions for a successful capital account liberalisation might themselves require the removal of capital account restrictions if they are to succeed. This undermines the sequencing argument: capital account liberalisation and the associated institutional and policy reforms should be seen as a package to be pursued concurrently. A prime example is the move from fixed to floating exchange rates. This, we have argued, is a necessary condition for capital account liberalisation. A well-functioning floating exchange rate requires a foreign exchange market of sufficient depth, including futures and swap markets. But it is difficult to see how this depth can be achieved in an environment in which capital controls remain in place. Both policies – capital account liberalisation and a move to a floating exchange rate – must, therefore, be pursued at the same time.

(b) Political economy considerations suggest that a staged approach may provide policy-makers with an excuse for prolonging bad policy. It is relatively easy for politicians, who are generally beneficiaries from the status quo, to agree in principle to reforms, but to emphasise the practical difficulties of satisfying the required preconditions. Sequencing considerations may also weaken the incentive to develop good policy. For example, we have already argued that capital controls can reduce the real interest rate, thereby cutting debt-servicing costs, and as a result weaken the incentive to refrain from a profligate fiscal policy. Sequencing arguments make sense if there is a genuine commitment to reform, but otherwise may be little more than a ploy for attracting assistance without implementing difficult policies.

The role of the IMF and other international organisations

Our assessment suggests that an orderly economic liberalisation is necessarily a complicated exercise, in terms of scope, sequencing and technical detail. Vines (1997, 2000) reviews four broad reasons why international institutions, including the IMF, are inevitably important as a source of research and policy advice on the relevant aspects of reform, such as current account liberalisation, industrial policy, financial market structure and regulation and the fiscal and monetary policy framework:

(a) Many national governments of poorer countries cannot afford or cannot get access to the resources required to design a comprehensive reform package. Thus the advice of international organisations becomes a form of technical assistance.
(b) There are significant economies of scale and scope in the provision of such analysis and this analysis is also an international public good (because the theory of macroeconomic policy is partly comparative).
(c) Agencies such as the IMF are uniquely placed to offer frank advice which stresses both weaknesses and required remedies.
(d) Agencies such as the IMF can develop an ongoing working relationship with a country to help it solve its problems, and to build policy credibility. This does not merely involve one-off advice, but continuing policy assistance.

The last three of these reasons mean that it is difficult to see how private suppliers could effectively provide the technical assistance to any large degree if it were not provided by international agencies. Economies of scale and scope, and the need for a continuing relationship, suggest that any attempt to substitute in this way would be dogged by market failure. Alternatively if the governments of advanced countries were to attempt to provide such advice directly, government-to-government, the result would be direct bilateral power relationships of a neo-imperialistic kind. The IMF is a multilateral institution. This gives it a legitimacy when it offers assistance in the solution of policy problems in developing countries.

Many may regard this view as simplistic and over-optimistic. The IMF has not always been perceived as a disinterested and dispassionate body which offers impartial advice to governments. Its detractors would tend to characterise it as an institution which is irredeemably wedded to a free market ideology and which uses crises to impose that model on governments which would prefer to operate according to more interventionist models. Such critics suggest that the location, the voting structure of the IMF and its recruiting policies make it unlikely that IMF advice could ever be dispassionate and certainly that it would never be seen as such. These concerns, whether or not justifiable, undermine the perceived legitimacy of the IMF. If we are correct in seeing an increased future role for the IMF as a persuader, with the implication that liberalisation policies will be more effectively 'owned', it is important that it addresses the legitimacy issue directly. Failure to do this will undermine its effectiveness and will reinforce the hands of its critics.

There is a role for other international organisations, as well as the IMF. But the various areas of required activity do not partition neatly among the relevant agencies. While the IMF may be the natural agency to lead on Central Bank conduct and organisation, the World Bank and the regional development banks may be the more appropriate lead agencies with regard to industrial policy. In development of domestic banking, there is a very clear role on which the International Financial Corporation (IFC) should be encouraged to lead.[8] The overall message, however, is that the long-run objective of capital account liberalisation increases the urgency of other reforms which are desirable on their own merits, and the various multilateral agencies should work together to encourage and assist governments in moving in this direction.

There is a clear need for further investment in research by the Fund and the other international institutions in order for them to be better able to provide this public good. We know much about the dangers and potential benefits of capital account liberalisation and we have identified broad conditions for an orderly and efficient liberalisation. However, there is much that we still need to learn about the detail. Fischer (1998, p. 8) remarks that: 'The difference between the analytic understanding of capital- versus current-account restrictions is striking. The economics profession knows a great deal about current-account liberalization, its desirability, and effective ways of liberalizing. It knows far less about capital-account liberalization. It is time to bring order to both thinking and policy on the capital account.'

Take, for example, the requirement for a reformed financial sector. Above we have identified the key priorities as: moving away from a system underpinned by guarantees to one based on prudential regulation; the development of modern methods of risk management; improved CARs; and enhanced loan-loss provisioning. There are many other requirements that could be added to this 'wish-list'. But such reforms are not achieved without cost and there are very significant practical problems in securing them (Garber, 1998). Some of these reforms are more important than others. And in no case is reform black and white: there is more than one model that can be followed. Individual countries come from a variety of starting points in terms of economic and institutional development and face different political and economic constraints. This suggests the sort of advice that is required must be extremely sophisticated and be tailored to the particular circumstances of each case. The IMF does not yet have the technical capacity to provide such advice to the extent required, and much more research, and capability building, is needed within the Fund.

The IMF's articles of agreement

As we noted in the introduction the IMF has, since 1998, been debating the stance it should take on capital market liberalisation. Two changes to the Fund's articles of agreement have been proposed: first, that its purposes should be

---

[8] The IFC is the part of the World Bank which lends to private sector corporations without any government guarantee. It also takes equity shares in private sector organisations.

extended to include the liberalisation of capital account transactions; and second, that it should be given jurisdiction over capital movements (IMF, 1997). Jurisdiction might be obtained by amending article VIII, which presently requires members to avoid restrictions on current payments, subject to the transitional arrangements outlined in article XIV. Extending the scope of this article to cover capital payments would mean that Fund approval would be required for both the maintenance of pre-existing capital account restrictions, under the transitional arrangements, and for additional temporary restrictions which might be required for prudential reasons or in the face of macroeconomic or financial instability.

We advocate a cautious 'yes' to the first proposal, but a firm 'no' to the second, at least for the time being. Our cautious approval of the first proposal stems from two roots. First, our assessment in this chapter of the pros and cons of capital liberalisation has led us to conclude that this should be one of the ultimate goals of economic policy. Amending the purposes of the IMF in this way would signal that a consensus existed surrounding this objective. Second, the promotion of capital liberalization is already a *de facto* purpose of existing IMF operations: as Polak (1998, p. 52) notes: 'the Fund has whole-heartedly embraced capital liberalization in its surveillance, financing, and technical assistance activities'. Formalising this would both clarify and solidify this commitment.

Our caution follows from our recognition that capital liberalisation forms just one part of a large set of reforms which developing countries should ultimately seek to embrace, and that many of these reforms are required either before, or concurrent with, capital liberalisation, in order for it to be successful. The removal of capital restrictions before these other reforms are in place is undesirable, and the promotion of capital account liberalisation should therefore be qualified. Furthermore, we have noted that capital liberalisation will increase vulnerability to financial crises, because, in particular, of the volatility of short-term capital flows. The recent experience of crises in East Asia and elsewhere has heightened this concern. This also underlines the importance of having an adequate mechanism for the resolution of crises when they do occur. The present international financial architecture is inadequate in this respect. In section 5 we discuss how we think it ought to be strengthened in order to provide such a mechanism.

Remarkably little has been published by the Fund, or by others, to suggest why it should be given jurisdiction over capital restrictions. The most common argument is that this will improve the credibility of the commitment by member countries to capital account liberalisation. Fischer (1998, p. 9) suggests that the acceptance of an extended article VIII by a member country would 'send a clear signal of its intentions to the international financial community, possibly strengthening thereby its access to international markets'. This strengthened access would presumably be manifested in a reduction in the premium demanded by international investors to compensate for the risk of additional capital restrictions being imposed. No attempt has been made to quantify the potential magnitude of this effect. However, its significance is questionable, because it is likely that those countries willing to accept such an amendment are those for which the risk premium is already small.

A further argument in favour of the extension of jurisdiction could be that it subjects the policies of the liberalising country to greater scrutiny. This would increase the transparency of these policies and so reduce uncertainty surrounding them. Quirk and Evans (1995) advance a further argument for extending the scope of article VIII, that it is desirable to treat current and capital payments consistently. They state that this would 'remove ambiguous administrative separations between the current and capital transactions that have on occasion impede elimination of controls on current account transactions' (1995, n. 28). They argue that this is an important reason why a number of countries is still subject to the transitional arrangements with regard to current account liberalisation.

On the other hand, there are at least two reasons why an extension of IMF jurisdiction to cover capital flows, either by an extension of article VIII or by some other means, would be undesirable:

(a) It could increase the pressure on the IMF to provide more generous financing when members face crises as the result of an unexpected outflow of capital. Extending the jurisdiction of the Fund to cover capital restrictions would create a responsibility to ensure that the liberalisation process was orderly and therefore an obligation to act if crises did occur. This is at a time when IMF funding is already widely regarded as being inadequate. The importance of this problem will depend, in part, on whether capital liberalisation makes crises more or less likely to occur. There are two opposing views here.[9] One holds that if capital liberalisation is undertaken in the right conditions the improved access to international capital markets will reduce the frequency with which the IMF is called upon to provide financing. The other, which we support, holds that, in practice, given the volatility of unrestricted capital flows, widespread capital liberalisation will make crises more likely, even if the liberalisation process is generally well managed. The East Asian crisis is at least *prima facie* evidence that the second view is correct, although this is tempered by the recognition that considerable mistakes were made in the liberalisations undertaken in that region.

---

[9] According to IMF (1997), the IMF Directors are themselves split on this issue.

(b) We have argued that capital liberalisation is just one element of a comprehensive liberalisation package. Managing this process and fitting the package of reform to the needs of a wide range of different member countries will require a level of expertise that does not currently exist anywhere, let alone at the IMF. This expertise must be developed within the Fund before any extension of its jurisdiction is considered.

Of these problems, (a) is probably the most serious. Even without any extension to the mandate of the Fund the trend growth in the volume of private sector capital flows suggest that the demands on its resources will grow over time. Consequently, the current political impetus is toward a reduction in its obligations, rather than an extension. In section 5 we argue for an alternative approach to the resolution of crises that would rely on standstills rather than the provision of huge loans by the IMF. Such a change would side-step the problem identified here, but as yet only modest progress has been made in this direction.

Problem (b) can, and should, be addressed over time. This ought to be a research priority of the Fund irrespective of whether it assumes jurisdiction over capital restrictions.

Polak (1998) argues that extending the Fund's jurisdiction to the capital account will be counterproductive. He argues that it will restrict the actions of the IMF staff and consequently inhibit the process of liberalisation. He states that: 'If given jurisdiction over such restrictions, the staff is likely to become the enforcer of the new legal code, making sure at each step that any policy it recommends or endorses can pass the test of the new Article. If not burdened with this legal task, the staff can be the unbiased adviser of member countries on the benefits and costs of capital liberalization and a reliable source of information about best practices in this field' (1998, p. 52).

On balance it would appear that the benefits from the extension of the Fund's jurisdiction are likely to be low, and the potential costs are currently large. At present, therefore, such a move would be unwise. Instead of assuming jurisdiction over capital restrictions the Fund should be restricted to the *advocacy* of orderly capital account liberalisation.

5 Conclusion

We live in a world in which international capital markets are becoming increasingly integrated. There are many advantages in this, as the experience of advanced industrial countries shows. In particular, we believe that capital market liberalisation is an important development objective at which all countries should aim. We see this as a necessary component in the development of a competitive and efficient financial sector and as the way out of endemic financial market repression. We see the beneficial effects of liberalisation as coming primarily via this route, rather than through possible effects on investment or by disciplining governments to adopt better macroeconomic policies.

Despite our enthusiasm for liberalisation, we acknowledge that the experience in East Asia during the 1990s suggests that we should pause before arguing that developing countries should rapidly move to embrace open international capital accounts. We have argued that, in the absence of the appropriate institutional reform, a move to capital account convertibility may not be welfare-improving and may increase vulnerability to financial crises. If and when crises do occur, the outcomes can be very costly. And if such crises are not well handled, they can also be politically destabilising, and can undermine support for the whole process of liberalisation and global integration. That will in turn reduce countries' growth prospects.

Capital account liberalisation should be regarded as one element of a wider package of economic reforms to which developing countries should aspire. The most important of these is the move away from fixed exchange rates to a freely floating regime, either on a stand-alone basis or as part of a currency union. In many ways, that is the more important reform, and capital account liberalisation should be placed in that context.

The IMF has an important role in the promotion of this economic reform and its purposes should be extended to include the liberalisation of the capital account so as to formalise this. Its jurisdiction should not, however, be extended at present to cover capital account restrictions. The most important contribution that the IMF can make in this context is by offering advice to governments and Central Banks based both on its extended experience and on a sound and impartial reading of relevant theory. But if this advice is to be accepted as impartial, the IMF will need to devote greater attention to ownership than has always been the case in the past. The objective must be that governments choose to liberalise their capital accounts because they perceive this to be in the long-term interests of their citizens, and not because this is imposed. In those circumstances, the IMF should stand ready to assist with the short-term costs that may be associated with liberalisation.

REFERENCES

Bevan, D., P. Collier and J. W. Gunning (1990). *Controlled Open Economies: A Neo-Classical Approach to Structuralism*. Oxford, Oxford University Press

Bosworth, B. P. and S. M. Collins (1999). 'Capital Flows to Developing Countries: Implications for Savings and Investment', *Brookings Papers on Economic Activity*, 1, 143–80

Collier, P. and J. W. Gunning (1999). 'Explaining African Economic Performance', *Journal of Economic Literature*, 37, 64–111

Cooper, R. (1998). 'Should Capital-Account Convertibility be a World Objective?', in S. Fischer *et al.*, 'Should the IMF Pursue Capital-Account Convertibility?', *Essays in International Finance*, 207, Princeton University
  (1999). 'Should Capital Controls be Banished?', *Brookings Papers on Economic Activity*, 1, 89–141
Corbett, J., G. Irwin and D. Vines (1999). 'From Asian Miracle to Asian Crisis: Why Vulnerability, Why Collapse?', in D. Gruen and L. Gower (eds.), *Capital Flows and the International Financial System*. Reserve Bank of Australia.
De Long, J. B., A. Shleifer, L. Summers and R. Waldmann (1990). 'Noise Trader Risk in Financial Markets', *Journal of Political Economy*, 98, 703–38
Deaton, A. (1992a). 'Saving and Income Smoothing in Côte d'Ivoire', *Journal of African Economics*, 1, 1–24
  (1992b). *Understanding Consumption*. Oxford, Oxford University Press
Dehn, J. (2000). 'Commodity Price Uncertainty and Shocks: Implications for Investment and Growth', D.Phil. thesis, University of Oxford
Diamond, D. W. and P. H. Dybvig (1983). 'Bank Runs, Deposit Insurance, and Liquidity', *Journal of Political Economy*, 91(3), 401–19
Diaz-Alejandro, C. (1985). 'Good-bye Financial Repression, Hello Financial Crisis', *Journal of Development Economics*, 19, 1–24
Dooley, M. P. (1996). 'A Survey of the Literature on Controls on International Capital Transactions', IMF Staff Papers, 43, 639–87
Dooley, M. P. and C. E. Walsh (1999). 'Academic Views on Capital Flows: An Expanding Universe', in D. Gruen and L. Gower (eds.), *Capital Flows and the International Financial System*, Reserve Bank of Australia.
Dornbusch, R. (1998). 'Capital Controls: An Idea Whose Time is Past', in S. Fischer *et al.*, 'Should the IMF Pursue Capital-Account Convertibility?', *Essays in International Finance*, 207, Princeton University
Eichengreen, B., P. Masson, M. Savastano and S. Sharma (1999). 'Transition Strategies and Nominal Anchors on the Road to Greater Exchange Rate Flexibility', *Essays in International Finance*, 213, Princeton University
Fane, G. (1998). 'The Role of Prudential Regulation', in R. H. McLeod and R. Garnaut (eds.), *East Asia in Crisis: From Being a Miracle to Needing One*. London, Routledge
Fischer, S. (1998). 'Capital Account Liberalisation and the Role of the IMF', in S. Fischer *et al.*, 'Should the IMF Pursue Capital-Account Convertibility?', *Essays in International Finance*, 207, Princeton University
Garber, P. M. (1998). 'Buttressing Capital Account Liberalisation with Prudential Regulation and Foreign Entry', in S. Fischer *et al.*, 'Should the IMF Pursue Capital-Account Convertibility?', *Essays in International Finance*, 207, Princeton University
Gilbert, C., G. Irwin and D. Vines (2001). 'Capital Account Convertibility, Poor Developing Countries, and International Financial Architecture', *Development Policy Review*, 19(1), 121–40
Giovannini, A. and M. de Melo (1993). 'Government Revenue from Financial Repression', *American Economic Review*, 83, 953–63

International Monetary Fund (IMF) (1997). *Annual Report for 1997*, Washington, DC, IMF

Irwin, G. and D. Vines (1999). 'A Krugman–Dooley–Sachs Third Generation Model of the Asian Financial Crisis', *Global Economic Institutions Working Paper*, 46, London Centre for Economic Policy Research

(2000). 'Government Guarantees, Investment, and Vulnerability to Financial Crisis', CEPR Discussion Paper, 2652, December; forthcoming in *Review of International Economics*

(2004). 'Preconditions for Capital Account Liberalisation: Lessons from East Asia', in C. Mayer (ed.), *Financial Instability*. Oxford, Oxford University Press, forthcoming

King, M. (1999). 'Reforming the International Financial System: The Middle Way', speech delivered to a session of the Money Marketers at the Federal Reserve Bank of New York, 9 September

King, R. G. and R. Levine (1993). 'Finance, Entrepreneurship and Growth: Theory and Evidence', *Journal of Monetary Economics*, 32, 513–42

Krugman, P. (2001). 'What Happened to Asia?', in G. Irwin and D. Vines (eds.), *Financial Market Integration and International Capital Flows*. Cheltenham, Edward Elgar

McKinnon, R. I. (1973). *Money and Capital in Economic Development*. Washington, DC, Brookings Institution

(1993). *The Order of Economic Liberalisation: Financial Control in the Transition to a Market Economy*, 2nd edn. Baltimore, MD, Johns Hopkins University Press

McKinnon, R. and H. Pill (1997). 'Credible Economic Liberalisations and Overborrowing', *American Economic Review*, 87(2), 189–203

Obstfeld, M. (1986). 'Rational and Self-Fulfilling Balance-of-Payments Crises', *American Economic Review*, 76(1), 72–81

(1991), 'The Destabilising Effects of Exchange-Rate Escape Clauses', NBER Working Paper, 3603

(1994), 'The Logic of Currency Crises', NBER Working Paper, 4640

(1995). 'Models of Currency Crises with Self-Fulfilling Features', NBER Working Paper, 5285

Polak, J. J. (1998). 'The Articles of Agreement of the IMF and the Liberalization of Capital Movements' in S. Fischer *et al.*, 'Should the IMF Pursue Capital-Account Convertibility?', *Essay in International Finance*, 207, Princeton University

Quinn, D. (1997). 'The Correlates of Changes in International Financial Regulation', *American Political Science Review*, 91, 531–51

Quirk, P. J. and O. Evans (1995). 'Capital Account Convertibility: Review of the Experience and Implications for IMF Policies', International Monetary Fund Occasional Paper, 131, October

Razin, A. and E. Sadka (1991). 'Efficient Investment Incentives in the Presence of Capital Flight', *Journal of International Economics*, 31, 171–81

Rodrik, D. (1998). 'Who Needs Capital-Account Convertibility?', in S. Fischer *et al.*, 'Should the IMF Pursue Capital-Account Convertibility?', *Essays in International Finance*, 207, Princeton University

Schneider, B. (2001). 'Issues in Capital Account Convertibility in Developing Countries', *Development Policy Review*, 19(1), 31–82

Shleifer, A. (2000). *Inefficient Markets*. Oxford, Oxford University Press

Shaw, E. S. (1973). *Financial Deepening in Economic Development*. New York, Oxford University Press

Stiglitz, J. E. (2002). *Globalization and its Discontents*. London, Allen Lane

Vines, D. (1997). 'The Fund, The Bank, and The WTO: Functions, Competencies, and Reform Agendas', Global Economic Institutions Working Paper, 26, London, Centre for Economic Policy Research

(2000). 'Reforming the Architecture of Global Economic Institutions: An Outline of the Issues', paper presented to the meeting on Reforming the Architecture of Global Economic Institutions, Bank of England, 5–6 May

Warr, P. (1998). 'Thailand', in R. H. McLeod and R. Garnaut (eds.), *East Asia in Crisis: From Being a Miracle to Needing One*. London, Routledge

Williamson, J. and M. Mahar (1998). 'A Survey of Financial liberalisation', *Essays in International Finance*, 211, Princeton University

Wyplosz, C. (1986). 'Capital Controls and Balance of Payments Crises', *Journal of International Money and Finance*, 5, 167–79

8　The resolution of international financial crises: an alternative framework

ANDREW G. HALDANE AND MARK KRUGER

1 Introduction

Since the mid-1990s, the incidence of financial crises among emerging-market countries appears to have increased (Hoggarth and Saporta, 2001). In response, governments and international financial institutions have worked intensively on ways to reduce the likelihood and virulence of crises. This is the debate on the so-called 'international financial architecture' (see, for example, Eichengreen, 2002, for an overview).

There is now a fairly widespread consensus within the official community on appropriate crisis-*prevention* measures (King, 1999; Eichengreen, 2002). For example, the best defence against financial crises is to establish sound macro-economic fundamentals and to have a credible policy framework in place to deal with economic and financial shocks. A broad international consensus has also emerged on the importance of prudent balance sheet management, with a particular focus on the balance sheet positions of governments and the financial system. Considerable work has also been done by international groups to establish codes and standards of best public policy practice. The official community should not be prescriptive about the adoption of standards. But it should promote transparency about the degree of country compliance with them (see Drage and Mann, 1999).

Even with such prevention measures in place, however, crises will still occur from time to time. Moreover, there is less consensus among policy-makers on appropriate crisis-*resolution* measures in these circumstances. This fact is well recognised by, among others, the IMF (Krueger, 2001). The IMF has responded

The authors wish to acknowledge the substantial input and involvement of Paul Jenkins, Senior Deputy Governor, Bank of Canada and Mervyn King, Governor, Bank of England. The chapter has also benefited from the comments and criticisms of a great many members of the official community and academe – too many to list in full here.

to crises by providing often large-scale lending packages, conditional on the implementation of macroeconomic and structural reform. These programmes are intended to offer bridging finance to the debtor. And this combination of reform plus bridging finance is in turn intended to help catalyse private sector capital flows.

But there is a concern that official lending on this scale may also undermine the incentives of debtors and creditors operating in international capital markets – a moral hazard risk. And the lack of *ex ante* clarity about the scale of official assistance represents an additional source of risk for borrowers and lenders operating in these markets. It may also serve to delay negotiations between debtors and creditors should repayment problems arise.

Against that backdrop, this chapter sets out an alternative framework for the resolution of international financial crises. The framework has the following ingredients. It is based on a presumption that multilateral official finance is limited in size. These limits mean that there would be some point at which the private sector would necessarily be involved in resolving crises.

The precise form of private sector involvement will depend on the crisis at hand. A range of private sector involvement options are possible, including voluntary debt rollovers and bond exchanges. From time to time, the crisis may necessitate the debtor calling a temporary payments standstill. This can be done in an orderly fashion, with support from the IMF, so as to benefit creditors as well as debtors. The framework allows for IMF lending limits to be breached in exceptional circumstances. But such exceptional financing would be subject to strict procedural safeguards.

In one sense, the proposal made here is a modest one because all of its elements already exist. The key difference is that here these elements are put together in the context of a sequenced and structured crisis resolution framework. Sequenced because the resolution of a crisis can be traced out as a chronological decision tree; and structured because the framework aims to align the incentives of all parties to a crisis. In this way, the incidence and cost of crises would potentially be reduced. The framework outlined has parallels, in some respects, with the proposal put forward by the IMF (Krueger, 2001).

The chapter is planned as follows. Section 2 briefly summarises the existing spectrum of proposals for resolving crises, while section 3 sets out some shortfalls in the current approach to crisis resolution by the official sector. Section 4 sets out the key ingredients of the alternative framework proposed here, including a discussion of possible criticisms of the proposal. Section 5 discusses the provision of exceptional finance, while section 6 draws together the key elements of the framework as a chronological sequence. Section 7 sets the proposal alongside the alternative model outlined by the IMF. Section 8 concludes.

2 A spectrum of approaches to crisis resolution

There has been intense debate among academics and policy-makers on the best approach to crisis-resolution. At one end of the spectrum, some have suggested that the IMF could provide emergency liquidity assistance in potentially unlimited amounts – an international lender of last resort (LOLR). At the other end, official finance is seen by some as part of the problem.

Fischer (1999) argues that not only is there a need for an international LOLR, but that the IMF has *de facto* taken on this role. He argues that it is not necessary for an international LOLR to be able to issue liquidity in order to be effective. What is needed, in most cases, is the reallocation of resources from liquid to illiquid entities. Since the IMF is akin to a credit union, potential borrowers have access to a pool of resources that the IMF can on-lend from member countries. In addition, Fischer notes that the IMF can borrow from the General Arrangements to Borrow (GAB) or the New Arrangements to Borrow (NAB), where necessary.

The International Financial Institutions Advisory Commission (2000), the 'Meltzer Commission', also recommends that the IMF act as an international LOLR (see also chapter 4 in this volume). Liquidity loans would have short maturity (120 days, with one rollover), be made at a penalty rate and be collateralised by a clear priority claim on the borrower's assets. Moreover, loans would be made only to countries that had met stringent preconditions, including on financial soundness.

Schwartz (2000) argues that official financial institutions engender moral hazard and so do more harm than good. She notes that the private sector successfully dealt with financial panics in the latter part of the nineteenth century by relying on clearing house loan certificates by private sector clearing houses. Thus, Schwartz recommends that 'in the interest of a more stable and more free international economy' the IMF be abolished, not reformed.

These approaches are unlikely to be optimal. Turning the IMF into an international LOLR is impractical as there is neither the capacity nor the political will to provide official money in unlimited amounts with the requisite speed. It is also undesirable because of the risk of moral hazard affecting both debtors and creditors. This would hinder the efficient intermediation of funds from developed to developing countries.

Equally, a world without official finance would also be suboptimal. This would ensure the maximum degree of private sector involvement. But crisis-resolution would come about through a combination of greater policy adjustment by the debtor and/or greater financing by the private sector. So output losses would be sharp and payment interruptions frequent and disorderly. Such an outcome would have adverse consequences for creditors as well as debtors – a deadweight cost. In short, it too would hinder the efficient functioning of the international financial system.

Between these two extremes, there is a middle way. This would recognise that modest amounts of official money can serve as a deterrent to self-fulfilling crises and provide time for policy adjustment. For example, the Independent Task Force sponsored by the Council on Foreign Relations (1999) argued that the IMF should return to normal lending limits for crises that do not pose a systemic threat. In exceptional circumstances, the IMF should turn to the NAB/GAB or a 'contagion facility'. And activation of the systemic facilities would require a supermajority decision by creditors.

3 The current framework for crisis resolution

Some progress has also been made by the official sector in cultivating that middle way. For example, the statement by the G7 at the Cologne Summit in 1999 set down some principles and tools for dealing with crises. By themselves, however, these principles and tools do not constitute a fully fledged framework for crisis-resolution. We know the ingredients of such a framework, but still lack a recipe for combining them. In this respect, we would highlight two aspects of the current framework that warrant attention.

First, there is a need for greater clarity regarding the amount of official financing. The size of official packages has varied considerably across recent IMF programmes. And in a number of recent large-country cases, normal IMF access limits have been breached, often by a significant margin. Too much discretion regarding official actions leads to confusion among debtors and creditors and time-consistency problems among policy-makers. Greater clarity about the scale of official financing would help to condition the actions and expectations of debtors and creditors about the roles they are expected to play in resolving crises.

Second, some of the crisis-resolution tools identified by the official sector have so far been under-utilised. One example would be the inclusion of collective-action clauses in bond contracts to facilitate debt restructuring. Another would be a payments standstill, which provides a debtor with temporary respite from debt payments and allows for an orderly work-out of debt problems. Too often in the past, sovereign default has been disorderly, with the work-out process slow, inefficient and inequitable. A better approach would recognise that default is a natural feature of the market mechanism, not something to be avoided at all costs. But it would seek to limit the costs of sovereign default when they do occur.

4 A clear framework

The framework presented here aims to strike a balance between official lending, debtor adjustment and private sector involvement, recognising that each has a role to play in the resolution of crises. But those roles and responsibilities need to be made clear *ex ante* to all parties. Indeed, this is precisely the role of a crisis-resolution framework.

The five key elements of this proposed framework are as follows:

(1) A presumption of limited official finance
(2) The nature of private sector involvement
(3) The role of standstills
(4) Standstill guidelines
(5) Potential costs of standstills.

A presumption of limited official finance

When crises strike, macroeconomic policies have to be adjusted to offset the adverse effects of shocks. But policy adjustment usually takes time. If policy is not credible, or if financial markets are impatient, then the prospect of adjustment may not be sufficient to change expectations. A country can fall victim to a self-fulfilling speculative attack.

Official money can help in these circumstances, serving as bridging finance during the period of domestic adjustment and helping catalyse private capital flows. But such lending needs to be limited, to prevent the adjustment incentives of debtors from being dented, or official money simply substituting for private capital flows. For this reason, there should be a clear presumption that 'normal' official lending limits apply in times of crisis.

Greater clarity about the limits on IMF lending would deliver three important benefits. First, it would reduce uncertainty, among both creditors and debtors, about the extent of the public sector contribution. Private creditors demand compensation for that uncertainty through a risk premium, which increases the cost of borrowing for emerging markets. A clearer framework for crisis-resolution would reduce that uncertainty premium, to the benefit of both debtors and creditors.

Second, limits would reduce the potential for the private sector to game the official sector into providing more money *ex post* than would have been optimal *ex ante*. The official sector has to strike a balance between the need to resolve the current financial crisis and the need to prevent future financial crises. In short, the official sector faces a time-consistency problem (Kydland and Prescott, 1977).

This balance between *ex ante* and *ex post* efficiency is familiar from a corporate bankruptcy context (Eichengreen and Portes, 1995). The IMF faces a similar dilemma (Miller and Zhang, 1999). As Rogoff (1999) argues, bailouts by the IMF encourage greater risk-taking by industrialised country banks, and those banks are also likely to take risks because of domestic support arrangements.

Policy-makers are, of course, familiar with the time-consistency problem. It crops up in all fields of public policy – fiscal, monetary, regulatory, etc. In response, they have often adopted clearer public policy frameworks. For example, in the monetary policy sphere, inflation targeting combines clarity about the objective of policy – the inflation target – with discretion about how best to achieve this target. It is a framework of 'constrained discretion', with clear roles and responsibilities for the different players. This helps mitigate time-consistency problems in monetary policy.

The adoption of a clear framework for crisis resolution could offer the international financial community similar time-consistency benefits. It would set out the presumptive constraints on official lending. And debtors and creditors would then have the discretion to operate in their own best interests, subject to these constraints.

Some have argued that the official sector should pursue a policy of 'constructive ambiguity' in the resolution of crises. An analogy is sometimes made with domestic lender of last resort facilities, where ambiguity is used to mitigate moral hazard. But international moral hazard can be mitigated in ways that do not introduce costly uncertainty into the framework for crisis-resolution – for example, by limiting lending.

Third, a related benefit of lending limits is that they would guard against moral hazard. Moral hazard applies to both debtors (by blunting incentives to undertake the necessary adjustment and reform) and creditors (by blunting incentives to undertake effective risk management). Moral hazard is clearly a question of degree. Every insurance contract possesses some degree of moral hazard. And the empirical evidence on the moral hazard effects of official lending is not conclusive (see, for example, Dell'Ariccia, Godde and Zettelmeyer, 2002). Nevertheless, anecdotal evidence of the importance of moral hazard is widespread. And the longer the current system of non-binding lending limits persists, the greater the scope for moral hazard to increase in the future.

The nature of private sector involvement

While there is broad agreement on the need for private sector involvement in crisis-resolution, there is still uncertainty about what precisely it means and how best to bring it about (Haldane, 1999).

Crisis lending by the official sector and private sector involvement are two sides of the same coin. So with limited IMF lending, private sector involvement would at some stage become an element in resolving all crises.

The precise form of private sector involvement is, above all, a choice for the debtor country, in consultation with its creditors. A spectrum of private sector involvement options is possible. Both voluntary solutions (such as bond exchanges and debt rollovers) and involuntary solutions (such as standstills) should be acceptable, in principle, by the official community. The role of the official sector is to make clear on what terms and conditions official finance will be available, and the limits of that finance. The debtor country must then decide for itself which option to take. The appropriate option will depend on the specifics of the crisis at hand.

In the majority of crisis cases, it should be possible for debtors to secure private sector involvement voluntarily, either by raising new money in the markets, or by reprofiling existing money in consultation with creditors. This has worked effectively in helping resolve crises in the past – for example, in Korea in 1997 and in Brazil in 1999. For countries with unsustainable debt burdens, market-based bond exchanges which write down the face value of debt outstanding – for example, as in Pakistan in 1999 and Ukraine and Ecuador in 2000 – are a second voluntary means of resolving crises.

On occasions, however, the combination of limited IMF lending and policy adjustment may be inadequate to mobilise sufficient private finance on a voluntary basis – for example, if capital flight is pervasive. In such situations, it would be counterproductive for the official sector to continue financing private capital flight. What is needed is some backstop measure to provide debtors and creditors with a breathing space to arrive at a cooperative outcome – a standstill.

The role of standstills

Standstills should not be construed as a way of relieving debtors of their obligation to service their debts in full and on time. Rather, they are a way of enhancing the effectiveness of the crisis management process. In particular, they offer three benefits.

First, they can promote creditor coordination. An orderly standstill can break the circuit of destabilising and, ultimately, self-fulfilling creditor expectations. By reducing creditor externalities, standstills can be a positive-sum game, advantageous for debtors and creditors alike. In a domestic context, Diamond and Dybvig (1983) show that allowing banks to suspend withdrawals can be a fully efficient mechanism for eliminating collective-action problems among creditors (see also Rogoff, 1999; Chui, Gai and Haldane, 2002).

Second, standstills can align creditor and debtor incentives. Creditors will be more willing to reach voluntary agreements quickly if there is a credible threat of a standstill. And debtors will be more willing to negotiate if they know that official monies are limited. So having standstills as a backstop should prevent the prolonged debt negotiations that have characterised a number of recent IMF programme cases. For example, in the case of Korea in late 1997, a large official assistance package did little to reduce capital flight and stabilise the balance of payments. It was only after 'the Federal Reserve Bank of New York called a meeting to convince key US banks that a rollover of their maturing interbank lines was in their own interest as not all of them could exit at the same time' that debtors and creditors were able to arrive at a solution (IMF, 2001).

Third, standstills can help ensure that payment stoppages are orderly. Standstills provide a safe harbour while debtors put in place remedial policy actions – for example, macroeconomic policy adjustment or debt restructuring. In this way, they are potentially useful both in cases where a country faces a short-term liquidity problem that necessitates the reprofiling of debt service, and in cases of unsustainable debt burdens where debt reduction is required.

The decision to call a standstill lies with the debtor. But the official sector can play a useful supporting role. Such support could take the form of the IMF's lending-into-arrears (LIA) – the provision of bridging finance. IMF lending would occur only under strict conditions, however, including the debtor negotiating with its creditors in good faith, creditors being treated equally, and the process having a definite time limit. That would ensure that debtors play fair during a standstill, neither calling them too often nor maintaining them too long. These guidelines would help ensure that a standstill was orderly.

Standstill guidelines

Standstill guidelines provide a framework for the resolution of sovereign debt problems. They are in some respects akin to bankruptcy procedures. For this reason, some have asked whether sovereign payments standstills should have a statutory basis. This would require a change in the law in all jurisdictions in which a debt contract might need to be enforced or by international treaty. The advantage of this is that it would confer legal protection on a debtor calling a standstill.

But changes in the law in many jurisdictions would also be a formidable exercise. Moreover, it is clear that countries, having sovereign rights, are different from corporations in several important respects. Sovereign debtors do not require a court's permission to call a standstill. Moreover, creditors cannot easily seize the domestic assets of a sovereign. Nor can they insist that a country's management be replaced.

Because of these differences, many of the benefits of a standstill can be achieved within a non-statutory framework, underpinned by a set of guidelines (see Council on Foreign Relations, 1999; Schwartz, 2000). These guidelines would then form the conditionality that applied to the IMF's lending-into-arrears. An illustrative set of guidelines might include:

1. *Transparency*. The debtor should communicate effectively by releasing all pertinent information to all creditors on a timely basis.
2. For the debtor to be bargaining in good faith, offers must be *reasonable*. Debtors that are illiquid should be offering rescheduling that maintains the value of their obligations in net present value (NPV) terms. If debt reduction is necessary, the amount of the haircut offered by the debtor should not be greater than necessary to achieve a sustainable medium-term debt profile.
3. Creditors should, as far as possible, be treated *equally*. This means that not only should individual creditors (foreign and domestic) within a class of instruments be treated the same, but also that holders of different instruments be treated according to the seniority of their contracts. A presumption of seniority should not be made where none exists in the debt contract.
4. *Net new money* should be granted seniority over existing claims, consistent with the 'superpriority' principle in a corporate insolvency context. Trade credit should be exempt from the standstill to help maintain production.
5. The process should be explicitly time-limited, to prevent debtors maintaining standstills too long. Should the time limit expire as a result of the debtor failing to submit a reasonable offer to creditors, then the guidelines will have been breached. If, however, the time limit expires as a result of some or all creditors failing to accept a reasonable offer made by the debtor, then the debtor is not in breach of the guidelines.

As long as the debtor is taking action that complies with the guidelines, the IMF should be willing to offer support by lending-into-arrears. With this framework in place, there would be incentives for debtors and creditors to reach timely agreement on a debt reprofiling. It would also be reasonable to hope that, for a debtor country following the guidelines, the risk of litigation from a creditor would be reduced. That is because creditors would know that when a debtor has followed the guidelines, it would be easier to persuade the courts to side with the debtor and not allow a minority creditor to grab a country's assets.

The *Elliot Associates* v. *Peru* case in 2000 shows that creditors can holdout from a negotiated agreement and press their claims through legal action. But it is far from clear that this case has set any legal precedent. And the experience of restructuring debt in Russia, Pakistan, Ukraine and Ecuador offers encouragement that litigation risk may not be that great. Either way, there is real merit in putting in place guidelines that could be used by courts in their interpretation of the behaviour of debtors and creditors.

Clearly, these guidelines would need to evolve in the light of experience, to ensure they strike the right balance between creditor moral hazard on the one hand (IMF loans financing capital flight) and debtor moral hazard on the other (debtors calling standstills too frequently or maintaining them for too long). But all regulation needs to be dynamic and responsive to the changing behaviour of market participants.

Potential costs of standstills

A number of potential costs of standstills have been identified. While they should not be taken lightly, many of these costs are more apparent than real.

One argument against standstills is that they undermine the primacy of contracts. This argument does not, however, hold up under close scrutiny. The presumption should always be that debtors meet their obligations in full and on time. But faced with a genuine liquidity shortfall or an unsustainable debt burden, meeting contractual terms may be impossible. In such cases, sovereign debtors need a safe harbour. Bankruptcy law provides this in a corporate context. Everyone accepts this as an important part of the capital market mechanism; it supports, not supplants, market forces. The same is true in an international context, where standstill guidelines can serve as surrogate bankruptcy law.

A second argument against standstills is that they may encourage debtors to default. Given emerging market economies' dependence on international capital, it seems unlikely that they would wilfully default on their obligations. Moreover, the IMF can play a useful role in guarding against strategic default, by refusing to lend-into-arrears to those countries (Gai, Hayes and Shin, 2003). The conditions attached to lending-into-arrears would also help ensure the debtor played fair during the standstill phase.

Some have argued that including standstills in the framework for crisis resolution might encourage investors to 'rush for the exit' at the first sign of trouble, thereby triggering a crisis. Investors with a short time horizon will always want to get out quickly, regardless of the institutional arrangements in place. Against this, the situation for relationship lenders, who value returns over the medium term, is quite different. A credible, well-managed standstill ought to enhance value for longer-term investors, by mitigating the costs of coordination failure. So the incentive for longer-term investors to rush for the exits will be reduced.

This would mitigate – and potentially offset – the negative consequences arising from the behaviour of skittish investors (Gai and Shin, 2002).

Others have argued that standstills may require capital controls to be enforceable, and that these are administratively impossible or extremely costly to impose. In the vast majority of cases, however, capital controls would not be needed to enforce a standstill; it would simply be a case of the sovereign ceasing payments temporarily. Occasionally, this moratorium may need to extend to the banking system. On rare occasions, when capital flight is large and persistent, capital controls may be required to provide a breathing space. But these cases would be the exception, not the rule. And because these controls would be temporary, their costs would not be punitive.

Another concern regarding standstills is that they might lead to contagion. Spillovers are a fact of life in a world of large, cross-border capital flows. The issue is whether standstills would worsen these spillovers. Orderly standstills, as part of a coherent crisis resolution framework, ought to mitigate uncertainties about the work-out process and preserve value. In this way, they may well relieve contagion risks by comparison with the counterfactual case of disorderly default.

An apparently powerful argument against standstills is that they may increase the cost of borrowing and reduce the flow of capital to emerging markets. This might happen, for example, because markets raise their perceived probability of a sovereign default. Given the high cost of borrowing for emerging markets, this argument is a potentially potent one. But it is only part of the story.

First, a lower volume of capital flow does not necessarily translate into lower welfare for a country (Gai and Shin, 2002). Before the Asian crisis, more capital flowed to emerging markets than could readily be absorbed. The bust that followed the boom was very damaging to the countries concerned. A lower but more stable flow of capital would have been welfare-enhancing (Penalver and Martin, 2001).

Second, even if aggregate capital flows are lower in a world of standstills, the composition of capital flows – less short-term and more long-term lending – is likely to improve. This improved composition of capital would reduce countries' susceptibility to future crises, by reducing the probability of capital flow reversals (Penalver and Martin, 2001).

Third, there are good reasons for believing an orderly framework for standstills will not raise the cost of capital for emerging markets. In pricing country risk, markets take account of three factors: the probability of a country defaulting; the recovery value in the event of a default; and a compensation for risk – a risk premium. An enhanced role for payments standstills might arguably increase the perceived probability of default (though it is possible that the expectation of a standstill could actually *reduce* the incidence of default). But against that, a predictable framework for crisis-resolution will increase the

recovery value on debt in the event of default and lower the degree of uncertainty regarding work-out procedures. In this way, the cost of capital for
sovereigns may well be reduced with a clear crisis-resolution framework in
place.

5 Exceptional finance

While the framework is founded on the principle of limited official finance,
exceptional events do sometimes occur. No rule or constraint is inviolable.
So there is a need to preserve the incentives and credibility of a system of
official lending limits, while allowing for a degree of flexibility to deal with
truly exceptional circumstances.

The IMF has long had the ability to lend beyond normal limits by invoking
an exceptional circumstances clause or, more recently, through the provision
of loans under the Supplemental Reserve Facility (SRF), a short-term facility
introduced in late 1997 in the wake of the Asian crisis. But procedural safeguards
on these facilities are limited and the definition of exceptional circumstances is
left vague. Procedural safeguards need to be buttressed.

One possible model of procedural safeguards for exceptional lending is the
US Federal Deposit Insurance Corporation (FDIC) Improvement Act of 1991.
The Act allows the FDIC to exempt a bank from 'least cost resolution' provisions
if it believes that the financial security of the United States is threatened and
FDIC assistance would mitigate adverse effects. This judgement would be made
by the Secretary of the Treasury, based on the recommendation of two-thirds of
the FDIC Board and the Board of Governors of the Federal Reserve, following
consultation with the President. The General Accounting Office is required
to review the basis for the decision *ex post* to ensure that regulators are held
responsible for the spirit of the Act (Bentson and Kaufman, 1998).

Similar rules for good governance can be developed for IMF lending in the
context of international financial crises. First, there is a case for identifying more
clearly than at present the circumstances that would justify a departure from normal lending limits. For example, one justification for exceptional finance could
be situations that threaten the stability of the international monetary system.
This is consistent with the rationale the IMF uses when it seeks supplementary
financing from the NAB countries.

Second, the mechanism for taking such a decision needs to be better defined.
A special IMF Staff Report could be prepared demonstrating that exceptional
circumstances exist. In addition, the Staff's findings would have to be confirmed
by a supermajority of the Executive Board. If a decision was taken to provide

exceptional financing, the Staff Report should be made public in the form of an open letter from the Fund's Managing Director.

Finally, those taking the decision to grant exceptional access would be accountable for their actions *ex post* and subject to an independent evaluation. This function could be performed by the Fund's new Independent Evaluation Office.[1]

6 A framework for IMF intervention

The flowchart (figure 8.1) is intended as a summary of the framework. It is shown as a decision tree, tracing out the chronology of crisis in terms of the options open to the debtor in moving from crisis to a sustainable solution.

Consider a stylised example. The first order of business would be an assessment of the country's debt burden. If a country's debt burden is not sustainable, then the provision of official finance risks worsening a country's financial position: the solution to the country's problem is less debt, not more. Moreover, since official creditors typically have seniority, this additional official finance reduces the value of existing private claims.

In assessing a country's medium-term debt sustainability, too much emphasis has in the past been put on the profile of the country's debt to GDP or debt service to exports ratios, with the debt burden judged to be sustainable if the ratios are falling over time. This sort of analysis says nothing about the sustainable level of these ratios (Cohen, 2000). Sustainability analysis should also assess sustainability thresholds.

If debt is unsustainable, creditors will be required to reduce their exposures in NPV terms. In these circumstances, it is important that there is an efficient means of organising creditor–debtor negotiations during the work-out. It is also important that creditor losses be allocated fairly. Standstill guidelines provide one means of ensuring that the debt work-out process is efficient, equitable and expeditious.

If the debt burden is sustainable, the presumption would be that normal IMF lending limits apply. Some countries may be eligible for the IMF's Contingent Credit Line (CCL), if they have satisfied the requisite *ex ante* conditionality. Other countries may be eligible for a StandBy Arrangement (SBA), in which case they would be required to abide by the requisite *ex post* conditionality. In

---

[1] The IMF Board has now agreed to tighten the criteria and procedures for exceptional access to IMF financing, in line with recommendations made here.

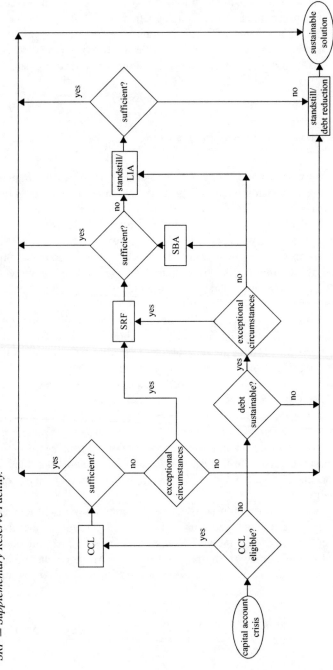

Figure 8.1 *Chronology of crisis-resolution*
Note: *CCL = Contingent Credit Line; LIA = Lending into Arrears; SBA = Standby Arrangement; SRF = Supplementary Reserve Facility.*

most cases, limited official assistance of this type would be sufficient to buy time for the country to overcome a crisis.

In more severe cases, however, official finance may not by itself be sufficient. The country may need to approach creditors in order to raise new money, or to work out a reprofiling of its existing debt service. Because the country's debt burden is sustainable, creditors would not suffer losses in NPV terms under such a rescheduling. So it should be possible to raise net new financing through market-based, voluntary procedures, such as debt rollovers, swaps and exchanges.

But if a voluntary agreement cannot be reached, or if capital flight is pervasive, the country has recourse to a standstill in order to halt the liquidity drain. The IMF can support the standstill by lending-into-arrears if the country is abiding by its standstill guidelines. The amount of official resources available under LIA would be limited to the amount not previously drawn under the SBA, so that there is an overall limit on access to IMF resources.

The presumption of normal limits applies to both SBA- and CCL-eligible countries. Additional financing would be available, but only under exceptional circumstances. These require additional justification. The additional resources would be provided under the Supplemental Reserve Facility (SRF). Funds available under the SRF are of shorter maturity and higher cost than under the SBA.

7 A comparison with the Krueger proposal

Krueger (2001) has proposed the creation of a Sovereign Debt Restructuring Mechanism (SDRM). The SDRM has some similarities with the international bankruptcy court idea proposed, *inter alia*, by Sachs (1994). It also has a number of similarities with the proposed framework here.

First, the SDRM is motivated by the need to reduce the excessive costs of disorderly sovereign default, as with the framework proposed here. Second, the mechanism is intended to alter the incentives of debtors and private creditors. Specifically, it is designed to encourage debtors to seek an earlier restructuring of their debts when these are unsustainable, by offering an orderly legal mechanism for operating this and by limiting IMF lending. Third, a centrepiece of the SDRM proposal is a temporary standstill on payments, allowing the debtor a breathing space to restructure debts and put in place remedial policies. Fourth, the SDRM provides for IMF lending during the standstill phase. All of these features are replicated in the framework here.

A number of operational features of the SDRM have yet to be decided. This would include the role played by IMF in activating the mechanism and in approving any restructuring. It is already clear, however, that the SDRM proposal differs from the framework proposed here in at least two important respects. First, the SDRM is intended to be a statutory framework, underpinned by domestic legislation or an international treaty. This is justified by concerns about creditor litigation and free riders. The framework here is founded instead on non-statutory principles which serve as the conditions on lending-into-arrears, and which are intended to shape the incentives of creditors to mitigate litigation or free riding.

Second, the SDRM is intended to apply only to countries whose debt burden is unsustainable and hence needs to be written-down. The framework here would be used for these unsustainable country cases, but also for countries facing a short-term liquidity problem. In this respect, the SDRM is a less all-embracing proposal than the one outlined here; it would deal with none of the pseudo-liquidity crisis cases which have been much in evidence in recent years.

These may, however, be differences of emphasis rather than principle. For example, a non-statutory standstill mechanism underpinned by principles could be seen as a staging-post en route to a fully-statutory framework. And an SDRM, once established, could be applied to a widening array of crisis cases – both solvency and liquidity – if it was found to be an effective means of dealing with collective-action problems among creditors. So it is possible – though by no means assured – that the two frameworks could converge in practice. Either way, the SDRM proposal is a bold idea whose merits and demerits deserve to be debated actively.[2]

8 Conclusions

There is both a need and a desire for greater clarity in the framework for crisis-resolution. A clear understanding of the respective responsibilities of the private and official sectors is fundamental in this regard. A central element in shaping private sector expectations is knowledge that the official sector will behave predictably. Constraints on IMF lending are a key step in that direction. They ensure that private sector involvement is a crucial part of crisis resolution. And they help encourage debtors and creditors to seek cooperative solutions to crisis.

In resolving crises and securing private sector involvement, the official sector must decide how much official finance will be made available and on what conditions. The debtor country must then decide which option to follow. One such option is a payments standstill. The official sector should stand ready to

[2] Despite the mothballing of the IMF's SDRM proposal at the Spring meetings of the IMF in April 2003.

support standstills if they are implemented in an orderly fashion. In exceptional circumstances, it may be necessary to breach normal lending limits. But such financing would be subject to stringent safeguards. A framework with these characteristics – constraints, clarity and orderliness – has the potential to reduce the incidence and cost of crises.

REFERENCES

Bentson, G. and G. Kaufman (1998). 'Deposit Insurance Reform in the FDIC Improvement Act: The Experience to Date', Federal Reserve Bank of Chicago, Economic Perspectives, Second Quarter

Chui, M., P. Gai and A. Haldane (2002). 'Sovereign Liquidity Crises: Analytics and Implications for Public Policy', Journal of Banking and Finance, 26, 519–46

Cohen, D. (2000). 'The HIPC Initiative: True and False Promises', OECD Development Centre Technical Paper, 166, September

Council on Foreign Relations (1999). Safeguarding Prosperity in a Global Financial System: The Future International Financial Architecture, Report of an Independent Task Force. New York: Council on Foreign Relations, October, http://www.cfr.org/public/pubs/IFATaskForce.html

Dell'Ariccia, G., I. Godde and J. Zettelmeyer (2002). 'Moral Hazard and International Crisis Lending: A Test', IMF Working Paper, WP/02/181

Diamond, D. and P. Dybvig (1983). 'Bank Runs, Deposit Insurance and Liquidity', Journal of Political Economy, 91, 401–19

Drage, J. and F. Mann (1999). 'Improving the Stability of the International Financial System', Financial Stability Review, 6, 4–39

Eichengreen, B. (2002). Financial Crises and What to Do About Them. Oxford, Oxford University Press

Eichengreen, B. and R. Portes (1995). 'Crisis What Crisis? Orderly Workouts for Sovereign Debtors', Centre for Economic Policy Research

Fischer, S. (1999). 'On the Need for an International Lender of Last Resort,' revised version of address to American Economic Association, IMF website, www.imf.org

Gai, P., S. Hayes and H. S. Shin (2003). 'Crisis Costs and Debtor Discipline: the Efficacy of Public Policy in Sovereign Debt Crises', Journal of International Economics, forthcoming

Gai, P. and H. S. Shin (2002). 'Rushes for the Exit', Bank of England, mimeo

Haldane, A. G. (1999). 'Private Sector Involvement in Financial Crisis: Analytics and Public Policy Approaches', Financial Stability Review, 7, 184–202

Hoggarth, G. and V. Saporta (2001). 'Costs of Banking System Instability', Financial Stability Review, 10, 148–65

International Financial Institutions Advisory Commission (2000). Report of the International Financial Institutions Advisory Commission, Washington, DC, http://www.house.gov/jec/imf/ifiac.htm

International Monetary Fund (2001). 'International Capital Markets Developments, Prospects, and Key Policy Issues', September

King, M. A. (1999). 'Reforming the International Financial Architecture – the Middle Way', Financial Stability Review, 7, 203–11

Krueger, A. (2001). 'International Financial Architecture for 2002: A New Approach to Sovereign Debt Restructuring', speech at the National Economists' Club Annual Members' Dinner

Kydland, F. E. and E. C. Prescott (1977). 'Rules Rather than Discretion: The Inconsistency of Optimal Plans', *Journal of Political Economy*, 85, 473–92

Miller, M. and L. Zhang (1999). 'Sovereign Liquidity Crises: the Strategic Case for a Payments Standstill', Centre for the Study of Globalisation and Regionalisation, Working Paper, 35/99

Penalver, A. and B. Martin (2001). 'The Effect of Payments Standstills on Yields and the Maturity Structure of Debt', mimeo

Rogoff, K. (1999). 'International Institutions for Reducing Global Financial Instability', *Journal of Economic Perspectives*, 13(4), 21–42

Sachs, J. A. (1994). 'Do we Need an International Lender of Last Resort?', Harvard University, mimeo

Schwartz, A. J. (1998). 'Time to Terminate the ESF and the IMF', *Foreign Policy Briefing*, 48, The Cato Institute

Schwartz, S. L. (2000). 'Sovereign Debt Restructuring: A Bankruptcy Reorganization Approach', *Cornell Law Review*, 85, 956–1034

9 Whose programme is it? Policy ownership and conditional lending

JAMES M. BOUGHTON AND ALEX MOURMOURAS

1 Introduction

IMF lending to countries is generally conditional on the government and Central Bank carrying out specified policies and achieving specified outcomes. Some of these conditions might be prerequisites for an initial disbursement, while others will be requirements for subsequent drawings on a standby arrangement. In discussions of the appropriate conditions, IMF and country officials often disagree, sometimes diametrically. Economic programmes supported by IMF resources usually are negotiated compromises between the policies initially favoured by the Fund and those favoured by the country's authorities. In some cases, having gone through this process of negotiation, the authorities might be reasonably happy with the outcome and may be said to 'own' the programme even though it was not their original preference. In other cases, they might be swallowing a bitter pill simply because it is the only way to get the IMF to cough up the money. This chapter tackles two questions raised by the distinction between 'owned' and 'imposed' outcomes. Is the distinction empirically meaningful? If so, what can be done to operationalise it?

First, it is necessary to define 'policy ownership'. Several definitions have been offered in the literature, but it is not easy to devise a definition that is empirically relevant. For a government to own a set of policies does not require that officials think up the policies by themselves, nor that the policies be independent of conditionality. What it does require is for the owner to appreciate the benefits of the policies and to accept responsibility for them. Ownership may therefore be defined as in IMF (2001c, p. 6):

The views expressed in this chapter are those of the authors and should not be ascribed to any institution. We thank Mark Allen, Pat Conway, Chris Gilbert, Nadeem ul Haque, Anna Ivanova, Mohsin Khan, Wolf Mayer, Cyrus Rustomjee, Sunil Sharma, David Vines and John Williamson for helpful comments, conversations and correspondence. All remaining errors are our own responsibility.

225

Ownership is a willing assumption of responsibility for an agreed program of policies, by officials in a borrowing country who have the responsibility to formulate and carry out those policies, based on an understanding that the program is achievable and is in the country's own interest.

The first challenge in making this concept operational is that it is not directly observable. A judgement about the extent to which ownership is present is a judgement about the state of mind and degree of internal commitment on the part of the country's officials. Inferences can be drawn from behaviour, but the evidence is unavoidably indirect and incomplete. If a government does not carry out a policy despite making a commitment to do so, weak ownership is only one of several possible causes. Circumstances might have changed and made a different policy preferable, key agencies may have lacked the administrative or technical capacity to implement the policy, or political conflicts may have arisen that prevented the government from acting.

A second challenge is that ownership is dynamic. The IMF lends to countries, but it negotiates with individuals in governments. Those individuals might at one stage be highly antagonistic to the idea of changing their policies, but that does not preclude the possibility that they will change their minds, nor that the lineup will change. An operational approach to ownership must include an analysis of processes of dialogue, negotiation and signalling that could strengthen ownership over time.

A third challenge is that there are many potential owners. When a country requests financial assistance from the IMF, discussions on policy conditionality typically take place in the country between a staff mission team and a team of officials led by the Finance Minister. Officials from other ministries and the Central Bank may also be involved, and it is common for the head of government to be engaged to some extent. Non-governmental organisations (NGOs) representing the interests of labour or industry or advocating policies favouring the poor, the environment, or other worthy causes under the banner of 'civil society' might also participate in discussions and help draft policies.[1] It is never the case that all of these participants will agree to a particular policy package. The critical mass of agreement at which country ownership is broad enough to be operationally meaningful may be very difficult to determine.

On a theoretical level, the relevance of policy ownership has been examined primarily in the context of agency models. If governments act on behalf of the country as a whole, it is straightforward to analyse welfare maximisation as a function of preferences subject to constraints. If interests are heterogeneous and multiple parties influence the outcome, then a more complex game must be analysed. Empirically, a key issue in the literature has been the relationship

---

[1] Broad participation is an explicit goal in low-income countries that qualify for long-term financing on concessional terms from the Fund's Poverty Reduction and Growth Facility (PRGF).

between external conditionality and domestic ownership in the ways they influence the ability or willingness of a country's authorities to carry out policy reforms. Those two aspects are taken up next.

2 Ownership and economic welfare

Lack of ownership is variously attributed to incongruities between the IMF's and member countries' objectives, to domestic divisions and heterogeneity within the recipient countries and to lack of economic understanding by policy-makers, the public, or the IMF. The key to sorting out these factors is to focus on the links between a recipient country's people, its government and the goals being pursued by the Fund. Recent political economy models explore these links and provide useful insights into the relationships among ownership, conditionality and welfare.

One fundamental purpose for which the IMF was created was to ameliorate the negative externalities that inappropriate national policies inflict on other countries. As stated in article I of the Fund's charter, the purpose is to give members the 'opportunity to correct maladjustments in their balance of payments without resorting to measures destructive of national or international prosperity'. When that phrase was articulated, in 1944, the concern was that countries that were unable to finance a balance of payments deficit would be forced to contract domestic demand excessively (destructive of national prosperity) or devalue excessively, raise tariffs, or introduce exchange or trade restrictions (possibly destructive of international prosperity). Financial assistance from the IMF would permit a more orderly adjustment. Subsequently, conditionality was introduced and refined to ensure that this orderly adjustment would occur. Even if governments of borrowing countries are perfectly maximising the long-run welfare of the country, the broader international perspective of the Fund may result in conflict.

In addition, domestic political systems are imperfect. Governments have interests separate from those of the people at large, and information about what the people really want and what is best for them is limited.[2] These imperfections open opportunities for the government to pursue its own interests and for special interest groups (SIGs) to influence the government. The political economy literature suggests two main channels through which interest groups influence the government. One is to contribute (make payments) to the government in anticipation of desirable policy decisions. This is the usual assumption in the

---

[2] See Drazen (2000, especially chapter 7) on the role of conflicts of interest and heterogeneity in analysing political economy issues in macroeconomics.

economics branch of the political economy literature, most notably in the work of Gene Grossman and Elhanan Helpman (1994, 2001). The other channel is for SIGs to inform the government about what impact different policies will have, the strength of support for a particular policy, etc. The political science branch of the political economy literature generally treats this channel as more important than outright contributing. At any rate, interest groups play an important role in inhibiting ownership and should be accounted for in a model of the ownership/conditionality nexus.

The influence of SIGs on programme ownership and implementation is well recognised in the academic literature and at the IMF.[3] From the work of Mancur Olson (1982, 1993) we know that opposition to welfare-improving change arises endogenously in the reform process. This point is well illustrated by considering the consequences of providing infant industry protection (Dixit, 2001, p. 6). Typically the original intent behind tariffs is to provide domestic industries breathing room to become competitive in world markets and to provide the 'infant governments' of countries with under-developed tax administrations with a convenient and effective tax vehicle. Yet, once in place tariffs often lead to the creation of ongoing lobbies favouring continued trade protection, with adverse consequences for resource allocation, economic growth and public welfare.[4] State enterprises and farms in transition and developing countries provide another example of the power of organised lobbies to resist socially beneficial reforms. In many countries, these organisations were transformed by their managers into 'rent-generating machines', diverting resources from producers or consumers for the exclusive benefit of small groups of politically connected people. Ominously, these special interests – including those controlling oil, natural resources and other wealth – sometimes turn against reforms even if they are pro-market in general, when they fear that their privileged positions and capacity to earn rents are under threat.[5]

These two dimensions of conflict, stemming from international and domestic sources of heterogeneity, require careful analysis if IMF-supported programmes are to be appropriately designed. This requirement is particularly relevant when programmes include major structural reforms, which inevitably have

---

[3] On the role of vested interests in blocking reforms, see Krueger (1974), Havrylyshyn and Odling-Smee (2000), IMF (2001c) and Odling-Smee (2001). Country ownership is discussed by Dixit (2000), IMF (2001c) and Khan and Sharma (2001).

[4] The theory of special interest group influence in trade and structural policies is developed in Grossman and Helpman (1994, 2001) and Dixit, Grossman and Helpman (1997). Models in which lobbies resist the adoption of new technologies, resulting in depressed welfare and lower growth, are developed by Krusell and Rios-Rull (1996); Bridgman, Livshits and MacGee (2001); and Prescott and Parente (2000).

[5] Dalmazzo and de Blasio (2001) develop a formal model and conduct tests of the influence of firms controlling oil wealth.

concentrated negative impacts on some sectors' interests. Recent political economy models allow us to analyse how SIGs may use their power to prevent a national consensus for reform from coalescing. This work also suggests ways for policy-makers and the IMF to build ownership over time and to avoid the fragilities that sometimes characterise the process. The view of conditionality that emerges is one of a commitment device that reform-minded governments can effectively use to increase their leverage with domestic opponents and push through policies that might not otherwise be approved (Vreeland, 2000).

Common agency models

The political economy literature has recently turned to analysing IFI lending and conditionality using as an organising framework the theory of common agency (or multi-principal games). The ownership implications of this framework may be illustrated by reference to two models. Allan Drazen (2001) considers government decision-making in the presence of domestic veto players *within* government – a positive approach developed in political science to study policy-making in different forms of political organization.[6] Wolfgang Mayer and Alex Mourmouras (2002) analyse government policy choices in the presence of private SIGs using the menu auctions approach of trade theory and public finance.[7] Both classes of models illustrate how competing domestic and international considerations influence the cost-benefit calculations of policy-makers in strategic (game-theoretic) settings.

The key to both approaches is that governments pursue multiple objectives, of which enhancing public welfare is only one. Narrower pursuits, such as the collection of political contributions, are also important. Hence, policy choices reflect the concerns of diverse constituencies inside and outside of government. Within the public sector, the role of parliament, regional and local authorities and other constitutional players is clearly important in implementing reforms. Outside government, the views of a multitude of domestic and international players must also be taken into consideration. Governments need to contend with active domestic SIGs representing the interests of labour and industry, as well as civil society and other domestic NGOs. In addition, governments are influenced by bilateral donors and international agencies, including the IMF,

---

[6] The theory of veto players was developed by UCLA political scientist George Tsebelis in the mid-1990s. Tsebelis (2001a, 2001b) presents the theory and applies it to the European Union.

[7] The basic reference on common agency theory and menu auctions is Bernheim and Whinston (1986). Grossman and Helpman (1994, 2001) and Dixit, Helpman and Grossman (1997) apply the theory to policy issues in international trade and public finance. Dixit (2001) draws implications.

the World Bank, the World Trade Organization (WTO), regional development banks and the European Union.

In a political economy equilibrium, government decision-makers must strike a balance between these competing influences. The outcome can be described as the equilibrium of a non-cooperative game[8] involving the authorities, the IMF (or, more generally, an IFI) and the veto players or private SIGs. While the objectives of the IMF may diverge from those of its borrowers by being more long-run and international in scope, this does not lead to negative consequences for the country or the international community. Appropriately designed, conditionality can overcome domestic divisions and be effective despite less than full national ownership and the differences between IMF and country objectives.

In order for conditionality to be effective, it must be consistent with – indeed, be part of – the recipient country's domestic political economy equilibrium. This equilibrium is determined by the strategic interactions between the government and various collective or individual stakeholders in the public sector whose consent is needed for reforms to be implemented. The number and identity of these key players depends on the form of a country's constitution and political organisation. In presidential systems, the legislature (one or two chambers) and the independently elected chief executive are veto players.[9] In parliamentary systems, where the executive is selected by the parliament, veto players are the parliamentary parties (or their coalitions) whose agreement is required for policy changes to be implemented. In addition to these institutional and partisan veto players, other potential veto players are the courts or specific individuals, such as army officials.

The power and influence of veto players are shaped by the constitutional and institutional rules governing their interactions with the executive, including the procedures determining the interaction of the presidency and the legislature, the sequencing of moves, agenda control and the rules of voting and vetoing in the legislature and the presidency. Awareness of these rules and procedures helps the IMF and other IFIs ensure that assistance programmes will succeed. Moreover, in general, policy stability increases, and reforms that change the status quo are harder to achieve, the larger is the number of veto players in a political system and the greater is the ideological distance among veto players (Tsebelis, 2001a, 2001b). Hence, in determining the nature, sequencing and timing of reforms, IMF-supported programmes may need to take into account these and other details of political economy, including, for example, whether

---

[8] As modelled, the game is technically non-cooperative, but in practice the process of interaction is cooperative through repeated plays of the game.

[9] In presidential systems the congress is the agenda setter since it makes take-it-or-leave it offers to the president. The president can accept that offer or veto the bill, in which case some qualified majority can overrule the veto.

the president has line item veto power, absolute and qualified (super) majority rules, abstentions, filibusters, and the like.

Outside the government, the support or acquiescence of key private actors in recipient countries may also be important for the success of reforms. This is illustrated in the political contributions framework which, in contrast to veto player theory, abstracts from government heterogeneity and views the executive as a unitary actor subject to influence by private SIGs. Mayer and Mourmouras apply the political contribution framework to the relations between IFIs and their member governments.[10] The analytics of the model and the main results are presented in the appendix. In the basic solution of this model in which the IFI is not involved, the recipient country government is concerned with the impact of its choice of economic policy distortions on national welfare and political contributions, ignoring the externalities that its choices generate for the rest of the world. The policy-maker's choice of economic policy distortions maximises its objective function, which differs from national welfare by an amount equivalent to the political contributions it receives from an organised domestic interest group. In the domestic political equilibrium the government balances its marginal benefit from political contributions against the marginal damage to national welfare caused by higher distortions. The more vested interests benefit from distortions, or the less representative the government is, the higher will be the equilibrium level of policy distortions, which may generate large distortions to its neighbour's welfare or even the welfare of the international community as a whole if the country is systemically important.

The involvement of the IMF may improve the quality of policies when recipient governments are constrained by the influence of private SIGs. Mayer and Mourmouras (2002) derive a role for IFI involvement under specific (and plausible) assumptions about the sources of conflict of interest between the borrowing government and the IFI. At the root of the international dimension of conflict of interest is the assumption that the IFI is a public interest institution while, as discussed above, the recipient country government cares about domestic welfare but is also subject to influence by SIGs. Specifically, the Mayer–Mourmouras view of the IMF as a costless institution that maximises a weighted sum of creditor and borrower country welfare is consistent with Thomas Willett's (2000) 'soft core' public choice approach to modelling the IMF. Under this assumption, IMF conditionality is justified by cross-border externalities associated with wrong national policies. The influence of domestic SIGs on the policy choices of the recipient government is a second reason for IFI involvement. Even if a borrowing country is so small that its choices result

---

[10] Lahiri and Raimondos-Möller (2000, 2001) have used the political contributions framework to study the interactions between donors and recipients in the presence of lobbies in the donor and recipient country.

in negligible cross-border externalities, IMF assistance and conditionality act as a countervailing force against the pernicious influence of domestic SIGs, enabling the government to select policies characterised by fewer distortions.

The nature of conditionality attached to the Fund's financial assistance affects the degree of ownership in important ways. Consider first hypothetical loans (or grants) provided without a quid pro quo on adoption of different policies. Unconditional assistance is the least intrusive form of involvement by an international institution in the affairs of a sovereign nation and therefore maximises government ownership of actual policies. It also improves welfare relative to the level attainable without assistance. But even if financing were provided without strings, it would alter the government's incentives. Because distortions normally reduce the effectiveness of aid, more aid raises the marginal damage of distortions on social welfare, resulting in improved choice of policies. If the Fund were to take into account the government's policy reaction function, it would choose an amount of assistance that puts the world economy on the highest welfare contour attainable given that assistance is provided unconditionally.

Unconditional lending, however, does not exhaust the gains from trade in the relationship between the Fund and the recipient government. More formally, the Mayer–Mourmouras model shows that unconditional aid does not maximise the joint welfare of the IFI and the recipient government; conditional lending improves policy outcomes relative to unconditional lending. But whereas this improvement results in more effective use of IFI resources, it is achieved at a price. As explained in the appendix, with conditional aid, the IFI is injected more deeply in the affairs of the recipient country since it must now make the magnitude of its assistance contingent on the government's choice of economic policies. In the language of game theory, the IFI becomes a second principal in a common agency problem in which the two principals – the IFI and the domestic interest group – jointly attempt to influence the government's choice of economic policies. In equilibrium, in addition to the domestic tangency condition discussed above, the marginal rates of substitution between disbursements and distortions must be the same for the IFI and the government. The international tangency condition demonstrates that the conditional assistance equilibrium is Pareto efficient while the equilibrium with unconditional assistance is not. But whereas the IFI and the world as a whole are better off providing assistance conditionally, the government is better off with unconditional assistance. (The marginal effect of conditionality on the country's aggregate welfare is ambiguous in this model.)

The preceding welfare results are subject to an important caveat. Mayer and Mourmouras (2002) incorporate an important asymmetry in their model. Whereas the IFI is portrayed as a benevolent agent, governments that borrow from IFIs are assumed to be conflicted agents subject to multiple influences. It may be objected that this asymmetry, which drives some of the welfare results, is artificial.[11] At least two additional distortions may be empirically important. First, voting in IFIs is weighted by formulas that strengthen the influence of wealthier countries. The weights in the global welfare function being maximised by the institution will to some extent reflect that distribution of power.[12] Second, the governments of industrial countries are not immune from political pressure by SIGs, including notably by lobbyists for powerful industrial and agricultural interests. IFIs are not likely to be able to fully resist that chain of influence. To the extent that IFI policies are distorted by narrow self-interests or by political influences from creditor countries or SIGs that care disproportionately about their own welfare, the welfare justification for IFI conditionality will be weakened. These issues, however, lie beyond the scope of this chapter.

State capture

A key issue facing multilateral and bilateral official creditors is when to cut off sovereign lending in cases of pervasive government failures. In the political contributions model, state capture is usually assumed to be partial, in which case IFIs may continue working with recipient governments in spite of the presence of active interest groups opposing reforms. Continued IFI engagement is warranted as it results in improved welfare for the world economy. This result does not hold when government failure is complete and results in misappropriation of foreign assistance funds.

A good example of this approach is the model presented by Christopher Adam and Stephen O'Connell (1999), which assumes that the government is wholly dominated by a SIG that uses the state's coercive powers to redistribute resources to its members.[13] Donors allocate exogenous amounts of budgetary resources to domestic public spending and foreign aid so as to maximise a weighted sum of domestic and recipient country general welfare. The difference in objective functions between the unrepresentative government and the donor

---

[11] The assumption that the IFI seeks to maximise global welfare while the borrowing government has distorted interests has been challenged in the literature. For example, 'hard core' public choice analyses sometimes view IFIs as budget maximizers (see Vaubel, 1996).

[12] This observation is not intended to imply that a one-country-one-vote system, such as that used in the UN general assembly, would produce a 'better' reflection of global welfare. In the absence of universal democracy, all assessments of global governance contain an inherently arbitrary element.

[13] This assumption is also made by Boone (1996) and McGuire and Olson (1996). In practice, higher transfers to favourite groups may be manifested in inefficient and irrational composition of government expenditure, including favouritism in state employment, and inefficient and inequitable patterns of spending on government-provided services across regions.

creates a conflict of interest. This resource allocation problem can be stated in terms of a set of indifference curves that describe the tradeoffs to the donor of different values of the aggregate tax rate and transfers to the favorite group (Adam and O'Connell, 1999, p. 23). The government imposes proportional taxes and spends on essential goods and services. It also may make lump-sum transfers to its favoured group, but not if the group is a very large portion of the population. The government's indirect utility function depends on the tax rate and the aggregate transfer to the favoured group. It sets these two parameters to maximise the welfare of the favoured group. But because it takes into account the reaction of the public to high tax rates, the tax rate is not confiscatory – a result reminiscent of the political economy equilibrium of the Meltzer–Richard (1981) model of taxation and redistribution. If the size of the favoured group is above a threshold size, then the deadweight loss from raising taxes to effect transfers is too high to make the process worthwhile. In other words, a government need not be fully representative for explicit transfers to favoured groups to be eliminated in equilibrium.

When the state is fully captured by special interests, aid resources intermediated through the government do not get channelled to tax reduction or other public welfare-improving uses. In these cases, unconditional aid would collapse. This can be seen by referring again to the Adam–O'Connell model. Although unconditional aid lowers the net public spending requirement, it is 'wasted' in additional transfers to the favoured group when the government is sufficiently unrepresentative. If the donor, which knows the type of the recipient country government, correctly anticipates this outcome and values alternative (domestic) uses of the aid resources sufficiently, it will provide no aid whatsoever. To avoid the collapse of aid, the government needs to be sufficiently representative: in this case, a small amount of aid will reduce the tax rate without initiating transfers.

A practical implication of the political contributions approach is that the limitations of unconditional aid to unrepresentative governments can be alleviated through conditionality aimed at reducing distortions. Similarly to the models discussed above, the gains from external assistance can be represented by a contract curve representing the locus of tangencies of the indifference curves of the donor and the recipient – that is, the combinations of transfers to the favoured group and the aggregate tax rate in the aid recipient country that leave each player on the same level of welfare. For given donor and recipient objective functions, the location of the equilibrium point on the contract curve after conditional aid allocations depends on the nature of the strategic interaction, whether it wastes resources, the relative bargaining powers or threat points of the two parties, etc. Conditionality prevents a collapse of aid when recipient governments are not sufficiently representative, reduces the distortionary tax rate and achieves constrained Pareto optimal allocations. If the donor has substantial bargaining power, aid is also accompanied by a reduction in the transfers to favoured groups. In the opposite case, transfers to favoured groups may actually increase.

Time-inconsistency problems provide conditionality with an additional and quite important role. In practice, governments are unable to commit *ex ante* not to tax capital income. Since a capital levy on investment income involves a zero excess burden *ex post*, even a representative government will face incentives to tax the results of productive investment at prohibitive rates once investment is in place. Anticipating this, the private sector will invest even less in the productive technology than in the 'commitment' equilibrium analysed so far. Condition-ality can help by making aid contingent on the adoption and maintenance of non-extortionary taxation policies that mimic the pre-commitment outcome.

A final aspect of intertemporal non-cooperative games to consider is the possibility of spontaneous or induced evolution of cooperation between self-interested players. Unlike the two-period model analysed by Adam and O'Connell, Avinash Dixit (2001) analyses a model of indefinitely repeated interactions in a country with a divided polity. Two self-interested groups alter-nate in power according to an exogenous Markov transition probability matrix. The group controlling the government has the power to decide on the alloca-tion of national resources. It could decide to use its capture of the state to grab as much for itself, or it could adopt a more cooperative stance and share re-sources with the other group. Because of the repeated nature of this interaction, groups have incentives to cooperate that do not exist in the one-shot game. Such self-enforcing intergroup cooperation is more likely the greater is each group's patience (i.e. the lower is each group's subjective rate of time preference) and the greater is each group's risk aversion. Cooperation is more likely the greater is the likelihood of switch in power by either party. While some persistence in power is consistent with the emergence of spontaneous cooperation, such an outcome is made impossible if one or both groups have a highly persistent lock on power. Although Dixit does not discuss the implications of his model for foreign aid, an obvious inference is that conditional assistance has the capacity to strengthen the parties' incentives to cooperate.

Adaptation or confrontation?

The models sketched out above all imply that the effectiveness of financial as-sistance from the IMF can be enhanced by conditionality, assuming that the conditions are appropriate in light of domestic realities. How, then, can the IMF achieve this happy outcome? In broad terms, the Fund has two options. First, so long as it does not compromise the safeguards for its financial resources, it can strive to adapt its conditionality to accommodate the domestic political constraints faced by governments. Alternatively, it can try to design or support programmes that tackle the distortions caused or magnified by SIGs through additional conditionality. The dilemma between accommodation and directiveness is a classic issue in the foreign aid literature.[14] The choice of strategy requires careful judgements, which can be made only on a case-by-case basis. Starting in the mid-1980s, the IMF gradually shifted to a more directive approach, driven by concerns about inadequate results in past programmes and poor governance and corruption in some recipient countries. The resulting intensification of the scope and detail of conditionality, though it probably succeeded on its own terms, has raised concerns both inside and outside the institution about the effects on domestic ownership of reforms. At present, the momentum is shifting toward a more accommodative stance: not to weaken conditionality but to raise the probability of successful implementation. The test of the effort to streamline and narrow the focus of conditionality will be whether borrowing countries effectively take up the challenge to design and implement their own policies within a broadly conceived strategy.

The desirability for Fund-supported programmes to be tailored to countries' circumstances requires a rethinking of whether first-best programmes – perhaps those favoured by IMF staff – are optimal when subjected to the domestic political economy constraint. In practice, this might imply a need for the Fund and the international community to adopt a gradual approach to supporting efforts to loosen the domestic constraint. Fund-supported programmes are much more likely to be interrupted in countries with a higher initial budget deficit, which is significantly positively correlated with the strength of special interests.[15] These findings suggest that many programme failures may be attributable to strong special interest groups – whether in the government, the parliament or the private sector – that prohibit broad ownership and block reforms. In 'questionable ownership' cases in which the IMF is nonetheless determined to remain involved, an accommodating strategy would aim to build ownership by demonstrating the broad benefits of reforms, educating policy-makers and the public, and gradually weakening the SIGs' hold over power and influence.

The connection between accommodation and gradualism requires some qualification. Gradualism will be inappropriate if pressure groups likely to oppose reforms are not organised (in Olson's, 1965, terminology, these groups are latent) at the outset of the reform effort. In such cases, reforms should proceed quickly so as to not allow latent pressure groups time to get organised. If pressure

---

[14] We are indebted to Pat Conway for bringing to our attention these hypotheses, which have a long history in economic development. The third alternative – to simply ignore SIGs – can be dismissed as it would likely lead to programmes that were ill-suited to particular country conditions and hence more likely to fail.

[15] Ivanova *et al.* (2001) find that successful programmes started with substantially smaller budget deficits (2.5 per cent of GDP) as compared with unsuccessful ones (4.8 per cent).

groups are organised at the outset of the programme, then gradualism may be a more appropriate strategy. To see this, consider the SIG's net welfare, defined as gross utility (or rents) derived from policy distortions, net of the contributions to the politicians required to bring them about. This welfare function is monotonic in the level of policy distortions. In other words, assume that SIGs are better off when distortions are high than when they are low. At an unchanged SIG political contribution schedule, each IFI-supported reform programme would gradually erode the SIG's political influence. By allowing the government to select a political equilibrium involving fewer policy distortions, IFI-supported reforms that help assure the acquiescence of SIGs result in lower welfare for the lobbies' members, which might induce members to opt out of participating in the SIG and paying the dues necessary to sustain it over time. Moreover, since the optimal level of political contributions is increasing in the level of policy distortions, a decline in distortions – at an unchanged contribution schedule – will lead to fewer contributions by the SIG, which benefits the country as it lowers the realised level of political rents and corruption. Of course, opposing forces are also at work. At each play of the domestic political game, the SIGs must consider how much of a contribution to make to induce the government to choose an equilibrium in which their preferences are not ignored. It is conceivable that this would result in equilibrium SIG contributions that increase as policy distortions are reduced. It is an open question for future research to assess the conditions needed to bring about the virtuous cycle described here.

Another insight of common agency theory has to do with the tension regarding the policy instruments to achieve programme goals. Tariffs, export taxes and other inefficient policy tools are resisted by IFIs because they are detrimental to aggregate domestic and international welfare. Common agency theory, however, suggests that SIGs have good reasons to prefer such tools and are likely to put pressure on policy-makers to maintain them. Key to understanding why special interests may prefer to use economically inefficient means of taxation and redistribution is the classical proposition in the normative theory of second best from public finance. This proposition (Diamond and Mirrlees, 1971) states that the government can achieve its socially optimal pattern of redistribution by taxing final goods only, even in second-best situations. Taxes and subsidies on intermediate inputs that distort production decisions are inefficient. In the common agency approach to public finance, however, the Diamond–Mirrlees result does not necessarily hold, simply because SIGs may prefer inefficient policy instruments in order to increase the benefits from their political relationship with the government.[16]

---

[16] Dixit, Grossman and Helpman (1997) construct a positive model of taxation and redistribution in which SIGs prefer such inefficient tax instruments. As stated by Grossman and Helpman (2001, p. 279): 'the less economically efficient are the tools of redistributive politics, the better is the bargaining position of the organized interest groups vis-à-vis the policymaker.'

Countries' incentives to opt for inefficient means of taxation and redistribution could be ameliorated by a country making commitments to international organisations (such as the IMF or the WTO) to eschew inefficient policy tools. Such decisions, however, are endogenous and require that the government's valuation of the benefits outweighs the short-run political costs. Alternatively, if the country is in a dire enough crisis, IFIs could confront the government with a take-it-or-leave-it proposal that proscribes inefficient policy instruments. But if domestic conditions are not dire, then more accommodative strategies may be needed.

3 Ownership and conditionality: empirical evidence

Finding empirical support for the role of ownership, as noted in the introduction, is difficult because ownership cannot be directly observed or measured and because it is dynamic and often fragile. These features make assessment of programme ownership a subjective exercise. The empirical literature has relied on case studies and econometric evidence that use proxies to evaluate the importance of ownership. While both approaches have well-known limitations, together they present a convincing case that ownership is crucial for programme implementation. The studies illustrate the obstacles to national ownership caused by domestic divisions owing to powerful interest groups inside or outside government, and political and electoral constraints, including from the possible short-term adverse impacts of reforms on vulnerable groups. The evidence also demonstrates what it takes to build durable coalitions that are successful in pushing reforms through, including dialogue, negotiation and decisive political leadership.

A number of case studies were developed for the external evaluation of the Fund's Enhanced Structural Adjustment Facility (ESAF) (Botchwey et al., 1998) and for the IMF's 2001–2 conditionality review (IMF, 2001c). Both groups of studies present an interesting variety of national experiences in developing ownership of reforms in Fund-supported programmes. Some cases illustrate the numerous difficulties in establishing and maintaining a broad and deep enough level of domestic support for reform programmes. Zimbabwe is a case in point. Starting in the late 1980s and into the early part of the 1990s, the government was motivated to pursue economic policy reforms following its unfavourable previous experience. While policy advice and financial assistance from the Fund and other IFIs seemed to be helpful in these circumstances, national commitment to reforms was not deep-rooted. Programme implementation and the effectiveness of international assistance were compromised soon after powerful groups in the business community, the government and the universities asserted themselves actively against the reform process. The situation did not improve, and Zimbabwe sank into a deep crisis.

Some transition countries in the Commonwealth of Independent States (CIS) have also experienced repeated difficulties in achieving the political consensus needed to undertake much-needed structural reforms throughout the 1990s. The experience of these countries provides a good example of the power of SIGs in blocking reforms. While the degree of commitment to macroeconomic stability was reasonable in the chaotic macroeconomic environment that followed the collapse of central planning, the governments in these countries were often divided on the advisability of the structural reform agendas of IMF-supported programmes. Pro-reform coalitions, which included key economic officials in government, were supported by the Fund and other IFIs. IFI-supported programmes in the CIS pushed hard to implement extensive reform agendas aimed to counter the influence of special interests. The modernisation of the public finances and the rationalisation of tax and expenditure policy and management were key in this regard. But while structural fiscal and other reforms have improved the situation, progress remained uneven. Programme measures were sometimes reversed or not fully implemented, and the implementation of institutional and structural reforms proved to be one of the most difficult tasks in these countries. The incomplete structural reform agenda remains a key obstacle to private business growth and employment creation in some CIS countries.[17]

One critical reason why these reform efforts were not more successful was the ambivalence of the top political leaders and resistance by other senior politicians and government bureaucrats, who were influenced by enterprise and collective and state farm managers and other members of the nomenklatura. The anti-reform forces often joined ranks in the legislatures and were able in several instances to slow down, block, or reverse IFI-backed reforms.[18] This alliance of private SIGs and conservative elements in the political leadership even managed in some instances to threaten capture of the state through their control of crucial sectors of the economy, their evasion or avoidance of taxation, and other privileges. While IFI-supported programmes eventually resumed, they often included lengthy lists of prior actions and other measures aimed to restore failed reforms in previous programmes, with limited success (see below).

---

[17] As stated by Odling-Smee (2001): 'Some countries in the region are stuck half-way along the transition process . . . Partial and halting reforms have allowed new (and sometimes old!) elites to gain control over productive assets, and they have then successfully used the state as a means to preserve their position by ensuring that they continue to receive privileges. This situation, which occurred to varying degrees in the countries of the region, had the most serious costs when it perpetuated an antiquated industrial structure and prevented the establishment and development of new businesses.'

[18] See, for example, Åslund (1999) and Hellman and Kaufmann (2001).

Some other cases provide evidence of how domestic political divisions can be overcome and what the Fund can do to help catalyse reforms. Uganda and Bulgaria are noteworthy examples. The Ugandan government gradually adopted more stable and market-oriented policies in the late 1980s, abolishing price controls, liberalising the foreign exchange market and privatising state enterprises. These changes were implemented after a lengthy public debate and were supported by the Fund through its own financial assistance and catalytic effects, which facilitated additional aid from other creditors and donors. In Bulgaria, a protracted crisis that led to hyperinflation in 1997 was instrumental in overcoming the influence of special interests and creating the national consensus needed to back difficult structural reforms. Following the acute crisis, the authorities, backed by the entire political class represented in parliament, were much more willing to tackle the structural economic problems at the root of previous reform failures. The IMF and other donors provided external backing at the critical moment. The support of the international community combined with broad national ownership to result in a successful programme that put the Bulgarian economy on a sound footing. Inclusive public debates sanctioned by the country's top leadership can be key to promoting broad ownership and effective programme implementation. This is underscored by the positive experience of several successful home-grown reform programmes that were implemented on government initiative. In addition to Uganda, these cases include Vietnam, Eritrea, Burkina Faso and Mozambique.

In econometric studies, ownership is assessed indirectly by relating programme success to indicators of political openness and unity (i.e. the absence of major obstacles to reform) and administrative capacity (i.e. the presence of an ability to formulate and implement the government's own programme). This literature originally examined the impact of ownership indicators in the context of multilateral grants or long-term concessional loans. More recently, this methodology has been applied to multilateral official financing more generally. The key finding in all studies is that the effectiveness of IFI-supported programmes depends systematically on a small number of domestic political economy indicators. Once these political economy conditions are taken into account, initial and external economic conditions or IFI effort do not seem to matter very much.

Two empirical studies are particularly revealing. The first, by the World Bank's Operations Evaluation Department (World Bank, 1999), examined a large number of projects supported by the Bank. It found that project outcomes (as measured by several objective and subjective indicators) were positively correlated with the government's commitment to each project. The second study, by David Dollar and Jakob Svensson (2000), used econometric methods appropriate for discrete choice variables to examine the causes of success or failure of about 200 Bank Structural Adjustment Programmes (SAPs).[19] The Operations Evaluation Department had rated about a third of these programmes as unsuccessful. Dollar and Svensson related programme outcomes to political economy indicators, donor inputs and initial domestic and external economic conditions in a probit regression. Since donors are likely to expend more resources to salvage programmes that are failing, the study carefully took into account – by means of instrumental variable techniques – the endogeneity of donor inputs. Dollar and Svensson found that domestic conditions conducive to reform were systematically related to programme success. Programmes were more successful in countries that were politically stable, not severely divided ethnically and whose governments were democratic and had not been in power for long. On the other hand, once the endogeneity of Bank effort was taken into account, there seemed to be little independent relationship between programme success and Bank inputs in preparing and monitoring programmes.[20]

Several studies at the IMF indicate that qualitatively similar conclusions apply to Fund-supported programmes. Mauro Mecagni (1999) examined the causes behind major disruptions in about thirty ESAF programmes. He showed that interruptions depended primarily on domestic factors and that programme design could not have prevented these unfavourable outcomes. A staff study, IMF (2001a, 2001b), employed a newly constructed index of structural programme implementation and found that the extent of implementation of structural conditionality was not related to the number of conditions in Fund-supported programmes. Aleš Bulíř and Soojin Moon (2002) studied the determinants of fiscal developments in countries after the expiration of their IMF-supported programmes. They documented that medium-term fiscal prospects were driven by initial disequilibria and subsequent economic shocks. Structural conditionality, whether measured by interruptions, the number of conditions in programmes, or their implementation record did not seem to matter at the margin. Alun Thomas (2002) examined the impact of imposing more prior actions for the success or failure of Fund-supported programmes. He found that when political economy variables were controlled for, using more prior actions did not improve the

---

[19] These are examined in more detail in IMF (2001a), annex I, and IMF (2001c). A third paper, by Burnside and Dollar (2000), examined relationships among aid, economic policies and real growth in *per capita* GDP. It concluded that aid had a positive impact on growth in developing countries that have good fiscal, monetary and trade policies but little effect in the presence of poor policies.

[20] As discussed above (see the discussion of time-inconsistency problems), and as emphasised by Dollar and Svensson (2000), these results should not be interpreted to mean that conditionality is superfluous. Conditional external assistance is an effective commitment technology in countries where reform programmes and the governments supporting them lack full credibility.

implementation of Fund-supported programmes. Valerie Mercer-Blackman and Anna Unigovskaya (2000) studied a sample of transition economies and found that programme implementation was related to economic growth. They argued that these correlations were due to a third factor – government commitment to reforms – that was positively related to both.

Another recent study (Ivanova *et al.*, 2001) tested directly for the importance of domestic divisions in limiting ownership. These authors applied the Dollar–Svensson methodology to a sample of 170 Fund-supported programmes, and tested for the direct influence of divisions due to special interests on programme prospects. Once again, when political economy variables were controlled for, Fund effort and conditionality and initial conditions did not seem to matter for programme implementation. Several political economy variables related to domestic divisions affected programme implementation. First, the strength of special interests in parliament was significant in almost all specifications: the more powerful special interest groups were in the parliament, the less likely it was that the Fund-supported programme would succeed. Second, a high degree of political cohesion increased the probability of successful programme implementation. This underscores that the interaction between the government and parliament is an important consideration when evaluating programme ownership and the probability of programme success. Third, too much or too little ethnic diversity was bad for reforms.[21] Fourth, political instability negatively affected the probability of programme success. Fifth, effective government bureaucracies tended to cushion the effect of political instability during times of government change. Sixth, the government's length of tenure did not seem to be a direct cause of programme failure; and finally, democratically elected chief executives do not improve a programme's chances of success once domestic political economy conditions are taken into account.[22]

4 An action plan for strengthening ownership

Two broad lessons for enhancing ownership emerge from the review of the political economy literature. First, the IMF must understand the domestic political economy and tailor the content of the reform programmes it supports to these realities. Cookie-cutter approaches will not do. This point is, of course,

---

[21] In a nutshell, too much diversity generates social conflict, while too little diversity generates inertia in policy-making. The turning point varies between 43 per cent and 51 per cent, which is close to the estimates obtained by Dollar and Svensson (2000) for Bank-supported programmes (44–49 per cent).

[22] Programme implementation was also related to macroeconomic performance, in terms of average changes in inflation, the ratio of reserves to imports and the real exchange rate.

well understood at the Fund. The institution has always been careful to take the individual situation of each country into account in the design of its policy and financing packages. But current efforts aim to apply best practices more systematically. Several aspects of this effort are described below.

A second lesson is that the IMF's process of interaction with borrowing countries matters for a programme's national acceptance and eventual success. Achieving a critical mass of ownership in favour of reforms in the presence of a plethora of players with stakes in the outcomes requires a careful process of interaction and negotiation. As a result of the delicate nature of the domestic coalitions that must support a programme, ownership of reforms is both dynamic and fragile – a lesson demonstrated by the case studies summarised above. While opposition to reforms from entrenched interests or a lack of *ex ante* measures to protect and compensate those temporarily hurt by reforms can weaken ownership and compromise programme implementation, an effective dialogue between the IMF and the country's authorities and an effective process of public information can help build and sustain national ownership in the face of shocks and temporary setbacks.

On a practical level, enhancing ownership means designing the Fund's interactions with member countries so as to give as much flexibility and empowerment to the authorities as possible, maximising ownership while adhering to the Fund's core objectives. Three specific aspects of this process may be noted. One is giving borrowers greater control over the agenda. The degree of ownership, the effectiveness of conditional assistance programmes and the distribution of the surplus from the political relationship between the IFIs and member governments depend on the timing, control of the agenda, the nature of the negotiation process and the extent to which the IMF (rather than its membership) controls the use of its assistance funds. Another is to build a relationship of trust with authorities, in the context of ongoing regular surveillance and during negotiations on the use of Fund resources, and by promoting economic education and understanding. The Fund may also need to 'sell' programmes more effectively. Inadequate economic education could be overcome through public outreach and through promotion of economic literacy. A third aspect is to help nourish domestic coalitions for reform. Such coalitions (and those against reforms) are endogenous and evolve over time and help determine the domestic political economy balance. This balance could also be altered by aligning the Fund with 'progressive' constituencies internationally (Birdsall, 2000).

As the review of the political economy literature illustrates, an important question for the Fund is how to interact with borrowers when ownership is in question or when time constraints limit time-intensive approaches to building ownership. One option is selectivity: where a threshold of ownership is not present, the Fund could limit its financial involvement but continue with surveillance, analytical work and advice. Such an approach would strengthen the signalling value of conditionality and the Fund's catalytic function. Over time, economic education (including through the Fund's training programmes) could result in better understanding of the Fund's positions.[23] Lack of Fund support for incumbents who are against reforms would weaken their hand and strengthen domestic coalitions favouring reforms (including inside government). Clearly, greater selectivity and conditionality should be applied if domestic corruption is high and government intermediation of IFI assistance is inefficient. But the danger of carrying this approach too far is that it could inject the Fund into domestic political debates in ways that would be counterproductive and violate the principle of uniform treatment of members.

The Fund and other IFIs have already taken steps to ensure that their assistance programmes provide benefits that extend beyond narrow interests in or out of government and reach the broader public in recipient countries. The Fund and the World Bank have adopted broad participatory processes for the drafting of Poverty Reduction Strategy Papers (PRSPs) as the basis for lending to low-income countries. Possibilities for similar approaches in other borrowing countries are under discussion. These processes aim to enhance national ownership of reforms through broader public participation and improved self-monitoring. In addition, IFIs have responded to instances of corruption and misreporting by imposing stricter financial safeguards on the Central Banks that are repositories of IFI resources. Strict monitoring by the Fund of the uses which governments make of savings from debt relief under the Heavily Indebted Poor Countries (HIPC) initiative helps ensure that resources are used to increase pro-poor spending on public education and health. Development aid is channelled, where possible, through private suppliers in foreign countries through established public and transparent procurement methods that reduce the possibility of rent-seeking and corruption.

Looking ahead, several additional steps could be taken in accord with the findings reviewed in this chapter. The following measures, which are currently being considered (IMF, 2001c), would help ensure that the Fund's financial assistance is deeply rooted in domestically owned programmes:

- First, the Fund can insist that a country seeking financial assistance has a viable plan of its own for resolving its problems. For the Fund to provide an initial draft of letters of intent setting out policy intentions is efficient in a sense, but the practice may seriously undermine ownership.
- Second, when the Fund provides policy advice to countries in need of assistance, it should provide the authorities with as wide a range of options as possible. A feeling of being hemmed in by limited options from the Fund is

---

[23] The aid effectiveness literature has reached similar conclusions. See Dollar and Svensson (2000).

one of the most frequently made complaints from governments of borrowing countries.

- Third, the Fund can promote flexibility in programme design by basing its conditionality more on achievement of broad outcomes than on detailed policy actions ('outcomes-based conditionality') and by permitting more flexibility in the timing of disbursements linked to structural reforms ('floating tranches').
- Fourth, the Fund may need to broaden its capability to analyse issues of political economy, in addition to its highly regarded abilities at technical analysis. What forces are likely to block reforms, and how can coalitions for reform be reinforced?
- Fifth, the Fund could devote more effort to providing technical support for capacity building in developing countries.
- Sixth, the Fund can support country-led communications strategies outside the formal negotiation process, to promote understanding of the basis for reform programmes in the countries concerned.
- Finally, systematic and thorough *ex post* reviews of why programmes succeeded or failed can help generate a growing body of knowledge regarding the separate contributing roles of ownership, implementation capacity, technical programme design, and other elements in the process.

To conclude: is policy ownership an operational concept? On the surface, a negative answer might seem appropriate, if only because ownership is not directly observable or measurable. But the larger message of this chapter is that ownership is operationally important and may even be the most critical determinant of programme success. That conclusion is supported by a host of theoretical models, and it is consistent with a sizeable body of indirect empirical evidence. If that premise is accepted, then the next logical question is: what can be done to promote and enhance national ownership of reforms? Fundamentally, what case studies suggest is that ownership depends on *processes*. Engaging a wide range of officials, market participants, and civil society organisations at an early stage of the reform process is an element of programme design that has taken on increasing importance in recent years, and that must be given further prominence.

The IMF often must work under intense time pressure to complete programme negotiations quickly enough to resolve crises and restore market confidence. In such circumstances, it is not surprising that the design of optimal economic policies to recommend to the authorities might take precedence over the time-consuming process of building a domestic consensus for reform. Nonetheless, one message emerges clearly from the theoretical models and empirical studies summarised above. Successful implementation of economic reforms – indeed, economic success – depends on national ownership, and ownership depends on successful processes in which every key participant is fully empowered.

Appendix Vested interests in a positive theory of IFI conditionality

International and domestic conflicts of interest are at the root of ownership problems in reform programmes supported by IFIs. Mayer and Mourmouras (2002) present a framework for thinking about the resolution of such conflicts. They model assistance by the IMF and other international financial institutions (IFIs) using the menu auction approach developed by Bernheim and Whinston (1986) and applied to the political economy of trade by Grossman and Helpman (1994, 2001).

In this framework, the government of a country that receives assistance from the IMF is also subject to political influence by a domestic SIG.[24] Specifically, the SIG makes contributions to incumbents that may be used to finance re-election campaigns or even politicians' personal expenditures. At any rate, the presence of a SIG generates a domestic conflict of interest. International conflicts of interest may also be present if countries receiving IFI support are systemically important, in which case their policy choices generate international spillovers. In these circumstances, recipient governments balance the marginal benefit from political contributions against the marginal damage to national welfare caused by higher distortions, but are likely to ignore the systemic impacts of their actions. The IMF, on the other hand, internalises the externalities of the government's policy choices on the world economy. Its assistance aims to tilt the recipient government's cost-benefit calculations. How effective such assistance is in achieving better policies depends on the process of interactions between the IMF and the government and between the government and domestic SIGs.

Formally, there are three players in the model: the incumbent government (G) in charge of economic decision-making, a domestic special interest group (SIG), and an international financial institution (the IMF). The SIG influences the incumbent's economic policy choices through its financial contributions to the government. These contributions are side-payments that do not enter the government's budget constraint. The IMF is a benevolent institution that safeguards the welfare of creditor and recipient countries alike. It influences policies by providing conditional financial assistance to the government in support of economic reforms. This assistance is channelled in socially beneficial ways and

---

[24] As discussed in section 2, this approach is complementary to that followed by Drazen (2001), who provides a political economy analysis based on veto player theory.

its repayment is assured by assumption. In a politico-economic equilibrium, the government's economic policies are shaped by the strategic interaction of all three players.

National welfare after IMF assistance has been released but before it has been repaid (W) depends on the amount of assistance from the IMF (T) and the quality of economic policies ($\omega \geq 0$ is an index of policy distortions). IMF assistance raises welfare in the recipient country directly, but at a decreasing rate: $W_T > 0$, $W_{TT} < 0$. Raising economic policy distortions lowers welfare at an increasing rate: $W_\omega < 0$, $W_{\omega\omega} < 0$. Higher distortions also reduce the effectiveness of IMF assistance, $W_{T\omega} < 0$. As explained more fully in Mayer and Mourmouras (2002), if the rate of repayment of IMF funds is b, the present value of repayments of IMF loans is bT. Net national welfare, after a country has received and repaid IMF assistance, is then $Y(\omega, T) = W(\omega, T) - bT$.

The IMF maximises net national welfare in the borrowing country and the rest of the world, denoted $I(\omega, T; \gamma, b) = \gamma Y(\omega, T) + Y^*(\omega, T)$, where $\gamma \geq 0$ is the weight the IMF attaches to the national welfare of the borrowing country. $Y^*(\omega, T) = W^*(\omega, T) + bT$ is net welfare in the rest of the world, after IMF loans have been disbursed and repaid, while W^* is the rest of the world's welfare after the IFI's lending but before repayment. Since IMF lending is financed by the rest of the world, donors incur financial costs by providing assistance, so that $W_T^* < 0$ and $W_{TT}^* < 0$. Recipient country policies may affect welfare in the rest of the world. If a country is 'systemically' important, an increase in its policy distortions could affect welfare in the rest of the world: $W_\omega^* \leq 0$, $W_{\omega\omega}^* \leq 0$.

The government's objective function (G) depends on the general welfare of its people and political contributions from the SIG, $G(\omega, T) = C(\omega) + aY(\omega, T)$, where $C(\omega)$ is the contribution schedule which the lobby offers the government contingent on the adoption of distortionary policies and $a \geq 0$ is the government's concern for national welfare. The SIG's objective function is $V(\omega) = U(\omega) - C(\omega)$, where $U(\omega)$, its welfare before contributions, increases at a decreasing rate with the degree of distortions ($U_\omega > 0$, $U_{\omega\omega} < 0$). In addition, it is assumed that $U_\omega(0) + aW_\omega(0, 0) > 0$, which guarantees that some distortions are present in equilibrium when the IFI is not active. As explained in Grossman and Helpman (2001, pp. 232, 266), the analysis of common agency games focuses on subgame-perfect Nash equilibria that are compensating (or truthful). The SIG's equilibrium contribution is compensating if in response to an increase in policy distortions the lobby raises its contribution by an amount equal to the additional distortions' marginal utility: $U_\omega(\omega^o) = C_\omega^o(\omega^o)$. In the absence of any IFI involvement, the domestic political equilibrium is a positive level of distortions ω^{-I}, assumed unique, and a truthful contribution schedule $C(\omega)$ such that $U_\omega(\omega) = aW_\omega(\omega, 0)$ when evaluated at ω^{-I}. In equilibrium, the government's policy choice maximises its political support. This entails equating the marginal benefit of distortions (in terms of increased political

Figure 9.1 *Equilibrium with conditional and unconditional IFI assistance*

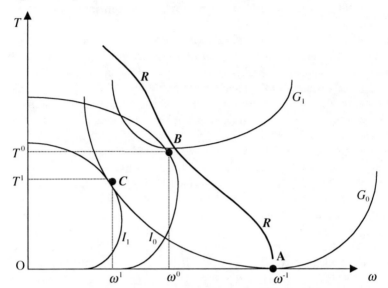

support from the SIG) with the marginal cost of distortions to aggregate welfare. This equilibrium is shown at point C in figure 9.1, where the superscript $-I$
indicates the absence of IFI involvement. See Mayer and Mourmouras (2002)
for more details.

When the IFI is active, its strategic interaction with the government and
the SIG must be considered. Mayer and Mourmouras (2002) model the interaction between the government, the IMF and the SIG as a non-cooperative,
multi-stage game. They consider two types of equilibria, corresponding to offers of unconditional and conditional assistance. As discussed in the main text,
unconditional assistance is the least intrusive form of involvement by an international institution in the affairs of a sovereign nation and, as such, it maximises
government ownership. When assistance is provided without explicit policy
conditions, the IMF does not make its offer contingent on the receiving government's pursuit of distortion-reducing economic policies. It does, however,
take into account the government's reaction to the availability of unconditional
assistance. Given these reactions, the Fund offers an amount of assistance that
maximises its utility. Formally, the political equilibrium with unconditional assistance is the outcome of a three-stage game. In stage one, the IMF decides
on the total amount of economic assistance. In stage two, the SIG chooses its
contribution schedule. In stage three, the government selects the distortion-
creating economic policies. The model is solved working backwards, by first
focusing on stages two and three to determine the government's choice of ω

in the presence of the influence-seeking SIG, given the amount of assistance made available by the IMF. In stage one, the IMF's choice of assistance is determined, given the government's policy response to alternative assistance levels.

Unconditional assistance does not mean the IMF can safely ignore domestic political realities.[25] Efficiency in the allocation of its resources requires the Fund to be familiar with how the authorities react to assistance even if it is provided without strings and is channelled in socially beneficial ways. Varying the level of IMF assistance alters the government's incentives as it affects the marginal damage of distortions on national welfare. Specifically, in setting its level of unconditional assistance, the Fund must obtain information on how the recipient government's domestic political economy constraint $U_\omega(\omega^o) = -a W_\omega(\omega^o, T)$ is affected by assistance. This constraint always binds in equilibrium. Although social welfare is maximised at $\omega = 0$, the government chooses a positive value of ω, and this choice varies with the level of assistance. It can be shown that higher assistance improves policies. An increase in assistance makes policy distortions costlier in terms of social welfare. Formally, the government's reaction function $d\omega^o/dT = -a W_{\omega T}(\omega^o, T)/[U_{\omega\omega}(\omega^o) + a W_{\omega\omega}(\omega^o)]$ is downward-sloping. The locus of choices of economic policy distortions traced by varying the amount of assistance is the downward-sloping government reaction function RR (figure 9.1). The slope of the reaction function depends on how much the government is concerned for the general public's welfare and how detrimental distortions are to the effectiveness of assistance. If the IMF takes into account the government's policy reaction function, RR, it will choose an amount of assistance T_o that puts it on the highest attainable welfare contour, namely I_0 at point B.

In practice, the Fund's offers of assistance are contingent on the incumbent government's pursuit of distortion-reducing economic policies. Conditional assistance turns the IMF into a principal in a common agency problem. The government's choice of economic policies is a subgame-perfect Nash equilibrium of a two-stage game between the government, the IMF and the SIG. In the first stage of the game, the IMF and the SIG set their compensating assistance and contribution schedule, respectively. In the second stage, the government selects the degree of policy distortions taking as given each principal's contribution schedule. Uniqueness of the equilibrium is guaranteed by selecting contribution and assistance schedules that are compensating. Compensating equilibria equate each principal's marginal benefit (cost in the case of the Fund) from additional distortions to its marginal cost in terms of additional contributions (assistance).

---

[25] In addition, the IMF must also worry about members' repayment difficulties, which Mayer and Mourmouras (2000) abstract from.

Compensating equilibria do not waste resources. In equilibrium, the joint welfare of the government and the interest group and the government and the IMF is maximised. If this were not true, the lobby or the IMF could offer the government alternative contribution and assistance schedules that would be mutually beneficial. In equilibrium, the marginal rates of substitution of the IMF and the government must be equal. This results in an 'international tangency condition' (point C in figure 9.1) between the indifference curves of the IMF and the government. This tangency pins down the government's choice of economic policy distortions and the level of IMF assistance. The equilibrium depends on all the 'deep parameters' of preferences of the government, the SIG and the IMF, including the magnitude of the marginal damage to the rest of the world from increased distortions, the weight of the borrowing country in the IMF's objective, and so on.

Two key questions are the aggregate effectiveness of conditionality and its impact on each player's welfare. These questions can be addressed by comparing the amount of IMF assistance, the resulting level of distortions and the welfare effects of IMF assistance under the alternatives of conditional and unconditional assistance. Regarding the first question, the main result is that the conditional assistance equilibrium is Pareto efficient while the equilibrium with unconditional assistance is not. At the international tangency condition, all mutually advantageous trades between the IMF and the recipient government have been exhausted, taking into account the reactions of the domestic SIG. But whereas the IFI is better off providing assistance conditionally, the government is better off with unconditional assistance. Note, however, that while conditionality results in more effective use of IFI resources, it is achieved at a price. With conditional assistance, the Fund is injected more deeply in the affairs of the recipient country as it becomes an active participant – a second principal – in the domestic political economy game.

The effectiveness of IMF assistance also depends on its form, whether loans or grants, as reflected in the value of $0 < b < 1$. Raising the value of b amounts to a reduction in the rate of subsidisation. Mayer and Mourmouras (2002) show that conditional grants are the most effective form of assistance from the point of view of the IMF. If the IMF cares for the recipients at least as much as for the creditors, reducing the rate of subsidisation raises policy distortions in the assisted countries. Formally, $dI/db = T(W_T + W_T^*)/(W_T - b) < 0$ if $\gamma \geq 1$. This result must be interpreted with some care. First, conditional grants are not 'free'. They are contingent on recipients achieving measurable results in reducing their policy distortions. No assistance is forthcoming if recipients deviate from agreed policies. Second, the result is derived in a perfect information, one-period model. It states that if the world lasted only one period, then the IMF's assistance would be most effective if it were provided in the most direct way. It is not likely to come out of a dynamic model of the 'revolving nature of Fund resources' in which the IMF must maintain an adequate capital base and in which the identity of future borrowers is not the same as the identity of present borrowers.

REFERENCES

Adam, C. S. and S. A. O'Connell (1999). 'Aid, Taxation and Development: Analytical Perspectives on Aid Effectiveness in Sub-Saharan Africa', *Economics and Politics*, 11, 225–53

Åslund, A. (1999). 'Why Has Russia's Economic Transformation Been So Arduous?', Carnegie Endowment for International Peace, paper prepared for the Annual World Bank Conference on Development Economics, Washington, DC, 28–30 April; available at http://www.ceip.org/files/Publications/econwn9.asp?from=pubauthor

Bernheim, B. D. and M. D. Whinston (1986). 'Menu Auctions, Resource Allocation, and Economic Influence', *Quarterly Journal of Economics*, 101(1), 1–32

Birdsall, N. (2000). 'The World Bank of the Future: Victim, Villain, Global Credit Union?', remarks delivered at 'Promoting Dialogue: Global Challenges and Global Institutions', Washington, DC, American University, 13 April; available at http://www.odc.org/commentary/bird-au.html

Boone, P. (1996). 'Politics and the Effectiveness of Foreign Aid', *European Economic Review*, 40, 289–329

Botchwey, K., P. Collier, J. W. Gunning and K. Hamada (1998). *External Evaluation of the ESAF: Report by a Group of Independent Experts*. Washington, DC, International Monetary Fund

Bridgman, B. R., I. D. Livshits and J. C. MacGee (2001). 'For Sale: Barriers to Riches', University of Minnesota and Federal Reserve Bank of Minneapolis, manuscript, January

Bulíř, A. and S. Moon (2003). 'Do IMF-Supported Programs Help Mark Fiscal Adjustment More Durable', IMF Working Paper, 03/38

Burnside, C. and D. Dollar (2000). 'Aid, Policies, and Growth', *American Economic Review*, 90, 847–68

Dalmazzo, A. and G. de Blasio (2001). 'Resources and Incentives to Reform: A Model and Some Evidence on Sub-Saharan African Countries', IMF Working Paper, WP/01/86, June; available at http://www.imf.org/external/pubs/cat/longres.cfm?sk=15168.0

Diamond, P. and J. Mirrlees (1971). 'Optimal Taxation and Public Production: I. Production Efficiency, and II. Tax Rules', *American Economic Review*, 61, 8–27, 261–78

Dixit, A. (2000). 'IMF Programs as Incentive Mechanisms', International Monetary Fund, mimeo, June

(2001). 'Some Lessons from Transaction-Cost Politics for Less-Developed Countries', Olson Memorial Lecture delivered at the University of Maryland, 26 October; available at: http://www/bsos.umd.edu/umccc/olson_memorial_lecture_series_schedule.htm

Dixit, A., G. M. Grossman and E. Helpman (1997). 'Common Agency and Coordination: General Theory and Application to Government Policy Making', *Journal of Political Economy*, 105(4), 752–69

Dollar, D. and J. Svensson (2000). 'What Explains the Success or Failure of Structural Adjustment Programs?', *Economic Journal*, 110, 894–917

Drazen, A. (2000). *Political Economy in Macroeconomics*. Princeton, NJ, Princeton University Press

(2001). 'Conditionality and Ownership in IMF Lending: A Political Economy Approach', paper presented at the 2nd Annual IMF Research Conference, 29–30 November

Grossman, G. M. and E. Helpman (1994). 'Protection for Sale', *American Economic Review*, 84, 833–50

2001, *Special Interest Politics*, Cambridge, MA: MIT Press

Havrylyshyn, O. and J. Odling-Smee (2000), 'Political Economy of Stalled Reforms', *Finance and Development*, 37(3); available at http://www.imf.org/external/pubs/ft/fandd/2000/09/havrylys.htm

Hellman, J. and D. Kaufmann (2001). 'Confronting the Challenge of State Capture in Transition Economies', *Finance and Development*, 38(3); available at http://www.imf.org/external/pubs/ft/fandd/2001/09/hellman.htm

International Monetary Fund (IMF) (2001a). 'Conditionality in IMF-Supported Programs – Policy Issues', 16 February; available at http://www.imf.org/external/np/pdr/cond/2001/eng/policy/index.htm

(2001b). 'Structural Conditionality in IMF-Supported Programs', 16 February; available at http://www.imf.org/external/np/pdr/cond/2001/eng/struct/index.htm

(2001c). 'Strengthening Country Ownership of Fund-Supported Programs', 5 December; available at http://www.imf.org/external/np/pdr/cond/2001/eng/strength/120501.htm

Ivanova, A., W. Mayer, A. Mourmouras and G. Anayiotos (2001). 'What Determines the Success or Failure of Fund-supported Programs', paper presented at the 2nd Annual IMF Research Conference, 29–30 November

Khan, M. S. and S. Sharma (2001). 'IMF Conditionality and Country Ownership of Programs', IMF Working Paper, 01/142, October; available at http://www.imf.org/external/pubs/cat/longres.cfm?sk=15374.0

Krueger, A. (1974). 'The Political Economy of a Rent-Seeking Society', *American Economic Review*, 64(3), 291–303

Krusell P. and J.-V. Rios-Rull (1996). 'Vested Interests in a Positive Theory of Stagnation and Growth', *Review of Economic Studies*, 63, 301–29

Lahiri, S. and P. Raimondos-Möller (2001). 'Poverty Reduction with Foreign Aid: Donor Strategy under Fungibility', Working Paper, University of Copenhagen, 28 March; available at http://www.econ.ku.dk/prm/revfung.PDF

(2000). 'Lobbying by Ethnic Groups and Aid Allocation', *Economic Journal*, 110, 62–79

Mayer, W. and A. Mourmouras (2002). 'Vested Interests in a Positive Theory of IFI Conditionality', IMF Working Paper, 02/73

McGuire, M. and M. Olson (1996). 'The Economics of Autocracy and Majority Rule', *Journal of Economic Literature*, 34, 72–96

Mecagni, M. (1999). 'The Causes of Program Interruptions', in H. Bredenkamp and S. Schadler (eds.), *Economic Adjustment and Reform in Low-Income Countries*. Washington, DC, IMF, 215–76

Meltzer, A. and S. Richard (1981). 'A Rational Theory of the Size of Government', *Journal of Political Economy*, 89, 914–27

Mercer-Blackman, V. and A. Unigovskaya (2000). 'Compliance with IMF Program Indicators and Growth in Transition Economies', IMF Working Paper, WP/00/47; available at http://www.imf.org/external/pubs/cat/longres.cfm?sk=3491.0

Odling-Smee, J. (2001). 'Belarus: Recent Experience and Challenges Ahead', speech given at the Belarusian Academy of Management, Minsk 6 November

Olson, M. (1965). *The Logic of Collective Action*. Cambridge, MA, Harvard University Press

(1982). *The Rise and Decline of Nations*. New Haven, CT, Yale University Press

(1993). 'Dictatorship, Democracy and Development', *American Political Science Review*, 87(3), 567–76

Prescott, E. C. and S. L. Parente (2000). *Barriers to Riches*. Cambridge, MA, MIT Press

Thomas, A. (2003). 'The Use of Prior Actions in Fund-Supported Programs', Working Paper, International Monetary Fund, forthcoming

Tsebelis, G. (2001a). *Veto Players: How Political Institutions Work*. Princeton, NJ, Princeton University Press and Russell Sage Foundation, forthcoming; available at www.polisci.ucla.edu/tsebelis

(2001b). 'Veto Players and Institutional Analysis', Department of Political Science, UCLA, manuscript; available at www.polisci.ucla.edu/tsebelis

Vaubel, R. (1996). 'Bureaucracy at the IMF and the World Bank', *The World Economy*, 19(2), 195–210

Vreeland, J. R. (2000). 'The IMF: Lender of Last Resort or Scapegoat?', Department of Political Science, Yale University, manuscript, April

Willett, T. D. (2000). 'A Soft-Core Public Choice Analysis of the International Monetary Fund', Claremont McKenna College and Claremont Graduate University, manuscript, October

World Bank (1999). 'Higher-Impact Adjustment Lending: Initial Evaluation', Operations Evaluation Department, Report 19797, Washington, DC, The World Bank

10 The IMF and East Asia: a changing regional financial architecture

GORDON DE BROUWER

1 Introduction

The financial crises of 1997 and 1998 have had a profound effect on East Asia's view of international financial and monetary arrangements, including the role of the International Monetary Fund (IMF) in international policy dialogue and financial cooperation.[1] There has been a tectonic shift in the policy landscape of the region.[2] While there are differences between and within countries, no longer is East Asia content to rely almost exclusively on global forums, mechanisms and institutions; it now wants to develop a complementary regional structure. The process of developing a regional economic and financial architecture may be in its early stages but the political and policy dynamics under way make it irreversible.

There are many elements to the expansion of regional arrangements – ranging from strengthened policy dialogue, greater financial cooperation, deeper economic and trade integration and even common currency arrangements. Much of the content of the evolving debate and policy on regional financial arrangements

I am grateful to Peter Drysdale, Jeff Frankel, Prasanna Gai, Chris Gilbert, David Vines and many (anonymous) officials from the region for their comments and feedback. The views and opinions expressed here, and any errors and inaccuracies made, are my own. Comments and corrections are welcome.

[1] The East Asian region includes China, Hong Kong SAR, Japan, Korea and Taiwan, the 10 ASEAN countries (Brunei, Burma, Cambodia, Indonesia, Laos, Malaysia, the Philippines, Singapore, Thailand and Vietnam) and Australia and New Zealand. The latter two countries are included because they are deeply economically integrated with the region, in both trade and in finance, and have a long history of policy interaction with many countries in the region: this was acknowledged by Japanese Prime Minister Koizumi's inclusion of them in his January 2002 Singapore speech outlining his vision of an East Asian Community.

[2] It is an over-simplification to say that a region as large and diverse as East Asia has any particular view, but that does not mean it is not possible or incorrect to attempt to describe broad sentiment at times.

is tied directly to the region's discontent with the IMF and its concomitant, disillusion with the way the United States dealt with the financial crisis in East Asia. It is also motivated by a profound sense that deep economic and financial integration in East Asia can be of substantial benefit, both nationally and internationally, to countries in the region. At the same time, the European experience is seen as compelling.

The IMF is widely seen in East Asia as having performed poorly in the financial crises of 1997 and 1998, although its performance did improve later in the crisis and it is credited with being more responsive to the region's concerns since then. The Fund's sins in East Asia are perceived by its critics to be many: it initially interpreted the crisis incorrectly, it forced countries to adopt macroeconomic and structural policies which did not support confidence and recovery,[3] it was rigidly ideological in its analysis of hedge funds and initial dismissal of the possibility of destabilising speculation in financial markets,[4] and it was not able to garner the support of the United States and Europe in dealing with the crisis at critical stages in 1997 and 1998. Rather than being credited as a key independent player, it was seen as US-run and dominated, ideological and inflexible, and obsessed with protecting its own bureaucratic interests.[5]

Despite this experience, there is no appetite in (most of) the region for doing away with the Fund. It plays far too valuable a role: it is a key resource for technical assistance and analysis; it is essential in dealing with broad-based or global financial crises, including securing private sector involvement; it is a useful tool for politicians to push domestic reform; it provides a voice for smaller countries at the global level; and it is a key device in securing US and European interest in the world outside their borders and immediate regions. But there is a profound sense in much of East Asia that international financial policy-making and cooperation cannot proceed only on the global level; it must be complemented by strong well-designed regional financial arrangements. These financial arrangements encompass strengthened policy dialogue, financial cooperation and perhaps common currency arrangements in East Asia.

This chapter analyses the regional financial architecture that is emerging in East Asia. It looks first in section 2 at the motivation for the new regional financial architecture. There is a layering of reasons behind the push for strengthened regional financial arrangements, with complex economic, strategic and chauvinistic components. The interplay of these factors has changed since mid-1997, with some of the bite of the emotionally charged elements moderated by the practicalities and broader strategic interests of the region. Understanding the motivation is important in deciding how to respond to the new Asian

---

[3] For references and the IMF staff's explanation and defence, see Boorman *et al.* (2000).

[4] See chapter 3 in de Brouwer (2001). As shown by its *Capital Market Reports* in 1999 and 2000, the Fund, or parts of it, may have subsequently become less sceptical.

[5] It is hard to source public quotes by officials along these lines, but this was certainly the private sentiment of many officials in the region.

regionalism: opponents who summarily dismiss it are likely to fuel the fire because they ignore crucial strategic and chauvinistic elements at play. The aim in section 2 is to characterise the general views of the region (and not the author's own opinion).

Section 3 looks in more detail at the policy agenda on regional financial arrangements. It examines the development of policy dialogue in the region and critically assesses the value of regional policy dialogue and the functioning of these forums. It then critically examines regional financial cooperation, looking at what is meant by 'financial cooperation', whether it should be regional or global, and what the state of play is in East Asia. It briefly looks at the issue of common currency arrangements. Section 4 concludes the chapter.

2 Motivation for a new regional financial architecture

The debate about regional financial arrangements is complex. The motivation for the new regional financial architecture has economic, strategic and chauvinistic dimensions. I briefly consider these in turn.

Economic reasons

The economic rationale for new regional financial arrangements has two main aspects.

The first is the perceived need for a mechanism for *regional* financial support to prevent or resolve financial crises. This is meant at least to supplement global mechanisms, if not to replace them in certain circumstances. The focus here is on the perceived failures of the IMF. It is probably correct to say that there is broad consensus within East Asia that the IMF rescue packages for Thailand, Korea and Indonesia suffered from flaws in terms of their involvement and their conditionality.

One strategic aim of IMF membership for many countries is to secure the interest of the United States and other 'big' countries in their circumstances. This is especially important since capital account crises are now so large that they are beyond the direct resources of the Fund and rely on broader official support through bilateral loans.[6] Indeed, the IMF normally relies on other international

[6] A total of $17.1 billion, $36.2 billion and $58.9 billion were committed to Thailand, Indonesia and Korea, respectively, in 1997 and 1998. The IMF components were $3.9 billion, $11.2 billion and $20.9 billion, respectively. The World Bank was also involved in these programmes but its involvement seems to many to be beyond the scope of its charter. The size of the financing requirements also raises the need for private sector involvement in the prevention and resolution of financial crises.

financial institutions and bilateral supporters in its country programmes in order to demonstrate wider endorsement of the policy measures in them.[7] There is a sense in the region that the IMF was not successful in securing US interest and involvement early enough in 1997. The United States, for example, did not contribute bilaterally to the Thai package, although it did later commit to the Korean and Indonesian packages (although the second line of defence was not drawn on in either case). Indeed, the only countries to be involved bilaterally in all three East Asian packages were two countries in the region: Australia and Japan.

The other flaw in the IMF packages was the nature of conditionality. There are two dimensions to this. One is that the nature of the crisis was not well identified early enough by the Fund. Looking at Thailand, the initial IMF policy diagnosis and assessment were that it was a conventional demand management problem – excessively easy fiscal and monetary policy and deteriorating current account – requiring a general policy tightening. But what was happening was not a current account crisis but joint capital account and financial system crises – requiring supportive fiscal policy and not prolonged tight monetary policy. The Fund took a long while to change its view (February 1998 in the case of Thailand), longer than occurred in the region,[8] and this took a long while to filter through to policy change at the national level. The other dimension was the focus on deep extensive structural reform as part of the conditionality for an IMF package, and the at-times naïve way reform was implemented.[9] While such reform is no doubt desirable and important, requiring immediate wholesale structural adjustment in an exchange rate crisis may not be realistic.[10]

Whatever the merit of the criticisms and notwithstanding the fact that many in the region do understand, and were involved in promoting, the use of such packages as a vehicle for pursuing domestic economic and structural reform, the IMF packages and reactions are widely thought to have exacerbated, rather than alleviated, the crisis at critical times in 1997 and 1998. If the global mechanism embodied in the IMF does not work as well as expected and cannot be fully remedied, the view in much of the region is that action has to also be taken at the regional level to prevent and manage financial crises.

The second economic motivation for regional financial arrangements focuses on exchange rate arrangements in East Asia. The causes of the east Asian financial crisis were many, and one aspect that has received considerable attention in East Asia, and Japan in particular, is the heightened vulnerability to external

---

[7] See Costello (1999).

[8] This is based on the author's discussions with policy-makers in the region. See also Grenville (1997, 1998) and Macfarlane (1997a, 1997b).

[9] An oft-quoted example is the closure of sixteen banks in Indonesia in November 1997. It led to widespread panic because depositors feared that this was just the start of a wave of closures.

[10] See, for example, Yoshitomi and Ohno (1999).

shocks caused by implicit dollar pegging in a number of crisis-affected economies, notably Thailand but also Indonesia and Korea.[11]

As the dollar appreciated relative to the yen and Mark from the mid-1990s onwards, the implicit dollar peg meant that these countries' currencies also appreciated relative to the yen and mark. Their export competitiveness weakened and their current account positions deteriorated, making them vulnerable to downward pressure on the exchange rate and susceptible to economic and financial shocks and changes in market sentiment. Had these countries tied their exchange rate, even loosely, to a basket peg – meaning some weighted combination of the dollar, yen and Mark (now euro) – they would have experienced less appreciation of the effective exchange rate and hence been less vulnerable in 1997.

This is not merely of historical interest. The argument goes that these same countries have now returned to an implicit dollar peg, at least to some extent.[12] If these countries are not genuinely floating their currencies as they say they are (because of the 'fear of floating'), then the rationale for a basket peg currency arrangement is even greater. Given the rise in intra-regional trade in non-Japan East Asia, some also argue that the weights in the basket peg should be common for the region, or some subset of it. But others fear that a basket peg would be too slow to respond to changes in economic fundamentals and so would be subject to speculative attack.

Strategic factors

While these economic reasons are important in their own right and warrant serious analysis, they mask the strategic plays by countries in the region. It is much easier and less threatening to use arguments about economics than arguments that make explicit strategic regional and global positioning in the debate about regional arrangements.

Dealing with the United States . . .

The central play is directed at the world's sole superpower, the United States. It has the dual aims of using regional arrangements as a bulwark against US economic influence in the region and balancing US influence in global policy-making forums like the IMF.

---

[11] See, for example, Ito, Sasaki and Ogawa (1998), Kawai and Akiyama (2000), Kawai and Takagi (2000), Yoshino, Koji and Suzuki (2000) and Williamson (2001).

[12] See Ogawa (2000) and Kawai (2001). De Brouwer (2002a) looks at alternative explanations.

Many of the arguments raised about the IMF's performance before and during the east Asian financial crisis are criticisms of US policy and power and how they were exercised. The IMF is widely seen by policy-makers and academics in East Asia as a US-run institution:[13] the United States has effective veto power over key decisions in the Executive Board; the IMF's head office is in Washington, DC only a few blocks from the US Treasury; and the powerful First Deputy Managing Director (who does many of the sensitive negotiations) is a US citizen often with close links to the US Treasury.

If the region believed that the United States was sufficiently responsive to its needs and aspirations and that it had an effective voice in the IMF, then the enthusiasm for regional financial arrangements, especially in terms of regional financial cooperation, might be weaker. But it does not.

This needs to be spelled out a bit more. The east Asian financial crisis had a radical effect on the region's perception of the United States as a reliable partner *in the domain of international finance*. The emphasis is intentional. A number of countries regard the United States as their primary partner in security and many regard the United States as a leading partner in trade and investment.[14] The region recognises and values the unique contribution the United States makes to maintaining security and stability in East Asia. There is no appetite to reverse this. But this does not mean that they are satisfied in all dimensions of international relations. While East Asia is heterogeneous and there are differences of opinion and emphasis between and within countries, the common view in East Asia is that the region was not well served in 1997 and 1998 by its reliance in international finance on the United States. Consider three examples that are in the minds of policy-makers in the region.

First, Thailand felt 'betrayed' by the United States.[15] Thailand allowed itself to be the platform for the United States in the war against communism in Vietnam but the United States did not offer bilateral financing support during the crisis. Indeed the US Treasury was perceived by some in Thailand to be bent on exposing weaknesses in that country even if that meant inducing a crisis in a traditional ally. Thais resented the apparent ready willingness of the United States to help 'bail out' South Korea, which is of clear strategic importance to the United States, but not Thailand.

Second, there is a perception in the region that the United States took advantage of the crisis to undermine Suharto's rule in Indonesia in January 1998 and was willing to do the same in Malaysia to undermine Mahathir later that year.[16] The United States was seen as being willing to undermine undemocratic

---

[13] See, for example, Lee and Yang (2001).

[14] See, for example, Yamamoto, Thiparat and Ahsan (2001).

[15] This is how a pro-US senior Thai journalist described local sentiment to the author.

[16] This is the assessment of a variety of senior officials across the region based on their discussions with some senior members of the US Administration in 1998.

regimes even at the risk of great economic and social cost. The robust and fulsome assertion of democracy in Cambodia, Indonesia, South Korea, the Philippines, Taiwan and Thailand in the past few decades shows just how much East Asia values democracy. But the region also places a high premium on political stability, especially in large heterogeneous nations like Indonesia, and there was deep bewilderment and disillusion with the perceived words and deeds of parts of the US Administration.

Third, countries were upset at the time by the United States' apparent two-faced position on hedge funds. On the one hand, the United States vigorously denied that the New York-based macro hedge funds and proprietary trading desks of international investment banks and securities firms played any particular destabilising role in Asian currency and equity markets in 1997 and 1998, in spite of the size and concentration of those positions and evidence of market manipulation.[17]

But, on the other hand, it organised a bailout of Long Term Capital Management (LTCM) because of the concern that unwinding that hedge fund's positions could have a negative impact on US financial prices, markets and institutions in September 1998. This sounded a touch inconsistent to east Asians long-lectured by the US Treasury and Federal Reserve about the evils of cronyism and dangers of moral hazard; the inconsistency led to talk in the region about the capture of US policy-making by Wall Street.

Some in the region also felt this to be implicitly racist or at least anti-Asian, as discussed in the next subsection on the chauvinistic motivation for east Asian regionalism. The 1998 IMF study on hedge funds was also viewed widely in the region as a whitewash of the issues (a sentiment which is most strongly felt in Malaysia and Thailand).[18]

It is understood in East Asia that US policy-making is divided between the Administration and Congress, and achieving consensus is especially difficult when different and antagonistic political parties occupy each seat of power. This was certainly the case in 1997 and 1998: not only was Congress very reluctant to support the Clinton Administration but the antipathy of many members of Congress to bailouts by the IMF, let alone the United States, was at its peak. The D'Amato amendment, passed by Congress after the Mexico crisis, also prohibited the US Treasury from using the Exchange Stabilisation Fund (ESF) at the time of the Thai rescue package, but had expired by the time of the Korean and Indonesian packages. It may be true that the Administration could not have supported Thailand (and Indonesia) more even if it had wanted to. But to the region, this just shows more starkly the unreliability of existing mechanisms and the consequent need for some sort of additional regional mechanism.

---

[17] See Financial Stability Forum Working Group on Highly Leveraged Institutions (2000).
[18] See de Brouwer (2001).

These criticisms are made notwithstanding the region's recognition of the central importance of the United States in the world economy and the fact that sustained strong US economic growth in the aftermath of the crisis provided much-needed external demand for Asian goods and services. While the increase in the US current account deficit at the time was welcomed in East Asia, it is viewed in the region as more the outcome of US policy-makers letting their own economic expansion continue to run than explicitly deciding to underpin East Asia's economies. The fact that US economic growth helped underpin East Asia was a happy coincidence.

The challenge for the region is how to maintain US economic and strategic involvement in East Asia but at the same time secure the sort of engagement in international financial policy-making that it wants from the United States. One way to do this is to emphasise that economic prosperity and security in East Asia are unambiguously in the US interest, and that, consistent with the express policy aims of the Bush Administration,[19] it is time for the region to be more self-sufficient in providing a market-oriented economic and financial infrastructure for itself. The regional financial architecture should be marketed as an example of East Asia being willing to take on its financial responsibilities, and the possibility of overlapping regional and global institutions or frameworks should be seen constructively as a device for avoiding excessive concentration of power in one institution.[20]

The sense after the crisis that the United States was an unreliable partner in matters to do with international finance spilled over automatically into disillusion with the IMF. The region does not feel that it can exercise its voice within the IMF, and so the region's 'problems' with the Fund cannot be readily addressed through normal processes.

There is a strong feeling in the region that it is wronged by the under-representation of Asia and over-representation of Europe in the Executive Board of the Fund.[21] There is little expectation of remedying this: why would the Europeans, especially the small countries, ever agree to reduce their influence? Japan also feels excluded from the US–Europe 'agreement' that the Managing Director of the Fund be European and the First Deputy Managing Director be American. Japan's nomination of its former Ministry of Finance Vice-Minister for International Finance, Dr Eisuke Sakakibara, as a candidate for Managing Director in 1999 was an assertion of its discontent.

---

[19] See Rice (2000).

[20] Loosely analogous to the aim of balance enshrined in the separation of powers in the US constitution. This is an argument that was used, for example, by Federal Reserve Chairman Greenspan in 1999 against the consolidation of prudential supervision in the United States into one institution.

[21] Based on GDP, Europe is over-represented by about 6 per cent in IMF quotas, while Japan and the United States are under-represented by 12 and 9 per cent, respectively. The Dutch, Saudi Arabian and Belgian constituencies are the most over-represented in terms of IMF quotas.

There is also a sense in non-Japan East Asia that one reason the United States has been able to dominate the IMF and other forums is because in the past Japan has not spoken up for the region as loudly as it could have. Observers of the IMF note that one aspect of the Fund is that it is a device for the major economies to champion the interests of their regions. The United States and Europe have long been robust supporters in a range of forums for Latin America and for developing Central and Eastern Europe and North Africa, respectively.

But Japan is not seen as having done this to the same extent for East Asia. Whatever the reasons – the legacy of colonialism and war, Japan's dependence on US security, a preference for consensus, the diversion of policy-makers' focus to domestic economic problems . . . – the result is that East Asia's champion has let itself be squeezed out. This has certainly started to change in the past few years but requires effort and persistence to remedy. There are also concerns that Japan's focus on regional financial architecture signals that it is less prepared to work in reforming global forums and representing the region's interests in them.

. . . and asserting national interests

But the strategic play is not only about giving the region a stronger voice in global affairs and limiting the hegemony of the United States. It is also very much about who has a voice and perhaps the strongest voice in regional arrangements. In other words, the play is not just about limiting the influence of the United States in the region but also about asserting a country's own influence.

The interests of countries in the region vary, but they tend to coincide in the promotion of regionalism and its embodiment, regional financial cooperation. Take three examples: Japan, China and ASEAN.

Japan is concerned with its place in the world. The 1990s have had a profound effect on that country's self-confidence. At the end of the 1980s, Japan felt that it was poised to become the world's leading economy: its assets were highly priced, its banks looked like they were about to dominate world finance, and its manufacturers were leading global industrialisation. The collapse of its asset price bubble and world financial empire and a decade of stagnation and four recessions have undermined its confidence in its ability and its future. The dominance of the dollar, the introduction of the euro and the deepening of European economic and financial integration have left Japan with a deep sense that it is losing its place as a key G3 economy. At the same time, the rise of China gives it the fear of losing its economic pre-eminence in East Asia.

This has meant that Japan has tried to assert a greater role in regional in-frastructure. The Miyazawa Plan for the recovery of crisis-affected economies, the proposal for an Asian Monetary Fund, the proposal for a common basket exchange rate peg arrangement for some ASEAN countries and the detail of the

ASEAN + 3 Chiang Mai swap agreement have all been led by Japan.[22] These have been proposed and argued on their perceived intellectual merits but they also meet Japan's strategic aim of entrenching itself permanently as the centre of regional arrangements.

The basket peg arrangement, for example, is proposed as a way to minimise the effects of volatility in the G3 countries' exchange rates on developing East Asia. But it is also anticipated that one effect of the arrangement – greater stability against the yen – will encourage more trade, investment and financial transactions to be conducted with yen. That is, it supports Japan's commitment to internationalise the yen, commensurate with its status as a G3 economy.

China is also aware of its growing status in the regional and world economy. While it opposed Japan's proposal in 1997 for an Asian Monetary Fund, largely because it was suspicious about Japan's motivation, it has since supported (or at least not vetoed) greater regional financial cooperation. China has judged that such cooperation is not only a useful balance against US financial power but enables it to secure a stronger strategic position at the centre of the region. China's proposal for an AFTA–China Free Trade Agreement is part of this play for greater political influence in the region.

Regional cooperation, especially ASEAN + 3, also provides China with a valuable forum for dialogue with Japan and Korea through additional bilateral and trilateral meetings on the fringe of the ASEAN + 3 meetings. The + 3 (that is, China, Japan and Korea) dialogue is also seen as a major advantage from the viewpoint of Japan and Korea, and was a primary goal in setting up ASEAN + 3.

From the ASEAN point of view, the regional arrangements are a substantial advance in outside recognition of ASEAN as a political entity, rather than merely as another collective expression for Southeast Asia. Aware that they are 'small' relative to the big economies of Northeast Asia, the ASEAN countries are keen to develop a subregional entity which can have more weight in dealings with the 'big three'.[23]

The promotion of these varying strategic interests within East Asia has gravitated towards a common agenda for stronger regional arrangements, financial and otherwise. While it means that there is now genuine support for deeper cooperation and integration in East Asia, it does reveal two vulnerabilities (which are not necessarily unique to the region). First, consensus based on reconciling competing strategic interests means that agreed outcomes tend to the lowest common denominator. As will be discussed in section 3, reaching agreement has been time-consuming and progress has been modest. Second, the consensus

---

[22] A swap involves exchanging domestic currency for a fixed amount of foreign currency, typically US dollars, for a fixed period at a predetermined price.

[23] At the same time, they are wary of being swallowed up by the big three.

is fragile to changes in how countries, especially the key players, perceive their strategic interests. This is not to say that arrangements made so far will come undone but it does mean that the path forward is not fixed; it could advance rapidly and substantively or it could progress no further for a while.

Chauvinistic motivation

Given the tumultuousness and nature of events in the past few years, it is not surprising that there has also been a chauvinistic and emotional element in the development of east Asian regionalism. This was most intense during and immediately after the crisis, but it still persists to some degree.

The crisis damaged the region's confidence and ego, not only by the terrible economic and social damage it caused but also by the exposure of flaws in domestic systems and policies and the reliance of the region on outside influences, especially the United States and the IMF. The ability of the region to come together so quickly and fulsomely to support Thailand (when the United States refused to) is a matter of regional pride. But parts of the region also feel shame that it did not have the comprehensive internal resources and wherewithal to deal with the crisis on its own, as the Europeans did in 1992.[24] The desire to both feel and assert a confident and capable east Asian identity is strong and is the rallying cry for building regional institutions.

The emotional intensity of this desire was exacerbated by the interaction between east Asian and US policy-makers during the crisis. The sense in East Asia was that US and other western policy-makers regarded East Asia's commitment to market-oriented economic and financial processes as weak. The region felt that its policy-makers were viewed by outsiders as relatively unreliable, opportunistic, inferior and incapable.

An example of this is the assessment by Eichengreen and Bayoumi (1999, pp. 361–4) that East Asia does not meet the necessary *intellectual* preconditions for regional integration. They argue that, in Europe, 'the ideal of integration is intimately connected with the liberal and democratic principles of the Enlightenment and has roots in centuries of history . . . [B]y 1945 the intellectual preconditions for European integration were in place', to be ignited by the 'spark of the Marshall Plan' into a regional commitment and agenda to cooperate at the deepest levels, including the unprecedented action of granting supranational authority to regional entities.

---

[24] See Kim, Ryax and Wang (2000) and Kim and Yang (2001). The EMS and East Asian crises were, however, different types of crisis requiring different policy responses; the former was a monetary crisis, the latter a financial crisis.

They argue that East Asia could not be more different. Not only does the region lack the necessary 'political solidarity and cohesion', but internal resistances to integration in East Asia are substantial and overwhelming. In the case of Europe, such resistances were 'overcome partly by the intervention of an outside agent, the United States' but this is missing in East Asia's case. They characterise East Asia as dominated by a colonial and insular military tradition, ideological conflict (communist China versus market-oriented economies elsewhere), and a complete unwillingness to allow outside parties to interfere in domestic affairs.

Indeed, they go on to say that East Asia is inherently incapable of substantive regional integration:

At a deeper level, East Asia lacks a Benthamite/Rousseauan/Saint-Simonian heritage of collective democratic governance through integration, As Katzenstein puts it, 'the notion of unified sovereignty . . . central to the conception of continental European states, does not capture Asian political realities'. As in China today, the regions resist the attempts of the center to exercise its politics through the operation of political and legal institutions. The idea of a centralized state with a monopoly of force that regiments its citizens through the superimposition of a common set of institutions is a European conception, not an Asian one. Asian civil society is structured by ritual, ceremony, and economic networks more than by military force or the rule of law. The notion of strong, cohesive nation-states in the Western mode being foreign to Asia, it is unrealistic to speak of pooling national sovereignties which do not exist. (1999, p. 363)

This type of assessment has not been well received in East Asia.[25] It is seen as a selective and glorified reading of European history and an assertion of European superiority. It is also seen as a subjective caricature which is far removed from the reality of modern East Asia. It is intellectually flawed in its assertion that there is only one institutional route to integration – the European way of creating (what are viewed from the outside as bloated, self-interested, poorly governed) regional bureaucracies, rather than regional cooperative policy-making supported by flexible secretariats. While there is no doubt considerable work to be done in strengthening markets and policy dialogue and cooperation in the region, it is wrong to say that it cannot be done in East Asia.

The nature of cross-Pacific dialogue has also encouraged Asian chauvinism. At times, US officials and economists have talked down to and hectored their east Asian colleagues.[26] And at times, they have delivered their message

---

[25] See, for example, Kim, Ryou and Wang (2000). They summarise the views of 'western scholars' and say that, '[n]evertheless, regional financial arrangements could be structured and executed so as to be complementary to the role of the IMF'.

[26] See Yamamoto, Thiparat and Ahsan (2001). This is not just felt with respect to the Americans. Some in the region also find the ASEM discussions a little one-sided at times, with the perception being that the Europeans are there to teach and the Asians are there to learn, rather than a focus on genuine dialogue and exchange.

aggressively. This has created bad feeling and been counterproductive to the willingness of the recipients to accept – and be seen to accept – the message, even if they agree with its substance.

3 The policy agenda

Dissatisfaction with the international and regional financial architecture after the crisis has set off a new programme for integration and cooperation in East Asia. This has three main elements: policy dialogue, financial cooperation and common currency arrangements. Consider these in turn.

Policy dialogue

The crisis revealed a number of weaknesses in the structure and nature of official policy dialogue on economics and finance in the region. Most strikingly, it showed the lack of a regional forum for comprehensive and substantive discussion of economic and financial issues and for the advancement of regional interests in global forums and institutions.

The need for such a forum is largely viewed as self-evident in the region. In the first place, it brings policy-makers together at the political and official level to talk, develop trust, and assess the economic and policy structures in place. It allows consensus views to be formed (or not, as the case may be) and for these to be presented beyond the region.

This might be important in expressing the region's views in global forums and in defending the region's interests in international policy-making. This is important because other regions – Europe, the Americas, Africa and numerous subcontinental groupings – have at various times used their group in order to increase their influence. Indeed, it is difficult to see how other regions could oppose the principle of enhanced regional policy dialogue in East Asia when they have themselves used their own groupings to influence policy.[27]

A regional policy forum is also important in deepening outsiders' understanding of the region. Region insiders have a comparative advantage over region outsiders in understanding the structure and operation of economies and policy structures in the region; it is hard to dispute the claim that the deepest understanding of the east Asian economies resides in East Asia, not the United States or Europe.

[27] See Henning (2002).

A number of forums for officials from East Asia to meet and discuss issues of common concern were well in place before the crisis, including meetings of the APEC finance ministers and officials, ASEAN finance ministers and officials, the EMEAP Central Bank governors, deputies and officials and the Four Markets Group. Table 10.1 provides a summary. Some of these forums, like APEC, have comprehensive regional participation and also include countries outside the east Asian region. The coverage of these policy forums also varies. APEC and ASEAN Finance Ministers cover a wide range of economic and financial issues in their meetings. Others are more specialised: EMEAP is focused on central banking matters (like financial markets, payments systems and supervision) and the Four Markets Group is focused on financial markets and institutions.

But none of them meets the need of East Asia for a regional forum which is comprehensive in membership and coverage, discusses the key issues in a substantive and frank manner and has the strong political support essential to influencing global institutions and policy-making.

APEC, for example, is a useful forum for identifying agreement and commitment in the Asia-Pacific region and for commissioning policy work and analysis. But its size makes it less useful as a forum for informality and extended negotiation, and the inclusion of the United States and others means that it is not an east Asian forum. The smaller specialist forums, like EMEAP and the Four Markets Group, include only regional economies, but their role is in promoting specialist discussion in the region. They also tend to be removed from the political process: being 'outside' the political orbit means that they can more readily concentrate on issues of policy substance rather than political form, but they also then tend to lack direct political influence and support.

Two new forums for policy dialogue were established as a result of the crisis. The Manila Framework Group (MFG) was established in November 1997 by a number of APEC members to progress financial cooperation and surveillance in East Asia. The MFG is a framework designed as a mechanism for regional surveillance, economic and technical cooperation, strengthening the IMF's capacity to respond to financial crises and developing a cooperative financing arrangement to supplement that of the IMF.[28]

By the end of 2001, there had been nine meetings of the MFG. Participants say that the value of the MFG lies in the frankness and coverage of dialogue between policy-makers. But many participants also feel that the discussion is one-sided, in the sense that they are subject to scrutiny by the United States and the IMF but not the other way round. And the participation of the United States and Canada means that it does not meet the aspirations of East Asia for a separate

[28] See the statement, 'A New Framework for Enhanced Asian Regional Cooperation to Promote Financial Stability', www.mof.go.jp/english/if/if000a.htm.

Table 10.1 *Fora for economic policy dialogue in East Asia*

Group	Established	Members	Authorities	Coverage
APEC	1989–95	Australia, Brunei, Canada, Chile, China, Hong Kong SAR, Indonesia, Japan, Korea, Malaysia, Mexico, New Zealand, Papua New Guinea, Peru, Philippines, Russia, Singapore, Taiwan, Thailand, United States, Vietnam	Ministries of Finance and Central Banks, IMF, World Bank, Asian Development Bank	All economics and finance
ASEAN	1967	Brunei, Cambodia, Indonesia, Laos, Malaysia, Myanmar, Philippines, Singapore, Thailand, Vietnam	Ministries of Finance and Central Banks	All economics and finance
ASEAN + 3	1999	Brunei, Cambodia, China, Indonesia, Japan, Korea, Laos, Malaysia, Myanmar, Philippines, Singapore, Thailand, Vietnam	Ministries of Finance and Central Banks	All economics and finance
EMEAP	1991	Australia, China, Hong Kong SAR, Indonesia, Japan, Korea, Malaysia, New Zealand, Philippines, Singapore, Thailand	Central Banks	Financial markets, payments system, bank supervision
Four Markets	1992	Australia, Hong Kong SAR, Japan, Singapore	Ministries of Finance and Central Banks	Financial Markets
Manila Framework (MFG)	1997	Australia, Brunei, Canada, China, Hong Kong SAR, Indonesia, Japan, Korea, Malaysia, New Zealand, Philippines, Singapore, Thailand, United States	Ministries of Finance and Central Banks, IMF, World Bank, Asian Development Bank	Economic surveillance and technical cooperation

Notes: APEC Trade Ministers first met in 1989 but APEC Finance Ministers first met in 1995; APEC stands for Asia Pacific Economic Cooperation; ASEAN stands for Association of South East Asian Nations; EMEAP stands for Executive Meeting of East Asia Pacific.

regional forum. The MFG has not been at the forefront of regional thinking about cooperative financing arrangements: it has considered the development of cooperative financing arrangements in the past few years but ASEAN + 3 remains the preferred focus of most participants.[29]

The ASEAN + 3 heads of state first met as such on 28 November 1999 and issued a 'Joint Statement on East Asia Cooperation', calling for strengthened policy dialogue and collaboration, among other things.[30] The value of ASEAN + 3 is that it is closer to being a regional forum and has strong political support. But it is still in its early days. Participants say that it is yet to achieve the openness and coverage in discussion that characterises other policy forums. And its regional coverage is not uniform, in the sense that it does not include regional economies such as Taiwan, Hong Kong SAR, Australia and New Zealand.

For greater financial collaboration in the region to be effective, it must be associated with improved policy dialogue and a willingness frankly to discuss key issues, including the policy stance and state of play in member economies. The tradition of not interfering in the domestic policies of countries in the region, especially in ASEAN but also in China, is a challenge to building effective meaningful policy dialogue in East Asia. But it is one that is on the minds of policy-makers and more thought is being given to ways to improve the effectiveness of dialogue.

There is interest in looking at the experience of other regions in building up policy dialogue, as shown by the discussions between East Asia and Europe in ASEM. The European experience does shed some light.[31] For example,[32] developing and maintaining close working relationships between policy-makers has been important in promoting effective policy dialogue. Policy meetings in Europe in the first few decades of the post-war period were dominated by many of the same people, and this served to promote effective working relations,

---

[29] See the Chairman's Summary of the 8th Finance and Central Bank Deputies' Meeting of the Manila Framework Group, 8–9 March 2001, Beijing, available at www.mof.go.jp/english/if/if037.htm and the Press Release of the 9th Meeting of the Manila Framework Group on 4–5 December 2001.

[30] This and some other ASEAN + 3 statements are available at www.mofa.go.jp/region/asia-paci-asean and at the ASEAN website, www.aseansec.org.

[31] The way in which groups of countries develop policy dialogue depends in part on the issues that they meet to discuss and in part on the history of their interaction. What works in one case may not work in another. East Asia is different from Europe: economic development is a key priority in a region as diverse as East Asia; openness and market orientation are essential to a region like East Asia which depends on broad-based world economic growth; and the history of interaction in East Asia is different from that of Europe.

[32] See Wyplosz (2001), Rollo (2001) and Pisani-Ferry (2001).

trust and a common vision. In this respect, duplication and overlap in forums, especially at early stages of region-building may be a useful tool.

One feature of the dialogue forums that 'worked' in Europe was that the chair of the forum did not rotate between members (every six months in the typical pattern) but was fixed for a relatively long period of time. Another feature that 'worked' in OECD discussion has been the use of an independent outside chair, namely the IMF Chief Economist, to open and lead discussion on economic and financial issues. It may also be the case that widening the membership to other economies in the region may change the dynamics of policy dialogue, as well as make it fully representative of the east Asian region.

Building up well-functioning forums for policy dialogue can take a long time. It is not a linear process and it is unreasonable to expect perfection at the start. Europe's experience in building regional policy dialogue was piecemeal and iterative. Policy-makers were opportunistic in the sense that they took advantage of opportunities to strengthen dialogue when they arose. The approach in East Asia has been, and is most likely to continue to be, similar in this respect. The process is likely to be messy, with progress going back and forth. But it is now under way and the commitment to it is strengthening.

Financial cooperation

The financial crisis led to a deep shift in the thinking within the region about the need for substantive forms of regional financial cooperation. The disillusion with the Fund's performance during the crisis has meant that some reliance on regional mechanisms is inevitable. This has been underpinned by high expectations but poor progress in international forums in dealing with key issues about the international financial architecture that are important to East Asia, such as private sector involvement, highly leveraged institutions and destabilising speculation, and reform of the IMF.[33]

One purpose of strengthening policy dialogue in East Asia has been to determine the structure, conditions and eligibility criteria for regional financial cooperation. The ideas have ranged anywhere between the two extremes of no regional financial architecture, with only a reliance on IMF facilities and the New Arrangements to Borrow (NAB), to only a regional architecture for financial support, thereby dropping the IMF out altogether.

---

[33] See Kim, Ryou and Wang (2000), SaKong and Wang (2000) and de Brouwer (2001). Following interventions by Anne Krueger, the First Deputy Managing Director of the IMF, the prospects for setting up mechanisms for private sector involvement in financial crises now seem brighter.

What is financial cooperation?

The debate and policy action are still at a relatively preliminary stage. In part, this is because policy-makers are still coming to grips with the aims of regional cooperation. Financial cooperation, be it regional or global, can be of three broad types. It can be a mechanism for providing very short-term temporary liquidity support, say because of a mismatch in funding.[34] The amounts in this case are likely to be small.

Or it can be a device for preventing crises: a financial crisis is more likely to occur, among other things, the weaker are economic fundamentals and financial structures. Much of the work on crisis-prevention has focused on reducing domestic vulnerabilities, reflected in the IMF's focus on developing and implementing standards for reporting and policy.

Crisis-prevention measures also include making more funds available to deal with crises. In standard models, strong fundamentals are associated with the stock of foreign currency reserves.[35] Building up the armoury of reserves through access to IMF facilities or bilateral swap arrangements – which are essentially one country lending its foreign exchange reserves to another – can be a device to prevent a crisis from occurring. This is most likely to work in a country where the economic fundamentals are broadly okay, so that the signal that the increase in reserves gives about the fundamentals is an accurate and credible one. The amounts required in this case are likely to be large.

There is another, more recent dimension to financial cooperation to prevent contagion. Even countries with fairly sound economic and financial structures may be adversely affected by changes in investor and speculator sentiment due to weakness in another country.[36] The possibility of contagion led the IMF to establish a new lending facility in 1999, the contingent credit line (CCL), which is available to countries in good economic condition which experience investor reversals because of a crisis elsewhere.

Financial cooperation can also be directed at resolving a financial crisis once it has begun. In this case, credit is provided to a country to boost its reserves to meet international payments, subject to conditions set by the lender. This sort of financial cooperation is designed to restore market and investor confidence

---

[34] The distinction between funding a short-term liquidity shortfall and preventing a financial crisis may be an artificial one: it is hard to see how in practice a country can have a short-term liquidity problem in international payments without generating a financial crisis.

[35] See Obstfeld (1996) and Corsetti *et al.* (2000).

[36] See Dornbusch, Park and Clasessens (2000). This does not imply that the events of 1997 and 1998 were due only to contagion; see de Brouwer (1999, 2001). There is also considerable debate between economists about the existence and prevalence of contagion; see, for example, Bordo and Murshid (2000), Edwards and Susmel (2000) and Rigobon (2001).

and underpin economic recovery. This is standard IMF fare and, as shown by the financial crises in 1994, 1997 and 1998, the amounts required are likely to be large.

Should financial cooperation be regional or global?

The substantive issue facing East Asia is how regional financial cooperation fits in with multilateral mechanisms centred on the IMF. Is regional cooperation designed to provide temporary liquidity support, prevent financial crises, or help in the resolution of these crises once they have begun? The merits of regional, as opposed to global, mechanisms need to be spelled out with respect to each of these types of financial cooperation.

The simplest case of financial cooperation is the provision of short-term liquidity support to cover a temporary shortfall in funds. This type of funding need is not generally provided by the IMF[37] and is typically provided by regional networks, such as through bilateral or regional swaps. In this respect, there is no inherent tension between regional and global financial temporary liquidity support arrangements. In fact, well-structured regional arrangements are important because they reduce the risks of a crisis caused by a short-term liquidity shortfall. Moreover, the policy dialogue that accompanies these arrangements helps increase intra-regional understanding of economies and markets.

The more complex cases are the crisis-prevention and crisis-resolution processes. At the risk of over-simplification and caricature, there are three standard arguments against regional processes in East Asia for financial cooperation.

The primacy of global cooperation
The first is that regional processes undermine global processes. The strong statement of this view is that the existence of any other financial support mechanism weakens the global mechanism.

The primary concern is that regulatory arbitrage will occur and weaken global systems. If the terms and conditions of the regional support mechanism differ from the IMF facility, then the putative borrower will seek the loan with the best terms (like lower interest rate and longer repayment schedule) and easiest conditions (less reform, easier policy stance). If the terms and conditions are easier on regional loans than on IMF loans,[38] then there will be a general

---

[37] IMF lending for a liquidity squeeze depends on the nature and size of the shock. The Compensatory Financing Facility (CFF), for example, is available to countries which experience a sudden shortfall in export earnings or increase in the cost of food imports caused by fluctuating world commodity prices. See the IMF website, for example at www.imf.org/external/np/exr/facts/howlend.htm, for a summary of the IMF lending facilities.

[38] This is the standard assumption, but it is just an assertion. See Henning (2002) for an interesting discussion.

weakening of conditionality and a drift away from the IMF and global cooperation. A subsidiary argument is that when crises occur across a mix of regions, the costs of coordination and risk of inconsistent outcomes are higher.

The counterargument made in East Asia proceeds as follows. The starting premise is different: there should be no presumption that a global arrangement is better than a regional arrangement in all cases. The criterion to judge which arrangement is better is that which best achieves the aim of preserving stability, not whether it is global or regional. For example, if the terms and conditions set by the IMF are inappropriate while those set by the regional body are appropriate, then the regional arrangement is preferred, all else given. And as for the argument that it is easier to preserve consistency at the global level, it is hard to make the claim that the IMF stands above political pressures and is always consistent in its programmes.

These are reasonable counterarguments. It cannot be assumed that regional arrangements in East Asia would be inherently worse than IMF arrangements: it ultimately depends on how the institutions and instruments of cooperation are organised in practice. There are five dimensions to this.

First, the crucial issue is whether regional or global frameworks have a comparative advantage in delivering appropriate conditionality. There is no doubt in most people's minds that the IMF made serious errors of judgement in the crisis. This is well-worn ground. The issue from here on in should not be payback: the past is past. It should be whether the IMF is more likely to repeat the same kind of mistakes again in the future and whether a regional arrangement is likely to do any better. Frankly, this is impossible to answer since it depends on too many unknown factors.

One factor is the level of knowledge and understanding about east Asian economies, markets and political processes. There is considerable technical knowledge, data and analytical power at the Fund but this does not mean that it has a solid understanding and experience with economic, institutional and market processes in the region. This sort of knowledge is generally found at the national and regional level.

The issue then is whether the regional body has sufficient expertise, experience, and 'distance' to marshal the resources, frame the conditions of the package and set them with the borrowing country. Moreover, the IMF has broad and extensive experience when it comes to dealing with financial reform after a crisis and facilitating the write-down of existing debt; more than a regional body would ever have. The conundrum is that the IMF may be more likely to be able to impose policy conditions in a package and provide expert advice in resolving the crisis than a regional body, but that the regional body is likely to better understand the economy, institutions and markets.

Another factor is the nature of the institution making the decision. One criticism of the Fund is that its view of the world – how it interprets a crisis and the policy that it recommends – changes slowly. This is exacerbated by its bureaucratic structure and size: the institutional view is a highly persistent reaction to the past. A regional institution which is less bureaucratised (like a secretariat) may be more flexible. It also depends on the intellectual bias or culture of the institution. Some criticise Fund economists as being too ideological and fundamentalist about markets. But the criticism of a regional body is that its intellectual culture may over-state the institutional differences in Asia at the expense of economic forces. There is also the problem of whether a large regional body would be able to attract the quality of staff and policy formation that global institutions, like the IMF and World Bank, can.[39] Another factor is whether countries are more likely to take ownership of reform if it comes from within the region or without. These are clearly open questions.

Second, regional arrangements are adequate if there are sufficient pressures in place to ensure that the public monies used to fund regional financial support are responsibly allocated – in short, that they are provided subject to terms and conditions. It would seem, on balance, that sufficient pressures do exist in East Asia. Most countries in the region are democracies and policy-makers are sensitive to their civic responsibilities and pressure from the electorate, especially after the large-scale exposure of official corruption and featherbedding of recent years.

The likely lender countries – China, Japan and Korea – have no appetite for wasting their own funds, as shown by the strict terms and conditions that they have attached to the network of ASEAN + 3 bilateral swaps (discussed on p. 279 below). The public in many countries is not prepared to accept it. The public mood against bank bailouts in Japan, for example, has made politicians unwilling to use public funds to buy out banks' bad debts: they are not going to tolerate their money being used to bail-out some other country.

Third, the relative merit of global and regional mechanisms depends on the effectiveness of governance over the lending intermediary – the IMF at the global level and, say, an Asian Monetary Fund at the regional level. It is not clear which provides the best governance mechanism. Governance by member governments of IMF staff and management through the Executive Board is weak.[40]

---

[39] The Asian Development Bank (ADB), for example, has many excellent and capable professionals, but it is generally regarded as less prestigious than the World Bank and unable to attract the same quality of staff.

[40] The weakness of the Executive Board in monitoring staff and management and leading the Fund's policy-making is a serious and complex issue. On the one hand, governance is weak because management and staff bypass the Board. For example, management use 'side-letters' in packages that the Board does not review, although these are now used less than before the crisis. Management also at times pre-empt the Board in critical matters, as occurred with the

The role of east Asian governments in the governance of the IMF is also weak. This is in part because the voting power of Fund members and constituency representation on the Executive Board is biased towards Europe, the Middle East and Africa, at the expense of East Asia, especially Japan. But it is also because some east Asian countries do not take advantage of their position to be actively involved and lead discussion in meetings, for any number of reasons – resentment, a distaste for directness or confrontation, relatively poor English-language skills, a poor grasp of the issues, or a reluctance to take a global rather than regional or national perspective.[41]

Whether governance would be better at the regional level is an open question. It depends on some critical factors. If regional arrangements are centred in a large bureaucracy with policy-making powers (akin to the IMF), then the institution is likely to be harder to govern by national governments. If it is more like a well-run secretariat (perhaps akin to the way Andrew Crockett ran the Bank for International Settlements (BIS)), then governance and control of policy are easier since policy-makers at the national level retain control over the policy agenda and its implementation. East Asian policy-makers are much more inclined to secretariat-type regional institutions. On the other hand, effective governance also requires policy-makers to participate actively and openly in governing forums.

Fourth, the ability of an institution to garner broader international interest and support is a crucial element in organising a rescue package. The IMF failed to garner additional support from the United States for Thailand (and Indonesia). This weakened the credibility of the programme and was the impetus for Japan's proposal for an Asian Monetary Fund in September 1997. A regional fund is one way to lock-in regional support. And it may also be a high-profile device to influence the IMF and other country lenders.

Fifth, regional lending facilities may in fact be more effective than global arrangements in preventing crises because of contagion. The IMF's Contingent Credit Line (CCL) facility was designed to prevent contagion: a country with

---

Russian emergency package in 1998. There is widespread dissatisfaction at the Board with the narrow policy options and limited information presented to it by staff. But, on the other hand, the Executive Board does not exercise its duties as well as it could. Some Board members are appointed for convenience, seniority or prestige rather than on merit. Some members of the Board have leaked sensitive material for political gain, which led to the use of side-letters in the first place. And, from the management point of view, there is little appetite at the Board for taking responsibility and making decisions. The effectiveness of the Board ultimately depends on the commitment of national governments to the Fund.

[41] See Stanley Fischer's (2001) exhortation to Asian policy-makers to improve the quality of their representatives on the Executive Board and engage more with IMF staff and management at the Executive Board.

reasonably good fundamentals would sign on to the facility to boost its reserves position in the event of financial contagion. But it has not been activated since it was introduced in 1999. There are two main reasons for this. In the first place, countries which meet the entry criteria are concerned that signing up to the facility would send a bad signal to financial markets, force up borrowing costs and even start a crisis. They are also afraid that exiting the facility, especially if they are forced to because they no longer meet the entry criteria, would create a loss of market confidence in them and also create a crisis. The problems with the CCL are the signals created by entry and exit, rather than the facility itself.

A regional financial arrangement which is available to members when they face contagion may overcome this problem. There is no adverse signal from entry or exit since there is no entry or exit from access to the facility: funds can be disbursed immediately on approval by the regional body (and at the discretion of the regional body). The credibility of the facility would depend on the credibility of the regional body. One way of acquiring credibility would be to allow for the IMF to make a statement of support of the regional action, if it considered this to be appropriate.

Put together, these five considerations suggest that there is a complementarity between global and regional arrangements. On the one hand, global arrangements allow policy-makers to deal consistently with crises. They create distance between the borrower and lender so the risk of the lender being 'captured' by the borrower is smaller. And international institutions have the requisite expertise to deal with the aftermath of a crisis. On the other hand, the best understanding of countries in a region resides in the region. Regional arrangements are more likely to prevent countries slipping through the global net because they are not important enough to the United States or Europe. And preventive arrangements at the regional level might be more effective than those at the global level, like the CCL.

This goes some way to addressing the question implicit in this analysis of whether an Asian Monetary Fund could have dealt better with the crisis than the IMF.[42] It is a natural question to ask but it is also a nonsense question because

---

[42] Some would argue that a regional fund would have made the crisis worse by weakening the commitment to reform and by raising the stakes in the game. On the latter point, the macro hedge funds faced no external financing constraints from the investment banks and securities firms that funded their short speculative currency positions in 1997 and 1998, and could have increased their positions as the level of reserves increased (Financial Stability Forum Working Group on Highly Leveraged Institutions, 2000; de Brouwer, 2001). Whether this would have happened is unknowable, and would probably have depended on the credibility of the regional fund and package.

the counterfactual is unknowable. There is no way of providing a firm answer one way or the other.

The crisis could have been handled better. There is widespread agreement that the Fund made some serious errors in terms of judging the nature, effects and severity of the crisis, and the policy recommendations to deal with it, including tight fiscal and monetary policies and excessive focus on structural defects in the economy in an exchange rate crisis. Others, including those in the private sector, also made these mistakes.

But could regional policy-makers left to their own devices have done better? The exchanges between officials in the region and those at the Fund and elsewhere outside the region are not on the public record. But those involved say that there were serious representations to those outside the region from senior officials within the region about these matters from the start of the crisis. If these views had influenced thinking outside the region, the effects of the crisis might have been dampened. If there had been a regional fund and this perception had influenced its thinking then things may have been better.

But new problems could have arisen, especially if only a regional fund were involved – such as resource constraints in a widespread regional crisis, finding sufficient expertise in the region to deal with the financial and institutional problems, and ways to involve private sector institutions from outside the region (like US and European banks) in crisis-resolution. The set of criticisms in the counterfactual might have been very different.

Resource constraints
The second argument against regional financial cooperation is that the region would not have the resources to deal with a regionwide shock because countries would need their own reserves and would not be able to share them. If all countries were affected or if a major financial shock were to hit the principal lenders in the region and limit their ability to lend, then the regional arrangement might not work.

The counterargument made in East Asia is that this means that global arrangements and regional arrangements must be complementary. It is not a case of 'either/or'. In some situations, a regional response may be appropriate and in some cases, such as a major regional or cross-regional crisis, a global response through the IMF would be appropriate. Even in the latter case, coordinated regional support as a first- or second-line defence may be important in putting an adequate financing package together.[43]

---

[43] See Parkinson, Garton and Dickson (2002) for a discussion on first- and second-tier financing.

Inadequate policy dialogue

The third argument against regional support arrangements is that the policy dialogue processes needed to underpin successful financial cooperation are too weak in East Asia. Countries in the region are not willing to expose themselves to surveillance and monitoring of domestic economic conditions and policy by their peers. This is particularly so with ASEAN's policy of non-interference in its members' domestic policy, including in both public and private discussion.

This was probably right before the crisis, but while it remains a serious issue things are starting to change. Policy-makers understand that policy dialogue has to be strengthened and improved, and there is now increasing political will to do this. They also realise that progress is piecemeal, uneven and iterative. It will take a while but it is unreasonable to expect all the pieces to be in place immediately.

Whatever the case, the real test of any regional arrangement will be in how it performs in future financial crises. There are arguments for and against regional financial arrangements of various sorts and it is not possible to conclude which is right on the basis of the arguments alone. It really depends on how they are implemented. Global and regional cooperation can be effective and stabilising or it can be ineffective and/or destabilising. The proof of the pudding is in the eating.

The effectiveness of financial cooperation at both the regional and the global level depends in part on how cooperation is structured. This includes not just the terms and conditions of the support lending, but also the institutional and dialogue forms in which it is activated. In practice, the evaluation of the instruments cannot be isolated from the institutional structures in which they are nested.

As a final comment, the success or otherwise of regional financial cooperation should be measured by how the regime as a whole prevents or resolves future financial crises in East Asia. The focus should *not* be whether regional mechanisms and institutions are established. Minimising crises is the matter of substance; creating mechanisms is a matter of form.

One hope of the talk and action on regional policy dialogue and financial cooperation is that it will influence global policy dialogue and financial cooperation. A new entrant makes the 'market' for dialogue and cooperation contestable and may change the reaction of incumbents. The formation of regional dialogue and cooperation was driven by deep dissatisfaction with the IMF's performance in 1997 and 1998 and the perception that US support was unreliable. Developing regional processes is partly aimed at changing the reaction function of the IMF and other countries, to make them consider the needs and characteristics of the region and to recommend and apply appropriate policies. But the 'threat' of entry is probably not sufficient to do this; actual entry may be required to change the reaction of the IMF and major countries outside the region.

The state of play in financial cooperation in East Asia

The first proposal for greater regional financial cooperation as a result of the crisis occurred fairly early, when Japan proposed an Asian Monetary Fund in September 1997. Japan was willing to commit half of the proposed $100 billion AMF. This proposal soon failed in the face of opposition by the United States, because of perceptions that it would undermine the IMF, and China, because it was suspicious of Japan's intentions.[44] What has eventuated so far in terms of financial cooperation has been much more modest.

There have been two developments in regional financing initiatives since 2000, both under the umbrella of the Chiang Mai Initiative (CMI) of May 2000. The first is the expansion of the ASEAN swap arrangement established in August 1977. Under this arrangement, the five original ASEAN members agreed to provide up to $40 million to other members. This amount was obviously too little to be of help except for minor liquidity shortfalls. It has been used only four times and was not used in the 1997–8 financial crisis.[45] The ASEAN swap arrangement was widened to all ASEAN members and increased to $1 billion in May 2001. The expanded arrangement is still too small to deal with financial crises, but can be used for liquidity shortfalls.

The second development is the establishment of a full series of bilateral swap and repurchase agreements between the ASEAN + 3 countries. The network of bilateral swaps in ASEAN + 3 were almost fully in place by mid-2003. The bilateral swaps are secured by government guarantees and range in amounts from $1 billion to $5 billion, and total to around $30 billion, 10 per cent of the swap can be allocated on the discretion of the lender and the remaining 90 per cent is allocated on the discretion of the lender and is subject to the borrowing country meeting IMF conditions for financing.[46] The swaps can be rolled over a specified number of times and the borrowing country is required to provide additional information regularly to the lending country.

In its current state, the CMI is far too small to be directed at crisis-prevention or crisis-resolution by itself. The total size of the bilateral swaps may sound large but, compared to the capital flows and size of speculative positions in

---

[44] Australia and Hong Kong also opposed the AMF proposal at the time.

[45] See Kim, Ryou and Wang (2000, pp. 29–30) for details.

[46] Including IMF conditionality was controversial but agreed to because it was thought important to link regional arrangements with global arrangements and ensure that appropriate conditionality is applied. This helps establish the credibility of the system and assuage concerns that regional arrangements are designed to subvert global arrangements.

place in 1997 and 1998 it is not.[47] The short positions on the baht alone in mid-1997, for example, were about $27 billion, the size of the Bank of Thailand's foreign exchange reserves. The size of the short positions on the Australian dollar, Hong Kong equities and Hong Kong dollar, New Zealand dollar, ringgit and Singapore dollar in mid-1998 are thought to have been roughly about $47 billion. The size of the short positions on the yen in mid-1998 are thought to have been between $200 and 300 billion. And the size of these positions was endogenous to the exchange rate policy and level of reserves at the time.[48]

The CMI in its current form can be used in conjunction with an IMF facility to minimise a financial crisis. And it can be used by itself to fund a temporary shortfall in liquidity between a member country, which may help avoid a crisis. The CMI is widely seen as only the first step in the process of regional financial cooperation and is due for review by the ASEAN + 3 in 2004.

The target of a number of countries is to create an Asian Monetary Fund-type institution which could be a first port of call in dealing with financial crises within the region. For most, if not all, countries, an AMF is seen as complementary to the IMF's regional and global responsibilities but would also be independent of the IMF. It is widely recognised that it will take time to develop and that progress towards it is not likely to be smooth since it depends on the sustained convergence of competing strategic interests in the region and the formation of consensus. The response of the United States is also important.

One intermediate step has been proposed by Korea. Kim, Ryou and Wang (2000) have proposed an Asian Arrangements to Borrow (AAB). The AAB would operate analogously to the New Arrangements to Borrow (NAB) and General Arrangements to Borrow (GAB),[49] which provide a mechanism for the IMF to supplement its resources for lending in a financial crisis. The AAB would be a regional mechanism for creditor countries to contribute to a pool of funds that could be disbursed under specific terms and conditions to east Asian countries facing or experiencing financial crisis. They propose that the AAB be managed within the region.

The proposal needs refinement. For example, the trigger for the AAB is not well defined. Kim, Ryou and Wang (2000) say that the AAB is a device to prevent a crisis and suggest that it could be triggered when a country with sound fundamentals experiences a large currency depreciation, say 20 per cent.

---

[47] See Financial Stability Forum Working Group on Highly Leveraged Institutions (2000) and de Brouwer (2001).

[48] The main macro hedge funds involved in these positions had essentially limitless access to fund their positions (Financial Stability Forum Working Group on Highly Leveraged Institutions, 2000). Their positions would most likely have been larger had reserves positions and the commitment to maintain exchange rates at prevailing levels been greater.

[49] See Kim, Ryou and Wang (2000) and www.imf.org/external/np/exr/facts/gabnab.htm.

But this is probably already too late. It also leaves open what is meant by 'sound fundamentals'.

Common currency arrangements

The third leg in regional financial arrangements is the adoption of some kind of common currency arrangement within East Asia or some subset of it. Common currency arrangements range from common basket pegs (to the dollar, yen and euro) and regional currency units (a weighted sum of regional convertible currencies) to formal currency union. While there is regional consensus on strengthening policy dialogue and financial cooperation, there is no consensus on common currency arrangements.

There is a wide mix of views about common currency arrangements in the region. Japan is a strong proponent of common basket pegs.[50] Korea favours the use of an Asian Currency Unit, not only for its perceived stabilising effect but because it does not concentrate decision-making and seigniorage returns on Japan.[51] ASEAN has also commissioned research on whether ASEAN should have a common currency.[52]

While the general view is that cooperative or common currency arrangements are still some time off, they are increasingly being thought of as a long-term policy aim. Deepening and developing regional policy dialogue and financial cooperation are important to the way in which common currency arrangements will evolve in East Asia. Strengthening financial cooperation is seen as particularly important in this respect since exchange rate cooperation must be backed by unequivocal financial cooperation if it is to work. At this stage, such commitment does not exist in the region.

The IMF will be included in the analysis of these issues but the degree to which the region seeks its advice and involvement will ultimately depend on the stance it takes on these issues. The IMF seems to be attracted largely to a bipolar view of the suitability of exchange rate regimes, and that the room for intermediate exchange rate regimes exists but is small.[53] There is, in particular, little support among Fund staff for common pegged exchange rate systems

---

[50] See Goto and Hamada (1994), Ito, Ogawa and Sasaki (1998), Council on Foreign Exchange and Other Transactions (1999), Kawai and Akiyama (2000), Kawai and Takagi (2000), Murase (2000), Ogawa (2000), Ogawa and Ito (2000), and Yoshino, Koji and Suzuki (2000). Dornbusch and Park (1999), Williamson (1999, 2001) and Kwan (2001), are also supportive. See de Brouwer (2002b) for an alternative view.

[51] See Kim, Ryou and Wang (2000), Moon, Rhee and Yoon (2000), Ryou and Kim (2001), and Moon and Rhee (2002).

[52] See Bayoumi and Mauro (1999).   [53] See Mussa *et al.* (2000) and Fischer (2001).

because experience with such regimes is that they tend to come undone in a costly manner. While many in the region agree with this – and so regard formal currency union in the longer term as the more viable common currency arrangement – others, especially in Japan, do not.

4 Conclusion

The financial crisis – and particularly the way in which it was dealt with by the IMF and the United States – has been a key force behind the assertion of the new Asian regionalism and its talisman, new regional financial arrangements. This has been boosted by Europe's experience with monetary union and by increasing trade openness and integration in East Asia.

Over the past few years there has been a clear shift in policy preferences to strengthen regional policy dialogue, create new forms of regional financial cooperation – including using new instruments for cooperation, developing regional financial markets and establishing new institutions for cooperation – and think more seriously about common currency arrangements in East Asia, or at least part of it.

Stronger regional financial arrangements are mostly viewed in East Asia as being complementary to global financial dialogue and cooperation, embodied in the IMF. The IMF is still seen to be an important and necessary institution, not least in being there to provide assistance in large or global financial crises but also in giving countries a voice in international policy-making and securing greater interest from the United States and Europe in events beyond their own regions. But it failed the critical test in 1997 and 1998 in providing expert policy direction and in garnering international support. Regional initiatives are a way to deal with this failure.

The two crucial elements of developing regional financial arrangements at this stage are strengthening policy dialogue and deepening financial coopera-tion. Strengthening policy dialogue is important in its own right: it improves understanding of regional economies and markets and gives the region a stronger voice in global dialogue and policy-making. It also is a necessary condition for effective financial cooperation.

Developing new forms of regional financial cooperation and support is also important in helping protect the region from further crises. At the most ele-mentary level, arrangements to deal with temporary liquidity shortfalls are not comprehensively provided at the global level but can be at a regional level.

There are usually three arguments made against regional support arrange-ments: they can weaken global arrangements, especially with respect to terms and conditions; they are too limited to deal with large regional or global crises and can cause coordination problems and inconsistency; and they need to be backed by adequate policy dialogue and surveillance processes. But none of these arguments is decisive.

First, the presumption that global arrangements are necessarily better than regional ones must be tested by actual circumstances. The IMF did poorly in the east Asian financial crisis on a number of fronts. But, having accepted this, it is time to move on and look to the future with balance. Global arrangements have particular advantages in creating a bit of distance between borrower and lender and in providing expertise in dealing with problems in financial institutions and firms after the crisis. Regional arrangements have particular advantages in understanding economic processes in the affected countries better, ensuring that someone is interested even if the United States and Europe are not, and in providing a practical way to deal with localised contagion. They may also be a substantial boost to the Fund's financial resources. By increasing the contestability of policy advice and action, they may affect the reaction of the IMF in future crises and improve international involvement and terms and conditions. Global and regional arrangements, properly structured, should be seen as complementary.

Second, large regional or global crises cannot be prevented or resolved just at the regional level and so there is a first-order argument for global arrangements, as exist with the Fund. Again the aim of regional arrangements should not be to supplant the Fund but to complement it.

Third, strong effective policy dialogue, including surveillance, is necessary for well-functioning arrangements for financial support. The region is not there yet, but policy-makers understand this and are working to improve dialogue. This will take time, as will the evolution of working financial support arrangements.

Progress on strengthening regional financial arrangements has been modest. Policy dialogue has been expanded through the Manila Framework Group and ASEAN + 3 Finance Ministers' meetings, although both forums have different relative strengths and weaknesses. Financial cooperation has been expanded through the ASEAN + 3 framework, expanding ASEAN swaps and introducing a comprehensive network of bilateral swaps between ASEAN + 3 countries, which aggregate to about $30 billion. While important symbolically as a first step in ASEAN + 3 cooperation, the amounts involved are too small to use in a financial crisis.

There is still a long way to go in developing regional policy dialogue and financial cooperation, let alone common currency arrangements, in East Asia. The path of financial and economic integration is not predetermined. The ultimate form and substance of regional financial arrangements is highly contingent on future circumstances and the willingness of countries in the region to engage and cooperate with each other. The process is iterative and messy. But it is underway, and the policy and political dynamic behind it is irreversible.

As regional financial arrangements progress, a major challenge for the region is to articulate and then actualise the sort of relationship it wants with the IMF. While resentment and disillusion with the Fund still runs deep – although less intensely than in 1997 and 1998 – the region needs to think pragmatically and strategically about the issue. The IMF is an essential part of the global financial architecture. Regional mechanisms and institutions can be an important complement to global ones but it is unrealistic to expect them to fully replace them. Developing regional policy-making at the expense of better global policy-making may be ultimately self-defeating: the more the region disengages from global processes and the IMF, then the less likely is the IMF to be suitably responsive to the conditions and needs of the region in future crises. A regional financial architecture is most unlikely to have the financial and technical capacity to deal with every financial crisis that affects East Asia. To be most effective, the development of a new regional financial architecture has to go hand-in-hand with renewed commitment to, and the exercise of leadership in, the Fund by the region.

REFERENCES

Bayoumi, T. and P. Mauro (1999). 'The Suitability of ASEAN for a Regional Currency Arrangement', IMF Working Paper, WP/99/102

Boorman, J., T. Lane, M. Schulze-Ghattas, A. Bulir, A. Ghosh, J. Hamann, A. Mourmouras and S. Phillips (2000). 'Managing Financial Crises: The Experience in East-Asia', IMF Working Paper, WP/00/107, June

Bordo, M. D. and A. P. Murshid (2000). 'Are Financial Crises Becoming Increasingly More Contagious? What is the Historical Evidence on Contagion?', NBER Working Paper, 7900

Corsetti, G., A. Dasgupta, S. Morris and H. S. Shin (2000). 'Does One Large Soros Make a Difference? The Role of a Large Trade in Currency Crises', Cowles Foundation Discussion Paper, 1273. New Haven, CT, Yale University

Costello, P. (1999). 'Australia and the IMF', Annual Report to the Parliament Under the International Monetary Arrangements Act 1947, Canberra, Australian Government Printing Service

Council on Foreign Exchange and Other Transactions (1999). 'Internationalisation of the Yen for the 21st Century', available at www.mof.go.jp/english/if/elb064a.htm

de Brouwer, G. J. (1999). *Financial Integration in East Asia*. Cambridge, Cambridge University Press

  (2001). *Hedge Funds in Emerging Markets*, Cambridge, Cambridge University Press

  (2002a). 'Debating Financial Markets and Policies in East Asia', chapter 1 in G. de Brouwer (ed.), *Financial Markets and Policies in East Asia*. London, Routledge, 1–16

(2002b). 'Does a Formal Common-Basket Peg in East Asia Make Economic Sense?', chapter 12 in G. de Brouwer (ed.), *Financial Markets and Policies in East Asia*. London, Routledge, 286–314

Dornbusch, R. and Y. C. Park (1999). 'Flexibility or Nominal Anchors?', chapter 1 in S. Collignon, J. Pisani-Ferry and Y. C. Park (eds.), *Exchange Rate Policies in Emerging Asian Countries*. London, Routledge, 3–34

Dornbusch, R., Y. C. Park and S. Claessens (2000). 'Contagion: Understanding How It Spreads', *World Bank Research Observer*, 15(2), 177–97

Edwards, S. and R. Susmel (2000). 'Interest Rate Volatility and Contagion in Emerging Markets: Evidence from the 1990s', NBER Working Paper, 7813

Eichengreen, B. and T. Bayoumi (1999). 'Is Asia an Optimum Currency Area? Can It Become One? Regional, Global, and Historical Perspectives on Asian Monetary Relations', chapter 21 in S. Collignon, J. Pisani-Ferry and Y. C. Park (eds.), *Exchange Rate Policies in Emerging Asian Countries*. London, Routledge, 347–66

Financial Stability Forum Working Group on Highly Leveraged Institutions (2000). Report, available at www.fsforum.org

Fischer, S. (2001). 'Asia and the IMF', remarks made at the Institute of Policy Studies, Singapore, 1 June, available at www.imf.org/external/np/speeches/2001/060101.htm

Goto, J. and K. Hamada (1994). 'Economic Preconditions for Asian Regional Integration', in T. Ito and A. Kruger (eds.), *Macroeconomic Linkage: Savings, Exchange Rates, and Capital Flows*. Chicago, University of Chicago Press, 359–88

Grenville, S. A. (1997). 'Asia and the Financial Sector', *Reserve Bank of Australia Bulletin*, December

(1998). 'The Asian Economic Crisis', *Reserve Bank of Australia Bulletin*, April

Henning, C. R. (2002). 'East Asian Financial Cooperation After Chiang Mai', Washington, DC, Institute for International Economics, *Policy Analyses in International Economics*, 68, September

Ito, T., E. Ogawa and Y. N. Sasaki (1998). 'How Did the Dollar Peg Fail in Asia?', NBER Working Paper, 6729

Kawai, M. (2001). 'Recommending a Currency Basket System for Emerging East Asia', paper presented at a conference on Regional Financial Arrangements in East Asia, organised by the Australia–Japan Research Centre, Australian National University, 12–13 November

Kawai, M. and S. Akiyama (2000). 'Implications of the Currency Crisis for Exchange Rate Arrangements in Emerging East Asia', Washington, DC, World Bank, mimeo

Kawai, M. and S. Takagi (2000). 'The Strategy for a Regional Exchange Rate Arrangement in Post-Crisis East Asia: Analysis, Review and Proposal', Washington, DC, World Bank, mimeo

Kim, T. J., J. W. Ryou and Y. Wang (2000). 'Regional Arrangements to Borrow: A Scheme for Preventing Future Asian Liquidity Crises', Seoul, Korea Institute for International Economic Policy

Kim, T. J. and D. Y. Yang (eds.) (2001). *New International Financial Architecture and Korean Perspectives*. Seoul, Korea Institute for International Economic Policy

Kwan, C. H. (2001). *Yen Bloc: Toward Economic Integration in Asia*. Washington, DC, Brookings Institution Press

Lee, H. H. and D. Y. Yang (2001). 'Reforming the International Financial Architecture', chapter 1 in T.-J. Kim and D. Y. Yang (eds.), *New International Financial Architecture and Korean Perspectives*. Seoul, Korea Institute for International Economic Policy, 9–33

Macfarlane, I. J. (1997a). 'Statement to Parliamentary Committee', *Reserve Bank of Australia Bulletin*, November

   (1997b). 'The Changing Nature of Economic Crises', *Reserve Bank of Australia Bulletin*, December

Moon, W. S. and Y. S. Rhee (2002). 'Foreign Exchange Market Liberalisation in Korea: Past and Future Options', in K. T. Lee (ed.), *Globalization in the New Millennium*. London, Routledge

Moon, W. S., Y. S. Rhee and D. R. Yoon (2000). 'Asian Monetary Cooperation: A Search for Regional Monetary Stability in the Post-Euro and Post-Asian Crisis Era', *Bank of Korea Economic Papers*, 3(1), 157–93

Murase, T, (2000). *Ajia Antei Tsuukaken: Yuroo ni Manabu Yen no Yakuwari (The Asian Zone of Monetary Stability: Lessons from the Euro and Role of the Yen)*. Tokyo, Keiso Shobo

Mussa, M., P. Masson, A. Swoboda, E. Jadresic, P. Mauro and A. Berg (2000). *Exchange Rate Regimes in an Increasingly Integrated World*. Washington, DC, IMF, April

Obstfeld, M. (1996). 'Models of Currency Crises With Self-Fulfilling Features', *European Economic Review*, 40(3–5), 1037–47

Ogawa, E. (2000). 'East Asian Countries Return to the Dollar Peg Again?', Tokyo, Hitotsubashi University, mimeo

Ogawa, E. and T. Ito (2000). 'On the Desirability of a Regional Basket Currency Arrangement', Hitotsubashi University, mimeo, March

Parkinson, M., P. Garton and I. Dickson (2002). 'Regional Financial Arrangements: What Role in the International Financial Architecture?', paper presented at the CCER Peking University/AJRC ANU Conference on Deepening Financial Arrangements in East Asia, Beijing, 24–25 March

Pisani-Ferry, J. (2001). 'The European Experience with Regional Financial Arrangements', powerpoint presented at a conference on Regional Financial Arrangements in East Asia, organised by the Australia–Japan Research Centre, Australian National University, 12–13 November

Rice, C. (2000). 'Campaign 2000: Promoting the National Interest', *Foreign Affairs*, January–February

Rigobon, R. (2001). 'Contagion: How to Measure It?', NBER Working Paper, 8118

Rollo, J. (2001). 'Monetary Cooperation and Policy Dialogue: The European Experience', powerpoint presented at a conference on Regional Financial Arrangements in East Asia, organised by the Australia–Japan Research Centre, Australian National University, 12–13 November

Ryou, J. W. and T. J. Kim (2001). 'The Choice of Exchange Rate Regime and Capital Mobility: An Emerging Market Economies Perspective', chapter 4 in T. J. Kim and

D. Y. Yang (eds.) (2001), *New International Financial Architecture and Korean Perspectives*. Seoul, Korea Institute for International Economic Policy, 87–108

SaKong, I. and Y. Wang (2000). *Reforming the International Financial Architecture: Emerging Market Perspectives*. Seoul, Institute for Global Economics and Korea Institute for International Economic Policy

Williamson, J. (1999). 'The Case for a Common Basket Peg for East Asian Currencies', chapter 19 in S. Collignon, J. Pisani-Ferry and Y. C. Park (eds.), *Exchange Rate Policies in Emerging Asian Countries*. London, Routledge, 327–43

(2001). 'The Case for a Basket, Band and Crawl (BBC) Regime in East Asia', in D. Gruen and J. Simon (eds.), *Future Directions for Monetary Policies in East Asia*. Sydney, Reserve Bank of Australia, 97–112, available at www.rba.gov.au/PublicationsAndResearch/Conferences/2001

Wyplosz, C. (2001). 'A Monetary Union in East Asia? Some Lessons from Europe', in D. Gruen and J. Simon (eds.), *Future Directions for Monetary Policies in East Asia*. Sydney, Reserve Bank of Australia, 124–55, available at www.rba.gov.au/PublicationsAndResearch/Conferences/2001

Yamamoto, T., P. Thiparat and A. Ahsan (2001). *America's Role in Asia: Asian Views*. San Francisco, The Asia Foundation

Yoshino, N., S. Koji and A. Suzuki (2000). 'Basket Peg, Dollar Peg, and Floating: A Comparative Analysis of Exchange Rate Regimes', Tokyo, Keio University, mimeo

Yoshitomi, M. and K. Ohno (1999). 'Capital Account Crisis and Credit Contraction: A New Nature of Crises Requires New Policy Papers', ADBI Working Paper, 2

11 The role of the IMF in developing countries

GRAHAM BIRD AND PAUL MOSLEY

1 Introduction

As originally envisaged, the International Monetary Fund (IMF) had three functions. It was an adjustment agency providing advice on balance of payments policy, a financing agency providing short-term liquidity to countries encountering balance of payments problems and finally an agent for managing the Bretton Woods international monetary system, which was based on an adjustable peg exchange rate regime. However, after the early 1970s, the Fund lost most of its systemic role. As flexible exchange rates replaced fixed ones, the Bretton Woods system as originally conceived broke down. Private capital markets began to provide balance of payments financing and regional monetary arrangements – particularly in Europe – began to shift attention away from the Fund. With these developments the dominant theme of the 1960s – the global adequacy of international reserves – diminished in significance and the Fund was effectively marginalised.

But at the same time as it was losing its systemic role, the Fund was gaining another one as it became heavily involved with lending to developing countries, and then countries in transition (CITs). Indeed, the Fund ceased lending to industrial countries altogether. Particular episodes saw it lending to highly indebted developing countries – especially those in Latin America – in the aftermath of the 1980s Third World debt crisis, to CITs as they embarked on the move to market-based systems at the beginning of the 1990s, to Latin America again during the Mexican peso crisis in 1994–5, and to Asian economies, Brazil and Russia during the financial crises of 1997–9. Throughout the whole period, the Fund also persistently lent to low-income countries, such as those in Africa.

An earlier version of this chapter was presented at the Development Studies Association conference in London, November, 2000. The authors are grateful to all those who have offered comments.

It has been largely in the context of its dealings with developing countries and CITs that the Fund has been exposed to pressure to limit or even curtail its operations, coming from both ends of the political spectrum. From the right, critics have claimed that the Fund acted in a way that postponed the debt relief required to solve the 1980s debt crisis; that support for transition economies initially came too late, but was then too generous to sustain fiscal discipline; that the bailing out of commerical lenders during the Mexican crisis created a precedent that served as a serious moral hazard during the subsequent East Asian crisis; and finally that, in the case of East Asia, conditionality was ill-designed, inappropriate and excessive. In the meantime, NGOs have attacked the Fund from the left, arguing that its policies of budgetary restriction have exercised a negative impact on development, particularly in Africa and transitional economies.

While lending to low-income countries involves quantitatively small amounts of finance, this cannot be said of the loans to Mexico, South Korea, Brazil and Russia. Indeed, these large loans put considerable strain on the Fund's own liquidity during 1998 and 1999, and led first to calls to increase the Fund's lending capacity and raise quotas, and second to a series of reassessments of the Fund's activities and proposals for reform. Among these, the most influential is likely to be the report of the International Financial Institution Advisory Commission (the Meltzer Commission), established by the US Congress (United States, 2000), which published its findings and proposals in March 2000 (see also chapter 4 in this volume). However other reports have been produced by 'task forces' sponsored by the Council on Foreign Relations (CFR) and the Overseas Development Council (ODC).

All three reports are critical of the *status quo* and advocate a narrower role for the IMF.[1] Thus the CFR Task Force recommends that the 'IMF should focus on monetary, fiscal and exchange rate policies plus financial-sector surveillance and reform and stay out of longer-term structural adjustment'. It advocates greater rewards for joining the 'good housekeeping club', with the IMF lending on 'more favourable terms to countries that take effective steps to reduce their crisis vulnerability' but the Report also argues that the IMF 'should adhere consistently to normal lending limits' as a way of reducing the moral hazard associated with its lending, and should turn to 'special contagion funds' only when a country is an 'innocent victim' of crises elsewhere.

---

[1] Other influential commentators have made a similar case. Former US Treasury Secretary, Larry Summers, has argued that 'the Fund should focus on its core competency of preventing crises [by collecting, assessing and sharing financial information] and mitigating them if they occur [by providing short-term financing for countries threatened by balance of payments problems, financial contagion or market panics] . . . The IMF should not be a source of low-cost financing for countries with ready access to private capital, or long-term welfare that cannot break the effect of bad policies' (Summers, 1999).

In common with the CFR Task Force the ODC Task Force also argues that events and reforms have pushed the Fund in the direction of dealing with problems, such as poverty and growth, for which it was not originally designed and is unsuited. It was these issues that, according to the ODC Report, dictated a long-run role for the IMF in developing countries; captured most recently by the Fund's involvement in the Heavily Indebted Poor Country (HIPC) initiative on debt reduction and, in relation to this, the replacement of the ESAF with the Poverty Reduction and Growth Facility (PRGF), the purpose of which is 'to support programmes to strengthen substantially and in a sustainable manner [qualifying low-income members'] balance of payments position and to foster durable growth, leading to higher living standards and a reduction in poverty'. As the ODC Report observes, 'one of the key changes from ESAF is that the complementarity of macroeconomic, structural and social policies will now be given greater recognition'. However the Task Force argues that this has transported the IMF into policy areas where there is little scientific consensus and has hindered the effectiveness of the institution, by discouraging early referral by countries and by sending out negative signals to foreign investors. According to the ODC Report the far-reaching conditionality that this involvement has brought with it is unlikely to be accompanied by governmental commitment, and for this reason, 'conditionality has, far more often than not, proven to be an ineffective way of influencing policy in the medium to long term . . . [it] has not been effective in promoting structural and institutional reform'. The ODC Report argues for moving the PRGF to the World Bank with the IMF retaining responsibility for short-run macroeconomic management.

The Meltzer Commission is more critical of the IMF's role in developing countries. It argues that conditionality has been ineffective across the board. Thus the Report says that accusations need to be 'taken seriously', that 'the IMF wields too much power over developing countries' economic policies', that 'G7 governments use the IMF as a vehicle to achieve their political ends', that 'the IMF's doctrines that are the basis for its guidance are inappropriate' and that 'the IMF relies too much on mandates and conditional lending dictated from abroad and too little on credible long-term incentives that encourage local decision-makers to act responsibly and reform domestic regulations, laws, institutions and practices'.

It also stresses heavily the moral hazard argument, claiming that IMF lending has encouraged over-lending by private capital markets. Because of its long-term lending to developing countries the Commission claims that 'the IMF's role now conflicts with other international financial institutions'. Although making a series of recommendations, the major thrust of the Report is that the IMF should discontinue long-term lending to developing countries and focus instead on short-term crisis lending. According to the Meltzer Commission the PRGF should be abandoned. Current conditionality should be replaced with financial and fiscal requirements that would have to be met before any country had access to Fund loans. The Fund should concentrate on emergency lending at penalty rates.

While differing in significant ways, all three reports agree that the IMF should reverse the trends of the last few years and withdraw from long-term lending to developing countries. The essence of the argument in each case is that IMF conditionality, particularly in the context of the ESAF, has been ineffective, that there is a serious moral hazard issue associated with IMF lending, and that in addition to this the World Bank is better equipped to undertake a long-term development lending role because of its superior institutional knowledge of development issues. Unanimity might initially be taken to imply that the argument for such a change is utterly compelling. But is it? Has the Fund's involvement in developing countries been as negative as the three Reports suggest? And if it has, is the appropriate policy response to return the Fund to its traditional role of providing short-term finance to countries in balance of payments crisis where, if conditionality is retained, it will focus on conventional macroeconomic stabilisation policies? Is it reasonable to assume that the World Bank or bilateral aid donors will be more effective than the IMF in providing support for structural adjustment? These are difficult questions to answer authoritatively. However, it is possible to discuss them in the context of the available empirical evidence, and this is what we seek to do in this chapter. Throughout we endeavour to maintain a distinction between the Fund's role in the better-off developing countries of Latin America and East Asia and its role in low-income countries to which the PRGF relates. Some discussions of the Fund unwisely blur this distinction.

The lay out of the chapter is as follows. Section 2 provides brief statistical evidence and analysis of the IMF's involvement in developing countries. Section 3 explores in more detail some of the analytical issues which lie behind IMF lending to developing countries. Section 4 examines the IMF's response to the balance of payments problems that have faced developing countries. Section 5 takes up some of the key analytical issues and criticisms raised in the debate about the IMF's role in developing countries and assembles empirical evidence in an attempt to make a judgement on them. In the light of this, Section 6 articulates an alternative policy direction which does not involve the Fund reverting to an exclusively short-term lending role.

2 The statistical background

Table 11.1 provides an indication of the IMF's involvement with developing countries by giving a snapshot of programmes existing in 1999. Table 11.2 puts this data in perspective by showing how IMF lending to developing countries varied during the 1990s.

Table 11.1 *Purchases and loans from the IMF, financial year ended 30 April 1999 (millions SDRs)*

Member	Reserve tranche[a]	Standby/ credit tranche	EFF	CCFF	Total purchases	ESAF loans	Total purchases and loans
Albania	–	–	–	–	–	12	12
Algeria	–	–	84	–	84	–	84
Angola	20	–	–	–	20	–	20
Antigua and Barbuda	1	–	–	–	1	–	1
Argentina	145	–	–	–	145	–	145
Armenia	–	–	–	–	–	21	21
Azerbaijan	11	–	11	56	78	20	98
Bahrain	1	–	–	–	1	–	1
Bangladesh	35	98[b]	–	–	133	–	133
Belarus	27	–	–	–	27	–	27
Benin	4	–	–	–	4	4	8
Bolivia	11	–	–	–	11	17	28
Bosnia and Herzegovina	12	24	–	–	36	–	36
Brazil	216	7,055[c]	–	–	7,271	–	7,271
Bulgaria	44	124	157	–	325	–	325
Burkina Faso	4	–	–	–	4	13	17
Burundi	5	–	–	–	5	–	5
Cambodia	6	–	–	–	6	–	6
Cameroon	13	–	–	–	13	54	67
Cape Verde	1	–	–	–	1	–	1
Central African Republic	4	–	–	–	4	8	12
Chad	4	–	–	–	4	17	20
Comoros	1	–	–	–	1	–	1
Congo, Republic of	7	7[d]	–	–	14	–	14
Côte d'Ivoire	22	–	–	–	22	40	62
Croatia	26	–	–	–	26	–	26
Czech Republic	57	–	–	–	57	–	57
Djibouti	–	3	–	–	3	–	3
Dominican Republic	15	40[b]	–	–	55	–	55
Ecuador	21	–	–	–	21	–	21
El Salvador	11	–	–	–	11	–	11
Equatorial Guinea	2	–	–	–	2	–	2
Eritrea	1	–	–	–	1	–	1
Ethiopia	9	–	–	–	9	15	24
Gabon	11	–	–	–	11	–	11
Gambia, The	2	–	–	–	2	3	5
Georgia	10	–	–	–	10	28	38
Ghana	–	–	–	–	–	41	41
Guinea	7	–	–	–	7	12	19
Guinea–Bissau	1	–	–	–	1	–	1

Table 11.1 (*cont.*)

Member	Reserve tranche[a]	Standby/ credit tranche	EFF	CCFF	Total purchases	ESAF loans	Total purchases and loans
Guyana	6	–	–	–	6	9	15
Haiti	–	15[b]	–	–	15	–	15
Honduras	–	48[b]	–	–	48	60	107
Indonesia	–	1,468	3,124	–	4,591	–	4,591
Iran, Islamic Republic of	105	–	–	–	105	–	105
Jamaica	18	–	–	–	18	–	18
Jordan	12	–	22	34	69	–	69
Kazakhstan	30	–	155	–	184	–	184
Kenya	18	–	–	–	18	–	18
Kiribati	–[e]	–	–	–	–[e]	–	–[e]
Korea	–	3,031[f]	–	–	3,031	–	3,031
Kyrgyz Republic	6	–	–	–	6	30	36
Latvia	9	–	–	–	9	–	9
Lesotho	3	–	–	–	3	–	3
Lithuania	10	–	–	–	10	–	10
Macedonia, FYR	5	–	–	–	5	9	14
Madagascar	8	–	–	–	8	–	8
Malawi	5	–	–	–	5	13	17
Mali	6	–	–	–	6	21	27
Mauritania	4	–	–	–	4	–	4
Mexico	208	–	–	–	208	–	208
Moldova	8	–	25	–	33	–	33
Mongolia	4	–	–	–	4	–	4
Mozambique	7	–	–	–	7	13	20
Myanmar	18	–	–	–	18	–	18
Nepal	5	–	–	–	5	–	5
Nicaragua	8	–	–	–	8	65	73
Niger	4	–	–	–	4	10	14
Nigeria	118	–	–	–	118	–	118
Pakistan	69	–	19	353	441	38	478
Palau	1	–	–	–	1	–	1
Panama	14	–	30	–	44	–	44
Papua New Guinea	9	–	–	–	9	–	9
Peru	43	–	–	–	43	–	43
Philippines	62	387	–	–	449	–	449
Romania	69	–	–	–	69	–	69
Russia	408	–	1,943[g]	2,157	4,508	–	4,508
Rwanda	5	–	–	–	5	24	29
St. Kitts and Nevis	1	2[b]	–	–	2	–	2
St. Lucia	1	–	–	–	1	–	1
Samoa	1	–	–	–	1	–	1
São Tomé and Principe	–[e]	–	–	–	–[e]	–	–[e]

(*cont.*)

Table 11.1 (*cont.*)

Member	Reserve tranche[a]	Standby/ credit tranche	EFF	CCFF	Total purchases	ESAF loans	Total purchases and loans
Senegal	11	–	–	–	11	18	29
Seychelles	2	–	–	–	2	–	2
Sierra Leone	7	12[d]	–	–	18	–	18
Slovak Republic	25	–	–	–	25	–	25
Solomon Islands	1	–	–	–	1	–	1
South Africa	126	–	–	–	126	–	126
Syrian Arab Republic	21	–	–	–	21	–	21
Tajikistan	7	–	–	–	7	40	47
Tanzania	13	–	–	–	13	65	78
Thailand	127	400	–	–	527	–	527
Togo	5	–	–	–	5	–	5
Trinidad and Tobago	22	–	–	–	22	–	22
Uganda	12	–	–	–	12	17	28
Ukraine	94	–	357	–	450	–	450
Uruguay	–	114	–	–	114	–	114
Uzbekistan	19	–	–	–	19	–	19
Vanuatu	1	–	–	–	1	–	1
Vietnam	22	–	–	–	22	–	22
Yemen	17	–	20	–	37	80	117
Zambia	31	–	–	–	31	10	41
Zimbabwe	23	39	–	–	62	–	62
Total	**2,657**	**12,868**	**5,947**	**2,600**	**24,071**	**826**	**24,897**

Notes:
[a] Includes reserve tranche purchases made in connection with the use of same-day SDR borrowing arrangement by members paying the reserve asset portion of their quota increase.
[b] Emergency natural disaster assistance.
[c] Includes purchases of SDR 6.5 billion under the Supplemental Reserve Facility (SRF).
[d] Emergency post-conflict assistance.
[e] Less than SDR 500,000.
[f] Includes purchase of SDR 2.85 billion under the SRF.
[g] Includes purchase of SDR 675 million under the SRF.
Source: IMF, *Annual Report*, 1999.

Although no attempt is made here to supply a detailed analysis of Fund lending to developing countries, a number of points are noteworthy.[2] First, the Fund has lent to both better-off developing countries and the poorest low-income countries; some of the latter, in particular, have been in a position of having almost quasi-permanent programmes with the IMF. Second, in quantitative terms,

---

[2] See Bird (1995) for such an analysis.

Table 11.2 *Outstanding IMF credit, by facility and policy, financial years ended 30 April 1992–1999 (in million SDRs and percentage)*

	1992	1993	1994	1995	1996	1997	1998	1999
			Millions SDRs					
Standby arrangements[a]	9,469	10,578	9,485	15,117	20,700	18,064	25,526	25,213
Extended arrangements	8,641	9,849	9,566	10,155	9,982	11,155	12,521	16,574
Supplemental Reserve Facility	–	–	–	–	–	–	7,100	12,655
Compensatory and Contingency Financing Facility	5,322	4,208	3,756	3,021	1,602	1,336	685	2,845
Systemic Transformation Facility	–	–	2,725	3,848	3,984	3,984	3,869	3,364
Subtotal (GRA)	**23,432**	**24,635**	**25,532**	**32,140**	**36,268**	**34,539**	**49,701**	**60,651**
SAF arrangements	1,500	1,484	1,440	1,277	1,208	954	730	565
ESAF arrangements[b]	1,646	2,219	2,812	3,318	4,469	4,904	5,505	5,870
Trust fund	158	158	105	102	95	90	90	89
Total	**26,736**	**28,496**	**29,889**	**36,837**	**42,040**	**40,488**	**56,026**	**67,175**
			Percentage of total					
Standby arrangements[a]	35	37	32	41	49	45	46	38
Extended arrangements	32	34	32	28	24	28	22	25
Supplemental Reserve Facility	–	–	–	–	–	–	13	19
Compensatory and Contingency Financing Facility	20	15	12	8	4	3	1	4
Systemic Transformation Facility	–	–	9	10	9	10	7	5
Subtotal (GRA)	**87**	**86**	**85**	**87**	**86**	**85**	**89**	**90**
SAF arrangements	6	5	5	3	3	2	1	1
ESAF arrangements[b]	6	8	9	9	11	12	10	9
Trust Fund	1	1	–[c]	–[c]	–[c]	–[c]	–[c]	–[c]
Total	**100**	**100**	**100**	**100**	**100**	**100**	**100**	**100**

Notes:
[a] Includes outstanding credit tranche and emergency purchases.
[b] Includes outstanding associated loans from the Saudi Fund for Development.
[c] Less than 0.5 of 1 per cent of total.

Fund lending to developing countries is heavily concentrated, with most of its financial support going to a small number of countries. Swings in Fund lending to developing countries are largely explained by whether loans are currently being made to one of the larger developing countries. Third, the Fund's involvement geographically spans the whole developing world.

Investigation of IMF lending to developing countries as a group (Bird, 1995) shows that it largely reflects the course of balance of payments deficits, and variations in access to private international capital. Developing countries turn to the IMF when they encounter balance of payments deficits that they are unable to finance adequately by borrowing from private creditors.[3]

In seeking areas of consensus from the studies that empirically investigate the use of IMF resources Bird (1996a) concludes that the Fund is a more important source of finance for relatively poor and low-growth countries, that it is more likely to have programmes with countries that have recently been involved with it, that exchange rate over-valuation has a positive and significant effect on borrowing from the IMF, and that international reserve holdings have a significant negative effect on the demand for Fund arrangements. Similarly, while all countries turning to the IMF have to demonstrate a balance of payments need, a current account deficit by itself does not provide motivation for seeking Fund support. The mere existence of a current account deficit does not automatically imply that a country will turn to the IMF; it is a necessary rather than sufficient condition.

Data from the IMF's *World Economic Outlook* reveal the persistence of current account balance of payments deficits among developing countries. But some of these enjoy better access to international capital markets than others and are therefore in a stronger position to finance current account deficits. Thus better off or middle-income developing countries do not tend to use the Fund for as long as they are deemed creditworthy by international capital markets. It is only when this creditworthiness evaporates in the midst of an economic crisis that they borrow from the Fund. For low-income countries the situation is different. For the most part these countries have little access to private international capital and therefore have a more enduring relationship with the IMF as a creditor. The statistical picture is therefore inconsistent with the idea that developing countries as a group are queuing up to borrow from the IMF. Borrowing from the Fund is in itself an indication that alternative options do not exist.

Tables 11.1 and 11.2 also show that institutionally IMF lending to better-off developing countries is usually channelled through conventional short-term

---

[3] Killick (1997) provides a detailed empirical examination of the circumstances in which countries negotiate programmes with the IMF. Another useful analysis of this issue may be found in Santaella (1995). Recent empirical evidence relating the determinants of borrowing from the IMF is surveyed in Bird (1996a).

standby arrangements or medium-term (Extended Fund Facility) (EFF) programmes, whereas lending to low-income countries usually occurs through the longer-term and concessionary Enhanced Structural Adjustment Facility (ESAF), now re-named the Poverty Reduction and Growth Facility (PRGF).

3 Analytical issues

The connection between current account balance of payments deficits and borrowing from the IMF warrants further discussion. There are two issues. First, what determines whether a country with a current account deficit turns to the IMF for support? Or, to put it slightly differently, what determines whether a current account deficit is a cause for concern? Secondly, why is it that current account deficits appear to be characteristic of many developing countries?

The conventional wisdom is that current account deficits are not a problem provided they are 'sustainable'. Sustainability depends partially on whether the causes of the deficit are temporary and self-correcting, and partially on whether the deficits may be financed by decumulating international reserves or by public or private capital inflows from abroad. A cyclical rise in import demand or a fall in export demand may therefore not create problems if countries hold an adequate cushion of international reserves or have access to international borrowing. More permanent changes in the terms of trade may not be a problem if they can be neutralised by changes in the value of the exchange rate or if domestic resources are mobile. Deficient domestic saving need not be a problem if it can be augmented by foreign saving and if the deficiency is cyclical.

A central feature of sustainability therefore relates to reserve levels and creditworthiness. Large holdings of international reserves mean that a country can sustain a current account deficit over a limited period of time until reserves have fallen to a threshold level at which a currency crisis is set off. Highly creditworthy countries may attract capital inflows over the reasonably long run and may therefore be able to sustain current account deficits over the long run as well. The US current account deficit during the 1990s was not widely perceived as a problem because of strong capital inflows – indeed one interpretation is that it is strong capital inflows that contribute to the current account deficit by driving up the exchange rate. Similarly the current account deficit in Thailand up to the mid-1990s was not of immediate concern for as long as capital was flowing into the country in volumes that not only financed it but allowed international reserves to be accumulated. It was only when these inflows were reversed and reserves fell sharply that a crisis occurred.

These observations allow countries to be classified according to how likely it is that they will need financial support from the IMF. Industrial countries have diversified product mixes, tend to be economically adaptable and have good access to international capital. They are therefore unlikely to encounter the kind of balance of payments crises that drive them to the Fund. Emerging economies may have economic structures that are less diversified and less easy to adjust and their access to international capital may be time-variant. They tend to be susceptible to capital volatility. As a consequence they may avoid the IMF for protracted periods of time but then may be forced to turn to the Fund in the midst of a crisis. Low-income countries tend to have a high degree of export concentration and are therefore exposed to export instability. They find it difficult to adjust quickly to changes in their terms of trade, frequently hold low levels of international reserves and have poor access to private international capital, relying more heavily on official inflows of capital. As a consequence they may be expected to be more regular users of IMF credits.

From one point of view one might expect poorer countries to be capital importers and richer countries to be capital exporters. Domestic saving might in principle be expected to be relatively low in developing countries and the return to investment relatively high. Current account balance of payments deficits in effect then simply mirror capital inflows and from this angle may be viewed as little cause for concern. Again, however, the key point relates to sustainability. The IMF becomes involved with developing countries when their current account balance of payments deficits become unsustainable. In these circumstances the policies supported by the Fund are aimed at creating or re-creating sustainability. In principle this may be achieved by increasing capital inflows, or by reducing current account deficits to a level that is consistent with existing inflows of capital, or, of course, by some combination of the two.

The IMF talks about its 'three-pronged' approach. One prong relates to the management of aggregate demand. The second relates to structural adjustment, designed to raise aggregate supply. And the third relates to attempts to catalyse other capital inflows. But what is the reality? At the time that the IMF becomes involved in a country there is likely to be a binding constraint in terms of external financing. The emphasis therefore falls on adjustment. But structural adjustment tends to be a long-term process and may even require some short-term increases in government expenditure to improve the economic infrastructure. In the midst of an economic crisis it is therefore likely that aggregate demand management will be at the core of adjustment. If a current account balance of payments deficit reflects an excess of aggregate demand over aggregate supply and if, in the short run and with a binding constraint in terms of external finance, aggregate supply cannot be increased, the apparently unassailable logic is that aggregate demand will have to be compressed. But is a policy response based on this logic likely to be effective and efficient in developing countries?[4]

---

[4] A similar approach based on national income identities is captured by $X - M = (S - I) + (T - G)$ where S is saving, T is tax revenue and G is government expenditure. This approach focuses

Compressing aggregate demand may indeed so reduce the demand for imports that the current account balance of payments 'strengthens'. But how big does the compression in aggregate demand have to be? Such a policy may work only at a high cost in terms of sacrificing domestic policy objectives. Furthermore, there are uncomfortable consequences of a demand-side approach. Depressing private sector investment and the capital component of government expenditure are likely to have an adverse effect on economic growth and future period income. An 'improvement' in the contemporary current account may be bought at the cost of a deterioration in the future. It is in this sense that balance of payments policy may have a negative growth effect. But to avoid this effect, demand compression will need to focus on consumption and the current component of government expenditure, and policies directed towards these goals are likely to encounter severe political resistance. For these reasons an adjustment strategy based on deflating domestic aggregate demand is likely to be abandoned by governments as soon as possible.

Even expenditure-switching balance of payments policies, such as exchange rate devaluation, may be less effective in countries where markets are ill developed and the price elasticities upon which the policies depend are low. Supply-side measures which have the effect of increasing price elasticities of both demand and supply may be an appropriate precursor to devaluation. In this context, longer-term structural policies may be needed in order to make the traditional policies of economic stabilisation work better. Monetary policy, fiscal policy and exchange rate policy encounter problems in developing countries that are more pronounced than those encountered in industrial economies because of ill-developed financial markets and the volatility of tax revenue and government expenditure. It is generally more difficult for developing countries to control the supply of money and the fiscal balance. Moreover, where these policies lead to falling real wages and increasing income inequality it may be expected that they will lead to greater social conflict, which will also undermine their effectiveness by reducing their political acceptability. Such policies may therefore need to be accompanied by others that enhance the scope for managing potential resistance. This may in turn necessitate protecting expenditure on primary health and education, providing social safety nets and avoiding, as far as possible, policies that are notoriously regressive such as indirect taxation.

Placing excessive emphasis on demand management tools in developing countries may therefore encounter strong political and social resistance and eventually fail. There is a need to build up consensus in favour of economic

---

on deficient private sector saving and fiscal deficits as the proximate causes of current account balance of payments deficits. While policy in the long run might focus on increasing S and T, short-run adjustment will tend to focus on cutting consumption, investment and government expenditure.

reform and to avoid conflict. Enhancing adjustment capacity will in turn raise the credibility of stabilisation measures with beneficial effects on capital inflows. Moreover, since it is easier to manage adjustment in an environment of economic growth it is also important to emphasise this as much as possible; not least because economic growth presents the opportunity for offsetting the effects of demand-side policies on poverty.

The foregoing discussion suggests that developing countries may encounter balance of payments problems for reasons that are in part beyond their control. The problems may reflect structural deficiencies that are unlikely to be susceptible to rapid correction. However, with impaired access to private international capital and facing a binding external financing constraint, countries will be forced to opt for quick-acting policies that emphasise contracting aggregate demand irrespective of whether over-expansionary policies were a prime cause of their balance of payments deficits or not. Such policies may be effective at reducing deficits, but only at a cost in terms of economic growth and development. For this reason they may generate domestic political resistance and exhibit a high probability of breaking down. In these circumstances an infusion of liquidity will relax the external financing constraint, and a supply-side response to balance of payments deficits may become feasible. In principle, this may confer a number of advantages. First, it may work directly on the root cause of the problem. Second, it may allow conventional demand management policies to become more effective in the future. And, third, it may provide a better opportunity for mitigating political resistance to reform. Both the economic and social capacity to conduct balance of payments correction may therefore be enhanced. However, if private capital markets will not provide the finance does this justify a role for the IMF or the World Bank?

4 The response of the IMF

Historically the IMF's response to the balance of payments problems of developing countries has been to assemble an array of facilities through which it lends to them and provides adjustment advice. Starting initially from a position where it argued that developing countries were adequately served by conventional standbys, the Fund subsequently introduced the Compensatory Financing Facility (CFF) to deal with the problem of export shortfalls, the Buffer Stock Financing Facility (BSFF) to help deal with the problem of export instability, the Extended Fund Facility (EFF) to encompass medium-term adjustment, the Structural Adjustment Facility (SAF) and the ESAF to deal with longer-term structural adjustment in low-income countries, and most recently the Contingent Credit Lines (CCLs) to help offset liquidity shortages during financial crises. Along the way, these facilities have on occasion been modified. Thus,

having been liberalised in the mid-1970s, the CFF was then changed to involve greater conditionality and to cover other shocks such as sharp increases in global interest rates, becoming the Contingent and Compensatory Financing Facility (CCFF). It has more recently been reverted to its original role (Bird, 2001).

Some of these facilities have been more heavily used than others (Bird, 1995). Over recent years, most drawings on the IMF by developing countries have occurred either through the EFF or the ESAF, and have taken place in circumstances where private capital markets were not prepared to lend. Drawings under the CCFF and BSFF have been much more modest, indeed sometimes non-existent, and this has led to the abandonment of the BSFF and changes to the CCFF.

Since the 1970s it is difficult to find any protracted period when the institutional arrangements through which the IMF lends to developing countries have been in steady state. The ESAF provides a case in point. Starting life as the SAF it was soon extended. It was then subject to periodic reviews, one of which was conducted by external assessors. In 1999 it was modified and renamed the Poverty Reduction and Growth Facility (PRGF).

It is not difficult to see how these institutional arrangements may have been designed to address the analytical issues raised in section 3. The Fund would no doubt claim that it has the institutional paraphernalia necessary to deal with the various balance of payments problems faced by developing countries, whether in terms of domestic economic mismanagement, external shocks or the need for longer-structural adjustment.

It is also true that as the purview of the Fund has extended, and in particular as it has begun to see balance of payments problems in a longer-term perspective, it has become increasingly involved in development issues. It is in this context that it has been exposed to the criticisms summarised in the introduction. But are the criticisms based on secure analysis and evidence? Should the IMF seek to extricate itself from its long-term involvement with developing countries and in particular low-income countries?

5 Key issues: empirical evidence

In this section we focus on a number of issues which lend themselves to empirical analysis and have a strong bearing on criticisms of the Fund's role in long-term lending to developing countries outlined earlier. First, does IMF lending lead to a moral hazard problem? Second, has conditionality been effective or ineffective in developing countries? Third, has the IMF encroached excessively into the territory of the World Bank and bilateral aid donors where it is at a comparative disadvantage? Would the World Bank and aid donors do a better job than the IMF?

The IMF and moral hazard

An early variant on the moral hazard theme was that governments in developing countries were encouraged to mismanage their economies and to create balance of payments deficits in order to gain access to concessionary IMF lending (Vaubel, 1983). However, empirical analyses of the economic characteristics of countries turning to the Fund are inconsistent with this view since exogenous factors are found to play a key role. Furthermore, the frequent existence of spare lending capacity in the Fund over the years suggests that conditionality has effectively policed any potential moral hazard problem. Even the highly concessionary ESAF has not always been heavily used by countries experiencing balance of payments problems, suggesting that its tight conditionality has had a discouraging effect on potential borrowers (Bird, 1995).

The more recent version of the moral hazard argument against IMF lending, as articulated in the Meltzer Report, is that it is the implicit insurance that it provides and the related prospect of being bailed out that encourages private creditors to over-lend. This then leads to financial problems which themselves lead to the Fund becoming involved. It is largely on the back of this argument that the Meltzer Commission claims that the problem of moral hazard 'cannot be overstated'. But surely it can. The argument came into vogue only after the Mexican peso crisis. For many years prior to that the IMF had been lending to developing countries and yet no one had claimed that this induced excess private inflows. Even if this was because of the general use of capital controls, empirical analyses of private capital flows suggest that they are influenced as much by 'push' as by 'pull' factors and that the prospective involvement of the IMF is not a significant factor or indeed one that would necessarily exert a positive effect on capital inflows. The probability of IMF involvement presages crisis; why should private creditors want to lend to potential crisis countries when the chances are that they will fail to escape the crisis scot-free? The Fund's reluctance to bail out Russia in 1998 has been seen as a further counterweight to the moral hazard problem. Moreover, to some the moral hazard critique of the IMF is little more than the conventional argument against lenders of last resort.

Although much has been made of the moral hazard argument there is little if any secure empirical evidence upon which to judge it. Where evidence is offered it is usually anecdotal and unscientific. In a minority report, some members of the IFIAC assess the view that 'moral hazard is the dominant problem facing the global financial system' in the following way:

The problem with this view is that there is no – repeat, no – empirical support for it. The majority argument that the Mexican support package caused the East Asia crisis is pure theory and, indeed, theology.

In isolated studies that have sought to test for moral hazard little or no support for it has been found. Willett (1999) finds no evidence to suggest that over-lending has been concentrated in the categories of capital flow where bailing out is most likely. Lane and Phillips (2000) test to see whether events affecting the likelihood or availability of Fund support affect interest rate spreads on emerging market bonds. They find that 'only 2 out of 22 episodes examined ... show behaviour of interest rate spreads consistent with moral hazard' and point out that 'even for these events, the behaviour of interest rates is difficult to separate from other contemporaneous events and from turbulent market condi-tions more generally'. While acknowledging the limitations of their study, they conclude that 'moral hazard created by the IMF is actually not very significant compared with numerous other factors affecting asset prices and interest rate spreads'.

Moreover, for low-income countries private capital flows in general are much less important than they are for a few 'emerging' economies. Instead these countries tend to rely more heavily on foreign aid and for them the moral hazard argument is irrelevant. Thus the Meltzer Commission's claim that the IMF has in effect encouraged over-lending by private capital markets is yet more difficult to sustain in the case of low-income countries.

If there is anything in the moral hazard argument, it might be more that countries do not appear to be penalised for failing to complete IMF-sponsored programmes. Failure to finish one seems most likely simply to lead to another – so where is the incentive to implement the agreed economic reforms? There is strong empirical evidence of this recidivist tendency, in particular among low income countries. (Bird, Hussain and Joyce, 2000). But it is inappropriate to draw the inference that the IMF should therefore stop lending to these countries; the appropriate inference might rather be that a different economic therapy is needed.[5]

Has conditionality been effective?

The answer to this question is central to the debate about the Fund's role in developing countries. If IMF conditionality had proved unambiguously and universally effective across an entire range of criteria the case for change would be weakened, if not undermined; although it could still be argued, of course,

---

[5] In any case the lender of last resort (LOLR) function, which is the one on which the Meltzer Commission says the Fund should focus, itself involves moral hazard, and there is reason to believe that relying on prudential standards, as the Commission advocates, will be less effective at policing it than the conditionality that it argues should be abandoned.

that there is scope for further improvement. If, on the other hand, conditionality had been equally clearly ineffective then the case for change would be strengthened; although this would not necessarily imply that conditionality should be abandoned or that the Fund should withdraw from long-term lending. However the reality is more nuanced. Thus with access to the same research findings, Haque and Khan (1998) claim that conditionality 'on balance' works while the Meltzer Commission claims that it doesn't. The inconsistency may be resolved by observing that conditionality has 'worked' according to some criteria but not according to others. It would therefore appear premature to draw firm conclusions on the effectiveness of conditionality at this stage (Bird, 2001). According to the available evidence IMF programmes seem to be associated with some improvement in the balance of payments, but perhaps a decline in investment and economic growth at least in the short run.[6]

However, we still do not know some rather important things about conditionality. First, does its effectiveness depend on the degree to which programmes are implemented? An answer to this question is important because it would indicate whether conditionality is well designed. An affirmative answer would suggest that conditionality does have appropriate design features and does make a positive difference. The trouble is that very few studies have examined this issue and from those that do there is no consensus.[7]

A second question is whether different types of conditionality have different effects. While the Meltzer Commission is critical of IMF conditionality *en bloc*, the ODC Task Force is critical of conditionality only in the context of the ESAF and structural adjustment. What does the evidence on the effectiveness of the ESAF tell us? Here again there is considerable disagreement. Early internal reviews of the ESAF were generally positive (Schadler *et al.*, 1993). However outsiders criticised the methodologies used and the conclusions drawn (Killick, 1995a). An external review commissioned by the Fund was also critical of the

---

[6] One of us explores these issues in some depth elsewhere and the arguments are therefore not replicated here (Bird, 2001). Assessing the effectiveness of conditionality on key macroeconomic variables is methodologically difficult because of the counterfactual problem. But in addition to this, answering the question of whether IMF programmes work requires a stricter definition of the criteria against which this can be judged. Poor rates of programme completion, high rates of IMF recidivism and a weak catalytic effect of IMF programmes on other capital flows could be used as evidence to suggest that conditionality is ineffective. But this does not necessarily imply that it should be abandoned. Instead these features of conditionality may help to delineate ways in which it should be reformed. In the text of this chapter we focus on the effectiveness of IMF conditionality in the context of the ESAF since this has been the facility most used by the low-income countries with which we are most concerned.

[7] Killick (1997) reports that he finds no statistically significant support for the idea that implementation makes a positive difference. Conway (1994), on the other hand, argues that his evidence suggests that it does. However there are methodological problems with both of these studies and at present there is simply no evidence upon which we can rely.

design of the ESAF (Botchwey *et al.*, 1998) and members of the review team have gone on to offer further critical assessment (Collier and Gunning, 1999), arguing that the ESAF has had little impact on poverty reduction and has tended to result in a tapering out of foreign aid.[8] The difficulties in assessing the track record of ESAF are nicely captured by an investigation that shows that while by using a modified control group to model the counterfactual, results are generated that suggest statistically significant beneficial effects of ESAF programmes on output growth and the debt-service ratio over the period 1986–91, diagnostic tests cast doubt on the reliability of the estimates (Dicks-Mireaux, Mecagni and Schadler, 2000).

Further evidence on the effectiveness of ESAF conditionality based on control group comparisons is presented in table 11.3. The results reported here compare the performance of a sample of countries that received ESAF credits from the Fund in the mid-1990s with a control group selected to be similar apart from their lack of Fund involvement.[9] Economic growth is found to be higher in the ESAF group, with the difference in the sample means being significant at the 1 per cent level. This confirms one of the findings in the study by Dicks-Mireaux, Mecagni and Schadler (2000) for an earlier period reported above. Leading on from the discussion in section 3 table 11.3 also provides results which seek to find out the association between ESAFs and the distributional stance of macroeconomic policy, as an indicator of the extent to which economic reform might exacerbate social conflict – and the Observer Human Rights Index – as an indicator of the government's ability to manage social conflict. Countries with ESAF programmes are found to have a more 'pro-poor' mix of stabilisation policies and greater 'social capacity'. Whatever the causal relationship, ESAF programmes seem, according to these data, to be associated

[8] Collier and Gunning (1999) criticise the ESAF because of what they see as its 'flawed design'. They claim that ESAF programmes have sometimes had 'adverse consequences for the poor either directly through reducing incomes, or indirectly through reductions in social provision'. However their principal criticism relates to the sequencing of reform rather than the content. Too much early attention has been paid to financial liberalisation, so they claim. They also argue that ESAF conditionality has transferred sovereignty away from governments in a 'dysfunctional' way and that inadvertently ESAF programmes have resulted in a misallocation of aid. ESAF support, so they claim, has tended to go to countries with poor policies where it is unlikely to reduce poverty. Countries complying with ESAF conditionality will tend to find aid tapering out.

[9] Details relating to the control group are available from the authors. Again it may be worth emphasising that control group comparisons are only one, albeit imperfect, way of constructing a counterfactual. Clearly it is impossible to select countries that are identical in all respects other than the involvement of the IMF. Thus it remains scientifically unsound to claim that differences in performance can be unambiguously attributed to IMF involvement. However, the difficulty is that there is no way of perfectly capturing the counterfactual; other methodologies encounter their own problems. By exercising care in choosing the control group and by interpreting the results as merely indicative rather than definitive, our intention is to provide at least some empirical evidence pertaining to the track record of the ESAF.

Table 11.3 *ESAF countries and control group: Fund agreements, economic performance and indicators of 'social capacity', 1995–1999*

Country	Date of most recent Fund agreement and type of agreement	Mix of stabilisation instruments[a]	Social capability indicators:[b] AM	Social capability indicators:[b] Obs	Growth 1995–9[c]
ESAF countries (average *per capita* GDP = \$426)					
Uganda	ESAF IV (1994)	6.4	−1.22	20.0	6.3
Malawi	ESAF IV (1994)	3.7	−1.57	13.7	6.0[d]
Tanzania	ESAF II (1993)	5.1	−1.22	22.4	1.7[d]
Mozambique	ESAF IV (1996)	7.1	. .	16.2	6.1[d]
Nicaragua	ESAF I (1994)	6.5	0.88	27.7	2.5[d]
Bolivia	ESAF IV (1994)	4.7	−0.35	21.2	2.4[d]
Albania	ESAF II (1995)	1.8	. .	38.6	5.5[d]
Vietnam	ESAF II (1994)	7.2	−0.49	29.7	5.7
Sri Lanka	ESAF III (1995)	1.4	0.35		3.6
Pakistan	ESAF I (1994)	1.3		56.5	2.2[d]
Zimbabwe		1.8	0.14	18.9	0.9
Ethiopia		3.2	−0.99	12.2	3.0
Bangladesh		2.7		30.5	
ESAF countries average		**3.8**		**24.7**	**3.1**
Non-ESAF countries (average *per capita* GDP = \$497)					
Nepal		3.1		27.4	
Sierra Leone		1.9		14.4	
Eritrea		0.6			2.1
Rwanda		2.3		26.3	. .
Sudan		0.8	−0.64	46.2	2.5
Haiti		1.4		25.3	
Vanuatu		1.1			0.5
Tonga		0.9		9.1	−2.5[d]
Congo (Dem. Rep.)		0.4		42.5	−4.5
Congo (Rep.)		0.2		41.1	
Non-ESAF average		**1.3**		**31.7**	**−0.4**
t-stat[e]		**4.23**[**]		**1.29**	**4.13**[**]

Notes:
** The control group is selected to have similar income and other initial conditions to the ESAF group, except for the fact of not receiving ESAF support. For this purpose, the countries of the control sample are selected pairwise in relation to countries within the treatment sample (e.g. Ethiopia is matched with Eritrea, Uzbekistan is matched with Albania, etc.).
[a] This is defined as ratio of real devaluation to increase of indirect tax rates, 1994–9.
[b] AM = Adelman–Morris index of social capacity; Obs = Observer Human Rights Index.
[c] Start date of the 5-year period is 1995 or year after inception date of ESAF (if different)
[d] Denotes data for 1995–8 only.
[e] T-statistic is defined for difference between sample means and is calculated

$$\frac{X_1 - X_2}{\dfrac{\sqrt{(S_1^2 + S_2^2)}}{(n_1 \quad n_2)}}$$

with measures that minimise social conflict by avoiding regressive policies and also with the creation of the social capacity required for managing structural reform and facilitating macroeconomic stabilisation. Although not in any way definitive, this evidence is consistent with the argument that the ESAF has been associated with effective pro-growth policies and policies which create an economic and political environment in which adjustment and stabilisation may be achieved on a long-term basis.

What does this imply? Perhaps it implies that a degree of agnosticism is appropriate in discussing the effectiveness of long-term lending to developing countries by the Fund. There is enough evidence to make a case that the ESAF has been relatively effective in facilitating economic growth and in helping to build up social capacity. It is through economic growth that developing countries will eventually become less reliant on the Fund (Bird, 1996a) and it is by building up social capacity that the scope for effective economic management may be raised on a sustainable basis. Long-term lending by the IMF may therefore be helping to create the conditions in which traditional stabilisation measures may be made more effective. A broader political economy assessment of the ESAF which goes beyond the conventional criteria for evaluating success and examines the social and therefore political environment in which economic adjustment is to be pursued may suggest that the facility has made a positive contribution. Abandoning the PRGF, and refocusing on conventional short-term standbys based on the management of aggregate demand could, in isolation, lead to a loss of effectiveness, not only because the economic conditions would be less conducive to its success but also because the political–social capacity to sustain the related policies would be in place to a lesser extent, and indeed might be damaged by too abrupt a process of stabilisation. The argument is not that macroeconomic stability is inappropriate, clearly it is. But in many developing countries macroeconomic stabilisation may be best achieved in the kind of economic and social environment which long-term lending by the IMF may be helping to create.

But what about relocating it into the World Bank as the ODC Task Force suggests? If there is a justification for structural adjustment, should it be the World Bank rather than the IMF that is institutionally responsible for encouraging it? Or should it be left to domestic governments supported by foreign aid donors?

Has the IMF encroached too much into the territory of the World Bank and aid donors?

It is certainly true that it is in the context of long-term lending and structural adjustment that the overlap between the IMF and the World Bank has become greater than was envisaged when the institutions were originally established. In terms of institutional design this implies various options (Bird, 1993, 1994). The CFR Task Force, the IFIAC and the ODC Task Force all favour placing long-term lending to developing countries more firmly and exclusively under the auspices of the World Bank and aid donors; the IFIAC stresses in addition the importance of encouraging private capital flows. Apart from arguing that the IMF has been ineffective in this role, the Reports claim that the World Bank and aid donors will perform the role better, because they possess more experience in the microeconomics of economic development. As noted above, by focusing on the correction of fiscal imbalances exclusive of aid flows, some commentators have argued that IMF conditionality under the auspices of ESAF loans has had the undersirable effect of tapering out foreign aid at exactly the time that it is most needed (Collier and Gunning, 1999). However the Reports almost seem to take it for granted that long-term lending and structural adjustment will be better conducted by the Bank and by aid donors.

Is this a reasonable presumption? There are a number of counterarguments. First, the World Bank's track record on structural adjustment has been criticised in many ways, ranging from design, to implementation and effectiveness (Mosley, Harrigan and Toye, 1995). Even where countries are seen as pursuing appropriate policies, researchers have found this to be generally unconnected with World Bank lending (Burnside and Dollar, 1997; Collier and Dollar, 1998; Dollar and Svensson, 1998). Second, if, as the ODC Task Force suggests, there is no consensus on issues affecting economic growth and development, it may be unrealistic to expect the World Bank to be any more successful than the IMF in identifying the correct policies. Certainly the Bank has been much criticised for what some have seen as its over-enthusiastic support of market-related policies, economic liberalisation and openness. There is legitimate doubt about whether the World Bank's approach to development is the one best suited to all developing countries (Mosley, 2000a). Third, where economic reform needs to combine macroeconomic stabilisation with economic adjustment, can it be confidently expected that the World Bank will come up with the appropriate blend of policies? Perhaps moving the PRGF to the World Bank, as the ODC Task Force suggests, will downplay too much the stabilisation element of reform, even though the ODC expects the IMF to take the lead in this component of programmes. Will such an institutional re-orientation really result in better-designed programmes? Or does improving the design of policy depend on more fundamental issues; in particular on gaining a better understanding of economic growth and development and of what policies are superior in different contexts? In any case, since lending under the PRGF is guided by a poverty-reduction strategy paper in which both the IMF and the World Bank are involved alongside the relevant government, civil society and the private sector it may be that whether the PRGF is formally lodged with the IMF or the World Bank is something of a 'red herring'.

Fourth, an important question when discussing the effects of IFI involvement in developing countries is their effect on other capital flows. Is World Bank involvement likely to be more effective than IMF involvement in encouraging private capital markets and aid donors to lend? Again, the available empirical evidence suggests not. There is no evidence to support the idea of a significant World Bank catalytic effect (Bird and Rowlands, 2001) and, although the evidence suggests that the IMF's impact is weak, there is at least some empirical evidence to suggest that it is positive, whereas in the case of the development banks it is negative (Rodrik, 1996). Managers of mutual funds and pension funds certainly report that they pay more attention and attach greater weight to IMF programmes than to those of the World Bank (Bird and Rowlands, 2000). Moreover, to the extent that it exists, the catalytic effect of IMF lending seems to be strongest in terms of official flows. Indeed, it has been in the context of ESAF that this form of catalysis has been most significant (Bird and Rowlands, 2000b). This is inconsistent with the idea that the IMF drives aid out at precisely the time that it is needed.

Indeed, a counterclaim can be made. Empirical evidence has usually found the macroeconomic effectiveness of aid to be weak; not even significantly different from zero. Part of the explanation for this could be that aid has been used to finance excessive fiscal deficits. There is therefore a moral hazard problem with aid. More recent evidence suggests, however, that aid is effective when combined with a good policy environment (including the avoidance of large fiscal deficits) and with strong social capacity to accommodate economic reform.[10] This is where the IMF may make a contribution. The evidence reported in the previous subsection combined with evidence presented in table 11.4 suggests that through the ESAF it may have had a positive impact. Foreign aid may therefore be most effective when combined with appropriate IMF conditionality.

[10] The literature on aid effectiveness is very large. Burnside and Dollar (1997) provide evidence to suggest that aid when combined with a good policy environment is effective, although additional research suggests that this environment does not depend on World Bank structural adjustment. More recently Hansen and Tarp (2000) have cast doubt on the view that aid works only where policies are 'good'. Their key result establishes a link between aid effectiveness and not the conventional index of good policy, but rather the Adelman–Morris index of social capacity. This provides further empirical support for the argument that the building up of social capacity, which may be assisted by the ESAF and PRGF, according to the results reported in the text, is important for the long-term economic success of developing countries. Foreign aid alone, however, clearly does not guarantee it. Aid flows are generally inversely correlated with tax effort. Poor countries can become trapped in a vicious circle in which aid dependence is both the consequence and the continuing cause of an inability to build up a democratic, accountable political system (Moore, 1998).

Table 11.4 *ESAF borrower countries and control group: IMF agreements, aid, taxation and private investment*

Country	Most recent IMF agreement: date and type	Aid flow/GNP Ratio 1997	Aid flow/GNP Change since 1990	Tax revenue/GDP Ratio	Tax revenue/GDP Change since latest IMF agreement	Private foreign investment/GNP Ratio	Private foreign investment/GNP Change since 1990
ESAF countries							
Uganda	ESAF IV (1994)	12.8	−3.4	11.2	+4.0	2.7	+2.4
Malawi	ESAF IV (1994)	13.7	−15.1			0.1	
Tanzania	ESAF II (1993)	13.9	−16.4	11.1	+0.6	2.1	+2.0
Bangladesh		2.3	−4.6			0.2	+0.1
Mozambique	ESAF IV (1996)	29.6	−16.0			1.0	+0.5
Nicaragua	ESAF I (1994)	22.7	−18.3	23.9	+3.8		
Bolivia	ESAF IV (1994)	9.2	−3	15.0	+3.2	10.2	+14.4
Albania	ESAF II (1995)	6.7	+6.1	16.6		1.7	+0.6
Vietnam	ESAF II (1994)	4.2	+0.1			7.7	+7.7
Sri Lanka	ESAF III (1995)	2.3	−7.0	18.5	0.0	3.7	+3.4
Pakistan	ESAF I (1994)	1.5	−0.5	12.9	−1.8	3.3	+3.0
Ethiopia		15.8	+4.7	11.9	+8.5	0.1	+0.4
ESAF countries, average		**11.2**	**−5.8**	**15.1**	**+2.6**	**3.0**	**+3.4**
Non-ESAF countries							
Sierra Leone		16.0	+7.9			0.2	−4.5
Eritrea			+14.8			0	0
Rwanda		11.6	+18.2			0.05	
Sudan				6.7	−0.8		
Congo (Dem. Rep.)				4.9	−0.3	0	
Burkina Faso		12.3	+3.3			0	
Congo (Rep.)		9.9	+4.8			0.05	
Uzbekistan		0.5	+.02			1.4	+1.8
Vanuatu							
W. Samoa							
Haiti		11.8	+6.0	8.1	+2.4	0.1	−0.6
Nepal		8.3	−3.5			0.6	+0.4
Average, non-ESAF countries		**10.0**	**+6.4**	**6.5**	**+0.6**	**0.3**	**−0.6**
t-statistic for difference between sample means		0.34	3.75	3.58	1.98	2.87	4.25

Sources: IMF, *World Economic Outlook* and (for tax data) *Government Finance Statistics Yearbook*; data on timing of IMF agreements are also from IMF *Annual Report*; private investment data from World Bank, *World Development Report 1999/2000*, tables 1 and 21.

Aid without IMF conditionality may be less potent in improving economic performance. In any case, given evidence of a positive correlation between IMF lending and aid, there is reason to believe that without IMF conditionality aid flows will decline.

So where does this leave us? The stark reality is that there is no sharp dividing line between development and the balance of payments and therefore no equivalently clear delineation between the World Bank and the IMF. Developing countries often have long-term balance of payments problems and the IMF is a balance of payments institution. Overlap cannot be avoided. Drawing on the evidence above gives no compelling reason to believe that phasing out the role of the IMF in long-term lending to developing countries and building up the role of the World Bank will necessarily have beneficial consequences. Relying more heavily on aid donors to provide long-term finance could be unwise given the track record of aid and could simply be unrealistic given the political economy of aid and declining trends during the 1990s. Moreover it is rather inconsistent for the IFIAC to recommend a greater reliance on bilateral aid because of increasing political influences over IMF lending. While this could make the politics involved in international lending more overt it would almost certainly increase the degree to which financial assistance depends on politics.

6 Concluding remarks

A series of influential reports have been published which advocate that the IMF should withdraw from its long-term lending role in developing countries. Sometimes more explicitly than others they suggest that the World Bank and aid donors should take over – or take back – this role.

However, there is a counterview that has not been represented but deserves attention. This is that criticisms that the Fund has been ineffective in its development role can be taken too far. Given the nature of balance of payments problems in developing countries that frequently arise from chronic debility on the supply side just as much as from over-expansion of aggregate demand, the modifications that the Fund had made to its lending facilities and in particular the ESAF have been qualitatively appropriate. Although Fund conditionality can certainly be criticised on various grounds (Bird, 1996, 2001) there have been signs that the Fund is responding to such criticism. Thus the PRGF makes an attempt to encourage ownership of related economic programmes. Lack of this and a related lack of commitment has sometimes been seen as an important reason why conditionality has at best had muted effects in the past.[11]

---

[11] In this chapter we have avoided a detailed discussion of IMF conditionality, the theory behind it and the ways in which it might usefully be reformed. Bird (1996b) provides an overview

Traditional demand-side policies will not deal with supply-side weaknesses. Structural adjustment may itself be required in order to make economic stabilisation measures more effective. Moving back to basics could therefore simply lead to greater IMF recidivism, with developing countries turning to the Fund time and again for emergency assistance and failing to escape from their fundamental economic difficulties. Moreover there is some empirical evidence to suggest that the IMF's long-term lending has had beneficial effects on economic growth, on strengthening the underlying fiscal position and on creating a social capacity for maintaining sustained stability.

Critics have therefore tended to be unduly harsh in their judgements of the IMF, and an agnostic position may be better warranted from a measured assessment of the evidence. Furthermore they have been unduly optimistic about the prospects for improvement simply by handing over the Fund's development role to the World Bank and aid donors. There are problems with World Bank conditionality as well as with IMF conditionality and the World Bank may be less effective at influencing private capital markets. Foreign aid encounters a moral hazard problem by allowing fiscal laxity. It may fail to correct underlying fiscal imbalances unless accompanied by IMF conditionality. Aid combined with IMF involvement may be more effective than aid on its own.

In the cases of the CFR Task Force and the IFIAC the focus has been on the better-off developing countries, on the economic crises that befell Mexico, East Asia, Russia and Brazil during the 1990s and the threats to systemic stability. An argument can certainly be made (and of course challenged) that the Fund over-lent in these cases and engaged in excessive conditionality. But it would be a mistake to treat all developing countries alike and to advocate systemic reform on the basis of experience in a few countries.[12] The majority of IMF programmes are with low-income countries which do not threaten the stability

of issues surrounding conditionality and discusses some proposals for reform. Mosley (1987) provides an early analysis of conditionality in the context of a bargaining model and goes on to develop a simple theoretical framework within which the theory underlying conditionality may be conceptualised (Mosley, 1992). Analyses of the effectiveness of conditionality which emphasise the degree of commitment to policy reform and the idea of 'ownership' include Bird (1998) and Killick (1997). In similar vain Collier *et al.* (1997) offer a wide-ranging critique of conditionality. It should be underlined that to argue that the IMF should continue to play a role in developing countries is not to endorse the *status quo* but rather to argue that more may be achieved by evolutionary reform along the lines that have been seen over recent years than by a more radical discrete institutional reorganisation which seeks to reallocate roles on the basis of a distinction that is unavoidably blurred.

[12] These richer developing countries place time-variant claims on the IMF's resources as their creditworthiness with private capital markets comes and goes. When it 'goes' the IMF becomes involved in emergency lending in the context of currency crises. Given the Asian crisis in 1997–8, it is unsurprising that this aspect of IMF activity has received most attention and is certainly the focus of the Meltzer Commission and the CFR Task Force. It is in the context of these crises that much has been made of the moral hazard associated with IMF lending. Although in quantitative

of the international financial system and whose economic problems are significantly different from those found in Mexico, Brazil or South Korea. Given the economic size of low-income countries, IMF lending to them does not absorb many resources relative to the total budget of the Fund. It would be misguided for the IMF, which has begun to see itself as the 'best friend of the poor' (Michael Camdessus, UNCTAD conference, Bangkok, 13 February 2000) and to devise (in conjunction with the World Bank) a coherent approach to structural balance of payments deficits, to be forced to abandon these advances as a by-product of concern over systemic financial instability. A number of poor countries have begun to emerge into a process of sustained growth under the tutelage of the ESAF/PRGF (Bolivia, Ghana, Lao PDR, Tanzania, Uganda, Mozambique) with consequent benefits for their trading partners. If this process is abandoned, the IMF's balance sheet would not improve; the poor would lose out; and, because of this, the rich countries might ultimately lose out as well. A more holistic approach to the protection of the international monetary system which showed a greater awareness of the problems faced by poor countries would assist both these countries and their creditors. Such an approach would tend to lead to a rather different future for the IMF than the one envisaged by the CFR Task Force, the Meltzer Commission and even the ODC Task Force. Although the outcome could involve an element of institutional overlap, it could also be more effective for all parties.

REFERENCES

Bird, G. (1993). 'Sisters in Economic Development: The Bretton Woods Institutions and Developing Countries', *Journal of International Development*, 5(1), 1–25

(1994). 'Changing Partners: Perspectives and Policies of the Bretton Woods Institutions', *Third World Quarterly*, 15(3), 483–503

(1995). *IMF Lending to Developing Countries: Issues and Evidence*. London, Routledge

(1996a). 'Borrowing from the IMF: The Policy Implications of Recent Empirical Research', *World Development*, 24(11), 1753–60

(1996b). 'The IMF and Developing Countries: A Review of the Evidence and Policy Options', *International Organisation*, 50(3), 477–512

terms such programmes dominate Fund lending they represent only a very small proportion of its activity in terms of the number of programmes. A case may be made that lending to these richer countries has been excessive and that loans could be better provided by other agencies (Bird and Rajan, 2000) and that the Fund should concentrate on encouraging private capital markets to lend to these countries, bailing in rather than bailing out private lenders. (For a discussion of these issues see, for example, Eichengreen, 1999; Bird, 1999.) For the poorest countries of the world and in the near term the IMF may need to substitute for private capital and it is to these countries that the analysis in this chapter primarily relates.

(1998). 'The Effectiveness of Conditionality and the Political Economy of Policy Reform: Is it Simply a Matter of Political Will?', *Journal of Policy Reform*, 1, 89–113.

(1999). 'Crisis Averter, Crisis Lender, Crisis Manager: the IMF in Search of a Systemic Role', *The World Economy*, 22(7), 955–75

(2001). 'IMF Programmes: Do They Work, Can They Be Made to Work Better?', *World Development*, 29(11), 1849–66

Bird, G., M. Hussain and J. P. Joyce (2000). 'Many Happy Returns?: Recidivism and the IMF', Wellesley College and University of Surrey, unpublished paper

Bird, G. and R. Rajan (2000). 'Is There a Case for an Asian Monetary Fund?', *World Economics*, 11(2), 135–44

Bird, Graham and Dane Rowlands (1997) 'The Catalytic Effect of Lending by the International Financial Institutions', *The World Economy*, 20(7), 967–95

(2000). 'The Catalyzing Role of Policy-Based Lending by the IMF and the World Bank: Fact or Fiction?', *Journal of International Development*, 12, 951–73

(2001). 'World Bank Lending and Other Financial Flows: Is There a Connection?', *Journal of Development Studies*, 37(5), 83–103

(2002). 'Do IMF Programmes Have a Catalytic Effect on Other International Capital Flows?', *Oxford Development Studies*, 30(3), 229–49

Botchwey, K., P. Collier, J. W. Gunning and K. Hamada (1998) *External Evaluation of the Enhanced Structural Adjustment Facility*. Washington, DC, IMF

Burnside, C. and D. Dollar (1997). 'Aid, Policies and Growth', World Bank Policy Research Working Paper, 1777; *American Economic Review*, 90(4), 847–68

Collier, P. and D. Dollar (1998). 'Aid Allocation and Poverty Reduction', World Bank, mimeo

Collier, P., P. Guillaumont, S. Guillaumont and J. W. Gunning (1997). 'Redesigning Conditionality', *World Development*, 25(9), 1399–1407

Collier, P. and J. W. Gunning (1999). 'The IMF's Role in Structural Adjustment', *Economic Journal*, 109, F634–F652

Conway, P. (1994). 'IMF Programmes: Participation and Impact', *Journal of Development Economics*, 45, 365–91

Council on Foreign Relations (1999). *Safeguarding Prosperity in a Global Financial System: The Future International Financial Architecture*, Report of Independent Task Force, Washington, DC, Institute for International Economics

Dicks-Mireaux, L., M. Mecagni and S. Schadler (2000). 'Evaluating the Effect of IMF Lending to Low-Income Countries', *Journal of Development Economics*, 61, 495–526

Dollar, D. and J. Svensson (1998). 'What Explains the Success or Failure of Structural Adjustment Programmes?', World Bank Policy Research Working Paper, 1998

Eichengreen, B. (1999). *Towards a New International Financial Architecture*, Washington, DC, Institute for International Economics

Hansen, H. and F. Tarp (2000). 'Aid Effectiveness Disputed', *Journal of International Development*, 12(3), 375–98

Haque, N. and M. Khan (1998). 'Do IMF-Supported Programmes Work? A Survey of the Cross Country Empirical Evidence', *IMF Working Paper*, 98/169

Killick, T. (1995a). 'Can the IMF Help Low Income Countries? Experiences with its Structural Adjustment Facilities', *The World Economy*, 18(4), 603–16.

(1995b). *IMF Programmes in Developing Countries*. London, Routledge

(1997). *Aid and the Political Economy of Policy Change*. London, Routledge

Lane, T. and S. Phillips (2000). 'Does IMF Financing Result in Moral Hazard?', *IMF Working Paper*, 00/168

Moore, M. (1998). 'Death Without Taxes: Democracy, State Capacity and Aid Dependence in the Fourth World', in M. Robinson and G. White (eds.), *The Democratic Developmental State: Politics and Institutional Design*. Oxford, Oxford University Press

Mosley, P. (1987). 'Conditionality as Bargaining Process: Structural Adjustment Lending, 1980–86', *Essays in International Finance*, 168, Princeton University

(1992). 'A Theory of Conditionality', in P. Mosley (ed.), *Development Finance and Policy Reform*. London, St Martin's Press

(2000a). 'Globalisation, Economic Policy and Convergence', *The World Economy*, 23(5), 613–34

(2000b). 'The IMF after the Asian Crisis: Merits and Limitations of the Long-Term Development Partner Role', University of Sheffield, Economics Discussion Paper, 2000:8, March

Mosley, P., J. Harrigan and J. Toye (1995). *Aid and Power: the World Bank and Policy-based Lending*, 2nd edn. New York and London, Routledge

Overseas Development Council (2000). *Task Force Report: The Future Role of the IMF in Development*. Washington, DC, ODC

Rodrik, D. (1996). 'Why Is There Multilateral Lending?', in M. Bruno and B. Pleskovic (eds.), *Annual World Bank Conference on Development Economics*, 1995. Washington, DC, World Bank, 167–93

Santaella, J. (1995). 'Four Decades of Fund Arrangements: Macroeconomic Stylized Facts Before the Adjustment Programmes', IMF Working Paper, 59/74

Schadler, S. *et al.* (1993). 'Economic Adjustment in Low Income Countries: Experience under the Enhanced Structural Adjustment Facility', Washington, DC, IMF Occasional Paper, 106

Summers, L. (1999). Speech at London Business School; available at www.lbs.ac. uk.news-events . . . scripts.summers

United States (2000). *Report of the International Financial Institution Advisory Commission* ('Meltzer Report'). Washington, DC, US Department of the Treasury

Vaubel, R. (1983). 'The Moral Hazard of IMF Lending', *The World Economy*, 6, 291–304

Willett, T. (1999). 'Did the Mexican Bailout Really Cause the Asian Crisis?', *Claremont Policy Briefs*, March

12 Argentina and the Fund: anatomy of a policy failure

MICHAEL MUSSA

1 Introduction

In the sad economic history of Argentina since the 1950s, the 1990s encompassed a remarkable transition. Rising from the ashes of yet another episode of economic chaos and hyper-inflation at the end of the 1980s, the surprisingly orthodox policies of the new Perónist President, Carlos Menem, brought a decisive end to decades of monetary instability and launched the Argentine economy into four years of unusually rapid expansion. Those economic policies featured a hard peg of the Argentine peso at parity to the US dollar, backed by the Convertibility Plan, which strictly limited domestic money creation under a currency board-like arrangement. Many doubted whether the new policy regime would survive, especially as tensions rose during the 'tequila crisis' initiated by the Mexican devaluation of December 1994. But it did survive; and after a sharp recession in 1995, the Argentine economy resumed rapid growth from late 1995 until the spillover effects of the Brazilian crisis hit Argentina in late 1998. Indeed, with most of the economies of emerging Asia collapsing into crises from mid-1997 to early 1998, Argentina became the darling of emerging-market finance – able to float large issues of medium- and longer-maturity debt on world credit markets at comparatively modest spreads over US Treasuries. And, in the official international financial community, especially the International Monetary Fund (IMF), many of Argentina's economic policies were widely applauded

The material in this chapter draws heavily on the author's study, *Argentina and the Fund: From Triumph to Tragedy*, Policy Analyses in International Economics, 67, published by the Institute for International Economics, Washington, DC, July 2002. The author would like to thank his colleagues at the Institute for International Economics, especially C. Fred Bergsten, Morris Goldstein, Bill Cline, and Ted Truman, as well as several former colleagues at the International Monetary Fund, for their useful comments on earlier drafts of this chapter. The views expressed are his own and do not necessarily reflect those of the Institute for International Economics or of the IMF where he served as a member of the staff from September 1991 through September 2001.
© Institute for International Economics

and suggested as a model that other emerging-market countries should emulate – international approval that was dramatised by President Menem's triumphant address to the IMF/World Bank Annual Meeting on 4 October 1998.

Barely three years later, Argentina's decade-long experiment with hard money and orthodox policies ended in tragedy, with the freezing of bank deposits in early December 2001 leading to riots that brought an end to the Presidency of Fernando de la Rúa. Official sovereign default and abandonment of the Convertibility Plan were then announced by President Saa, who served only a few days, and were confirmed by his more durable successor, Eduardo Duhalde. Subsequently the Argentine economy, already in its fourth year of recession, continued to spiral rapidly downward, with real GDP at mid-2002 falling to about 25 per cent below its peak of 1998. Eight months after the initial deposit freeze, the domestic banking system remains effectively closed, with no indication of when it may resume something approaching normal operations. The peso has lost about 70 per cent of its value against the dollar. Economic and financial chaos banished from Argentina since the hyper-inflation of 1990 have returned, and there is a real threat that hyper-inflation itself may soon return unless the Argentine authorities can re-establish and maintain credible monetary and fiscal discipline. With default on its sovereign external debt, the darling of emerging-market finance was transformed within barely two years to the world's leading deadbeat.

Focus on the role of the Fund

These developments, of course, mainly concern Argentina and its people. The policies that contributed importantly to the success of Argentina's stabilisation and reform efforts from 1991 to 1998 were the policies adopted and implemented by the Argentine government, generally with broad popular support. Similarly, the policies pursued in the face of deepening economic difficulties after 1998 and subsequent to the collapse of late 2001 were those determined by the Argentine authorities. Thus, the primary responsibility for what happened in Argentina, both good and bad, and the primary responsibility for what will happen going forward must lie with Argentina and its government.

However, the international community played a significant role in the economic evolution of Argentina during the 1990s; and it should seek to play a constructive role going forward. Indeed, the purpose of this chapter is primarily to examine the role of the IMF, and of the international community more broadly, in Argentina's transition from triumph to tragedy during the 1990s.

The Argentine case is particularly revealing because the Fund was deeply involved with Argentina for many years before the emergence of the present crisis. In this important respect, Argentina is different from most other cases where the Fund has provided exceptionally large financial support. Virtually continuously throughout the 1990s, Argentina operated under the auspices and close scrutiny of a Fund-supported programme. In contrast, in other cases where the Fund provided exceptionally large support (Mexico in 1995; Indonesia, Korea and Thailand in the Asian crisis; Brazil in the crisis of late 1998 and early 1999), a Fund-supported programme was started only after the crisis was already under way. Thus, any failures of the Fund in the pre-crisis period were those of its relatively low-intensity surveillance activities. For Argentina, the failures of the Fund are clearly associated with the core of the Fund's most intense involvement with a member – when it is providing financial assistance and when the policies and performance of the member are subject to the intense scrutiny of Fund conditionality. Leaving aside Turkey where the outcome is not yet clear, the only other case of exceptionally large Fund financing to a member already operating under a Fund-supported programme was Russia in the summer of 1998. But in Russia the Fund (and the rest of the international financial community) faced the new challenge of assisting a country involved in the transition from a socialist to a market economy and there were intense political concerns in the Russian case that spread well beyond the economic and financial sphere. For Argentina, these additional concerns were by no means as intense. Moreover, in Russia and in the countries caught up in the Asian crisis, the key policy issues involved deep problems of structural reform (including problems of the financial sector) that went beyond the Fund's established areas of competence. In contrast, the economic issues that Argentina needed to confront were primarily in the areas of fiscal, monetary and exchange rate policy – the traditional bread and butter of Fund policy concerns. Thus, to the extent that the Fund got it wrong, or failed to get it right, in Argentina, this is likely to be revealing of particularly deep-seated deficiencies.

Necessarily, the emphasis here must be on issues where the Fund got it wrong in Argentina. This does not imply that the Fund got it completely wrong or that the Fund, rather than the Argentine authorities, was primarily responsible for the ultimate outcome. However, the end result in Argentina has clearly been a disaster of considerable magnitude, and no reasonable person should believe that substantially better outcomes were not achievable under realistic alternative economic policies if they had been implemented sufficiently early and appropriately vigorously. In view of the Fund's deep and continuing involvement with Argentina's economic policies, its financial support for those policies and the confidence in and praise for those policies that the Fund so often expressed, it follows that the Fund must bear responsibility for the mistakes that it made in this important case; and must be prepared to recognise and learn from these mistakes.

I shall argue that the Fund did make at least two important mistakes in Argentina: (1) failing to press the Argentine authorities much harder to have a more responsible fiscal policy, especially during the high-growth years of the early through the mid-1990s; and (2) extending substantial additional financial support to Argentina during the summer of 2001, after it had become abundantly clear that the Argentine government's efforts to avoid default and maintain the exchange rate peg had no reasonable chance of success. I shall also suggest that there were three other important issues where it might reasonably be argued that the Fund got it wrong, but where in view of the Fund's particular mandate and responsibilities *vis-à-vis* its members, it took the right position: (1) the initial scepticism in the Fund about the desirability and viability of the exchange rate peg before the 'tequila crisis'; (2) the Fund's subsequent support for the Argentine decision to maintain the peg; and (3) the decision by the Fund in December 2000 (formally approved by the Executive Board in early 2001) to organise a large international financial support package to assist Argentina at a time when a number of competent observers were concerned that such a large support package was not appropriate.

To develop the basis for the analysis of these issues, it is essential to review key aspects of the economic evolution of Argentina over the 1990s. In particular, because sovereign default was clearly a critical factor in provoking the catastrophe, it is important to understand how the Argentine government proceeded from a situation of apparent solvency, reflected in its ability to float large volumes of debt in international financial markets, to the point where it could no longer service its obligations. In this context, especially given the Fund's traditional emphasis on fiscal probity, it is important to discuss what the Fund was saying and doing as Argentina's fiscal situation deteriorated. It is also clear that Argentina's Convertibility Plan played a central role in the crisis. Accordingly, it is critical to examine both how the Convertibility Plan contributed to the initial success of Argentina's stabilisation and reform efforts and why it ultimately collapsed in tragedy. And, as with Argentina's fiscal policy, it is important to discuss what the Fund was saying and doing about Argentina's monetary and exchange rate policy, both as the crisis loomed and at an earlier stage when a more orderly shift away from the Convertibility Plan might have been undertaken.

During 2000 and 2001, as the threat of a catastrophic crisis deepened, the Argentine government undertook increasingly urgent and desperate measures to try to head off the crisis. The Fund supported these efforts with exceptionally large financial packages, despite the deep concerns of many in the international community about the usefulness and appropriateness of such packages. These efforts clearly failed catastrophically – giving rise to the question of whether they were wise in the first place, or whether an earlier decision to accept the inevitable might have led to a less disastrous outcome. Looking to the future, it is also relevant to examine what lessons the Argentine case may teach for how the Fund financial support should be used in other actual or potential crises – hopefully to secure less catastrophic outcomes.

2 An unsustainable fiscal policy

Several factors contributed to the remarkable transformation of Argentina from an apparent paragon of economic reform and stabilisation in 1997–8 to the tragedy unfolding in that economy in 2001. If Argentina had a more flexible economy, especially in its labour markets, the economy would have been more able to adapt to the rigors of the Convertibility Plan; unemployment would have been lower; growth would have been stronger; fiscal deficits would have been smaller; and interest rates would have been lower because creditors would have had more confidence in the capacity of the Argentine government to service its obligations. If the US dollar had not been so strong in recent years, Argentina would have had a more competitive exchange rate *vis-à-vis* its important European trading partners, contributing to both somewhat better growth and a better balance of payments. If Argentina had not suffered the external shock from the collapse of Brazil's crawling peg exchange rate policy, one of the important causes of Argentina's recession during 1999–2001 would have been removed; and this would have had favourable consequences in several important dimensions. Or, if Argentina had decided in 1997 or 1998 that the Convertibility Plan had fulfilled its purpose and the time had come to shift to a more flexible regime for exchange rate and monetary policy, it might have been better able to manage the difficulties of 1999–2001. In sum, if things had broken more in Argentina's favour, this surely would have helped to preserve the success and avoid the tragedy of Argentina's stabilisation efforts.

Enumerating the many things that contributed to Argentina's tragedy, however, should not obscure the critical and avoidable failure of Argentine economic policy that was the fundamental cause of disaster – namely, the chronic inability of the Argentine authorities to run a responsible fiscal policy. This is an old and a sad story for Argentina. To satisfy various political needs and pressures, the government (at all levels) has a persistent tendency to spend significantly more than can be raised in taxes. When the government can finance its excess spending with borrowing, it borrows domestically or internationally from wherever credit is available. When further borrowing is no longer feasible (either to finance current deficits or roll over outstanding debts), recourse is found in inflationary money creation and/or explicit default and expropriation of creditors. This is what happened during the Alfonsin presidency, culminating in

Figure 12.1 *Real economic indicators, Argentina, 1960–1991*
Note: The bars trace real GDP growth (left axis) and the line traces real GDP
(right axis).
Sources: IMF World Economic Outlook *database; Economic Ministry of Argentina.*

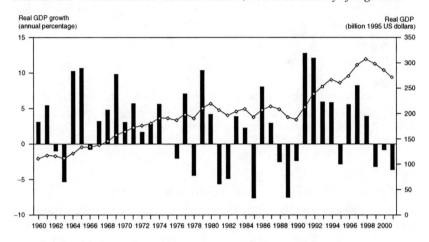

the hyper-inflation of 1990. With some differences in the details but none in the central substance, it is also what happened in the events that culminated in several earlier financial crises during the preceding fifty years.

This is what happened again during the 1990s. To appreciate what happened, it is useful to recall that the 1980s were a very poor decade for the Argentine economy (see figure 12.1). Indeed, the index of real GDP reached its peak for the decade in 1980, then declined by 10 per cent by 1985, and subsequently recovered to just below its 1980 peak in 1987. A deep recession followed, amid financial instability that culminated in the hyper-inflation of 1990, with real GDP ultimately falling more than 10 per cent below its 1987 level. The inflation at the end of the 1980s wiped out much of the domestic currency debt of the Argentine government, leaving the US dollar-denominated external debt as the bulk of the $80 billion face value of debt outstanding in 1990. The face value of the debt was reduced by about $10 billion in the Brady bond restructuring of early 1993. This left the Argentine government with a debt to GDP ratio of 29 per cent in 1993.

The Convertibility Plan was introduced at the start of April 1991. As is often the case with exchange rate-based stabilisations, it helped to bring both a precipitous reduction of inflation, down to the low single digits by 1993, and a remarkable rebound in economic activity, with the index of real GDP rising by 28 per cent cumulatively between 1990 and 1993. Not surprisingly, with such a spectacular recovery of the economy, the Argentine government was able to run a fiscal policy that avoided increases in the outstanding stock of government

Table 12.1 *Argentina, selected data, 1993–1998*

Year	1993	1994	1995	1996	1997	1998
GDP, $billion	237	257	258	272	293	299
Real GDP, % change	5.7	5.8	−2.8	5.5	8.1	3.9
Central govt budget balance, % of GDP	0.9	−0.5	−1.4	−2.2	−1.6	−1.3
Consolidated govt budget balance, % of GDP	−0.2	−1.7	−3.4	−3.3	−2.1	−2.1
Total public debt, % of GDP	29.2	31.1	35.9	37.7	38.9	41.4

Sources: Nominal GDP and percentage change in real GDP (calculated) from IMF, *International Financial Statistics Yearbook 2001*; other data from IMF Press Release, 96/15, 12 April 1996 and from IMF Public Information Notice (PIN), 00/84, 3 October 2000.

debt. However, the growth rates of the Argentine economy during the initial years of recovery from the disaster of the 1980s were clearly not sustainable, and the real test of Argentine fiscal policy would come when economic growth slowed to a more sustainable pace – as occurred during the five years between 1993 and 1998.

Table 12.1 presents some relevant data. Using the annual average data on which this table is based, the change between 1993 and 1998 corresponds essentially to the change over the five years from mid-1993 (after the Argentine economy was past the initial stage of very rapid recovery) to mid-1998 (before the Argentine economy fell into the recession at the end of the decade). This five-year period includes the sharp recession associated with the 'tequila crisis' of 1995, as reflected in a 2.8 per cent year-on-year decline of real GDP between 1994 and 1995. Otherwise, however, the Argentine economy enjoyed quite strong growth, as well as very low inflation, during this period. Indeed, notwithstanding the 'tequila crisis' recession, Argentina's real GDP advanced at an annual average rate of almost 4.4 per cent between 1993 and 1998. Aside from brief growth spurts in recoveries following financial crises, this growth record was the best performance of the Argentine economy since the 1960s, as illustrated by looking at real GDP growth of the Argentine economy on a five-year moving average basis in figure 12.2. With the GDP deflator rising less than 3 per cent cumulatively between 1993 and 1998, the rise in nominal GDP was only modestly larger than the rise in real GDP, but still recorded a solid cumulative gain of 26 per cent between 1993 and 1998.

How was Argentine fiscal policy performing during this period of generally superior economic performance? The central government budget balance (as a share of GDP) was the measure usually given greatest importance in Fund programmes. The central government budget recorded a small surplus in 1993 and was in moderate deficit thereafter. Taken at face value, these budget results

Figure 12.2 *Real GDP growth, Argentina (five-year moving average), 1964–2000*
Sources: Economic Ministry of Argentina; author' calculations.

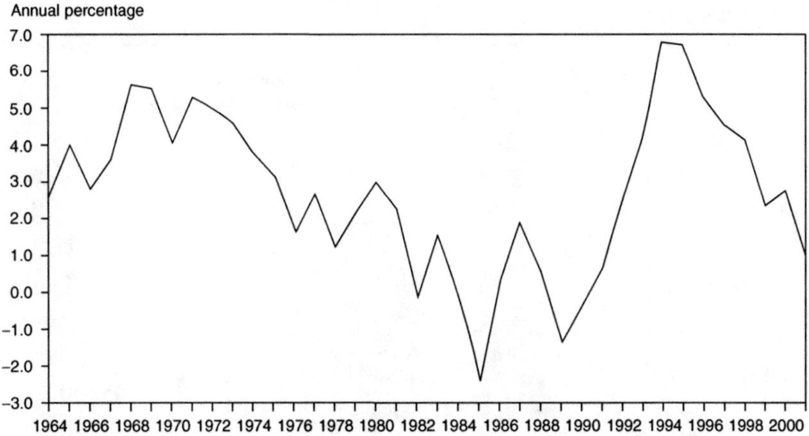

do not look too bad, especially if one recognises that the 'tequila crisis' recession tended to boost the deficit in 1995–6.

However, even restricting attention to the central government, the fiscal outcome in these generally high growth years was significantly worse than it initially appeared. From 1993 through 1998, the Argentine central government realised $3.1 billion of non-recurring revenues from the proceeds of privatisation and another $1.4 billion of capital account revenues that offset what would otherwise have been an increase in the government debt of another 2 per cent of GDP. More importantly, the Brady bond restructuring involved a substantial back-loading of interest payments. This is reflected in the fact the central government's interest payments on its external debt rose from $2.552 billion in 1993 to $6.445 billion in 1998. A modest part of this nearly $4 billion increase in interest expenses is attributable to increases in the stock of debt between 1993 and 1998; but most of it reflects deferral of interest expenses that was effectively a disguised form of government borrowing. The further increase in interest expenses on the external debt up to $10.175 billion by 2001 also partly reflects the effects of deferring earlier interest expenses.

Moreover, much of Argentina's fiscal problems (particularly in the 1990s but also at earlier times) arose from inadequate fiscal discipline in the provinces for which the central government ultimately had to take responsibility. Indeed, the Argentine system – enshrined in the Constitution and in decades of practice – was fundamentally one where the provinces retained much of the initiative and incentive for public spending, but the responsibility for raising of revenue and payment of debt was passed off largely to the central government. The operation of this system of fiscal irresponsibility is reflected in the figures for

324   **Michael Mussa**

Figure 12.3 *Fiscal deficit and change in public debt, Argentina, 1994–1998*
Source: Economic Ministry of Argentina.

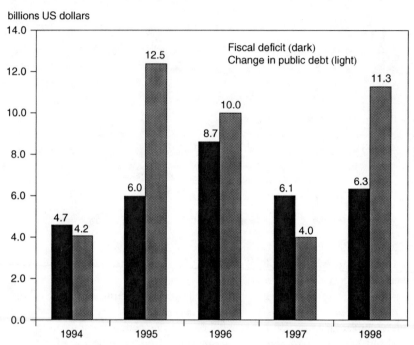

the consolidated government budget balance, which incorporates all levels of government. Every year the budget balance for the consolidated government is significantly worse than for the central government alone.

If public sector borrowing in a given year corresponded to the consolidated government deficit in that year, as one might naïvely expect from standard accounting principles, then the cumulative increase in the public debt over several years would correspond to the cumulative consolidated government deficit over those years. In fact, the ratio of total public debt to GDP in Argentina rose from 29.2 per cent to 41.4 per cent between 1993 and 1998 – an increase in the debt to GDP ratio of 12.2 percentage points. This looks quite close to the sum of the consolidated budget deficit to GDP ratios over this period – either 12.8 per cent including 1993 or 12.6 per cent excluding 1993. However, the denominator in the debt to GDP ratio, nominal GDP, rose 26 per cent between 1993 and 1998; and this should have depressed the gain in the debt to GDP ratio by about 7 percentage points below the sum of the deficit to GDP ratio results for these years. Why not? Because the Argentine public sector engaged in a good deal of borrowing that was not included in the budget, as illustrated in figure 12.3.

For some purposes, such as judging the likely effect of deficit spending on aggregate demand, it may be appropriate to exclude some components of public sector borrowing from a relevant measure of the budget deficit. To assess overall budget discipline and fiscal sustainability, however, public debt is public debt, and all of it counts. Thus, at the bottom line, the fiscal results for the Argentine public sector during 1993–8 show an increase in the debt to GDP ratio of 12 percentage points. If Argentine fiscal policy produced this large an increase in the debt to GDP ratio during a period of superior economic performance, what might it reasonably be expected to produce in less favourable circumstances?

Indeed, as already noted, Argentina's fiscal performance in 1993–8 was actually worse than suggested by this rhetorical question. During this period, Argentina's fiscal performance benefited from the Brady bond deal in terms of the back-loading of interest payments, as well as the Argentine government's receipt of significant privatisation and other capital revenues that were fully counted on budget. In sum, during 1993–8, when the Argentine economy was generally performing very well and the government was receiving substantial non-recurring revenues from privatisation and enjoying other temporary fiscal benefits, the public sector debt to GDP ratio nevertheless rose by 12 percentage points. This clearly was not an adequately disciplined or sustainable fiscal policy.

As most industrial countries have government debt to GDP ratios above 50 per cent and some above 100 per cent, it might reasonably be asked why a debt to GDP ratio of just over 40 per cent was worrying for Argentina. There are at least five important reasons.

First, unlike some industrial countries that successfully carry much higher debt to GDP ratios, Argentina has had little success in raising tax revenues (including social security contributions) of more than 20 per cent of GDP, compared with nearly 50 per cent of GDP in several European countries. Indeed, in Argentina, the provinces are perennially in deficit and, from time to time, have called on the central government to assume responsibility for their debts. Thus, as a practical matter, any revenue of the provinces is committed to spending, and little of it is likely to be available for debt service. This means that the tax base that realistically might be available to pay debt service is the tax revenue of the central government, less the substantial funds that were legally required to be transferred to the provinces.

Second, with most of its government debt denominated in foreign currency and with much of this debt held externally, Argentina faced the dual challenge of persuading creditors that it was capable both of raising fiscal revenues sufficient to service its debt and of being able to convert these revenues into foreign exchange with an exchange rate that was rigidly pegged to the US dollar. In addition, the Argentine private sector had significant external foreign currency debt which required foreign exchange for its servicing. Indeed, Argentina's total external debt rose massively from \$62 billion at the end of 1992 to \$142 billion by the end of 1998 – more than doubling during a period when Argentina's nominal GDP rose by about a quarter. Traditionally, export receipts are taken as a measure of the foreign exchange earnings that might be available to service a country's external debts. As is the case with many countries that substantially reduce their barriers to external trade, Argentina's trade expanded rapidly between 1993 and 1998, with both exports and imports doubling. The rapid expansion of exports helped to limit the rise in the external debt to exports ratio. Nevertheless, at over 400 per cent, this ratio was exceptionally high relative to that of most countries – at a level that often signals substantial risk of an external financing crisis that can be resolved only through a debt restructuring.

Third, it is not just the level of the government debt (relative to GDP or tax revenues or exports) that matters, it is also how the debt has been behaving. If Argentina had stabilised its debt to GDP ratio for some time, under both good and bad economic conditions, then a debt to GDP ratio around 40 per cent might not have been so worrying. However, a debt to GDP ratio that rose from 29 per cent of GDP to 41 per cent of GDP during general good economic times was surely a worrying signal of incapacity to maintain reasonable fiscal discipline, especially for a country that had a record of persistent difficulties in this area.

Fourth, emerging-market countries in general, and Argentina especially, were potentially vulnerable to external economic shocks that might impair fiscal sustainability at debt to GDP ratios far lower than those of industrial countries. Indeed, this is what happened. Events surrounding the collapse of Brazil's crawling exchange rate peg in early 1999 had important negative spillovers for Argentina. Real GDP contracted 4 per cent between 1998 and 2000. The price level also fell, with the result that nominal GDP dropped 4.9 per cent between 1998 and 2000. In this weak economic environment, despite some efforts at fiscal consolidation, the budget deficit widened. With public debt rising and nominal GDP falling, the debt to GDP ratio jumped from 41 per cent in 1998 to 50 per cent in 2000. With recession and deflation continuing in 2001, the economic and political environment for fiscal consolidation was clearly becoming even more difficult; and there was real reason to fear that the public debt was on an unsustainable upward spiral.

Fifth, as an emerging-market country with a substantial external debt, Argentina was clearly vulnerable to changes in financial market sentiment. Aside from brief interruptions during periods of general market turmoil, Argentina would probably be able to maintain necessary access to external financing – so long as financial markets believed that Argentina was a good credit risk. However, Argentina's long record of periodic financial crises and debt restructurings was not reassuring. If market sentiment ever shifted to an expectation of significant risk that Argentina might default, market access would be cut off and that expectation would soon become self-fulfilling.

3 The Fund and fiscal policy

What was the Fund's role in the fiscal failures of the Argentine government? Certainly, the Fund did not explicitly encourage the Argentine government to run substantial fiscal deficits leading to a substantial build-up in public debt relative to GDP. But, this is not the central issue. The central issue is why the Fund failed to use the leverage that it typically has over a country operating under the auspices of a Fund-supported programme to press for a more prudent fiscal policy that would have created less danger of a devastating financial crisis – taking due regard of the risks and vulnerabilities to which Argentina was otherwise exposed.

Part of the answer is that in the period from 1991 through the start of the 'tequila crisis', fiscal policy was not the Fund's most urgent concern about Argentina. The excess of government spending over recurring revenues was modest and was partly financed by privatisation receipts and other sources that did not lead immediately to increases in debt; and the level of government debt was not threatening. The central concern was that the exchange rate, which was pegged at parity to the US dollar in nominal terms, was becoming over-valued in real terms because inflation in Argentina (although dramatically reduced) remained above US inflation. Also, as the Argentine economy recovered from the economic impact of hyper-inflation, domestic expenditure rose sharply, contributing to a growing current account deficit. The key concern was that if the capital flows to Argentina that were financing the current account deficit began to reverse or even slow down significantly, a foreign exchange crisis would likely ensue.

The devaluation of the Mexican peso in mid-December 1994 supplied the trigger for just such a crisis as the so-called 'tequila crisis' rapidly spread to Argentina. In this crisis, the Fund supported Argentina's successful efforts to maintain its exchange rate peg. The policy response included a moderate tightening of fiscal policy intended to both contribute to a reduction in the current account deficit and reassure Argentina's creditors. When the actual fiscal deficit began to exceed the programme targets during 1995 because of a weaker than expected economy, the Fund insisted on some further tightening measures, but showed unusual flexibility (by past Fund standards) in allowing an upward revision of the deficit target. In my view, this was the right approach. Provided that the confidence of Argentina's creditors was reasonably well maintained, it did not make sense (in the face of a weaker than projected economy) to insist on substantial further fiscal tightening to stay within the original target allowed for the fiscal deficit.

Unfortunately, however, the Fund's flexibility in allowing an upward revision of the fiscal deficit target in the face of a weaker than expected economy was not applied symmetrically. Starting in late 1995, the Argentine economy began three years of very rapid recovery, significantly more rapid than was assumed in setting the (nominal) fiscal targets for the Fund-supported programmes in this period. Normally, one should have expected that the Argentine government's fiscal deficit would have come in well below the permitted target – which, as always in Fund programmes, was clearly defined as a ceiling for the fiscal deficit that was not to be exceeded and not as an objective to be hit exactly. However, the deficit never came in well below the target; generally it was just below or even slightly above the permitted limit. Indeed, during the five-year period from 1995 through 1998, the deficit of the Argentine government was within the quarterly limits prescribed at the beginning of each year under the IMF-supported programme less than half of the time. More than half of the time either waivers were granted for missed fiscal performance criteria, or these criteria were met but only after they had been revised upward, or the violations (at the ends of some years) were simply ignored by the Fund and effectively swept under the rug. During 1995, when the recession turned out to be steeper than assumed at the start of the Fund-supported programme, there was plausible reason to grant waivers and make upward adjustments to the deficit limits, rather than to try to force sharp additional fiscal tightening to meet the originally prescribed programme targets.

At other times, however, when the Argentine economy was generally growing strongly, it is difficult to understand why the Fund did not make active use of its conditionality to press the Argentine government to run a more responsible fiscal policy. Rather, to avoid embarrassing the Argentine authorities, the Fund placed little emphasis on Argentina's transgressions of the initially specified fiscal targets, especially in public. And the fiscal targets were significantly less demanding than they appeared to be (even allowing for stronger than expected economic growth) because they conveniently ignored substantial amounts of government borrowing that were viewed by the Argentines as off-budget.

All of this was quite different from what happens when the Fund wants to make a point and to press a programme country to strengthen its policies and, as a consequence, there are delays in completing programme reviews and in concluding negotiations for new programmes or the later phases of established programmes. In sum, the failure of the Argentine government to run a suffi-ciently prudent fiscal policy that effectively restrained the increase in public debt when the Argentine economy was performing well was surely a key – arguably, the key – avoidable policy problem that ultimately contributed to the tragic collapse of Argentina's stabilisation and reform efforts. The Fund's tepid efforts to press the Argentine government to run a more responsible fiscal policy appear to be more a part of this problem than a part of its solution.

In mitigation, it should be noted that after successfully navigating the strains of the 'tequila crisis', Argentina was widely seen as one of the most successful emerging-market economies. Its economic policies were widely praised in the official international community. Indeed, as a hero of successful economic stabilisation and reform, President Menem was accorded the unique honour of appearing jointly with President Clinton to address the IMF/World Bank Annual Meeting in Washington in October 1998. Private financial markets also roared their approval by financing large amounts of Argentine borrowing at attractive spreads relative to most other emerging-market debtors, with the EMBI + spread for Argentina typically running well below the average spread for all emerging-market borrowers from 1997 through 1999. These favourable assessments reflected the important successes that had been achieved by Argentina's stabilisation and reform efforts in the 1990s, after many decades of dismal policies and performance. Indeed, with the collapse into financial crisis of many previously successful Asian emerging-market economies in 1997–8 and the developing difficulties in Russia and Brazil, Argentina stood out as one clear success story. With the Fund under widespread criticism (rightly or wrongly) for its involvement in Asia, it was particularly gratifying to be able to point to at least one important programme country where the Fund appeared to be supporting successful economic policies. In this situation, there was probably even more than the usual reluctance for the Fund to be the skunk at the garden party by stressing the accumulating failures of Argentine fiscal policy.

4 The role of the Convertibility Plan

The Convertibility Plan adopted in early 1991 played a central role in both the success of Argentina's stabilisation and reform efforts during the past decade and their ultimate tragic collapse. The essential objective of the plan was to end decades of financial and economic instability by ensuring that Argentina would have sound money. This was to be accomplished by linking the value of the domestic currency at one-to-one with the US dollar, with the guarantee that pesos could be exchanged for dollars at will. The Argentine Central Bank was given independence from the government, under the mandate that it maintain convertibility by holding dollar reserves against its domestic monetary liabilities (currency and commercial bank reserves). This 100 per cent reserve requirement could be relaxed to 80 per cent in emergency situations declared by the government, and the Central Bank could then hold up to 20 per cent of its assets in government debt. Otherwise, the Central Bank was prohibited from printing money to finance the government. These features were meant to provide credible assurance that the persistent Argentine problem of rapid inflation generated by monetisation of fiscal deficits could not be repeated under the Convertibility Plan.

Figure 12.4 *Real effective exchange rate, Argentina, 1980–2001*
Note: The real effective exchange rate index is based on the consumer price index.

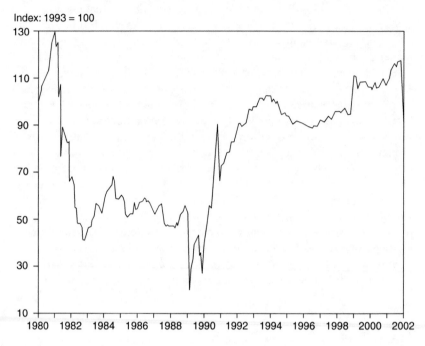

Index: 1993 = 100

Beyond the Convertibility Plan itself, the Argentine government undertook important measures to assure a sound banking system, especially after the 'tequila crisis'. Commercial banks were privatised and most of these banks were taken over by large foreign banks from Spain and the United States. Commercial banks were required to be well capitalised and prudently managed; and, after 1995, they were encouraged to arrange foreign lines of credit that could be drawn in the event of a foreign exchange crisis. Commercial banks could do business in either dollars or pesos, but generally maintained a reasonable balance between assets and liabilities denominated in the two currencies, and the banks were further protected by the government's guarantee of convertibility of pesos into dollars. (The strength of the banks, however, would be seriously undermined if the government defaulted on the substantial volume of claims held by banks, or if the Convertibility Plan collapsed and led to defaults by Argentine borrowers on their dollar-denominated loans from banks.)

As is often the case with exchange rate-based stabilisation efforts, particularly from situations of hyper-inflation, the Convertibility Plan performed very well initially. With the new peso rigidly pegged to the dollar, the inflation rate collapsed from 4,000 per cent per year to single digits in less than three years.

Figure 12.5 *Argentina's current account balance, 1980–2001*
Source: Economic Ministry of Argentina.

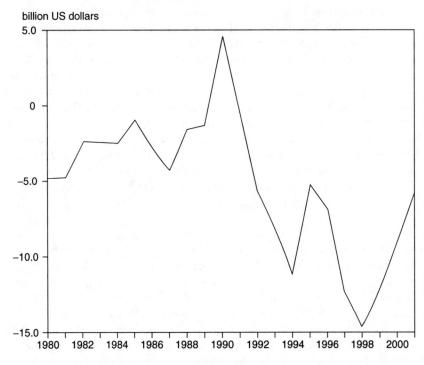

With reasonable assurance of monetary stability, the Argentine economy re-covered rapidly from the economic devastation wrought by hyper-inflation. As noted earlier, however, the real exchange rate appreciated and the current ac-count moved into significant deficit, as illustrated in figure 12.4 and 12.5. This was a pattern common in exchange rate-based stabilisations, often leading to foreign exchange crises and the collapse of stabilisation efforts. The Fund was rightly concerned that this problem might also engulf Argentina's Convertibility Plan.

The crucial test of the Convertibility Plan came in the 'tequila crisis' of 1995. Here, the strengths of the plan, in contrast with many efforts at exchange rate-based stabilisations, made themselves apparent. The government used the emergency provisions to relax the constraint of 100 per cent foreign currency reserves, and this allowed the Central Bank of Argentina some room to avoid as tight a monetary policy as would otherwise have been forced by the loss of reserves. Nevertheless, monetary conditions were tightened considerably and interest rates rose to substantial premia over corresponding US rates.

Commercial banks came under significant pressure as high interest rates and a weakening economy undermined credit quality, and deposits flowed out of the banking system because of fears of bank failures or possibly of a break in the exchange rate peg. A few small banks did fail, but the banking system as a whole, notably all of the large banks, survived the pressures of the crisis – crucial evidence of both the importance and the success of the measures that had been undertaken to strengthen the banking system. In addition, Argentina had good luck externally: the US dollar depreciated sharply in early 1995, improving Argentine competitiveness in European markets; the Brazilian real strengthened markedly, improving Argentine competitiveness relative to that key trading partner; and interest rates in US capital markets fell back as it became clear that policy tightening by the US Federal Reserve was at an end and a shift toward easing (which began in the summer of 1995) might be in store. Were it not for the substantial improvements in bank soundness and for the external good luck, the Convertibility Plan might not have survived the 'tequila crisis'.

After the test of the 'tequila crisis', some might argue that the time was ripe for an orderly exit from the Convertibility Plan. The main benefits of an exchange rate-based stabilisation had already been achieved, and many of the foundations for monetary stability without an exchange rate peg had been put in place. Argentina was surely not part of an optimum currency area with the United States, as the Argentine economy was subject to much different shocks than the US economy and the monetary policy appropriate for Argentina did not generally coincide with that appropriate for the United States. Moreover, by this stage, Brazil was Argentina's largest trading partner, and a potential collapse of Brazil's exchange rate-based stabilisation effort was an important risk for Argentina and its Convertibility Plan. Clearly, looking back with the knowledge of recent developments, one would have to say that an earlier and more orderly exit from the Convertibility Plan would have been preferable to the present tragedy.

On the other hand, there were sound reasons for the Fund to continue to support the Convertibility Plan in the years after the 'tequila crisis'. The Argentine government was determined to preserve the Convertibility Plan, and the Convertibility Plan undoubtedly enjoyed wide and deep popular support in Argentina. After enduring decades of financial instability, punctuated by occasional financial crises, most Argentines were particularly appreciative of the stability that had been produced by the Convertibility Plan. Some, of course, recognised that the constraints imposed by the Convertibility Plan had important costs. In the 'tequila crisis', unemployment rates rose substantially, and remained relatively high in the subsequent recovery. There was great pressure to bring down domestic costs, particularly in industries exposed to external competition; and this resulted in downward adjustments in nominal and real wages. Workers in the affected industries, many labour union leaders, and some politicians (especially in the Perónist party) were not happy. However, to the extent that Argentines more generally were concerned with these problems, they did not necessarily attribute them to the Convertibility Plan; and, in any event, they were not inclined to abandon the Convertibility Plan with the risk that implied to financial stability and to the value of their own savings.

Indeed, among the supporters of the Convertibility Plan, there were those who saw that one of its important benefits was to force painful but necessary changes on the Argentine economy. After decades of protectionism and other government interventions to support specially favoured sectors of the economy, the institutions of Argentine labour markets needed to become more flexible and the Argentine economy needed to become more efficient. From this perspective, the Convertibility Plan, which enjoyed broad and deep political support, provided the political leverage to achieve these desirable results.

Inside the Fund, sympathies undoubtedly lay with those who wanted to reform the Argentine economy in directions that would better allow it to reach its full productive potential. The Argentine authorities who wished to preserve the Convertibility Plan also appeared to be inclined in this direction. More importantly, consistent with its Articles of Agreement (specifically article IV, section 2), the Fund was constrained to accept the basic exchange rate strategy chosen by the duly constituted authorities of Argentina, so long as that strategy had at least a reasonable chance of success.

Up to as late as mid-2001, it was not clear that the Convertibility Plan was doomed to collapse. If sufficiently forceful measures had been undertaken early enough, the difficulties of the Argentine economy during 1999–2001 would not have been entirely avoided, but the outcome of the crisis could have been much more favourable under plausible alternative scenarios that included preservation of the Convertibility Plan. True, one might argue that Argentina would have been better off in the long run without the Convertibility Plan than under this plausible alternative scenario. But the fundamental choice of Argentina's monetary policy framework and exchange rate regime was a choice for the duly constituted government of Argentina. The Fund could advise on the relative merits of different policy regimes and their relevance to Argentina. However, under the principles that govern the behaviour of the IMF as a voluntary association of its sovereign members, the basic choice of regime is a decision of the member – at least up to the point where the chosen regime has no reasonable chance of success under policies that could plausibly be implemented.

Thus, while an independent observer might reasonably conclude that rigidities of the Convertibility Plan deserve relatively more weight, and the failures of Argentine fiscal policy correspondingly less weight, in the blame for the tragedy that ultimately befell Argentina, this is not the relevant perspective from which to view the role of the Fund. For the Fund, the relevant question was – given the choice of Argentina to adopt and maintain the Convertibility Plan – what other policies were necessary to make the stabilisation and reform effort a success? Given the Convertibility Plan, failure to run a sufficiently prudent fiscal policy would likely prove a fatal error. The Fund, having accepted Argentina's choice to maintain the Convertibility Plan, had the responsibility to press very hard to avoid this fatal error.

5 Policy options as Argentina moved toward crisis

It is difficult to know at what point an economic catastrophe for Argentina became inevitable. The collapse of Brazil's exchange rate-based stabilisation effort, the Real Plan, in early 1999 was an important negative shock for Argentina. This was well understood in global financial markets, and interest rate spreads on Argentine bonds rose along with (although not as much as) Brazilian spreads as doubts about the sustainability of the Real Plan deepened in the autumn of 1998 and early 1999. When the collapse came in mid-January 1999 and intense financial turmoil continued in Brazil for another month, the spillover effects effectively shut Argentina out of global financial markets. However, as the situation in Brazil calmed down during the spring of 1999 (with the aid of exceptionally adept management of Brazilian monetary policy by the new Central Bank governor), Argentina regained access to global credit markets, and usually on relatively attractive terms.

The success of Argentina in floating substantial amounts of sovereign debt in global credit markets during much of 1999 and the first half of 2000 testifies both to the special conditions in those markets and to the Argentine authorities' particularly deft management of the public debt. With the advent of the euro (and in anticipation of that event) interest rates for previous high-yield borrowers within the euro area converged downward toward the yields of the lowest-rate borrowers. This left a clientèle of investors in the euro area with potential interest in higher-yielding instruments. Argentina was quick to exploit this market opportunity. The Argentine debt managers were also careful to avoid excessive reliance on short-term debt or on floating interest rate instruments. Financial markets undoubtedly respected and probably rewarded Argentina's prudent debt management policies.

Argentine debt management also benefited from a good domestic market for Argentine government debt. Confidence in the Convertibility Plan and in the measures to ensure a sound banking system clearly contributed to a massive reflation of domestic credit. As domestic financial institutions are important holders of sovereign debts, this credit reflation created an important domestic market for government debt. In addition, the creation of funded pension plans (that invested heavily in Argentine sovereign debt) expanded the domestic market for such debt. The existence of a substantial and relatively stable domestic market of Argentine government debt was also presumably reassuring to international investors and tended to support their demand for Argentine instruments.

Other developments were less reassuring. President Menem's quest for a constitutional amendment that would permit him to run for a third consecutive term was clearly not a spur to determined efforts at fiscal consolidation, from the start of his second term in 1995 through much of his final year in office (which ended in December 1999). After this possibility was finally laid to rest, election-year concerns further depressed the normally low level of interest that most Argentine politicians, at all levels of government, attached to measures of fiscal prudence. Meanwhile, the continuing recession in the Argentine economy (which began in late 1998) was depressing tax revenues and increasing demands for compensatory social spending – thus contributing to an already difficult environment for efforts to rein in the fiscal deficit.

Conditions deteriorated during the second half of 2000 as the recession continued and as turmoil within the administration of President de la Rúa (including the resignation of the Vice President) both inhibited decisive action and undermined confidence. Analysts of the Argentine economy who (with some exceptions) had remained supportive of the longer-run viability of the government's finances through 1999 began to turn pessimistic, and the possibility of a default on Argentina's sovereign debt was openly discussed.

At the Fund as well, concerns mounted about the deteriorating situation in Argentina as the recession deepened and the government debt continued to grow. By October it appeared that the (not overly ambitious) fiscal deficit target in the Fund-supported programme for the end of 2000 might well be missed. Even if this embarrassment was somehow avoided (or swept under the rug as on two earlier occasions), it was clear that the Argentine government would face severe difficulties in meeting its financing requirements for 2001; the possibility of sovereign default loomed.

Because the sovereign debt of Argentina was mainly fixed rate and medium term, it did not face the challenge of rolling over large amounts of short-term debt or the threat that the budgetary effect of an upward spike in interest rates would suddenly make the fiscal situation unsustainable. However, with little prospect of generating substantial primary surpluses that would pay off much of the debt as it matured, the Argentine government did face a large continuing need to refinance its large debt. For each of the five years from 2001 through 2005, projected financing requirements were around \$22 billion – under the (optimistic) assumption that the fiscal deficit could be contained to a level that roughly stabilised the debt to GDP ratio. Domestic sources might reasonably be expected to supply about half of the necessary financing. The remainder would need to come from external sources.

By late 2000, the Argentine sovereign was the largest emerging-market borrower on international credit markets, with outstanding obligations amounting to slightly more than 20 per cent of the entire asset class. Shrewd debt management had enabled the Argentine sovereign to float substantial new debt issues on international markets in 1999 and 2000. But the market was becoming saturated. With rising doubts about Argentina's ultimate ability and willingness to service its debts, the government needed to demonstrate its capacity to restrain its appetite for public borrowing to within reasonable limits before international credit markets would willingly take on additional exposure – or even agree to roll over most of their maturing claims.

For the Fund, the deteriorating situation in Argentina in the autumn of 2000 presented a critical challenge. An important emerging-market country was already in deep economic difficulty and was potentially on the threshold of sovereign default and financial chaos. A star pupil that the Fund had praised and supported as a model of economic stabilisation and reform was in danger of turning into a basket case.

By November, Argentina appeared likely to breach the revised fiscal performance criteria for year-end 2000 (which the Fund had already agreed in September to change to accommodate a larger deficit). This could have provided a plausible excuse for the Fund to announce a suspension of its financial support for Argentina in late 2000 – as had been done with a number of countries whose Fund-supported programmes had gone persistently off track. However, the failures of Argentina to achieve the agreed fiscal objectives of its Fund-supported programme in 2000 (as in 1999) were, to a considerable extent, attributable to the weaker than expected performance of the economy. For a country of the importance of Argentina that was making some constructive efforts to address its policy deficiencies, it would have been unusual – but not unprecedented – for the Fund to announce publicly a suspension of its support. However, unlike many countries where the Fund had announced interruptions in its financial support, Argentina appeared to be particularly vulnerable to potentially catastrophic consequences. Announcement of a suspension of Fund support might well provoke a financial crisis that would lead to sovereign default, a collapse of the Convertibility Plan and financial and economic chaos. The Fund (and the international community more broadly) needed at least to consider other options.

One approach would have been to continue with an essentially standard Fund-supported programme. Levels of official financial support would be within the normal boundaries for such programmes; that is, up to 100 per cent of Fund quota (about $2.5 billion) from the Fund plus additional moderate amounts from the World Bank and the Inter-American Development Bank. The policies under the programme would involve preservation of the Convertibility Plan (by choice of the Argentine authorities) and would emphasise efforts at fiscal consolidation to contain borrowing public needs, reassure private creditors and maintain market access.

The main difficulty with this approach was that, by late 2000, it seemed unlikely to succeed because participants in international financial markets would see that it was clearly inadequate. Under this approach, Argentina would need to access international credit markets for substantial amounts of financing during 2001, even if it succeeded in achieving the fiscal objectives in a reasonably tough adjustment programme. With financial markets sceptical about Argentina's medium- and longer-term fiscal sustainability, if such large-scale private financing were available at all, it would probably be only on terms so onerous that they would confirm market fears about fiscal sustainability. The likely outcome would be that Argentina would be forced into sovereign default and probable collapse of the Convertibility Plan some time in the first part of 2001.

A second approach would have been to conclude that because of the continuing recession and the lack of political support, there was no realistic hope that the Argentine government could implement a fiscal policy that would avoid a messy sovereign default. Further official support for Argentina, within reasonable limits for such support, would not be adequate to avoid default. Instead, Argentine authorities should be advised that further official support would be available only on the condition that Argentina reach agreement with its private creditors that would substantially reduce its financing requirements in coming years – to an extent that would provide credible assurance that official support advanced by the Fund and other agencies would be repaid in a timely manner. Necessarily, this rescheduling of private credits could not be entirely voluntary, as private creditors would be required to accept significant modifications of their existing claims that would reduce their market values. On the other hand, private creditors would benefit from the likelihood of a more favourable long-run outcome made possible by the continuation of official support (contingent on write-downs of private credits) and by the conditionality applied to the behaviour of the Argentine authorities.

The main argument in favour of this second approach was that by late 2000 it was already likely that, sooner or later, Argentina would need to restructure its outstanding private credits in a less than fully voluntary manner. The alternative course, relying on further fiscal tightening to contain government borrowing and regain market confidence, might succeed, but the likelihood of such success was limited. Accordingly, it would be better to accept the damage likely to accompany any involuntary restructuring at a time when Argentina still had ample reserves, as well as additional support from the Fund and the official community, that could be used to help contain the damage from such a restructuring. In particular, if debt restructuring were pursued at this stage, there was at least some hope that the Convertibility Plan could have been preserved, or that the mess associated with its collapse could be managed somewhat better than actually turned out to be the case.

Moreover, the second approach would have been consistent with the principles enunciated by the Fund's Ministerial Committee, the IMFC, at its meeting in Prague in September 2000. Once it became clear that a country could not reasonably be expected to continue servicing its private credits on their contractual terms, the Fund would continue to provide financial support only on the condition that a country seek a reasonable understanding with its private creditors that would reduce debt-service requirements to sustainable levels.

On the other hand, it had to be recognised that any effort by Argentina to restructure its private credits in a non-voluntary manner would be viewed as a *de facto* sovereign default and would likely be very messy. Very likely, in the face of *de facto* sovereign default, the Convertibility Plan would become untenable. The government's credibility would be seriously damaged, including the credibility of its commitment to maintain the Convertibility Plan. This would probably lead to a run out of domestic money and bank deposits, leading to sharp declines in limited foreign exchange reserves and to a severe contraction of domestic credit. The solvency of, and confidence in, the domestic banking system would also be seriously impaired by *de facto* sovereign default, both from the direct effect of reductions in the value of government securities held by banks and from the effects of deposit runs and credit contraction as Argentines fled from all domestic assets of questionable value (including dollar-denominated deposits in Argentine banks).

Thus, a decision by the Fund in late 2000 to press Argentina into a debt restructuring that would have amounted to a *de facto* sovereign default would have been a very weighty matter. The Argentine government was dead set against such action. Argentina's private creditors would have been outraged. Nevertheless, some in the official community appeared to favour this approach, or something close to it. This included those who were deeply opposed to large packages of official financial support, those who were especially (in my view, excessively) concerned with the possible moral hazard effects of such packages and those who strongly favoured the substantial involvement (and punishment) of private creditors as an essential counterpart of official efforts to help resolve major international financial crises.

Inside the Fund, however, there was little enthusiasm for this approach. Some recognised that there was a significant risk of sovereign default, collapse of the Convertibility Plan and financial chaos (while others merely shuddered at such possibilities). But in the autumn of 2000, the Argentine situation was not seen as without realistic hope of a better outcome – especially if Argentine policy could be put on a better path. Sovereign default is an exceptionally serious step that should be taken only as a last resort. Sovereign default is also properly the decision of the government involved: and the Fund (and the international community) should not press for such a decision except when there is clearly no other viable alternative. Similarly, reneging on the Argentine government's solemn commitment to maintain the Convertibility Plan was not something that the Fund could reasonably advise (under the threat of suspension of Fund support) so long as there was a reasonable chance that the system could be preserved and the Argentine authorities desired to pursue that chance.

The third approach – the approach actually adopted – was to proceed with a Fund-supported programme for Argentina for 2001 with levels of support substantially greater than in standard Fund-supported programmes (to be achieved by a substantial augmentation of the large support already committed by the Fund under the existing three-year Standby Arrangement). As in the first approach, the policies under the programme would emphasise fiscal consolidation, in both the deficit targets to be achieved for 2001 and in more fundamental measures (including better discipline on deficit spending by the provinces) to ensure fiscal sustainability in the longer term. The deficit target would be set so as to carefully balance the need to keep borrowing within responsible limits and show credible actual progress in achieving essential fiscal discipline against the very real economic and political difficulties of fiscal consolidation in a deepening recession. Official financing would be sufficiently generous to meet virtually all of Argentina's projected external financing requirements for 2001, assuming that the programme's fiscal objectives were met. Official financing would be available on a more limited basis to meet part of projected external financing needs for the subsequent two years. (The headline figure for financial support associated with the programme was almost $40 billion, with about $14 billion from the Fund, $5 billion from the Inter-American Development Bank and the World Bank and $1 billion from the government of Spain. According to the Fund press release (01/3 of 12 January 2001), the package also included 'about $20 billion of financing from the private sector that relies on a market-based, voluntary approach intended to complement Argentina's objective of accessing international capital markets as soon as confidence returns.' This money, however, was not effectively committed to support Argentina; it was likely to come only if the programme succeeded.)

The objective of this third approach was to give Argentina one last chance to avoid the catastrophe likely to ensue from sovereign default and a probable collapse of the Convertibility Plan. Success was not assured even if the Argentine government lived up fully to its policy commitments; and was highly doubtful if there was any substantial policy failure, especially in the critical fiscal area. But at least the international community, led by the Fund, was pledging a level of financial support that offered a further window of opportunity to demonstrate a willingness and ability to pursue the difficult measures necessary to attain fiscal sustainability. Also, the international community would be sending an important signal by pledging support to Argentina on a scale similar to that of other important countries that had faced severe international financial crises in recent years; whereas significantly less generous support for Argentina would likely be seen as quite a negative signal. Moreover, from the perspective of the Fund, a substantial support package for Argentina could be seen as consistent with the general principle of 'uniformity of treatment', which is one of the basic tenets that is supposed to govern all of the Fund's activities. Unless Argentina was, for some substantive reason, significantly less deserving than other members that had received large support packages or could reasonably be judged to be significantly less likely to succeed in its stabilisation efforts, the principle of 'uniformity of treatment' argued that Argentina should be given a last chance to avoid catastrophe – with a level of international support (subject to appropriate conditionality) consistent with that made available in other roughly similar cases.

In retrospect, as the Argentine case has ended in sovereign default and a messy collapse of the Convertibility Plan, one might reasonably argue that an earlier move toward this alternative would have done no harm and might have done some good. The latter would be the case if the resources from the international community used to attempt to avoid the collapse were instead conserved to help deal with its consequences, or if the collapse would have been better managed if undertaken in an earlier, better-planned manner. Indeed, I shall argue below that one of the important costs of the (in my view, misguided) decision to augment Fund support for Argentina in the summer of 2001 was precisely that this support was wasted in what was already clearly a lost cause. Was this not also the case with the decision in December 2000 that initiated Fund support for Argentina on an exceptional scale? Was not that key decision also a serious mistake?

The answer depends primarily on the assessment, in late 2000, of whether Argentina still had a realistic chance of avoiding *de facto* sovereign default and a likely collapse of the Convertibility Plan – which would surely have very dire consequences including a potential collapse of the financial system – and whether the Argentine authorities were prepared to pursue policies that offered reasonable hope of realising that chance. While sceptical that the chance of success was as great as 50 per cent, my view was (and is) that in late 2000 there still was a reasonable chance that what would otherwise be an economic and financial disaster of great magnitude could have been avoided – if the Argentine government had assiduously implemented fiscal measures that reassured private creditors about longer-term debt sustainability.[1]

---

[1] Contrary to normal practice and protocol in the Fund, I was not kept informed about discussions with the Argentine authorities in November and December 2000 and was not consulted by Fund management in advance of its decision to recommend a large assistance package for Argentina. Accordingly, the view that I now take of that operation is not influenced by the position that I took in my official capacity at the time.

Figure 12.6 *Interest rate spreads on Argentine sovereign debt and the Emerging Markets Bond Index, 1996–2001*
Note: End-of-month values.
Source: Economic Ministry of Argentina.

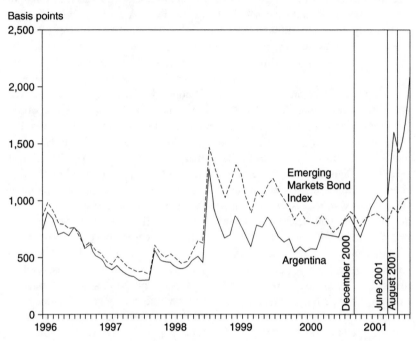

Evidence supporting this assessment included the fact that Argentina still had ample international reserves, with a significant margin above the size of the domestic monetary base. Indeed, the loss of reserves that Argentina sustained between late summer and mid-November 2000 was recovered as negotiations on a new Fund-supported programme progressed. Also, despite a modest downturn from October to December, deposits in Argentine banks remained near their peak level and, in light of the weak economy, signs of stress in the banking system were quite limited. There had been no major runs on Argentine banks or other clear signs of a domestic collapse of confidence in the sustainability of the Convertibility Plan or in the solvency of the government. Externally, there was the hope in late 2000 that the evident slowdown in the US economy might lead to both an easing of monetary policy in the United States and a downward correction of the US dollar against the euro, both of which would help Argentina (as had happened in the 'tequila crisis' in 1995).

In international capital markets in late 2000, interest rate spreads on Argentine sovereign debt had risen to about 750 basis points above US treasuries, up from about 550 basis points a year earlier, as illustrated in figure 12.6. And interest rate spreads on Argentine bonds in late 2000 had risen modestly above the average spread for emerging-market borrowers. This indicated rising concern about fiscal sustainability in Argentina, but not yet firm conviction that sovereign default was virtually inevitable. In fact, Argentina had survived the Brazilian crisis of late 1998 and early 1999 when spreads on Argentine sovereign debt had briefly breached 1000 basis points and subsequently rose briefly to 800 basis points on two occasions, before falling back to more moderate levels.

Indeed, relatively straightforward calculations indicate that at interest rate spreads of 500–600 basis points, Argentina's debt dynamics might have been sustainable under achievable degrees of budget discipline; whereas at persistent interest rate spreads of 1,000 basis points or more, the situation would be virtually hopeless. Formally, the condition of fiscal sustainability – that the ratio of pubic debt to GDP should not be rising persistently – may be stated as the condition that the ratio of the primary budget surplus to GDP, b, must be greater than or equal to the ratio of debt to GDP, d, multiplied by the difference between the interest rate on government debt, r, and the growth rate of the economy, g: that is, b must be greater than or equal to d times $r - g$. For Argentina in 2000–1, the ratio of public debt to GDP was about 50 per cent, and for reasons already discussed, persistent increases above this ratio were not sustainable. Interest rates on medium-term US Treasuries in late 2000 were running around 5.5 per cent, implying that with a spread of 550 basis points above US Treasuries, r would be about 11 per cent. At this level of interest rates, prior experience suggests that the Argentine economy would probably be able to grow at a moderate pace, with little or no price inflation – say, a growth rate of nominal GDP, g, of 4 per cent per year. All of this suggests that a primary budget surplus, b, of about 3.5 per cent (equal to 50 per cent times the difference between 11 per cent and 4 per cent) would have been required for fiscal sustainability. A primary fiscal surplus of 3.5 per cent of GDP would have been ambitious in an Argentine economy mired in deep recession. However, a successful effort to produce a consolidated budget surplus of 2 per cent of GDP in the midst of recession might have established market confidence about what would be achieved in more normal economic circumstances.

In contrast, at interest rate spreads of 1,000 basis points above US Treasuries, r would have been at least 15 per cent. At this level of interest rates, it would have been difficult to achieve much real growth in the Argentine economy, and deflation probably would continue at a modest pace. This suggests that g, the growth rate of Argentine nominal GDP, would have been about zero. Under these conditions, the primary budget surplus, b, must be at least 7.5 per cent of GDP (equal to 50 per cent times 15 per cent minus zero) to achieve fiscal sustainability. It is inconceivable economically, and especially politically, that Argentina could have achieved a primary budget surplus of near this magnitude; and the economic effect of attempting to do so would likely have deepened the recession. Thus, sustained interest rate spreads above 1,000 basis points would be a clear signal that Argentina was headed for sovereign default.

With interest rate spreads rising to 750 basis points in late 2000, there was an urgent need for action to persuade financial markets that the Argentine government would find its way out of its fiscal difficulties and thereby induce a reduction in interest rate spreads to a level more plausibly consistent with fiscal sustainability and with economic growth. But the situation did not appear hopeless. With determined action by the Argentine authorities and a pledge of substantial support from the Fund and the international community, there was still a realistic chance of success. However, if these efforts faltered or failed and interest rate spreads rose significantly, this would signal an irreparable loss of market confidence, and the game would almost surely end in tragedy.

Two other approaches to Argentina's difficulties might also have been considered in the autumn of 2000. President Menem and some in his administration had mused about moving from the Convertibility Plan to full dollarisation – that is, replacing the peso completely with US dollars. However, President de la Rúa and his Administration did not favour this approach. Even if moving to dollarisation had been feasible and potentially desirable, it would have been inappropriate for the Fund to press a sovereign member for such a fundamental change in its monetary regime. Another approach would have been a very big bailout that would have provided the Argentine government with guarantees of official support sufficient to cover its prospective financing requirements for several years, with repayment spread out many years into the future. However, this would have meant a substantial escalation in the magnitude and duration of official financing packages, and there was no support for this among the major countries that provided the Fund's resources. Indeed, following the controversies over previous large support packages, there was a consensus to move in the other direction – toward more modest amounts of official support and toward more consistent efforts to involve private creditors in the resolution of financial crises, including, when necessary, through involuntary sovereign debt restructurings.

6 Desperate efforts to avoid collapse

Argentina enjoyed a very brief period of respite in early 2001. On 3 January, Argentina got a boost as the US Federal Reserve cut US short-term interest rates and signalled the likelihood of further cuts. On 12 January, the Fund's Executive Board formally approved the augmentation of the Fund's Standby Arrangement for Argentina and authorised immediate disbursement of about $3 billion. Aided by these developments, spreads on Argentine sovereign debt fell to about 650 basis points, and the Argentine authorities took advantage of renewed access to international credit markets to float a large euro bond issue.

Unfortunately, however, Argentina's respite was short-lived. Political turmoil in Turkey helped to undermine confidence in that country's efforts to defend its crawling peg exchange rate, which collapsed in a messy crisis in February; and contagion from this crisis was reflected in an increase in spreads for the Argentine sovereign. More importantly for Argentina, things were not going well at home. Fiscal results for the Argentine government for the fourth quarter of 2000 would likely reveal failure to meet the fiscal targets for end-year 2000. This failure might, once again, be swept under the rug. But, with revenues coming in well below programme assumptions (due partly to the recession and partly to deteriorating tax compliance) and expenditures not particularly well contained, by February, fiscal results for the first quarter of 2001 also appeared at risk of exceeding programme targets; and this would be impossible for the Fund to ignore. The deteriorating fiscal situation led to renewed concerns about Argentina in financial markets and to a renewed widening of spreads. The likely need to adopt additional measures of fiscal tightening to meet programme targets heightened political tensions with the Perónist opposition in the Argentine Congress, with provincial political leaders and within the Argentine government.

With dissension in the Argentine cabinet focused on Economy Minister Luis Machinea, President de la Rúa decided (in February) to make a change in the head of his economic team. The well-known, University of Chicago-trained, Argentine economist Ricardo López-Murphy was selected as the new Minister of Economy. Within days, he proposed new measures of fiscal consolidation, focused on sharp reductions in public spending, to address the Argentine government's deteriorating fiscal position. Argentine politicians of all parties and ranks were outraged, including most of López-Murphy's fellow ministers. The President refused to back his new Economy Minister and sided with the vast majority of Argentine politicians.

In my view, this event marked the effective end to any realistic hope that the Argentine government would address its fiscal difficulties with sufficient resolve to avoid sovereign default and its attendant chaos. In February, interest rate spreads on Argentine sovereign credits rose to 850 basis points and generally fluctuated between this level and 1,050 basis points through the spring. At this level of spreads, there was little hope either that the Argentine economy could begin a sustained recovery or that the debt dynamics of the Argentine sovereign could be put on a sustainable path. Moreover, it was becoming increasingly clear that resolution of Argentina's potentially unstable debt dynamics through fiscal tightening was neither politically feasible nor economically sensible. On the political side, fiscal tightening is particularly difficult when a country is already in deep recession, and especially so in the Argentine system where the provinces can easily undermine austerity efforts at the central government level. On the economic side, fiscal tightening in the midst of a deep recession tends to forestall economic recovery, which is essential to put debt dynamics on a sustainable path. Recognition of these difficulties made financial markets particularly sensitive to both political difficulties in achieving fiscal austerity and to adverse news on the performance of the Argentine economy. Once financial markets became persuaded that Argentina had no viable way out of this predicament, fears of sovereign default would become self-fulfilling.

After the departure of López-Murphy, President de la Rúa next called on the legendary Domingo Cavallo, author of the Convertibility Plan and genuine hero of Argentina's stabilisation and reform efforts in the early 1990s, to resume his old post of Economy Minister. With his characteristic energy, Minister Cavallo rapidly secured parliamentary approval for wide (but not unlimited) powers of the president to enact economic measures by decree. Eschewing the López-Murphy approach of fiscal consolidation through expenditure restraint, Cavallo focused primarily on taxes. A financial transactions tax (initially at a 0.25 per cent rate and later raised to a 0.4 per cent and then a 0.6 per cent rate) was introduced to raise significant additional revenue. Some other measures sought to raise revenue, while others sought to spur investment and growth at the expense of revenues. The overall intended effect was to raise revenues – not enough to reach the original deficit targets for the first quarter of 2001, but enough to suggest that an upwardly revised deficit target for the second quarter could be met and that the original deficit target for the end of 2001 could still be attained.

In evaluating these measures *vis-à-vis* the agreed objectives in the Fund-supported programme, the Fund's decisions were governed by its long-standing policies and practices. It is not infrequent that Fund-supported programmes go 'off track' and fail to meet their previously agreed objectives (spelled out in Fund conditionality). When this happens, the member is almost always allowed to propose corrective policies which, if they offer the reasonable expectation of returning performance to the original programme objectives, lead to a Fund decision to continue scheduled disbursements under the programme. This is what happened for Argentina. In view of the new fiscal measures, violation of the fiscal target for the first quarter of 2001 was waived and the disbursement for that quarter (after a short delay) was made. The fiscal deficit target for the second quarter was revised upward somewhat, while the original fiscal deficit target for end 2001 (of $6.5 billion) was maintained.

Notably, the key issue of whether the Fund-supported programme for Argentina still had any realistic chance of avoiding *de facto* default and a likely collapse of the Convertibility Plan was not seriously addressed at this time. This was consistent with Fund practices going back fifty years. By the decision taken by Fund Management in December 2000 and ratified by the Executive Board in early January 2001, the Fund was effectively committed to continue disbursements under the programme for Argentina so long as the Argentine authorities were making reasonable efforts to meet their policy commitments under that programme. By March 2001, financial markets had apparently concluded that these efforts no longer had much chance of success; and this conclusion would very likely prove to be a self-fulfilling prophecy. Nevertheless, the Fund could not reasonably back out of a commitment it had already made to support Argentina's efforts to avoid a disastrous financial and economic crisis.

In the face of deteriorating market confidence during the spring of 2001, Minister Cavallo pursued numerous new initiatives. These initiatives were often announced without consulting in advance with the Fund or even with most of his own staff. Actions in three areas are particularly noteworthy. In mid-April, Cavallo suddenly announced a change in the Convertibility Plan. Rather than being pegged one-to-one to the US dollar, the peso would instead be pegged 50 per cent to the dollar and 50 per cent to the euro. Initially the new exchange rate would apply only to international trade transactions (and not to capital flows or services), and would be implemented by a system of taxes on imports and subsidies to exports in order to avoid creating a 'multiple exchange rate practice' that violated Argentina's commitments under the Fund's articles of agreement. Because Argentina trades about as much with the euro area as with the United States, the economic rationale for this initiative is an arguable issue. However, the effect on confidence in financial markets of the announcement of a change in the Convertibility Plan was clearly quite negative – at a time when confidence in financial markets was of critical importance for Argentina.

A second Cavallo initiative of spring 2001 concerned the Argentine Central Bank and its governor, the widely respected Pedro Pou. Governor Pou was not a fan of Minister Cavallo's efforts to adjust the Convertibility Plan or his desires to reduce the liquidity reserves that banks were required to hold and thereby have the Central Bank pursue a more accommodative monetary policy by stretching the limits of what was allowed under the Convertibility Plan. Both issues were debatable as to their economic merits. But the decision on these issues was within the province of the independent Central Bank, and Governor Pou was well within his legitimate authority to determine the decision – subject to his interpretation of the requirements of the Convertibility Plan. As an important guarantee of the effective independence of the Central Bank, its governor could be removed only for cause, not at the whim of the Economy Minister or even the president. Cause was conveniently found; Governor Pou was accused of serious misconduct by failing to prevent certain money-laundering transactions by some Argentine branches of foreign banks. Whatever the merits of this accusation, it achieved its desired effect in securing the removal of Governor Pou. However, the effective independence of the Central Bank was clearly compromised and confidence in financial markets was further undermined, dealing another blow to confidence both domestically and internationally.

The third, and perhaps most important, Cavallo initiative was the large swap of Argentine government debt that was carried out at the end of May. This swap was voluntary, at least from the perspective of external holders of Argentine sovereign debt; it was not carried out under the threat of default – although worries about possible default clearly depressed the market value of Argentine sovereign debt at this time. The effect of the swap was to exchange nearly $30 billion of face value of Argentine sovereign debt (including about $8 billion held externally) with interest and principle payments heavily concentrated in 2001 through 2005 for sovereign debts with interest and principal payments concentrated in later years.

The debt swap was characterised as an important success by the Argentine government and its financial advisers (who earned substantial fees). It was a success at least in the limited respect that a substantial volume of debt was offered for exchange by both Argentina's domestic and foreign creditors. Indeed, an upward move in interest rate spreads attributable to fears that the offered swap would be a market flop was at least briefly reversed when the volume of tendered securities proved larger than expected.

However, a proper analysis of the effects of the swap for Argentina cannot be based on whether its creditors found the terms of the swap sufficiently attractive to motivate them to tender. Rather, the swap was a good deal for Argentina only if the benefits from the reductions in debt service during 2001–5 outweighed the costs of the additional debt service obligations in later years. This, of course, is not a simple arithmetic comparison. With positive interest rates, the net (undiscounted) cost of a swap that lengthens the average maturity of the debt (by about three years in the case of the Argentine swap) will be positive even for a deal that is quite beneficial from an Argentine perspective. The issue is how high a price is being paid to achieve a given increase in the maturity of the debt.

At the time when the swap was carried out, the interest rate spread of Argentine sovereign bonds over US Treasuries was between 900 and 1,000 basis points, corresponding to an interest rate on Argentine sovereign debt of between 15 and 16 per cent. Because holders of Argentine debt already had the opportunity to trade in the market Argentine debt of lower maturities for debt of higher maturities at these interest rates, they surely would not voluntarily accept an officially sponsored swap at less attractive terms. Consistent with this fact, in the swap, the Argentine government achieved a reduction in its debt service obligations between 2001 and 2005 of only about $12 billion, at the expense of additional debt service obligations of about $66 billion in the years beyond 2005.

Not surprisingly in view of the level of market interest rates, it takes a discount rate of over 16 per cent to make the present value of this swap break even from the Argentine government's (and citizens') perspective. This is a very high discount rate to apply for a country that (under the assumption the Convertibility Plan is maintained) is not likely to enjoy an annual growth rate of GDP (measured in US dollars) that consistently exceeds 7 per cent. Indeed, as argued previously, interest rates for the Argentine sovereign of 16 per cent (interest rate spreads of above 1,000 basis points) were not consistent with positive growth of the Argentine economy or with debt sustainability. By pursuing and accepting a debt swap on such onerous terms, the Argentine government was effectively declaring that it shared the market's assessment that sovereign default was virtually inevitable. Thus, the debt swap on these terms is properly viewed as an act of desperation by a debtor who is prepared to promise almost anything in the longer term for relatively modest debt-service relief in the nearer term.

The Fund issued a very brief public statement that 'welcomed . . . the announcement by the Argentine government of the successful conclusion of the debt exchange offer'. In the circumstances, it could hardly have done otherwise. However, beyond this brief public statement, there was broader effort by the Fund staff to analyse the consequences of the debt swap in depth and reach conclusions concerning its costs and benefits for Argentina. Notably, in much of this effort there was a tendency to portray the debt swap in the best possible light for the Argentine authorities who had undertaken it, rather than to recognise the simple truth that modest short-term debt-service relief had been secured at very high cost in terms of longer-term debt-service obligations. This was symptomatic of the general tendency in the Fund to try to see things in the best possible way from the perspective of the member and its authorities.

Chutzpah

After brief respite following the introduction of new measures to improve the fiscal balance and agreement on a somewhat revised programme with the Fund (and disbursement of the tranche of Fund support due for the first quarter), sharp upward pressures on interest rate spreads for Argentine paper re-emerged in late June and July. One worry was that tax revenues were coming in below forecast, raising concerns that even the revised fiscal targets for the second quarter might not be met. Probably more important, large-scale withdrawals of deposits from Argentine banks, which had been halted and partially reversed in the spring, resumed in July as Argentines became increasingly concerned about a possible breakdown in the Convertibility Plan. Also, the Argentine government was running very short of cash – a fact that the general public may well have surmised from widespread reports of delays in government payments, including transfers to provincial governments. With deposit runs accelerating and interest rate spreads spiking to 1,500 basis points above US Treasuries, something needed to be done quickly, or the game was about to end.

Through leaks to the local press, the Argentine government circulated the story that the Fund would accelerate its normal schedule for (favourable) consideration of its disbursement of about $1.25 billion, based on satisfactory performance through the end of the second quarter. More important, the Fund would augment this disbursement with an addition of about $8 billion. Financial markets reacted positively to this news and the bank runs slowed. A little later on, Cavallo announced that in conjunction with the augmented Fund support, the Argentine government would pursue a more ambitious fiscal policy – with the objective of reducing the fiscal deficit to zero from then onwards. However, announcement of a zero-deficit plan did not assure its approval or, even more importantly, any realistic chance of its successful implementation. With the Argentine economy already in deep recession and spiralling downward under the pressure of crushingly high interest rates, the massive additional fiscal tightening needed to achieve a zero deficit was neither politically acceptable nor economically sensible. By the summer of 2001, the Argentine government was clearly trapped with no viable avenue of escape.

Nevertheless, Cavallo pressed on with his initiative in classic Cavallo style. The suggested augmentation of Fund support was announced without consultations with the rest of the Argentine government. Even some key Cavallo aides were taken by surprise. There were no prior consultations with the Fund, nor any prior indication of support from the Fund for a substantial augmentation of its lending. Indeed, the goal of Cavallo's tactic was to force the Fund to augment its lending by creating a *fait accompli*. Financial markets and Argentine citizens reacted favourably to the announcement of augmented Fund support. If they were disappointed that this support was not forthcoming, the Fund (and the international community more broadly) would be seen to be responsible for the consequences.

For those not familiar with how the Fund normally operates, it may be difficult to understand how great a perversion of its policies and principles was perpetrated in this incident. The Fund is not an aid agency; it does not give money to countries to ease their economic and financial distress. The Fund lends money to countries in support of a well-defined set of economic policies, especially monetary, fiscal and exchange rate policies. The objective of such lending is to assist the country in meeting its international payments obligations, while that country is undertaking policies that give credible assurance that payments imbalances will be corrected – in a manner that avoids, to the extent possible, damage to national and international prosperity. To merit Fund support, a critical requirement of any policy programme is that it must provide reasonable assurance that the resources lent by the Fund will be repaid in a timely manner.

In recommending a Fund-supported programme for approval by the Fund's Executive Board, the Managing Director certifies that he is confident that the policies promised by the national authorities in the Letter of Intent to the Fund will be responsibly implemented and that under these policies there is credible assurance that the Fund will be repaid. The amount of resources pledged by the Fund to support a member's policies and the phasing of their disbursement is determined by the Managing Director (as his recommendation for approval by the Executive Board) at the end of negotiations over the programme, based on his assessment of the country's financing need and of the strength of the country's policy programme. It has never been acceptable for a country to decide by itself the size of support it will receive from the Fund and seek to impose its wishes through the *fait accompli* of a public announcement.

The Fund's emergency assistance to Russia during the summer of 1998 is a case in point. The Fund had an ongoing programme with Russia, within the standard limits of Fund financing. During the first half of 1998, Russia's financial situation deteriorated sharply as the current account went into deficit (due partly to weakening world oil prices) and interest rates on the government's domestic currency debt escalated as creditors became increasingly worried about potential default. The policy performance of the Russian government under the Fund-supported programme since early 1996 had been – to put it politely – less than entirely satisfactory, especially in controlling the fiscal deficit. Nevertheless, Russia was clearly a very important case, and there were important reasons, perhaps more political than economic, to give its government a last chance to avoid the chaos likely to result from devaluation or default. The Managing Director of the Fund, Michel Camdessus, took the initiative. He proposed a large augmentation of the Fund's support for Russia (beyond normal access limits) and arranged with the Fund's leading members to activate the General Agreements to Borrow (GAB) in order to supply the Fund with additional liquidity to underwrite the operation. For its part, the Russian government was required to strengthen its policy programme, especially in the fiscal area. Indeed, before the approval of the augmented programme and disbursement of the initial tranche of augmented support (about $5.5 billion out of a total of about $15 billion), the Russian government was required to implement a number of prior actions, including passage of certain legislation by the Russian Duma. When the Duma refused to pass two key measures, the Managing Director cut back the size of the initial disbursement by about $800 million. Neither the Russian government nor many of its political supporters were pleased with this decision, and financial markets reacted negatively. But the Managing Director had the authority to set access to Fund resources (subject to later approval by the Executive Board), and he was determined to show that the Fund was serious about its conditionality in a situation where determined action by the authorities was absolutely essential to restore market confidence and to provide some hope for the success of the programme.

For Argentina, the December 2000 support package (approved by the Executive Board in January 2001) involved a large augmentation to an already existing Fund-supported programme, beyond the normal limits of access. Similar to the July 1998 package for Russia, this December 2000 package for Argentina was supposed to support a last chance to strengthen its policies and avoid a catastrophe. By the summer of 2001, that last chance effort was clearly failing. Yet, at its own initiative, the Argentine government was insisting on substantial additional support for a second last chance – perhaps to be followed by more last chances down the road.

Not only was the procedure unusual, the outcome – a Fund disbursement of over $6 billion (announced in August and formally approved in early September), with a pledge of $3 billion more to support an unspecified debt restructuring – was extraordinary in both its size and in the lack of any reasonable justification. The disbursement was the second largest in Fund history. About $1.25 billion was the amount due for Argentina upon successful completion of the review of its performance through the end of the second quarter. Argentina reportedly met the quantitative criteria of the Fund-supported programme, most importantly keeping the fiscal deficit within the revised limit permitted for that quarter. But, the target on the cash deficit was met with the aid of substantial payment arrears: tax rebates under the VAT and export incentive schemes were delayed; transfers due to the provinces were withheld; payments for government wages, pensions and health and welfare benefits were deferred. Under the Fund's traditional three-monkeys approach to assessing a member's performance – hear no evil, see no evil, speak no evil – such transgressions would often be ignored. As with the disbursement in May, the long-standing Fund policy of continuing disbursements under an already agreed programme (provided that the member is meeting the explicit requirements of Fund conditionality) might reasonably have justified proceeding with the already scheduled disbursement of about $1.25 billion.

On the other hand, the Fund's decision on disbursement of the scheduled tranche was supposed to be based on a 'programme review' which, in addition to a narrow appraisal of the satisfaction of quantitative performance criteria for the end of the second quarter, generally called for a forward-looking assessment of whether the programme was on track and likely to meet its objectives at least through the end of the programme year. With the Argentine economy performing well below the economic assumptions of the programme, with interest rate spreads at levels (about 1,500 basis points) that clearly implied deepening recession and continuing deflation and with no realistic chance of actually implementing fiscal measures that would (in these economic circumstances) come close to achieving the year-end deficit limits, an honest forward-looking assessment would have concluded that the programme was headed irreparably off track. Such an assessment, perhaps reinforced by some critical reference to the substantial payments arrears that were used to meet the formal performance criteria for the end of the second quarter, ought to have sufficed to overturn the usually strong presumption that the Fund would continue with scheduled disbursements under an already established programme (subject to nominal compliance with the explicit performance criteria).

More important, large augmentation (the disbursement of an additional $5 billion and the pledge of $3 billion more to support debt restructuring) clearly called for a *de novo* assessment of the entire Argentine programme – as was done at the time of the December 2000–January 2001 decision to augment substantially Fund support for Argentina. Was there a reasonable expectation that the Argentine authorities would be able to implement the policies to which they were committed under the programme; and, if so, was there a reasonable expectation that the programme would succeed, especially in the key requirement that Argentina would be able to repay the Fund in a timely manner?

Arguably, in December 2000, it had been possible to answer these critical questions in the affirmative. Interest rate spreads for the Argentine sovereign had risen sharply to about 750 basis points, up from about 550 basis points a year earlier. With the commitment of a new, large package of international support, with determined and credible actions of the Argentine authorities to contain this deficit within responsible limits and with some good luck (such as a shift by the US Federal Reserve toward monetary easing), there was at least a reasonable chance that a disastrous default and likely collapse of the Convertibility Plan might be avoided. Financial market confidence in Argentina could improve, allowing renewed market access at significantly reduced interest rate spreads. With capital market access restored and interest rates reduced, economic recovery could begin and fiscal sustainability could be achieved with a politically feasible degree of budgetary restraint. Indeed, as noted earlier, in January 2001, after formal approval of the new international support package and a clear signal of a shift toward ease in Federal Reserve policy, Argentina appeared, at least briefly, to be moving along this desirable course.

By August 2001, however, prospects for a favourable outcome were pure fantasy. In contrast with the situation eight months earlier, successive runs on Argentine banks had reduced bank deposits by more than $10 billion, see figure 12.7. Also, as illustrated in figure 12.8, Argentina had suffered substantial losses of foreign exchange reserves (after deducting inflows of reserves from disbursements of Fund support). Most importantly, interest rate spreads for the Argentine sovereign had risen persistently above 1,000 basis points and were generally fluctuating in the range of 1,300–1,600 basis points. This implied nominal interest rates for the Argentine sovereign (which generally set the

Figure 12.7 *Total bank deposits, Argentina, 1996–2001*
Source: Central Bank of Argentina.

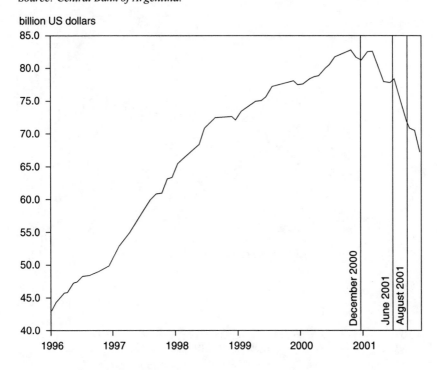

billion US dollars

lower bound for other Argentine credits) of 18–22 per cent, with real interest rates even higher due to deflation. Economic recovery was impossible in this situation: and nominal GDP would surely continue to contract even more rapidly than real GDP, implying significant increases in the debt to GDP ratio even if, by some miracle, the government budget were brought into overall balance. The Argentine government's fiscal policy, with its increasing reliance on unsustainable payments arrears, clearly could not meet its targeted objectives. The political consensus to raise the huge primary surplus that would be required to demonstrate sustainable debt dynamics in these circumstances was, quite understandably, nowhere apparent and never likely to materialise. Substantial reserve losses had already occurred, and further bank runs were a continuing threat. An emergency injection of another $6 billion of cash from the Fund was urgently needed to just stave off immediate default and keep the farce going for another few months. If announcement of a large package of international support had helped to bring only brief respite in the relatively favourable circumstances of January, it was absurd to believe that a more modest augmentation of that package by another $5 billion–$8 billion would somehow produce a miracle

Figure 12.8 *Foreign exchange reserves, Argentina, 1996–2001*
Source: Central Bank of Argentina.

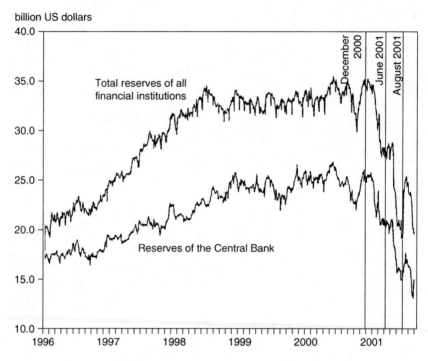

billion US dollars

in the clearly desperate circumstances of August. Looking at the facts, a wide range of analysts outside of the Fund (and several inside the Fund) – often with differing views on many issues – clearly concluded that for Argentina, the game was over. Only a fool would conclude otherwise.

Why, then, did the Fund, and the international community more broadly, acquiesce in this folly? Inside and outside of the Fund, there was rightly a great deal of concern about the deteriorating situation in Argentina and about the disaster that would accompany a sovereign default and a likely simultaneous collapse of the Convertibility Plan and the Argentine financial system. Also, Argentina was generally seen as a country deserving of sympathy and support; and the Argentine authorities were certainly willing to draw on this sentiment. President Bush publicly expressed the concerns of the US government and its support for further assistance to Argentina. Prime Minister Blair travelled to Argentina to emphasise similar views on part of the United Kingdom. Chancellor Schroeder voiced the concerns and support of Germany, as did senior political leaders from many other European countries. And, beyond the genuine sympathy that was felt for Argentina, there was undoubtedly the desire, both inside and outside the Fund, to avoid the appearance of responsibility for Argentina's collapse.

In fact, however, the Fund's large September disbursement would do no more than postpone the catastrophe in Argentina by three months. This was known or should have been apparent to the top officials in the Fund and among the Fund's major members who together determined how the Fund would respond to Argentina's request for augmented support. Here there was a failure of intellectual courage – to face up to the realities of the situation in Argentina – and a failure of moral courage – to take the difficult decision to decline substantial additional support to policies that no longer had any reasonable chance of success.

Indeed, even as the Fund's August augmentation was arriving (in early September), the tragic end for Argentina's efforts to avoid default and preserve the Convertibility Plan was drawing near. Parliamentary and provincial elections in mid-October turned control of the national legislature and of most provincial governorships over to the opposition Perónists. That meant even less political support for austerity measures needed to implement Cavallo's zero-deficit policy at the central government level. Negotiations with provincial governors for their necessary contribution to greater fiscal austerity bogged down. Tax revenues dwindled as economic activity continued to shrink and tax avoidance and evasion (always a favourite sport in Argentina) escalated, encouraged by the government's increasing dereliction of its own payments' obligations. In world financial markets, the value of Argentine sovereign bonds plummetted further, with spreads over US Treasuries rising above 2,000 basis points.

By mid-November, the cash position of the government was again becoming precarious. In the last week of November, the run on Argentine banks escalated, reaching nearly $1 billion per day. With foreign exchange reserves down to $15 billion (barely enough to cover domestic currency in circulation), the end had come. The government was forced to close the banks and announce that when they reopened, cash withdrawals would be limited to $250 per week. This was described as a temporary measure, for up to three months, but Argentines generally realised the truth. The Convertibility Plan was finished. The banks were bust. Depositors would be lucky if they ultimately got anything near the book value of their claims. In the streets of Buenos Aires, pesos exchanged for dollars at a discount of about 25 per cent; across the Rio de la Plata in Montevideo, the discount was about 50 per cent.

After more than three years of recession, with unemployment at nearly 20 per cent and rising, deprived of access to their bank deposits and with the value of the domestic currency rapidly depreciating in the black market, the Argentine people had finally had enough. Riots in the provinces spread to the capital. Stores were looted. Banks were ransacked. Foreign-owned businesses were attacked. In efforts to restore order, nearly thirty people died. Recognising that his efforts had failed, Minister Cavallo resigned, and President de la Rúa soon followed.

7 Some lessons from Argentina's tragedy

It is impossible to know at what point sovereign default and a likely collapse of the Convertibility Plan became unavoidable. Perhaps it was already too late by the autumn of 2000. But surely, the ultimate tragic collapse was not preordained from the time that Argentina's stabilisation and reform efforts began a decade earlier. The Convertibility Plan clearly implied a very rigid framework for Argentina's exchange rate and monetary policy. This limited the options available to respond to adverse shocks such as those associated with Brazil's exit from its exchange rate-based stabilisation effort. It also meant that if developments ever did lead to a collapse of the Convertibility Plan, the consequences for the financial system and the Argentine economy were likely to be significantly more catastrophic than with a less rigid exchange rate and monetary policy regime. However, the fundamental cause of Argentina's tragedy was not primarily the Convertibility Plan. Rather, it was the large and persistent excess of public spending over recurring revenues that led to an unsustainable accumulation of public debt and ultimately to sovereign default that fatally undermined the basis for Argentina's financial and economic stability – and would have done so under virtually any conceivable monetary policy and exchange rate regime.

Of course, the long recession that began in late 1998 made containment of Argentina's fiscal deficit and build-up of sovereign debt more difficult – both economically and politically. But, as emphasised earlier, the fiscal problem started much earlier. If during each year of the 1990s the primary balance of the entire Argentine government had been, on average, 2 per cent of GDP better, the cumulative effect (including reduced interest expense) would have reduced Argentine sovereign debt in 2001 by about $60 billion. This would have removed any serious concerns about sovereign default and would have allowed significantly lower interest rates and a much better environment for economic recovery. Indeed, even moderately vigorous and realistic efforts of fiscal consolidation beginning with the recovery from the 'tequila crisis' would probably have done the job. For example, an improvement in the primary balance of 1 per cent of GDP in 1996, 2 per cent of GDP in 1997, and 3 per cent of GDP in 1998 should have been economically and politically feasible during these rapid growth years; and holding on to an established fiscal improvement of 3 per cent of GDP should have been achievable in the more difficult period of 1999–2001. This improvement in fiscal policy would have reduced Argentine debt in 2001 by about $40 billion (below the actual level), and would have provided a convincing demonstration over six years of a capacity to run a more responsible fiscal policy. This should have been enough to remove serious doubts about fiscal sustainability. Thus, the margin between sustained success of Argentina's stabilisation and reform efforts of the 1990s and the tragic collapse at the end of 2001 was far from insurmountable.

The key lesson that obviously follows from this conclusion is the vital importance of seriously addressing important policy problems while they are still manageable. This is especially true with respect to persistent fiscal deficits during periods of relatively good economic performance. Such deficits tend to build up to severe problems of fiscal sustainability that materialise when economic performance slackens. Emerging-market countries that have histories of fiscal imprudence and financial instability, that finance themselves to a significant extent in foreign currencies and that have or may develop over-valued exchange rates are particularly vulnerable to this problem.

Brazil and Turkey (in addition to Argentina) are important current examples of this phenomenon. From the perspective of Fund involvement, these two cases differ from Argentina in that the build-up of debt occurred largely before Fund programmes were established (for Brazil, in November 1998 and for Turkey, in January 2000) or were the consequence of subsequent recognition of fiscal losses that had been effectively incurred before these programmes were established (including the large costs of bank restructuring in Turkey). Thus, the failures of the Fund to discourage more effectively these build-ups of government debt can at least partly be explained by the relative weakness of Fund surveillance as a means for persuading countries to maintain more responsible policies – as compared with the greater leverage that the Fund has over a country, like Argentina, that is operating under the auspices of a Fund-supported programme. Nevertheless, the lesson is clear that the Fund should use whatever leverage it does have to press countries to run responsible fiscal policies in relatively good times in order to lessen the risk of potentially very serious difficulties when economic conditions turn less favourable.

A second important lesson for the Fund from the Argentina case concerns the grave difficulties and risks of dealing with situations where a country may face an imminent need to default and/or to restructure its debt in a less than fully voluntary manner. As discussed above, Argentina reached this critical point by late 2000; and by the summer of 2001, Argentina was beyond the point where there was any reasonable chance that sovereign default–restructuring (and a probable collapse of the Convertibility Plan) could be avoided.

I have argued that the Fund was correct in December 2000–January 2001 to commit substantial additional financial support to Argentina to provide one last chance for Argentina to demonstrate sufficient fiscal discipline to persuade financial markets of its longer-term fiscal sustainability. If the effort succeeded, there would clearly be large benefits. There were also clearly significant risks that the effort would fail, leading probably to an even messier and more costly default–restructuring, and leaving Argentina with significantly greater obligations to the Fund and other official lenders. A responsible decision by the Fund to proceed with a large international support package in this situation had to be based on a reasoned assessment that the benefits of success weighted by the chance of success were greater than the costs of failure weighted by the chance of failure. In future similar situations (such as Brazil in the summer and autumn of 2002), a similar analysis needs to be applied – with honest assessments of the benefits and costs of success and failure and of the relative chances of these two outcomes.

I have also argued that the decision to augment substantially Fund support for Argentina in August–September 2001 was a serious mistake – indeed, the most serious single mistake during the ten years that I spent on the Fund staff. By this point, there simply was no reasonable chance that the augmentation of Fund support would bring success. Indeed, beyond delaying the collapse by three months, Argentina was not helped. The end result was that external assistance that was potentially far more valuable in helping to contain the damage once a *de facto* sovereign default had occurred was instead squandered in a futile effort to avoid the inevitable, leaving Argentina with an unnecessarily large burden of servicing its obligations to the Fund.

In addition, a last opportunity to persuade the reluctant Argentine authorities to face unpleasant realities and prepare for a potentially more orderly (although still difficult and dangerous) retreat was lost. In fact, through the autumn of 2001, until early December, the Fund maintained a dialogue with the Argentine authorities on the assumption that the measures needed to implement Cavallo's zero-deficit policy (including the cooperation of the provinces) might somehow be implemented and that Fund disbursements related to performance through the third quarter and year-end 2001 might be made (possibly with waivers or under somewhat revised performance criteria). Perseverance by the Fund in this charade clearly did not encourage the Argentine authorities to face up to the reality of their situation and to the painful but necessary decisions implied by this reality. Moreover, the new government that took over in late 2001 undertook several measures (especially those related to the banking system) that made the crisis even deeper and more difficult to manage. At least some of this policy mismanagement might have been avoided if the Fund had pressed the Argentine authorities, at an earlier stage, to plan and pursue a more orderly approach to debt restructuring, revision of the Convertibility Plan and management of the inevitable problems in the financial system.

Looking to the lessons on how to handle future similar situations, it is clear that the Fund (and the international community) need to establish better procedures for decisions concerning large provisions of official support to emerging-market countries. A key requirement must be that the country receiving such support have a reasonable expectation of achieving a viable external payments position including, if necessary, through rescheduling of its existing private credits, in order to assure that official financial support can be repaid in a timely manner. In fact, under its Articles of Agreement, this is a fundamental requirement for the provision of Fund financing – that it be temporary and subject to adequate safeguards to assure that it is temporary. In meeting this essential requirement in situations similar to that in Argentina, the Fund and the international community need to be sensitive to three special problems.

First, the assumption in Fund-supported programmes is that the responsible officials of a country will pursue the best interests of their country. However, while many officials would be indignant at any questioning of this assumption, the fact is that officials are agents of the citizens whose interest they are supposed to represent – and the interests of these agents can and do sometimes diverge from those of an average citizen. Normally, such divergences may not be an important problem for Fund-supported programmes; and it is difficult to conceive of an alternative assumption on which the Fund could normally operate. However, for a country on the verge of a financial crisis, it is essential to recognise that the interests of officials in power may diverge significantly from those of the average citizen. Avoiding a crisis benefits both officials and citizens; but a moderately costly crisis may not be much better for officials (who will lose their positions and reputations) than a much deeper and more costly crisis. Putting off a crisis until after an election may benefit officials more than average citizens, even if the ultimate costs of the crisis are significantly enlarged. Thus, government officials (like private business leaders) often have an incentive to 'gamble for resurrection' even if the odds of success are relatively poor.

Second, officials who are fighting hard to avoid a crisis often have an overly optimistic view of their chances of success. This is a common psychological phenomenon. When you are fighting hard for a good cause, it is difficult to believe anything other than that you will succeed – despite what others may say about the odds against you. Indeed, from many discussions in which high officials have vigorously and conscientiously insisted that their exchange rates were not over-valued and their fiscal positions were sustainable, I believe that a distorted view of reality is more important than the divergence of interests between officials and ordinary citizens in explaining why governments generally wait too long and incur excessive costs by delaying decisions to devalue or to restructure.

Third, these problems on the side of the borrowing country are reinforced by the tendency in the Fund and the official community to want to avoid any apparent responsibility for an unpleasant and difficult decision. As former Budget Director and CEA Chairman, Charles Schultze wryly observed, the fundamental rule in Washington is: 'Do no visible harm.' This rule applies on 19th Street as much as at the White House or on Capitol Hill. The result is that in cases like Argentina in 2001, there is an tendency for the Fund and the international community to bow to requests for further official support in the unrealistic hope that a crisis may somehow be avoided (rather than only briefly delayed).

In my view, there is no complete solution to these three problems nor a perfect way to address the larger issue of which they are a part – the proper principles, procedures and practices to govern the provision of international support to emerging-market countries facing severe payments difficulties. In particular, reflecting concerns about the asserted problems arising from large official support packages for Mexico in 1995, Thailand, Korea and Indonesia in 1997–8 and Russia and Brazil in 1998–9, there are several proposals to put an end to, or at least seriously curtail, such large-scale, conditional IMF lending. High officials in many industrial countries (including the Bush Administration), as well as the new Managing Director of the Fund, indicated their support or sympathy for such proposals. Now it is clear that these proposals have been repudiated by actual practice – with the participation and active encouragement of a number of governments that had earlier voiced opposition or scepticism about large support packages. In 2001–2, Argentina, Turkey, Uruguay and Brazil have all been granted exceptionally large packages of official support (mainly from the IMF). Indeed, relative to GDP, IMF support committed to Turkey is the largest in history, followed by Uruguay. In absolute amount, IMF support recently committed to Brazil sets the all-time record, followed by Turkey, and with Argentina not far behind. Thus, at this stage, it seems essential to recognise that there will be occasions when the international community will want to consider large official support packages for emerging-market countries that are well beyond the normal access limits for Fund financing.

However, sensible and constructive action is such cases is seriously impaired because there is no consistent set of principles that appears to govern decisions concerning the provision and operation of these large official support packages. And, this problem has got worse, not better, in 2001–2 – with the mess in Argentina dramatically illustrating the problems that arise when decisions are made in the absence of a reasonable framework. Granted, important differences among individual cases preclude precise rules to resolve all critical issues in particular cases. But, going into any specific case, such as Argentina in late 2000–early 2001, it should be possible to set the basic guidelines for dealing with that case in a manner that is broadly consistent with how other cases have been and will be treated.

These guidelines should include an understanding of the maximum support that the official community might provide to the country, taking account of the possibility that the official community may, in some circumstances, want to augment the level of support that is initially committed. There should also be an understanding of the feasible policy undertakings by the country that would justify a substantial (but less than maximum) commitment of official support to be disbursed in appropriate instalments. If the country's payments problems do not appear to be solvable under feasible policies with a plausible (but less than maximal) commitment of official support, then an alternative strategy involving devaluation and/or debt restructuring is called for as a condition for the initial commitment of official support. In addition, it should be clearly understood from the start that if, as the situation develops, things go badly because of inadequate policy implementation or other adversities, then further disbursements of official support are likely to be suspended. In this situation, if feasible policy adjustments appear unlikely to put the country on a sustainable payments path (possibly with some augmentation of official support but not above the pre-established maximum), then a shift to an alternative strategy to establish payments viability, involving devaluation and/or debt restructuring, would be become necessary for resumption of official support.

This basic approach has been applied successfully in several cases of exceptionally large Fund-supported programmes. For example, in Korea in December 1997, it rapidly became apparent that (as I had forecast), the initial commitment of official support and the policy efforts of the Korean authorities were insufficient to stem a rapid outflow of capital – mainly from the rundown of credit lines to Korean banks from major international banks. No feasible actions by the Korean authorities or plausible augmentation of official support would solve this problem. On Christmas Eve, the policy strategy was changed; the principal private lenders to Korean banks were officially encouraged to roll over their exposures and a system was established to monitor these rollovers. Although the Korean economy continued to contract through the winter and spring of 1998, the external payments crisis was successfully contained, and Korea was able to rapidly regain market access and enjoy a quite spectacular economic recovery.

Brazil in 1998–9 is another example. The Fund programme agreed in November 1998 committed about $40 billion of official support to Brazil, with about $10 billion to be disbursed immediately. The Brazilian authorities insisted on the preservation of their crawling peg exchange rate regime, without any modification, despite clear indications that the Fund would have preferred a step devaluation, an acceleration of the crawl, or a move to floating. The Brazilian authorities pledged to adopt several important fiscal measures, including measures requiring Congressional approval, that would raise the primary budget surplus to over 3 per cent of GDP. They were given latitude to use up to about $10 billion of their reserves if needed to keep the exchange rate within the crawling band. Some doubted whether this effort would succeed; my view was that the chances were about 50 per cent, assuming a high likelihood that the Brazilians would actually implement their policy commitments. In the event, there were legislative delays and a couple of key fiscal measures failed to secure Congressional approval. Confidence which was boosted by the announcement of the international support package in November began to wane, reserve out-flows accelerated, and by the year-end it was clear that Brazil would not meet its commitments under the IMF programme. The exchange rate peg collapsed in mid-January. The Fund made it clear that a resumption of international support required a substantial modification of the original policy strategy, including a floating exchange rate, a temporary tightening of monetary policy to resist over-depreciation of the exchange rate and contain inflationary pressures, and vigorous implementation of measures to achieve the agreed fiscal targets. Thus, in this case, the 'stop-loss' element in the initial Fund programme worked as intended – when the programme went seriously off track and was beyond repair, an alternative policy strategy was adopted.

In late 2000, it was understood that, even with a large Fund-supported pro-gramme, there was significant risk that Argentina might not be able to avoid a disastrous crisis. There was not, however, clear understanding of the need for a 'stop-loss' trigger that would force a shift to an alternative policy strategy if the preferred strategy was not working. Thus, at the behest of the Argentine author-ities, whose interests and perceptions of reality were distorted by impending catastrophe, the Fund continued to extend and expand its support even after any reasonable chance of success had vanished. The fact that Argentina faced more dire consequences from a shift to an alternative strategy to assure payments viability than Korea in 1997–8 or Brazil in 1999 can partly explain – but not excuse – the reluctance of the Fund (and the international community) to see the issue clearly and act appropriately. In general, the tougher the situation, the greater is the premium on clarity of vision and forcefulness of action. In other tough situations, the Fund has done better; and it should have done better in Argentina. With better guidelines concerning how to handle potential cases of exceptionally large Fund support, and with more effective adherence to such guidelines, mistakes like those the Fund made in Argentina in 2001 should not be repeated.

13 Countries in payments' difficulties: what can the IMF do?

ANDREW POWELL

1 Introduction

There are several different strands in the current economic literature regarding the role of IMF. In this chapter, I develop one particular theme, namely the role of the IMF in assisting countries that have serious international payments difficulties. One characterisation of this debate is that between the 'moral hazard' school and the 'liquidity' school. The former stresses the classic perverse incentive problem created with insurance-type interventions in capital markets leading lenders to bet on being 'bailed out' at some future date if things go wrong – especially in countries that might be considered 'too big to fail'.

Adherents to this school point to the sheer size of IMF-led packages to emerging economies, the very low emerging-market spreads after the assistance to Mexico in 1995 and the 'lending boom' to emerging economies, including the Asian economies, that then followed as evidence of the potential importance of moral hazard. In figure 13.1, we plot the EMBI spread from 1994 as an illustration.[1]

Some have labelled this as a 'theory of plenty': a theory of too much private lending, on the one hand, and too little discipline on the other. This lack of discipline might result in countries contracting large amounts of debt (either in the public or private sectors or in the private sector with implicit or explicit guarantees) while, at the same time, failing to address structural weaknesses or not adjusting quickly enough to negative shocks as they arise.

According to this school of thought, the role of the IMF must then be very limited. Lending instruments and IMF programmes should be designed to reduce

I would like to thank Leandro Arozamena, Michael Gavin and Federico Sturzenegger for their tremendous help in writing this chapter. I would also like to thank Christopher Gilbert and David Vines for detailed comments on an earlier draft and for excellent advice on editing. Naturally all mistakes remain my own.

[1] The EMBI is JP Morgan's 'Emerging Market Bond Index'.

Figure 13.1 *Overall and Argentina EMBI spread, 1994–2001*
Note: EMBI = JP Morgan's Emerging Market Bond Index

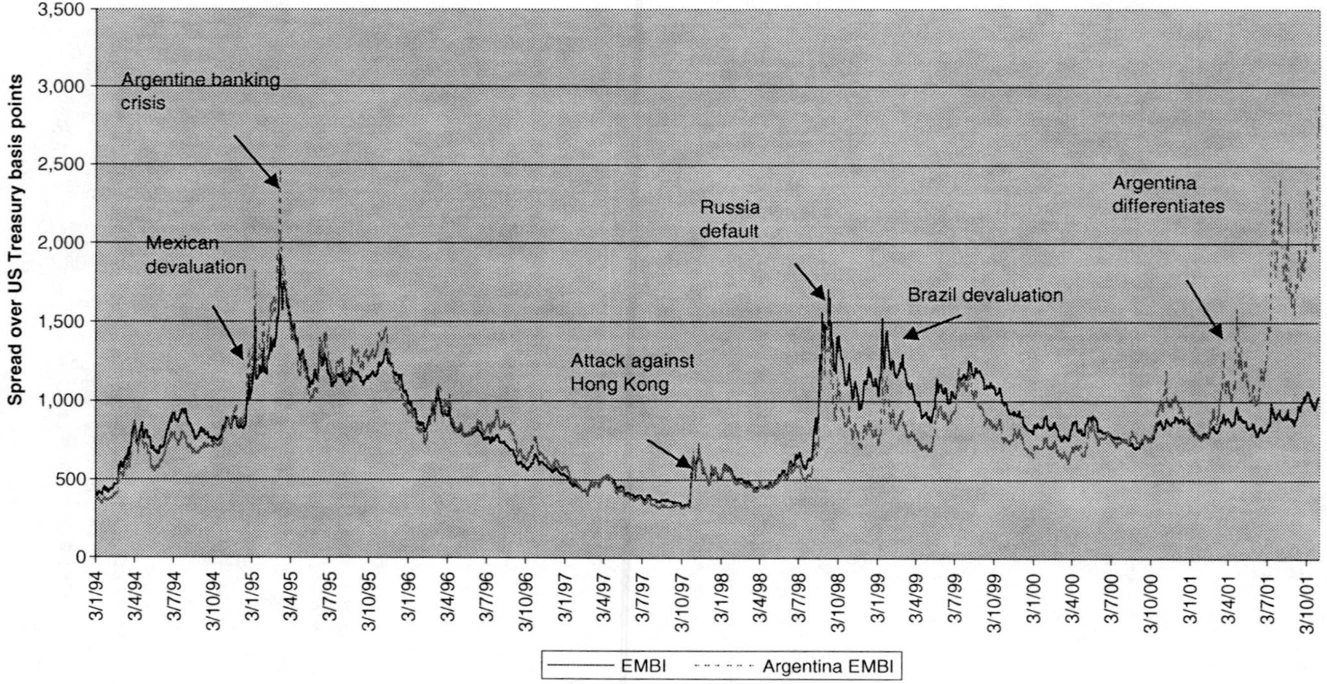

'moral hazard' as far as possible. The emphasis is then on how to resolve cases of countries with payments difficulties with minimum official involvement and higher degrees of private sector involvement (PSI). A payment difficulty is essentially a problem between a country and its private creditors.

The second school stresses failures in international capital markets. In particular, adherents point to asymmetric information between lenders and borrowers and coordination failures between lenders, giving rise to potential problems of multiple equilibria. According to this school, financial markets may be subject to inherent instability and consequent 'runs' which may prove extremely costly for the countries concerned. Such theories might be labelled 'too much instability'. Evidence includes lending booms and subsequent 'sudden stops' in capital flows (as non-residents attempt to 'run' and residents attempt to place funds abroad), the volatility of emerging-economy risk spreads and the apparent frequency of recent financial crises.

Proponents of this view tend to believe that while countries that suffer 'runs' may have structural weaknesses that make them more vulnerable to 'attack', nevertheless there is a tendency that the 'punishment' is worse than the 'crime' and hence there is an 'over-shooting' of relative prices and stocks causing grave damage to the countries that are 'hit' and disrupting international markets more generally through 'contagion'. Further evidence in favour of this view is the high (unexplained) correlation between emerging-country bond spreads.

In this view of the world, the role of the IMF is to attempt to stabilise capital markets and to make them work more smoothly. The IMF should, according to adherents of this view, act essentially as a provider of liquidity. Indeed, simply the credible promise of liquidity should eliminate the desire of investors to 'run'. The IMF may also act to coordinate lenders, at a minimum providing a focal point for expectations, and hence potentially affecting equilibrium selection. More directly, through both its informal powers of persuasion and more formal conditionality, the IMF may also affect the perceptions of atomistic investors and also reduce problems of lack of discipline as stressed by the moral hazard school. The IMF may also act as an 'honest broker' attempting to ameliorate problems of information asymmetry between borrowers and lenders which again, it might be argued, lead to unstable outcomes.

These appear to be quite opposite views of the world and hence somewhat difficult to reconcile. However, I will argue that both schools are right, and moreover, that they may be right simultaneously. In particular, I build on previous work and develop a very simple game-theoretic model that encompasses both views of the world. I show that depending on particular assumptions, the world may indeed be characterised by both views simultaneously. Indeed, I suggest that it is precisely because both schools are right simultaneously that the task of the IMF is made so difficult and, unfortunately, potentially without a clear normative solution.

Different waves of thought flowing through the IMF, and through its political masters, often prompted by events, may of course lead to particular policy approaches being adopted and outcomes generated. Unfortunately, such perceived changes in policy direction may serve only to increase the inherent instability of international capital markets. Hence, if this chapter does have a normative message it is an appeal for distance from dogmatic discussions of either one view or the other and a call for revision of the international financial architecture built on the recognition that both views have validity.

Given this reality, more creative thinking may be required to find a better way to manage these problems – including, for example, the need to consider changes in institutional structures. I use the results of the modelling exercise to comment on some of the recent debates regarding reform of the 'international financial architecture'. In particular, I consider the role of collective-action clauses in bond contracts and the recent (or revived) proposals for a bankruptcy procedure for countries. The model yields interesting and new interpretations for these proposals.

It is likely, however, that particular events will continue to shape policy changes in the months and years to come. At the time of writing the first draft of this chapter, Argentina was attempting to restructure, in an orderly fashion, its foreign-held public sector debt to avoid explicit default. This attempt failed – or never really got off the ground. At the end of 2000 a large IMF support package was agreed but subsequently Argentina backtracked on a proposal to cut politically sensitive public expenditure, adopted more heterodox economic policies to the displeasure of the IMF and country risk soared to over 1,000 basis points (see also chapter 12 in this volume). It is argued that at that point the IMF had a decision to make – either it had to support Argentina strongly or withdraw. In fact, it did neither – the perception was one of vacillation. The model presented in this chapter provides an explanation as to why first Argentina deviated to a more risky strategy and secondly why the IMF vacillated, being caught between the discomfort at continuing support to a country adopting more risky strategies (that subsequently made the default more painful) and the knowledge that withdrawal would no doubt have prompted a private sector run and the default that Argentina was trying to avoid.

The IMF did finally withdraw support and the feared private sector run did indeed take place. The banking and exchange controls, put in place as a consequence of the run, were an important element in bringing down the de la Rúa government at the end of 2001. At the time of writing this second draft, Argentina has devalued and defaulted. Formal negotiations between Argentina and her foreign private creditors have yet to begin and indeed I argue below that a game is continuing. On the one hand, the IMF and world leaders, concerned that new money might simply put off needed reforms and new promises might not be kept, have called for a 'sustainable solution' from Buenos Aires. On the other hand, President Duhalde has suggested that a sustainable solution may not be possible without international support. This is not the place to discuss solutions to the Argentine crisis. Suffice to say that the Argentine authorities are caught between the negative political and economic effects of the banking controls, and the fear that lifting these controls without an agreement with the IMF might provoke a 'run' on the currency and worsened monetary instability. The exchange rate dived to around 4 pesos to one dollar (from 1 to 1 in January) as the private sector found ways to 'run' to dollars despite the controls in place. The exchange rate subsequently recovered but, at the time of writing, is now around 3.7 pesos to the dollar, with banking controls and a more explicit Central Bank intervention policy still in place.

The chapter is organised as follows. In section 2, I review briefly some recent strands of the more theoretical debate regarding the role of the IMF. In section 3, I develop a simple model of the interaction between the IMF, a country and the private capital markets. In section 4, I relate the results of this modelling exercise to the current debate regarding reforming the international financial architecture. In section 5, I use these antecedents to then focus on the case of Argentina and the difficult role of the IMF as the country's situation became more fragile. Section 6 concludes.

2 The role of the IMF: selected themes in the current academic debate

A set of interesting papers has proposed different roles for the IMF in models of sovereign lending. The three potential roles reviewed here are the IMF as 'auditor' versus the IMF as 'enforcer' versus the IMF as a 'fund', a potential provider of money or the promise of money.

Dooley and Verma (2003) focus on the potential role of the IMF as a type of contract-enforcer. In their model, in the event of default, the IMF enters with an exogenous probability and enforces a sharing of future country output between borrowers and lenders. In the absence of the IMF, there is a costly renegotiation process and hence the role of the IMF is to reduce the probability of a large sunk cost that would be implied by costly renegotiation.

It is interesting to note that in this model there is an optimal value of the probability of IMF intervention between zero and one. In other words, it appears to be optimal for the IMF to intervene unpredictably. In a further extension to the model, the authors claim that in a world where contracts are supported by reputation and not 'gunboat' diplomacy, then the role of the IMF as the 'enforcer' of contracts may be redundant.

A second approach considers the IMF not as an enforcer of contracts but as an auditor. This is the focus of a paper by Gai, Hayes and Shin (2001). In this latter paper, there is a tradeoff whereby, as IMF intervention improves information and hence reduces the probability that borrowers are faced with large renegotiation costs, *ex ante* lenders are less willing to lend. This tradeoff is referred to by the authors as the 'whistleblower' versus the 'fireman' role of the IMF. In their setup, the IMF is generally bad for lenders as the 'fireman' reduces the *ex post* cost of resolution and hence reduces the stock of debt that can be supported in equilibrium – following Dooley (2000) – and this unambiguously reduces lenders' welfare. However, for borrowers the IMF may imply a net benefit, as improving the information available to lenders reduces the inefficiency of the information asymmetry and this can outweigh the costs of the lower level of debt.

Gai, Hayes and Shin (2001) also consider an IMF that acts unpredictably (which they refer to as 'case-by-case') but in their setup conclude that this will make lenders better off and may make borrowers worse off relative to the regime where the IMF follows a specific policy rule. It is in effect an intermediate model between a version with no IMF and the full IMF model. This contrasts with the Dooley and Verma (2003) result where an unpredictable IMF as enforcer may actually be the optimal policy. Of course the IMF is doing different things in the two cases, so perhaps this difference is not too surprising.

The IMF clearly has other roles, too, apart from that of 'enforcer' or 'auditor'. Specifically the IMF also provides money or promises of money. This role can protect borrowers against coordination problems between lenders. If the IMF offers standby arrangements then this may prevent costly self-fulfilling-type runs. This is the approach taken by Gavin and Powell (1999). However, the price for such liquidity protection may be moral hazard, thus allowing borrowers or lenders to take greater risks actually making 'fundamental'-type runs more likely. Gavin and Powell (1999) argue that private sector standbys (contingent facilities) might also provide countries with the same type of liquidity protection and that if these are correctly priced (i.e. assuming that there are no information problems), then these may serve to restrict moral hazard.

In what follows I present a very simple model where the IMF only plays a role of providing money or the promise of money – following previous work by Gavin and Powell (1998). It also turns out, in this very simple approach, that the IMF may end up playing unpredictably, which following Gai, Hayes and Shin (2001) may also be thought of as a 'case-by-case' strategy or its close cousin – the 'Constructive Ambiguity' doctrine of Central Banks (see also Fischer, 1999).

3 A simple model

In this section, I describe a very simple model to fix ideas. The model can be thought of as a three-player game where the actors are (1) the country,

Figure 13.2 *The game in extensive form*

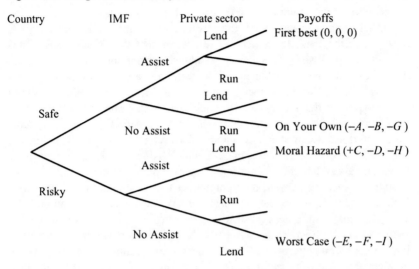

(2) the IMF and (3) private sector lenders. In what follows we consider different temporal structures of the game. Let us suppose for simplicity that we restrict the potential actions of each to a bivariate decision. In particular, that the country must decide a Safe or a Risky strategy, the IMF must decide whether to Assist or Not Assist and the private sector must decide whether to Lend or to Run.

A game with the IMF, a country and private investors

This game with three players, each with two possible actions, has eight potential outcomes. We represent the game in extensive form in figure 13.2. However, in what follows we restrict the outcomes in a way that depends on some other features. Let us assume that there is a simultaneous game between the IMF and the country and that then the private sector conditions its decisions on the outcome of that game and in particular, on what the IMF does. This intertemporal structure can be justified in at least two different ways. First, the private sector is making decisions every second in real time, whereas IMF and country policy discussions have more of a defined structure and timetable. Second, the private sector is composed of many different actors and may be thought of as incapable (or less capable) of making any commitment. Hence, its actions must be conditioned on the actions of others. However, as we discuss below, one interpretation of the current debate is precisely to attempt to change the intertemporal structure of this game. We therefore explore different sequential structures below. It should come as no great surprise that the results are highly sensitive to the particular assumed intertemporal structure.

Furthermore, we assume that the private sector's actions crucially depend on those of the IMF. In particular, we assume that the private sector Runs unless the IMF Assists. This may seem a harsh assumption, but it makes little difference if instead we say that there is a greater probability of the private sector running without IMF assistance so long as that greater probability results in expected payoffs that satisfy certain conditions which we outline below. Hence, while this particular assumption is harsh, weaker assumptions along the same lines would lead to similar results and it does reflect reality in a way that the IMF, and the country, must take into account. We discuss this more extensively below and also relate the assumption to the case of Argentina.

At least two more theoretical interpretations for this assumption are available. First, as discussed above, the private sector has a severe coordination problem and hence may Run unless the IMF 'coordinates' in some fashion or by Assisting the IMF directly rules out a 'Run' equilibrium through its promise of liquidity. A second interpretation is that there is some (unmodelled) information problem and the private sector trusts only the country (and the IMF), if the IMF puts down its own money rather than simply indulges in 'cheap talk' without committing resources. The assumption, that the private sector 'Runs', without IMF assistance, is how the 'liquidity' school argument is introduced into this version of the model. With this assumption there are then only four relevant outcomes (as in the standard prisoner's dilemma), as the private sector's action is determined by the actions of the IMF.

As there are only four outcomes that depend on the actions of the country and the IMF, we can also represent the model in a two by two matrix as in figure 13.3. We label the four potential outcomes: 1 First Best, 2 On Your Own, 3 Moral Hazard and 4 Worst Case. These labels refer to some general notion of world welfare and not the payoffs of particular players. The First Best is a case where the country plays Safe, the IMF Assists and the private sector Lends. The Worst Case is when the country plays Risky, the IMF does Not Assist and the private sector Runs. A third outcome is where the country plays Safe, the IMF does not Assist and the private sector Runs which we label as 'On Your Own'. It might also be referred to as the case where the discipline of the IMF and the private sector is most fully operating. The final outcome is that where the country plays Risky, the IMF Assists and the private sector Lends. This, we refer to as the Moral Hazard case.

Discussion of the payoffs

The equilibrium of this game naturally depends on the assumed payoffs. As the actions of the private sector are assumed to follow those of the IMF, it is only

Figure 13.3 *The game: a simplified form*

	IMF Assist	IMF No Assist
Country Safe	First Best (0, 0)	On Your Own (−A, −B)
Country Risky	Moral Hazard (C, −D)	Worst Case (−E, −F)

the payoffs of the IMF and the country that matter. Assume that the base case is the First Best and the payoffs, for both the country and IMF, are zero. We will write the payoffs as a vector with the first element, the payoff to the country and the second, the payoff to the IMF. Hence the payoffs are $\{Country, IMF\}$ = $\{0, 0\}$ in this case.

In order for there to be a moral hazard problem it must be the case that, given the IMF is Assisting, the country will prefer not to play Safe but would rather play Risky. We assume then, following the 'moral hazard school' that in the Moral Hazard outcome the payoffs are $\{C, -D\}$ with $C, D > 0$ where we assume that the country is better off and the IMF is worse off relative to the base case.

In the 'Worst Case', the country plays Risky, the IMF does Not Assist and the private sector Runs. Here we assume the payoffs are $\{-E, -F\}$ where E, $F > 0$. We assume that $-D < -F$ or, in other words, for the IMF, the Moral Hazard outcome is worse than the 'worst case' outcome. One interpretation of recent lobbying of the 'moral hazard' school economists is precisely to ensure that this is the case. We discuss this particular issue further on p. 380 as we note that recent authors have suggested otherwise (see Eichengreen and Ruhl, 2000). For the country, however, the Worst Case outcome is the worst of all i.e. $-E$ is the lowest payoff the country may receive.

Finally, in the On Your Own outcome the payoffs are $\{-A, -B\}$ $(A, B > 0)$ and we assume that $-E < -A$. In other words, for the country, while this outcome is clearly worse than the First Best, if the IMF is not Assisting, On Your Own is preferred to the Worst Case. Hence, if the IMF does Not Assist, it is then better for the country to play Safe and not Risky. This clearly makes sense thinking about lender Moral Hazard – or, in other words, that the risky strategy is that the country is contracting too much debt at too low an interest rate as lenders believe that there is a high probability of them being 'bailed out'. We also assume that the payoff to the IMF here is $-B$ where $B > 0$. This implies that if the country is playing Safe, then the IMF would prefer to Assist than to Not Assist.

Discussion of potential equilibria

If the country and the IMF are acting simultaneously, with the payoffs as defined above, it is simple to see that this game has no Nash equilibrium in pure strategies. In particular, start from the First Best. If the IMF is Assisting, the country then prefers to play Risky so the country prefers the Moral Hazard solution to the First Best. But if the country is playing Risky then the IMF prefers to Not Assist and hence prefers the Worst Case to Moral Hazard. However, if the IMF is Not Assisting and the private sector Runs, then the country prefers to play Safe (i.e. the country prefers On Your Own to the Worst Case) but then if the country is playing Safe, the IMF should Assist and we are back to the First Best. Hence, there is no Nash equilibrium in pure strategies.

However, it is well known that in such a situation there is at least one equilibrium in mixed strategies where the IMF plays randomly between Assist and Not Assist and where the country plays randomly between Safe and Risky. In particular, suppose that the probability that the IMF plays Assist is p and the probability that the country plays Safe is q. It follows that, given the payoffs there is a particular pair of probabilities, p and q, that make the Country indifferent between playing Safe and playing Risky and that make the IMF indifferent between Assisting and not Assisting, respectively. This probability pair then defines the mixed-strategy equilibrium.

To find the probability, p, that the IMF Assists in this equilibrium, consider the position of the country. To ensure that the country is indifferent between playing Safe and Risky, it must be the case that the expected payoff to the country from playing Safe, calculated using the probabilities of the IMF playing Assist or not, is equal to the expected payoff to the country of playing Safe, again weighted by the probabilities of the IMF Assisting or Not Assisting. In mathematical terms:

$$p0 + (1 - p)(-A) = pC + (1 - p)(-E)$$

It then follows by rearranging this equation that:

$$p = \frac{E - A}{E - A + C}$$

The existence of 'moral hazard' is critical in the explanation of why there is no equilibrium in pure strategies and only in mixed strategies. If there were no 'moral hazard' then C would not be positive but would be zero or negative (C is the payoff to the country if it plays Risky given that the IMF Assists). If there was no moral hazard present, then the probability p would be unity (or would not be well defined as it would be greater than one) and, if the other payoffs remained unchanged, the First Best would then be a pure-strategy equilibrium.

In similar vein, the probability that the country plays Safe, q, can also be found by considering the position of the IMF. The IMF will be indifferent to Assisting and or not Assisting if its expected payoff from playing Assist is equal to the expected payoff of Not Assisting: i.e. if:

$$q0 + (1 - q)(-D) = q(-B) + (1 - q)(-F)$$

Rearranging this equation we find that:

$$q = \frac{D - F}{D - F + B}$$

It is easy to check from our assumptions regarding payoffs above that $0 < p < 1$ and $0 < q < 1$.

There are various interpretations of this mixed-strategy equilibrium. First, the IMF and G7 have consistently stated their preference for a 'case-by-case' approach to countries with international payments' difficulties and that has indeed been the norm in practice. There is a close analogy here between the 'case-by-case' approach applied to countries and the apparent affinity for 'Constructive Ambiguity' of Central Banks when it comes to helping banks in distress.

There are at least two interpretations of the reasons why 'case-by-case' or 'Constructive Ambiguity' may be useful. One is that the world is just too complex to write down the right set of rules and hence flexibility is required to deal with particular cases as they arise. This might be referred to as the 'incomplete contracts' view. However, the other interpretation is that 'case-by-case' or 'Constructive Ambiguity' really implies unpredictability. As we show in the game above, if there is 'moral hazard', and other conditions are met, then unpredictability may be necessary for there to be an equilibrium. Under this interpretation, to ensure an equilibrium the IMF must never Assist with certainty, and the country will respond by never being absolutely clear that it will play Safe in order for each to be content given the strategy of the other.[2]

A second interpretation of mixed play is that players actually choose a pure strategy but there is some uncertainty about what the other player will do.

---

[2] In Gavin and Powell (1998), we developed a slightly more complex model with imperfect information where the IMF prefers a mixed-strategy equilibrium to a Nash equilibrium in pure strategies where the IMF always Assists in the case of a systemic problem and never Assists in the case of an individual problem, giving a slightly different interpretation of the Constructive Ambiguity doctrine. See Fischer (1999) for a further discussion of the analogy between 'case-by-case' and the 'Constructive Ambiguity' doctrine of Central Banks and the interpretation that such approaches are in part designed to control 'moral hazard'.

That is to say, as Binmore (1992) puts it, 'each player chooses, *as though* their opponents were playing mixed strategies. Insofar as any mixing occurs it happens within players' heads'.[3] A third interpretation is that, while the equilibrium is in mixed strategies, players may take time to get there. Players will note changes in opponents' actions over time, which may of course depend on the changes in other players' actions, and attempt to infer if players are then playing in pure or mixed strategies and assess the relevant probabilities. Over time, if the mixed-strategy equilibrium is stable, then there will be a convergence to the probabilities in that equilibrium but the outcomes observed will reflect this convergence process. Loosely speaking, players might then be thought of as playing a set of 'disequilibrium' pure strategies that, over time, converge to the mixed-strategy equilibrium.[4]

I remain agnostic as to the particular interpretation of the mixed-strategy equilibrium. However, the important point is that given the payoffs, the mixed-strategy equilibrium is the only Nash equilibrium to this game.

It is interesting to note that the probability that the country plays Safe depends on the relationship between $(D–F)$ and B: the payoffs to the IMF. If $(D–F)$ is large, relative to B, then the probability that the country will play Safe, in this mixed-strategy equilibrium, increases. This means that if the Moral Hazard outcome is very bad for the IMF compared to the Worst Case outcome (this is summarised by the difference, $D-F$), then the probability that the country plays Safe rises in equilibrium. On the other hand if $(D-F)$ is reduced, then the probability that the country plays Safe diminishes.

The welfare of the country in the mixed strategy equilibrium is equal to $(1 − p)(−A)$ or $−AC/(E − A + C)$.[5] This is increasing in E but decreasing in A and C. This implies that, for example, increasing E (i.e. making $−E$ more negative, making the Risky strategy combined with non-assistance from the IMF more painful for the country), would actually increase country welfare in the equilibrium – as the IMF would have to Assist more frequently for an equilibrium to be found. This is somewhat analogous to the result that increasing the pain of a country in default might actually make a country better off, *ex ante*, as it would support greater private lending, although the mechanism for this result here is quite different.

---

[3] This is known as 'purification' of a mixed-strategy Nash equilibrium (see Binmore, 1992, p. 51).

[4] Binmore (1992) illustrates this possibility with an example where players are fully rational but myopic. In his words: 'Players always choose a pure strategy that maximises expected payoffs given their beliefs. But their beliefs change as they observe their opponent's play. In the long run, their beliefs converge on the Nash equilibrium of the game' (see Binmore 1992, pp. 404–8).

[5] Note that in the Nash, mixed-strategy equilibrium, the country is indifferent to playing Safe or Risky by definition and so the payoff to the country can be calculated as simply the payoff to playing Safe.

While the equilibrium of this game is in mixed strategies, *ex post* after the dice are rolled, particular outcomes will be observed. These outcomes may result in a higher or a lower welfare for each player *ex post* compared to the *ex ante* welfare of the mixed-strategy equilibrium. In particular, if the IMF Assists the welfare of the country is either C or zero depending if the country ends up playing Risky or Safe, respectively. These welfare levels are clearly higher than $(1 - p)(-A)$, the *ex ante* welfare level of the mixed-strategy equilibrium while if the IMF does Not Assist the country's welfare levels are lower (either $-A$ or worst of all $-E$).

As noted in the introduction, a common argument is that after the Mexican 'bailout', international capital markets were affected by severe moral hazard. Some have even gone as far as to blame the Asian crisis on such moral hazard and hence the very low risk spreads 'post-tequila' in 1996–7.[6] More recently, there has been a focus on attempting to limit this moral hazard and hence greater pressure to restrict IMF action.

This story can be rationalised easily within the context of the simple model above. After Mexico, it might be hypothesised that the dice were rolled and the 'moral hazard' outcome observed. This outcome then consisted of countries adopting a more Risky strategy, the IMF Assisting through large packages and the private sector Lending. Subsequently, one interpretation might be that various lobbying activities by moral hazard school economists have attempted to increase D-F – or, in other words, that the IMF has a lower relative payoff to the Moral Hazard outcome versus Not Assisting if the country plays Risky. These lobbying activities may then be rationalised as attempts to increase the probability that countries play Safe. From the above it follows that if D-F is raised then this increases q, the probability that the country plays Safe in the Nash equilibrium.[7]

An additional step to the game might be added where the private sector *ex ante* (i.e. before the game analysed above has started) offers a standard debt

---

[6] Mussa (chapter 12 in this volume) also suggests that the IMF was not tough enough on Argentina during the 'good times' of 1996–7 and some might even go as far as to blame the Argentine crisis on 'moral hazard', too. After all, if Argentina's fiscal policy was characterised by a chronic lack of fiscal responsibility, as Mussa suggests, then lender 'moral hazard' must be one candidate explanation for the low risk spreads at that time.

[7] Naturally the actual outcome of the game here is random and is in some sense then less interesting. The story relates to how the probabilities in that equilibrium might change as the payoffs change. An important distinction is whether the outcomes are random ones from some probability distribution or whether they are changing pure strategy equilibria. Binmore (1992) defines a 'kibitzer' as someone who watches a game but does not play, but by some rule of nature is always more expert than the actual players themselves. He then goes on to note how kibitzers may interpret different games. A kibitzer, who observes a game where players are playing randomly, may of course think that he is observing a pure-strategy Nash equilibrium when in fact he is observing just one potential outcome of mixed-strategy play (see Binmore, 1992, n. 5, p. 397).

contract to the country. The 'fair' interest rate on this contract (say, fixed such that expected returns to the private sector *ex ante* are zero or the same as some opportunity cost of funds), will reflect the potential outcomes of the mixed-strategy equilibrium weighted by their respective probabilities. Given that in the mixed-strategy equilibrium there is a positive probability (namely $p(1-q)$) of the Moral Hazard outcome, the *ex ante* 'risk spread' will then reflect to some extent, 'lender moral hazard'. *Ex post*, the private sector will win or lose relative to this 'fair interest rate' depending on the observed outcome of the roll of the dice and which particular outcome is observed.[8] Private Sector Involvement, in its broad sense, might then be defined as any outcome where the private sector loses according to this measure.

Repeating the game: the opportunities for cooperation

Let us now consider what might happen assuming the above one-shot game is repeated. In the one-shot game, the only equilibrium was one in mixed strategies. As discussed above, if the IMF offers Assist the country would prefer to play Risky but if the country plays Risky the IMF would prefer to play Safe but in that case the IMF would prefer to Assist. As it was assumed that the country could not commit to play Safe if the IMF offered Assist (moral hazard), then the First Best was not an equilibrium and given the assumed structure of payoffs there was indeed no pure strategy equilibrium available.

However, in a repeated version of this game there may be an opportunity for cooperation developing between the IMF and the country. Note that the best outcome for the IMF is the First Best. Suppose that the IMF offers the First Best but with the threat that if the country deviates (and plays Risky to obtain the Moral Hazard outcome), then the IMF will respond with the Nash (mixed-strategy) equilibrium forever. As we had before, the payoff to the country in the Nash equilibrium is equal to $(1-p)(-A)$ and the country is then clearly worse off than that in the First Best, which is equal to zero. It is possible then, that the First Best can be attained through this approach.[9]

---

[8] I am indebted to Leandro Arozamena, Christopher Gilbert and David Vines for pointing this out.

[9] As is well known this is only one potential 'cooperative' outcome of many. The IMF might, for example, use On Your Own forever as the threatened trigger punishment strategy where the IMF does not Assist and the Country prefers to play Safe. On Your Own in this game is the country's security level (or Max-Min) in the sense that it gives the best payoff for the country assuming that the IMF will always choose the worst action for the country given the country's choice. There is no claim to uniqueness here. Another issue is whether the assumed trigger strategies are non-renegotiable. We do not discuss these issues further here and leave the analysis of a proven non-renegotiable punishment strategy for future research (see Fudenberg and Maskin, 1986).

In this example, the country must weigh up the welfare of staying in the First Best forever, which is equal to zero, versus the alternative of deviating and obtaining the payoff, C, from the Moral Hazard outcome for one period and then the welfare of the mixed-strategy equilibrium for the rest of time. The First Best can then be supported if:

$$C + \frac{\delta}{1-\delta}(1-p)(-A) < 0$$

where δ is the discount factor of the country and hence the second term on the left-hand side gives the payoff to playing the Nash equilibrium forever, discounted by one period. Substituting for p in terms of the payoffs and rearranging, this yields the following condition for the First Best to be supported:

$$\delta > 1 - \frac{A}{C+E}$$

By our original assumptions $A, C, E > 0$ so we know that this gives a threshold discount factor of less than one.[10] The larger is C (the payoff from deviating and obtaining the Moral Hazard outcome for one period), then the higher is the threshold discount factor – or, in other words, if C is large then the country must weight future payoffs more highly for the First Best to be supported. This is because increasing C increases the reward from deviation. The threshold discount factor also rises if E is increased. If the country's pain from playing Risky and the IMF not Assisting is greater, then as the welfare in the Nash equilibrium rises, the discount factor now has to be greater to support the First Best.

Suppose that default occurs only when the country plays Risky and the IMF does Not Assist,[11] where the payoff to the country is equal to $-E$ such that in fact $-E = yG - (1-y)H$ where $(1-y)$ is the probability of default $(0 < y < 1)$ and H $(H > E > A)$ is the cost of default.[12] Perhaps, somewhat surprisingly

---

[10] We note that if $C + E > A$, then the threshold discount factor is greater than zero, too, although there is no obvious reason why that is the case. If then C or E are sufficiently small or A sufficiently large (subject to the restrictions to obtain the unique Nash mixed-strategy equilibrium), any positive discount factor would support the First Best.

[11] In other words if the country plays Safe we assume that the technology is such that the country is protected from insolvency and if the IMF Assists but the country plays Risky (the moral hazard outcome) then we assume that the IMF bails out the country if there are insufficient resources (or unwillingness) to pay private creditors.

[12] This may be motivated by saying that there is a probability y of a good outcome from the Risky strategy in which case the payoff is $+G$ and a probability of $(1-y)$ of a bad outcome, in which case the country defaults, and the cost of default is then represented by $-H$. This structure may be motivated either within an 'ability to pay' – or a 'willingness to pay' – type model of default. In the latter case, given the bad outcome (and the lack of IMF Assistance), it would be in the best interest of the country to default rather than, say, pursue some very costly adjustment.

then, if default is made less costly (H is reduced such that $-H$ is less negative), then the First Best has *more* chance of being supported in the sense that the threshold discount factor increases.[13] This simple model then provides some interesting results which we follow up on below in a discussion on the reform of the international financial architecture.

However, it also raises some difficult questions. Suppose the probability of avoiding default in the case of Risky play and not obtaining IMF assistance, y, is a stochastic variable with some persistence over time and that even if the IMF and the country are in the First Best the value of this probability and its stochastic process are known. For example, it is likely that y will be highly correlated to country fundamentals such as growth or the country terms of trade. Substituting in for y and rearranging the equation for the threshold value of the discount factor, above, this can be re-expressed as a threshold value for $1 - y$, the probability of default in the case of Risky play and no IMF Assistance. It then turns out that for the First Best to be supported:

$$1 - y < \frac{G - C + {}^A/_{1 - \delta}}{G + H}$$

As $H > E > A$, it follows that $H < {}^A/_{1-\delta} - C$ and hence this gives a threshold value for $1 - y$ which is less than one. As long as the numerator is positive it is also greater than zero (this might be thought of as a limit on how large C can be in relation to G and A to control the incentives to deviate). Now, if the probability of default in the case of Risky/No Assist, $(1 - y)$, rises to a level exceeding this threshold then the country will deviate to the Risky strategy. The intuition behind this is that as the probability of default in the Risky/No Assist outcome rises, and hence the payoff for the country in that outcome is made worse, the probability that the IMF will Assist in the mixed-strategy equilibrium must rise (for there to be an equilibrium which makes the country indifferent between Safe and Risky). This then means that the *ex ante* welfare of the mixed-strategy equilibrium for the country increases and hence the First Best has less chance of being supported. To put it another way, as country fundamentals suffer, the country can expect a greater probability of IMF Assistance in the non-cooperative mixed-strategy equilibrium and hence the incentives to cooperate to achieve the cooperative First Best are eroded.

Now consider the case of a country with deteriorating fundamentals sinking deeper towards payments' problems. As the threshold value of $(1 - y)$ is less than one, it is very likely that at some point before default this value will be breached and the country will deviate to the Risky strategy.

---

[13] We have to be careful here as if the cost of default is reduced such that $-E > -A$, then the nature of the equilibrium changes and indeed, all else remaining the same, the Worst Case becomes a pure-strategy equilibrium. This possibility becomes important in section 4.

To put it simply, before a country defaults, it is likely that it will deviate. One characterisation of this result is that it supports the idea that countries will 'gamble for resurrection' before they actually default.

This raises some interesting issues. Consider the position of the IMF. Faced with the possibility of deviation to a risky strategy before default is called, an interesting question is whether the IMF should not attempt to anticipate this set of events.

The difficult issue is then at what point should the IMF itself decide to switch to the mixed-strategy equilibrium. If y follows some stochastic process over time related to country fundamentals and the IMF today knows the conditional distribution of y before each one-shot game is played, should the IMF play with the mixed-strategy equilibrium if the expected value of $(1 - y)$ next period, conditional on information at time t, is above the threshold level? Or perhaps the IMF should take a 'Value at Risk' approach with a rule that it should withdraw support if there is a probability greater than X per cent, that $(1 - y)$ will pass the threshold next period and that the country will deviate?

However, if the country knows the rule by which the IMF will withdraw support based on its prediction of the future value of $(1 - y)$, then surely the country should *anticipate* the IMF's actions, and may then wish to deviate one period earlier. We may then find, depending on the starting conditions, that the whole repeated game may unravel such that the First Best was not attainable in the first place. We leave a rigorous analysis of these complex issues to further research but note that the decision of whether and when the Fund should withdraw support to a country with an increasing probability of a payments' problem and the effect that the anticipation of that decision may have on a country's policy framework is both a complex and a very real issue. It is one that comes out very clearly indeed from the discussion of the Argentine case below.

4 The current debate on the reform of international financial architecture

The simple model outlined above sheds light on some recent discussions regarding the reform of the international architecture. In particular in this section, I focus on arguments related to collective-action clauses in bonds, other issues regarding private sector involvement (PSI) and the possibility of establishing a bankruptcy procedure for countries.

Eichengreen and Ruhl (2000) perhaps represents the most forcefully argued paper in favour of collective-action clauses in bond contracts and indeed their arguments stem from a simple game, taken from Eichengreen and Ruhl (2000), which is similar to the one-shot game presented above. The essential difference is in the assumptions regarding payoffs; in particular, these authors assume that, in the end, the IMF prefers the 'Moral Hazard' to the 'Worst Case' outcome. They defend this position arguing that if the IMF does not Assist, then the ensuing crisis will be so bad for the country and potentially for international capital markets that it is not credible for the IMF to state that they will Not Assist given that the IMF has the country's interest and the stability of international financial markets at heart. The equilibrium in their game is then similar to the 'Moral Hazard' outcome in our game above. Eichengreen and Ruhl (2000) then argue in favour of reducing the costs of a country declaring default through the addition of 'collective-action clauses' to bond contracts. These contracts allow for a more orderly re-negotiation such that a default can be resolved more easily and is then presumably less costly for the country. They argue that if this change were made then the IMF's payoffs would change and hence the Moral Hazard outcome would no longer be the equilibrium. Indeed, in the context of their model they argue the equivalent of the First Best would become the pure strategy equilibrium.

Eichengreen and Ruhl (2000) assume that the addition of 'collective-action clauses' would imply that the 'Worst Case' is not such a bad outcome for the IMF. Their optimistic view is then that if the Worst Case outcome is now preferred to the Moral Hazard one by the IMF, then the country will choose the Safe strategy and hence we get the First Best. However, these are precisely the assumptions we have made above which imply that there is no pure strategy equilibrium.[14] Moreover, the introduction of collective-action clauses may change the payoffs such that the country would now prefer the 'Worst Case' to 'On Your Own', i.e. it might make $-E > -A$ ($E < A$) in the game above. If this is the case, then adding collective-action clauses may make the Worst Case the only pure-strategy equilibrium. To put this another way, if adding collective-action clauses makes countries prefer to play Risky rather than Safe (assuming no IMF assistance), because, say, default has now become less costly, then neither the IMF nor the private sector will lend. Of course, this simply reflects the standard tradeoff versus the cost of *ex post* default and the willingness of lenders to advance credit *ex ante*.

---

[14] One might interpret the game in Eichengreen and Ruhl (2000) as giving the first move to the country. Then, if the country knows that a Risky Strategy will be answered by Not Assist from the IMF, the country may well prefer to play Safe. However, this sequential play order supposes that the country can commit to its Safe strategy. This seems highly unrealistic. The country clearly has an incentive to claim it will play Safe, get IMF Assistance and then actually play Risky. The sequential structure offered in this chapter appears more realistic and then, in the one-shot game, the addition of collective-action clauses either simply ensures the unique mixed-strategy equilibrium as depicted above – or, in an extreme case where the cost of default is reduced sufficiently, then the Worst Case will become a pure strategy equilibrium.

However, the repeated game presented above suggests a new interpretation of the potential value of collective-active clauses. Suppose that these clauses do reduce the cost of default, H, which then reduces E (i.e. they make $-E$ less negative – or, in other words, make the Risky strategy for the country, combined with Not Assist from the IMF, less painful). This reduces welfare in the Nash (mixed-strategy) equilibrium (as it reduces the probability of IMF Assistance in that equilibrium) and hence increases the amount of 'punishment' that the IMF can inflict. It therefore makes it more likely that the First Best will be attained. In other words, collective action clauses may reduce the threshold discount factor required to ensure that the country does not want to deviate.

Roubini (2000), in his comprehensive PSI survey, claims the value of collective-action clauses may be overdone but does not contemplate the kind of repeated game advanced here. Moreover, Roubini suggests that if the IMF can commit to make only limited Assistance then perhaps the country will prefer to play Safe and not Risky ($C < 0$ in the game above), so the moral hazard problem goes away. And of course the private sector will then Lend, so a modified 'First Best' with limited IMF Assistance may then become a pure-strategy equilibrium.

In similar vein, Haldane and Krug (2000) have argued that there should be a strong presumption of limited IMF and official resources. In their view, the problem has been a lack of clarity regarding official policies. They state that while some might think of this lack of clarity as 'Constructive Ambiguity', for them it has resulted in the assembly of very large packages that have then given the wrong signals to the private sector regarding the probability of being bailed out. Moreover, the authors state simply that there is no longer a political will for such large packages going forward.

The Haldane and Krug (2000) view might be considered as a criticism of the mixed-strategy equilibrium in the one-shot game analysed – one interpretation of which is indeed Constructive Ambiguity. They argue for a clear statement about how much IMF or official money is available and for clearer rules regarding how such money may be made available to borrowers. The authors also support the idea of a standstill and lending-into-arrears such that the borrowing country can, for a time, cease to service an 'unsustainable debt' but the IMF can continue to Assist assuming that the country has adopted the right policy framework (playing Safe).

While I have sympathy for attempting to develop greater clarity for official policy, it seems very unlikely, within the context of the one-shot game set out above, that a clear (credible) commitment from G7 and the IMF that there is only so much on the table, and a clear message that the private sector would have to have a much larger involvement in crisis-resolution, would resolve the strategic problem as analysed. Indeed, it seems more likely that such a policy would tend to provoke a Run from the private sector making the 'punishment' worse than the 'crime'. Further, it would surely aggravate rather than solve the coordination problem in the private sector.

A possible defence of the Haldane and Krug (2000) view is to interpret their position as wishing to reduce C (*the payoff* to the country from the Moral Hazard outcome) within the context of the repeated game. This then reduces the welfare to the country of the Nash (mixed-strategy) equilibrium. If this could be achieved, all else being equal the First Best is now more likely to be attained – in the sense that it will be attained for lower values of the country discount factor. However, this assumes that the limited IMF assistance is sufficient to ensure that the private sector does not run even when the IMF is assisting.[15]

While the depiction of the private sector is very stylised in the above game, the strategic coordination problem within the private sector is a very important element of the story. The model, and the mixed-strategy equilibrium, illustrate that the IMF is caught between the potential moral hazard if it Assists and a private sector Run if it withdraws, then making the 'punishment' worse than the 'crime'. This raises the question as to whether there are other devices to ensure lender coordination that would then make IMF withdrawal less costly for the country, possibly altering the game above. Indeed, this is perhaps the strongest argument in favour of private sector contingency lines. Gavin and Powell (1999) suggested that a private sector contingent credit line can be seen precisely as a coordinating device among private sector creditors and hence might well play such a role.[16] However, in practice such a line is likely to remain relatively small. In the case of Argentina a contingent line stood at less than $5 billion at the time of its use, and though while successfully used, could be thought of only as coordination between a rather small subset of lenders.

Standstills can also be thought of as another type of coordinating device. Contingent credit lines might be thought of as *ex ante* coordination by lenders (i.e. before any contractual default had been declared), whereas standstills are a type of *ex post* coordination. As analysed by Gai, Hayes and Shin (2001) they

---

[15] One view is that in the face of a liquidity run partial help is pointless in that unless the assistance is complete the 'Run' from the private sector will not be halted. Either the promise of liquidity provision is complete, through a very large package, or not. Roubini (2000) suggests however that in a game with multiple equilibria, then there may be a role for partial assistance in order to influence equilibrium selection.

[16] Some doubt that private institutions would actually satisfy their contractual obligations in times of stress while others have suggested that private banks may hedge their exposures such that liquidity is not actually increased at the time the facility is used. The successful triggering of the Argentine facility in August 2001, in conjunction with an IMF package, when the country had no access to other private credit, may now serve to dilute some of these criticisms. However this limited line could not prevent the subsequent run, default and devaluation driven by more fundamental concerns.

may indeed have a useful role to play in terms of crisis resolution. However, as noted by Roubini (2000), the existence of an explicit standstill policy may provoke the 'run' *ex ante*. The combination of a more comprehensive contingent credit line *ex ante and* an explicit standstill policy *ex post* may be a superior alternative.

Indeed, while the introduction of collective-action clauses, and a clearer message regarding the (limited) funds available from the IMF and other lenders, may make the First Best more likely to be attained and the use of creditor coordination devices might alleviate to some extent the problems of the private sector 'Run', as illustrated in the repeated game model presented in this chapter, the repeated game model also highlights a fundamental problem which none of these particular advances in architecture is likely to solve. That problem is that if a country is in the unfortunate position that its fundamentals are deteriorating such that default is becoming more and more probable, then at some point it is likely to have the incentives to deviate to Risky play and hence the IMF will be forced to respond with the mixed strategy. The problem that at some point deviation is likely to occur before default appears to require deeper changes in institutions.

Indeed, this more fundamental problem provides an interesting defence for the rekindled interest in the idea of a bankruptcy procedure for countries. Anne Krueger has explicitly proposed such a policy.[17] Suppose that we start in the First Best of the repeated game. Krueger argues that it must be the country that is to decide whether it enters into a bankruptcy procedure or not. A bankruptcy procedure might then be thought of as an additional action available to the country. The payoff to the country in the bankruptcy procedure would, on the one hand, reflect the degree of protection from creditors afforded to the country while, on the other hand, the country would no doubt suffer from the stigma that entering such a procedure would elicit *and* would suffer from additional controls and monitoring that such a procedure might entail. Let us assume that this payoff is then under the control of the international community and could be managed as a function of the probability of default.

As the probability of default increased the bankruptcy procedure could be designed to become relatively more attractive to the country such that, at the point where the probability of default in the Risky/Non-Assist outcome hits

---

[17] As Krueger (2003) states: 'As you know, we consider that a statutory framework could most effectively be established through the Sovereign Debt Restructuring Mechanism, using an amendment to the Fund's Articles. The Fund has been asked by the International Monetary and Financial Committee – which is made up of twenty four Ministers of Finance – to develop a concrete proposal for a statutory mechanism, and to report to the Committee's next meeting in April. Our proposal has been developed with the enormous benefit of extensive dialogue with the private sector, workout professionals, academics, and official community.'

its threshold value, choosing the bankruptcy procedure would be slightly more attractive for the country than deviating to the Risky strategy. A bankruptcy procedure designed in that fashion might then keep the country playing Safe until the point at which the procedure was chosen. This line of argument might be used to place a lower and an upper bound on the attractiveness how generous or painful the bankruptcy procedure should be for the country. Note that the payoff to the country from the First Best is zero such that at the point where the country prefers to play Risky, the payoff from deviating is just above zero. At the point where otherwise the country would deviate, the bankruptcy procedure must also give a payoff of just slightly above zero. It goes without saying, though, that, until that point, choosing default should never be more attractive than continuing with the First Best, i.e. it should attract a payoff of less than zero.[18]

Now, compared to the case considered above, where a country is almost certain to deviate before default is called it is not obvious that introducing a bankruptcy procedure is worse for the private sector. As suggested by Krueger (2003), the bankruptcy procedure is a type of coordination device. In the absence of such a procedure, the prediction of the model above is that a country will deviate to Risky play before it defaults, the IMF will respond with play consistent with the non-cooperative mixed-strategy equilibrium and at some point IMF Assistance will be withdrawn and the private sector will Run. While some lucky private creditors may get out in time, as the Run itself is very harmful to the country, the *ex ante* prospects for private investors – who in general will not know whether they will get out in time or not – may actually be better with the bankruptcy procedure in place. With a bankruptcy procedure designed according to the ideas here, the country would chose the procedure *before* it deviates to Risky play and before the withdrawal of IMF Assistance. From the standpoint of the private sector whether this is better or not will depend on a tradeoff, between, on the one hand, the probability of getting out in time (in the absence of the procedure during the 'Run') and the haircut applied to the wider set of investors caught in the bankruptcy procedure. The latter may turn out to be better for the private sector and hence the argument that the private sector may reduce the amount of credit to a country if such a procedure is introduced loses much of its force.

Note also that, for the IMF, if the country deviates to Risky play this is a highly negative outcome. In the First Best the IMF obtains a payoff of zero whereas if the country deviates this becomes $-D\left(1 + {\delta(1-q)}/{(1-\delta)}\right)$ which is

---

[18] It is assumed here that the country cannot deviate to Risky play and then opt for the bankruptcy procedure. This implies that while the country is the one that asks for the procedure to be implemented there must be a decision-making body (the IMF, or another) that decides whether the procedure is appropriate or not and one of the criteria for that decision must be whether the country has maintained appropriate (Safe) policies.

clearly negative. This suggests that the international community should also be willing to invest something in the bankruptcy procedure. As discussed above, such a procedure would have to afford the country a payoff slightly higher than zero at the point where the country would otherwise deviate. Given that if the country does deviate then this is a bad outcome for the IMF, there should be some resources that the IMF would be willing to make available to the country to provide the right incentives to chose bankruptcy over deviation in those rare and unfortunate circumstances.

5 On the case of Argentina

The Argentina crisis backs up both the assumptions and the predictions of the model discussed above. It also helps provide an interesting, if very painful, illustration of the current deficiencies in the 'international financial architecture'. This is not the place for a detailed discussion of the history of the Argentine crisis. In box 13.1, I present, in highly schematic form, three mutually reinforcing hypotheses regarding the roots of the crisis. Suffice to say in my view the crisis was a result of a fairly complex set of factors including bad luck, a required adjustment of the current account which due to domestic inflexibility provoked recession but which was largely completed through 2000, a required but modest fiscal adjustment that was not achieved, and very bad politics (see Powell, 2003). This account contrasts with that of Mussa (chapter 12 in this volume) that emphasises the fiscal dimension. My intention here is to focus instead on the game between the IMF, the country and the private sector as Argentina entered into payments problems as an illustration of the ideas discussed above.

Box 13.1 Three hypotheses regarding the roots of the Argentine crisis[a]

Fiscal and debt sustainability

Argentine debt reached 46 per cent of GDP by the end of 2000, not large by European standards but some argued too much for an emerging country of Argentina's characteristics. Fiscal irresponsibility is the explanation favoured by Michael Mussa in chapter 12 in this volume. However risk spreads on Argentine bonds were about 670 basis points in mid-February 2001 reflecting an average market view that there was some risk of default, but not certainty. Wall Street economists were clearly divided. JP Morgan in September 2000 suggested the debt story was 'Much to do about not so much'. Lehmann Brothers suggested the situation was unsustainable.[b]

Competitiveness, external shocks, the exchange rate, inflexibility and the sustainability of the current account

The debt position was more clearly unsustainable if Argentina could not grow. Recession started in the third quarter of 1998 (although there was growth in late 1999). Through 1998, Argentina suffered from a fall in the terms of trade, the rise in the US dollar and the fallout in emerging-market risk spreads after the Russian default (increasing interest payments to external debtholders) and, in January 1999, the Brazilian devaluation. With a fixed exchange rate and inflexible formal labour markets, one view was that Argentina could adjust only through recession and deflation. On the other hand, exports grew every year during Convertibility except 1999 after the devaluation of the real, albeit from a small base. A broader question was whether the current account was sustainable. Foreign direct investment remained buoyant, private sector foreign assets had grown to over $100 billion and returns on those assets could have resulted in substantial inflows if repatriated, and during 2000 an increasing amount of debt, issued abroad in foreign currency, was transferred to domestic pension funds and banks. In Powell (2003) I argue that although the trade balance needed to adjust through 1999, by the end of 2000 this adjustment was near complete. On this view the current account was not so far from sustainability as to explain what was to follow.

Political risk

Argentine politics has been extremely messy, and this severely affected economic management from 1998. Ex-President Menem's power waned during his second term, leading to a period of very factious politics. The 1999 election campaign saw President Duhalde suggesting that the external debt should be renegotiated and ex-Minister Cavallo, an architect of the currency board, apparently suggesting that the peso could float. The 'Alianza' government of ex-President de la Rúa was perceived as fragile in part because of the fragile nature of the alliance and the fact that it lacked an outright majority in Congress. Fights within the alliance and political scandal dogged 2000, culminating in the resignation of the Vice-President towards the end of the year. January–April 2001 saw three different Economy Ministers with López-Murphy being ousted after a political storm created by his proposed fiscal adjustment package. Political scandal remained and an acrimonious battle between then Minister Cavallo and Central Bank President, Pedro Pou, led finally to the latter's ousting. This, plus Cavallo's idea to include the euro in the currency board basket (arguably a political rather than an economic event), sent country risk soaring. The interaction between the electoral system, the structure of political parties and the federal nature of the country made for continuous divisions within and between parties, and between the federal and provincial governments and arguably contributed to a high cost of government, few incentives to improve the quality of public services (lack of accountability), possible corruption and difficulties in maintaining fiscal discipline (see Calvo and Abal Medina, 2001).

Notes:

[a] Powell (2003) conducts a Vector Autoregression (VAR) econometric analysis and finds support for the view (a) that these hypotheses were mutually reinforcing and (b) that there were multiple equilibria. In particular higher risk spreads fed through to lower bank deposits, higher political risk (measured as a published political risk index constructed monthly) and weaker tax revenues that fed back to higher risk spreads.

[b] See 'Argentina's Debt Dynamics: Much ado about not so much', JP Morgan Market Brief, September 2000 and Lehman Brothers, 'Global Weekly Economic Monitor', March 2001, section entitled, 'Argentina: Speaking the Unspeakable'.

In December 2000, Argentina obtained a very significant support package from the IMF and from a set of private sector creditors. This package was known as the '*blindaje*' and was essentially seen as a stand-by to protect against possible exclusion from capital markets to create confidence ('*blindaje*' implies armour plating or defensive protection against an attack). The authorities claimed that the total package stood at close to $40 billion. With the *blindaje* in place, country risk fell to around 700 basis points over US Treasuries. This level of country risk reflected 'average market opinion' that the risk of default was significant but clearly less than unity. It is a maintained hypothesis of the discussion to follow that (a) default and devaluation were not inevitable at this stage and (b) this agreement represented a 'cooperative' First Best, in terms of the repeated model, where Argentina had agreed to a set of Safe policies and the IMF was Assisting.[19]

However, even with the *blindaje* in place, the real economy did not appear to improve and, if anything, deteriorated in the first quarter of 2001. Moreover, there was continued political squabbling within the governing alliance in

[19] An alternative interpretation of the risk spreads is of course that default was already deemed inevitable but that the Fund or others would bail out international investors.

Figure 13.4 *Argentina EMBI + and banking sector deposits, January 2001–October 2001*

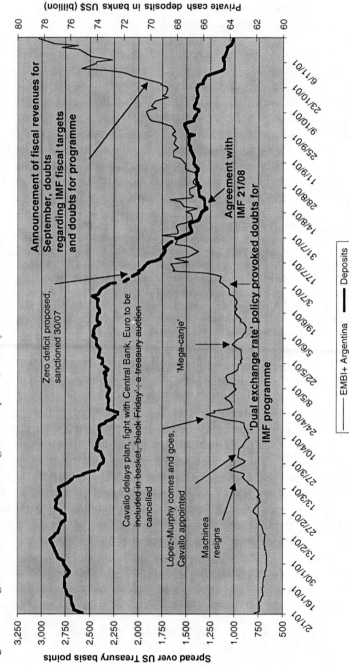

part regarding the promises made to the IMF. This resulted in the March 2001 resignation of Economy Minister Luis Machinea and then, only a few days later, of his replacement Ricardo López-Murphy who was himself replaced by Domingo Cavallo after only a very short term in office. Announced policy oscillated wildly from the orthodox fiscal rectitude of López-Murphy to the heterodoxy of Cavallo. Cavallo's policies included the introduction of the euro into the currency basket against which the peso was pegged, subsidies to particular industries and a relaxation of banking regulations. The resultant uncertainty was heightened by the eventual departure of Central Bank President, Pedro Pou, after a 'political inquiry' that was widely regarded as undermining the Central Bank's legal independence. Country risk soared to over 1,000 basis points over US Treasuries.

The decision of President de la Rúa not to support the López-Murphy fiscal adjustment package may be seen as having marked the political limit to fiscal adjustment through cutting nominal expenditure. In my opinion, a relatively modest fiscal adjustment might well have sufficed to restore confidence at that time.

However, in the language of the repeated game outlined above, the country had reached its limit with respect to 'Safe' policies. With the $40 billion IMF-sponsored *blindaje* in place, but the real economy still not responding and default probabilities rising, the incentives were in place to deviate to a more Risky strategy – to attempt to 'get the economy moving'. This Risky strategy consisted of relaxing banking regulations, the introduction of subsidies aimed at particular sectors of the economy, the proposal to include the euro in the currency board peg and the subsequent introduction of a *de facto* dual exchange rate through a set of subsidies and tariffs based on the dollar–euro exchange rate.

With country risk soaring to over 1,000 basis points in April, the IMF also had a decision to make. The choice was between support for Argentina by strongly restating its commitment to the *blindaje* and essentially saying that the private markets were wrong, or withdrawal on the basis that it disagreed with the sacking of López-Murphy and the subsequent change in course in Argentina's economic policy (see figure 13.4). In fact the IMF did neither. The perception from Buenos Aires was that the IMF vacillated.

It is clear that, with the country having deviated to Risky play, the IMF was caught precisely as represented in the payoffs to the non-cooperative, one-shot game discussed above. On the one hand, the IMF was surely uneasy continuing to support a country following a set of policies that the Fund did not support (see Mussa, chapter 12 in this volume). On the other hand, the Fund was most definitely aware that if it withdrew support then this might very well provoke a private sector run and almost certain default and devaluation. As represented in the one-shot game, there is no pure-strategy equilibrium to this game and, with no cooperative solution available, vacillation was indeed the equilibrium response!

The game above also contains a highly stylistic interaction between the decisions of the IMF and the private sector. This suggested interaction is amply backed up by the Argentine case. In Buenos Aires, each new policy announcement was analysed in detail from the standpoint of whether this would, finally, create a rupture with the IMF or whether the IMF would continue to support. The importance of this cannot be over-stated as a common view at the time was that if the IMF withdrew then this would create the conditions for a run on the banks and hence that source of financing for the government would be eliminated.

The announcement of the *de facto* dual exchange rate regime in July 2001 was, for many, the final straw that could have provoked the withdrawal of the IMF. If the IMF had indeed interpreted the measure as a dual exchange rate then it might have been very difficult to maintain support (see Mussa, chapter 12 in this volume). As it turned out, the Argentine authorities argued successfully that it was not a dual exchange rate, as the policy operated through export subsidies and import tariffs, but the speculation regarding the withdrawal of the Fund was enough to create the conditions for a run on the banks in July and August.

This bank run was very clearly arrested by the final IMF package signed in August 2001. This package came as a surprise to many. In the spirit of the repeated game above it simply reflected the IMF's mixed-strategy play. The sequence of speculation regarding IMF withdrawal, bank run and then IMF Assistance and the bank run being stopped backs up very clearly indeed the stylised assumptions regarding the dependence of private sector decisions on IMF action in the model and the 'coordinating' role of the IMF. Finally the Fund did indeed withdraw support and that withdrawal did indeed help to create the conditions for a final major run on the banks of November 2001. This run sparked the banking controls that helped to bring down the de la Rúa government and subsequent default and devaluation.

It can be argued that a 'game' between the IMF and Argentina, similar to that depicted above, continues today (May 2002). Indeed, at the time of writing the Argentine authorities are actively seeking assistance from the IMF and other multilaterals. Presidents Bush and Aznar and other world leaders have asked Argentina to present a 'sustainable plan' indicating implicitly that (only) if such a plan were forthcoming from Buenos Aires would international assistance become available. President Duhalde's reply was that in his opinion only with international assistance would a plan from Buenos Aires be sustainable. President Duhalde's remark is no doubt based on the view that the private sector will fail to have confidence and invest unless an agreement with the IMF is in place. However, if international assistance is given up-front, then the IMF most likely calculates that Argentine politicians will have reduced incentives to carry through the required reforms.

In other words, with Assistance comes Moral Hazard but if no Assistance is forthcoming, the Argentine government believes that it is impossible to stop the private sector from running further. The authorities are then caught between the negative effects of the banking sector controls and the fear that lifting them, with no IMF agreement in place, might create a run on the currency and very significant monetary instability. The continuing lack of a pure-strategy equilibrium is then still evident. Moreover, now that Assistance has been withdrawn and the 'punishment' of the mixed strategy has been dissipated, it appears very difficult indeed to regain the cooperative First Best outcome. Unfortunately, Argentina may have to resolve this crisis on its own, such that it has something to lose to make the removal of IMF support a tangible punishment before the First Best is once again supported.

What might have been different if a bankruptcy procedure for countries had existed? Following the arguments above, for such a procedure to be effective, the country should have preferred that alternative rather than deviating to the Risky strategy in the first half of 2001. If this route had been taken, then the bank runs of July and November, and the build-up of public sector debt within the domestic banking system that occurred during 2001, might have been avoided. Arguably, more Argentine debt might have remained with foreigners (who effectively transferred debt to Argentine residents through 2001) and it is possible that a default might have then created more contagion. However, the debt would have been widely held and it is unlikely that this would have been a serious problem. The main point is that had domestic institutions been stronger at the time of default the new economic direction of the country could have been developed from a much stronger position. As it happened, the weakening of the banking system through 2001, the banking system runs the banking controls and the asymmetric pesification created large redistributions and losses which remain to date the source of considerable friction and are preventing a final resolution of the crisis. It does seem that a more managed process would have been highly beneficial in managing the default and securing a more rapid recovery.

6 Conclusions

In this chapter I have focused on the role of the IMF in countries facing international payments difficulties. I have suggested that the two main opposing schools of thought on this role – namely, the moral hazard school and the liquidity school – are both correct and moreover that they are both correct simultaneously. Unfortunately, this implies – and this is the main argument of the chapter – that the role of the Fund is an extremely difficult one, as a one-shot game between the Fund, the country and the private sector appears to have no pure-strategy equilibrium. The Fund cannot give unconditional support without generating moral hazard but if it does not give support the coordination problem within the private sector may lead to a 'run' and a liquidity crisis (on top of any fundamental problems). The only Nash equilibrium in a one-shot game is with the Fund hedging its bets by unpredictably giving support and the country then, only with some probability, adopting a 'Safe' policy.

However, in a simple repeated game framework, it may be possible for cooperation to develop. In particular the IMF can offer the First Best (where the IMF Assists, the country plays Safe and the private sector Lends), but threaten that if the country deviates to Risky play then the result will be the Nash (mixed-strategy) equilibrium thereafter. Under this view, a country should not deviate unless the country's discount factor is too low.

In a discussion linking the results of this simple game to the recent discussions on PSI, a number of conclusions emerge. First, there is a view that multilateral funds, for bailouts, should be strictly limited. On the one hand, this runs the risk of creating the conditions for a private sector Run. However, the policy might be rationalised in the repeated game version of the game as this may reduce the welfare of the country in the Nash (mixed-strategy) equilibrium and hence permit the IMF to inflict greater punishment and hence create a greater chance of the First Best being supported.

It is also argued that in the one-shot game, introducing collective-action clauses in bond contracts may simply ensure that the only equilibrium is the mixed-strategy one – or, if default if made much less costly, may even imply that the Worst Case (of no IMF Assistance, Risky country play and the private sector Running) becomes a pure-strategy equilibrium. However, interestingly collective-action clauses may be rationalised in the repeated game framework. Surprisingly, perhaps, if we assume that the introduction of such clauses reduces the pain of countries from playing Risky and the IMF not Assisting (the outcome where default is most likely), then this reduces the (*ex ante*) welfare of the country in the Nash (mixed-strategy) equilibrium and hence allows the IMF to impose greater punishment. Hence there is again a greater chance of the First Best being supported.

However, a close analysis of the repeated game shows that as the probability of default rises at some point the country will have the incentive to deviate to Risky play. This implies that countries will generally deviate before they default. This problem will not, it seems, be solved by attempting to make international assistance more rule-bound or by introducing collective-action clauses.

However, the introduction of a bankruptcy procedure as a new potential action for the country, that is slightly preferred by the country than deviation to the Risky strategy, just at the point where otherwise the country would deviate, might provide the best potential solution to this problem. The bankruptcy procedure should not, of course, otherwise be more attractive for the country than the First Best. This approach may yield some bounds to the attractiveness or pain that such a bankruptcy procedure should entail for an unfortunate country in such a desperate position.

A review of the role of the IMF in Argentina serves to illustrate many of these issues. While the chapter remains agnostic with respect to the causes of the crisis, there was clearly a failure to find an orderly solution to Argentina's external debt problem. While this has not appeared to create significant international financial contagion, it has led to a very severe crisis in Argentina and led to a set of questions regarding the role of the IMF.

The interpretation offered here is that, at the start of 2001, default was not inevitable. Indeed, let us assume that Argentina was trying to implement Safe policies at the time and the Fund was assisting consistent with the First Best. However, having secured IMF Assistance at the end of 2000, Argentina adopted a set of more Risky policies to the displeasure of the Fund – largely in an attempt to get the economy moving. Around May 2001, country risk had risen to 1,000 basis points and the IMF had a decision to make: support the country strongly, implicitly saying that the markets were wrong, or withdraw. The perception from Buenos Aires was that the Fund vacillated. The IMF was caught between continuing support for a country adopting a set of policies it became increasingly uncomfortable with (moral hazard) and the knowledge that if it withdrew support then it would provoke a Run from the private sector that would most certainly herald the default that Argentina was trying to avoid. This is precisely the structure of payoffs in the (one-shot) model presented and the equilibrium play is then in mixed strategies – vacillation. The Fund finally did withdraw its support, and that most certainly was an important factor in triggering the run from the banking sector and from Argentine bonds pushing country risk from levels of around 1,400 basis points to over 3,000 in November 2001.

While the Argentine crisis was most certainly home-bred, deriving from a mixture of bad luck (negative shocks), required adjustment of the current account and the fiscal accounts and bad politics, the crisis also serves to show the dilemma facing the IMF in these situations. Criticisms of the particular policies of the various decision-makers in the IMF at the time appear to miss the point. More importantly, there is a need to analyse more carefully the nature of the underlying game. As discussed extensively above, the interaction of moral hazard plus the severe private sector coordination problem makes the role of the IMF an extremely delicate one.

Unfortunately, the one-shot game appears to be one with no pure-strategy equilibrium and a cooperative solution to the repeated game is likely to break down as default approaches – at least given the current institutional arrangements and standard financial contracts. Some creative thinking is required to give countries in such unfortunate situations an alternative that does not constitute a 'bail out' for private sector creditors, that protects countries from the excesses of liquidity type 'runs' and that gives, as far as possible, incentives for countries to maintain safer policies that will ensure a more rapid recovery after default.

REFERENCES

Binmore, K. (1992). 'Fun and Games: A Text on Game Theory'. Lexington, MA, D.C. Heath

Calvo, E. and Abal Medina J. M. (eds.) (2001). 'El federalismo electoral argentino', INEP-Eudeba, Buenos Aires

Dooley, M. P. (2000). 'Can Output Losses Following International Financial Crises be Avoided?', NBER Working Paper, 256–72

Dooley, M. P. and S. Verma (2003). 'Rescue Packages and Output Losses Following Crises', in M. P. Dooley and J. A. Frannel (eds.), *Managing Currency Crises in Emerging Economies*, Chicago, University of Chicago Press

Eichengreen, B. and C. Ruhl (2000). 'The Bail-In Problem: Systematic Goals, ad hoc Means', NBER Working Paper, 7653

Fischer, S. (1999). 'On the Need for an International Lender of Last Resort', *Journal of Economic Perspectives*, 13(4), 85–104

Fudenberg, D. and E. Maskin (1986). 'The Folk Theorem in Repeated Games with Imperfect Public Information Discounting or with Incomplete Information', *Econometrica*, 54, 533–56.

Gavin, M. and A. Powell (1998). 'Domestic and International Lender of Last Resort: Constructive Ambiguity and Cheap Talk', Central Bank of Argentina, mimeo

    (1999). 'Should the International Lender of Resort be Privitized?', Central Bank of Argentina, mimeo

Gai, P., S. Hayes and H. Shin Song (2001). 'Crisis Costs and Debtor Discipline: The Efficiency of Public Policy in Sovereign Debt Crises', Bank of England Working Paper, 136

Haldane, A. and M. Krug (2000). 'The Resolution of International Financial Crises: Private Finance and Public Funds', available at www.bankofengland.co.uk

Krueger, A. (2003). 'The Need to Improve the Resolution of Financial Crises: An Emerging Consensus', Address to the Harvard University Business School's Finance Club, Boston, 27 March 2003; available at www.imf.org

Powell, A. (2003). 'Argentina's Avoidable Crisis: Bad Luck, Bad Economics, Bad Politics, Bad Advice', in Brookings Trade Forum 2002, Washington, DC, Brookings Institute

Roubini, N. (2000). 'Bail In, Burden Sharing, Private Sector Involvement in Crisis Resolution and Constructive Engagement of the Private Sector. A Primer: Evolving Definitions, Doctrine, Practice and Case Law', Stern School of Business, New York University, mimeo

14 Accountability, governance and the reform of the IMF

NGAIRE WOODS

1 Introduction

To be effective, the IMF and its activities must be transparent to the public, accountable to its members, and responsive to the lessons of experience and outside evaluation. (G7 Communiqué, 15 April 2000)

Over the 1990s, in an effort to improve both its effectiveness and its public image, the IMF began to take steps to make itself more transparent, more accountable and more participatory. This chapter investigates how accountable the institution has become and what 'accountability' might and should mean for an international institution such as the IMF. Curiously, although great strides have been made in improving transparency and in better understanding concepts of participation and ownership in the implementation of the institution's programmes, a rigorous definition and concept of 'accountability' has been slow to emerge. Indeed, most contemporary proposals for the reform of the institutions use the term regularly without ever developing who should be accountable to whom and for what.

Section 2 of the chapter discusses why accountability is now so prominently on the agenda and why the traditional structure of the IMF no longer meets expectations as to how accountable the institution should be. Section 3 examines the demands of new actors to hold the institution better to account, focusing in particular on the rise of non-governmental organisations (NGOs) and their engagement with the IMF. Section 4 critically examines the role of the United States in reforming the Fund and evaluates the recommendations of the Meltzer Commission. Section 5 examines how we might more rigorously consider the flaws and solutions to improving the accountability of the IMF, analysing the

With many thanks to Christopher Gilbert, Devesh Kapur and Stephan Haggard for their extremely helpful comments on an earlier draft of this chapter.

steps already being taken in the IMF. Conclusions are offered in the final section 6.

2 Why rethink the accountability of the IMF?

Accountability has sprung onto the agenda of global governance for three interrelated reasons. First the demands of globalisation have foisted *new roles* on international institutions. As other chapters in this volume demonstrate, the IMF is no exception. Since the debt crisis of the 1980s the institution has expanded its role and the breadth of its conditionality so as to affect a wider range of people, groups, and organisations than ever before. One result has been to create *new actors* demanding a voice and a capacity to hold the institution to account. The demands of these new actors reflect *heightened expectations* about public institutions and accountability which form a third driving force for change. An increase in global communication and political activity, alongside a wave of national and international democratisation, has fuelled expectations about public and global institutions and placed them under unprecedented scrutiny. A spotlight has been cast onto the IMF, revealing a number of inadequacies in its core structure – now some fifty years old and in need of review.

At its creation, the accountability of the IMF probably reasonably matched its functions and structure. It was created as a mutual organisation coordinating exchange rates and offering assistance for temporary balance of payments difficulties. It was not a development agency using the resources of wealthy countries for development in poorer countries. Its mandate did not require extensive policy advice or engagement with wider society within member countries. As a monetary coordinating agency, the IMF dealt (as its articles of agreement provide) with the Treasury, Central Bank or other fiscal agency of member countries. Likewise, each member was represented (whether directly or indirectly) on the governing boards of the Fund by officials from these agencies. This structure remains in place today.

In theory, all member governments can hold the IMF to account through the Board of Governors which meets once a year and gives broad guidance, or through the Executive Board which supervises day-to-day operations of the agency. This structure ostensibly holds to account the staff and management of the organisation. However, several serious flaws in this form of representative accountability have emerged over time.

First, the Executive Board of the IMF is no longer adequately representative. The membership of the IMF has trebled, leaving most countries indirectly represented even when the Board is directly discussing programmes immediatly affecting them. The only countries directly represented on the Executive Board are China, France, Germany, Japan, Russia, Saudi Arabia, the United Kingdom, and United States, all other countries are grouped in constituencies which elect one Executive Director whom any one government cannot subsequently dismiss or replace (unlike the governments enjoying direct representation). This means that most national governments have only the weakest link to the formal deliberations and decision-making processes of the institutions. For example, twenty-one anglophone African countries are represented by one Executive Director and an Alternate Director.

Further exacerbating the lack of voice of many members of the IMF is the fact that voting power on the Boards of the institutions is unequal, and indeed has become more unequal over time. Originally, steps were taken to ensure some equality among members by allocating each member an equal number of 'basic votes' (Gold, 1972, pp. 18, 173–4; Horsefield, 1996). In 1955, these 'basic votes' comprised 14 per cent of all votes, yet today they comprise only about 3 per cent of votes in the Fund. The twenty-one African countries mentioned above collectively have a voting share of 3.26 per cent.

The unequal voting power of members is calculated according to a 'quota' determined by formulae which attempt to translate relative weight in the world economy into a share of contributions, votes and access to resources. The determination of quotas is (and always has been) a highly politicised process – as reflected in discussions ensuing from the review of quota formulae in 2000 – (IMF, 2000; Jadhav, 2000; Van Houtven, 2001). In addition to a lack of voting power, many of the smaller and poorer members of the IMF have little capacity to exercise informal influence throughout the institution through lobbying, independent research and policy advocacy.

A second major flaw in the accountability structure of the IMF is the weakness of the Executive Board in holding staff and management to account. In part this is due to the demands placed on Executive Directors who face a daunting number of country programmes, technical issues and policy decisions about which they must brief themselves and prepare statements. This problem is magnified where Executive Directors are in the job for only a short time. However, equally if not more limiting of the role of the Executive Board is the approach of the staff and management. Here we find that internal disagreements are seldom divulged to the Board; rather, staff and management tend to attach 'considerable importance' to presenting a unified view in Board discussions. This dynamic was underscored by an external evaluation taken of the IMF's surveillance function (IMF, 1999, p. 34).

A final very obvious flaw in the IMF's accountability is the lack of an open and transparent process of appointment for the senior management of the organisation. The present procedure embodies neither a guarantee of political representation nor of technical excellence. Rather a fifty-year-old political compromise means that the Managing Director is appointed according to the wishes of Western European members and the Deputy Managing Director according to US preferences (Kapur, 2000; Kahler, 2001). Following the fiasco of the last appointment where Germany's first favoured candidate failed to win support from other major shareholders, a Committee was established to review the procedure. However, it would seem that little change is in the offing since neither the US nor European members can agree to give up their special privilege in this regard.

The problems of accountability highlighted above have all been magnified by the increase and transformation of the IMF's activities. The institution is no longer only engaged in monitoring exchange rates and other specific macroeconomic policy targets. Rather it engages in negotiations with member governments which cover virtually all issues of economic policy-making – and indeed beyond, including 'good governance' standards for the rule of law, judicial reform, corporate governance, and so forth. This new wide-ranging domain of advice and conditionality means that decisions undertaken by the IMF directly affect (and demand compliance from) a new range of policies, people, groups and organisations within member countries.

Yet the IMF was not created, nor structured, to undertake nor to be accountable for such wide-ranging activities. It was created to deal with a narrow, clearly stipulated range of technical issues. For this reason, its constitution stipulates that it must deal with member countries only through their Treasury, Central Bank or other fiscal agency. In turn, this means that the IMF is making these agencies formally accountable for policies which should properly lie within the scope of other agencies, and for which those other agencies are domestically accountable. A policy affecting subsidies or distribution in healthcare, for example, we would expect to be the responsibility of the Minister of Health whom we could expect to be answerable to voters and his or her society at large. Yet, as the Fund has intruded further into these kinds of decisions it has created formal and enforceable lines of accountability with the Finance Ministry or Central Bank which over-ride other agencies and local or democratic accountability.[1]

A further implication of the new wider ambit of Fund programmes negotiated through the Finance Ministry or Central Bank is that domestic political struggles become distorted. In theory, different agencies within government compete for and debate competing priorities and goals. However, where Fund conditionality affects these priorities it can heavily sway these debates, subjecting broad areas of policy to the narrower focus, priorities and analysis of the Central Bank and Finance Ministry – even though neither necessarily have the desire, mandate, accountability, nor expertise to evaluate and formulate policy

---

[1] Of course, the external line of accountability does not always produce the outcomes desired by the international leading agencies, as argued by Paul Collier (1999).

in respect of these broader issues. In a subtle way, this point is underscored by a remark in the External Evaluation into IMF Surveillance, where the evaluators found that 'the most favourable appraisals came from those whose lines of work bore close similarities to the Fund's – Central Banks, and, to a lesser extent, finance ministries' (IMF, 1999, p. 35). Turned on its head, this statement emphasises the degree to which the Fund's core mandate remains that shared with central bankers. Yet at the same time, the institution is now formulating directions for policy in areas outside of this formal mandate and expertise. In so doing Fund staff are attempting to broaden consultations and contacts within member countries even though formal lines of accountability remain fixed. This in itself, however, is not without additional problems of accountability for the institution.

3 The inclusion of new actors in the work of the IMF

The IMF has always had significant (even if not formal) relations with private sector actors. In recent years it has begun to foster relations with another group of non-state actors: non-governmental organisations (NGOs). In part this is because the IMF now faces grassroots NGOs claiming to represent people whose lives and livelihoods are being directly affected by its actions and policies. In part it is also because the institution needs the compliance of these actors if Fund policies and programmes are to be successfully implemented within countries.

At the global level the Fund has also become porous to new actors. Transnational advocacy NGOs have injected their concerns as to particular principles, values, future generations and other factors which they believe are not otherwise adequately expressed or debated in the international system. Global environmental protection serves as one example, poverty reduction is another. These transnational NGOs argue that they must be heard at the global level because national-level politics is so often over-ridden by the new intrusiveness of international organisations.

Various international economic organisations have responded to these claims by taking steps towards including or consulting with NGOs more regularly. At the same time, robust arguments have been made within the IMF for keeping NGOs out. The core traditional argument is that all member states are already represented in the governing boards of the organisations. The appropriate place for NGOs lies in domestic political debate. To open any international institution up to special-interest pleading would erode the legitimacy and interstate structure of the organisations. Curiously, the same arguments could (and perhaps should) be voiced in respect of private sector actors, yet they are not.

It is worth noting that in reality the scope for NGO activity in the IMF has increased, but it is both partial and limited. Executive Board members and staff within the Fund now consult with lobbying organisations in Washington, DC, with grassroots organisations in member countries, trade unions, church groups, and such like. These contacts are taking place at regional, country and local levels. IMF resident representatives are being told to seek out and maintain such contacts. At the annual and spring meetings the institution has been actively involved in more dialogue and meetings with a select group of transnational NGOs.

In addition to these measures which increase transparency and consultation towards certain kinds of NGOs, the IMF (and World Bank) have also opened up participation by non-state actors at the local level, such as in the poverty-reduction strategy paper process (PRSP) which requires countries seeking enhanced debt relief to consult nationally in formulating strategies for poverty reduction.

Two kinds of problem emerge in respect of accountability, given this new relationship between the Fund and NGOs. These problems relate to whom the NGOs represent and to whom they are accountable. The issues are somewhat different in respect of engagement with local grassroots NGOs and transnational advocacy organisations.

Local or Southern NGOs are stakeholders in Fund policies in a fairly straight-forward sense of the term where they represent groups directly affected by the new more intrusive programmes and policies of the international economic organisations. Indeed the agencies themselves recognise this, putting great emphasis on the need to ensure ownership and participation by such local groups if their programmes are to be effective. Broadly put, to fulfil its new role the Fund now realises it needs to win the hearts and minds of people, not just persuade governments to sign agreements.

The resulting relations being developed with local NGOs introduce questions such as how and with which local NGOs does the IMF choose to work, to whom are they accountable and with what implications for local politics and accountability. Ideally, the actions of international economic institutions should work through and reinforce local mechanisms of accountability. However, local accountability may or may not be improved by using NGOs. There are some instances where using NGOs bypasses government institutions and in so doing risks thwarting 'institution-building', 'state modernisation', and indeed, even democratisation itself, particularly in fragile democratising states (Abugre and Alexander, 1998).

Nonetheless, the vociferous debate about NGOs and their lack of accountability risks being over-played in the context of local NGOs. Certainly they now have access to more information: and transparency is a powerful step towards holding governments and institutions accountable. NGOs are also, with government approval, consulted more regularly. However, even with the new inspection procedures of the World Bank and IFC/MIGA where local NGOs now have access to new complaints procedures, they have not effected a transfer of decision-making power or substantial influence. This might be contrasted to the much greater influence that has been gained by Northern NGOs. Indeed, it has been argued that local NGOs and their governments should work together more effectively so as to counter the growing power of Northern NGOs (Abugre and Alexander, 1998).

Most transnational NGOs do not claim to be directly representative of local peoples affected by international institutions. Rather, they set out to represent and uphold concerns, principles and standards which affect such groups. If we ask to whom transnational NGOs are accountable, the answer lies in: their membership (actual and potential and predominantly Northern); their major funders and/or clients (which may include governments and corporations); and their NGO or 'local' partners (some of which may be in developing countries). It is probably fair to say that most Northern-based NGOs are primarily (and formally) accountable to their membership and funders. For this reason, a long-standing concern about these NGOs is that their activities further magnify the voice and influence of industrialised countries' peoples and governments in international debates and institutions which already disproportionately represent the industrialised world. The fact that 87 per cent of the 738 NGOs accredited to the Ministerial Conference of the WTO in Seattle were based in industrialised countries gives some substance to this concern.

The difficulty for critics is that while the work of many NGOs has undoubtedly magnified the influence of already powerful constituencies, they have also used their influence with the US government (both Congress and the Executive) and other G7 governments, effectively to campaign for greater transparency, disclosure and new forms of accountability which are of interest to all stakeholders (see below). That said, however, there is a legitimate fear here that in further exhausting the little time key policy-makers within the international economic institutions have for consultations, these NGOs are yet further closing-out the opportunities for smaller developing countries to have input. A broader lesson to be drawn highlights the dangers of simply opening up to NGOs without considering issues of accountability more rigorously. As has been argued in a World Bank Working Paper, 'enhancing participation' will not necessarily ensure that disempowered stakeholders acquire a voice. Rather it can simply magnify the voice of those who are already powerful within domestic institutions (Viera da Cunha and Junho Pena, 1998).

In summary, some NGOs have acquired more of a voice in the IMF. However, none has acquired a formal participatory role in decision-making. This remains the preserve of national governments who can, of course, choose to permit their own NGOs to take up such a role. Transnational NGOs have sought and succeeded in gaining more of a place in informal consultations with the IMF and they have secured this place by their successful campaigning for more transparency and information from the organisation. The question of which NGOs are gaining influence as a result of these reforms and what that infers for accountability requires ongoing scrutiny, and will be further discussed below.

4 The role of the United States in reform and the report of the Meltzer Commission

The member government to whom the IMF is most accountable is undoubtedly the United States. This is not only due to the fact that the United States has the largest share of voting power within the organisation. It is also because the institution is situated at the heart of US government in Washington, DC, its staff are mainly US-trained and the United States pours significant resources into its representation and advocacy in the IMF. Further enhancing the influence of the United States is the fact that other members of the institution, and its staff and management, actively court the favour of the US Executive and Congress. These attributes give the United States a disproportionate capacity (compared to all other members) to hold the organisation to account, as illustrated in the 1997 Eleventh Quota Review. In those negotiations, the US Congress, with no consultation with other governments, succeeded in setting down unilateral terms for change in the IMF in return for a quota increase (Locke, 2000).

One specific aspect of the late 1990s US Congressional negotiations on increasing the Fund's resources was the establishment of a Commission in November 1998 to consider the future roles and structures of the IMF, the World Bank and other institutions. The subsequent Meltzer Commission Report focused heavily on improving the accountability of the agencies, listing among its five core aims no less than three which deal with accountability:

(2) increasing transparency of aims, decisions, and financial statements, and accountability for achievements and effectiveness
(3) relying more on incentives and local decision-making and much less on programmes and conditions imposed by multilateral agencies
(5) increasing incentives for institutional reform, expansion of markets, and prompt provision of reliable information about economic, financial, and political changes.

This report is worth further consideration for it highlights important contradictions and problems within the approach of US NGOs and government towards accountability (see also chapter 4 in this volume).

The Commission made several direct criticisms of the IMF's accountability. Overall it argues that the governance structure of the IMF makes it insufficiently independent to pursue *bona fide* economic objectives and insulates it from proper accountability: 'the IMF's management and oversight board are not distinct, its deliberations are not public, and formal votes are rare. If the G7 finance ministers can agree on a policy that they wish to pursue, for whatever reason, they can use the IMF as the instrument of that policy' (IFIAC, 2000, p. 40).

Two things are highlighted in this analysis. First, as this chapter has already argued, the existing structure of a representative Executive Board does not adequately hold the institution to account. Secondly, the G7 have such controlling influence in the organisation that they can use it as an instrument of their own policies. This point is correct and highlights the need for greater developing country voice, voting power and capacity to hold the institution to account. Yet the ensuing discussion of the Meltzer Commission proposes no remedies for this. Rather it focuses on further cementing the ways in which US policy-makers might hold the institution to account, highlighting for example that the use of the IMF has 'bypassed the appropriations process in the US Congress and foreign parliaments, a process that is the centerpiece of democratic government' (IFIAC, 2000, p. 28). The problem here is that a further emphasis on the accountability of the IMF towards the US Congress and parliaments of other G7 countries is likely to further exacerbate the core problem of the institution's inadequate accountability to its most affected developing country members.

In respect of developing countries, the report argues that the IMF has 'undermined national sovereignty and often hindered the development of responsible, democratic institutions that correct their own mistakes and respond to changes in external conditions' (IFIAC, 2000, p. 30). Furthermore, the IMF permits particular policy-makers to exact concessions from their legislatures, shifting power in a way which distorts the constitutionally established system of checks and balances (IFIAC, 2000, p. 38). These are strongly made points and again echo arguments already made in this chapter. Not only does the IMF's representative structure inadequately permit developing countries to hold the institution to account, its work within developing countries erodes the capacity of local actors to hold policy-makers to account. Yet the Commission recommends little to deal with this specific problem.

The Commission makes a number of recommendations in respect of the transparency of IMF governance. For example, the Report proposes reform of the Fund's accounting procedures and publication of full details of IMF assistance to each country as well as of article IV consultation reports. These measures are already ongoing and undoubtedly enhance the extent of information available to stakeholders about the work of the staff and management of the institution. Further to this, the Commission recommends the taking and recording of votes at Executive Board meetings and the publication of summaries of meetings after a reasonable lag. This proposal will be further discussed below and would undoubtedly enhance the accountability of the institution to people living within its member countries, making more information available about what government representatives were doing within the IFIs. Such proposals have been made by other eminent commentators on the IMF (De Gregorio *et al.*, 1999).

Curiously in respect of the flaws in representative accountability of the IMF, the Report not only proposes little remedy but if anything proposes to exacerbate the deepest flaws. The analysis of the Commission highlights failures on the part of both the IMF and the World Bank to take into account governments, peoples and societies within developing countries. Yet the Report makes no proposals to redress the imbalance in the representation of developing countries within the IMF which leaves the US and other G7 countries with commanding influence. Nor does the Report propose ways in which developing country governments and societies could have more input into the formulation of IMF-backed policy proposals or hold the institution better to account. Rather the Report advocates that its own unilateralist agenda towards the IMF be adopted and that the United States uses its power within the organisation further to alter and reduce the IMF's role.

The contradiction within the overall recommendations for the IMF is apparent when we consider that the Commission did not consult developing countries affected by the IMF in formulating its recommendations. The proposal reflects the Commission's genesis as a creation of the US Congress. It rightly (in those terms) reflects the views and interests of a US constituency. However, as such it is on weak ground proposing that certain measures ought to be imposed on other countries. In so doing the Commission underscores the problems of accountability which its own analysis highlights. If the Meltzer Commission proposals were to be foisted on the IMF, this would impose on developing countries measures which did not enjoy the uncoerced agreement of legislatures nor the participation, consultation and ownership of recipient countries which the Report calls for.

The failure to consider more deeply how to remedy these gaps is one which runs through much of the literature on reforming the IMF. In large part this undoubtedly reflects the political obstacles which confront any change in the distribution of power within the institution: states are loath to give up power or privilege in their international relations. The frustrated efforts to reform how the Managing Director is selected (mentioned above) are a testimony to these obstacles. Nevertheless, there are other ways in which the IMF can and is being made more accountable.

5 Critically rethinking how to make the IMF more accountable

This chapter has argued that until recently the IMF's claim to being an accountable institution has been based heavily on its constitutional limits and its representative governing boards. The Constitution of the organisation – its articles of agreement – has ostensibly limited its activities, setting out and de-limiting its structure, main objectives and functions. However, as argued above, this has not prevented a huge expansion in the role of the institution. The Board of Governors and the Executive Board of the organisation are supposed to en-sure that member governments enjoy oversight and overall control. Yet, as also argued above, serious flaws have emerged in this form of representative ac-countability in an organisation whose role has been expanded and transformed. This underlines the core questions as to whom and how the IMF might be accountable.

This chapter has already alluded to the arguments for throwing open the doors to as many new actors and participants as possible. This might loosely be referred to as 'democratising the IMF'. A plethora of NGOs, independent experts and other non-state actors would all gladly step more closely into the deliberations and work of the institution. Critics of such a move argue that the IMF has been efficient and successful precisely because it has been a small, tightly disciplined organisation, contrasting the Fund with the more diffuse, unwieldy and thereby (in their terms) inefficient agencies of the United Na-tions (and, indeed, the World Bank). Certainly it is true that increasing par-ticipation and enhancing accountability incurs costs: both in terms of budget and in terms of efficiency. These costs are too often overlooked by reform-ers. However, it is also true that the IMF's *modus operandi* can no longer be assumed to be maximally efficient and effective. Indeed, several aspects of it have been put into question by the institution itself in a search for greater impact and success in promulgating and ensuring policy reform in member countries. In seeking to improve the performance of the institution, concepts such as greater participation and ownership are now running rife throughout the organisation.

In terms of accountability we need carefully to consider the issue of partici-pation. Participation does not necessarily ensure more or better accountability. As mentioned above, enhancing participation might well simply magnify the voice and capacity to hold to account of those who are already controlling the organisation. Furthermore, opening up the doors to increasing participation does not necessarily ensure that policy-makers are held to account for specific processes, advice or outcomes. This fact is highlighted in debates about the role of elections in holding governments to account. It is often assumed that politi-cians and officials in democracies are held accountable by direct elections. However, the evidence shows that citizens rarely use their votes to sanction officials for abuse, neglect, or incompetence (or, indeed, to reward the oppo-site). Rather voters often use elections to express party loyalty or enthusiasm for a future set of policies (Przeworski, Stokes and Manin, 1999). Further-more, voters seldom have the requisite information or capacity to follow up information they do have. In the words of one scholar, the control of politicians by voters faces 'problems of information, monitoring, and commitment' (Maravall, 1999). For these reasons, elections and representative politics on their own are not adequate forms of accountability within national political systems.

At the international level, representation is yet less direct and participation is even more partial. Indeed, even if every government in the world were democratically elected, it would not follow that their voters had a capacity to hold them to account for pushing or supporting particular policies in the IMF. Gaps in information and access to the informal debates and lobbies within the institution further exacerbate these problems. However, this does not mean that the IMF cannot be more accountable. Rather, it means we must examine other forms of accountability alongside changes in its formal representative structure.

The most useful examples to examine are the ways governments are held accountable at the national level. There are several kinds of institutions which can ensure that political actions are predictable, non-arbitrary and procedurally fair, that decision-makers are answerable, and that rules and parameters on the exercise of power are enforced. This kind of accountability is sometimes referred to as 'horizontal accountability' (Schedler, Diamond and Plattner, 1999). In domestic politics courts, ombudsmen and other agencies assume some of these tasks. For example, judges may play a role in reviewing official decisions, overturning them, or sanctioning the officials responsible. Legal action can be taken against public officials proffering professional judgements without due diligence. Media exposure, public debate, parliamentary scrutiny and checks and balances with the agencies of government all play some role.

A clear prerequisite for these forms of horizontal accountability to be effective is information and some degree of transparency: public officials or agencies must provide information about their actions and decisions, as well as justifications to the public and to any relevant specialised agencies to whom they must account. Equally important in ensuring the accountability of public officials are ongoing processes to monitor compliance and enforce the limits, rules and norms which circumscribe the exercise of official power.

This approach to accountability gives us a useful yardstick to measure many of the contemporary reforms which are being undertaken in the IMF and proposed by other academics (see Bradlow, 2001). It highlights the importance of information and transparency, monitoring and enforcement in ensuring accountability, and in these areas several important steps have been made as the institution has come to recognise the need: 'to provide accountability to the organisation's shareholders and the public for the results of its activities in the absence of market criteria by which to measure its effectiveness' (IMF, 2001).

Improvements in transparency

Transparency refers to the recording, reporting and publishing of information about the processes, decisions and outcomes of the institution. Although it is a cornerstone of accountability, the IMF has long expressed strong reasons for limiting transparency. The reasons have included the need to protect proprietary or confidential information, the costs of publishing extensive information and a belief that openness would adversely affect decision-making processes – for example, by entrenching people in particular positions that they have to account for afterwards to those they represent outside the walls of the meeting.

Many of the objections to greater transparency have been gradually waning in the IMF as previously perceived dangers have been recognised as over-stated. Indeed, when one compares the information the IMF now makes available to that of a decade ago it is not an exaggeration to say that a revolution has occurred. Where previously most of the institution's documentation was inaccessible to anyone outside the walls of the institution, the Fund now publishes most of its research and a substantial amount of documentation regarding its work with individual countries on its website. At the same time, the IMF is now pressing government members to permit greater disclosure and publication of policies and agreements made with the IMF (which are confidential if the government so wishes). The results of these changes include the publication of information such as Public Information Notices (PINs) following about 80 per cent of the IMF's article IV consultations (surveillance), and publishing Letters of Intent (LOIs) and related country documents that underpin Fund-supported programmes with respect to about 80 per cent of requests for or reviews of Fund resources.

The most noticeable gap in the transparency of the IMF concerns decisions taken by the Executive Board (as mentioned in the previous section). The minutes of Board meetings are not published. Votes are not taken and therefore cannot be recorded or publicised. This is a significant omission for an institution which purports to be representative and whose member governments claim to be accountable to their own people. It is extremely difficult to hold one's government to account for a collective decision if the government's role in that decision is not known.

The countercase is often made that the secrecy of Board deliberations and members' positions reinforces the 'collegiality' of the Executive Board and its capacity to make good technical decisions by consensus. There are two issues at stake here. First, would an open voting process heighten political obstacles to making good technical judgements? Second, would an open, recorded process quash frank and open discussion? The latter point was raised and tested in the United Kingdom when the decision was taken to publish both the minutes and votes of the Monetary Policy Committee (MPC) of the Bank of England shortly after their meetings. Far from reflecting worst fears, the result has not been to shut down real debate and to limit discussion. To cite an expert outsider's assessment gleaned from conversations with the members of the committee: 'Discussions were said to be lively and well focused on the relevant information and the decision to be made, with ample opportunity for examining key issues and for airing a full range of views by all MPC members' (Kohn, 2000, p. 2).

The deeper objection to recorded voting on the Board of the IMF is that this would result in Board members playing to a domestic audience even more than they may currently do and Board members would be more often mandated by their governments to vote in particular ways. Practically speaking, this argument is easy to over-state for only eight member countries have their own representative who can be mandated to vote in a particular way. All other countries are in constituencies and must rely on one representative to aggregate and represent their collective interests. More broadly, however, this objection to recorded voting takes us to the essence of accountability and how and why the Fund should be held to account. On one view the IMF is a technical organisation like a Central Bank which needs to be collegial and insulated in order to make good decisions. On this reasoning, the institution should be accountable for its outputs – the quality of its decisions – but not necessarily in respect of the inputs and process by which it makes decisions. However, this chapter argues that the IMF is a political, multilateral organisation with a mandate which extends beyond that of any Central Bank. Indeed, this is reflected in its representative structure and the obligations spelt out for the Fund in its articles of agreement. It is for this reason that greater accountability of the institution's decision-making processes is necessary.

Improving evaluation and monitoring

Along with transparency, evaluation and monitoring are core elements of accountability. The IMF finds itself under increasing pressure from shareholders and members as well as outside NGOs and critics, to evaluate their operations and effectiveness in a more thorough, effective and public way. Since 1996, the Fund's work has been evaluated in three ways: self-evaluation (by operational staff) at the behest of management; internal evaluation (by the Office of Internal Audit and Inspection, OIA); and external, independent evaluations by outside experts (such as the evaluations of ESAF, surveillance work and research activity). In 2001, the IMF established an Independent Evaluation Office to undertake further evaluation.

The new Independent Evaluation Office (IEO) has been created with four purposes: enhancing the learning culture of the IMF and enabling it to better absorb lessons for improvements in its future work; helping build the IMF's external credibility by undertaking objective evaluations in a transparent manner; providing independent feedback to the Executive Board in its governance and oversight responsibilities over the IMF; and promoting greater understanding of the work of the IMF.

The IEO is independent from management and staff of the IMF. It is not independent from the Executive Board, rather it operates at 'arm's length' from the Board. It is headed by a Director who is appointed by the Executive Board for a period of four years (renewable for a further three years and who cannot be appointed to the IMF Staff at the end of his term). Although there is a 'strong presumption that the IEO reports will be published promptly after consideration by the Executive Board' (within the constraints of market sensitivity), in exceptional circumstances the Executive Board can also decide not to permit publication of IEO reports.

Overall the weakness of monitoring and evaluation in the IMF to date has been that all too often reports and reviews are ignored and not followed up. This was highlighted by the specially formed Evaluation Group of Executive Directors in the IMF who noted the lack of follow-up and monitoring of changes and reform subsequent to any evaluation (IMF, 2001) and in the purposes of the new IEO which include better absorption of lessons for improvements (as above). Many both within and outside of the IMF believe that publishing critical evaluations of the organisation is one way to ensure that findings get some public attention and external pressure for change which can help to overcome inertia or vested interests. As yet, however, the IMF does not publish all evaluations of its work. For example, the work of the Office of Internal Audit and Inspection (OIA) is not published, nor are all internal evaluations undertaken by operational staff. Obviously without publication not just of activities but of independent assessments of what the organisation is doing, it is difficult for the public to judge how well or poorly the Fund's responsibilities are being discharged and equally difficult for outsiders to offer support to insiders who recognise the need for change. For this reason enhanced monitoring and transparency are critically intertwined.

Although there are many positive aspects to enhanced monitoring and transparency, they are not unproblematic for all members of the IMF. Indeed, many of the under-represented developing countries mentioned in earlier sections of this chapter have consistently opposed reforms in these areas. Their opposition raises an important question as to whether increased information and monitoring can, in and of themselves, help people in developing countries hold the IMF to account. The answer depends heavily on the capacity of developing countries to absorb, publicise and act on information.

When information is released into the public domain, it needs to be picked up and publicised by NGOs, the media, politicians and others at the national level and subsequently translated into governmental and non-governmental pressures on the international organisation. The problem for developing countries is that they see this occurring much more in industrialised countries. The result is to increase the influence of industrialised countries through informal channels and thereby further marginalise the influence of developing countries. Unsurprisingly, then, they have opposed increased transparency and monitoring. Blanket opposition, however, cuts off an important longer-term goal of holding these institutions better and more equitably to account and obscures some of the more subtle issues and tensions about transparency and evaluation with which all members of the IMF need to engage.

At the heart of transparency and evaluation are choices and tradeoffs as to which kinds of information are collected by whom and how, since for obvious practical reasons not all information can be collected and released about all activities. Too often arguments for transparency are made without reference to who will bear the costs and what are the opportunity costs to monitoring particular activities. Yet these choices create advantages for some and disadvantages for others. For example, consider the choice between collecting elaborate forms of data which might assist in economic modelling, and collecting simpler forms of data which might be adequate for local development planning. The choice has implications for both cost and for the capacity of local agencies to aggregate the information. In respect of the costs of evaluation within the IMF, it is worth underscoring that borrowing members bear most of the cost of increased transparency and monitoring through increased loan charges – a point which underlines the need for borrowing members to be engaged in deciding transparency and monitoring for what and for whom.

More judicial-style accountability?

Absent from the IMF's present reform agenda is a more active form of accountability such as the judicial-style accountability used in national governments where tribunals, ombudsmen and review panels offer affected parties redress. The object is to ensure that an agency acts within its powers and in keeping with its own operational rules. A judicial-style panel or agency can examine specific actions or decisions taken by an institution in order to adjudicate whether or not some breach has occurred. Often in the case of courts, tribunals or ombudsmen there are few direct powers positively to direct a wrongdoing institution to take some alternative course of action. Rather, the process draws attention to a breach of rules and can result in agencies being asked at least to reconsider their decision.

The World Bank Group has already moved in this direction. In 1993 an Inspection Panel was created by the Executive Board of the World Bank to service the IBRD and IDA. The Inspection Panel can receive complaints from any group able to show that: (1) they live in the project area (or represent people who do) and are likely to be affected adversely by project activities; (2) they believe that the actual or likely harm they have suffered results from failure by the Bank to follow its policies and procedures; (3) their concerns have been discussed with Bank management and they are not satisfied with the outcome. A three-person Inspection Panel has powers to make a preliminary assessment of the merits of a complaint brought by a group, taking into account Bank management responses to the allegations. Subsequently, the Panel can recommend to the Board that a full investigation be undertaken, and make recommendations on the basis of such a full investigation. The Executive Board retains the power to permit investigations to proceed, and to make final decisions based on the Panel's findings and Bank Management's recommendations.

It is worth noting that this form of accountability requires institutions to develop and publish detailed operating principles and procedures for which they can subsequently be held to account. A different model exists in another part of the World Bank Group. In 1999 a Compliance Adviser/Ombudsman's office (CAO) was set up after consultations with shareholders, NGOs and members of the business community to service two other agencies within the World Bank group: the International Finance Corporation (IFC) and the Multilateral Investment Guarantee Agency (MIGA). The aim of the CAO is to find a workable and constructive approach to dealing with environmental and social concerns and complaints of people directly impacted by the IFC and MIGA-financed projects. The CAO or ombudsman and her staff are independent of the Bank and IFC and report directly to the President of the World Bank. The emphasis of the office's work is on dialogue, mediation and conciliation. The CAO has the power to make recommendations but not to act as 'a judge, court or policeman'.

There are several obvious limits to these measures of judicial-style accountability. First, not everyone is in an equal position to use the procedures available, not just in bringing formal complaints but in ensuring that the threat of such actions keeps officials of an institution within their powers and rules. In several cases going to the Inspection Panel people in developing countries have relied on Northern NGOs to assist in funding and presenting their case. This leads critics to allege that the work of accountability tribunals is skewed in favour of issues and areas of most concern to people within industrialised countries, as expressed through Northern NGOs, leaving unserviced those people in the developing world who have not attracted the attention of such NGOs. A further risk is that the outcomes of a formal process such as the Inspection Panel may well end up being shaped more by the needs of Northern NGOs to garner publicity through confrontation and showdown, rather than by quiet measures which more modestly improve the lives of those directly affected. This critique has been made of the World Bank Inspection Panel's investigation into the China Western Poverty Reduction Project (Wade, 2000).

A second limitation on judicial-style accountability is that the process can be used to attack good decisions which suffer a minor technical flaw in respect of the rules. It can also be long, costly and time-consuming, diverting resources away from the central purposes of the institution. For this reason the threshold or cause for complaint which can spark a full inspection or action is crucial.

A final important limitation in judicial-style accountability is that the process examines whether an institution has adhered to its existing policies and operational rules. It does not examine or adjudicate the quality or purposes of those policies or rules. Judicial-style accountability does not substitute or offer recourse against the responsibility of decision-makers to make good policy or rules. It cannot prevent or call to account bad decisions being made within the rules. This means that accountability for the quality of the rules themselves has to be achieved through some other means.

Notwithstanding the limits of judicial-style accountability, these new mechanisms within the World Bank Group have responded to a public demand and expectation that people directly affected by the actions or policies of international institutions be able to hold those institutions to account. It is unlikely that the IMF will be able to resist pressures for some form of equivalent redress. An alternative to the judicial-style panels already discussed which has been proposed by one academic would be to set down a standard of professional responsibility for the staff and management of the IMF, not unlike that which accountants, auditors and other professionals face, thereby creating the possibility for affected parties to hold the staff professionally accountable for the quality and diligence of their advice (Raffer, 1999). Although Kunibert Raffer makes the proposal in respect of the IBRD, one can see obvious parallels in the IMF where countries are regularly expected to rely on IMF estimates and calculations. Such a proposal is highly unlikely to receive a favourable reaction from staff and management who might face such actions but it pinpoints three critical issues. First, what is the basis of IMF estimates and calculations: to what extent are they technical and professional judgements and to what extent are they political compromises? Second, to what extent should countries rely on these estimates? And finally, what responsibility should the institution bear for mistakes, misjudgements or miscalculations?

6 Conclusions

This chapter has argued that two kinds of accountability within the IMF need to be improved. First the representative accountability of the institution needs to be updated to take account of its new role in the world economy. Secondly, the horizontal accountability of the IMF – the capacity of other actors to ensure that the institution works effectively, fairly and within its jurisdiction – can and should be further enhanced. On the latter issue, the chapter underlined measures already being undertaken in the IMF and indicated further ways in which the 'horizontal' accountability of the institution can and should be improved, bearing in mind the costs and tradeoffs inherent in enhancing transparency, evaluation and judicial-style accountability. Further reform would both respond to public demands for greater accountability which are spread throughout both developed and developing countries, and contribute to improving the effectiveness of the work of the IMF.

The representative accountability of the IMF is more difficult to remedy. It requires an improvement in the voice and participation of developing countries. It bears noting that here transparency, information-sharing and further evaluation are not enough. Many of the processes within the IMF are informal with consultations and consensus-building going on behind the scenes and long before formal meetings of the Executive Board. For this reason a developing country or group of developing countries wishing to hold others to account needs to be privy to much which cannot be recorded and circulated as a publication. Active and informed participation is vital for full and accurate information as to substance as well as process.

The kind of participation which would enhance accountability is worth an additional comment in this conclusion. The IMF and World Bank have themselves emphasised the need to 'secure broad-based participation and ownership in the process of strategy development and implementation' (IMF/World Bank, 2001). This is the kind of participation needed at Board level if developing countries are to play a role in holding the institution to account. As found by researchers evaluating the PRS process, *ad hoc* information-sharing and consultations do little to enhance accountability. Institutions which permit participation in the processes of priority-setting, policy-making, implementation and monitoring in an ongoing and continuous way are vital (SGTS, 2000).

Representative reform within the IMF requires overhauling not just the voting structure but the decision-making processes of the institution. The goal has to be, to quote an evaluation of multi-stakeholder processes in global governance, that all members 'feel that they have access to the process, that their voices are fully heard, and that their participation in the deliberations is meaningful' (Dubash *et al.*, 2001, p. 4). Only in this event will the demands of a minimal representative accountability be met.

REFERENCES

Abugre, C. and N. Alexander (1998). 'Non-Governmental Organisations and the International, Monetary and Financial System', *International Monetary and Financial Issues for the 1990s, IX*. Geneva, UNCTAD, 107–25

Bradlow, D. (2001). 'Stuffing New Wine into Old Bottles: The Troubling Case of the IMF', *Journal of International Banking Regulation*, 3(1), 9–36

Collier, P. (1999). 'Learning from Failure: The International Financial Institutions as Agencies of Restraint in Africa', in A. Schedler, L. Diamond and M. Plattner, *The Self-Restraining State: Power and Accountability in New Democracies*. Boulder, CO, Lynne Rienner.

De Gregorio, J., B. Eichengreen, T. Ito and C. Wyplosz (1999). *An Independent and Accountable IMF*. London, ICMB and CEPR.

Dubash, N. K., M. Dupar, S. Kothari and T. Lissu (2001). 'A Watershed in Global Governance?: An Independent Assessment of the World Commission on Dams'. Lokayan, World Resources Institute

Gold, J. (1972). *Voting and Decisions in the International Monetary Fund*. Washington, DC, IMF

G7 (2000). 'Statement of G7 Finance Mininsters and Central Bank Governors', Washington, DC, 15 April, LS-556

Horsefield, K. J. (1996). *The International Monetary Fund, 1945–1965: Twenty Years of International Monetary Cooperation*, 1. Washington, DC, IMF

IMF (1999). 'External Evaluation of IMF Surveillance', Report by a Group of Independent Experts, Washington, DC, IMF

   'Report to the IMF Executive Board of the Quota Formula Review Group', Washington, DC, IMF, 28 April

IMF/World Bank (2001). 'Poverty Reduction Strategy Papers – Progress in Implementation', Annex 2: Guidelines (paper prepared by the staffs of the IMF and the World Bank, Washington, DC, 20 April

   (2001), *Review of Experience with Evaluation in the Fund (Prepared by the Evaluation Group of Executive Directors)*. Washington, DC, IMF

International Financial Institution Advisory Commission (IFIAC) or Meltzer Commission Report (2000). *Final Report and Transcripts of Meetings and Hearings*. Washington, DC; available at http://phantom-x.gsia.cmu.edu/IFIAC

Jadhav, N. (2000). 'IMF Quota Formulas and Mechanisms: A Developing Economy Perspective', paper prepared for G24 Technical Group Meeting, Lima, 1 March

Kahler, M. (2001). *Leadership Selection in the Major Multilaterals*. Washington, DC, Institute of International Economics

Kapur, D. (2000). 'Who Gets to Run the World?', *Foreign Policy*, 121, 44–50

Kohn, D. L. (2000). 'Report to the Non-Executive Directors of the Court of the Bank of England on Monetary Policy Processes and the Work of Monetary Analysis', Bank of England, 18 October

Locke, M. (2000). 'Funding the IMF: The Debate in the US Congress', *Finance and Development*, 3, 56–9

Maravall, J. M. (1999). 'Accountability and Manipulation', in A. Przeworski, S. Stokes and B. Manin, *Democracy, Accountability, and Representation*. Cambridge, Cambridge University Press, 154–96

Przeworski, A., S. Stokes and B. Manin (1999). *Democracy, Accountability, and Representation*. Cambridge, Cambridge University Press

Raffer, K. (1999). 'Introducing Financial Accountability at the IBRD: An Overdue and Necessary Reform', Department of Economics University of Vienna, unpublished manuscript

Schedler, A., L. Diamond and M. Plattner (1999). *The Self-Restraining State: Power and Accountability in New Democracies*. Boulder, CO, Lynne Rienner

SGTS & Associates (2000). 'Civil Society Participation in PRSPs', *Report to the Development for International Development, 1: Overview and Recommendations*. London, SGTS, October

Van Houtven, L. (2001). *Governance of the International Monetary Fund: Decision Making, Institutional Oversight, Transparency and Accountability*, Washington, DC, Per Jacobssen Foundation

Viera da Cunha, P. and M. Valeria Junho Pena (1998). 'The Limits and Merits of Participation', World Bank Working Paper, 594; available at http:/econ.worldbank.org/docs/594.pdf

Wade, R. (2000). 'A Defeat for Development and Multilateralism: the World Bank has been Unfairly Criticised over the Qinghai Resettlement Project'; full manuscript unpublished, short version published in *Financial Times*, 4

15 The IMF at the start of the twenty-first century: what has been learned? On which values can we establish a humanised globalisation?

MICHEL CAMDESSUS

It is a distinct privilege for me to have been invited by the manager of the Cyril Foster Fund at Oxford University to give this year's lecture.[1]

Of course, the impressive list of my predecessors for the occasion makes me very modest, as I am far from displaying comparable talents and achievements. But I also feel immensely rewarded by what is very peculiar in this invitation: the wish of Mr Cyril Foster that such lectures deal with the 'elimination of war and the better understanding of the nations of the world'. To devote our thoughts to these two essential objectives of humanity could bring us to the heart of the intense debate we are having now, all around the world, about globalisation. This is a debate about its opportunities, of course, but also its risks, which are so clearly demonstrated by the new breed of economic crises the world suffered during the 1990s, the instability of the world finances, the threat of marginalisation of the most vulnerable and rising inequality.

This debate about globalisation is striking by its intensity and even more by the contrast between the optimism of officials in charge who pretend that their efforts to adapt the system to the new realities should end up by making globalisation an opportunity for all and the total rejection of this view by many protesters in our streets, including here, I suspect. Beyond this contrast, one cannot but recognise the depth of the 'malaise' of a significant part of world public opinion, which suspects that the problems we are now confronted with are deeply related not so much to institutions or procedures but to the very values founding our civilisation. If this is even partly true, then what is needed is much more than the business-as-usual commitments of ministerial communiqués.

It is no wonder then if, in the rhetorical deluge that globalisation has generated recently, one of the few declarations that have gone truly to the heart of the matter

[1] 2000 Cyril Foster Lecture, University of Oxford, delivered 9 November.

was made by Václav Havel, the President of the Czech Republic and the hero of the 'velvet revolution' of 1989. President Havel delivered this message in September 1999 to Ministers of Finance, Central Bank governors and bankers of the world, on the occasion of the annual meetings of the IMF and the World Bank in Prague:

We often hear about the need to restructure the economies of the developing or the poorer countries and about the wealthier nations being duty-bound to help them accomplish this. If this is done in a sensitive manner against a backdrop of sound knowledge of the specific environment and its unique interest and needs it is certainly a worthy and much needed effort. But I deem it even more important that we should begin to also think about another restructuring – a restructuring of the entire system of values which forms the basis of our civilization today. This, indeed, is a common task for all. And I would even say that it is of greater urgency for those who are better off in material terms.

This will hardly ever happen unless we all find, inside ourselves, the courage to substantially change and to newly form an order of values that, with all our diversity, we can jointly embrace and jointly respect; and, unless we again relate these values to something that lies beyond the horizon of our immediate personal or group interest.

But how could this be achieved without a new and powerful advance of human spirituality? And what can be done, in concrete terms, to encourage such an advance?

'A new order of values we can jointly embrace and jointly respect' . . . which values?

Let me tell you very frankly that this was a question I had with me, during thirteen years, when meeting with so many leaders of the world with so different cultural background, telling me their anxieties, the apparently intractable problems of their societies, their dreams of an always elusive renaissance.

As this chapter is about what has been learned during that period, let us concentrate on that level of concern, forgetting for a while more technical issues of financial architecture. Which values must we promote if we are determined to make sense of our history? Which values should guide us as the new century unfolds? Well, when trying to draw the conclusions of so many conversations and exchanges, at times quite intense, I end up with three values: the sense of global responsibility, solidarity and a worldwide sense of citizenship:

- a sense of global responsibility for all countries, and all of us, to contribute to the human success of globalisation
- solidarity to alleviate and ultimately to eradicate poverty and
- a new sense of citizenship to back a new global governance.

No doubt you will immediately see how crucially linked these three values are to elimination of war and the better understanding of the nations of the world.

1 A sense of global responsibility

The world was confronted during the 1990s with a new breed of economic crisis.

The Mexican crisis, and much more evidently the Asian crisis, were unlike any seen before. Crises of this new type explode on the open capital markets, arise from complex dysfunctions and are much less exclusively macroeconomic in nature. They quickly take on systemic proportions, and can be checked only through the immediate mobilisation of massive financing. Take the three major Asian crises, for example: Thailand, Indonesia and Korea. Dealing with them meant dealing with a three-dimensional problem: a dimension, obviously, of macroeconomic imbalances, along with massive outflows of short-term capital; an acute crisis in the financial sector, reflecting institutional and banking practice weaknesses; and a much more fundamental crisis in the economic management model to which the previous success had complacently been attributed, but which was quite simply in conflict with the new demands of a globalised economy. I am thinking here of unhealthy – I would even say incestuous – relations among corporations, banks and government. This third dimension, which the students in Djakarta shouted down with cries of corruption, collusion and nepotism, implied that fundamental reforms were immediately required. It would have been out of the question for the IMF to provide massive financial assistance in the absence of a body of measures or rules that would lead to greater transparency, better management and anti-corruption efforts. These reforms are now under way: some have already produced their expected positive results; others, which are tackling deeply rooted problems, will take more time, but are resolutely being applied.

It is clear that the multi-faceted factors behind today's economic crises have been evident – *mutatis mutandis* – in a good many other cases: in Japan, where the abundance of reserves averted a more open crisis; and in Russia, of course, on a grand scale. As we well know, these symptoms exist in differing degrees almost everywhere. So what, then, are the lessons we can learn from this new breed of crisis? Well, basically, that whether a country is large or small, any crisis can now become systemic through contagion on the globalised markets. Domestic economic policy therefore must, now more than ever, take into account its potential worldwide impact; a duty of universal responsibility is incumbent upon all. Every country, large or small, is responsible for the stability and quality of world growth.

This adds a new dimension to the duty of excellence that is required of every government in the management of its economy. I use the word 'excellence'; I could also say 'absolute rectitude'. Globalisation is a prodigious factor in accelerating and spreading the international repercussions of domestic policies – for better or worse. No country can escape, and all should be fully aware of this.

This is why the IMF, in the dialogue it holds with each of its member countries, from the largest to the smallest, places such an emphasis – now in the context of globalisation – on three points:

- rigour and transparency in overall economic management
- growth that is centred on human development and
- government reform, and all that that implies in terms of seeking public sector efficiency, appropriate regulation, emphasis on the rule of law, independence of the judiciary, anti-corruption measures, etc.

The aim of an international financial organisation in making such suggestions is not so much to seek balanced books at all costs, important as that may be, but rather to encourage countries to discover and realise what their global responsibilities imply and what the consequences are of the two-way relationship between integrity of monetary and financial management and poverty reduction. Without a credible prospect of reducing poverty, policies promoting monetary and financial integrity have little chance of enduring, and without integrity in monetary and financial management, any efforts to reduce poverty will be protracted, at best. Laying the groundwork for participatory development and eradication of poverty are decisive factors of sustainability. The necessary popular support for a lasting stabilisation and reform effort cannot be counted upon, unless the whole population, including the poorest, is able to have its say on the policies adopted and of course benefits from them.

This two-way relationship is part of an emerging more comprehensive development paradigm of which moral values are an integral part. It must be supported. Let me emphasise two of its key features.

First, a progressive humanisation of basic economic concepts. It is recognised that the market can have major failures, that growth alone is not enough and can even be destructive of the natural environment or precious social goods and cultural values. Only the pursuit of high-quality growth is worth the effort. What is such growth?

- growth that can be sustained over time without causing domestic and external financial imbalance
- growth that has the human person at its centre, that is accompanied by adequate investment, particularly in education and health, to take full advantage of the tremendous leverage of human capital for future growth
- growth that, to be sustainable, is based on a continuous effort for more equity, poverty alleviation and empowerment of poor people and

- growth that promotes protection of the environment, and respect for national cultural values.

This is what IMF and World Bank programmes are, more and more, and must be after.

Second, at a deeper level, we observe in recent approaches a striking and promising recognition of a convergence between a respect for fundamental ethical values and the search for efficiency required by market competition. We can see now a far wider recognition:

- that participatory democracy – that major conquest of the twentieth century over colonisation, totalitarianism, and cronyism – can maximise the effectiveness of sound economies
- that transparency, openness and accountability are basic requirements for economic success
- that combating collusion, corruption and nepotism is now recognised as a legitimate concern for the international financial institutions
- that systematically dismantling the state is not the way to respond to the problems of modern economies; rather we must aim for a slimmer yet more effective state, able to provide the private sector with a solid framework in which the rule of law could prevail, on a level playing field.

All of this is tantamount to recognising that economic progress is strongly dependent on the basic value of responsibility: the sense that each is responsible for the advancement of all, and on the harmony of social relations at national level and peace internationally. This should, in the end, allow each country to play a greater positive role for the prosperity of the global economy. This cannot but give more relevance, more importance than ever, to the mandate of surveillance of the IMF and to its broadening to the whole financial sphere. As the Asian and the other countries were not only the actors of the so-called 'Asian crisis' but also the victims of something wrong in the working of the international financial system, one of the fields to which a sense of global responsibility must be applied is the correction of these deficiencies, what we, somewhat pretentiously call 'the financial architecture'.

Equally important is to observe that international financial flows have become mainly private now, with an enormous potential to contribute to a more efficient financing of productive investments. But for this to happen we will need also to see that a sense of global responsibility is demonstrated not only by governments but also by all the other key actors: enterprises, financial institutions and all components of civil society: labour unions, NGOs, religious organisations, etc. All of them can play an important role for the success of the newly emerging paradigm in humanising globalisation. This new paradigm, rooted in fundamental human values, coupled with a better ability to prevent and manage crises, could be a distinct and positive chance of our times: provided we are able to take full advantage of it and of the new opportunities for growth created by the revolution in information technology, to overcome the ultimate systemic threat: poverty.

2 Solidarity to fight poverty

'The ultimate systemic threat': these words are from Angel Gurria, Minister of Finance of Mexico.

When considering all the positive dynamics at work in our world, the slowness of progress in reducing poverty appears all the more unacceptable. I need not describe in graphic terms the extent of present human deprivation – you know them at least as well as I.[2]

The widening gaps between rich and poor within nations, and the gulf between the most affluent and most impoverished nations, are morally outrageous, economically wasteful, and potentially socially explosive.[3] Now we know that it is not enough to increase the size of the cake; the way it is shared is deeply relevant to the dynamism of development. If the poor are left hopeless, poverty will undermine the fabric of our societies though confrontation, violence and civil disorder. If we are committed to the promotion of human dignity and peace, we cannot afford to ignore poverty and the risks it entails for peace. We all must work together to relieve all this human suffering. This is what solidarity means: solidarity, an obvious central value for a unifying world. But the fight for peace and solidarity must go hand in hand as peace is an inescapable precondition for durable economic progress. We have heard that development is another name for peace. Why do we forget the converse: that peace is another name for development? When considering the tragic situation of an impressive part of Africa, where at least one-third of the countries are directly or indirectly involved in

---

[2] More than 1.2 billion individuals live on less than $1.00 a day; more than 1.4 billion have no direct access to drinking water; 0.9 billion are illiterate; and 0.8 billion suffer from hunger or malnutrition.

[3] Jim Wolfensohn, President of the World Bank, put that in very striking terms in his Prague address in September 2000: 'We live in a world scarred by inequality. Something is wrong when the richest 20 per cent of the global population receive more than 80 per cent of the global income. Something is wrong when 10 per cent of a population receive half of the national income – as happens in far too many countries today. Something is wrong when the average income for the richest 20 countries is 37 times the average for the poorest 20, a gap that has more than doubled in the past 40 years. Something is wrong when 1.2 billion people still live under less than one dollar a day and 2.8 billion still live on less than 2 dollars a day.'

military or civil or ethnic tribes conflicts, how could we entertain any illusion that progress in human conditions is achievable if these conflicts are not brought to an end? Ideally, as Cyril Foster would have put it, war should be eliminated; but at least there must be a major effort – well beyond what we see today – to reduce tensions and to prevent new wars from being started. I know, of course, that any suggestion of this kind runs the risk of being met with scepticism, if not cynicism. Nonetheless, as the lives of so many people – so many children – are at stake, not to mention the chances of improving their human condition, I have no hesitation in reiterating several suggestions that have been made to contain the arms trade and military expenditures:

- restraining the sales of military equipment to sensitive regions
- abolishing the provision of export credits for military purposes
- following the recommendation of Secretary General, Kofi Annan, to adopt national maximum levels for military expenditure that should not exceed 1.5 per cent of GDP in Africa, and might often be lower
- cooperation in the interdiction of the smuggling of raw materials and natural resources to finance armed conflict and
- broadening the UN register on military exports to involve many more countries and to cover small arms and ammunition.

We must endorse these suggestions. Just think how many ploughshares could be forged with such an oversupply of swords!

If through a diversity of initiatives of that kind better prospects for peace can emerge, then good windows of opportunity for development could appear. But many other conditions will have to be put in place for its process to become effective. Here, the poor countries themselves are on the front line. Already many of them have been showing what can be done when the ultimate objective is human development. Their experience suggests an approach for each country with five components.

First, country-driven strategies that make poverty alleviation the centrepiece of economic policy, together with a renewed emphasis on rapid growth led by the private sector.

Second, sound macroeconomic policies are fundamental and will lead to high rates of saving and efficient investment in both physical and human capital.

Third, the promotion of the free market and an outward orientation of economic policies – which are sometimes called the first generation of reforms: trade and exchange liberalisation; improving incentives by rolling back price controls and subsidies; reforming public enterprises; and strengthening financial systems are all elements.

Fourth, the web of laws, regulations, standards and codes that support the functioning of markets. It is all summed up in two key concepts – transparency and good governance. These 'second-generation reforms' are not abstract concepts that can await more auspicious times; they are essential building blocks of a successful market economy. The more they overlap with the first generation of reforms, the better.

Fifth, a strong social component – well-targeted and cost-effective social safety nets, a shift in public spending toward basic social services in education and health care and efforts to provide income-earning opportunities for the poor.

But if the content of a programme is important, the degree of national support for it matters even more. It need hardly be said that a programme will work only if the country wants it to work; not just the government, but the people and organisations within the society. In short, success lies in national 'ownership' of the policies, through a participatory approach that engages civil society in a constructive dialogue. Absolutely central to the spirit of what the Bretton Woods institutions are doing now is to make sure that the country is in the driver's seat of the process. And the rest of the world should then be ready to move promptly when these countries indicate that they need support. How can development partners support the efforts of the poorest countries? Let me point to three areas.

First, on the trade front, by assigning the highest priority to providing unrestricted market access for all exports from the poorest countries, including the heavily indebted poor countries (HIPCs), so that these countries can begin to benefit more deeply from integration into the global trading system.

Second, by working strenuously to encourage flows of private capital to the emerging and lower-income developing countries, especially foreign direct investment (FDI) with its twin benefits of new finance and technology transfers.

Third, by their financial support. Allow me to be somewhat more explicit on that point, as we are dealing here with an issue which goes much beyond – important as it may be – the simple provision of badly needed financing. It is an issue deeply related to the basic fabric of a unifying world community, to the mutual trust among its members which implies that we ensure that giving one's word means just that. Over the 1990s, we have witnessed two rather paradoxical phenomena. On the one hand, while the industrial countries have happily been collecting their peace dividends, they have steadily reduced their official development assistance, falling further and further short of the target of 0.7 per cent of GDP that all – with the exception of the United States – had pledged for themselves for the year 2000. At the same time they have pledged, alongside the developing countries and transition economies, at one world conference after another, to promote measurable and achievable human development objectives. One can remember the Copenhagen Declaration, in which we promised to reduce by half the number of people on this planet living in abject poverty by 2015. We should also remember the conferences in Rio,

Jomtien, Cairo, Rome and Beijing, where we promised to achieve at least seven other objectives during this period:

- reduction by half of the number of people suffering from hunger or malnutrition (Rome)
- universal primary education in all countries (Jomtien, Beijing and Copenhagen)
- reduction of infant and child mortality by two-thirds (Cairo)
- reduction of maternal mortality by three-quarters (Cairo and Beijing)
- universal access to reproductive care and counselling through primary health services (Cairo)
- reversal of the current rate of destruction of the environment and
- elimination of the disparity in access to primary and secondary education for girls and boys by 2005.

Imagine for a moment that these pledges were actually fulfilled. What a giant step this could be toward a better world, what a giant step it would be toward improving the lot of the most disadvantaged among the poor – women and children! But many of the world's top leaders are losing sight of these pledges, as I myself have had occasion to observe. I am therefore very pleased that they have agreed that each year, at the G7–G8 meeting, they will look at a detailed report by the main institutions concerned evaluating their progress toward these goals and, if there are delays, they will reflect on the measures to be taken to define a new path to achieve them. This is only a small step, but it shows us, above all, how fragile our collective commitments are, and how small the chances are that they will be fulfilled without a universal mobilisation of public opinion, as has been the case with the Jubilee 2000 campaign. If I were asked what should now be the theme of a new campaign, I would say: we must undertake to ensure that the pledges made in our name are fulfilled.

I asked the heads of state of the G7–G8 to make the first decade of the twenty-first century the decade of fulfilment of past pledges. The key is clearly our solidarity but what is needed is something that is also fundamental in human relations: abiding by one's word. If we allow cynicism to prevail in this area, we may as well give up the dream of progressing to a more fraternal global society. This is a matter of great urgency. I see the time soon coming when we will be told that, considering the amount of time we have lost since these pledges were made, the targets are no longer attainable. We have not reached this point yet, but the situation is urgent. We need a jolt of responsibility and solidarity, and indeed the case is overwhelming. The ODA contribution of industrial countries is now down to 0.23 per cent of their GDP against a target of 0.7. We have frequently surpluses in the budgets, growth is high, the opportunities are there to be shared, etc.

Two other current initiatives could make a big difference:

- The first is the vigorous implementation of the debt reduction operations for the HIPCs. Reaching the end of the 2000 deadline should in no way reduce the urgency put on that issue. We should go on pressing for the quick adoption of any necessary measures for the interested countries to benefit fully from debt reduction. The measures to be taken by industrial countries to open fully their markets to their products should be given, of course, the highest priority, together with the provision of financial backing for this initiative, without forgetting that this should in no way be seen as a substitute for new financial flows.
- The second is the vigorous implementation of the new joint strategy by the IMF and the World Bank, aimed at making poverty-reduction the centrepiece of their joint strategies in the seventy-five poorest countries. Assume for a moment that recipient and industrial countries alike take our seven pledges seriously. This could trigger a kind of virtuous circle that could generate additional growth over and above current trends, as long as this effort develops in the context of programmes focusing on high-quality growth implying bold reforms, including reforms of public institutions and methods of government. One can easily imagine the many synergies which could develop in such a framework: synergies between social spending and growth, between education and participatory democracy, between the education of girls and the ability of women to control their own lives, and so forth. Such synergies would increase the chances of reaching the higher level of national growth which will be needed to reduce poverty by the pledged proportion. Moreover, acceleration of growth of the developing countries can make a powerful contribution to the prosperity of the whole world community. This should be the contribution of the developing countries themselves, as they have also subscribed to these seven pledges, and they of course have the primary responsibility for their own human development.

Having touched these key aspects of the fight against poverty, let me underline that what we are referring to here is not just our obligation of generosity toward a world much poorer than ours but to the very fabric of a world which is now one: a fabric crucially dependent on elimination of war, respect for pledges and active support for those anxious to stand on their own feet.

Beyond this major issue of poverty, we know only too well that in the world today many people feel that they lack control over their own destiny, and fear that there is no legitimate authority to deal with problems that are increasingly taking on worldwide dimensions: threats to the environment, drugs, corruption, crime, money laundering, etc. For these issues as for poverty, I do not see how we can overcome them without tackling the problem of world governance.

3 World governance

No doubt, the time has come to ask ourselves if we are effectively creating the institutional conditions that will enable us better to protect ourselves as a group against collective risks on a global scale, and together to obtain a clearer view of our common destiny.

To be sure, what is currently being accomplished with the available resources by the UN, the Bretton Woods institutions and all forms of bilateral and multilateral cooperation is not negligible, and it is probably for that reason that the Asian crisis and its aftermath did not turn into the major systemic crisis that loomed in 1998. But we all feel that we could do better. In that, we need to urgently revisit the broad issue of world economic governance. This is not a reference, of course, to some kind of world economic government, but only to the more limited ambition of finding a global response to inescapable global problems. The task is, nevertheless, monumental (see appendix).

We are the first generation in history to be confronted by the need to organise and manage the world, not from a position of power such as Alexander's or Caesar's or the Allies' at the end of the Second World War, but through a recognition of the universal responsibilities of all peoples, of the equal right to sustainable development and of a universal duty of solidarity and cooperation. The challenge is to find mechanisms for managing the international economy that do not compromise the sovereignty of national governments, that help the smooth and effective working of markets, that ensure international financial stability and that offer solutions to problems that transcend the boundaries of the nation-state and to which we are now responding very unsatisfactorily by frequently over-stretching institutions. A tall order indeed!

To understand this challenge, we need merely compare our world to the world in 1945. Each country has now achieved sovereignty, each wants to shoulder its full responsibility in the face of global problems, and we know full well that the effective participation of each country is key to the proper functioning of the 'Global Village'. What is more, while globalisation has until now operated at the whim of more or less autonomous financial and technological forces, it is high time that we take initiatives so that progress toward world unity can be made consistently and in the service of humankind. All this requires institutions that can facilitate joint reflection at the highest levels, whenever needed, and that are capable of ensuring that globalised strategies are adopted and followed when it appears that problems can be dealt with effectively only at the global level. Clearly, we need to be imaginative enough to visualise the institutions that would best serve the global commonweal – or, at least, to make the necessary changes in the institutions created in San Francisco and Bretton Woods.

The problems are serious, and they are many. I would like to mention just three of them: first, lack of appropriate institutions in new fields of major global concern; second, coherence and fair representation in international economic decision-making; and third, political responsiveness.

The problem of lacunae in the present system of world governance is the most straightforward – though this does not mean that there is readiness to solve it. Problems which threaten us every day now were unknown or were unimportant fifty years ago when the system was established. The most striking case is the environment: a problem of worldwide dimension *par excellence*.[4] Whatever the merits of those in charge in the UN family, what we have now is not sufficient.

Whatever our reluctance to add to the bureaucratic apparatus of the UN, it is crystal clear that the world will have – the sooner the better – to face this unjustifiable lacuna, a lacuna on which public voices remain generally silent and which is brought to our minds, but so far to no avail, only when a major environmental catastrophe takes place.

Together with the environment, anti-trust and migrant-worker issues would also justify the creation of freestanding bodies at a global level. Needless to say, the cost of establishing such institutions could be offset at least partly by further streamlining the system in other fields.

Second, the lack of coherence. It can be exemplified, in decision-making at world level, by the failure in Seattle to launch the millennium round of trade negotiation. Where is the incoherence? On one hand we have the far-reaching decision by governments, in the framework of the Bretton Woods institutions, to reduce significantly the debt of thirty-five or forty heavily indebted poor countries. On the other hand, these same governments have failed – in the framework of the WTO – to launch a trade round which could at least partly eliminate trade barriers to the exports of these countries. It is the latter that has the greater long-term potential for lifting the poor out of poverty through export-led growth. This failure, unless quickly reversed, will make a mockery of a decision on debt that is otherwise of significant dimensions. This lack of co-herence calls for a framework in which leaders at the highest political level could define strategies on issues whose multi-faceted aspects are dealt with presently in different bodies governed by different ministerial membership, making the adoption of compromise solutions on issues such as the 'social clause' or the environment in the narrow framework of trade negotiation extremely difficult.

Let me be blunt. We cannot rely on the G7 to make such strategic decisions: a body where China, Indonesia, Brazil, Nigeria – to name just a few – are not represented has not the legitimacy for that. We must then add here a missing dimension of fairness in representation. To my judgement, a modest step in

---

[4] See appendix for a list of major global environmental problems.

that direction could consist of replacing the G7 Summit every two years by a meeting of the heads of state and government of the countries – approximately thirty at any one time – who have Executive Directors on the Boards of either the IMF or the World Bank. This would be more thoroughly representative of the entire membership of 182 countries than any of the presently available formulas. As it would be attended by the heads of the two Bretton Woods organisations, the ILO, the WTO and the Secretary General of the United Nations, it would offer a way of establishing a clear and strong link between the multinational institutions and a representative grouping of world leaders with the greatest possible legitimacy. This idea has been floated but so far apart from some sympathetic murmurs of interest, I do not see distinct signs of movement in that direction in the ranks of major G7 bureaucracies; but this could be a useful item, together with several other suggestions, for discussions in forthcoming G7–G8 summits.

Equally urgent – with little progress so far – is the issue of the 'political responsibility' of international institutions including the IMF. Too often they are portrayed as unaccountable technocracies. The truth is that they are responsible and accountable to their member governments, and that, for instance, in the IMF all decisions have to be approved by the Executive Board of twenty-four members, representing 182 countries. May I mention that every single loan, including of course the controversial loans in Asia and to Russia, has had – I am proud to say – the overwhelming support of our member governments. The problem is not that institutions are not accountable, but that they are not seen to be accountable, and that some member governments from time to time find it convenient not to express their public support for actions they have supported in the Executive Boards. Part of the problem is that member governments have until recently been reluctant to publish their agreements with the institutions, heightening the perception that they are not accountable. But, as far at least as the IMF is concerned, efforts at making the institution more transparent are now bearing fruit. Greater openness will help ensure its legitimacy as well as its effectiveness in improving the quality of policy debate and democratic participation in member countries, and at the same time it will help the international capital markets become more efficient.

But it is also important to ensure that the IMF is seen, far more visibly, to have the legitimate political support of its shareholders. One reform that I supported before leaving the IMF would respond to this problem. It would entail transforming the IMF's advisory ministerial committee – until recently called the Interim Committee, renamed in September 1999 the International Monetary and Financial Committee – into a decision-making council for the major strategic orientations of the world economy. Far from leading to an undue politicisation of the IMF, this would simply, in the eyes of the public, place responsibility squarely where it already rests. This would help. But governments remain to be convinced.[5]

Under this heading of world economic governance I have reported only timid reform ideas. Much more far-reaching initiatives, I am sure, will have to be considered soon, but too little support is at this stage being demonstrated for that. While a coalition of forces coming from very different horizons – protectionist, 'sovereignist', and all those for which globalisation must simply be rejected – try to oppose any movement in that direction, a new sense of world citizenship has not yet emerged around the commonly held values in our world. I think that this will be necessary if humanity is to become better aware of, and to assume responsibility for, the global aspect of its destiny, by providing the world with the necessary institutions. This will be necessary also if we are to be sensitive to the so frequently expressed fear outside America that the treasures of local cultures and traditions are at risk of being overwhelmed by the strongest. One of the most pressing responsibilities of the international community will be to make sure that just the opposite occurs, and that local cultures are given a new stronger chance to contribute their uniqueness to a unifying world.

As a matter of fact, the great hopes we have for the twenty-first century – to see human development truly served by the globalised process that is unifying the world – will not come to full fruition if new generations of opinion-makers do not deliberately accept this responsibility of endowing public opinion with a global consciousness. A new kind of citizenship must be created, not simply a vague cosmopolitanism, but a genuine citizenship at all levels: local, regional, national and global.

Affirming this does not take anything away from the need better to structure the world architecture, to create regional organisations where they are still lacking and to strengthen the political dimension of the regional economic organisations already in place, such as the European Union. The more we see the need to consolidate or vest new responsibilities in world bodies, the more it is

---

[5] I will not elaborate on many other suggestions for improvement of world governance which are already at different stages of discussion in different forums:

- Adapting a WTO – made universal in its membership – to the new dimension of its tasks (E-commerce and other issues,) including in their ethical dimensions, the fight against corruption, etc.
- In the framework of the IMF, to move toward an orderly and well-sequenced liberalisation of capital accounts, recognition of the Fund's role as a lender of last resort (LOLR) and strengthening of the framework for dealing with commercial debt crises.
- Strengthening of the mechanism for checking that international ODA pledges are fulfilled.
- Strengthening regulations and supervisory bodies for all kinds of financial transactions to contain risks and moral hazard, and to make the competence of these bodies universal so as to deal with the black holes created by the existence of offshore financial centres.

necessary, as well, to let them know that their contribution can only be subsidiary and ensure that everyone understands that nothing can be accomplished at the global level unless it is taken up at the grassroots level and supported by initiatives of the entire institutional chain, initiatives in which the NGOs will play an ever-greater role. Responsible citizenship at all levels must be one of the key values of the twenty-first century.

Having borrowed from Václav Havel the basic inspiration for these remarks, let me conclude by submitting to your attention his conclusion at the opening of the ministerial debates in Prague:

Given this state of affairs, to my mind, we have only one possibility: to search, inside ourselves as well as around us, for new sources of a sense of responsibility for the world; new sources of mutual understanding and solidarity; of humility before the miracle of Being; of the ability to restrain ourselves in the general interest and to perform good deeds even if they remain unseen and unrecognized.

He mentioned 'humility before the miracle of Being' and 'the ability to restrain ourselves in the general interest' but also a sense of responsibility for the world and solidarity. As far as the new kind of citizenship I tried to outline here, you will all agree, I presume, that Václav Havel provided the world with more than a lesson to be learned, in fact a perfect embodiment of it.

Appendix Six global environmental problems

1. Depletion of the ozone layer. So far, the Convention for the Protection of the Ozone layer, together with the Montreal Protocol, have proved to be the most successful international environmental agreements in spite of the remaining open issues.
2. The global climate is changing in consequence of the so-called 'greenhouse effect'. The framework Convention on Climate Change and the Kyoto Protocol are the first important international steps to reduce the emission of greenhouse gases worldwide. But the final success of these efforts to protect the climate will depend on future negotiations.
3. The conservation of biological diversity is a common concern of mankind. So far, the Convention on Biological Diversity has not been able successfully to protect endangered species.
4. Desertification and drought have been recognised as problems of global dimension. The Convention to Combat Desertification alone is not sufficient to solve this problem.

5. International waters are threatened especially by water-quality degradation and over-exploitation of marine resources. No single international body or mechanism has been set up to regulate the use of international waters and coordinate activities meant to conserve marine ecosystems.
6. Last but not least, our forests need to be protected. No legally binding international agreement at the moment copes with the problem of deforestation.

Index

Printed in the United States
101890LV00002B/26/A